THE DEVELOPMENT OF
CHILDREN'S THINKING

Sara Miller McCune founded SAGE Publishing in 1965 to support the dissemination of usable knowledge and educate a global community. SAGE publishes more than 1000 journals and over 800 new books each year, spanning a wide range of subject areas. Our growing selection of library products includes archives, data, case studies and video. SAGE remains majority owned by our founder and after her lifetime will become owned by a charitable trust that secures the company's continued independence.

Los Angeles | London | New Delhi | Singapore | Washington DC | Melbourne

JEREMY CARPENDALE
CHARLIE LEWIS
ULRICH MÜLLER

THE DEVELOPMENT OF
CHILDREN'S THINKING
ITS SOCIAL AND COMMUNICATIVE FOUNDATIONS

Los Angeles | London | New Delhi
Singapore | Washington DC | Melbourne

Los Angeles | London | New Delhi
Singapore | Washington DC | Melbourne

SAGE Publications Ltd
1 Oliver's Yard
55 City Road
London EC1Y 1SP

SAGE Publications Inc.
2455 Teller Road
Thousand Oaks, California 91320

SAGE Publications India Pvt Ltd
B 1/I 1 Mohan Cooperative Industrial Area
Mathura Road
New Delhi 110 044

SAGE Publications Asia-Pacific Pte Ltd
3 Church Street
#10-04 Samsung Hub
Singapore 049483

Editor: Amy Jarrold
Editorial assistant: Katie Rabot
Production editor: Imogen Roome
Marketing manager: Lucia Sweet
Cover design: Wendy Scott
Typeset by: C&M Digitals (P) Ltd, Chennai, India
Printed in the UK

Figure 7.2: Kanzi, language-reared male bonobo, converses with Sue Savage-Rumbaugh in 2006 using a portable "keyboard" of arbitrary symbols that Kanzi associates with words. Photo distributed on Creative Commons Attribution-Share Alike 4.0 International license.

Figures in Chapter 10 are courtesy of Karen Shimmon.

Library of Congress Control Number: 2017942223

British Library Cataloguing in Publication data

A catalogue record for this book is available from the British Library

ISBN 978-1-4462-9563-2
ISBN 978-1-4462-9564-9 (pbk)

For Hannah, Max and Deb (JC)

For Rosie, Tom, Camilla, Lyndsey, Laurie and to the
memory of Tony (1949–2015) (CL)

For Benjamin, Emily, Nathaniel, and Nadia (UM)

CONTENTS

List of figures   xi
About the authors   xiii
Acknowledgements   xv

1 **Introduction: What is Human Thinking and How Does it Develop?**   **1**

1.1 What is this book about? A quick survey of the following chapters   2
1.2 Criticism, debate, and worldviews   4
1.3 Views of knowledge: constructivism   10
Summary and conclusion   10

2 **The Role of Biology in Psychological Development**   **13**

2.1 Nature, nurture, and forms of interaction   15
2.2 Genetics, epigenetics, and developmental psychobiological systems 26
2.3 Neuroconstructivism: shaping neural pathways through experience   29
2.4 Relations between psychology and neuroscience   31
Summary and conclusion   33

3 **Constructivist Approaches to Children's Thinking**   **35**

3.1 Piaget's biography and his quest: how does knowledge develop?   37
3.2 Four factors in development   42
3.3 Developmental progress: Piaget's equilibration theory   43
3.4 Understanding Piaget's stages   44
3.5 Evaluating criticism of Piaget's theory   52
Summary and conclusion   58

4 Sociocultural Approaches to Children's Thinking   61

4.1 The social origin of the mind   61
4.2 Sociocultural approaches: Lev Vygotsky   62
4.3 Research evaluating Vygotsky's hypotheses   70
4.4 Vygotsky and Piaget   77
Summary and conclusion   79

**5 The Development of Communication and Social Understanding
in Infancy**   81

5.1 Early steps in social processes: infant–caregiver interaction and early
development of communication   83
5.2 Sharing a focus on an object: joint visual attention   87
5.3 Following gaze direction: the eyes as windows on the soul?   89
5.4 From gaze following to gestures: the emergence of intentional
communication   91
5.5 Gestures based on head movements and signing   95
Summary and conclusions   96

6 Theories of Communication and Social Understanding in Infancy 99

6.1 Beginning with the individual   100
6.2 Beginning with social activity: 'In the beginning is the deed' 109
6.3 Imitation, culture, and pointing   117
Summary and conclusions   119

7 Animal Communication and Human Language   121

7.1 The evolution of meaning and language   122
7.2 Can animals be taught languages?   129
7.3 Implications of research on animal communication: the role of meaning   139
Summary and conclusions   141

8 Language in Human Communication and Thinking   143

8.1 Theories of language   145
8.2 Continuing debates between followers and critics of Chomsky   148
8.3 The child's search for meaning in language   157
8.4 The meaning of meaning   160
Summary and conclusion   163

9   How Children Learn the Meaning of Words   **167**

9.1 Grasping the meaning of words   167
9.2 What do babies need to know before they can learn words?   168
9.3 Theories of word learning   177
9.4 The social-pragmatic account of early word learning   181
Summary and conclusion   186

10   How Children Come to Control Their Behaviour   **189**

10.1 Executive function: the skills and how they fit together   191
10.2 Methodological issues in the analysis of executive function   196
10.3 The nature of executive function: biological and social explanations   200
10.4 Theoretical issues   207
Summary and conclusion   209

11   Understanding the Social World   **213**

11.1 A brief history: from perspective taking to false belief understanding   215
11.2 Further development in social understanding: beyond (false) belief?   217
11.3 Theories of social cognitive development   222
11.4 Recent research and two current theoretical debates   225
11.5 Social cognitive neuroscience: neurons and knowledge   229
Summary and conclusion   239

12   Social Interaction, Language, and Social Understanding   **243**

12.1 The influence of the social context   244
12.2 Language and social understanding   251
12.3 Language, minds, and social understanding: theoretical issues   258
12.4 Social understanding and children's social lives   262
Summary and conclusions   266

13   Moral Reasoning and Action   **269**

13.1. What is morality?   270
13.2 The dimensions of morality   272
13.3 Jean Piaget's theory of moral development   275
13.4 Lawrence Kohlberg's theory of moral development   279
13.5 Criticisms of Kohlberg's theory   285
13.6 Social-cognitive domain theory   290
Summary and conclusions   292

14 Recent Issues in Moral Development **295**

14.1 Emotions and morality 296
14.2 Morality and neuroscience 301
14.3 Evolution and morality 305
14.4 The development of prosocial behaviour: helping and cooperating 307
Summary and overall conclusions 314

References 321
Subject Index 375
Author Index 381

LIST OF FIGURES

5.1	Reid & Striano's (2005) study	88
5.2	Amanda Woodward's attention task	91
6.1	The modelling of the three facial gestures in Meltzoff and Moore's 1977 study of 12- to 21-day-old infants	104
6.2	Two of the conditions in Povinelli's research with chimpanzees	107
7.1	Demonstration by Georgia Tech University of Computing	127
7.2	Kanzi examining a network of lexigrams	133
10.1	Six boxes test for working memory	191
10.2	Materials used for the Day-Night task (Gerstadt, Hong, & Diamond, 1994)	192
10.3	Typical materials used for the card-sort task	193
10.4	The Tower of London task	194
10.5	The 'unity with diversity' model of executive function (Miyake et al., 2000)	195
10.6	An EEG net with 128 channels	202
11.1	Jastrow's duck-rabbit	221

ABOUT THE AUTHORS

Jeremy I. M. Carpendale is Professor of Developmental Psychology at Simon Fraser University, Canada. He has published in the areas of cognitive, social cognitive, and moral development. His work focuses on the nature and development of thinking about social and moral matters and the role of language and social interaction in such development. He is author of *How Children Develop Social Understanding* (2006 with C. Lewis) and editor of several books, including *Social Life and Social Knowledge: Toward a Process Account of Development* (2008 with U. Müller, N. Budwig, & B. Sokol), *The Cambridge Companion to Piaget* (2009 with U. Müller & L. Smith), and *Self- and Social-Regulation: Social Interaction and the Development of Social Understanding and Executive Functions* (2010 with B. Sokol, U. Müller, A. Young, & G. Iarocci).

Charlie Lewis is Professor of Family and Developmental Psychology at Lancaster University, United Kingdom. His research focuses on both preschoolers' social cognitive skills and the influence of family factors on the nature and development of these skills. He has written or edited 16 books and several research papers on cognitive, social cognitive, and social development not only in typical children, but also in atypical populations, particularly children with autism. His current research includes studies on the development of executive function skills in preschoolers and children with developmental difficulties.

Ulrich Müller is a Professor of life-span development in the Department of Psychology at the University of Victoria. He currently serves as Department Chair. His research focuses on the development of self-regulation, the contribution of self-regulation to psychological adjustment and academic achievement, and the impact of parent–child interaction on the development of self-regulation. He was awarded the Early Scientific

Achievement Award from the Society of Research in Child Development in 2005. He has published widely in journals such as *Child Development*, *Developmental Psychology*, and the *Journal of Experimental Child Psychology*. He is co-editor of several books, including the *Cambridge Companion to Piaget* (2009), *Self-Regulation and Auto*nomy (2013), *Social Life and Social Knowledge* (2008), and the prestigious *Handbook of Child Psychology and Developmental Sciences, Vol. 2: Cognitive Processes* (7th edition, 2015).

ACKNOWLEDGEMENTS

Many people have contributed in diverse ways to this book. We especially want to thank Rosie Smith for her careful reading of the chapters. We have learned from colleagues too numerous to name but in particular Jeremy would like to acknowledge Michael Chapman, Michael Chandler, and Denis Krebs. Charlie was inspired by John and Elizabeth Newson and John Shotter. Both Jeremy and Ulrich would like to acknowledge Bill Overton. We thank Katie Twomey for her analysis of Chapter 9. Questions from our students as well as colleagues have been very helpful in fully articulating the views in the book. We also want to thank the parents and children who generously participated in our research. In particular, we want to acknowledge inspiration from our children who continually remind us of both the complexity of development and the enjoyment of human engagement. Jeremy would like to acknowledge the influence of discussions with Deb O'Connor.

INTRODUCTION: WHAT IS HUMAN THINKING AND HOW DOES IT DEVELOP?

LEARNING OUTCOMES

By the end of this chapter you should:

- Be aware of the topics covered in this book.
- Understand that theories are based on sets of preconceptions.
- Understand the differences between the two worldviews on which many theories are based.
- Be aware of the complexity of how knowledge is acquired and the constructivist view of this process.

As humans we can plan for the future and reflect on the past with pride or regret. We can talk to others about topics ranging from the weather and gossip about friends to the state of the world and what we can do about it. We can reflect on our role in society and how we might improve life for others. How is all of this possible? Although other species are intelligent in many ways, they do not seem to engage in such complex activities. How is it that we as humans have come to understand something about our universe and the life history of stars, as well as reflect on our own intelligence? This is the overall question we explore with its many dimensions. How do human forms of thinking develop? This question, or at least some aspects of it, motivates the careers of many scientists. We will address aspects of this question in our book.

Humans like to think of themselves as a very successful species because they have spread across all of the continents on the planet, and thrived in diverse environments. There is a common perspective that the evolutionary process led from lower to higher forms of life, culminating in human beings, who are ranked on top of all these forms of life. Yet, it is difficult to establish criteria for success and evolutionary progress (for a discussion see Nee, 2005; Rosslenbroich, 2006). It also remains to be seen how long term our success will be, or whether we will continue to ignore signs that we are rapidly making our environment inhospitable for us. Whether humans turn out to be a flash in the pan, destroying what we need to live, is debatable. Kurt Vonnegut (1991, p. xi), the author of several bestselling novels, was not optimistic. He suggested that 'If flying-saucer creatures or angels or whatever were to come here in a hundred years, say, and find us gone like the dinosaurs, what might be a good message for humanity to leave for them, maybe carved in great big letters on a Grand Canyon wall? Here is this old poop's suggestion: WE PROBABLY COULD HAVE SAVED OURSELVES, BUT WERE TOO DAMNED LAZY TO TRY VERY HARD ...' (original emphasis). As humans we have used our cognitive abilities to construct technologies that have advanced our ability to rapidly change our environment. But we don't always consider the consequences.

Fundamental to our argument in each chapter is that it is important to take a developmental perspective in order to fully explain aspects of being human such as thinking, language, perception, emotion, and abnormal behaviour. To study development is not to assume that skills come online and need no explanation. The processes involved help us to understand the origins and nature of skills like thinking. There are also practical implications that follow from understanding typical development because this can shed light on cases where there are problems with development as well as having implications for education.

1.1 WHAT IS THIS BOOK ABOUT? A QUICK SURVEY OF THE FOLLOWING CHAPTERS

This book examines key theories and research on how children's thinking develops. A way to frame this question is in terms of how the world comes to be meaningful for children through their biologically embodied interaction with the world and other people (Marshall, 2016). This broad question divides into multiple issues, and we bring out the significance of developmental changes in childhood by organising this book around a series of questions. Questions or problems always come first for scientists, and the same should hold in education. We feel that students need to know why a problem is important. In fact, we often need to be reminded of the significance of everyday experience: this is because 'It would hardly be fish who discovered the existence of water' (Kluckhohn, 1949, p. 11). Fish are supported by and immersed in water, and therefore would take it for granted without noticing it, just as we humans live *in* language, social interaction, and culture, and, therefore, may have difficulty noticing these aspects of our lives. We take aspects of our world like language for granted, so it is hard to reflect on how language actually works. Ironically, it actually takes skill to notice what is always right in front of us.

We review topics that are usually considered separately, like cognitive development, infant communication, language, social cognitive development, and moral development. This separation of topics follows from a particular theoretical framework, or set of presuppositions, according to which each is viewed as separable from the rest. From our perspective, however, they are fundamentally interrelated and should be presented together. Indeed we go further, to argue that thinking cannot be adequately explained by only focusing on individual minds because the very ablty to think is socially constituted. By this we mean that when we talk about the development of thinking we highlight the crucial role of social interaction, charged by emotion, in this process. The sequence of chapters which follows attempts to unravel the interrelations among the topics covered, as well as describing the research in each 'area' of understanding. Yes, we discuss topics like 'language' or 'moral reasoning' in separate chapters, but we affirm here that we treat these as being part of the same process.

To reflect upon how approaches to development differ, in this chapter we discuss the preconceptions on which two contrasting worldviews are based. We do so by briefly describing the focus of the forthcoming chapters. These sets of preconceptions or views regarding the nature and development of knowledge are referred to as worldviews (Overton, 1991; Overton & Reese, 1973). Any theory in psychology is based on assumptions about our biological level of functioning, but these can originate in radically different theoretical frameworks. In order to evaluate current claims it is necessary to know something about recent developments in biology, which we discuss in Chapter 2. According to a popular claim, infants are born with ready-made ways of thinking. By contrast, current work in biology suggests that this is implausible. Instead, because of the large extent of plasticity in human neural development, ways of thinking and neural pathways are shaped through experience. Therefore, it is essential to study the dynamic interplay between biological functioning and sociocultural context, and to investigate the role of the child's activity in cognitive development. This leads to the chapters on cognitive development in which we review relevant theories dealing with the development of knowledge.

A question that arises from this discussion concerns the nature and development of meaning on which human thinking is based. In the first group of chapters (3 and 4), we examine how infants and young children come to understand the world in their everyday lives. They do so by learning how to interact and how to interpret others' contributions to interaction. We focus on a theory which has dominated developmental psychology over the past ninety years but which has been misunderstood and played down in recent years. This theory considers how knowledge and thinking develop within the child's everyday experience. As a result, it takes an action-based, embodied approach to understand how the emergence of knowledge and thinking must be viewed in terms of the individual's interactions with the world. It begins with simple sensory and motor activity as well as very primitive feelings and experience with others. We then broaden the focus to consider the role of wider social processes in the child's construction of knowledge. In this discussion we will raise questions such as the importance of preschoolers' talk to themselves in order to reflect on how this might provide insights into how cognitive development takes place.

If social experience is vital in cognitive development how does this process occur? The next group of chapters (5–8) home in on the development of communication and language. To understand how this happens we return in each chapter to views of meaning and its development. This section starts with how infants come to master communicative skills involving gestures such as pointing (Chapters 5 and 6). We continue by review-ing research and theories on language development, using animal communication as a means to investigate the nature of human languages (Chapter 7). The next two chapters (8 and 9) then examine how learning to use sentences and grasp the meaning of words is part of the process by which young children make sense of everyday interactions.

The analysis of language development provides a platform for the next topic, which is how children develop higher-order cognitive processes, currently referred to as executive function (Chapter 10). This is often studied as a window into the workings of the mind-brain system. Yet we suggest that if we wish to understand how children come to gain high-level control over their actions, we need to examine the social constitution of these executive function skills.

In the next group of two chapters (11 and 12) we consider children's thinking about the social world. This is often termed 'social cognition', but recent research on this topic has labelled it 'theory of mind'. However, we prefer the more theoretically neutral description, 'the development of social understanding'. In reviewing research on how children develop social understanding it is important to consider the evidence of strong links to language. Making sense of this research requires examining conceptions of mind and meaning. A crucially important aspect of the vast topic of social understanding is morality – concerning how we treat others. Moral development is the topic of the last two chapters in the book (13 and 14), where we discuss what morality is and how it develops.

It is our conviction that, in order to understand development more fully, we need to approach it from a multidisiplinary perspective. Humans are both biological entities and a highly social species. Consequently, in this book we draw on many other disciplines in addition to developmental psychology, including cognitive science, philosophy, linguis-tics, biology, neuroscience, evolutionary theory, primatology, sociology, anthropology, and history.

1.2 CRITICISM, DEBATE, AND WORLDVIEWS

In each of the various areas of research reviewed in this book, there is by no means com-mon agreement about the interpretation of the empirical evidence. Instead, competing theories have been proposed to explain the research findings, and there is thus consid-erable debate. A careful and critical evaluation of research and theoretical positions is crucial to the scientific enterprise because science is about testing ideas as well as adding to knowledge. The way to build on others' thinking is through careful analysis, which can involve criticism, correction and extension. In the words of Alexander Pope:

> Trust not yourself; but your defects to know,
>
> Make use of every friend – and every foe
>
> *(Essay on Criticism*, 1711, Part II, p. 69)

In other words, critics help in building sound theories by pointing out flaws that need to be addressed. Historians (Kuhn, 1962) and philosophers of science (Popper, 1934/59) have long pointed out that science is a process of continued questioning of competing theories and hypotheses. Developmental psychology is no exception to this rule.

When you come to analyse the theories that we describe, it is essential to be aware of the assumptions on which they are based. Theories are based on sets of preconceptions, known as worldviews. It is important to be aware of these assumptions and the fact that they should be critically evaluated.

For over a century (indeed much longer) 'popular' accounts of psychology have depicted development as either the unfolding of inborn or 'innate' skills, or as a blank slate upon which behaviours are shaped by parents and caregivers. We group these together into one worldview because contemporary nativist and empiricist theories view the mind as funda-mentally passive. The mind is conceived of as being a container for mental contents (e.g. beliefs, ideas, representations). The content arrives in the mind through a causal process: the input (e.g. sensory stimulation) triggers a causal process that activates the mental content, which, in turn, causes an output (e.g. movements). A person's mental contents, or ideas, are just the effects of stimuli external to the mind and the mechanical operations or com-putations triggered by those stimuli. Meaning resides in the mental content; it needs to be accessed by the individual and can then be shared with others. Empiricist and nativist theo-ries lack the idea of an active agent who produces meaning in his or her interactions with the world; the 'person as agent becomes superfluous' (Judge, 1985, p. 51). Sharing the assump-tion that the mind is passive, the difference between empiricist and nativist approaches then boils down to the issue of whether the computational machinery that intervenes between input and output is innate or learned based on experience.

Both nativism and empiricism start from the taken-for-granted adult experience of hav-ing a mind that is private and accessible only to the self. Meaning is encapsulated in the mental content of the individual mind. From a developmental perspective, the problem that the child then faces is how to understand and communicate with others. This perspec-tive has various names. It has been referred to as Cartesian after the philosopher René Descartes (1641/1960), who famously articulated this position in a series of 'meditations' or reflections on the mind. However, this view has an even longer history and can be traced back to Saint Augustine's *Confessions* written a thousand years before Descartes (Wills, 2001). Augustine (354–430 CE) wrote about what he imagined had been his experience when he was an infant. He claimed to recall that he faced the problem of trying to communicate his desires such as his hunger to others. What Augustine referred to is nowadays known as an individualistic or cognitive perspective. This is based on the assumption that the starting point of development is the individual's subjective experience. Given subjective experience, the individual must infer and construct his or her understanding of others and the world. This perspective has been termed 'a split position' because it assumes that the child is encapsulated in his or her own subjective experience and thus separated from others and the world (Overton, 2015). The problem that follows from these starting assumptions concerns how to figure out that the other bodies observed also have minds like oneself. This is known as 'the problem of other minds' in philosophy. For example, this problem arises for Descartes (1596–1650) when one had to figure out whether the sight of something that looked like a person was really a human being or just an automaton (which were very popular in his lifetime):

> So I may by chance look out of a window and notice some men passing in the street, at the sight of whom I do not fail to say that I see men …. And nevertheless: what do I see from this window except hats and cloaks which could cover automata? (Descartes, 1960, p. 89: first published in 1641)

A next step is to assume that this problem from philosophy is exactly the problem that young children face in coming to understand their social world. This is a taken-for-granted, static, approach and it results in various theories regarding how children come to understand their social world (see Chapters 5, 10 and 11). This set of preconceptions affects the way all of the topics in this book are investigated.

The Saint Augustine/Cartesian/split/cognitivist approach assumes that there is already a world, adult-like and ready-made, that the child then has to make sense of from a somewhat detached perspective, like an interested observer. This is epitomised by the frequent references to the idea of the child-as-scientist (Gopnik, 1996), in which the detached child observer makes hypotheses about the world. This individualistic approach has been common in psychology and many, but certainly not all, approaches in cognitive science. If the mind already exists ready-made then this not completely a developmental approach, because the child is assumed to be a scientist from the start.

The second, contrasting, range of theories is based on an alternative worldview beginning from the assumption that the person is always actively directed to and immersed in the world. According to this view, mental contents are not something that occur to the person because they are triggered by some input, but instead the person actively creates these contents in the context of his or her goal-directed pursuits. Furthermore, by virtue of being related to the world, the person is also always directed toward others, and meaning and mental content emerge in the context of social interaction that revolves around objects in the world. Proponents of this view suggest that development starts with the infant's actions or interactions because, they argue, it is inappropriate to presuppose that the newborn infant can 'think'. In order to understand how cognitive processes develop, it is essential to start with the baby's actions in the physical world. Later gestural communication develops as infants learn about their social world. Language is then built on this early communication and linked to the development of social understanding, including moral development. Such approaches are less well represented in most textbooks.

One way to introduce this alternative worldview is to consider Donald Winnicott's (1964) famous statement that there is no such thing as a baby. His point in making this apparently outlandish claim is that the baby does not and cannot exist in isolation. Instead, she is embedded in a complex web of interrelations with other people – indeed these are vital for the infant's very survival. Parents and other caregivers structure the new baby's life (although by crying, fussing, and filling diapers [nappies] babies also structure their parents' time). So Winnicott's point is that it becomes difficult to draw a clear boundary between parent and child (he wrote exclusively about the mother as he lived in a more sexually divided and sexist historical period). For example, the infant's line of vision and her focus of attention is determined by how she is held. This experience results in her learning about certain aspects of her world and this, of course, shapes her neurological development. From this perspective we write about bi-directional processes in which each actor (e.g. parent and child) influences the other's actions and elicits particular experiences (e.g. an infant looking at the adult's eyes may elicit a busy parent's interaction, albeit unknowingly).

From this perspective, infants develop an understanding of the world within their embodied interaction with the physical and social world. Over repeated episodes they develop expectations about what will happen in particular interactions. That is, they learn the interactive potential of their world, including that of other people. Thus, they anticipate how others will respond to their actions and they learn how to coordinate their actions, like cooing, with parents, and engage in the turn-taking sequences of language. Taking the infant's action and interaction as a starting point, these theories are based on what is often termed 'a process-relational worldview'. They are also referred to as action-based, constructivist, relational, embodied, enactive, or interactive theories. We tend to label this approach as 'a relational developmental systems perspective', partly because of the link to developmental systems theory in biology. This is an attempt to avoid the dictomomy between biological and social factors discussed further in the next chapter.

To sum up the section so far: many authorities in developmental psychology argue that the first worldview described above is a taken-for-granted perspective of seeing babies as separate from the world (Lerner, Agans, DeSouza, & Hershberg, 2014: Overton, 2015). The second perspective (process-relational) is that taken by a researcher who has stepped out of the armchair/philosopher perspective to look closely at what is actually happening. That is why the focus is on the process of how we can explain the outcome. Thus, the second perspective would describe the philosophical assumptions of the first as 'adultocentric' as it posits a baby (or child or adult) as somewhat detached from the world. The second perspective depicts itself as more complex and embedded in social relationships, and it is the worldview we emphasise in this book.

Let us illustrate how topics look from these two contrasting perspectives. Suppose we consider one of the topics in this book: how children learn about other people and develop social understanding. Well, one idea might be that babies see other people walking around doing things and they have to figure out that these bodies are not just robots and that they have minds and thoughts just like the baby's own thoughts. That is, it is assumed that infants face the problem described by Descartes in the quotation cited above – 'the problem of other minds'. For philosophers this might seem reasonable and it is a common view based on ancient ideas. But it assumes the infant or child has knowledge of their own inner states, a first-person, subjective experience, and the problem they are faced with is figuring out other people. This perspective is taken by Temple Grandin (e.g. 1986) in an exercise to understand her own autism.

However, if the baby is trying to figure out other people and perhaps wonders if they also have minds, then this perspective actually already implicitly assumes that the baby has a mind and can think to begin with. So it has already been smuggled in the mind when that is what it was supposed to explain. In fact, the whole way of setting up the problem the baby faces also smuggles in possible answers. This is why it is essential to examine the assumptions that theorists begin with. If we just begin from those assumptions without examining them we are doing philosophy and theory, but it is just invisible.

Another topic with which to illustrate the contrast between worldviews is the development of communication, a crucial and central topic in this book and in understanding human development. In studying the development of communication we could ask, 'what is communication for?' The obvious answer might seem to be 'to express ourselves!' However, we should more cautiously recognise that this already presupposes a mind with something to say, something to express. So this sidesteps the actual problem of explaining development. As described in Chapter 5, from the perspective of the process-relational worldview, the development of communication can be explained through the increasing coordination of activity between infant and adult.

The two families of theories, or worldviews, also differ significantly regarding the role biology is assumed to play. For example, there have been many recent claims that knowledge and thinking are innate or 'hardwired'. In order to be able to critically evaluate such claims we will review recent work on genetics, neuroscience, and evolutionary theory in the next chapter. Such work suggests that it is a long process to get from genes to thinking, and that claims of thinking being 'hardwired' may not be biologically plausible. This suggests that the meaning of the term 'innate' needs to be more carefully examined. From the perspective of the second group of theories, biology plays an equally important, but different, role. From this perspective, the meaning on which human forms of thinking is based emerges from social activity, and therefore cannot be purely individual. Biology plays a crucial role in these approaches in structuring the experience through which children develop, and patterns of neural interconnectivity are formed within such activity. In other words, the point is not simply a rejection of an individualistic approach to be replaced by purely social approach, which is equally problematic. Instead a third option is a relational constructivist approach in which biology and social levels are interwoven and cannot be clearly separated. In the context of biology, this approach is referred to as Developmental Systems Theory. From this perspective, the biological characteristics of the human infant elicit the social and emotional interactivity in which humans develop.

In explaining the development of children's thinking, a relational developmental systems approach includes all levels from the biology of genetics and neuroscience to the forms of interaction children are engaged in – this is a cell-to-society, and genes-to-justice approach. This sort of approach is becoming influential in cognitive science in general. It is present in developmental psychology, both in classical theories and current approaches, but it is under-represented in most textbooks (Lerner et al., 2014: Overton, 2015). The idea of a system has a long history. For example, there are roots in Aristotle's view that the whole is more than the sum of its parts. This developmental approach also has a long tradition in the history of ideas with classic developmental theorists such as James Mark Baldwin, Heinz Werner, Jean Piaget, and Lev Vygotsky, as well as philosophers such as Charles Sanders Peirce, George Herbert Mead, and Ludwig Wittgenstein (see Bernstein, 2010; Overton, 2015).

Unfortunately, it is difficult to use only one name to refer to these two contrasting worldviews because any of these terms can be, and have been, used in multiple ways. Cognitivists describe themselves as constructivists, and individualists label relational-process thinkers as individualistic. Therefore, readers must gain some understanding of the two worldviews so that they can recognise these approaches independently of the labels used.

The centrality of relations can be found in a number of theoretical perspectives. In Western scholarship the focus tends to be on individualism and independence rather than interdependence, but at the same time the theme of the importance of communities and social networks can also be seen (Sprintzen, 2009). A relational approach is more central from the perspective of a Canadian First Nations worldview and approach to justice in terms of restoring healthy relationships (Ross, 2006). A relational view of justice has important implications for the law (Llwellyn, 2016), and a relational approach can also be applied to social policy and practice (Hankivsky, 2004).

Although there is concensus that social interaction is important, there are two ways of thinking about interaction. The first is that the starting point is the pre-existing environment and individual which then interact. In contrast, the second is that development is based on many levels of bi-directionally interacting factors and the environment and individual do not pre-exist separate from each other, instead, they mutually create each other. That is, from a relational perspective interaction is primary. From the perspective we take, children determine their environments due to their sensitivities, and their actions bring forth or elicit aspects of the environment in which they develop skills. These skills, in turn, can elicit more complex experience in which the child develops further.

We acknowledge that in grouping theories into two large families we are simplifying, and that in fact the situation is not so black and white. However, for our purposes here of introducing theories and worldviews we feel that it is a useful first step in learning about the development of thinking.

1.3 VIEWS OF KNOWLEDGE: CONSTRUCTIVISM

The two worldviews described above also entail contrasting views of knowledge, that is of how children come to understand the world they experience. Why should developmental psychologists be concerned with views of knowledge? Isn't it obvious that we just look at things and we learn about them? Although we have the experience of doing this, it is misleading and neglects the process infants may go through to develop such experience. This view that learning about the world is just a simple passive process of seeing follows from the individualist theories that we have described above, and is what the American pragmatist philosopher and educationalist John Dewey (for discussion see Bernstein, 2010, Chapter 3), criticised and labelled a 'spectator theory of knowledge'. It is also similar to what the Swiss scholar Jean Piaget (e.g. 1970) referred to as a 'copy theory of knowledge', That is, the idea that we learn about the world through passively forming copies of it. Reality is impressed on the mind – like the impression of light on the photosensitive film in a camera, or an impression on a wax tablet. The knower comes to understand the world simply through observation.

Children do learn about the world they encounter and they are born with important potentials for interacting with this world and learning. We do get better at interacting in the world. We do not constantly bump into things, for example, and our understanding of the spaces we move through is the result of several developmental achievements. We have learned through experience what happens as we act in the world. This view of how knowledge develops is *constructivism.* The child actively constructs the known world; the knower assimilates her experience to structures (i.e. repeats old skills and routines in different circumstances) and also accommodates (i.e. learns new ways of overcoming intellectual challenges). For example, a baby playing with a simple object such as a cup can discover what she can do with it. She can hold on to it and bring it to her mouth to suck and she begins to understand the cup in terms of these actions, of what she can do with the object, and so when she sees it she can anticipate the potential actions and results. The world is known through the organisation of activity (e.g. Müller, Overton, & Sokol, 1998). These views of knowledge and representation (i.e. how we acquire knowledge of the world) will be important in the rest of the book.

SUMMARY AND CONCLUSION

We have introduced the topics to be covered in the following chapters in this book. In reviewing these areas of research we introduce the various relevant theories, and discuss the debates surrounding them. We point out that these theories are based on sets of pre-conceptions, or worldviews, and theories can be evaluated based on the assumptions they start with. The theories in each topic area can be usefully grouped into two contrasting families. These worldviews underlie theories in each of the topic areas to be covered so they will come up again and again.

One worldview on which a family of theories is based starts from individual minds and then attempts to explain how such minds come to know about each other and the world. The contrasting process relational worldview starts from individuals in relation to others, and thus begins from the social process. From this relational developmental systems perspective the task is to describe how communication and minds emerge from this social process. This approach explains the mind in terms of thinking as the outcome of a social process.

FURTHER READING

Jopling, D. (1993). Cognitive science, other minds, and the philosophy of dialogue. In U. Neisser (ed.), *The Perceived Self* (pp. 290–309). Cambridge, MA: MIT Press.

Lerner, R. M., Agans, J. P., DeSouza, L. M., & Hershberg, R. M. (2014). Developmental science in 2025: A predictive review. *Research in Human Development, 11,* 255–272.

Marshall, P. J. (2016). Embodiment and human development. *Child Development Perspectives, 10,* 245–250.

2 THE ROLE OF BIOLOGY IN PSYCHOLOGICAL DEVELOPMENT

LEARNING OUTCOMES

By the end this chapter you should:

- Understand the debate regarding the roles of nature and nurture in development and views regarding how to resolve that debate.
- Be able to evaluate the biological plausibility of claims of innate knowledge, including whether cats raised with rats are good at hunting rats.
- Have an understanding of the role of genes in the human developmental system.
- Be aware of the study of epigenetics, regarding how genes are expressed, and the new field of sociogenomics concerning social influences on gene expression.
- Understand the distinction between predetermined and probabilistic epigenesis.
- Be aware of plasticity in brain development.
- Understand that genes don't completely determine brain development but, instead, neural pathways are shaped through experience.
- Be able to think about the relations between psychology and neuroscience, and the role of the brain in thinking.
- Be able to evaluate neuroscience approaches to development, contrasting approaches that interpret the brain as an information-processing device with current arguments and evidence that perception is best understood as action plans in the brain, consistent with an action-based constructivist approach.

One of John Lennon's teeth was recently purchased for over 30,000 dollars by a dentist who later revealed that he hopes to clone Lennon if DNA can be extracted from the tooth. He then plans to give guitar lessons to the cloned Lennon (*Rolling Stone*, 21 August 2013). Lennon had given an extracted molar, probably a wisdom tooth, to his housekeeper for disposal, but she kept it in her family and it was auctioned many years later (*Daily Mail*, 9 April 2014; *Huffington Post*, 25 August 2013). There are difficult ethical and legal issues with the plan to clone John Lennon and, ironically, even if this were possible, his well-known rebelliousness might well put an end to these carefully laid plans. But this story is of interest here because this idea does seem to follow from widespread claims made in the popular press about genes, and even in the scientific literature about innate abilities and 'hardwired' traits. This chapter is about why this whole process of getting from genes to the adult person is much more complex, and how a host of biological as well as social factors in addition to genes are crucial in understanding human development.

There are many current claims regarding the role of biology in explaining the development of thinking, and in order to understand and evaluate these positions, it is necessary to know something about current work in biology. This knowledge is essential in evaluating recent positions that appear to have a biological basis, such as claims regarding innate knowledge. We consider the biological plausibility of such views in light of current genetics and neuroscience.

It would be misleading to entitle this chapter 'Biological Approaches to Psychology' because any theory in psychology requires a biological side to the story. Theories, however, can differ radically in how these relations are conceptualised. The two worldviews (sets of philosophical preconceptions) introduced in the previous chapter influence thinking about biology in two ways that we discuss in this chapter. The first issue concerns the nature and development of human thinking and whether it is possible for knowledge and forms of thinking to be innate. From the perspective of the cognitivist or individualist worldview, claims are made that some aspects of knowledge are innate. In contrast, from the developmental or process-relational position, it is argued that forms of thinking develop. It is essential to be aware of the shift in biology in the last several decades. Developmental science is currently experiencing a shift in ways of thinking, moving away from a gene-focused view of instinct and innate knowledge, toward tracing the development of forms of activity and thinking emerging from biological characteristics in a bi-directional interaction with multiple levels of environment (Greenberg, 2014b; Lickliter & Honeycutt, 2015). Even a rudimentary understanding of genetics seems to indicate that it is an incredibly complex process in getting from genes to thinking and there is nothing predetermined in this process (Fisher, 2006; Meaney, 2010).

The second issue concerns the role of the brain in thinking. Obviously, the brain is essential in explaining human thinking. But given this, it is still possible to interpret the role of the brain in cognition in contrasting ways from the perspectives of different worldviews.

The cognitivist perspective assimilates neuroscience to the information-processing and computational view of the mind, according to which the brain is assumed to process input. The result is an output that we refer to as conscious experience or action. From the developmental or relational-process perspective, the brain as part of the nervous system is the organ that expands and makes more complex the child's relation to the world and allows for learning about the interactive potential of the world.

2.1 NATURE, NURTURE, AND FORMS OF INTERACTION

How thinking develops is the problem we grapple with in this book. In explaining the human ability to think, answers tend to fall into two types, focusing either on biological or social factors – nature or nurture. The study of human development is often cast in terms of a contrast between nature and nurture, a debate that was already ongoing among the ancient Greeks in the fourth and fifth centuries BCE (Karmiloff-Smith, 2015). Use of the terms and the separation between nature and nurture can be traced to 1582 when a British teacher, Richard Mulcaster, discussed the ways in which they work collaboratively in child development (West & King, 1987). That collaborative notion, however, was transformed when Sir Francis Galton (1822–1911), Darwin's cousin, set the terms in opposition to one another (i.e. nature vs nurture). This is the way they are more commonly conceptualised (Spencer et al., 2009). It is also part of how we often talk about children's characteristics concerning what they are born with compared to what they have learned.

Unfortunately, innateness is a rather ill-defined term that can have very different meanings. For example, Matteo Mameli and Patrick Bateson (2006) discuss 26 different definitions of innateness. Broadly, the most important conceptualisations in this context are that a trait can be considered innate (a) if it is not learned; (b) if it is present at birth; (c) if it is genetically determined; and (d) if it is highly heritable. However, as Mameli and Bateson show, none of these definitions identifies a coherent concept of innateness. The fact that a trait is present at birth does not rule out that it has been acquired in the course of prenatal development (Gottlieb, 1997; Spencer et al., 2009). The idea that innateness means that a trait is genetically determined is also too simplistic 'because no phenotype is such that only genes are needed for its development. Genes by themselves don't do anything' (Mameli & Bateson, 2006, p. 158). The idea that innateness implies a lack of learning suffers from the fact that learning is a diffuse and ill-defined notion. The problem with the idea of heritability is that it refers to the variability of a trait in a given population at a particular point in time. As a consequence, traits that are invariant in a population (e.g. walking on two legs) cannot be innate, and changes to the composition of the population can change the heritability of the trait in an organism – both notions that run counter to what we usually imagine when we think that some trait is innate.

Notwithstanding problems with the definition of innateness, the roles of nature and nurture in development remain a hot and controversial topic. Researchers argue that a particular amount of individual differences in a trait is genetic (Friedman et al., 2008), that a gene for a particular trait or disorder has been identified (Gopnik, 1990), and that a specific skill emerges so early in development or is so complex that it could not possibly be learned (Margolis & Laurence, 2013). Even though most researchers would assume that both nature and nurture play some role in development, there is still considerable difference between positions regarding how to conceptualise their relative importance and how to relate them to each other. On one hand, there are those who argue that it makes sense to quantify the contribution of genes compared to environment to individual differences in a trait (Plomin & Simpson, 2013). This field of study is called behaviour genetics or quantitative genetics, and uses research designs such twin and adoption studies. On the other hand, some maintain that it is not meaningful to separate genes and environment in order to calculate their relative contribution to individual differences because the two are inextricably linked (Meaney, 2010).

A different approach to studying the influence of nature on development is taken by molecular genetics, a field of study for the investigation of how DNA segments are associated with psychological characteristics. A number of different approaches are used to link heritable traits to variation in DNA. For example, linkage analysis tries to find variants of DNA sequence (markers) that co-occur with the presence of a disease in families with both affected and unaffected members. Linkage analysis has been successfully employed in the case of disorders that are caused by single mutations that have large effects (e.g. Huntington's disease, which emerges in middle age and leads to rapid cognitive decline and death), but it has not been successfully employed for more complex disorders that involve many genes with more modest effects (e.g. schizophrenia). A more powerful method to discover genes associated with particular traits or disorders is the genome-wide association (GWA) study. GWA studies use DNA microarrays containing probes for a million or more single-nucleotide polymorphisms (SNPs); nucleotides are the basic building blocks of DNA. Even though GWA studies have identified new locations of DNA sequence that are related to complex physical traits and disorders, the amount of variance explained by SNPs is rather small across studies, and SNPs identified for cognitive abilities and personality traits do not replicate across studies (Manuck & McCaffery, 2014). The small amount of variance explained by SNPs (even taken together, all relevant SNPs rarely explain 10% of variance in trait variation) has led to some disillusionment among proponents of molecular genetics. The difference between the small amount of variance explained by SNPs and the relatively large genetic influence (up to 80%) usually reported in behaviour genetics studies has been referred to as 'missing heritability problem' (Maher 2008). Several solutions to this problem have been suggested (Manuck & McCaffery, 2014); however, we think that it points to deep-rooted and incorrect assumptions about the functioning of genes and that a new way of thinking about the role of genes in development is required to solve this problem.

Researchers claiming that some forms of thinking are innate might appear to be providing a rigorous scientific and biological explanation of thinking. But the problem is that such claims depend on biological assumptions in getting from the functioning of genes to forms of thinking. In order to evaluate these claims, it is necessary to know something about biology. To give a bird's-eye view of the issue we can roughly group approaches to biology into two families. One is a gene-centred approach in which the claim is that forms of thinking are 'specified by our genetic program' (Pinker, 1997, p. 21). Here the idea is that genes contain a plan or program that determines developmental outcomes. Although phrases like 'genetically determined' are avoided these days, that idea may still lurk behind more ambiguous wording alluding to biological foundations or claims that infants are 'endowed' or 'equipped' with certain forms of knowledge. But the biological process resulting in whatever is being endowed tends to be left unspecified. The second approach is known as developmental systems theory, which we turn to below.

There has been considerable debate about the extent to which infants are born with knowledge ready to understand aspects of their world. Elizabeth Spelke and Katherine Kinzler (2007, p. 89) 'believe that humans are endowed with a small number of separable systems of core knowledge for representing objects, actions, number, and space', as well as possibly 'a fifth system for representing social partners' (see also Spelke, Bernier, & Skerry, 2014). Another approach also makes strong claims about thinking being innate, but argues that this thinking is more specific to solving particular problems. This approach is known as Evolutionary Psychology, according to which the human mind is claimed to consist of a large collection of innate modules that have evolved to solve particular problems that existed when humans were evolving in our ancestral environment (Cosmides & Tooby, 2013; Pinker, 1997).

Evolutionary perspectives on understanding and explaining human behaviour have been common in developmental psychology and informed the theorising of major developmental psychologists such as James Mark Baldwin (1896), Heinz Werner (1948), and Jean Piaget (1967/1971). However, what is referred to as Evolutionary Psychology is a more narrow research programme founded by Leda Cosmides and John Tooby that makes a number of problematic assumptions about the human mind and evolution. First, Evolutionary Psychology subscribes to the computational theory of mind according to which the mind is an information-processing system (a formal symbol manipulator). Second, it treats the mind as a collection of separate domain-specific, special purpose computational systems or modules. These include 'face recognition systems, a language acquisition device, mindreading systems, navigation specializations, animate motion recognition, cheater detection mechanisms, and mechanisms that govern sexual attraction' (Cosmides & Tooby, 2003, p. 63). Third, it considers the computational systems as adaptations, the result of random mutations that proved to be advantageous (i.e. enhanced fitness) and therefore were selected. Fourth, the computational systems have evolved to solve recurrent problems (e.g. food aversion, mate selection, way finding) that our ancestors, living in small hunter-gatherer bands, encountered during our evolutionary past in the Pleistocene conditions (a period that lasted approximately from 2,000,000 to 10,000 years ago), and they still guide our behaviour today, even if they may no longer offer a selective advantage in our present environment.

Evolutionary Psychology has been criticised for a variety of reasons (e.g. Sanders, 2013). First, it simply assumes that the computational mechanisms are considered as adaptations (Richardson, 2007), leaving them untestable and making further or deeper analysis very difficult. Second, the idea that the computational mechanisms are adapted to the Pleistocene has been questioned (Dupré, 2012). Third, the computational view of the mind has itself been criticised (e.g. Heil, 1981). Fourth, it has been pointed out that we do not know the world our ancestors inhabited and thus can only tell 'just-so-stories' about the recurrent problems they faced (Buller, 2005a). This characterisation is from Rudyard Kipling's (1902/1962) *Just So Stories*, a series of apocryphal children's bedtime stories purporting to explain 'how the lepoard got his spots' and 'how the camel got his hump' and so on. Finally, the empirical evidence produced by evolutionary psychologists to support their theory has been subjected to a scathing criticism (Buller, 2005a, b).

A final line of criticism directed at Evolutionary Psychology is that the notion of modularity is flawed (Prinz, 2006). The notion of modularity can be traced back to the nineteenth-century movement of phrenology and its founder Franz Joseph Gall. Gall argued that human faculties such as thinking or the love of offspring are located in particular areas of the brain and that the strength of the faculty was indicated by the size of the brain area. Gall's phrenology was soon discredited, but more recently Jerry Fodor (1983) revived the idea of modularity. According to Fodor, one essential feature of modules is that they are informationally encapsulated in that even if you know that your friend will not poke you in the eye, this information cannot stop you from automatically blinking in response to a finger approaching your eye. Although Fodor entitled his book *The Modularity of Mind*, he thought that peripheral (e.g. perception, motor processes) but not central (higher cognitive abilities such as thinking) processes are modular. Since Fodor's book, the notion has changed to include conceptual modules specialised for particular domains such as the physical world and the social world that are somewhat separate from other systems (Sperber, 1994). This position was expanded by Steven Pinker in his book *How the Mind Works*, in response to which Fodor – clearly unhappy with the idea of conceptual modules – published a book entitled *The Mind Doesn't Work that Way*. Although this is a complex debate that is difficult to summarise because there are many positions, the term is now used primarily to discuss claims of innate domain-specific knowledge, a position we evaluate in this chapter. However, the claim from Evolutionary Psychology is that these modules evolved to solve particular problems faced by our ancestors. But this assumption of the environment as presenting problems has been criticised by Richard Lewontin (1983/2001) who points out that organisms' characteristics influence the environment they experience. Furthermore, the notion of modules assumed by Evolutionary Psychology has been modelled on Chomsky's claims about language being based on an innate mechanism. However, Chris Moore (1996, p. 613) points out that it is difficult to argue that language evolved to solve a particular problem because it has many functions, such as:

Shall we have Chinese or Italian tonight? (foraging)

Has anyone ever told you you have beautiful eyes? (mating)

Look both ways before you cross the street (parenting)

NO TRESPASSING (territoriality)

In most of the areas of research covered in this book we describe how some researchers make claims about innate knowledge, that is, about infants being born with certain forms of knowledge such as concerning the social world (Gopnik & Wellman, 2012; Leslie, Friedman, & German, 2004; Onishi & Baillargeon, 2005) and morality (Bloom, 2010, 2014; Hamlin, 2013). Of course, researchers making such claims acknowledge that there must be further development. But these are still strong claims that are based on biological assumptions and therefore they need to be carefully evaluated.

Instead of being new, attempting to understand human development in terms of innate characteristics has a long history and it keeps re-emerging. The Hippocratic School of ancient Greece (i.e. followers of Hippocrates, the father of medicine, in the fifth century BCE) explained human development by assuming that the fertilised egg contains a miniature adult. This is not a truly developmental explanation because it claims that there is only an increase in size and fails to explain how structures form. Aristotle, however, questioned this and argued instead that structures gradually develop rather than being preformed. Of course, no one currently claims that there is a small person in an egg that just gets bigger, but the idea that the information for the adult is already contained in the fertilised egg in the 'genetic program' persists, and this is a variation on the ancient idea of preformationism (i.e. the belief that we are already formed and start as tiny versions of ourselves) (Lickliter & Honeycutt, 2009, 2015).

Some notion of innate knowledge or instinct has a long tradition that can be traced back at least 2,500 years to Greek literature (Beach, 1955). There is a history of this debate in various disciplines. The notion of instincts has also been long debated in psychology. In the late nineteenth century William James (1890) argued in *The Principles of Psychology* that instincts are important in understanding human psychology. The idea of innate instincts and biological maturation due to genes was thought to be a sufficient explanation for human development in the first half of the twentieth century, as proposed by Arnold Gesell (1945), but biological inheritance was rejected by John Watson (1924/1970) who emphasised learning instead. The idea of instincts to explain reoccurring patterns of activity re-emerged in ethology in the work of Konrad Lorenz and Nikolaas Tinbergen. In contrast, the biologist Daniel Lehrman (1953/2001) argued that instincts are not an adequate explanation, and, instead the development of the behaviour must be explained (a point we come back to below). In anthropology, Franz Boas and his student-colleagues Margaret Mead and Ruth Benedict also rejected instincts and emphasised the role of culture in human development (Laland & Brown, 2011). History is repeating itself, and once again claims of innate knowledge are re-emerging. This legacy still has an influence today, which is why this chapter is necessary at the beginning of the book.

It might seem reasonable to claim that babies are born with knowledge because isn't this the case with other species? A common example used by psychologists is that spiders are claimed to have innate knowledge of how to spin a web so why should it be surprising that human babies have innate knowledge? Well, ironically, claims about spiders knowing how to spin webs tend to be made with no reference to the scientific research on spiders. If we consider a group of spiders about which something is known, the story gets more complicated and more interesting. Portia spiders don't spin webs but they are known for their complex hunting strategies. Are these complex strategies innate? These spiders have tiny brains, literally the size of a pin. Their hunting behaviour is not based on innate knowledge but rather on the types of eyes they have and where these are located on their bodies. That is, the complex behaviours they exhibit have to do with the nature of their embodiment rather than innate knowledge (Barrett, 2011). So, is this ability to hunt innate? It depends on what is meant by innate. These spiders regularly show complex behaviours that emerge from their biological characteristics in interaction with their typical environments. That is, the behaviours regularly emerge in the spiders' developmental system.

Claims regarding innate knowledge rest on biological assumptions and it has long been argued that researchers making such claims should feel obliged to ensure that this assumed process is biologically plausible (Hebb, Lambert, & Tucker, 1971). However, the more that is learned about biology the less plausible a simple gene-based mechanism seems. Such claims fit with views about inheritance and brain development that were dominant in biology forty years ago. But they no longer fit with contemporary findings in developmental neurobiology. Instead, the more recent view in this subdiscipline is that human brains develop through a dynamic process involving the influence of experience (Stiles, 2009; Stiles, Brown, Haist, & Jernigan, 2015). In this chapter we aim to give readers enough knowledge of current relevant work in biology to evaluate claims that human infants are born with innate knowledge.

What is assumed in claims that some behaviour is innate? Consider an example suggested by Noam Chomsky (2007, p. 12). He stated that the 'pecking of a chicken' is an example of 'a genetically determined instinct'. This is because chicks don't seem to learn this action pattern, but all of them do it, so it seems that it must be 'genetically determined'. This claim seems reasonable because chicks start the coordinated actions of pecking and eating within a few hours of hatching – so early in life that it appears unlikely to be based on learning.

However, this is all speculation without being based on any empirical research, and indeed, without the awareness of previous findings on this topic. In fact, the Chinese comparative psychologist Zing Yang Kuo had already done the careful research in the 1920s and 1930s providing a complex developmental analysis, showing how this action pattern is not simply genetically determined. Kuo, working without the benefits of modern sensing equipment, came up with a method for examining development within the egg by creating a window in the shell in order to see the processes occurring within the egg. Through examining development in 3,000 live samples he found that this activity pattern emerges as the chick is developing in the eggshell. At about day 3 its heart starts beating, causing a head movement that sets up a motion resulting in the development of the pecking move-ment (Greenberg, 2014a). So, although genes are involved in everything, they alone do not determine this movement, and pecking movements would not necessarily emerge without the chick developing within the constraints of the eggshell along with the beating of the heart, among other factors (Greenberg, 2014a; Kuo, 1967; Lehrman, 1953).

What this example shows is that we should not be satisfied with simple claims that some traits are 'genetically determined' and instead it is important to trace very carefully the actual developmental emergence of a behaviour. This should perhaps be the mantra of developmental psychologists. The constraint of the eggshell is one level of the environ-ment experienced by the developing chick. For humans, especially, we need to be aware of the influence of levels of the social environment on development. It is crucial to think about the whole developmental system in which human infants develop.

Consider another example, also studied by Kuo, which is a step closer to social inter-action. It might seem that cats have an innate rat-killing instinct. However, Kuo found that kittens raised with rats don't kill rats. In fact, these cats may form emotional bonds with not only their rodent 'step-siblings' but also other members of that species. So, the pattern that cats raised in typical environments tend to kill rats is not the product of a simple instinctive impetus. As Kuo (1930, p. 35) put it, 'if one insists that the cat has an instinct to kill the rat, I must add that it has an instinct to love the rat, too'. A more com-plex developmental story is required to understand cats' hunting behaviour since simple biological maturation is not sufficient. This is certainly not to deny the role of biology in the typical emergence of this skill, but instead to point out the need for a more compre-hensive explanation (Kuo, 1930, 1938; Lickliter & Honeycutt, 2015).

When we encounter claims that a trait is innate this generally means a developmental account is not yet available. That is, we are owed an explanation (Lickliter & Honeycutt, 2009, 2015). But the problem here is that it is not usually understood this way. Instead, claims of innate knowledge tend to be accepted and thus they block further develop-mental research because they masquerade as explanations. They are non-developmental. Daniel Lehrman (1953) nicely showed the pitfalls of the nativist approach in his cri-tique of Konrad Lorenz's notion of instinct, and argued that taking a nativist position precludes the exploration of behaviour from a developmental process view. Lehrman pro-vided various examples that appear to support innateness, but actually do not. His main conclusion is that all of these supposedly innate behaviours are not actually tightly inte-grated and autonomously maturing, but instead are the result of a cascade of ontogenetic (i.e. developmental) processes such that the organism's developmental change (from one stage to the next) is the product of the interactions that occur between the organism and its internal environment. Current interactions link past developmental stages and future ones.

Any scholar, even those making very strong claims about genes determining traits such as Steven Pinker (1997), must acknowledge that the modules they claim do the thinking do have to *develop*. That is, there is general agreement that there is interaction between biology and the environment, and it is also frequently stated that the nature–nurture debate is over. But these issues still tend to arise even when they have been declared stone dead. What is needed to really drive a stake through the heart of this perpetual zombie is to leave our armchairs and take a close look at the interaction between biological and social factors (Oyama, 2000). This is because there are two ways to think about such interaction. One is to acknowledge that, of course, biology and the environment interact, but that they are pre-existing entities and it is possible to separate them, which means that it is also possible to consider roughly what percentage of each contributes to development or individual differences in development. Behaviour genetics takes this approach. Many researchers also continue to talk about the genes providing the blueprint and the environment doing the tweaking. In other words, there is an interaction between the two separate entities of nature and nurture. Although this may be an improvement, it shows that the dichotomy is not completely dead.

Nature–nurture debates are often presented as disputes between nativism and empiricism, between biology and a 'blank slate' view of the infant (Cosmides & Tooby, 2013; Pinker, 2002). However, as we have argued in Chapter 1, nativism and empiricism are not so different because they share the assumption that the mind is essentially passive. Furthermore, this way of setting up the debate is itself a problem because it already presupposes two separate entities that interact. It tends to be assumed that there are just two positions and the pendulum swings back and forth between them (Allen & Bickhard, 2013). Instead it is crucial to follow Allen and Bickhard's plea and get off the pendulum to take a different position, by setting up the problem in a different way. So, rather than solve the problem we must dissolve it.

Nature and nurture are abstracted out of relations through the use of these words. In fact, nature and nurture mutually create each other, so it is the many levels and types of relations of this mutual creation on which we should focus. Human infants have developed characteristics over nine months in the womb that set them up for further development; their sensitivities at birth create the environment they experience and that they elicit, and this experience then results in further biological development in a bi-directional manner. This results in a very different view of interaction. Developmental systems theorists try to do without the dichotomy by focusing on the relations rather than separable biological and social factors. That is, when we look closely at any aspect of development it is not possible to draw a clear line between biology and social factors because they mutually create each other in a bi-directional manner. If interaction is taken seriously and closely examined, then the notion of pre-existing entities starts to dissolve because biological characteristics result in a social environment in which neural pathways are developed and babies develop skills with which they can elicit more complex social experience and so on. This mutual influence of biological and social factors continues to interact bi-directionally so that it is not possible to ever clearly separate them. So, from this perspective, it is not possible to see where the biology stops and the social starts.

Infants 'create' their environment through their biological characteristics. This process is best understood by giving an illustration. Babies' visual systems determine what they can see. To cite two examples, the characteristics of human eyes draw infants' attention to eyes and faces, and they cry in response to discomfort. These biological characteristics develop in the womb, and that is another complex developmental story that, unfortunately, for reasons of space, we cannot cover in this book (Moore, Persaud, & Torchia, 2008). We can say that genes are involved as one essential part in the developing system, but only one part, and by themselves they do not determine or control anything. Instead many factors, including social experience influence gene expression, that is, the process by which information from the gene is used in the synthesis of a functional gene product (e.g. protein).

In fact, the more we learn about biology, ironically, the clear line between biology and social levels disappears, and it seems more accurate to say that 'nature is nurture' because social experience such as abuse or chronic poverty can cause biochemical changes to the DNA, resulting in differences in the activity of genes (van IJzendoorn, Bakermans-Kranenburg, & Ebstein, 2011, p. 309). Thus, according to Michael Meaney (2010), separating the influence of genes and environment is a 'rather arcane notion' (p. 41) that is 'inconsistent with even the most rudimentary understanding of gene function' (p. 69). Indeed, claims that genes cause outcomes such as conduct disorder 'drive many scientists slightly mad, since the data are merely correlational and do not imply a cause–effect relation between the genomic variant and conduct disorder' (p. 43).

We will go into further detail in the rest of the book, but for the moment even these very simple examples, overlooking layers of complexity, illustrate how the biology creates the social environment of the child and social experience influences biological development. It is not possible to neatly draw any clear line between the two. That is, the characteristics of the infant's biological embodiment influence the environment of development, the developmental niche in which the baby grows up.

When we consider the complexity of a child growing up it may be hard to avoid thinking that it must emerge from pre-existing information, and then naturally the question arises of where this information would be located. The answer seems to be in the genes, in a 'genetic program' that is set to unfold. It is difficult to avoid the tendency to think of complexity as being preformed somewhere, an assumption made by Parmenides three hundred years before Aristotle in the fifth century BCE. We need analogies to be able to break out of this pattern and think of the complexity of human thought as the regular outcome of a system of interacting factors. Instead of genes as 'blueprints' containing a plan or information for the construction of an individual, think of ecological succession as an analogy. Consider forests, for example.

> ## WHY IS THERE REGULAR DEVELOPMENT IN ECOSYSTEMS?
>
> Mature, old-growth forests on the Pacific northwest coast of North America tend to be primarily Western Hemlock and Western Red Cedar. This is a regular outcome of a complex process, but it is not pre-specified. After a forest fire the first plants to start recolonising tend to be fireweed and then small shrubs and gradually maple trees grow. The trees that can tolerate the shade under the maples tend to be hemlock and cedar. So, they grow and gradually become the dominant species. Thus, simplifying greatly, this type of forest is a regular outcome, given typical climate conditions (which are changing).

This analogy can be helpful in thinking about how something incredibly complex like a forest ecosystem, or a child, can be a regular outcome given typical conditions in the developmental system. That is, the usual outcome of a Hemlock–Cedar forest is expectable, yet it is not pre-specified. With this example we can see a complex system regularly emerging, but it is not pre-specified anywhere. The same goes for human developmental trajectories.

In order to understand the complexities of interaction in human development, it is helpful to think about specific aspects of the process. For instance, consider the simple everyday example of smiling, an incredibly important aspect of what it is to be human that is crucial for interpersonal emotional communication. The importance of smiling can be appreciated simply by paying attention to how we experience someone smiling at us. So, is smiling innate? It is found only in humans. Other great apes may sometimes raise the corners of their lips, but this is not responded to by others, so it does not appear to be a social signal in the way it is in humans. Smiling is also universal in the sense that all humans typically smile except in rare cases involving considerable neurological damage. Smiling also seems to have a universal meaning across cultures. If we walk down a street and someone smiles at us it affects us emotionally, and this would most likely be the same across cultures (Jones, 2008).

Newborn infants smile, even if they are blind, so this does not require any social experience or observation. However, the smiling of newborns is not the same as that of older infants. It is not really a social smile because they do so when sleeping or drowsy. Smiling while awake begins at about 4 to 6 weeks of age when it is in response to various actions of humans but also non-humans and even movements of non-living objects. That is, a baby may smile at a parent but also at a curtain being blown by the wind (Jones, 2008). So, smiling seems to be the result of a startle, a rapid change in the state of arousal. Smiling in adults is linked to happiness, although it has many social uses. Thus, the development of smiling turns out to be a complex interaction of biological characteristics and social experience. This is shown neatly in Viktoriya Wörmann's study of the emergence of an infant smile in relation to maternal smiling. The pattern was found at 6 weeks in Germany but not until 12 weeks in Nso infants in Cameroon (Wörmann, Holodynski, Kärtner, & Keller, 2014), presumably because the two cultures promote different patterns of adult–infant interaction. At 4 to 5 months, some infants smile when they are in face-to-face interaction, apparently as a social bid to try to restart the interaction with their mothers who were asked to hold a still face (Mcquaid, Bibok, & Carpendale, 2009; this is further discussed in Chapter 5). There is evidence of smiling that is influenced by the social context when children are somewhat older (i.e. between 8 and 12 months). At this point some infants smile while engaged with toys and then turn toward their mother while smiling. But some infants do so less when their mother is preoccupied. These are the same infants who also engage in other forms of early communication such as pointing, suggesting that smiling at this point is beginning to be a communicative act depending on their understanding of the social situation (Jones, 2008). Here we have only mentioned a few early steps in the development in complexity of this important human social act. As adults we are aware of the incredible diversity of forms of smiling in various social situations, and the social information communicated by the smile.

We have suggested that a shift is occurring in thinking about development, from a focus on DNA as determining developmental outcomes to an appreciation of multiple additional biological factors, to be discussed further in the following section. Interestingly, in developing a comprehensive theory of evolution, Jablonka and Lamb (2007) distinguish between four different, yet interacting, inheritance systems that stabilise development but also transmit variations on which selection processes can operate. Specifically, they argue that 'heredity involves more than DNA' (p. 357), and suggest that inheritance systems include, in addition to DNA, epigenetic inheritance and behavioural and symbol-based inheritance systems. Broadly, epigenetic inheritance (which we discuss below) refers to 'inheritance of phenotypic variations that do not stem from differences in DNA sequence' (Jablonka & Lamb, 2007, p. 357). The behavioural-based inheritance system involves socially mediated learning by means of which animals and humans generate traditions. For example, macaque monkeys on the small Japanese island of Koshima have learnt to wash sweet potatoes after this habit was introduced by a young female (but see Tomasello, 1999). The most important symbol-based inheritance system is language, which is also transgenerationally transmitted. Offspring also inherit the ecological niche from their parents. The ecological niche, in turn, influences the development and behaviour of the offspring. There are many examples of niche construction among animals – dam building among beavers, earthworms chemically altering the soil in which they live (see Odling-Smee et al., 2003) – but niche construction has taken on a qualitatively new level among humans.

From Jablonka and Lamb's theory emerges a fundamentally different view of the relation between biology and culture, and of the role of development in evolution. Biology and culture interact in complex ways, in phylogenesis as well as in ontogenesis. Humans, as well as other animals, create the environment in which they live and therefore the conditions to which they adapt. The transmission of these environments, behaviour patterns and symbol systems changes the environments faced by our genes (Henrich & Boyd 2002; Laland et al., 1999). At the same time, this may open the door for new evolutionary pathways for species that rely on social learning. Furthermore, developmental changes and learning can contribute to evolution as they may lead to innovations that are intergenerationally transmitted (Richerson & Boyd, 2005). Jablonka and Lamb (2007, p. 361) conclude that:

> genetic and cultural selective processes are important in human evolution, but they cannot be considered independently from the social construction processes at the individual and group levels that have been recognized and emphasized by the social sciences. Development, learning, and historical construction are central to the generation of cultural entities, to their transmissibility, and to their selective retention or elimination.

(Reproduced from Précis of Evolution in Four Dimensions, *Behavioural and Brain Science, Vol 30, Iss 4*, pp. 353–392, Dec 2007.)

2.2 GENETICS, EPIGENETICS, AND DEVELOPMENTAL PSYCHOBIOLOGICAL SYSTEMS

Claims of innate knowledge depend on assumptions that explanations focused on genes cannot account for complex traits or forms of thinking, let alone how we can conceptualise any emerging ideas about justice. Thus, to evaluate such claims it is necessary to know something about recent research on genetics and the biology of development. The evidence reviewed above doesn't support the idea of genes directing the show and determining the outcome. Instead, genes are a crucial part of a system and they are influenced in multiple ways in a bi-directional manner. In fact, genes can have separate, even opposite, effects in different cells, depending on other factors that are present in the cell's cytoplasm. For example, the activation of the glucocorticoid receptor gene promotes cell life in liver cells but causes the death of cells in the thymus (an organ of the immune system) (Meaney, 2010). Genes are part of a developmental system; they are influenced by other biological processes at the level of cells, tissues, and the organism as well as aspects of the environment (Gottlieb, 2007).

From the popular press it is easy to get the idea of genes as conductors, as carrying information or as blueprints making it possible to build an individual. This view of development might lead to the idea of trying to clone John Lennon mentioned at the beginning of the chapter. But DNA is actually an inert molecule, not a mastermind or a plan. It cannot turn itself on and off. That is done through signals that may come from within the cell or outside the cell, or even outside the organism. As one example of gene–environment interaction consider the important neurotransmitter serotonin – a neurotransmitter is chemical that transmits signals between neurons in the brain. Low levels of serotonin in humans are associated with depression and alcohol abuse (Gottlieb, 2007). The production of serotonin is associated with a gene, but it is not so simple because it also depends on the individual's social experience. Some Rhesus monkeys have a gene that is associated with behavioural difficulties due to low serotonergic function, but this only results in problems if the monkeys are raised by peers without mothers. In contrast, when these monkeys are raised by mothers the gene is not related to low serotonergic function (Gottlieb, 2007).

HIGH BLOOD PRESSURE IN RATS

As another example of gene–environment interaction consider a spontaneously hypertensive strain of rats (that is, they were bred to have high blood pressure). But these rats only have high blood pressure if they are reared by their hypertensive mothers. They don't develop hypertension if they are reared by a normal non-hypertensive female rat. Furthermore, normal rat pups don't develop high blood pressure if they are reared by the hypertensive mothers. Thus, the outcome of high blood pressure requires the gene and the environment, so it is the relationship between the mother and the pup that is crucial (Gottlieb, 2007).

In addition, aspects of the environment that may be important in development may be completely non-obvious aspects of experience. For example, if chicks are prevented from seeing their toes for the first two days after hatching they will not peck at and eat mealworms as normal chicks do (Gottlieb, 1991).

How about sex? Isn't that genetically determined? Well, it is in mammals but not in some reptiles. It depends on the temperature at which the egg is incubated. Furthermore, in coral reef fish, if a male dies one of the high-ranking females in the group turns into a male over two days, which keeps the sex ratio about the same in the social groups of coral reef fish (Gottlieb, 1991). As another example of the influence of the environment, the rate of adult sexual development is slower in female gerbils that were close to a male fetus during gestation, due to having been exposed to the higher level of testosterone produced by the male siblings, and this effect extends to the daughters of these gerbils (Lickliter & Honeycutt, 2009).

Claims about genes for certain traits such as aggression are common in the popular press. To study this in mice, a strain of mice was selected to be aggressive over 39 generations. So it would seem that these mice must have genes for aggression. But it turns out that they are only aggressive when raised in isolation. In contrast, when they were reared with other mice they were not aggressive, showing that it is not as simple as just having a gene for aggression (Gottlieb, 2007).

Timing is also of crucial importance in the developmental process. For example, the lethal deformation of lambs born with a single central eye occurs when pregnant sheep eat a particular type of lily, but only on day 14 of gestation, and only when the chemical in the lily interacts with the 'sonic hedgehog' protein, involved in regulating growth, produced by the sonic hedgehog gene. Only this interaction and timing of the process of development results in that particular deformity (Lewkowicz, 2011).

In different situations, the same genes can lead to different outcomes. For example, in a beehive, the queen and workers may have the same DNA but they are radically different—compared to the worker bees, the queen is a huge egg-laying machine. This difference is due to rearing and the food they are given. Furthermore, in the wake of discoveries regarding the interactive and bidirectional nature of the process of gene expression, even the idea of a gene is becoming more complex with discussion of the 'fluid genome', 'vanishing gene' (Ho, 2010), and 'relational gene' (Lickliter & Honeycutt, 2015).

It is now well known that aspects of the environment affect gene expression. For example, for rats stressed from sleep deprivation, the smell of coffee increases or decreases the expression of different genes. This changes the expression of proteins in the brain, some of which are known to have potential beneficial antioxidant and anti-stress functions (Seo, Hirano, Shibato, Rakwal, Hwang, & Masuo, 2008). In fact, there is now so much evidence that neurobiologists have moved on from the question of whether behaviour can affect gene expression, to the more interesting question of whether there are any behaviours that do not result in differences in gene expression (Stiles, 2009).

A new field is emerging known as *social genomics* concerning the study of how genes are differentially expressed in response to social experience (Slavich & Cole, 2013). For example, stress experienced by students preparing for examinations can result in changes in gene expression (Gottlieb, 2007). Even in plants, different genes are expressed in response to being attacked by different insects (Appel, Fescemyer, Ehlting, Weston, Rehrig, Joshi, Xu, Bohlmann, & Schultz, 2014).

The evidence that the activity of genes is influenced by many factors led Gilbert Gottlieb (e.g. 2007) to propose what he referred to as 'probabilistic epigenesis' in contrast to pre-determined epigenesis (the view that there is a one-way directional effect of the genes in determining development). Genes are critically important, but they are not the master conductor in charge. Genes function in a developmental system. They are an essential part of a process, but they are not sufficient by themselves to cause an outcome. Disorders such as Huntington's disease mentioned above – caused by single mutations with devastating effects – are rare. For the development of psychological functions of concern in this book, it is important to be aware of multiple factors as aspects of an interactive developmental system (Griffiths & Tabery, 2013; Jablonka & Lamb, 2005; Lickliter & Honeycutt, 2015).

Another source of inheritance in addition to DNA is the host of important biological factors inherited from the mother in the cytoplasm of the egg, including mitochondria, which provide the primary source of energy in the cell. In fact the embryo begins developing in a period of genetic inactivity during which time it depends on the mother's RNA and

DNA and other components in the cytoplasm of the egg until the embryo's own genome is activated (Charney, 2013).

Although the structural part of the DNA molecule is relatively stable over the lifetime of an individual and across generations, whether the genes are active is influenced by many factors. The study of how gene expression is influenced by various levels of the environment is referred to as *epigenetics*, which means 'above the genome' (Gottlieb, 2007). Epigenetic modification affects gene expression, but without altering the structural sequence of the DNA. One of the most common processes through which this occurs is *methylation*, a chemical process through which genes are silenced – 'a kind of cork on a bottle of champagne' (van IJzendoorn et al., 2011, p. 306). This is caused by experiences starting from fertilisation, and even earlier from the experience of the mother and father. Methylation locks genes in an 'off' position, effectively reducing gene expression and thereby protein production, and the methylation pattern is reproduced when genes are copied (van IJzendoorn et al., 2011). Some epigenetic marks that are influenced by the environment appear to be transmitted to the next generation. Thus, information is transmitted from one generation to the next without being encoded in the DNA.

As some geneticists have pointed out, we are sitting on parts of our body that could have been used for thinking or seeing. This is because although each cell in an individual's body contains the same DNA, it is expressed differently so that in one area of the body, such as the brain, a nerve cell (or neuron) will support memory, whereas in the adrenal gland a cell will produce the hormone cortisol (van IJzendoorn et al., 2011). This specialisation of cells is accomplished through silencing of some genes and increasing the expression of others.

Identical or monozygotic twins share 100% of their DNA. However, if the individuals have different experiences, their genes may be expressed differently. For example, a pair of monozygotic twins at 3 years of age had 1,000 genes with differential expression, and a pair of twins at 50 years had 5,000 genes that were expressed differently. This is referred to as 'epigenetic drift' (van IJzendoorn et al., 2011). In fact, even at birth monozygotic twins, with identical DNA, still may have differences in DNA methylation, probably from differences in the environment they experience in the womb (Marshall, 2015).

2.3 NEUROCONSTRUCTIVISM: SHAPING NEURAL PATHWAYS THROUGH EXPERIENCE

The dominant view fifty years ago was that brain development is the outcome of predetermined maturation based on gene expression and that this results in behaviour. More recently, this view has been challenged and neuroscientists have acknowledged the role of experience in brain development (Stiles, 2009; Stiles et al., 2015). One theoretical framework that emphasises the influence of multiple interacting levels of biological and environmental factors on brain development is neuroconstructivism (Mareschal, Johnson,

Sirois, Spratling, Thomas, & Westermann, 2007; Sirois, Spratling, Thomas, Westermann, Mareschal, & Johnson, 2008). Instead of being pre-programmed or preformed in some way, brains are constructed developmentally through ongoing interactions both within the organism and between the organism and the environment; that is, those aspects that are relevant for the organism (Oyama, 2000, p. 4). Neuroconstructivism thus represents a process-based account of brain development (Mareschal et al., 2007).

A typical adult human brain contains an estimated 100 billion neurons! The number of connections between neurons – synapses – is even more astronomical, estimated at 100 trillion connections! It has been argued that even if genes could specify neural interconnectivity, which they cannot, as reviewed above, there are simply not enough genes in the human genome to do this for the human brain (Mareschal et al., 2007). Humans have about the same number of genes as mice – not enough it seems to specify the incredible complexity of neural interconnectivity in human brains (Mareschal et al., 2007).

At birth, the structure of the brain is already formed in terms of differences between regions in density and type of neurotransmitters (see Stiles et al., 2015, on prenatal brain development). Patterns of neural interconnectivity, however, are shaped through experience. The number of synapses increases and then decreases as children lose synapses in response to experience. In this process the brain is sculpted through experience and different brain areas progressively specialise to take on particular cognitive functions (Johnson, Jones, & Gliga, 2015; Karmiloff-Smith, 2009, 2015; Mareschal et al., 2007).

The idea that the brain is shaped through experience is now generally accepted. Neurons form stronger connections through the process of firing together because the firing of a neuron results in gene expression and the production of a substance that is essential for the survival of neurons. This increases the chance for survival of the neurons and the connection between neurons. The more the neuron fires the more of this substance is produced, thus the greater the chance that the connection is strengthened and becomes part of a neural pathway (Stiles, 2009). This is a brief description of a very complex process that is played out in the formation of each of the trillions of connections between neurons – synapses – in the brain. Thus, brain development and behaviour are interdependent and bidirectional, and the notion of innate knowledge that is pre-specified and predetermined by genes does not fit with this understanding of brain development. This knowledge of current biology does not support claims that complex behaviours can be simply explained as being caused by genes. Instead, inheritance sets in motion a complex developmental process, which can result in regular outcomes given particular developmental systems (Stiles et al., 2015).

An example of the role of experience in shaping neural pathways is that when individuals are blind from an early age, instead of visual experience shaping the area of the brain that would be the primary visual cortex in sighted people, this area is activated by Braille reading (Mareschal et al., 2007) or hearing, allowing the person to hear echoes from sound bouncing off objects. The organisation of the cortical areas depends on the sensory inputs that are available, and these areas are not specialised at the start. But this does not imply a 'blank slate' position. Areas of the brain area are not equal; they differ in the structure of cells, types and densities of neurotransmitters, and so on. Thus, the language areas of the brain, for example, are not dedicated to language processing to begin with, but, in Elizabeth Bates's (1999, 2005) words, they usually 'win the language contract' because they are well suited to processing that sort of input (see Chapters 7 and 8).

Once we have an idea of how the human brain develops, it is still a step further to address the question with which we started the book. That is, how the world becomes meaningful for the child. Although neuroconstructivism is an important step in understanding brain development, it is not clear whether it can provide a way of understanding how the world becomes meaningful for the child (cf. Lickliter, 2008). That is because neural constructivism deals with the development of the neural substrate that supports psychological life, but not with psychological life and its development. To elaborate, we move to a discussion of the role of the brain in psychological experience.

2.4 RELATIONS BETWEEN PSYCHOLOGY AND NEUROSCIENCE

Neuroscience is often considered a science that produces hard facts. However, neuro-scientific findings must be interpreted and are understood through the lens of theoretical frameworks. In fact, controversies in neuroscience abound (Slotnick 2013). There are different ways of conceptualising the role of the brain in psychological experience and we examine this issue here from the perspectives of the two worldviews introduced in the previous chapter. We first consider how neuroscience is related to psychology from the perspective of the information-processing/cognitivist perspective. We then move to a view of the relationship between mind and brain from the perspective known as embodied cognition.

The cognitivist perspective has been heavily influenced by the idea that the mind works as a computer that operates on input (provided by sensory information) and computes some output (experience or action). In this context, the 'mental states' are identified on the basis of the type of causal and functional role they play in producing the output. For example, the desire to eat ice cream causes you, given appropriate sensory input (e.g. hot weather), to go and buy ice cream. An important feature of the cognitivist approach is that the computations or information processing can be realised in many different physical systems. The system does not have to be the brain but might as well be the hardware of a computer, a view which has inspired artificial intelligence. Cognitivism as a framework forces cognitive neuroscience into a Procrustean bed. This idea of forcing something into a framework in which it may not fit comes from Greek mythology. Procrustes, a son of Poseidon, invited travellers passing by to stay the night, but he only had one bed, so any visitor had to be made to fit, even if that meant stretching them or cutting off their legs. Because the physical basis of information processing did not matter for cognitivism, this approach resulted in de-emphasising and ignoring the actual details of neuroscience (Marshall, 2009, 2015). Furthermore, cognitivism focused on the bottom-up, input–output information processing, leading from perception to action.

There is increasing behavioural and neuropsychological evidence that the particular physical structure of the human body, including the brain, plays an important role in cognition, and that the bottom-up flow of information might be too simplistic because action influences perception (Marshall, 2009). That is, perception occurs in terms of action potential; we see objects and events in terms of what we can do with them. For example, when a ballet dancer watches a ballet performance, the motor areas associated with those dance movements are activated in her brain (Kinsbourne & Jordan, 2009). In addition, there is a growing body of evidence that conceptual knowledge, including language comprehension, is strongly influenced by sensorimotor experience (e.g. Glenberg & Gallese, 2012; Vainio, Symes, Ellis, Tucker & Ottoboni, 2008). For example, Glenberg and Kaschak (2002) asked participants to read sentences that implied motion either away from the body (e.g. 'Close the drawer') or motion toward the body (e.g. 'Open the drawer'). Participants were asked to verify the meaningfulness of the sentence by making arm movements away from themselves or toward themselves. Glenberg and Kaschak found that participants' responses were faster when the direction of the response matched the direction of motion implied in the sentence. Findings such as these have given rise to the view that cognition is embodied, i.e. grounded in sensorimotor experience (Barsalou, 2008; Gallese & Lakoff, 2005).

To account for these findings, a new theoretical framework has emerged that is termed 'embodied cognition'. The main thesis of embodied cognition is that 'many features of cognition are embodied in that they are deeply dependent upon characteristics of the physical body of an agent, such that the agent's beyond-the-brain body plays a significant causal role, or a physically constitutive role, in that agent's cognitive processing' (Wilson & Foglia, 2015: cited in https://plato.stanford.edu/entries/embodied-cognition/). In other words, embodiment refers to 'not just having, and acting through, some physical instantiation, but recognizing that the particular shape and nature of one's physical, temporal, and social immersion is what makes meaningful experience possible' (Anderson, 2003, p. 124). Furthermore, cognition is viewed as being a preparation for action. Whatever is happening in the environment will affect our cognition and our actions (Wilson, 2002). For example, when driving a motor vehicle we focus our actions on driving the car while we perceive changes in the driving environment. We map out our destination and are prepared to encounter obstacles such as traffic lights, pedestrians, and other motorists.

The embodiment approach with its emphasis on action and the dynamic interplay of perception, action and mental processes is consistent with the process-relational worldview. However, one critical issue concerns the way in which the brain should be conceptualised in the embodiment perspective. One tendency is to reduce the body and mind to the brain and treat embodiment from a purely neurophysiological perspective (Marshall, 2015). By doing so, however, meaning vanishes. This is because the functioning of the brain consists of patterns of activation that cause further patterns of activation and so on like an infinite row of falling domino pieces. The cyberneticist Heinz von Foerster (2003) pointed out that the 'language' of the brain consists of the firing of neurons. All we can hear are the 'clicks' of action potentials (if sufficiently amplified). For that reason, it would be a fundamental error to ascribe to the level of functioning of the brain terms such as meaning, thinking, or reasoning because these terms only make sense at the level of the person and not the brain. It is the person who thinks, perceives, feels, and acts. The brain is the part of the body which links the organism to the world. In fact, the brain creates loops between neural perceptual and motor pathways, and a more complex brain is the condition for the development of flexible and complex behaviour. Thus, from a process-relational view the brain is a necessary condition of psychological experience. However, psychological experience cannot be reduced to neural function but requires its own level of description and explanation. Indeed, the brain is part of the body and the body is part of a larger social context, and meaning arises within and through the interaction of the embodied interactions between person and world. Neuroscience provides an important part of this story, but only one part of the story. The neuroscience side of the story should be consistent and coordinated with the psychological and developmental perspective on the story. Ideally, both stories should complement and inform each other (Marshall, 2014, 2016).

The nervous system enables interaction and is also shaped through this interaction in a constant bidirectional process in which new skills open up new opportunities for interaction and further learning. The complexity of the human nervous system enables anticipation of the outcome of actions through linking neural activity and behavioural activity. This link between perception and action fits with the view of knowledge in the action-based and embodied approaches introduced in the previous chapter, and further explicated in the next chapter. This is the way to understand how the world becomes meaningful for the child. Emotions and interest develop and as the child learns what can be done with aspects of the world that acquire significance for the child she can anticipate what will happen next in good or bad ways. This process applies to the physical and social world. We explore this process of the child developing knowledge throughout the rest of the book.

A number of methodologies have been developed to study the structure and function of the human brain. In particular, various technologies make it possible to form images of activity of particular brain regions. Research with such neuroimaging procedures will be reviewed in Chapters 10 and 13.

SUMMARY AND CONCLUSION

In this chapter, we have considered relations between biology and psychology. We have examined claims that infants are born with innate knowledge, and suggested that such claims are inconsistent with current thinking in biology and developmental neuroscience. Current biology suggests that neural pathways are not pre-specified by genes and that instead there is a great deal of plasticity in development, meaning that neural pathways are shaped through experience. This means that thinking cannot be innate and that it is crucial to study the role of experience in shaping neural structures. We need a different level of explanation that is the focus for the rest of the book. Discussions from a developmental systems perspective suggest that debates about the roles of nature and nurture are based on a false dichotomy and that these are not clearly separable factors. Instead, it is more fruitful to consider the relations between them as they mutually create each other in a bidirectional manner within a developmental system. This is because infants' biological characteristics result in social experience, which, in turn, will feed back to and change biological characteristics.

From the starting point of describing or explaining human behaviour in terms of the neural activity involved, we still have to address the question raised in the first chapter regarding how the world becomes meaningful for children. Doing this requires setting development into a social and emotional context of embodied activity. Children act in a human world and discover the potential for interacting with the physical world. They are also embedded in the social and emotional world of their culture. Many other difficult and exciting questions are lurking as we move from biological factors as parts of a system of bidirectionally interacting factors to complex human activities such as thinking about justice. We turn to grappling with these questions in the remaining chapters in the book.

FURTHER READING

Gottlieb, G. (2007). Probabilistic epigenesis. *Developmental Science, 10*, 1–11.

Lickliter, R., & Honeycutt, H. (2015). Biology, development, and human systems. In W. F. Overton & P. C. M. Molenaar (vol. eds), *Vol. 1: Theory and Method*, R. Lerner (Editor-in-Chief), 7th edition of the *Handbook of Child Psychology and Developmental Science*. New York: Wiley Blackwell.

Mareschal, D., Johnson, M. H., Sirois, S., Spratling, M. W., Thomas, M. S. C., & Westermann, G. (2007). *Neuroconstructivism: How the Brain Constructs Cognition* (vol. 1). New York: Oxford University Press.

Stiles, J. (2009). On genes, brains, and behavior: Why should developmental psychologists care about brain development? *Child Development Perspective, 3*, 196–202.

Tallis, R. (2011). *Aping Mankind: Neuromania, Darwinitis and the Misrepresentation of Humanity*. Durham: Acumen.

Westermann, G., Mareschal, D., Johnson, M. H., Sirois, S., Spratling, M. W., & Thomas, M. S. C. (2007). Neuroconstructivism. *Developmental Science, 10*, 75–83.

VIDEO LINKS

Epigenetics: www.youtube.com/watch?v=9DAcJSAM_BA

3 CONSTRUCTIVIST APPROACHES TO CHILDREN'S THINKING

LEARNING OUTCOMES

By the end of this chapter you should:

- Be able to discuss the details of Piaget's view of how knowledge develops including the concepts of assimilation, accommodation, and equilibration.
- Understand Piaget's view of sensorimotor intelligence and its role in his theory.
- Distinguish physical knowledge and logical mathematical knowledge.
- Be able to describe concrete operational reasoning and formal operational reasoning.
- Be aware of some of the common criticisms of Piaget's theory, and responses to them.
- Be able to define horizontal décalage and understand whether it is a problem for Piaget's theory.
- Understand 'procedural décalage' and grasp the argument for this approach and problems with strategy.

The study of cognitive development covers a lot of ground, ranging from elementary cognitive processes such as recognition memory that humans share with other animals to uniquely human cognitive skills manifest in planning, decision making, reasoning, problem solving, and imagination. Consider, for example, the complex cognitive skills required for planning a surprise birthday party: you need to decide whom to invite, find a date that works for everyone, instruct the invitees to keep the party a secret, make arrangements for food and drinks, select and prepare party games, and so on. Such planning abilities make multiple demands and require the sequencing and coordination of different activities. Usually, these abilities are mastered by adolescence (unless there has been a severe head injury; Pentland, Todd, & Anderson, 1998).

There are various approaches to explaining how human cognition develops into the complex, uniquely human skills that we exercise so effortlessly in mundane contexts. These approaches differ markedly in the assumptions they make about what constitutes human knowledge, the knowing process, and the sources as well as the process of development. We review these approaches in the following chapters, starting with the constructivist or action-based approach in this chapter. There is a current transition in ways of thinking in developmental psychology toward considering the role of embodied activity in the development of thinking (Marshall, 2016). These approaches fall into the process-relational worldview discussed in Chapter 1 and are variously referred to as constructivist, action-based, enactive, interactive, or embodied. From the perspective of these approaches, a starting question is how does the world become meaningful for the child (Marshall, 2016)? There are a variety of constructivist theories in different areas of knowledge (e.g. Maturana & Varela, 1992; von Glasersfeld, 1995), but none is as comprehensive and well developed as Piaget's theory. For this reason, we focus on that theory in this chapter.

Constructivism, as an approach to the development of thinking, emerged over a century ago (e.g. Baldwin, 1897), but it is Piaget's work that has had an enormous and crystallising impact on developmental psychologists. Over the course of his long career, Piaget wrote some 100 books as well as 600 published papers (Archives Piaget, 1989). He and his collaborators designed and conducted countless experiments. His theory and experiments provided developmental psychologists with questions, as well as methods to address these questions. Indeed, according to one anonymous reviewer of an article on Piaget's theory, assessing his influence is like 'assessing the impact of Shakespeare on English literature or Aristotle on philosophy – impossible. The impact is too monumental to embrace and at the same time too omnipresent to detect' (cited in Beilin, 1992, p. 191). In contemporary developmental psychology, Piaget's importance is generally acknowledged, but at the same time his theory has been heavily criticised or even dismissed (Brainerd, 1978; Gelman & Baillargeon, 1983; for discussion see also Lourenço & Machado, 1996; Müller & Overton, 1998). We believe that this dismissal is largely based on misunderstanding Piaget. Instead, we argue that his theory is still relevant today, particularly as new approaches based on an action-based, enactive, embodied, and situated view of knowledge emerge and become the dominant view in cognitive science (Hutto & Myin, 2013). In this chapter we both present a summary of Piaget's theory and respond to some of the common criticisms, partly as a means of understanding his theory more clearly.

In the following sections, we present Piaget's biography, which provides some insights into the motivation underlying his work. Next, we discuss his conceptualisation of knowledge, and we argue that he addressed a crucial issue that is still relevant today. We then describe how he conceived of the process of development. Finally, we summarise the key features of his stages of cognitive development. Throughout the chapter we present and evaluate influential criticisms of his work.

3.1 PIAGET'S BIOGRAPHY AND HIS QUEST: HOW DOES KNOWLEDGE DEVELOP?

Jean Piaget was born in 1896 in Neuchâtel, Switzerland. As a child, he was interested in natural history and became such an expert on mollusks that he was offered a job as a curator of a museum, which he had to decline because he was still a schoolboy (Smith, 2009). In his youth his interest in science clashed with his religious beliefs (Vidal, 1994), resulting in the central issue of his life which was how to reconcile truth and value or science and religion (Chapman, 1988). When Piaget was in his late teens he had a break-down that we would now refer to as an identity crisis. He spent a year in the mountains in Switzerland, and during that time wrote a somewhat autobiographical novel about a young man facing a crisis and how he resolved it. Michael Chapman (1988, 1992) suggests that this resolution provided Piaget with a plan for his career.

Piaget earned a PhD in zoology when he was just 21. He then moved to Zürich, where he was influenced by the psychiatrist Eugen Bleuler, who coined the term 'schizophrenia', and his (to become more famous) assistant, Carl Jung. He moved to Paris to work in the laboratory of Alfred Binet where he was supervised by Théodore Simon, both of whom were pioneers in developmental and educational testing. There he interviewed children and became fascinated by the mistakes they made. His next move was to Geneva where he set up an interdisciplinary institute, involving education, philosophy, logic, sociology, biology, and mathematics. Piaget's long career extended to his death in 1980.

We now turn to the aims of Piaget's theory. These can be inferred from the term he used to describe his work: *genetic epistemology*. In this context, genetic does not refer to genes, as in current use, but, rather, to the origin and development of knowledge (genetic comes from the Greek, *genno*, meaning to give birth, as in the first book of the Bible, 'Genesis'). Epistemology usually refers to the study of the nature, sources, scope, and validity of knowledge, and is considered to be a branch of philosophy. Piaget tackled these venerable philosophical questions, but not in the way they are typically addressed by arm-chair philosophising. Instead, Piaget suggested that the observation of the development of knowledge in children can contribute to answering these questions.

So, what is the nature of knowledge and how is it acquired? A common answer is that knowledge arrives through our senses: we just open our eyes, information comes in, and we form some sort of copy of the world, which is what constitutes knowledge. But Piaget argued that this 'copy theory' is flawed because there is no way to check this copy against the world except by forming another copy, which also cannot be checked against reality (Chapman, 1999; Piaget, 1970). This would be like reading an unlikely story in the newspaper and wanting to check the truth of the story, but doing so by buying a second copy of the same newspaper. This clearly doesn't help to get us any closer to reality (Wittgenstein, 1968). The idea that knowledge arrives through our senses and that the mind just passively registers incoming information, associating it with information already stored, is a hallmark of empiricist theories of knowledge. In addition to criticising the copy theory assumption, Piaget also thought that his empirical research with children showed that this empiricist theory of knowledge is incorrect. He similarly criticised nativism (i.e. the idea that forms of knowledge are innate) on theoretical and empirical grounds. Instead, he described knowledge as developing rather than pre-existing in children.

Piaget's alternative to empiricism and nativism is constructivism. He proposed that 'in order to know objects, the subject must act upon them, and therefore transform them' (Piaget, 1970, p. 704). According to this view, knowledge does not pre-exist in the world to be imposed on children or copied by children, nor is it already innately prepared in the child. Instead, knowledge develops through the child coordinating her interactions with the world; the child comes to understand the world through learning what she can do with it (Piaget, 1954). In contrast to empiricism and nativism, Piaget conceived of the person as always actively interacting with the world. In infancy, this activity is manifest in concrete actions such as pushing objects, putting them together, taking them apart and so on. These 'sensorimotor' actions provide the foundation for all later stages of knowledge. Consequently, for Piaget, all knowledge ultimately is rooted in action (Müller, Sokol, & Overton, 1998; Piaget, 1970).

Perception is not the primary source of knowledge; instead it is subordinated to action in the sense that we perceive objects in terms of the actions they afford, that is what we can do with them, their potential for interaction. To quote Piaget, 'To perceive a house is not to look at an image which has just got into your eye, but to recognize a solid shelter for you to get into!' (Inhelder & Piaget, 1959/1969, p. 13).

KITTENS' EXPERIENCE AND THEIR DEVELOPMENT OF KNOWLEDGE

A classic study with kittens demonstrated the importance of actions in creating meaningful experience (Held & Hein, 1963). In this study, one kitten walked around inside a cylinder towing a second kitten in a basket, so that the second kitten saw exactly what the first kitten saw (i.e. patterns on the walls), but in contrast to the first kitten, the second kitten did not move herself (she was passively moved). When both kittens were tested the first kitten could, of course, coordinate what it could see with what it could do, but the second kitten could not. That is, when they were tested by holding them close to the edge of a table, the first kitten reached a paw toward it to step onto it but the second kitten did not.

A central tenet of Piaget's genetic epistemology is to anchor psychological development and functioning firmly in biology. Many theoretical approaches recognise the importance of biology – evolution, genes, physiology. But they differ greatly in how exactly they conceptualise the relation between biology and psychological development. Currently, a popular approach is to reduce psychological development to the unfolding of hereditary programs or to the maturation of particular areas of the brain (see Chapter 2). Piaget considered such reductionist approaches inadequate because they fail to capture essential characteristics of psychological functioning: the construction of meaning and the irreducibility of implication to causality (see below). That is, an explanation at the level of DNA and neurons does not fully answer the question posed above about how the world becomes meaningful for the child.

Piaget thought that the most fundamental aspect of life is that it is a self-organising system. Self-organising systems reproduce their organisation, in exchange processes with their environment, through interactions between their components, by following an internal dynamic. Machines, by contrast, are not self-organising systems because their reproduction is controlled by an external agent. From an evolutionary perspective, the continuously self-organising process leads to more complex organisms and the emergence of cognitive processes as tools to regulate the exchange with the environment. Piaget thus argues that cognitive processes are the outcome of and extend the processes of organic self-organisation by using and adapting to new circumstances the different systems of organic self-regulation that can be found on the genetic, physiological, and nervous levels. In support of this claim, he describes many functional and structural analogies between organic and cognitive functioning. Central among these analogies is the triad of assimilation, accommodation, and scheme.

Assimilation and accommodation at the psychological level extend the physiological interactions between the organism and the environment because their functioning no longer depends on the incorporation of material elements (e.g. a metabolic cycle that assimilates particular nutrients) but now incorporates informational content. Assimilation and accommodation maintain the equilibrium between an organism and its environment (Piaget, 1952). At the psychological level, *schemes* are structures composed of affect, sensation, motor movement, and perception. They are the child's repertoires of action that start with simple reflex actions which gradually become more complex. 'Assimilation' refers to the incorporation of new information into already existing schemes, a process of giving meaning to the content (Piaget, 1952, 1985). For example, when a baby grasps a rattle, the rattle is assimilated to her grasping scheme and thereby attains the functional meaning of being 'graspable'. Assimilation is thus the use of an existing psychological scheme; its functioning carries the history of the child's interaction with the world (i.e. objects) into each particular act. For example, an infant who has differentiated various ways of interacting with the rattle will have different action potentialities available compared to an infant who has not.

Schemes are structures with varying degrees of generality, so applying them to particular situations always requires an adjustment of the scheme. Accommodation or the development of a new way of interacting with an object thus particularises the general schemes, supplies them with specific content, and modifies them in doing so (e.g. the pre-existing grasping scheme needs to be modified, becoming more specific to take into account the particular spatial position of the rattle, its shape or 'graspability').

Piaget's concepts of assimilation and accommodation have been criticised as being vague. For example, David Klahr (1995, p. 369) stated with respect to Piaget's description of assimilation and accommodation, 'Although it has a certain poetic beauty, as a scientist, I do not understand it, I do not know how to test it, and I doubt that any two readers will interpret it in the same way' (see also Klahr, 1982). But in response to these criticisms, it should be pointed out that assimilation and accommodation describe general ways of interacting with the world. Assimilation emphasises the fact that living beings can never just passively encode information; instead what they do depends on their experience – they cast the net of their schemes out into the world and what they catch depends on the structure of the net. Reality can never be copied; rather, it is the child's understanding that emerges in her or his dynamic interaction with the world. In this sense, reality is a construction, and it is always structured by our knowledge schemes and action potential. Second, assimilation and accommodation also emphasise the continuity between biological and psychological functioning. However, Piaget did not simply reduce psychological to biological functioning; rather, he thought that the psychological level emerged from the biological level and continued the self-organizing activity at a higher, more complex level. In this manner, he avoided the trap of reductionism that views biology (genes, physiology) as the cause of psychological functioning, making it impossible to study meaning and reason. Third, assimilation and accommodation help to explain the direction of development. Development cannot consist of copying or slavishly adapting to the environment, but instead is a function of the existing organisation. In this context, accommodation leads to a differentiation of the existing organisation, and assimilation to hierarchic integration. For example, when infants modify the grasping scheme in response to the experience of clutching different objects, the action has differentiated into subclasses of grasping schemes. Accommodation can also explain the diversification of action and knowledge schemes. For example, when an infant, in her attempt to grasp a ball, accidentally touches it so that it rolls away, she becomes interested in exploiting this accidental discovery and repeating this action, now slightly pushing the ball. The pushing scheme becomes differentiated from the grasping scheme, thanks to infants' interactions in the world. The last example also illustrates Piaget's idea that children are curious and generally interested in whatever new events they encounter.

The two interrelated functions of assimilation and accommodation can be seen at multiple levels, from this example of action in infancy to adults' activity of learning a new dance with a partner. We accommodate if a misstep results in awkward coordination or toes trodden on. The process can also be seen in learning words. For example, a child might learn a word such as 'dog' but over-extend it to include other animals such as sheep and then accommodate in response to others' reactions. At the level of learning about theories, students might assimilate theories such as those of Piaget and Vygotsky to their previous ways of thinking, but if they realise that the theories are different they will need to accommodate (i.e. learn the differences), resulting in further understanding. Assimilation, in turn, leads to hierarchical integration by means of the coordination of independent schemes (Piaget termed this 'reciprocal assimilation'). For example, infants may use two schemes independently: opening a cupboard door, then grasping a pot. By coordinating or reciprocally assimilating these schemes, actions become hierarchically organised.

Piaget recognised that, compared to other species, humans are in a unique position. This, according to Piaget, is because evolution has led to an increasing disappearance of innate fixations that, in the case of human life, has resulted in a 'bursting of the instinct' (Piaget, 1967/1971, pp. 366–367). That is, unlike other animals, human beings no longer have a fixed, species-specific environment (Berger & Luckmann, 1966; Gehlen, 1940/1988; Herder, 1772/1967). Instead, human beings are left unfinished by design and must design themselves (Gehlen, 1940/1988). This openness to the world creates a space for extensive development and for the influence of social-cultural factors on this development to an extent that is unparalleled in other species. Indeed, this world openness is intrinsically connected to the fact that we are historical beings in the sense that understanding human development requires an understanding of its historical context. This connects Piaget's theory to sociocultural approaches such as Vygotsky's, which is discussed in the next chapter.

The important role of assimilation becomes evident in the context of understanding the relation between mind and brain. The notions of assimilation, meaning, and consciousness are closely interrelated in Piaget's theory. Assimilation confers meaning on objects and consciousness is a system of meanings. These meanings are related by implications and not causality. For example, the action of pulling a blanket upon which a rattle is placed in order to grasp the rattle shows that the infant understands that the spatial relation 'placed upon' implies that the rattle is drawn along, especially if the infant does not pull on the blanket when the rattle is placed next to it. By contrast, causal explanations apply to the level of the brain (e.g. the activation of neuron A triggered the activation of neuron B). Because implications and causal relations are qualitatively different, psychological processes and phenomena cannot be reduced to neurophysiological processes.

In summary, Piaget's genetic epistemology is rooted in biology but this is fundamentally different from contemporary reductionist theories. For Piaget, evolution does not lead to a passive adaptation of humans to the world. In contrast, the opposite must be explained: How humans come to live almost everywhere (have no specific habitat) and adapt the world, through technology, to themselves. This is only possible because evolution has led to a disappearance of instincts and an openness to the world requiring that humans construct their world. This is why Piaget emphasised activity and transformation to explain the fecundity and creativeness of human thought and action. Instead of reducing psychology to biology, Piaget thought that psychological levels of functioning emerge from (but remain rooted in) biological levels of functioning in a continuing process of self-organisation. This leads to increasingly complex forms of interaction between the organism/person and the world. Piaget also rejected the reduction of psychological processes to neuropsychological processes because this would eliminate meaning and necessary knowledge. This means that although neuropsychological processes are, of course, essential in the child's whole developmental system, the child's activity is also crucial in understanding how consciousness and meaning emerge from biological levels of functioning in a process of self-organisation.

3.2 FOUR FACTORS IN DEVELOPMENT

In explaining development, Piaget acknowledged that the classical factors of 'maturation' and 'experience' are important, but he argued that they are still not sufficient to explain development. That is, no matter how well a child is fed she will not merely mature into a normal human without experience – both physical and social (Piaget, 1970, p. 712). We refer here to four themes that he commonly returned to in his writing.

Piaget divided experience into experience of the physical environment and experience of social environment. Just simple experience is not enough. For him learning depends on the *development of structures*. The information may be there all the time, but children must have a structure to assimilate it to – to relate it to. This point is illustrated in Piaget's (1977) 'bottle study'. Children see water in various forms every day of their lives, such as lakes, rivers, baths, and so on, and its surface is always horizontal. Yet if they are shown a bottle half full of water that is then put in a bag and tipped on its side, and they are asked to draw a line on the bag indicating the surface of the liquid, young children tend to draw the line parallel to the bottom of the bottle (as it was when the bottle was standing up). It was not until the average age of 9 (in poorer sections of Geneva) that children got this right. Here the information was available all the time but what was needed was the development of a coordinate system outside of the bottle; that is, a frame of reference or sense of space. The younger children employ a coordinate system that is within the bottle and so their points of reference are the bottom of the bottle, which is why they draw the surface in relation to the bottom. So, it is not just a matter of passively recording information from the environment. Instead, a structure is needed to assimilate it to; that is, an understanding of the world.

To understand why activity was important for Piaget we should consider his idea of physical experience. Piaget thought that there are two types of experience with physical objects resulting in different forms of knowledge. Physical knowledge is knowledge that can be abstracted from objects, such as weight, colour, or other properties of the objects. This form of knowledge can be acquired through reinforcement, and thus it can be forgotten (extinguished). This knowledge is drawn from objects in the environment and can be acquired at any point in a child's development, and it does not change at later points in the child's development.

In contrast, *logical-mathematical* knowledge is not drawn just from objects, but, instead, from actions on objects. Logical mathematical experience involves the relationship between the child and the external world. It involves the child's actions on the world. For instance, Piaget (1977) gave the example of his friend who was a mathematician and remembered counting pebbles when he was a small child. He had placed 10 pebbles in a row and counted them from left to right and then from right to left, and was surprised and delighted that he always ended up with 10 no matter which way he counted them, even if he arranged them in a circle. That is, number is a property of the actions on the pebbles; the sum is independent of the order of counting. Logical mathematical knowledge concerns knowledge of relations and it cannot be acquired at any point in the child's development because the child needs the appropriate structures in order to assimilate this knowledge. This knowledge is not acquired through reinforcement, and thus it cannot be extinguished. Using the example of a child playing with pebbles, physical knowledge is of their colour, weight, texture, and so on, whereas logical mathematical knowledge is based on actions such as counting the pebbles.

The third factor for Piaget is *social interaction*. Of course, this is necessary and important but not sufficient, because first the child has to have already developed some way of making sense of what teachers are saying, and second it doesn't explain the origin of new knowledge. If development is just learning – that is from the social environment – then new knowledge at the societal level cannot be explained. It is commonly assumed that Piaget neglected social factors in this theory. In fact he assumed that they are obviously important, but he argued they are not enough to explain development.

Piaget argued that a fourth factor is necessary – *equilibration*. Other psychologists talk about the first three factors, but Piaget believed equilibration was the most important because none of the others are sufficient in themselves. For him development is a function of maturation, experience, and equilibration. Equilibration involves interaction between maturation and experience, organism, and environment.

3.3 DEVELOPMENTAL PROGRESS: PIAGET'S EQUILIBRATION THEORY

At each point in their development children are in a state of equilibrium with the environment, characterised by a particular balance between their activity and their effects on the world (i.e. do they accomplish what they set out to do?). Development is a process that leads to increasingly more stable (complete and consistent) forms of equilibrium; therefore, development is progressive and not mere change (e.g. a change from being tired early in the afternoon to being alert in the early evening). Piaget termed this process *equilibration* (see Piaget, 1985). The theory of equilibration takes a central place in his later work (see Müller et al., 2009) in which he focused in more detail on the specific processes involved in equilibration.

Equilibration is triggered by disequilibria – i.e. imbalances between the child's activities and environmental effects. For example, the child may encounter obstacles to her goals so that they cannot be reached (e.g. the cookie may be out of reach, the wind-up toy cannot be operated to make the interesting effect, the tower made of blocks tumbles over, the mother does not understand what the child is trying to communicate). Disequilibria can be momentary and can be removed with means already available to the child (e.g. she already knows how to climb a chair so she does so to reach the cookie). In such a situation, she does not create a more complex form of equilibrium; such a solution to the problem would not constitute equilibration. By contrast, when the child learns how to align the blocks properly so that the tower is more stable, she has modified and differentiated as well as coordinated her schemes, with the consequence that the tower will not fall over as easily in the future. These are the fundamental components of accommodation, discussed above. Because the child has now created a more stable form of equilibrium between herself and the world (the tower with respect to the laws of gravity), this case would constitute equilibration. Although Piaget identified several processes as playing an important role in the equilibration processes, his theory of equilibration remains unfinished (Campbell, 2009; Piaget, 1971, 1985).

3.4 UNDERSTANDING PIAGET'S STAGES

Piaget's theory is often associated with the term 'stages'. For him, these are not identified in terms of age. Rather, they describe forms of thinking and are defined in terms of the child's performance on particular tasks, analysed in terms of the operations and structure they require. He fully acknowledged that the age of acquisition of operations is highly variable and influenced by the amount of cognitive stimulation that the child experiences. Furthermore, as a biologist, he was interested in classifying forms of thought, and this led to his theory of stages. However, by focusing on his stage theory, contemporary developmental psychologists have overlooked that for Piaget the explanation of the development of these forms of thought was far more important than their description in terms of the approximate age at which a child can perform a particular function (although the description is the step that must occur prior to explanation). To explain the development of these forms of thought, Piaget formulated his theory of equilibration. Central to his approach was not the age at which the stages emerge but rather the mechanisms involved in developmental transitions. Each stage is a temporary equilibrium in the continual process of equilibration. As they build on each other, they constitute an invariant sequence. We next briefly describe the main characteristics of each stage (see Chapman, 1988; Müller et al., 2009).

Sensorimotor stage

Piaget (1952) termed the developmental period during approximately the first 18 months of life the *sensorimotor* stage. It plays a key role in bridging the gulf between the biological level of functioning and rational thought. Sensorimotor intelligence is the beginning of intelligence in practical, lived activity, which centres on the child's action on objects. Sensorimotor intelligence is a practical, embodied interaction with the world through perception–action cycles. At this stage, meaning is originally embedded in unreflective activities; objects have a functional, practical meaning, they are things at hand, utensils for practical use or manipulation.

It is difficult to understand what an infant's experience is like and to avoid assuming that it is like an adult's experience. To get an idea of how radical Piaget's theory is he argued that infants start off with no idea that objects continue to exist when they can't see them. The assumption of an external world that exists independent of us is such a central part of our understanding that it is hard to imagine that we were not born with this understanding and had to develop it (Piaget, 1970, p. 704).

The process of learning about the world consists of acting on it. Infants employ action schemes like sucking, pushing, hitting, and grasping to explore and manipulate the world. At the outset, the newborn has no self-consciousness and no clear awareness of what effects she produces through actions on the world compared to effects that occur independent of her actions. By coordinating her actions and applying them in the social domain (imitation), the infant gradually learns to distinguish between self, other persons, and the world. Piaget traced the process of differentiation and coordination of action schemes through several sensorimotor substages.

Piaget's methodology for studying infancy consisted of naturalistic observation undertaken with his wife of their three infants, and the use of minor manipulations or experiments. Piaget's three books on infancy, based on detailed observations of his own three babies, have been referred to as 'Three of the most remarkable and original documents in psychology' (Russell, 1978, p. 98). They are devoted to describing the beginning of intelligence in infancy. Advantages of this approach include that it is longitudinal and may lead to the discovery of phenomena that would not occur in an experiment. They knew their infants well enough to make inferences about the success or failure of an action. Also, Piaget was an excellent observer.

Piaget's substages of sensorimotor development

Each stage represents a higher level of organisation and adaptation (equilibrium) and is built on previous ones. The substages are not defined by age, but rather by the structure/pattern of the interaction. Piaget was interested in what is general about the development of intelligence, so the substages describe forms of interaction of increasing levels of complexity, not infants. Indeed individual infants might use forms of interaction from more than one substage.

Stage 1 (0–1 months): reflex activity. Infants' interaction at this first stage consists of general patterns such as sucking, rooting, grasping, touching, crying, movement of arms and legs. These are not fixed reflexes like sneezing because even at this stage infants get better at these skills, such as finding their mother's nipple for feeding.

Stage 2 (1–4 months): primary circular reactions. These reactions are referred to as primary because they are centred on the baby's body and circular because they form cycles of movements repeating something that happened by chance which has resulted in an interesting sensation. For example, an infant may grasp her foot by accident and repeat it in order to feel it again. These are simple acts such as thumb sucking, hand clasping, and foot grabbing that the infant repeats. The activity is not just automatic as in reflexes. The *coordination* of two schemes can be seen at this stage in which they are integrated into a single whole action (e.g. looking and grasping, or reaching and sucking). Repeating an action is done for its own sake and the goal is the activity itself that the infant is enjoying. These are patterns of activity that are repeated to experience the sensations that go with them.

Is this just a matter of babies forming associations? Piaget described it differently: 'It is this active relationship between the subject and the objects that are charged with meanings which creates the association and not the association which creates this relationship' (Piaget, 1952, p. 131). That is, it is because things come to have meaning for the infant that they form associations. The bottle comes to have significance for a baby and he may open his mouth. From this perspective, the beginning point is the activity and that is tied up with needs and interests. Babies are not just passive machines forming associations. Instead, they are actively exploring their world, enjoying or getting frustrated and so on.

Stage 3 (4–8 months): secondary circular reactions. Secondary circular reactions now involve events or objects in the external environment, unlike primary circular reactions, which are centred on the infant's own body. The infant is focusing on the external consequences of the activity, not just the activity as in primary circular reactions. For example, Lucienne at 3 months 5 days, lying in her crib, kicks her legs, which causes the bassinet to sway back and forth resulting in the movement of dolls hanging from the hood. That is, there is an *effect* of her action and she tries to recreate that effect by repeating the same action. This is the beginning of intention, which involves differentiation of means and ends, but it was not clear that Lucienne kicked in order to make the dolls move or whether kicking and smiling simply made up a reaction of pleasure. This is different from Stage 2 in which the infant is just concerned with the action but not the result. It is also different from Stage 4 because the goal is set after the fact and the infant just tries to recreate something that has happened by chance. The relations such as shaking to make something move were discovered by chance and repeated but were not constructed on purpose. It is not that the infant wanted to do something and then figured out how to do it; instead, she accidently did something that resulted in an interesting effect and then repeated it.

Stage 4 (8–12 months): Coordination of secondary schemes. In contrast to Stage 3, activity at Stage 4 is truly goal-directed because the means are now differentiated from their ends or the goal the infant is trying to achieve. For example, Laurent (7 months, 13 days) strikes his father's hand to move it in order to get at a box of matches. In another example Laurent is trying to grasp a piece of paper that is too high. He uses the scheme: 'pulling the string' (which he has often done before to get things) and the 'grasping' scheme when he can reach the paper. In these purposeful, goal-directed acts, means and ends are differentiated and two independent schemes are hierarchically coordinated, with one serving as the end, the goal (grasping the matchbox), and the other serving as the means (hitting Piaget's hand). The coordination of two or more action schemes is referred to as reciprocal assimilation. The schemes become more 'mobile' in the sense that they can be detached from their original contents and applied to other objects and situations. A limitation is that at this point babies can only coordinate familiar schemes.

Stage 5 (12–18 months): Tertiary circular reactions: 'the discovery of new means through active experimentation'. At Stage 5 infants discover some new effects of their actions and then they perform that action over and over again with variations and learn the results of this trial and error process (Chapman, 1988). For example, infants might experiment with dropping objects. At this stage they gradually change an action pattern to fit a particular situation. Whereas at Stage 4 the infant might have to give up if none of the familiar schemes work, at Stage 5 she will try different means. Infants discover some new effect that one of their actions has caused and repeat the action with variation to see what will happen.

Stage 6 (over 18 months): The invention of new means through mental combinations. At this stage, instead of a series of trials and errors, infants seem to arrive at the solution before they act. For example, Lucienne at 1 year, 6 months, 23 days, was pushing a doll's carriage but she bumped into a wall. She then pulled the carriage instead of pushing it, but this was awkward because she had to walk backwards. She paused, and then walked around to the other side of the carriage and pushed from there, apparently anticipating that this would work (Piaget, 1936/1952). At this stage, the child's interaction with the world can be described in terms of mentally coordinating schemes before she acts (Müller, 2009).

Stages in the development of the object concept

Piaget's (1937/1954) second book on infancy, *The Construction of Reality in the Child*, describes the process by which the infant comes to understand her world through developing an understanding of the interrelated concepts of objects, space, time, and causality. Of these concepts, we focus only on the object concept because of its importance and the amount of research on this topic. In general, the development of the object concept reflects a dramatic change in the infant's experience of the world: right after birth, everything is centred on the baby's own body, and at the end of the sensorimotor period, the infant understands herself as one object in the same space as other objects.

At Stages 1 and 2 infants show no special behaviour regarding objects, but their action still suggests some knowledge of objects. This is because even at two months an infant may continue to look toward where a person has disappeared, apparently expecting that person to reappear there. At Stage 3 an infant can find and retrieve an object if it is partially covered. Infants at Stage 4 can find *completely covered* objects but they make a curious kind of mistake known as the A-not-B error. Piaget had noticed this when he was watching a 10-month-old baby playing with a ball. The ball rolled under an armchair where the infant found it. The baby threw it again and it rolled under a sofa where he could not find it, and then he went back to look under the armchair. In the A-not-B task, developed based on Piaget's observations, an object is hidden in one spot (A) and the infant finds it there several times, and then it is hidden instead in a second location (B). Infants at Stage 4 tend to look in the first location under A. They do this even if they see the object hidden right before their eyes and even if the cover is transparent (Chapman, 1988; Harris, 1974). From Piaget's perspective, this error suggests that our experience of a world of objects that we take for granted is gradually constructed during infancy. His explanation was that infants at this age only have a partial understanding of the object as continuing to exist, and it is tied to the infant's own actions of finding it in the first location. The object is still not differentiated from their action. Objects become more independent for the baby if they can be grasped, sucked and looked at; they become externalised in relation to the infant, and so not just linked to her own action. At Stage 5 infants can follow an experimenter changing the location of an object (e.g. a key or a coin) from one cover to another if the object is visible. Not until Stage 6 can infants do this if the object is not visible because it is hidden in the experimenter's hand when it is being moved from one location to another.

Thus, sensorimotor intelligence is practical, action-based, lived knowledge based on richly coordinated action schemes. This action-based knowledge can be reformulated on the plane of thought (by simply thinking through a problem) without the actual manipulation of objects. This signals the emergence of representation at the end of the sensorimotor stage. From this action-based perspective, being able to represent (or re-present) an object is the result of having learned a whole series of potential action patterns in the context of interacting with that object. But this can result in egocentrism at first because the child is not very good at controlling transformations and must acquire a broader set of perspectives – i.e. become decentred.

Preoperational stage (2 to 7 years)

At the end of the sensorimotor period the child is no longer limited to thinking about what is right in front of her. She can now re-present objects that are not currently present. The practical understandings of objects, space, causality, and time, which children develop during the sensorimotor period, must now be gradually reconstructed at the representational level involving objects that are present as well as absent. This stage extends from about 2 to about 7 years, and is divided into the substages of preconceptual thought (approximately 2 to 4 years) and intuitive thought (4 to 6–7 years). The beginning of the preoperational stage is indicated by the emergence of the symbolic or semiotic function. According to Piaget, the semiotic function underlies children's abilities to engage in a number of different activities, such as imitation when the model being imitated is no longer present ('deferred imitation'), pretend play, drawing, and language. A limitation of preoperational thought is that while this form of thinking is no longer attached to particular objects or events (the here-and-now), children do not understand the difference between individual members of a concept and a general concept. For example, Piaget noted that his daughter Jacqueline, at the age of 31 months, said 'the slug' to refer to any slugs she saw when walking on a particular road every morning. She would say 'There it is!', and later on saw another slug a short distance away and said 'There's the slug again' (Piaget, 1945/1962, p. 225, Obs. 107). Piaget referred to this as a preconcept because Jacqueline had no clear understanding yet of individual members of a general class and particular objects in the class (Bibok, Carpendale, & Müller, 2009; Piaget, 1945/1962).

At the second, intuitive substage of preoperational thought, children develop the ability to relate two schemes at the symbolic level to each other. For example, in comparing the liquid in two differently shaped containers, children may use height in order to infer the amount of liquid but ignore the width of the container. Intuitive thought remains centred on one dimension at a time; children are not yet capable of relating two dimensions to each other.

Concrete operational stage (7 to 11 years)

Concrete operational thinking begins to emerge at about 6 to 7 years of age. According to Piaget, thought originates in actions such as putting similar objects together, and putting objects in one-to-one correspondence. At this stage children can solve problems without actually performing these actions; that is, these actions are interiorised and are what Piaget referred to as operations. These operations become coordinated and integrated into logical systems. As a result, children no longer focus (centre) on one aspect of a situation, and they can mentally reverse transformations that have occurred in reality. The coordination of operations into systems also leads to the emergence of logical necessity.

Piaget devised a variety of tasks to assess concrete operational thinking, many of them requiring understanding forms of conservation. Conservation refers to the understanding that a whole exists as a quantitative invariant and therefore remains intact even if its parts are rearranged. For example, in a conservation of length task two sticks of equal length are placed side-by-side, then an experimenter moves one so that the ends of the sticks no longer line up and asks the child if one is now longer. A child using preoperational reasoning will focus on one end and thus will claim that one is now longer. Being able to conserve length and use concrete operational thinking involves overcoming the misleading appearance and understanding that the sticks are still the same length. Passing a conservation of number task requires understanding that if a line of coins is rearranged by spreading them out, this does not change the number of objects even though it may appear to because the line is longer. A conservation of liquid task involves showing a child that two glasses contain the same amount of liquid and then pouring one of them into a tall thin glass. The experimenter then asks the child if one glass has more. Preoperational thinking consists of being misled by the appearance and claiming that one now has more, usually the tall glass because it is higher but it could also be the wide glass if the child focuses on that dimension. Concrete operational reasoning involves understanding that the amount of liquid is still the same because nothing has changed. To understand that the liquid has not changed, children need to coordinate transformations in two dimensions – the width and the height. An operative understanding of conservation is logical in nature; it is not acquired by simply repeatedly observing transformations. When Piaget discussed this development with Einstein, Einstein remarked 'It's more complicated than physics!' (Bringuier, 1980, p. 135).

Given his commitment to the idea that knowledge is not simply a copy of the world, Piaget believed that an *operation* is the essence of knowledge. To 'know' is to modify or to transform the object and understand the process of this transformation, and as a consequence also understand the way the object is constructed. For example, an operation would consist of grouping objects in a class to classify or order objects, put them in a series, or count or measure them.

Operations are never isolated. They are always linked and exist within a system of operations. For example, numbers exist in a whole system, so the ability to add and subtract applies to all sorts of numbers (Chapman, 1988). The concept of number develops; it is not innate or in the environment; it is in the child's action on the world. The actions of grouping objects together and separating them are the basis for children learning about addition and subtraction (Chapman, 1988). Physical actions such as putting together or taking apart become interiorised when children can understand the process without actually having to perform them and they are aware of the potential actions.

These forms of thinking are concrete; that is, children still reason in terms of objects, and so they are limited to reasoning in terms of concrete objects – and not in terms of hypotheses that can be thought about before knowing whether they are true or false.

Formal operational stage (12 to 15 years)

The last stage of cognitive development described by Piaget emerges during adolescence. Piaget and his collaborator Bärbel Inhelder studied *formal operations* by presenting children and adolescents with materials and asking them to discover scientific laws (Inhelder & Piaget, 1958).

PIAGET'S PENDULUM TASK

In the pendulum task children and adolescents were presented with a pendulum that they could manipulate by varying the length of the string, and using different weights. They were asked to figure out what factor determines the oscillation of the pendulum: the weight, the length of string, the height of dropping point, or the force of push? The adolescents formulated hypotheses and derived predictions, then tested them systematically by varying the factors one at a time. In this way they could exclude hypotheses that did not fit with their observations. Adolescents' approach demonstrates hypthetico-deductive reasoning, which Piaget viewed as an essential characteristic of formal operational thinking.

The ability to think of possibilities raises the potential to generate hypotheses, or possible solutions to a problem, and then deduction can be used to draw out the implications from the hypotheses. For example, the adolescents may have started out with the hypothesis that the length of the string determines the oscillation of the pendulum. If this were true, then the pendulum should swing faster with a short string and more slowly with a long string. At the same time, they realise that there are other factors (e.g. weight) that might also affect the oscillation of the pendulum. Thus, in order to arrive at a definite answer that it is only the length of the string that affects the oscillation of the pendulum, they have to vary the length of the string and hold the other factors constant (e.g. compare the frequency of oscillations for long and short strings, holding the weight, force of push, and height of dropping point constant). They must then repeat this process for all other variables to rule out that they may affect the frequency of oscillation.

This systematic experimentation and the isolation of variables is only possible because children start with mere possibilities and make deductions about what would happen if one of these possibilities were true. In Piaget's words, formal-operational thinkers subordinate reality to possibility – they start with a number of possible scenarios, deduce what would follow if one were true, carry out systematic experimentation to test their hypotheses, and then arrive at what actually is the case. In contrast, children at the concrete-operational level do not systematically vary one factor at a time because they cannot systematically consider the different possibilities and deduce what would be the case if they were true.

This form of thinking is called 'formal operations' because it involves a separation of the form from the content. Children can start with mere possibilities and then draw the necessary conclusions on the basis of these hypotheses.

However, not all adolescents pass Piagetian formal operational reasoning tasks, both within Western cultures as well as across other cultures. Piaget (1972/2008) considered three possible explanations for this finding. The first is that the speed of development at which individuals progress through the stages will vary depending on social environments that differ in intellectual stimulation. A second hypothesis is that adolescents differ in their talents and interests, and only those with aptitudes in physics and mathematics will pass formal operational tasks because the tasks Piaget used were logical-mathematical in nature. Therefore, literary, artistic, or practical adolescents may not pass them. But Piaget considered a third possibility most probable – all individuals develop formal operational thinking either between the ages of 11 to 15 or between 15 to 20, but they do so in their area of activity and expertise. Piaget used law as an example that contrasts with physics and mathematics, but activities such as mechanics, carpentry, baking, or farming could all involve hypothetical thinking in solving problems.

3.5 EVALUATING CRITICISM OF PIAGET'S THEORY

As well as being very influential, Piaget has also been highly criticised. When he was interviewed Piaget said that he was the most criticised author in psychology and he got through it alive (Bringuier, 1980). Much of this criticism, however, has been based on misunderstandings of his theory. What has been referred to as the 'received view' has become entrenched in textbooks and, unfortunately, this incorrect interpretation is all that readers may be aware of. But Piagetian scholarship has shown that this 'received view' and the criticisms based on it are flawed (e.g. Chapman, 1988). When Piaget was asked what he felt about the recognition he received, he said 'I'm pleased by it, of course, but it's pretty catastrophic when I see how I'm understood' (Bringuier, 1980, p. 54). Therefore, providing a contemporary account of Piaget's theory requires addressing common criticisms of his theory in order to facilitate a better understanding of his contribution. Because many of these criticisms are based on a misunderstanding of that theory, addressing these criticisms will provide us with the opportunity to clarify his theory.

Challenges to Piaget's views of the object concept

Challenges to Piaget's theory of infant development derive from the neonativist approach, which claims that infants have an innate core knowledge of the physical world (Spelke & Kinzler, 2007). There is no dispute regarding the importance of the ability to think about objects that are not in the immediate visual field. The object concept is of fundamental importance in our everyday lives; we can't conceive of thinking of the world without this concept. Instead, the controversy is over how and when this understanding develops. Piaget's view of how infants develop an understanding of objects has been challenged by Renée Baillargeon and others (e.g. Baillargeon, 1987, 2004, 2008). They argue that Piaget's method of assessment requires manual search and this could be too difficult for young infants, and therefore this method fails to reveal early knowledge of objects (Baillargeon, 1987, 2004).

In a well-known study, Baillargeon (1987) used the habituation–dishabituation technique, a method used for studying infants' perceptual abilities. Infants are repeatedly shown something until they are thoroughly bored with it; that is, they have habituated and stopped paying attention to it. Then they are shown something new. If the babies lack the ability to tell the difference they will continue ignoring it, but if they now pay attention again it shows that they have noticed a difference. From the increase in looking behaviour it can be concluded that they notice a difference, but not what that difference is. In Baillargeon's (1987) study infants were habituated to watching a screen move back and forward through 180 degrees like a 'drawbridge'. After this, a box was placed behind the drawbridge and the infants were shown either a possible event in which the drawbridge stopped at the box, or an 'impossible' event in which it seemed to pass right through the box, but in fact an unseen research assistant had surreptitiously removed the box. This method is known as the violation of expectation paradigm. The hypothesis was that if infants understand that objects are permanent they should be surprised if the drawbridge passes through the box, and this surprise would be shown by the infants looking longer in the impossible condition. As hypothesised, infants as young as 3½ months did look longer in the impossible condition.

Thus, Baillargeon claimed that Piaget had underestimated the age at which infants develop knowledge of objects. But this was not just a disagreement about age. Baillargeon argued that if infants were showing knowledge of objects this early they must be developing it through a different process from that suggested by Piaget, and therefore his account of object permanence that infants learned through action by coordinating sensorimotor schemes must be wrong. Recently, Baillargeon (2008, p. 11) has claimed that infants have an 'innate' 'principle of persistence, which states that objects persist, as they are, in time and space'. This idea resonates with those of other authors who argue for innate knowledge (Spelke & Kinzler, 2007). Baillargeon and others have also used many other research paradigms (see Chapter 10) in addition to the drawbridge series of studies, and similar claims have been made about these other lines of research. But here we focus on the drawbridge study because of the controversy and follow-up research it has generated.

Responses to challenges

Many textbooks stop the story at this point, claiming that Piaget's view of how and when infants develop an understanding of objects has been shown to be incorrect. However, these claims are very controversial and there are extensive responses to these challenges (e.g. Allen & Bickhard, 2013; Haith, 1998; Müller & Giesbrecht, 2008; Müller & Overton, 1998). Baillargeon's strong claims about infants' abilities are based on a particular inter-pretion of the differences in looking time: the infant's longer looking time in an impossible condition is interpreted as surprise, which is viewed as indicating that an infant realises a violation of the laws of physics has occurred. This 'rich' interpretation has been critiqued because all that is shown is that the infants notice a difference between the two conditions. For Baillargeon's argument to hold, looking longer must mean that they have the ability to reason, realise, generate expectations, and hence their surprise when the expectations are not fulfilled. But the looking time paradigm was developed to assess infants' sensory or perceptual capabilities, and its extension to the study of higher-level cognitive processes creates some obstacles (Haith, 1998; Haith & Benson, 1998).

Length of looking time indicates that infants notice a difference between conditions but this can be influenced by perceptual differences between conditions rather than knowledge of objects. Some studies suggest that longer looking time may be due to a perceptual prefer-ence for the impossible condition (Rivera, Wakeley, & Langer, 1999). Infancy researchers also know that both the novelty and familiarity of a new display influence infants' looking time. In general, after a few familiarisation trials infants prefer familiarity, but after more trials they prefer to look at something new, and this shift occurs more quickly if the dis-play is simple (and slower if the display is complex). In a series of studies Bogartz Shinsky and Speaker (1997) systematically varied familiarity and novelty, and on the basis of their results argued that these perceptual factors explained Baillargeon's results, not possibility or impossibility (Special issue of *Infancy* [2000]; Bogartz, Shinskey, & Schilling, 2000).

In a commentary on this research, Baillargeon (e.g. 2000) claims that there were subtle methodological differences in the perceptual display, such as the distance that infants sat from the screen, how brightly lit the room was, or the number of seconds between trials which resulted in not replicating her findings. But this argument fits better with the position that differences in looking times may be due to perceptual differences. If infants really understand object permanence it is not clear why these minor differences would make such a difference (see also Allen & Bickhard, 2013). Furthermore, if infants at 3 to 4 months know that objects exist, it is not clear why they still make the 'A not B error' even at 8 months. Baillargeon argues they have difficulty with means–ends reasoning. That is, they can't coordinate what they have to do (move the screen) to reach their goal (get the object). However, they handle means–end relations just fine in the A-trials, so this cannot be the critical feature for why they fail in the B-trials where they look in the wrong place (Müller & Overton, 1998).

It is important to be cautious about overly rich interpretations. Of course, we know that infants develop into adults, but we have to be careful to avoid excessive 'adultocentrism' – i.e. assuming that infants think in the same way as adults. It has been argued that neonativist research such as Baillargeon's is non-developmental, because it implies that the earliest suggestion of an ability is taken as indicating that the infant has mastered a concept (Haith 1998). Baillargeon's argument for rejecting Piaget's view only follows if his description of the substages of the development of object permanence is collapsed into a dichotomy: either an infant has object permanence or she doesn't. In fact, Piaget did not claim that very young infants had no idea of the external world. Even at Stage 2 infants have some knowledge of objects. Piaget observed his son at two months looking toward where his father had disappeared, apparently expecting him to reappear (1937/1954, pp. 8–9, Obs. 2). In developmental research, abilities are not either present or absent; instead different forms emerge in a developmental progression. So, it seems that Baillargeon's results are actually consistent with Piaget's observations!

So why spend so much time talking about object permanence? It is an important concept, a foundation of an understanding of our world. Also, this debate brings out more of what Piaget meant by knowledge and development, and the need to be aware of the assumptions that theories are based on (Müller & Giesbrecht, 2008). It shows the close connection between philosophical issues and developmental theory and research (i.e. the difficult philosophical question of knowledge and how it develops). Baillargeon claims to have demonstrated that infants continue to represent objects when they cannot see them, and believes that she is using the term 'representation' in the same sense as Piaget, but others argue that she is using it in a very different way (Müller & Giesbrecht, 2008). Part of the problem is what is meant by 'representation' – a word that is used in such different ways that James Russell (1992) called it a Humpty Dumpty term – that it can mean anything you want it to. However, developmentalists usually mean the ability to think about something that is not right in front of us. That is, the ability to 're-present'. Let's compare this view with Baillargeon's.

This debate has methodological dimensions but it also illustrates how research programmes are based on different worldviews. Baillargeon assumes the cognitivist worldview introduced in Chapter 1, which is based on an empiricist causal representational view of knowledge as passive and caused by perceptual information, which then enters a computational system. According to Baillargeon (2004, p. 422) what infants 'possess is an abstract computational system, a physical reasoning system that monitors physical events and flags those that do not unfold as expected for further scrutiny'. In other words, she does not take knowledge of reality as a problem. Knowledge is simply a matter of perception. Baillargeon does not explain how an infant's representation caused by perception is different from a camera's image, even if the information is then processed by 'an abstract computational system' (Bickhard, 1999; Heil, 1981).

In contrast, recall that Piaget starts from a critique of this passive view of knowledge, and begins from the contrasting worldview – a process-relational one according to which infants learn about the world through coming to anticipate what will happen when they act on it. Thus although adults and older children might feel they have knowledge of the world through perception, this is because they have gone through a gradual developmental process in the course of which the world becomes meaningful to them (Müller, 2009; Müller & Giesbrecht, 2008; Müller & Overton, 1998; Müller et al., 1998). This debate illustrates the fundamental differences between the two approaches to how the mind is conceptualised (Müller, 2009).

Procedural décalages: inconsistency in different forms of a task

A common criticism of Piaget presented in many textbooks is that he underestimated children's abilities because his tasks were too difficult. Much of this criticism was a misreading of work within the Piagetian tradition (Donaldson, 1978). It was argued that his tasks require memory and verbal skills that prevent researchers from assessing children's true competence. The solution suggested was to simplify the tasks. For example, it was argued that Piaget's conservation of number task with five objects was too complex and required performance factors such as memory and attention that are obstacles to assessing the child's ability. When the task was simplified to include only two or three objects it was found that preschoolers could pass the task, and thus it was claimed that this competency develops earlier than previously thought (Gelman, 1972). This inconsistency in reasoning on different forms of a task is referred to as *procedural décalage*. The simplified task, however, may be solved in a different way. Children can count the objects at a glance, called 'subitising'. That is, they can see immediately that there is the same number of objects in each row. But if they pass the task by subitising they are not conserving number. If children can pass the task with a different ability the task is no longer assessing what it was designed for. The conservation of number tasks were intentionally designed to assess the ability to overcome the misleading cue of the length of the rows in order to pass the task. The simplified version is measuring something different (Chapman, 1988). The focus is on the success or failure on the task, not on the form of reasoning used, which was what Piaget was interested in. The strategy of eliminating performance factors may change the competence assessed by the task, because the revised task may be solved with a different competence.

Horizontal décalage: inconsistency in forms of reasoning

Piaget is typically portrayed as a stage theorist who claimed that stages are general structures that define a child's behaviour in each area of cognitive functioning. Therefore, the authors of many textbooks claim that Piaget predicted consistency in reasoning within stages. That is, it is assumed that once a child can pass a concrete operational reasoning task she has reached that stage, and would then be expected to use that form of reasoning on all such tasks. This is *the received view* and it is also referred to as the *mental logic* interpretation of Piaget. It is assumed that Piaget believed that children solve concrete operational reasoning tasks such as those measuring transitivity by developing logical principles. In transitivity tasks, the child is shown three sticks and told that A is greater than B and B is greater than C. The child can therefore assume the transitive relation that A is necessarily greater than C. This is a logical principle that applies to length or weight or any other dimension, so that once a child understands this principle it would seem that she should be able to apply it to any problem of this form. However, children's behaviour is inconsistent. For example, a child may reason at a preoperational level on one conservation task and at a concrete operational level on another. This inconsistency in forms of reasoning across different tasks is referred to as *horizontal décalage* and is demonstrated by passing some concrete operational reasoning tasks while failing others. For example, children tend to pass the conservation of substance task at about 7 to 8 years, weight at 9 to 10 years, and volume at 11 to 12 years. Similarly, children pass transitivity of length problems before transitivity of weight problems. Consequently, it is argued that Piaget's theory is flawed because empirical evidence shows inconsistency in reasoning.

This conclusion depends on whether it is indeed true that Piaget's theory implies mental logic. However, this portrayal of Piaget's stage theory is utterly incorrect (Chapman, 1988; Lourenço & Machado, 1996; Smith, 1993). Piaget did *not* claim that stages are characterised by homogeneity. In fact, he often made the opposite point that variability should be expected (Chapman, 1988). Michael Chapman (1988) tried to find a clear statement from Piaget showing that he expected consistency in reasoning. But after searching through Piaget's books and articles, Chapman could not find such a claim; instead, he found that Piaget stated there is no reason to expect consistency and he reported inconsistency (horizontal décalage). Piaget's books (*The Origins of Intelligence in Children*; *The Construction of Reality in the Child*; *Play, Dreams and Imitation in Childhood*) sometimes gave examples of different stages of thinking from the same child. This shows that he was classifying forms of thought, not children as being 'in' or 'at' a stage. Furthermore, variability in children's performance on structurally similar tasks is entirely consistent with the basis of Piaget's claim that thought originates in action. Based on this assumption, cognitive structures should, at first, be linked to the context and the materials the child is working with. That is, cognitive structures cannot be separated from their content (the materials), and although structures involving different content (e.g. number and volume) may be of the same *logical* form, they develop independently in a *functional* sense through the child's activity with these different areas of content. For example, children could solve a transitivity of length task based on their experience of comparing sticks of varying length and coordinating these comparisons to reach the answer. Given enough experience they can solve the problem without actually physically doing the comparison. Although the same logical principle underlies transitivity problems involving weight, children's way of solving such tasks at the concrete operational level depends on their experience with such materials (Chapman, 1988).

This misunderstanding of Piaget's theory is due to a misconception of his view of stages, interpreting these as being the result of simple maturation. In contrast, for Piaget stages describe different forms of thinking. Thus, a child is not in a stage; rather she may use various forms of reasoning and it is those forms of reasoning that can be described in terms of stages. The *sequence* of stages or forms of thinking is important because each form of thinking builds on previous ones.

Criticism: did Piaget ignore social factors?

It is often claimed that Piaget ignored social factors and that his theory took an individualistic approach to studying the child interacting with the physical world – this is the image of a child playing by herself with pebbles on the beach and figuring out the concept of number. In fact, this is not correct. In his early work (e.g. 1928) Piaget argued that reasoning has a social origin in arguing with others. He continued to write about the importance of social factors (e.g. Piaget, 1950; 1977/1995), but this line of work was not translated until 1995. He also argued that although social factors are important they are not sufficient for a full explanation because they don't explain *how* new knowledge develops, nor how the child develops to the point at which she can learn about the knowledge available from others. Piaget (1932/1965, 1950) also argued that it was obvious that social experience was important, but it is necessary to go beyond this claim to explore the influence of different types of social relationships – a point we return to in the last two chapters of this book.

SUMMARY AND CONCLUSION

We have focused on Piaget's theory in this chapter as a prototypical theory of development based on a process-relational worldview, also referred to as a constructive, action-based account or embodied or enactive approach. His theory is astounding in terms of both its scope and depth. It addresses fundamental epistemological questions such as the relations between biology and cognition, cognition and affect, the social and the individual, and nature and nurture. He presented a systematic theory of the role of action and experience in development. In these respects, it is still unparalleled.

At the same time it is challenging to understand, and in order to do so it is essential to grasp the questions he was grappling with. Susan Carey (1985) and others point out that the changes in Piaget's thinking make the theory hard to pin down. Yet, his goal was to understand how scientific knowledge develops, and this involves how new knowledge develops as well as how it becomes rigorous. One way to approach this problem is to study how knowledge develops in children. Piaget was interested in what is general about how intelligence develops. Rather than focusing on individuals this means describing forms of thinking that are general steps on the way to more complex thinking. In doing so, he described a series of stages beginning with sensorimotor intelligence, followed by preoperational, concrete-operational, and finally formal operational thinking.

The next step is to study the development from one form of thinking to another. In explaining development, Piaget discussed the usual factors of maturation, experience with the physical and social world, but he argued that a fourth factor was required: equilibration. Assimilation and accommodation are the two interrelated aspects of this process. Assimilation involves applying a general scheme to a particular situation, and this always involves some adjustment, which is accommodation, the way in which a general scheme is modified. Assimilation carries the history of the child's interactions. That is, the child encounters situations and understands them in terms of what has happened before. Young children understand the world in terms of action potentials, things they could do with objects.

As well as being very influential, Piaget's work has also been heavily criticised. Many of these criticisms, however, were based on flawed interpretations of his theory. Thus, although some interpretations of his theory assume that he expected consistency in reasoning within stages, he actually expected horizontal décalages (inconsistency in reasoning across tasks). Hence the existence of horizontal décalages does not contradict his theory. He was also criticised for neglecting the role of social and emotional factors in development. Although he was aware of their importance, his own interests lay in other areas. Michael Chapman (1988) and others have defended his theory, but this doesn't mean that it is should not be the subject of criticism. He was constantly revising his theory. Like any other it should be criticised and improved, but in order to advance it the criticisms should be based on an understanding of his theory and goals (see Müller et al., 2009).

What is the future of Piaget's theory? Our presentation of his work in this chapter has just scratched the surface of his extensive investigations, and he continued developing new ideas even toward the end of his life when he was in his eighties. There is still continuing work on his theory. We have used his approach to the acquisition of thinking as a good example of an action-based view of development. He was concerned in particular with logical-mathematical knowledge, but the general approach to development can be applied in other areas beyond those that Piaget focused on. In other chapters in this book we consider approaches applying this view to communicative, social, and moral development. His work on moral development will be discussed in Chapters 13 and 14.

FURTHER READING

Carpendale, J. I. M., Müller, U., & Bibok, M. (2008). Piaget's theory of cognitive development. In N. J. Salkind (ed.), *Encyclopedia of Educational Psychology*, vol. 2 (pp. 798–804). Thousand Oaks, CA: Sage Publications.

Chapman, M. (1988). *Constructive Evolution: Origins and Development of Piaget's Thought*. New York: Cambridge University Press.

(Continued)

Lourenço, O., & Machado, A. (1996). In defense of Piaget's theory: A reply to 10 common criticisms. *Psychological Review*, 103, 143–164.

Müller, U., Carpendale, J. I. M., & Smith, L. (eds) (2009). *The Cambridge Companion to Piaget*. Cambridge: Cambridge University Press.

VIDEO LINKS

A not B error: www.youtube.com/watch?v=lhHkJ3InQOE

Piagetian tasks: www.youtube.com/watch?v=gnArvcWaH6I&feature=related

Piaget on Piaget, part 1: www.youtube.com/watch?v=I1JWr4G8YLM

Part 2: www.youtube.com/watch?v=Qb4TPj1pxzQ

Part 3: www.youtube.com/watch?v=x9nSC_Xgabc

Part 4: www.youtube.com/watch?v=cVSaEHhOEZY

4 SOCIOCULTURAL APPROACHES TO CHILDREN'S THINKING

LEARNING OUTCOMES

By the end of this chapter you should:

- Be able to define sociogenesis.
- Understand the details of Vygotsky's theory of the development of thinking.
- Understand the idea of the zone of proximal development, and how this follows from Vygotsky's view of the social origins of thinking.
- Be able to discuss Vygotsky's view of the role of language in the development of forms of thought, and how this is related to Piaget's views on the topic.
- Understand how the topic of the development of an understanding of numbers is approached differently from the theoretical perspectives of Vygotsky, Piaget, information-tion processing, and neo-nativist positions.
- Be aware of similarities and differences between Vygotsky's and Piaget's theories, and ideas about how they can be combined.

4.1 THE SOCIAL ORIGIN OF THE MIND

Sociogenesis refers to the idea that human minds originate within social processes. The view that thinking has social origins has a long history and is currently of great importance in developmental psychology. The currently best-known proponent of this view is the Soviet psychologist Lev Vygotsky. According to Vygotsky, all higher mental functions or complex thinking appear twice – first between people in social interaction (or, as he calls it, on the inter-psychological plane) and then within the person (or on the intra-psychological plane).

Although in psychology the focus has been on the work of Vygotsky, the idea of sociogenesis can be traced back to Marx and Engel's view that consciousness derives from the nature of materially grounded activities. It also has its roots in the work of the French psychologist Pierre Janet according to whom all higher mental acts have a social origin: 'All social conducts performed vis-a-vis others have their private repercussions. All things we do vis-a-vis others, we do them vis-a-vis ourselves; we treat ourselves as another' (Janet, 1928, p. 22; translated and cited in van der Veer & Valsiner, 1988, pp. 57–58). Furthermore, Janet seems to have been influenced by James Mark Baldwin (Valsiner, 2000), who started his career in Toronto, Canada, before moving to the US and then continuing his writing during his exile in Paris and Mexico City. One of Baldwin's key ideas was that the development of self-concept (ego) is intrinsically linked to the interaction with and understanding of the other (alter ego): 'The ego and the alter are thus born together' (Baldwin, 1906, p. 321; see Müller & Runions, 2003; Müller, Carpendale, Budwig, & Sokol, 2008). Elsewhere, Baldwin (1911, p. 281) wrote the following about development (or, in his terms, 'genetic conditions'): 'Work in social psychology has greatly modified the notion of the individual. The individual is found to be a social product, a complex result, having its genetic conditions in actual social life.' Thus, the idea of sociogenesis has a long complex history and it should not be attributed to the work of a single individual. In fact, it can also be traced to American philosophers such as George Herbert Mead writing in the early twentieth century in the United States (Valsiner & van de Veer, 2000). Mead's ideas, unfortunately, did not catch on even though they were available and did not require translation. Here, however, we focus on Vygotsky since he has had a greater influence on developmental psychology over the last half century. But his work should be considered in the broader context of the history of these ideas (Valsiner & van de Veer, 2000).

This chapter is divided into four sections. In the first, we introduce the general principles behind Vygotsky's theory. In the second we describe four key concepts in Vygotsky's account of development. In the third we examine the empirical evidence from studies that have attempted to test some of these central ideas of the theory. Finally, a brief section compares Piaget's and Vygotsky's theories as many developmental psychologists have misconstrued some of the points of comparison between them.

4.2 SOCIOCULTURAL APPROACHES: LEV VYGOTSKY

Lev Vygotsky was born in 1896, the same year as Piaget. Piaget's long career lasted over sixty years and ended just before his death at the age of 84. Tragically, Vygotsky died, at the age of 38 in 1934, of tuberculosis, which he contracted after nursing his mother and younger brother. As a youth he had been determined to go to university, but in tsarist Russia – because he was Jewish – he had to achieve a gold medal in gymnasium (similar to high school and first-year college in North America) by achieving the highest grades in all his courses. At that time only 3 to 5% of university students were allowed to be Jewish. Vygotsky did, in fact, earn a coveted gold medal, but unfortunately – just months before his examinations – the authorities changed the policy so that Jews would be admitted based on a lottery. Fortunately, Vygotsky was lucky and was admitted to university. He took a diverse range of courses, including medicine and law, as well as courses in philosophy, psychology, and education. It appears that he was going to both Moscow University and Shanyavsky University, and according to his daughter graduated from both in 1917 (Valsiner & van de Veer, 2000).

Unlike Piaget's background in biology, Vygotsky began his studies in art and literature. His interest in psychology was linked to his interest in theatre and literature, studying authors such as Dostoyevsky, and his Master's thesis was on *Hamlet*. Vygotsky even founded his own publishing house and published several books of poetry until they ran out of paper. He did not make the move to psychology until he was 27, and then he began teaching at the First Moscow State University. In 1925 he became very ill with tuberculosis and was in hospital for six months and in bed for several more. Two years later he was able to resume work but died in 1934. Vygotsky was a Marxist and welcomed the 1917 revolution. Yet, with Stalin's seizure of power the intellectual climate in the Soviet Union became increasingly restrictive, and his work was heavily criticised by the Soviet authorities in his final years.

In spite of his short career in psychology of about ten years Vygotsky accomplished a surprising amount of work. He held several academic positions, had a heavy teaching load, edited translations, worked as a clinical consultant for 'maladapted' children, and wrote most of his books and papers either when recovering from his illness in hospital, or at home in a tiny apartment with his two small children playing or sleeping (Valsiner & van de Veer, 2000). His best-known book, *Thought and Language*, was published after his death in 1934. It was not translated into English until 1962, with better translations in 1986 and 1987. In the early 1960s, his work started to have a great influence on North American psychology. Since then more of his writing has been published in six volumes of his collected works.

Vygotsky's claim that thinking originates in social activity is summed up in his 'general genetic law of cultural development' in the following often-cited quote (note that 'genetic' at the time Vygotsky was writing meant developmental and did not refer to genes):

Every function in the cultural development of the child appears on the stage twice, in two planes, first, the social, then the psychological, first between people as an intermental category, then within the child as an intramental category. (Vygotsky, 1997)

Vygotsky's genetic law implies that forms of thought are first external and social before becoming internal as they are gradually mastered by individuals. The law highlights Vygotsky's developmental process approach to psychology because he focuses on the process through which forms of thinking develop rather than just on the outcome. For Vygotsky (1981, p. 165), development is the 'conversion of social relations into mental functions', and so thinking is an activity that is first distributed between people, and gradually the child can take this over and master it as an individual process. The term 'internalisation' is used to refer to this movement from the external to the internal, to making an external social process internal in the sense that the individual can do it herself.

How should the process of internalisation be understood? One view is that it is a passive copying process whereby the child just 'soaks up' whatever she experiences through a form of mental imitation. This idea was prominent in the nineteenth-century accounts of human development (Danziger, 1985). Alternatively, internalisation is understood as an active process by means of which the child appropriates and transforms whatever information she is provided with by others.

Word learning is not just copying

Let us look at children's word learning. On the surface it appears that when your child uses the word 'dog' to refer to a four-legged furry creature, after you have taught her this word on numerous occasions, that she is just copying your verbal utterance. But when your child then creatively goes on to refer to cats, rabbits, and other four-legged furry creatures as 'dog', you notice that she has transformed the meaning of the word based on her own understanding.

Vygotsky appears to have understood internalisation in the latter, active, transformative sense (Valsiner & Lawrence, 1997). He believed that it was interpersonal activity (i.e. our social interactions and relationships) that created these internal processes. In the words of a colleague, 'the process of internalization is not a *transferral* of an external activity to a preexisting, internal plane of consciousness: it is the process in which this internal plane is *formed*' (Leontiev, 1981, p. 57).

It is important to be clear that this view is different from social learning theory according to which children learn from others through observation, imitation, and modelling (Bandura, 1977). Vygotsky argued that people were not just influenced by the social world. Much more than this is implied. Thinking is not just influenced by others; it is actually socially *constituted* because it is formed through social activities.

Vygotsky distinguished between three domains of inquiry and each of them is required to fully understand development. The first is evolutionary or phylogenetic. It concerns the evolution of the human species. Inquiry in this domain uncovers the potential for development. For example, the evolution of a large and complex brain does not, by itself, explain human thinking, but it provides the plasticity that is the condition for its development in a social context. The second domain concerns sociocultural and historical change. Inquiry in this domain examines how the cultural and historical time period can influence children's development. For instance, a research topic pursued in this domain is whether learning to read and write affects a child's cognitive development. The third domain is ontogenetic or individual development. To understand the development of human forms of thinking it is important to think of the child's evolved biological characteristics in the context of development within a social and cultural setting (Wertsch, 1985, 1991). The examples that Vygotsky explored here involved the gradual acquisition of language (1934/1986), memory and higher-level thinking skills (Vygotsky, 1978), which we now term 'executive function' (see Chapter 10).

So how does Vygotsky's theory work? To understand the processes that he proposes, we now turn to the three key features of his approach.

The zone of proximal (or potential) development

If thinking develops within social relations, then there will be a protracted time in the child's development when she will not perform particular tasks at the level of complexity of an adult. During this period she may succeed in solving a task when she receives help from others but she may not succeed without such support. This difference between how the child performs by him- or herself and with the assistance of others gives rise to the idea of the 'zone of proximal development' (ZPD), which is closely related to the movement from the interindividual plane to the intrapsychological plane. Exchanging the word 'proximal' for 'potential', as Luria did (Vocate, 1987), may be helpful in understanding this concept. The ZPD is defined as 'the distance between the actual developmental level as determined by independent problem solving and the level of potential development as determined through problem-solving under adult guidance or in collaboration with more capable peers' (Vygotsky, 1978, p. 86). This idea naturally follows from the idea that thinking develops from social activity. Specifically, the child will internalise and appropriate the more advanced problem-solving skills and strategies that others enact when assisting the child.

This approach also leads to a different way of thinking about assessing children's abilities. The standard approach to intelligence adopted by psychologists, like Francis Galton (1869), perceives this ability as unchanging and a reflection of our 'natural' or genetically endowed propensities. According to this view children's intelligence (known as 'IQ' or 'g') is assessed with tests that must be solved without assistance to allow for their true competence to be measured. Instead, Vygotsky recognised that two children may be at the same level of actual development, as assessed with a regular test, but they may differ in their level of potential development, as shown by giving them increasing social support. Accordingly, Vygotsky argued that children should not just be assessed by themselves but also under conditions in which they received assistance. The ZPD also reveals the functions that are only in the process of development but are not yet fully mature and mastered by individuals. Those functions are displayed when the child is assisted by others. Gradually she will internalise such skills and perform them without the assistance of others.

Psychological tools

Vygotsky introduced the distinction between 'elementary' and 'higher' mental functions. Elementary functions are derived from the natural or biological line of development. They are products of evolution and biologically explained. They include associative memory, classical conditioning (the propensity to make simple connections between events) and involuntary attention. Higher mental functions are the product of the social or cultural line of development. They involve more complex thought processes. For example, memory can be aided by various cultural products such as culturally derived sign systems like tying a knot in a handkerchief, making a shopping list or taking notes. A list of cultural devices that mediate the natural line of development from Vygotsky covers:

> language; various systems for counting; mnemonic techniques; algebraic symbol systems; works of art; writing; schemes, diagrams, maps, and mechanical drawings; all sorts of conventional signs. (Vygotsky, 1981, p. 137)

These psychological tools are used as a way of influencing the mind. They are social because they are not invented by the individual. Instead, they are products of socio-cultural evolution, and individuals are exposed to them through a culture – across generations or within a peer group. Since their primary function is communication, these tools will be shaped by the demands of conversational exchange. Thus, because mental processes originate in social activity they are 'quasi-social' in nature. Emerging from this social activity they become mastered by an individual. Thus, as a consequence of interaction, on the psychological plane, speech can take on an intellectual function in addition to communication.

These cultural products were not intentionally designed as tools for thinking. However, a current area of computer science, known as *information visualization*, is devoted to designing tools meant to assist in thinking and decision making in particular areas by presenting information visually in ways that facilitate thinking about it.

Thinking and speech

Language is the psychological tool to which Vygotsky devoted most of his attention. The ways in which talking and thinking are related have been discussed by philosophers for hundreds or even thousands of years. For example, in keeping with Vygotsky's ideas, Plato viewed thinking as being based on language. This approach contrasts with the computational approach to the mind, according to which language is just an input–output process, and does not play a role in the development and nature of thinking (Carruthers, 2009).

Vygotsky developed his view of the relation between language and thought in the context of a critical analysis of Piaget's early work. Piaget was the first researcher to pay serious attention to the fact that young children often talk to themselves and he considered whether it is important in children's development. In one of his first books (1923/1955), *The Language and Thought of the Child*, he called this type of speech 'egocentric speech' and described it as follows:

> [the child] does not bother to know to whom he is speaking nor whether he is being listened to. He talks either for himself or for the pleasure of associating anyone who happens to be there with the activity of the moment. This talk is ego-centric, partly because the child speaks only about himself, but chiefly because he does not attempt to place himself at the point of view of his hearer. Anyone who happens to be there will serve as an audience. The child asks for no more than an apparent interest, though he has the illusion ... of being heard and understood. He feels no desire to influence his hearer nor to tell him anything; not unlike a certain type of drawing-room conversation where every one talks about himself and no one listens. (Piaget, 1923/1955, p. 32)

Egocentric speech has a global communicative function (Piaget, 1962/2000, p. 248) but is not expressed in such a way that others could easily understand it because it is rooted in the child's own perspective. Piaget felt that egocentric speech is social, but not socialised or socially adapted as communication in which the interlocutors take each others' perspective: 'if an individual *A* mistakenly believes that an individual *B* thinks the way that *A* does, and if *A* fails to understand this difference between the two points of view, this is, to be sure, social behavior in the sense that there is contact between the two. But from the perspective of intellectual cooperation, such behavior is unadapted' (1962/2000, p. 248). For Piaget, egocentric speech reflects mainly the immaturity of the child's perspective taking; it does not have any specific adaptive function.

Piaget described three types of egocentric speech in children aged 4 to 7: '(1) *Repetition*: the child just imitates sounds or words from someone else; (2) *Monologue*: he child is talking to him- or herself while doing something (e.g. "Lev sits down at his table alone; "I want to do that drawing there ... I want to draw something. I do. I shall need a big piece of paper to do that." p. 37); and (3) *Collective Monologue*: the speech of one child seems to stimulate speech in another, but the remarks of the second child are not a meaningful response to the first child (e.g. "Pie: "Where could we make another tunnel?" Ah, here Eun?" Eun (responding egocentrically): "Look at my pretty frock"' (Piaget, 1923/1955, p. 76).

Vygotsky, in contrast, thought that egocentric speech serves an important function because it is a step in the development of thought. It is an external tool of thought (external because it is speech which the child both produces and hears), allowing children to regulate their own behaviour. In the course of further development, this speech goes 'underground' to become inner speech or verbal thought. As a psychological tool speech becomes an individual function but originates as a social function.

It might seem that there is a potential problem for Vygotsky's idea that at least certain forms of thought develop through the use of speech. One argument that is often used to support the claim that thought comes before and is independent of speech is the familiar phenomenon that we often experience of having difficulty finding the right words to express our thoughts. That is, sometimes we have a thought but we can't immediately come up with the right words to express it, and we have to struggle for a moment to find the best way to put that thought into words.

It would seem that this phenomenon would present a problem for Vygotsky because he seemed to be arguing that thought is some form of internal speech – it is speech that has gone 'underground' or has become 'internal' and is no longer spoken out loud. But there are two types of responses that Vygotsky might have given to this challenge. First, according to him, in the process of transformation from social speech to inner speech, the latter becomes *abbreviated* and simplified so that it almost becomes, in his words, 'thought without words' (Vygotsky, 19345/1986, p. 244). That is, it becomes shortened. When thought is shared with other people it must be expanded so that it is understandable, and this is when words must be chosen to fill out the thought.

What did Vygotsky mean by abbreviation, and how does this process work? In a conversation, we don't have to repeat everything that has been said, and what we say relies on things that have been said at the beginning of the conversation. In other words, we build up a certain amount of shared knowledge and so our utterances can be abbreviated because we rely on the assumption of that shared knowledge. If we were talking to someone who forgot everything that happened two minutes ago, we couldn't make this assumption and we couldn't abbreviate our utterances. In contrast, in the case of close friends who have a lot in common, even a short statement can convey a great deal of information, and it might take some time to explain the same thing to someone else.

ABBREVIATED SPEECH

This is what 'in jokes' are about. A group of people pick up on their meaning because they share knowledge. You can tell that an 'in joke' is very abbreviated because it would take some time to explain it to someone who is not in the group. Consider routine situations like an operating room, in which a surgeon can just say 'scalpel', or even just hold out her hand at a particular moment in the procedure. Or in the cockpit of an airplane on the final approach to land, a pilot could just say 'ten degrees of flap', or maybe even just 'ten degrees', and expect the other pilot to know what to do because it is a routine, shared activity.

In research on the pragmatics of language use, Grice (1975) described one of the implicit rules of conversation as giving the right amount of information – what is needed, not more or less. So, when there is a lot of shared knowledge or common ground, this implicit rule might lead to shorter utterances. This social process of not needing to give information that is already shared also applies at the level of the individual talking to herself, resulting in abbreviation.

The second type of response Vygotsky might have given to this challenge is that when he related verbal thought to language, he did not claim that all forms of thought depend on the latter: 'there is a vast area of thought that has no direct relation to speech' (Vygotsky, 1934/1986, p. 88). Language is not the only tool of thought, there are several other types of symbol or psychological tools, such as maps or images, or different kinds of pictures. Other languages such as mathematics or musical notation might also become tools for thinking. A calendar or filing systems could enable us to organise our thinking in particular domains, even if the calendar or clock is not present. These very concepts allow us to employ certain ways of thinking. As mentioned above, computer scientists in the field of *information visualisation* specifically design tools to facilitate thinking in areas of science ranging from understanding chemical processes to practical medical decision making such as how to treat stroke cases.

Many scientists have talked about the use of imagery in creative thinking. Ideas don't always come in the form of sentences. In some areas of computer science, people often work out ideas by sketching them. Scientists often talk about moments of inspiration in which they suddenly get a good idea or a solution to a problem they have been working on. This may come when they are having a bath or riding a bus. Physicists talk about the 3 Bs – the bed, the bath, and the bus. Einstein said that he had to be careful when he was shaving because that was a time when he sometimes had good ideas, and he had to be careful not to cut himself when he suddenly thought of something. It seems that people sometimes have a whole idea in a moment but it would take some time to explain it in words.

Vygotsky had read Piaget's book on the language and thought of the child when it was translated into Russian, but Piaget did not read Vygotsky's book until it was translated into English in 1962. The publisher, MIT Press, asked Piaget to write some comments on it that were distributed with the first edition. Piaget's response was re-translated by Les Smith and published in 2000 (see Piaget, 1962/2000). Even though it is still sometimes assumed that Piaget viewed egocentric speech as 'a developmental dead-end' (Fernyhough & Fradley, 2005, p. 104), he actually stated that he agreed with Vygotsky's hypothesis that egocentric speech is the basis for the development of inner speech as a form of thinking (Piaget, 1962/2000). But Piaget argued that in his original work he was hoping to discover a reliable measure of children's intellectual egocentrism in their speech. Although Piaget was sympathetic, he argued that Vygotsky had failed to recognise that the egocentricity of young children's minds is an obstacle to cooperation. He asked the question how can children cooperate if they are not able to see another child's point of view? This is an obstacle in cognitive development that must be overcome in order to achieve cooperative social interaction, which according to Piaget is necessary for the development of logical thought.

4.3 RESEARCH EVALUATING VYGOTSKY'S HYPOTHESES

Vygotsky and many of his colleagues and students in the Soviet Union conducted research on speech and thinking, but his work was banned there after his death, which made it difficult to pursue this line of research. After his work has been translated into English, many researchers, particularly in North America, followed up on his ideas. Several have referred to speech that the child uses for him- or herself as *private speech* rather than 'egocentric speech' because they felt that the later term carried with it theoretical baggage (Diaz & Berk, 1992). Certainly, children repair speech errors in speech that is clearly meant to be social more than they do in utterances they seem to be using to help themselves solve a task (Manfra, Tyler, & Winsler, 2016). However, there are problems with this name change because, according to Vygotsky's theory, this form of speech has a social origin, so it is difficult to draw a clear line between the social and the private forms.

A number of specific predictions follow from Vygotsky's view of the developmental link between speech and thinking. According to his theory, children learn to talk and then they begin to use speech as an external tool for thought. This implies that private speech has a social origin. To support this idea, increased social interaction should result in more private speech. Supporting Vygotsky's claim, when children have a friendly peer or adult nearby they tend to use more private speech when engaged in an activity such as drawing a picture compared to when they work alone (Berk, 1992). Furthermore, there tends to be less private speech in communities in which adults do not talk to children as much as in other communities (Berk, 1992).

Both cross-sectional and longitudinal studies have supported a hypothesis deriving from Vygotsky's theory that the development of private speech follows a quadratic function. This is often termed an inverted U-shape trajectory, as the curve on a graph with age along the horizontal axis looks like this: ∩. This pattern is predicted over the course of development, with no to very little private speech when children are very young, an increase in private speech into the preschool years, and the decline of private speech thereafter. This decline does not mean that children do not use speech to guide their thinking; rather it means that private speech has become inner, inaudible speech – in other words, that it has been completely internalised. Beyond these ages, older children and also adults may use private speech at times, particularly when a task is demanding.

Another quadratic pattern has been noted over a microgenetic time span when a child engages in a task or skill during which learning takes place. It has been predicted that private speech will be used when initially attempting a challenging task, and individuals tend to decrease in relying on external speech as they become proficient

(Behrend, Rosengren, & Perlmutter, 1989). A further question concerns whether the use of private speech helps in successfully completing tasks, or leading to improvements slightly later on as predicted by Frauenglass and Diaz (1985). Here just correlating task performance with the use of private speech is not the best method because challenging tasks may elicit more speech, and it is not necessarily the case that more speech is better. However, it does necessitate longitudinal research, intensive studies where it is hoped that the researchers will witness development occurring within each child and inferences are made about the nature of that change. This is the hallmark of what are termed 'microgenetic designs' (see Flynn, Pine, & Lewis, 2007).

Researchers since the 1980s have tended to set children from the age of 2 (and even adults; Duncan & Cheyne, 2002) a series of tasks of varying difficulty. These studies have long shown that when such activities are at or just above their level of competence, children use more private speech (Behrend et al., 1989). Children's use of private speech is experimentally manipulated to test whether encouragement to use private speech can be beneficial for their performance or discouraging its use can negatively affect that performance. To set up such research on private speech, researchers need to prompt children by giving them permission to speak out loud if they wish, as not to do so leads to few examples of this language (Frauenglass & Diaz, 1985). The research has produced results that repeat Behrend et al.'s finding that children use private speech primarily when a task becomes difficult (Winsler, 2009). Some studies support Frauenglass and Diaz's prediction that private speech will correlate with later success in a task (e.g. Azmitia, 1992). More recent research has been more equivocal. For example, Fernyhough and Fradley (2005) gave 5- to 6-year-olds trials of an advanced puzzle, known as the Tower of London, which assesses the ability to plan actions in a correct sequence. (This task is illustrated in Figure 10.4 in Chapter 10.) They set up the procedure by saying, 'Sometimes children like to talk aloud when they play this game. You can do that if you like. I bet in class you have to be quiet! While playing this game you can talk and say whatever you want to'. Like others, they found that private speech that was 'task relevant' (i.e. words referring to what they were doing or to the task itself) were used in trials at their level of competence (i.e. not too easy or too difficult). However, they did not show that this predicted later success. This association is not always present, but there are sufficient studies to show that it can be found (e.g. Bivens & Berk, 1990)

Recent research has explored the role of private speech in special populations in which language is a reason for membership in an atypical group. In particular, autism is a disorder identified by impairments in both social interaction and in communication, particularly spoken language. Research on this group shows that they tend to use less private language than controls and their performance on high-level tasks, like the Tower of London, seems to be similarly impaired. That there may be a causal connection is hinted at because when typically developing children are prevented from using private speech they did as poorly as the children with autism (Wallace, Silvers, Martin, & Kenworthy, 2009). In addition, children with autism spectrum disorder who can speak do seem to use private language in order to learn a complex task, and this correlates with success more than silent practice with a task (Winsler, Abar, Feder, Schunn, & Rubio, 2007). There is also evidence of deaf children using private signing. This is particularly the case when the parents are also deaf because this means that these children are exposed to a complex sign language earlier on compared to deaf children with hearing parents (Winsler, 2009). Finally, when children with Specific Language Impairment are encouraged to use private language while performing the Tower of London task, they appear to catch up to typically developing children in reaching solutions to the task (Aziz, Fletcher, & Bayliss, 2016). So, all this evidence from language-impaired groups seems to support the idea that private speech is helpful in children's mastery of complex cognitive tasks like planning.

Much of the research on private speech has followed Vygotsky's lead and focused on the role of speech in problem solving. This is an important area of investigation, but some examples of private speech seem to involve the control of feelings. The use of private speech in emotion regulation seems to have been overlooked yet would be a worthwhile direction to explore in future research.

Scaffolding

Vygotsky's ideas have been influential in developmental psychology in various ways. A concept that follows from his view that thinking originates in interaction with others is that some forms of interaction may be more beneficial than others in helping a child master a way of thinking. The term *scaffolding* refers to help provided by adults for children, or by an expert for a novice learning a new skill (Ninio & Bruner, 1978, Jerome Bruner died in 2016 at the age of 100). The metaphor refers to a temporary structure used to construct something, usually a building. Good scaffolding refers to help that changes in quality depending on what a child needs. That is, it provides appropriate assistance, tailored to children's needs at particular moments to help them overcome difficulties in solving problems. To begin with children depend on the structure provided by others, and then gradually take over this structure as they become more skilled. The support varies depending on what the child needs, from physical guidance to verbal support. Scaffolding can help children with various aspects of solving problems such as setting goals, regulating action, inhibiting responses that are not helpful in reaching the goal, organising actions, and selecting strategies. Adults can provide scaffolding in various ways such as giving hints or prompts or directing the child's attention. The idea follows from the notion of sociogenesis – the view that thinking is first observed in the interpersonal process between people before becoming a skill that individuals can engage in by themselves (Wood, Bruner, & Ross, 1976).

The idea of scaffolding has given rise to considerable amount of research. For example, in a study conducted by Saxe, Guberman, and Gearhart (1987), 2- and 4-year-olds and their mothers worked on simple numerical tasks such as counting the number of objects in an array or matching the number of objects in one array with those in another array.

The researchers were interested in the nature of the help the mothers gave their children. They found that mothers adjusted the level of help they provided relative to the abilities of the child. More explicit help was given to younger compared to older children. Mothers also adjusted their help depending on how successful the child was. If the child succeeded on a step the mother gave less help with the next step, but if the child failed she gave more help. Sensitive scaffolding like this has been found to be positively linked to children's cognitive development (e.g. Bibok et al., 2009; Hammond, Müller, Carpendale, Bibok, & Liebermann Finestone, 2012).

More broadly, Vygotsky's work has been the major influence on sociocultural or sociohistorical approaches to cognitive development (Gauvain & Perez, 2015; Rogoff, 2003). A major problem encountered by sociocultural theories is how to conceptualise the relation between individual or person and culture (Carpendale & Müller, 2004). One solution to this problem is to argue that culture is some sort of external variable that causally influences an individual's behaviour. If such a view is taken, culture is reified; that is, it becomes a thing by itself. A different, relational solution that is consistent with Vygotsky's active view of internalisation considers person and culture as co-constitutive (Lawrence, 2017; Mistry & Dutta, 2015; Valsiner, 2014): without culture there would be no person, and without person there would be no culture. Person and culture are co-creating each other. The developing person engages in routines, traditions, and rituals, and uses material objects and tools (including symbol systems), and thereby adapts to and becomes a member of society. Such an approach is captured by Rogoff's (1990) metaphor of development as apprenticeship in thinking. The sociocultural approach thus focuses on the activities that the developing child engages in with others because it is through those activities that a person becomes enculturated. In the process of enculturation, cultural resources and meanings are reconstructed and personalised, assimilated into the individual's beliefs, and become part of the personal meaning system of that individual (a personal culture; see Valsiner, 2014). In their actions and communications individuals then externalise their personal meaning system (which is cultural in origin), and thereby recreate the cultural meaning systems. Externalisation of personal culture can also lead to subtle changes in cultural beliefs, routines, and so on, which may, in turn, result in major cultural change. The cultural resources can also be rejected and cultural discourse be resisted, which may provoke an even more dramatic cultural change (Lawrence, 2017). By emphasising the agency of developing persons and the bi-directional, co-constructive nature of person and culture, the sociocultural approach overcomes the reification of culture.

By the numbers: contrasting theoretical perspectives on understanding numbers

One way to understand differing theoretical perspectives is to contrast their approach to how children develop an understanding of number. This is a unique area of study because number is the archetypal symbolic system – a human invention which allows us to consider Vygotsky's theory, particularly its connections with Piaget's theory, as well as alternative views. Different theories begin with different ways of setting up the problem. As mentioned in the previous chapter, Piaget was concerned with the generativity of cognitive development and the rigorous knowledge it results in. His theory focused on finding answers to the questions of how new knowledge develops and the issue of necessity, in the sense that at some point children realise that 2 + 2 is *necessarily* 4 (and check whether their calculator is broken in case it gives a different answer). It is not just that their teacher or parent says that this must be the case. Nor is it just a matter of memorising an answer like a phone number. Instead, once children understand number they know when answers are necessarily correct, and they can figure out all sorts of other questions, as for Piaget number is always a relational construct. They must, for example, understand the principle of cardinality, that to count a set of items the number of the last counted object is the set size. The number of objects relates to the number reached in counting them. Relations also operate in terms of the components of a set. For a child fully to understand that 2 + 2 = 4, she must also know that 4 – 2 is 2. In addition, numbers are constant; with four objects it is possible to count them in any order desired and the answer will always be the same: 4.

According to Piaget's constructivism, such an understanding of numbers develops through the child's action on objects. This knowledge is not present in the environment nor is it innate; instead, it develops through actions on the world. The mathematical operations of addition and subtraction develop from the child's actions of grouping objects together and separating them (Chapman, 1988). These operations are always linked and grasping one forms an integral part of understanding the other. That is, it is possible to add and then subtract. Numbers and operations that can be performed on them don't exist in isolation; they are part of a system, a whole network of potential actions. Multiplication and division are further operations based on adding and subtracting. This way of coordinating numbers and arithmetic operations in a systematic way results in necessity.

The socio-cultural approach to number emphasises the social and cultural practices that revolve around counting. Consistent with Vygotsky's idea of the movement from the social to the individual, the activity of counting and doing arithmetic is considered first as a social activity before children master it and can do it themselves, and later they can do it 'in their heads' – they no longer need to actually perform it by counting on their fingers and so on.

Activities with numbers vary across cultures. For example, the Oksapmin from a mountainous region in Papua New Guinea traditionally used a 27-body-part counting system before contact with Western cultures in the 1940s (Saxe, 2012). This system traditionally did not include arithmetic functions such as addition and subtraction, but with the introduction of currency and economic exchange and schooling some people did build on the system to perform arithmetic functions (Saxe, 2012).

A third theoretical perspective on children's understanding of mathematics is represented by the information-processing approach. Diverse approaches are grouped together under the umbrella term of 'information processing' (Munakata, 2006). One group of theories that are sometimes claimed to be information-processing theories are neo-Piagetian theories. Here the idea is to build on Piagetian theory and explain cognitive development in terms of an increasing capacity to hold information in mind and manipulate it. A common approach, however, within information processing is based on the metaphor of a computer as a model for the mind, involving input of information, manipulation, and finally output. Based on this perspective, one approach is to look for general changes across many different tasks in the speed of processing as children grow older. A more common approach, however, is to work on a detailed model of performance on one task. Because the information-processing approach treats the mind like a computer program, an obvious method that researchers pursue is to write programs with the goal of accounting for observed behaviour. For example, Robert Siegler (Siegler & Shrager, 1984) addressed the issue of children's mental arithmetic and wrote a computer program to model patterns of development. This is based on the assumption that the way children come up with answers when they are asked an arithmetic question is that they first encode the answer, then attempt to retrieve an answer from their memory of learned associations between questions and answers. It is assumed that these associations are just formed from the number of times children have heard the question and the answer together. So stronger associations will be formed if the child has heard the question and answer together many times, and the associations will be weaker the fewer times they have been heard together. If the association for the answer the child has to remember is too weak she will retrieve another one, and state the answer if she feels sufficiently confident about it. If the child does not feel confident then she will go to the fallback procedure of counting (Kail & Bisanz, 1992; Siegler & Shrager, 1984).

Siegler found high correlations between the output of the computer program and children's own performance. However, for some tasks it is possible to write more than one program, so it is not clear which one is better. Furthermore, we don't know if this is actually how children solve the problem. Although the program might describe some aspects of the way children learn about numbers and how they do arithmetic problems, it says nothing about what they actually understand if they have the correct answer so it only covers a small subset of the issues addressed by Piagetian theory. Piaget was particularly interested in how children justified their responses.

At the most general level, the idea of understanding thinking in terms of the processing of information is reasonable. Applied at the neurological level, it is possible to talk about light energy arriving at a person's eyes and being detected by cells in the retina which then transmit impulses through the optic nerve to the brain and the visual cortex. This can be described in terms of the transfer and processing of information. This is information in one sense of the word. It is also the way in which we can talk about a camera recording information. However, when we talk about a person thinking about or understanding a photograph or a scene, then a quite different meaning of 'information' is implied. The information is for the person meaningful – and this is clearly different from how the information is for the camera or the brain. The problem with the information-processing approach is that these two contrasting meanings of information are treated interchangeably and their difference is overlooked. Thus is it appears to be possible to get from the causal sub-personal level of the firing of neurons, to the personal level of the meaning the world has for an individual through a theoretical sleight of hand. But this means that the problem with which we started the book, of explaining how the world comes to be meaningful for the child, is sidestepped rather than dealt with.

Yet a different perspective on number is represented by the neonativist view that infants have an innate understanding of number (Wynn, 1992). In one study interpreted as providing evidence for innate knowledge of number, 5-month-olds were shown a stage with one doll; then a screen blocked their view and they saw an experimenter add a second doll behind the screen. Then the screen was moved and there was either one doll, which would be unexpected given the chain of events, or there were two dolls, which would be expected. The infants tended to look longer when there was one doll rather than when there were two dolls. This was interpreted as indicating surprise, suggesting that the infants understood something about number. A similar procedure was applied to study subtraction. In this study, infants were shown two dolls, and then they saw a doll being taken away from behind the screen; they tended to look longer if they saw two dolls on the stage when the screen was removed. These results were interpreted as showing that infants have an implicit understanding of addition and subtraction. Wynn (1992, p. 749) claims that her results indicate that 'infants possess true numerical concepts and suggest that humans are innately endowed with arithmetical abilities'.

These results have been critiqued on methodological grounds. For example, it is difficult to know exactly why infants look longer in certain situations. It is also not clear what kinds of skills these tests require. From an action-based perspective, before children develop an understanding of number they could still have some grasp of numerosity or quantity tied to the physical space the object takes up, and this could be how infants pass Wynn's task without needing a concept of number (Bibok et al., 2009). Furthermore, claims of innate knowledge have been examined in Chapter 2, and based on recent work in biology, we have argued that such claims are highly problematic.

We have barely scratched the surface of the complex area of research concerned with the development of mathematical reasoning (see Nunes & Bryant, 2015). New research in this area is primarily constructivist and explores the problems Piaget and his colleagues focused on (Nunes & Bryant, 2015). In our own work, we try to bring together the work of Piaget and Vygotsky within a social constructivist approach to number. In an earlier experiment, Frydman and Bryant (1988) asked children to associate two groups of numbers in one-to-one correspondence and then to divide them into separate piles. They obviously had the same number (to an adult) as each one in one pile has been matched to one in the other. Children were asked to count their set and were then asked 'How many are there in my set?' Rather than inferring the same number, the children counted the second set and Frydman and Bryant inferred that this demonstrated a lack of understanding that equivalent set sizes are equal. We wondered whether the children count the second set simply because that is what they do when working on number with an adult. To test this we set up a scene in which all children travel to school by bicycle, but the children are inside the school and cannot be seen. Even 4-year-olds could infer the number of children in the school after they had counted bikes (Muldoon, Lewis, & Towse, 2005).

How do children acquire the ability to make such comparisons? According to the information-processing and nativist accounts described above, they should do so by gaining experience of procedures like counting. However, Kevin Muldoon and Charlie Lewis found that in a longitudinal study procedural skills are not nearly as good predictors of an understanding of number as is the social interaction skill of being able to tell when another person is accurate or inaccurate in their counting and sharing (Muldoon, Lewis, & Berridge, 2007; Muldoon, Lewis, & Francis, 2007). These results suggest that the child comes to grasp number and numerical relationships as a result of daily interactions and negotiations over the distribution of resources and their related concepts of fairness (Muldoon, Lewis, & Freeman, 2009). This fits squarely with Vygotsky's idea of thinking originating in social interaction, as well as Piaget's belief that all numerical concepts are relational. Accordingly, there is a basic compatibility between the two theories. We turn to this issue next.

4.4 VYGOTSKY AND PIAGET

Many textbook authors present Piaget as concerned with individual children interacting with the world of physical objects – a single child playing with pebbles on the beach – and Vygotsky, in contrast, is typically presented as being concerned with the role of the social world in development. That is, they are often presented as polar opposites. It is ironic, therefore, that Vygotsky actually criticised Piaget for focusing *too much* on the social dimension. Vygotsky (1934/1986, pp. 51–52) summarised what he saw as 'the central flaws in Piaget's theory' by pointing out that it is 'the relations between a child and reality that are missed in his theory. The process of socialization appears as a direct communication of souls, which is divorced from the practical activity of a child.' Vygotsky only had access to Piaget's first few books. As we noted in the previous chapter, Piaget's later work was criticised for neglecting the social dimension of development, but this is partly because his later work on the role of social interaction in the development of knowledge was not translated until after his death (Piaget, 1995).

In fact, there are a number of similarities between Piaget and Vygotsky. Les Smith (1996a) put together what he called a 'Piaget–Vygotsky self-test' based on a series of 10 quotations from Piaget and 10 from Vygotsky. The task is to decide if a particular quotation is from Piaget or Vygotsky. This is surprisingly difficult even for scholars in the area, so don't worry if you find it hard.

CAN YOU TELL THE DIFFERENCE BETWEEN PIAGET AND VYGOTSKY?

The common view is that Piaget neglected social interaction, whereas it is important for Vygotsky, so consider the following and think about whether it is from Piaget or Vygotsky:

'Human intelligence is subject to the action of social life at all levels of development from the first to the last day of life.'

If we believe the standard textbook or 'received view' this quote must surely be from Vygotsky because it is all about the importance of social experience in development. But, in fact, it was actually Piaget who wrote this. Similarly, Piaget also wrote that 'Human knowledge is essentially collective, and social life constitutes an essential factor in the creation and growth of knowledge, both pre-scientific and scientific' (1996a, p. 109), even though this also sounds very much like Vygotsky's writing (Smith, 1996a).

As well as similarities, however, there is still an important difference between Piaget and Vygotsky concerning how new forms of thinking develop. They both suggested the same thought experiment: in a society of peers (i.e. children of the same age) would there be development (Smith, 1996b)? For Vygotsky, the answer would be 'no', there wouldn't be development because this occurs through interaction with an adult or more experienced peer. For Piaget, however, the answer would be 'yes', there would be development because even interacting with a peer who also fails to solve a problem but in a different way could possibly result in development (e.g. two children could fail a conservation of liquid task in different ways by saying that the liquid in a tall thin glass is more because it is higher or less because it is narrower). Nonetheless, Piaget would acknowledge that development in a society of peers may differ from typical development.

Integration of Piaget and Vygotsky: Chapman's 'epistemic triangle'

One way to integrate Piaget's and Vygotsky's theories was proposed by Michael Chapman (1991). Piaget had worked on the child's social experience in his early work, as well as the child's construction of knowledge of the physical world in his later work. But he did not explicitly integrate these lines of thinking. Vygotsky, on the other hand, is known for his emphasis on the social dimension. The metaphor of an epistemic or knowing triangle provides a helpful way of thinking about the development of knowledge as consisting of both the dimension of physical interaction and the dimension of social interaction. The triangle is formed by (a) the child's interaction with the physical world, and (b) communicative interaction with other people about (c) their interaction with the world of objects. This triangle applies to the case of the development of children's understanding of numbers in which they interact with objects and learn the cultural procedures for counting (see Muldoon et al., 2009, for example).

The development of this triadic interaction between self and other (i.e. another person) about objects in the world around us (what Chapman calls 'objects of knowledge' as they might refer to abstract properties) makes a good bridge to the next topic of infants' communicative and social development. Chapman's idea is that all knowledge develops in this triadic interaction. That is, children learn about the world not only through their interaction, but also from communicating with others about their experience with the world. Learning is a mix of not only interacting with objects (or later concepts) but also of communicating with others about their experience with those objects. In this way, it occurs through communication and cooperation with others. At the same time that children gain a new understanding of the physical world they also learn about the social dimension. In this way, the child grasps something about others' minds. For example, if the child has a different experience of the world compared to someone else then the child can learn that others may experience and interpret the world in different ways. As we will see in the following chapters on language, thinking, social understanding, and morality, the evidence suggests a need to theorise development in terms of the negotiations we make between our experience with areas of knowledge and our interactions and negotiations with others about that knowledge.

SUMMARY AND CONCLUSION

The idea that human forms of thinking develop within social relations has been an important influence in developmental psychology. Many thinkers have contributed to this idea. One of the key theorists on which this approach is based is Lev Vygotsky. According to him, forms of thinking emerge within social interaction and then individuals gradually master this social process. Only then can they use these forms in their own thinking. From this, it follows that as an individual masters a cognitive skill she will require less social support. The process of mastering forms of thinking is closely related to the ideas of a 'zone of proximal development'. Scaffolding is the process through which an adult or more expert peer can help a child master a way of solving particular tasks. Ideally it involves the more knowledgeable person giving just the right amount of support required to the less skilled one: more when needed and less when the individual can do it herself. Poor scaffolding could occur either by letting the child flounder by herself with no help or doing the task for her without letting her do what she can or structuring the moves that need to be made.

Vygotsky discussed social-cultural practices that can become tools for thinking. These could vary from filing systems to techniques for remembering. In particular, Vygotsky focused on language as a social practice that children first master as a means for communication and influencing others, and then use as a means of influencing their own thinking. Children talk to themselves and this is an external tool for thinking that gradually becomes internalised as a form of thinking – verbal thought or inner speech. This was initially referred to as 'egocentric speech' but it is now researched under the label 'private speech'.

Piaget is often contrasted with Vygotsky and they are depicted as taking opposite positions, with Piaget focused on children's interaction and developing knowledge of the physical world and Vygotsky emphasising social interaction. However, their theories are similar in many ways even though important differences remain. The integration of Piaget and Vygotsky is possible with Chapman's (1991) notion of an epistemic triangle.

This epistemic triangle, or triadic interaction, provides a bridge to the topic of the development of social understanding in infancy (Chapters 5 and 6); that is, thinking about the social world. This is still a form of cognition (thinking), but now instead of thinking about the physical world of objects the focus is on thinking about other people.

FURTHER READING

Gauvain, M., & Perez, S. (2015). Cognitive development and culture. In L. Liben & U. Müller (vol. eds), *Vol. 2: Cognitive Processes*, R. Lerner (Editor-in-Chief), 7th edition of the *Handbook of Child Psychology and Developmental Science* (pp. 854–869). New York: Wiley Blackwell.

Vygotsky, L. S. (1978). *Mind in Society: The Development of Higher Psychological Processes*. Cambridge, MA: Harvard University Press.

Vygotsky, L. S. (1986). *Thought and Language*. Cambridge, MA: MIT Press. (Original work published 1934.)

Wertsch, J. V. (1985). *Vygotsky and the Social Formation of Mind*. Cambridge, MA: Harvard University Press.

5 THE DEVELOPMENT OF COMMUNICATION AND SOCIAL UNDERSTANDING IN INFANCY

LEARNING OUTCOMES

By the end of this chapter you should:

- Be familiar with the two most studied forms of social understanding and preverbal communication in infancy: gaze following and pointing.

- Be able to describe the complexities of how this communication works and develops through infancy and toddlerhood.

- Be familiar with less well-researched communication strategies that infants develop.

- Be able to reflect on the role of very early social gestures, like pointing and shared visual attention, in the emergence of infants' and toddlers' thinking.

- Be familiar with other forms of communication, notably head movements and signing.

PREVERBAL COMMUNICATION

It's Max's first birthday. He's not talking yet but he is doing a lot of communicating with gestures such as pointing. Last night he pointed to something he wanted on the shelf and then he pointed to me, which I responded to as a request. At other times he uses his index finger just to point out things that he is interested in, like birds or trees. These are examples of communication in infancy before language, or preverbal (i.e. 'before words') communication.

The English word *infancy* has its roots in Latin, *in-fans*, meaning 'without speech'. However, before language emerges there is already much communication between the baby and her caregivers. This chapter is all about the important forms of communication that emerge in infancy, the period from birth up to about two years before infants develop a proficiency in language. Long before children can talk with others and answer questions about what they understand, they are already actively engaged in communicating and interacting through giving, showing, making requests, and coordinating attention and action with others through following gaze and pointing gestures. All of these social and communicative skills reflect forms of social understanding and are essential aspects of development.

Over the past thirty years, considerable research and theory have addressed the development of children's social understanding – an understanding of self and other people, which we explore further in Chapters 11 and 12 focusing on the later preschool years and beyond. However, debate has extended recently into studies of infant development because several researchers have pointed out that a number of skills emerge in infancy that already seems to reflect some form of social understanding. This is a return to a view held by many in the 1970s that there is a basic level of social understanding shown in infants' ability to engage in interaction with others which forms an essential human capacity. Indeed many key thinkers in the field of developmental psychology have suggested that the skills developed in the first year are crucial to the development of thinking (Bates, 1979; Trevarthen, 1979). Peter Hobson (2002) refers to this period as the 'cradle of thought' – the infants' social interactions and sharing of affect nurture thinking. The skills demonstrated by Max (described above) allow infants to learn language with which they will later develop a more sophisticated understanding of the social world (e.g. Bates, 1976; Carpendale & Lewis, 2015; Tomasello, 1995).

In earlier chapters, we have dealt with the way in which human infants learn about key aspects of their physical world. But other people are a huge part of early experience and children also have a great deal to learn about the social world. As well as learning about social experience, the skills children develop in social interaction help them to develop new cognitive skills. Much of the research attention in this area has focused on the development of gaze following and the use of gestures such as pointing. Gaze following is important because we often need to understand what another person is looking at when communicating with that person. You or I will naturally switch between looking at a speaker's direction of gaze and the object on which he is focused. Imagine that you are learning object labels in a foreign language and your teacher says 'boru', a word you have not heard before. To grasp what she is saying one clue would be to see whether she is looking at something that may be called a 'boru' – that is, something that you have not labelled before. She may indeed be pointing to help you. The ability to home in on a person's point while she is labelling something emerges around an infant's first birthday. Such skills are grouped as forms of *joint attention* usually this is joint *visual* attention. This chapter reviews these areas of research by exploring the details of two aspects of this skill.

> Video link to an example of joint attention: www.youtube.com/watch?v=tif4U3OjT2M

It might seem that the abilities to follow someone's gaze or pointing gesture are very simple and of only limited interest to psychologists. But it is how they fit into the child's developing social and cognitive skills that makes them important. Joint attention is closely related to emotions, language, and cognition. Imagine a toddler pointing something out to his father. This might be accompanied by a gaze at dad to see if he is looking at the identified object, followed by shared enjoyment – a mutual smile to indicate both pleasure in seeing an object and the joy of sharing. These social skills are a part of the process of becoming human, of entering the human world, and developing language, thinking, and a mind, as well as engaging in cooperation of various forms. Indeed, preverbal communication is linked to what is arguably the hardest problem in science, namely how meaning is conveyed in human forms of communication.

To address the learning objectives outlined above, this chapter divides into four parts. We first consider the building blocks of social interaction – the abilities found in very young infants that make them home in on social stimuli. Secondly, we describe two key forms of social understanding and communication in infancy because it is important to identify the nature and developmental sequence of preverbal communication. The third part examines how these preverbal skills develop, becoming more complex and feeding into communication based on language. Finally, in order to dispel any thoughts that pointing and shared visual attention are the only forms of joint attention in infancy, we briefly describe two other forms of nonverbal gesture that infants and their caregivers use to communicate before language emerges.

5.1 EARLY STEPS IN SOCIAL PROCESSES: INFANT–CAREGIVER INTERACTION AND EARLY DEVELOPMENT OF COMMUNICATION

Much of the research on infant cognitive development has focused on the months around infants' first birthdays because that is where the action seems to be in communicative development. Not only do children start to use social signals that we will focus on here, but also their grasp of spoken language becomes increasingly apparent at this time. To avoid being seduced by apparently miraculous transitions, it is necessary to be aware of what is happening in earlier months to set the stage for these emerging skills (de Barbaro, Johnson, & Deák 2013; Rossmanith, Costall, Reichelt, López, & Reddy, 2014).

What makes social interaction so special for infants? Human infants prefer to look at biological motion compared to other forms of motion, even at just a few days old (Simion,

Regolin, & Bulf, 2008). They even react differently to projections of faces shone through the abdomen into the womb than to stimuli that are as complex but are not faces (Reid et al., 2017). A preference for biological stimuli is also documented across other species such as monkeys, cats, and birds, suggesting that it has strong biological roots (Klin, Lin, Gorrindo, Ramsay, & Jones, 2009). Babies have a propensity to look at face-like displays rather than equally interesting patterns or scrambled faces (Fantz, 1961; Morton & Johnson, 1991), and are sensitive to eye gaze from birth (Farroni, Massaccesi, Pividori, & Johnson, 2004). Recent research has looked at the ability to discern human movements in point-light displays. Experimental videos were made by an actor wearing an electronic suit recording motion of body joints in three dimensions reduced to points of light. What appears on the video is a movement of lights that adults can see is of a human attempting to engage an infant with routines such as peek-a-boo or pat-a-cake. Typically developing toddlers preferred looking at the video right-side-up, rather than upside-down movies of the same action (Klin et al., 2009). Interestingly, unlike typically developing children, 2-year-olds who are later diagnosed with autism do not appear to recognise or prefer biological motion in these displays of point-lights (Klin et al., 2009; see Chapter 11). This difference in preference may create a very different environment for their further development and consequently sets them on a different developmental trajectory. That is, unlike typically developing infants, the outcome may be that these infants do not naturally follow eyes and faces, which are essential sources of social information.

IS ATTACHMENT THEORY IMPORTANT FOR OUR UNDERSTANDING OF CHILDREN'S THINKING?

It is essential to be aware that the developmental niche in which infants grow up is saturated with feelings. The strong emotional bonds that form between infants and caregivers over the first year of life are referred to as attachments, and are based on children's experience with their caregivers. John Bowlby (1958) observed that human infants go though a period between about 6 and 30 months when they require the care and proximity of one or two key people, known as 'attachment figures'. Attachment theory concerns the development and expression of an intense emotional relationship. Bowlby (1969) asserted that attachments are hugely influential on a child's thinking. Patterns of everyday love and care set up infants' expectations regarding how particular caregivers will typically respond to him or her (what Bowlby terms 'internal working models'), and these are hypothesised to form the basis of early thinking. They do so in two ways. In a negative sense, the ability to explore the environment is curtailed if a child does not feel secure and such a feeling is

(Continued)

generated within a close attachment relationship. A child who is insecurely attached does not have the confidence to explore the environment and meet the intellectual hurdles that we have written about in Chapter 3. Secondly, Bowlby proposed that a child learns crucial distinctions between self and others and between different types of emotional experience, and these form the building blocks for the cognitive developments that occur. His claims receive support from several studies discussed in this chapter.

How do infants become proficient social actors and how might their early social interactions help them develop more complex levels of thinking? Some early forms of interaction can indicate initial ways of understanding others. It is *within* interaction that newborns gradually learn about the pacing and content of interactions. This can be seen in an experimental procedure known as the *still face* paradigm in which mothers are asked to interact normally with their 4- to 5-month-old infant in a face-to-face situation for one or two minutes. The mothers are then asked to hold a still face for one minute, and finally to resume normal interaction. It is actually quite difficult for mothers to do this – that is, to refrain from interacting, and this shows how the interaction comes from both sides, and how it becomes expected and enjoyable. Some of the infants appear to use smiling as a social bid, attempting to draw their mothers back into the pleasurable game of responding to each other. This is seen particularly in those babies whose mothers respond contingently to their babies' actions (Mcquaid et al., 2009). A similar technique is to set up interaction between a mother and her baby via a live video link, which is then altered to replay earlier interaction which was therefore non-contingent (i.e. the mother's actions were out of sync with the infant's actions). When this happened babies at 2 months of age looked less at the screen, smiling dwindled from about 15% to almost none, and infants started frowning (Nadel, Carchon, Kervella, Marcelli, & Réserbat-Plantey, 1999). These pieces of evidence suggest that even with 2 months of interactive experience, infants have learned something about the nature and synchrony of social activity, like the role of smiling in this social engagement (see Chapter 11 for a discussion of emotional reactivity; also Shanker, 2004).

We have already mentioned young infants' sensitivity to eyes. This and other characteristics of the human face, the dark–light contrasts, symmetry, and movement of the eyes and lips, draw babies into attending to human social activity. Such cues alert us to the importance of the environment in which infants develop. This human developmental system consists of babies' everyday experience in their first months of life, which has long been a focus of theoretical interest (e.g. Baldwin, 1897). Whereas some animals are born ready to get up and run for their lives, human infants experience an extended period of helplessness (Portmann, 1944/1990). This biological characteristic means that human infants have to be looked after, necessarily resulting in the social environment in which they develop.

At the same time, human infants have relatively well-developed senses compared to other similar species. As a result, they are not able to get what they want, but they are cared for by others who can fulfil their desires. Babies' cries produce clear arousal responses including increased skin conductance (a sign of stress: e.g. Frodi, Lamb, Leavitt, Donovan, Neff, & Sherry, 1978) on those within hearing distance. The most typical response to crying is to pick up the infant (Bell & Ainsworth, 1972), although this is channelled through cultural norms. This action becomes rewarding because the best way to stop the crying is to hold and comfort an infant (Korner & Thoman, 1970). When chimpanzees are kept in a similar environment, being cared for by humans, they also experience the same problem of getting what they want from someone looking after them. In such settings, they usually develop pointing gestures to make requests for caregivers to get out-of-reach objects, whereas these types of gestures are not known to occur in the wild (Leavens, 2011).

As they are being cared for, infants learn about the activity patterns of others around them. They come to anticipate what is coming up next in the typical social routines they share with others. They learn to anticipate the reappearance of someone playing peeka-boo and to share emotion when they reappear unexpectedly (Bruner & Sherwood, 1976). Typical social routines may vary across most cultures, however. In Ecuador, many babies were swaddled on boards for over an hour, in an attempt to reduce their activity during the heat of the day, but this also reduces the propensity for interaction (Lewis, 1979).

Slowly but surely the dyadic interaction between infant and parent becomes triadic interaction involving objects as well. This consists of jointly structured actions that have a temporal sequencing and come to involve objects of shared attention. The adult and infant, from at least 12 months onwards, draw each other's attention to objects of common interest, so the 'triad' consists of infant, caregiver, and object. Sharing a toy or a book are common examples of this joint attention in some families and cultures. In one study charting parent–infant interaction between 3 and 12 months of age, Rossmanith et al. (2014) found that throughout this period mothers engaged their babies in book sharing. Interestingly, the infants used the book for social interaction except when they were about 7 to 9 months old, when they appeared to be solely focused on the book itself. In such routines infants learn where to look and about sharing emotions, excitement, and interest. Rather than emerging at the end of the first year (see next section), longitudinal studies of parent–infant interaction show that the infant's ability to switch between the mother and an object emerges slowly in everyday coordinated interactions with the parent attuning to subtle changes in this ability (de Barbaro et al., 2013). Other social routines may be more common than book reading across other cultures such as feeding or being picked up. This coordination can be seen even beginning at two months when infants are already learning to coordinate their actions with caregivers by stiffening their bodies when their caregiver is about to pick them up (Reddy, Markova, & Wallot, 2013).

At 6 months infants begin to understand others' reaching actions in terms of the person's goal of grasping an object (Woodward, 2013). Learning about this aspect of human activity seems to be facilitated by different forms of interaction. Infants at 7 months whose mothers were emotionally available in interaction tend to be better able to understand human action as goal directed. In a study by Maria Licata and colleagues, infants' temperament, working memory, and their mothers' level of education did not seem to be related to the infants' ability to understand goal directedness. Instead, it was having mothers who were emotionally available that was helpful. One possibility is that these mothers were good at facilitating their child's learning about actions and goals, perhaps through 'motioness'; that is, exaggerating and emphasising movement in order to draw the infant's attention and help them learn about the endpoints and outcomes of actions (Licata, Paulus, Thoermer, Kirsten, Woodward, & Sodian, 2014).

In this section we have focused on the social interactional skills that help to orientate infants towards both people as caregivers and the physical world. That is, infants start to reach for objects as they learn about them, and this developing interest feeds a desire for the objects as well as a desire to share them. Furthermore, we must consider that infants often reach toward objects of interest when their caregivers are present, so they can learn from the responses of others. Responses may include talking about the object or warnings like 'no' or 'hot'. We have given some hints at the relations between biological and social levels that are important during the first year of infants' lives in setting the scene for the development of communicative and social skills. That newborns cry, and cease crying when comforted, demonstrates biological mechanisms, which gradually acquire psychological meaning in terms of attachments and an infant's understanding of objects and people as predictable. These and other biological characteristics draw infants into an increasingly social world, which is the crucible of thinking.

5.2 SHARING A FOCUS ON AN OBJECT: JOINT VISUAL ATTENTION

How do children learn to use gestures to communicate? There are a number of skills in infancy that appear to involve some grasp of other people's perspectives. These activities have been labelled *joint attention* because they involve coordinating a shared focus on an object with an adult. This often, but not always, relies on vision. Joint attention begins to emerge in the months before and after infants' first birthdays. In the early months of life interaction is 'dyadic', usually involving face-to-face looking, cooing and smiling. Infants gradually become more engaged and move from interacting *dyadically*, with caregivers or objects, during the middle of the first year, to coordinating their own attention to objects with others' attention in *triadic* interaction towards the end of the first year (Chapman, 1991). One way to study this is to use the fact that infants' attention to a stimulus tends to dwindle as they become bored with it (habituation), and this contrasts with their tendency to pay renewed attention when they experience something new (novelty). This habituation–novelty procedure has been used a lot over the past fifty years to examine infants' early discrimination between different stimuli. For example, Vincent Reid and Tricia Striano (2005)

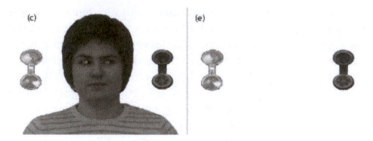

Figure 5.1   Reid & Striano's (2005) study

In this infants are habituated to the picture on the left (a woman looking at the darker object on her left [our right]) and then shown the toys alone (as in the picture on the right).

Republished with permission of John Wiley & Sons Inc., from Reid, M. V., & Striano, T. (2005). Adult gaze influences infant attention and object processing: implications for cognitive neuroscience, *European Journal of Neuroscience, 21*(6). Permission conveyed through Copyright Clearance Center, Inc.

showed infants a photo of a woman looking at one of two toys on either side of her, as shown in Figure 5.1C. Once the infant had habituated (lost interest) they replaced that picture with just the two toys (Figure 5.1E). Infants looked longer at the toy that the woman had *not* gazed at, showing that 4-month-olds are already using the other's eyes to guide them to objects of interest, and were now more interested in the object not already looked at by the woman and presumably the infant. Reid and Striano used a number of other trials as controls, like the woman gazing straight ahead and a toy containing the same shapes and colours of the stimuli in Figure 5.1E, and neither led to preferential looking when just the objects were presented.

Triadic interaction soon becomes more sophisticated. One early example of this is *social referencing*, which describes infants' tendency to look toward their parents when faced with ambiguous situations, such as being presented with a toy spider or needing to crawl across an apparent cliff in order to reach their parent (Walden & Ogan, 1988). If a parent, standing on the other side of the visual cliff (a clear sheet of plexiglass that can bear the infants' weight), smiles and looks happy, infants may go ahead and crawl across the surface over the apparent void. One interpretation is that they look to their parent for information regarding whether the ambiguous situation is safe. Such behaviour is sometimes considered to be an example of joint attention because infant and parent are both engaged visually in the same exchange. But it is not completely clear *why* babies look at their caregiver in this situation. Rather than trying to gain information, it is possible that they feel anxious and look toward their parent for comfort rather than information (Baldwin & Moses, 1996; Striano, Vaish, & Benigno, 2006). But, in this case, emotional comfort could be said to be a means of seeking information and a motivation to develop the skill of social referencing.

The first year of life is marked by the gradual increase in coordination of attention with others, using gaze following and communicative gestures such as pointing. These two social skills have received a great deal of research attention and we review them in this chapter. Most of the research on infant social understanding has focused on achieving joint visual attention. However, it is also possible to coordinate attention with other senses, using tactile or vocal cues, and this is necessary for blind children (Bigelow, 2003). It is possible that parents in some cultures might also rely on other cues. For example, the role of the postural position of the body such as leaning toward something may serve to orient interest toward particular objects (Akhtar & Gernsbacher, 2008).

5.3 FOLLOWING GAZE DIRECTION: THE EYES AS WINDOWS ON THE SOUL?

For adults, other people's eyes are incredibly important sources of information. They seem to reveal a lot about a person's character and intentions. Following the direction of someone's gaze indicates some understanding of other people, particularly that they attend to objects in the world. This understanding starts long before children can talk about beliefs and desires. Some researchers claim that following gaze indicates that infants understand the other is looking at something, which in turn is taken to indicate that they believe the viewer has a mental life (Meltzoff & Brooks, 2007). For adults this interpretation may be correct, but it should not be taken for granted in infants. Rather, it is important to take a developmental approach and examine how this skill begins and how understanding is achieved. We must be cautious about assuming that infants have an adult level of understanding. Gaze following has been reported in many other species. Chimpanzees are quite good at it (Call & Tomasello, 2008; Emery & Clayton, 2009), and even domestic goats follow the gaze of other goats who have been shown food by an experimenter (Kaminski, Riedel, Call, & Tomasello, 2005). This ability can provide important information about the possible location of food, but this does not necessarily reveal the same form of social understanding as in adult humans.

Some sensitivity to eyes is present even in newborn infants. Already at 2 to 5 days of age babies prefer to look at a face which is looking at them compared to a face with averted gaze, and they prefer open to closed eyes (Farroni et al., 2004). A range of biological characteristics may contribute to newborns' interest in eyes. The infant's visual system may be sensitive to the dark white contrasts that are seen in human eyes (Morton & Johnson, 1991). Human eyes are unusual compared to those of other species in that the dark iris is surrounded by a large white area of sclera, making the eyes highly salient and eye direction easy to detect (Kobayashi & Kohshima, 1997, 2001). This may make cooperative interaction easier for humans than other primate species (Tomasello, Hare, Lehmann, & Call, 2007), and facilitate their entry into the social world through drawing their attention to highly relevant sources of information. This starts infants on a pathway toward becoming experts on eyes and faces (Carpendale, Frayn, & Kucharczyk, 2017). Although the attention paid to eyes applies in typical development, infants who are later diagnosed as being on the autism spectrum display different reactions (usually avoidance), which may result in them starting on a different developmental trajectory (e.g. Jones & Klin, 2013; see Chapter 11).

When do infants start to follow others' gaze? Although this might seem like a straight-forward question, the answer given from research actually varies from the first few months of life to 15 months or more depending on the difficulty of the task. The experiment by Reid and Striano (2005) (see Figure 5.1) shows some ability at 4 months. Many skills are developmentally spread out, as we see in learning a language (see Chapters 7–8), or skiing or dancing to a high standard. In assessing infants' ability to follow gaze, the typical procedure is for the experimenter to be seated across from the infant who is sitting on her parent's lap. The researcher first makes eye contact with the infant, and then turns to look to one side of the room (Scaife & Bruner, 1975). The test is whether the infant follows the experimenter's gaze and looks toward what the experimenter is attending to. Passing the test depends on how easy the task is and on how strict the criteria are for passing (Carpendale & Lewis, 2006).

An especially easy set-up is when the object the adult looks at is close to the infant and in her visual field. In this setting, when an adult turns her head toward one of two close targets, even 3-month-olds may follow the experimenter's gaze and look in the right direction significantly more than to the incorrect target (D'Entremont, 2000). The adult's head turn is important as it cues the infant. These movements form signals that cue infants and they develop expectations that there will be something of interest in the direction of the movement (Corkum & Moore, 1998). This ability is extended to more distant objects by the age of 6 months, but infants do not always find the right object because they stop at the first one they see in that direction – a difficulty that is overcome by 12 months of age (Butterworth, 2001). At this age they can also crawl around a barrier to discover what an adult is looking at (Moll & Tomasello, 2004). Skill at gaze following continues to improve. From 12 to 18 months infants get better at following others' looks at objects located behind themselves, and rely more on eye direction rather than just head orientation (Moore, 2008).

Although the ability to follow gaze emerges early in development, this does not necessarily mean that babies understand the implications of this form of attention in terms of seeing or understanding. In a classic article with three experiments conducted by Amanda Woodward, 7-, 9-, and 12-month-old infants were habituated to seeing an actor reach toward one of two objects. Then a curtain was closed so that the position of two objects could be switched. Infants paid renewed attention when the actor reached for a new object even though the motion was the same, but they did not dishabituate (i.e. pay attention once more) to the actor reaching for the same object that was in a new location (see Figure 5.2 from Woodward, 1998). This suggests that the infants understood that there was a relation between the actor and that particular object. But in other conditions when the actor only looked at and did not grasp the object the 7- and 9-month-old infants did not pay more attention, suggesting they did not yet understand the actor's gaze toward the object in the same way they understood grasping in terms of a relation between the actor and the object. Between 9 and 12 months infants begin to understand gaze in terms of a relation between people and the objects they are looking at (Woodward, 2003).

Figure 5.2 Amanda Woodward's attention task

In this procedure infants are habituated to a reach towards the ball (panel A). After a brief pause (with a curtain closed between them and the scene) they see one of the reaches shown in panels B–D. They look longer at the reach to the bear at 9 months, whatever its location (panels C & D) (Woodward, 1998).

5.4 FROM GAZE FOLLOWING TO GESTURES: THE EMERGENCE OF INTENTIONAL COMMUNICATION

What use does the ability to follow someone's gaze serve? One goat following another's look may discover a new source of food, but this might not involve an inference – the direction of the goat's head might simply direct the onlooker. Yet, in humans following gaze soon becomes a form of *joint* attention, like social referencing and pointing gestures. These all involve the coordination of attention between an infant and an adult towards an object or event. But there are important differences among these activities. Social referencing and gaze following may involve information being conveyed in the sense that the infant faced with a need or desire to cross a visual cliff may get information from her parent, just as the goat 'follows' another goat's gaze. Gaze could also be used intentionally to convey meaning by catching someone's attention and intentionally directing it through eye movements, but this is more unusual. However, other more directive human forms of communication, like pointing, usually involve intentionally conveying meaning. We turn to this topic next.

Gestures: preverbal communication

For the two months before and after their first birthday, infants start using a range of gestures. These differ from one another and may develop in different ways. Some gestures, such as waving, seem to be learned partially through imitation and so may be culture-specific. In cultures where this is a common gesture, babies are not at first very good at accomplishing the physical motion of waving with their hand. Even at 22 weeks, some parents report observations of their babies attempting to imitate waving, but their hand motion is more like an arm flap or the opening and closing of their hand. Babies gradually master the hand movement for waving, but they still have to learn to use it in appropriate settings and grasp what the gesture means. Such understanding is achieved, at least partially, through the response infants get from others. Once mastered, waving can potentially be used in different ways. As well as indicating 'goodbye', Max used waving to convey different meanings, such as when a book was finished, or he had eaten his dinner. He even combined waving with pointing to the door, which could have meant that he wanted to go out. In another instance at 17 months he had lost a clear plastic toy in the bath, and while looking in the bath he waved, apparently meaning that it was gone.

Other gestures do not seem to be learned through imitation, but instead appear to be based on natural reactions, such as infants leaning or reaching toward what they desire. The 'arms up' gesture is common and is learned early, usually by 9 months (Lock, 1978). Here the infant raises both arms, either when it is clear that they are going to be picked up or if they want to be carried. Its origin seems to be in the natural reaction of reaching toward a caregiver. It has meaning for the adult because it is fairly obvious what the infant wants within a particular context. This shows how infants learn that their action has meaning for the adult and can be used to communicate intentionally.

The 'arms up' gesture is very interesting because infants do not see adults perform this action. How they learn to do this fits with George Herbert Mead's (1934) view that meaning already exists in social relations before children become aware that they are communicating. They gradually learn to anticipate what others will do in response to their action, and then they can intentionally communicate.

Pointing

Pointing gestures have attracted a great deal of attention in the research literature because, although appearing to be very simple social acts, they are an example of a complex human form of communication emerging very early in development (Bates, 1976; Werner & Kaplan, 1963). Infants typically start pointing around their first birthday, but this can vary from 8 to 15 months (e.g. Butterworth, 2003; Carpenter, Nagell, & Tomasello, 1998), and fully mastering the many uses of this skill is extended over many months.

Pointing is also linked to language. Children who point more than their age mates have larger vocabularies and they continue to develop larger vocabularies (Colonnesi, Stams, Koster, & Noom, 2010). For example, infants who point to many objects at 14 months tend to understand more words when they are 42 months of age (Goldin-Meadow, 2007). This might be because these children may elicit more talk from their parents about the objects and events they point to, or it could be that the pointing reveals a relatively advanced level of social understanding that continues to develop and is also manifest in language skills. These two possibilities are not mutually exclusive.

In contrast, lack of pointing seems to indicate difficulties with social cognitive development. Infants who are not pointing at objects to show them to an adult at 18 months are more likely to be later diagnosed with autism (Baron-Cohen, Allen, & Gillberg, 1992; Baron-Cohen et al., 1996).

The use of pointing gestures with an extended index finger is common but not completely universal across cultures, at least among adults (Wilkins, 2003). In some cultures pointing with an index finger is taboo, and other body parts are used to direct attention such as lip pointing. However, it seems that some way to direct others' attention would be required in typical human interaction, and so might be expected to be found across cultures. It is still not known whether infants in those cultures without pointing begin doing so with their index fingers, and then reach an age at which they learn that it is impolite and so stop. Alternatively, they may never use index finger pointing. However, we do know that cross-cultural research on the development of pointing has reported fairly consistent timetables of development of such communicative skills across diverse cultures (Carpendale & Wereha, 2013; Lieven & Stoll, 2013; Liszkowski, Brown, Callaghan, Kakada, & de Vos, 2012).

The *canonical pointing gesture* is an extended index finger with the other fingers curled into the palm and the arm extended. It is called 'canonical' (a term that derives from theology but in this case means 'prescribed') because it is accepted as the typical means of making the gesture. Extending the index finger has been observed in infants even between the ages of 9 to 15 weeks, but of course this is not yet used as a social act (Blake, O'Rourke, & Borzellino, 1994; Fogel & Hannan, 1985; Masataka, 2003). At that age, it does not convey meaning, it is a 'pointless point' (Lock, Young, Service, & Chandler, 1990). Children have to learn how to use their index finger to communicate. As we will show, this has to be based on a shared history of interaction.

An extended index finger can be used to touch objects and explore textures, conveying no message at all, but it can also be used to communicate almost limitless meanings. In a classic study, Bates, Camaioni, and Volterra (1975) categorised forms of pointing as falling into two categories: to make requests (*proto-imperatives*) and to direct attention (*proto-declaratives*). They defined *proto-imperative pointing* as 'the child's intentional use of the listener as an agent or tool in achieving some end'. In contrast, they referred to *proto-declarative pointing* as a 'preverbal effort to direct the adult's attention to some event or object in the world' (1975, p. 208). This categorisation system contrasts the instrumental use of the gesture with the enjoyment of others' attention. It has been an influential and useful way of categorising pointing gestures, but this system results in overlooking the vast diversity of social acts within these very broad categories (Carpendale & Carpendale, 2010; Carpendale, Atwood, & Kettner, 2013). More recently, other functions have been described. Experimentally it has been shown that 12-month-old infants will point to inform an adult looking for an object where it is located (Liszkowski et al., 2006). Pointing can also be used to ask a question (Begus & Southgate, 2012; Carpendale & Carpendale, 2010; Rodríguez, 2009), as well as to answer a question (Carpendale & Carpendale, 2010). The gesture may be used when an infant is attempting to elicit interaction about an object or event, or to indicate either the direction in which the infant is going or wishes to go, or where she wants to place an object. In addition, it can be used in combination with actions to make a request, such as by taking a book and pointing to the couch, or giving an adult a shovel and pointing to the garden (Carpendale & Carpendale, 2010; Carpendale & Lewis, 2015; Muñetón & Rodrigo, 2011). So, pointing comes to be part of a rich fabric of communication for toddlers.

Infants also have to learn about other people's use of pointing. In simple settings this may begin with some success before the first birthday. By the age of 14 to 18 months infants can understand that the same pointing gesture can convey different meanings depending on what has happened previously with that person.

UNDERSTANDING THE SAME GESTURE IN DIFFERENT CONTEXTS

That the same pointing gesture can convey different meanings was demonstrated in a study in which infants played different games with two experimenters. With one experimenter they put a puzzle together, whereas with the other experimenter they cleaned up the room. When the 'puzzle experimenter' pointed to a puzzle piece the infants tended to respond by placing it in the puzzle, whereas if the 'clean up experimenter' used exactly the same pointing gesture toward the puzzle piece they assumed she wanted them to tidy up and they put the piece away (Liebal, Behne, Carpenter, & Tomasello, 2009).

We hope to have convinced readers of the importance of the apparently simple act of pointing because it is an early example of the form of communication upon which human languages are based. Once children start using language, however, the complexity is overwhelming and it becomes difficult to be aware of how meaning works. With gestures before language, it is possible to get a glimpse of how children master human communication. That is, instead of getting lost in philosophical debates about the nature of meaning, it is possible to observe how babies progress through various forms of communication. So how does pointing develop, and how do children learn to use it to communicate in so many different ways, as well as understand other people's pointing gestures? There are a number of explanations for the development of pointing and social understanding in general. We address theories of social development at the beginning of Chapter 6 and will then return to explanations for how particular gestures like pointing develop. First, we need to examine other gestures that infants learn and understand.

5.5 GESTURES BASED ON HEAD MOVEMENTS AND SIGNING

Pointing is only one means of communicating without words. It is the most studied of joint attention gestures, but it is only one of a repertoire of skills that we employ effortlessly and which we can call upon either to emphasise a point or in circumstances where we cannot rely on verbal communication. In this brief section we summarise less well-researched forms of prelinguistic gestures to illustrate the diversity and complexity of nonverbal skills. That young infants pick these up in the course of their early interactions is a mark of both the mental agility of *homo sapiens* and the nature of their caregiving environment.

An under-explored set of gestures concerns communicative movements of the head. For example, indicating *yes* and *no* with head nodding and shaking would seem to be very useful gestures that we might assume to be necessary in typical human interaction. Interestingly, they develop later than pointing, typically after 16 months. This is surprising because to adults these gestures seem to be such simple and straightforward social acts (Kettner & Carpendale, 2013).

Although these gestures are not completely universal across cultures, they are quite common. Both Charles Darwin (1872/1998) and René Spitz (1957) proposed, in different ways, that nodding and shaking are based on infants' natural reactions that become transformed into gestures as a result of how parents respond to them. It is still not completely clear whether this is the case, especially for nodding to indicate an affirmative. Note that these gestures are culturally specific – a nod in Greece (or really a head back gesture but it can include a forward movement) means 'no', whereas a head shake in parts of India is often an affirmative. Nodding for 'yes' and using the word 'yes' develop later than the corresponding expressions for 'no', and so presumably the former is a more difficult social act to master. Before mastering these expressions of affirmation, various actions function to indicate that the infant does want what is being offered. For example, if an infant is asked 'do you want a cracker?' her excitement is shown, for example, by waving arms. So, her natural reaction of excitement indicates that she wants it, even if she does not yet say 'yes' or nod her head. Later in development she may say 'cracker' or use the baby sign for cracker or 'more', and later still respond with a 'yes' or nodding of her head (Kettner & Carpendale, 2013). One child in a diary study did learn nodding to indicate 'yes' early at 14 months through a form of teaching based partially on imitation, but within the social routine of responding to a question. His mother wanted him to learn to nod in order to avoid the frustration of figuring out what he wanted. So, when he was requesting something she asked him if this was what he wanted while holding out the object, modelled by nodding her head, and waited until he also nodded (Carpendale & Carpendale, 2010).

Finally, we should consider the issue of *baby signing*. There has been some suggestion that infants' early use of symbolic gesturing may facilitate their word learning (Goodwyn, Acredolo, & Brown, 2000). There is also popular interest in teaching infants to use 'baby sign', such as touching the fingers of both hands together as a sign for 'more'. This raises the question of whether this experience has a positive or negative impact on language learning. A training study found that teaching baby sign does not delay infants' use of words, but it also does not accelerate it (Kirk, Howlett, Pine, & Fletcher, 2013; see also Nelson, White, & Grewe, 2012). However, the mothers in the gesture training group were more responsive to their children and more likely to encourage independent action. Thus, baby sign may influence parent–child interaction and make communication easier. Learning it does not seem to improve language for infants who already experience a rich linguistic environment, but it might be helpful for infants who do not (Kirk et al., 2013), and it appears to increase parents' responsiveness to their children (Vallotton, 2012).

SUMMARY AND CONCLUSIONS

In this chapter, we have examined in detail the emergence of infants' social-communicative skills in the context of gaze following and pointing. These abilities develop through early social experiences. Engagement with others is facilitated by biological characteristics that draw infants and parents into interaction. We have reviewed some examples, such as being born less mature than other species, which results in helplessness. This provides a necessarily social environment because infants have to be cared for and face their caregivers regularly when being fed or being carried. The nature of human eyes and infants' visual systems are other examples of biological characteristics that draw infants into social engagement within which they learn about the social world and can then engage in more complex social interaction. These skills are normally discussed in books about 'social development'. From a relational developmental systems perspective, social interaction is the crucible of cognitive development.

Within interaction, infants learn to anticipate others' actions. These early social skills are shown in joint attention behaviours, usually involving vision. Social referencing (evident when infants look toward their parent in ambiguous and anxiety-provoking situations) is one example of infants' emerging social awareness. Gaze following, however, has attracted more research attention. Eyes carry huge significance in everyday interaction. This fascination with eyes begins soon after birth, most likely due to the nature of human eyes as well as infants' visual systems. Typically developing infants are attracted to eyes and become experts in the communication conveyed through eye gaze. This is a gradual process and they learn to become more skilled in locating what others are looking at. One controversial question is what do they understand about others when they can successfully follow their direction of gaze?

Although gaze following is an important social skill, it still differs from the use and understanding of gestures in prelinguistic communication. This is because actions like pointing or nodding are employed intentionally to convey meaning. Some gestures like the 'arms up' movement that many infants learn as a request to be picked up are based on the natural reaction of reaching toward their parent. It is a manifestation of their desire to be picked up, which would typically be responded to by their parent. Infants learn to anticipate this result and can then intentionally make a request to be picked up. This type of action is very common and appears early in development. Other gestures, like waving, are likely culturally specific conventions and so imitation must play some role in their development. However, infants still take considerable time to learn the appropriate social situation in which to use such gestures.

Among the many gestures infants master, pointing has been the focus of a great deal of research. Perhaps this is because it is an early developing gesture, emerging around 12 months of age, yet it can be used to convey so many different meanings. Many different functions of pointing have been described, particularly in order to make requests (proto-imperatives) and direct attention (proto-declaratives). Pointing is also associated with later language development, and social understanding more broadly. Infants who do not engage in proto-declaratives are more likely to be later diagnosed as being on the autism spectrum. Infants also master the skills needed to understand others' pointing gestures and that the same gesture used by different people or in different situations can convey completely different meanings.

On one hand, the fact that all of these complex social skills are mastered by infants who are years away from even being able to tie their own shoelaces seems amazing. But, on the other hand, in the context of everyday life, these skills seem totally natural and expectable. In fact, it is difficult to notice what is always right in front of us, and doing so takes some skill. After describing some examples of the social skills that young infants master, the next step is to explain how they develop. This is where theories come in and we examine these in detail in the next chapter.

FURTHER READING

Bruner, J., & Sherwood, V. (1976). Peek-a-boo and the learning of rule structures. In J. S. Bruner, A. Jolly, and K. Sylva (eds) *Play: Its Role in Evolution and Development.* Harmondsworth: Penguin.

Carpendale, J. I. M., & Carpendale, A. B. (2010). The development of pointing: From personal directedness to interpersonal direction. *Human Development*, *53*, 110–126.

Carpendale, J. I. M., & Lewis, C. (2006). *How Children Develop Social Understanding*. Oxford: Blackwell.

6

THEORIES OF COMMUNICATION AND SOCIAL UNDERSTANDING IN INFANCY

LEARNING OUTCOMES

Having read this chapter you should:

- Be familiar with and able to distinguish between the major theoretical accounts of how infants develop the ability to engage in prelinguistic forms of communication: the innate module, 'like me' and relational perspectives.

- Be able to apply these theories to the use of early gestures to understand how they develop.

- Be aware of how preverbal communication is thought to influence children's thinking.

- Be familiar with evidence of the emergence of gestures like pointing from various methodologies including experiments, diary studies, and cross-cultural comparisons.

- Be aware of the developmental changes in the sequencing of pointing gestures and referential looks to the other person across the second year of life: these help us to explain how joint attention skills develop.

This chapter builds on the summary of the research on infant preverbal communication in Chapter 5. We have seen that, long before they can utter a few words, infants are both attracted to other people and develop their own communicative skills within exchanges that occur as a result. In this chapter, we examine the explanations for how preverbal skills develop. A key question concerns how the emergence of joint attention occurs. As with other areas of development, several theories of the origins of communication have been proposed and there is much debate over the issue of how and why it occurs (e.g. Carpendale & Lewis, 2006; Flom, Lee, & Muir, 2007; Racine & Carpendale, 2007a, 2007b).

In the first section we briefly outline the theoretical perspectives that have received recent attention over the past twenty years. Although different from one another, they are each based on the claim that infants have a precocious grasp of the social world. The first suggests that nature does not leave this vital human skill to chance and we are born with an abstract representation of others' minds. We describe this perspective in more detail because it has received a lot of attention in the past ten years. The second seems more modest, that infants can make 'like me' comparisons, but the starting point of both perspectives is that the social world is understood by the individual making inferences about what is 'out there'.

We contrast these two perspectives in the third section with the process-relational approach, according to which an ability to use and understand communicative gestures is a hard-won achievement emerging from highly interactive social experiences. A description of these perspectives allows us to revisit the topics that were explored in Chapter 5 to consider the evidence on how shared visual attention and pointing skills emerge. This leads naturally into a consideration in the fourth and final section of two key types of evidence on the origins of infants' communicative skills before language. The first concerns whether there are cultural differences in the use and development of gestures. Secondly, we compare the skills of infants over the second year of life to argue that a skill like pointing unfolds gradually and consists of a number of developmental achievements. This incremental change supports a constructivist account of the emergence of skills that form the basis of communication and thinking.

6.1 BEGINNING WITH THE INDIVIDUAL

The innate module account

One group of approaches to explaining the development of social understanding begins with the individual mind as the starting point. Followers of this view have produced interesting research and interpreted their findings as suggesting that newborns can copy simple gestures like tongue protrusion, or 1-year-olds appear to expect others to act on what they know. There are various interpretations of this evidence but these authors share the assumption that some form of social understanding is innate. The claim that infants are born with social knowledge has propelled a group of developmental psychologists into the public eye. For example, Kristine Onishi and Renée Baillargeon (2005, p. 257) 'assume that children are born with an abstract computational system that guides their interpretation of others' behavior'. In a recent review of research on infants' social understanding, Baillargeon, Scott, and Bain (2016, p. 179) concluded that 'it seems clear that this core domain of causal reasoning depends on a content-rich, adaptive, neurocomputational system that begins to operate early in life (Cosmides & Tooby, 2013)'. We discussed Tooby and Cosmides' theory briefly in Chapter 2.

Similarly, Andrew Meltzoff (2011) argues that infants are born with early forms of social understanding on which later forms are based. Alan Leslie and his colleagues also claim that 'the concepts of belief, desire, and pretense [are] part of our genetic endowment' (Scholl & Leslie, 2001, p. 697) and 'Theory of mind is part of our social instinct, the product of core architecture for specialized learning' (Leslie et al., 2004, p. 531). The example below looks at a key piece of evidence in detail.

EXAMPLE: EVIDENCE FOR PRECOCIOUS SOCIAL UNDERSTANDING?

In 2005, Onishi and Baillargeon conducted an experiment which, they argued, shows that an understanding of the mind is innate. Infants were seated on their caregiver's lap at a table and watched a series of trials in which an actor opens a door on the other side of the table and places an object (a piece of plastic 'watermelon') in a green box and not a yellow box. In two additional trials the actor reaches into the green box. Then, in one condition, while the doors are closed and the experimenter cannot see, the melon moves from the green to the yellow box. The actor then returns and reaches for 30 seconds towards either the yellow box or the green box (where she put it). At 15 months infants look longer when she reached to the yellow box compared reaching to the green box. This longer looking time is interpreted as indicating surprise that the actor has reached toward where the object actually was rather than in the green box where she should believe it be, having left it there. A number of other conditions were in place to control for spurious reasons why infants may do this. So, for example, in a 'true belief' control where the actor sees the melon move from one box to another, infants look longer at a reach to the empty box – the opposite results to the reach in 'false belief' condition. Onishi and Baillargeon concluded that this experiment shows infants already possess a rudimentary understanding of others as agents.

This is an area of heated theoretical debate. Baillargeon (see Baillargeon et al., 2016 for a review) has conducted research with several other versions of this task and strengthened

(Continued)

her resolve that these looking patterns demonstrate innate propensities. However, there are several possible alternative interpretations and the jury is still out on whether these looking patterns reveal an early grasp of others' minds (Onishi & Baillageon, 2005), or a much simpler ability to follow simple behavioural rules without having to infer mental states (Ruffman, 2014) or expectations about typical human activity (Stack & Lewis; 2008). We discuss this experiment in Chapter 11.

On the basis of 'infant false belief' studies showing that even 10-month-olds appear to make fine distinctions that reflect an actor's agency (even a triangle chasing a square in an animation: see Surian & Geraci, 2012), many have concluded that 'The nativists won the battle over the newborn's mind' (Meltzoff, 2011, p. 51). However, as outlined below, we suggest that this claim is premature.

Of course, there must be a genetic and biological part to the story of how infants develop communicative and social skills, but these accounts can differ significantly. Claims that babies are born with innate knowledge might seem to be biologically based, and for that reason may appear to carry some weight. However, no details have been filled in yet, and to the contrary neuroscientists and geneticists argue that genes don't work that way and it is a long way from genes to traits (e.g. Fisher, 2006; Mareschal et al., 2007; Meaney, 2010). So, it is not clear that these claims are in fact biologically plausible (see Chapter 2). Given that there is a biological and genetic side to the story, there are still two families of approaches to fill in the details: gene centred or developmental systems. That is, one approach focuses on genes as an explanation, whereas another approach centres on biological differences, including genes that affect the social system in which the baby develops.

There is an additional problem when it comes to explaining a social skill like pointing, which involves intentionally conveying meaning. This form of communication is different from an evolved biological function. For example, poison dart frogs are brightly coloured and easy to spot (see, for example, https://en.wikipedia.org/wiki/Poison_dart_frog). This is because their distinctiveness indicates danger to potential predators. The more brilliant the colouring the more poisonous. This odd evolutionary quirk has helped these frogs survive. Human actions are different. Gestures like pointing can be used to convey almost limitless meanings (not just 'I'm poisonous!'). Given that the watcher has to interpret one of many possible meanings this skill must be based on shared experience in everyday routine interactions (e.g. Canfield, 2007; Goldberg, 1991; Wittgenstein, 1968).

It might seem obvious that the first step in science is to describe the question to be solved. What is less obvious, however, is that the way a problem is set up already brings in preconceptions that are rarely examined, and even smuggles in potential answers and methods along with the framing of the problem (Carpendale et al., 2013; Jopling, 1993). This can be illustrated within the current debate on infant social cognitive development.

For example, Leslie and colleagues (2004, p. 531) clearly set up the problem with the following claim:

> The fundamental design problem for a young brain that learns about invisible, intangible, abstract states like belief is being able to attend to such states in the first place. Without noticing these states, the brain could not learn about them.

On the surface this seems like an interesting perspective on the issue of how infants learn about the social world – indeed it seems exciting and taps into the neuropsychology fashion in psychology. Yet, there is something problematic about this way of setting it up. If these 'states' that 'a young brain' should attend to are 'invisible, intangible, abstract', then what exactly could the infant (or for these theorists, the infant's 'young brain') be born with that could allow it to notice these 'invisible, intangible' states? First, brains don't attend to things by themselves. Organisms with brains, and much more, attend to aspects of their world. Second, if they are 'imperceptible' and 'immaterial' then how can they be perceived? Infants must learn about others through what is observable. Furthermore, it is clear that children and parents actually have no difficulty knowing if a child is happy or upset or wants something, although figuring out exactly what she wants may not be so easy.

More broadly, Leslie et al. (2004) give a clear description of the problem as it is set up from the perspective of *one* theoretical approach. Although there is much debate about how this problem is solved by children, there is agreement within the theory of mind tradition that this is the problem children face in learning about other people. As mentioned in Chapter 1, this is a well-known issue in philosophy, articulated by Descartes, and known as the 'problem of other minds'. It suggests that humans (including children) are faced only with physical bodies, so the problem is how do we get below this 'surface' level to the 'deep' level of mental states?

The 'like me' account

Once Leslie et al.'s way of setting up the problem is brought into play, there are two general approaches to solve it. One approach is that the infant is assumed to make inferences about others' minds. This is the innate module account that is outlined in section 1.1, according to which children have the ability to draw inferences through implicit theory formation. To do so they need to be born with inferential 'mechanisms' or an 'abstract computational system'. The second approach is that the infant uses her own experience to understand others. Given that this involves imagining yourself in someone else's shoes, it is known as simulation theory, and there are various versions. A prominent view is Andrew Meltzoff's (2011) claim that infants are born with an innate ability to understand others as 'like me'. Given this understanding that the other people they see are like them they can then, according to Meltzoff, apply their own understanding of their self to other people. That is, this innate ability then allows infants to reason by analogy about others, and learn about the social world in this way.

These proposals follow from the problem of other minds set out by Descartes. It arises in the dualist or cognitivist worldview based on a preconception of beginning with the private individual mind in explaining social development. But because the mind is presupposed it cannot actually be explained. Instead it is already taken as given for the starting point.

Meltzoff's (2011) claims are based on research that he interprets as demonstrating new-born infants' ability to imitate facial expressions – neonatal imitation. From the 1970s onwards he has reported that newborns appear to imitate simple facial gestures like mouth opening and tongue protrusion (see the box). It was this research that led him to argue that infants are born with the ability to view others as 'like me'. Put more formally, they can understand others through reasoning by analogy. In Meltzoff's words:

> When infants see others acting similarly to how they have acted in the past – acting 'like me' – they make an attribution. They ascribe the internal feelings that regularly go with those behaviors, based on their self-experience. This gives infants leverage for grasping other minds before language can be used. (Meltzoff, 2011, p. 53)

That is, if they feel happy when they smile and they see others smile they could reason that those others are also happy.

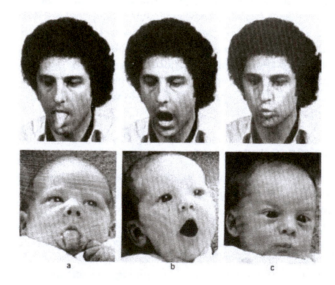

Figure 6.1   The modelling of the three facial gestures in Meltzoff and Moore's 1977 study of 12- to 21-day-old infants

a) tongue protrusion; b) mouth open; c) lip protrusion.

Reproduced with permission from Elsevier, Journal *Science*, 'Infants selectively encode the goal object of an actor's reach', October, 1977, Vol/Iss: 198 (4312) pp.75–78 (Image located on page 75).

EXAMPLE: CAN NEWBORN INFANTS COPY SIMPLE FACIAL GESTURES?

Some forty years ago Andrew Meltzoff and Keith Moore (1977) published an elegant study in the journal *Science*. For 15 seconds they modelled one of three facial gestures and one movement of the hand (tongue protrusion, mouth wide open, lip protrusion, and sequential finger movement) to very young infants and then showed a still face for 20 seconds (see Figure 6.1). In the latter period they assessed whether infants displayed the just-modelled gesture more than the others. This seemed to suggest their specific copying of the action just modelled.

The evidence that infants imitate a range of facial expressions has been debated and retested several times since and still remains controversial. It seems that newborns only reliably respond by sticking out their tongue at adults who do that to them. That is they only consistently match tongue protrusion not other facial expressions (Anisfeld, 1991, 1996; Anisfeld, Turkewitz, & Rose, 2001; Ray & Heyes, 2011). There has been even more controversy, however, regarding how to interpret this tendency to match tongue protrusion. Although Meltzoff claims that this is imitation others disagree. They argue that the appearance of imitation may well be accounted for by a simpler process. In fact, infants stick out their tongue in various interesting or arousing situations such as having their palms touched, the sight of a black pen or small ball looming and receding, or even short excerpts of music from *The Barber of Seville* (Jones, 2006). So, it has been argued that matching others' tongue protrusion could be explained as a simple response to something interesting (Jones, 1996, 2009). Another criticism of claims regarding neonatal imitation is that infants stop imitating in this way after two to three months and then they begin imitating again when they are about one year of age (Jones, 2007). Furthermore, newborn imitation has been observed in chimpanzees and rhesus macaque monkeys. Yet adult chimpanzees are not skilled imitators, modelling others' action only about 5% of the time, and adult rhesus macaques do not seem to imitate at all (Jones, 2009). More recently, an analysis of almost 40 studies concluded that of 18 gestures studied only tongue protrusion is replicable, and even this could be explained by rapid learning rather than the infant making 'like me' judgments and copying (Ray & Heyes, 2011). However, the debate does on. Since Ray and Hayes' large-scale analysis Nagy, Pilling, Orvos, and Molnar (2013) published data suggesting an imitation effect in the first week of life. Despite this evidence, it has been hard to provide conclusive support over the past forty years of experimentation for the strong claim that infants are born with the innate knowledge necessary for imitation.

The idea that infants draw on their own experience in order to understand others is also proposed by Michael Tomasello and his colleagues. For this group 'infants begin to understand particular kinds of intentional and mental states in others only after they have experienced them first in their own activity and then used their own experience to simulate that of others' (Tomasello, Carpenter, Call, Behne, & Moll, 2005, p. 688). Tomasello and Carpenter (2013) more recently have clarified their view and claimed that this ability does not depend on reflection. They state that

> when the infant understands that someone 'sees' something, all she knows about seeing is her own experience of seeing, and so that is what she takes the other to be doing. There is no reflection on her own mental states involved. (2013, p. 402)

Tomasello and Carpenter do not attribute infants with a level of understanding claimed in the innate module view, but they do assume that they have an ability to apply their own experience to others. Adults and older children can draw on their own experience to understand others, although we may resort to this skill only rarely. But this does not mean that infants can do this. Other species, such as cats, dogs, and frogs, also have the experience of seeing, in the immediate sense of the term, but this does not mean they are able to use this experience to understand others. Doing so requires a different form of experience beyond the immediate lived experience (Baldwin, 1906; Carpendale & Lewis, 2015b). We must be cautious not to attribute an adult level of understanding, which is a developmental outcome, to infants (e.g. Hobson & Hobson, 2011; see also e.g. Carpendale & Lewis, 2004, 2010, 2015a; Hobson, 2002).

The process that Melztzoff and Tomasello claim explains social development in infancy is also known as the 'analogical argument' – that infants can compare their own with others' actual (Meltzoff) or hypothetical (Tomasello) perspectives. Theories based on this analogical argument have long been criticised for already assuming, rather than explaining, key aspects of social development. This is because they assume that infants can distinguish themselves from others in order to reason analogically and apply their own experience to others (Müller & Carpendale, 2004; Müller & Runions, 2003; Scheler, 1913/1954; Zahavi, 2008). Logically, this kind of reasoning could not allow infants to develop the idea of self and other: it is simply there. It therefore already presupposes what must be explained. Once children have this distinction then they might be able to reason by analogy in some cases, but they cannot form this distinction through analogy.

Tomasello has been largely interested in explaining the development of joint attention in infancy. He argues that there is a '9-month revolution' when skills like showing objects to caregivers and then pointing emerge. He claims that these concern infants' understanding of others as intentional agents with goals, and that these joint attention skills are manifestations of the same underlying insight (Tomasello, 1995a, 1999): 'manifestations of infants' emerging understanding of other persons as intentional agents whose attention and behavior to outside objects and events may be shared, followed into, and directed in various ways' (Carpenter, Nagell, & Tomasello, 1998, p. 118). This prediction is supported by Carpenter et al.'s report that evidence of different joint attention behaviours appears to be correlated with one another, although the correlations they found were not as strong as they had expected. Other researchers have not found correlations between similar behaviours (Slaughter & McConnell, 2003), such as responding to and initiating joint attention (Mundy et al., 2007) and pointing and gaze following (Brooks & Meltzoff, 2008). The complexity and variability of joint attention skills and their inter-relations are evident when they are assessed weekly in longitudinal research (Striano, Stahl, & Cleveland, 2009). There are even mixed results on the question of whether infants' understanding of others' pointing precedes their own use of pointing gestures. Some researchers find that infants first follow pointing before producing it (Bruner, 1983; Carpenter et al., 1998), whereas others find the opposite relation (Desrochers, Morissette, & Ricard, 1995; Murphy & Messer, 1977). But to assess infants' understanding of a gesture it is important to know whether they grasp the reason the other is pointing, or if they are just following a pointing gesture (Behne Liszkowski, Carpenter, & Tomasello, 2012).

Even if correlations were found among many joint attention behaviours, Chris Moore (1998) has argued this would not necessarily mean that all infants' pointing gestures are based on an insight about other people. Babies may learn various gestures in different ways. If we consider their use of the 'arms-up' gesture mentioned above, for example, this gesture could develop into a request to be picked up. A full developmental account would explore in detail how this request emerges. If such a skill appears gradually then we would expect it to start as just reaching toward a parent, before learning to anticipate a response, and becoming able to engage in intentional communication (Lock, 1978; Service, Lock, & Chandler, 1989).

In this section we have explored current versions of simulation theory – that infants either naturally understand others' actions in terms of their own experience (Meltzoff),

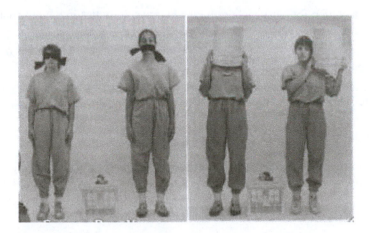

Figure 6.2   Two of the conditions in Povinelli's research with chimpanzees

If chimps are aware of another's perceptual stance they should gesture for the food on the unturned basket to the person who can see them, but they do not.

Image courtesy of Daniel Povinelli.

or they learn to do so at around 9 months of age (Tomasello). Tomasello's claim is based on the idea that skills emerge together. When things look similar on the surface we tend to assume they are similar, but this is not always the case. Young infants can follow gaze, but Daniel Povinelli (1999) has shown that chimpanzees can also do this. However, he then went on to show in a careful series of experiments that these chimpanzees still did not know much about attention. For example, they were just as likely to beg for food from an experimenter who had a bucket over her head or her eyes closed as from an experimenter with her eyes open (Figure 6.2). The chimpanzees could learn to beg from the right person, but it took many trials. This seems surprising because young children figure this out right away.

Shared intentionality

Shared intentionality is a concept currently drawn on by Tomasello and his colleagues in making sense of social understanding. According to Tomasello and Carpenter (2007, p. 121), 'Shared intentionality, sometimes called "we" intentionality, refers to collaborative interactions in which participants share psychological states'. Tomasello bases his analysis on the fact that communication between humans is very complex and assumes that it involves a sophisticated understanding of others' perspectives. How does this develop in children? In this quotation shared intentionality is presented as a *description* of cooperative activity, but in many analyses like this there is a shift to taking it as an *explanation* for such interaction. He considers collaborative interactions to be

- 'an adaptation for participating in collaborative activities involving shared intentionality' (Tomasello et al., 2005, p. 690);
- 'the underlying psychological processes that make these unique forms of cooperation possible' (Tomasello, 2009, p. xiii);
- or 'a suite of social-cognitive and social-motivational skills that may be collectively termed shared intentionality' (Tomasello & Carpenter, 2007, p. 121).

Tomasello asks

- 'what does the individual bring to the interaction that enables her to engage in joint attention in a way that other apes and younger children cannot?' (2014, p. 152).

His answer is

- 'that something like recursive mind-reading or inferring – still not adequately characterized, and in most instances fully implicit – has to be part of the story of shared intentionally' (p. 152).

If we look at these examples of Tomasello's theory closely we can see the underlying assumptions. By using terms like 'adaptation' and 'underlying psychological processes' he takes a cognitivist perspective for granted, naturally shifting from *describing* a form of interaction to *explaining* it as the result of the cognitive processes that make it possible. In the last quotation he clarifies that the infant's cognitive skills are sophisticated. To have 'recursive mind-reading' skills, babies need to be able to keep their own mental state in mind and bring it to the fore to compare with that of the other interactant. However, this sort of approach then runs into the problem of explaining where these cognitive processes come from. As yet Tomasello has not provided an adequate developmental account, in part because if the very young infant can do this there is not much to explain in terms of later development (Carpendale & Lewis, 2015b).

6.2 BEGINNING WITH SOCIAL ACTIVITY: 'IN THE BEGINNING IS THE DEED'

In this section we build up an alternative perspective, the relational framework, which more closely resembles the position taken by developmental psychologists over the past century. This approach takes the opposite approach to those in the first two sections and assumes that social relations are the *origin* of cognitive skills rather than the other way around (Mead, 1934). That is, for Mead and others it is not the cognitive skills of shared intentionality that make interaction possible; rather that it is through social relations that individuals develop communication, language, thinking, and mind (see Carpendale & Lewis, 2015a, 2015b). Put another way, the cognitivist position of Tomasello and the other authors we have referred to has been described by Peter Hobson (2002) as a 'joining-together' approach because the starting assumption is that infants just experience other bodies and have to infer minds – a view inherited from Descartes' 'problem of other minds'. The contrasting approach, which we favour, is a 'differentiating-out' approach because it begins with infants' experience and how they gradually learn about aspects of this experience, including other people, and in this way develop distinctions.

The alternative to theories such as those of Meltzoff and Tomasello, which have been referred to as providing 'rich' interpretations of infant behaviour, is a more traditional developmental perspective termed a 'lean' approach, as it does not presuppose that the infant has more than a few simple behavioural skills to respond to cues in the environment (e.g. Moore & Corkum, 1994). According to this latter perspective, there is much that children learn about others in the process of interaction. The origin of social understanding is in the social relations within which infants learn to anticipate human activity.

The relational framework begins from the infant's experience (Baldwin, 1906; Hobson, 1993; Piaget, 1954; Vygotsky, 1978; Werner & Kaplan, 1963). Infants can respond to others' attitudes without yet having a conception of what those attitudes are. Social understanding is grounded in interpersonal relatedness. This is known as a sensorimotor account of developing social skills based on a relational constructivist worldview (Bibok, Carpendale, & Lewis, 2008; de Barbaro, et al., 2013; Mascolo & Fischer, 2015; Moore, 1998). By sensorimotor, Jean Piaget meant an account that is based on the infant's activity (see Chapter 3), which naturally gives rise to experiences with objects and people that gradually come to be understood. The term 'relational constructivist' identifies that such learning occurs in interaction with others.

There are several relational constructivist accounts of how infant social understanding develops. Moore and Corkum (1994; Corkum & Moore, 1995, 1998; Moore, 1998, 1999) provide a leaner interpretation, asking the question 'how do we come to understand that self and others are the same kind of psychological entity?' (Moore, 2006, p. 206). They argue that infants come to engage in joint visual attention, mainly because their attention is coordinated with adults'. They learn to share attention through instrumental learning or cueing by the adult, without having yet developed an understanding of attention. Rather than joint attention necessarily revealing infants' understanding of other people's attention, Moore and Corkum (1994) suggest that understanding others is constructed within this interaction. From this perspective, the problem is to integrate information from first- and third-person perspectives (Barresi & Moore, 1996).

From a constructivist approach to knowledge, infants learn about what they can do with the world (see Chapter 3). They learn the interactive potential of aspects of the world. And since other people are a large part of an infant's world they learn about what people do and how people respond to them, and through this process also learn to communicate intentionally. Given this examination of general theories of infant social development, we now turn to the development of gestures, and to pointing in particular, described in detail in Chapter 5, in order to show how this emergence of shared attention takes place.

From joint attention to joint action and communication

The focus of this chapter and the previous one has been on research on joint attention, which is usually achieved visually. It is on how infants learn to coordinate their attention with others and look at the same thing. But how do they develop social and communicative skills, and enjoy sharing attention with others to objects and events? We need to move from coordinating attention to an account in which the shared nature of communication is clearly captured. Consider some examples of learning about a routine social activity in which communication works through a shared understanding of familiar social situations:

- *A toddler at 13 months walked to the apartment door and held his foot over his shoe, vocalising to get his father's attention.* This functioned as a request to go for a walk because this is the beginning of the action routine that leads to the everyday social activity of going for a walk.

- *A 14-month-old walking to the park held out his hand toward his uncle as they got to the curb, which was a big step down for a toddler.* This action functioned as a request given the well-known routine during walking to the park.

- *In the context of a meal, his mother was feeding him, then he took the spoon and used it himself, and then he gave the spoon to his uncle.* The toddler expected this to be understood as a request to be fed. (All these examples are from Carpendale et al., 2013.)

These are all interactions involving a shared understanding of what is coming up next. Infants can anticipate what will happen because they become familiar with routines, and they know what to expect when they initiate an activity. Thus, a history of joint action can be the foundation for communicating. Such a history is a necessary outcome of our human embodiment, the fact that we are bodies moving in space and time (Canfield, 2007; Carpendale & Wereha, 2013; McDonough, 1989; Mead, 1934; Wittgenstein, 1968). At the same time, many of our gestures are culturally constrained – in some societies it is more appropriate to be taken for a walk, helped to overcome a hurdle or fed than in others.

YOUR STUDY OF POINTING

If you know a child aged 10–14 months (you may have a relative or friend with one), ask them to note when the infant first uses a point and how this skill develops or, better yet, observe the child yourself. Often toddlers will start pointing at everything (they seem to be getting the point!). Careful observation will identify whether the infant just points or whether she then looks at the adult to see if that person is sharing attention. This look is a crucial landmark in the development of gestures as it is one source of evidence revealing a greater sophistication in the child's communicative skills.

Getting the point: explaining how pointing develops

We now return to examining specific views regarding how babies learn to point (see Chapter 5). Various theories have been proposed to explain this crucial development. One of the hypotheses for pointing considered by Tomasello is that it is based on infants' insight regarding others as intentional agents with attention that can be directed (Tomasello, Carpenter, & Liszkowski, 2007). However, we have already reviewed criticism of the explanation for the development of such an insight. As an alternative, in this subsection we consider various constructivist accounts of the developing skill.

The idea that pointing might originate in a reaching action and that it is 'nothing but an abbreviated grasp movement' (Werner & Kaplan, 1963, p. 78) has a long history going back to the end of the nineteenth century (Wundt, 1973), and Guillaume (1926/1971) and Vygotsky (1978) in the 1920s. In Vygotsky's words (1978 [written before his death in 1934], p. 56, emphasis in original):

> Initially, this gesture is nothing more than an unsuccessful attempt to grasp something, a movement aimed at a certain object ... placed beyond his reach; his hands, stretched toward that object, remain poised in the air. His fingers make grasping movements. At this initial stage pointing is represented by the child's movement, which seems to be pointing to an object – that and nothing more. When the mother comes to the child's aid and realises his movement indicates something, the situation changes fundamentally. Pointing becomes a gesture for others. The child's unsuccessful attempt engenders a reaction not from the object he seeks but *from another person*.

As the child learns about the reactions her action elicits from others, there is a change in the function of the physical movement from being directed toward the object to being aimed at other people. The general idea of pointing gestures emerging from natural non-communicative actions or reactions being transformed into a social action has been proposed in different ways by many scholars (e.g. Bates, 1976; Shinn, 1900; Werner & Kaplan, 1963). Vygotsky's (1978) specific proposal in the quotation above considers requests. This explanation might account for the development of a request, but it would still be necessary to explain why infants change from a grasping action to using their index finger. Some infants do learn how to make requests with an abbreviated grasping movement consisting of opening and closing their hand with their arm extended (Carpendale & Carpendale, 2010). Also, Vygotsky's account does not explain the use of pointing for other functions such as declaratives and asking or answering questions. Still, the general idea of a non-communicative action becoming communicative may hold.

Others have argued that pointing may first emerge as an action that orientates the self, and it later becomes a social act that can be used for a variety of social functions (Bates, 1976) – this is why so many infants seem to go through a stage of pointing at everything even if they think they are alone. In diary observations of an infant, Shinn (1900/1975) noted a transition from exploration with the index finger of close objects to more distant objects that interested the infant. A number of researchers have also noted that babies seem to use their index finger to explore objects (Bates et al., 1975; Carpendale & Carpendale, 2010).

The above accounts of the origins of communicative pointing in initially non-social activity have provoked much research over the past century. Bates et al. (1975; see also

Bates, 1976) found that the infants in their diary study first used the pointing hand configuration non-communicatively. They suggested that social pointing has its origin in the initially non-social use of the index finger for finger tip exploration. In a recent case study based on diary observations, the infant being observed seemed to use the pointing hand configuration first in fingertip exploration, and then as part of his own orienting activity toward objects of interest, before gradually learning about the social significance that his action had for others, and then learning to use it as a social act (Carpendale & Carpendale, 2010).

Since the heyday of behaviourism in the mid-twentieth century, researchers have attempted to show that pointing is an activity that is gradually 'shaped' from early attempts. Indeed, chimpanzees acquire gestures in this way through social shaping, a process which is referred to as 'ontogenetic ritualisation' (Halina, Rossano, & Tomasello, 2013; Plooij, 1978). Shaped gestures are learned through others' responses to the natural actions of infant chimpanzees. Michael Tomasello (2003) acknowledges that it is possible that some human infants may learn to point in this way, especially before 12 months.

Individual case studies help to inform us about the complexities of a child's possible routes into using particular gestures. Elizabeth Bates and her colleagues (1975) traced the emergence of pointing from earlier forms of interaction. In their classic diary study, Carlotta moved from physical contact with an adult to other ways of getting attention such as smiling, laughing, and eye contact (1975, p. 216). She discovered she could attract adult attention by showing off and repeating behaviours that had previously been successful in attracting attention. She then learned to show an object to obtain attention (Bates et al., 1975, p. 216). Bates et al. (1975, p. 213) noted that 'The mutual joy taken in such interactions provides the first loop in the construction of declarative communication: the formulation of social interaction as goal in itself'. This is a crucial insight into how the infant's emotions can structure the form of interaction in which communication develops. Infants may hold an object out to an adult, at first with no intention of handing it over. From Bates et al.'s perspective, showing is an earlier phase in developing the social skill of directing attention. Infants learn that giving an object is a way to engage with an adult. So, if they want to interact but have no object they might run to get one. 'Giving' and 'taking' are actually complex social acts full of precision timing (e.g. show, check the other is looking and 'sharing the gesture', extend arm, release object when the other has grasped the object, share the meaning of the exchange), and these social acts are imbued with cultural meaning. It might, therefore, be better to describe the early steps in the development of such social skills more neutrally as 'the transfer of objects' (Clark, 1978). When showing an object to someone, Carlotta might drop the object into his or her hand, but this often happened when she was distracted by something else rather than obviously intending to give the object. It is often hard to know exactly when an infant is showing an object or giving; instead it seems to be a gradual transition (Bates et al., 1975).

What *is* pointing and how does it develop? There is evidence that infants at 10 to 11 months who experience more interaction around holding out and giving objects to their parents used more pointing gestures at 12 months, suggesting that this interaction is important in the development of pointing (Cameron-Faulkner, Theakston, Lieven, & Tomasello, 2015). Showing and giving have also been observed in some corvids (members of the crow family, including jays and ravens), so this skill may not be unique to our species. Ravens seem to use declarative gestures to show objects (like a piece of moss, a small stone, or a twig with no functional utility) to other ravens. These 'may function as "testing-signals" to evaluate the interest of a potential partner or to strengthen an already existing bond' (Pika & Bugnyar, 2011, p. 1). In ravens it is possible that these patterns of interaction might develop because they are attracted to objects and may learn that other ravens also tend to be attracted to them. They can learn to use such objects with the anticipation that it may attract others. This is an example of a distant species performing gestures that resemble those of humans, but there are clear differences. Let's return to Bates's case example.

Carlotta had developed a pointing scheme in non-communicative situations when examining 'small book figures, and orienting toward novel and interesting sounds and events' (Bates et al., 1975, p. 217). But in these episodes she was not seeking the attention of adults because she might do this when she was alone in a room and unaware that she was being observed, or gestured when others were present but she did not turn to look toward them.

More recent accounts of this skill follow Jerome Bruner's (1975) claim that it is because we are such a social species that we come to use pointing. The mutual joy in interacting with each other and sharing attention could be the foundation for many social routines. For example, in a diary observation a 12-month-old held out a shovel and his enjoyment was clear in his smile as he looked at his adult caregivers. This mutual joy forms the foundation for declaratives. Although it is possible to describe early pointing as providing or requesting information, for infants this may not be clearly separable from their enjoyment in engaging with others, so observers can label the pointing 'declaring' but it may be primarily for the enjoyment of sharing in the moment (Bates et al., 1975, p. 209). Another situation where pointing emerges in the context of an emotion is when a toddler is trying to reach a goal and cannot achieve it. In this situation, the toddler is frustrated because he cannot get what he desires. Requests of various types may develop when a baby's desire for something is manifest in his action, like leaning or reaching toward a parent, or reaching toward an object. Requesting in this kind of situations depends on the baby developing, and understanding, the interaction potential of an object (i.e. knowing what to do with the object being requested), the ability to reach, and so on.

Emotions play an essential role in structuring the forms of interaction in which infants learn routines, and displays of enjoyment and other feelings develop further within such interaction (Bates et al., 1975; Leavens, Sansone, Burfield, Lightfoot, O'Hara, & Todd, 2014). The social routines that babies learn are based on emotions of different sorts. Greeting, for example, is based on the mutual joy of a parent and infant seeing each other, and this develops over the first few months as they form emotional bonds (Canfield, 2007).

In summary, the explanations for pointing discussed in this section revolve around the natural emergence of this hand configuration in interaction to which adults respond. Through this process infants learn about the communication that is already present in the interaction. In this way, they come to intentionally communicate with pointing gestures and learn to use these to perform a variety of social acts.

The roots of prelinguistic communication

As mentioned above, after the age of 12 months infants start to use pointing gestures for many different functions (e.g. Carpendale & Carpendale, 2010). For example, Carlotta extended her use of pointing from directing attention to making requests, such as for a glass of water. Other diary studies have documented many other uses of pointing for asking and answering questions (Carpendale & Carpendale, 2010). Infants also show increased flexibility in the use of other gestures. For example, we have mentioned Max's use of waving to indicate that he had finished his food, or finished the book he was looking at, and when combined with pointing, to indicate wanting to go outside (see Chapter 5). How can this be explained? Is this based on an insight about other people and is it evidence for such an insight? From one perspective it could be seen as evidence of a '9-month revolution' (e.g. Tomasello & Carpenter, 2013), supporting the claim that infants begin to understand others as intentional agents with attention that can be directed. But what exactly is this insight and how does it develop?

An alternative interpretation is that this ability is based on the practical understanding of social situations. Piaget's (1936/1952) description of the development of sensorimotor intelligence characterises sub-stage 5 as involving the use of new ways to achieve familiar goals (see Chapter 3). That is, action patterns that have been developed in one setting can be extended and tried out in others. This description of the process of cognitive development also applies to infants' developing understanding of interacting with other people. This step in social understanding is what Shinn (1900/1975) termed 'combining habits'. The infant attempts to reach a goal by trying out all of the actions that have worked previously. Piaget referred to this as 'generalising assimilation'; that is, learning an action pattern in one setting and trying it out in another. By generalising their action schemes to new situations, infants may even expect their actions to affect other people in a specific way. In any case, what we propose here is an action-based interpretation of behaviour that may create the impression it is based on insight.

In describing the development of pointing, Bates et al. (1975, p. 217) note 'a peculiar transition period' during which Carlotta seemed to be combining action sequences. She would first orient toward the interesting object or event and point. Then she would swing around and point toward the adult with the same gesture, and then return to looking and pointing at the object. Later, this sequence became smoother with pointing toward the object while turning to look at the adult. Since Bates et al. discussed this sort of observation of pointing toward an adult it has rarely been mentioned in the literature. Franco and Butterworth (1996) observed this form of pointing in 10-month-olds but not older infants, and Matthews, Behne, Lieven, and Tomasello (2012) mention in a footnote that this type of observation was not coded. In our view, this type of pointing has significant implications for theories of the development of pointing. Part of this form of pointing is pointing directly at another person (Carpendale & Carpendale, 2010). If infants understand others as intentional agents it is not clear why they would perform this action. But it is consistent with the view that pointing is at first associated with infants' own attention and orientation to the world before becoming more clearly social and used to direct others.

If pointing is used to direct attention then it might seem necessary to look at the other person. This is what is referred to as visual 'checking'. Pointing without looking might seem to show a lack of understanding that it is essential for the other person to notice the gesture. But in some settings, such as book reading, joint engagement might be taken for granted by the infant. Bates et al. (1975) note that one of the children in their study appeared so confident of her mother's attention that she only checked she had her mother's attention if her 'command' was not responded to. It is also possible that checking might just be looking at the parent for other reasons, such as emotional comfort, making sure the parent is still there, or to see what will happen next.

One experiment in particular charts the emergence of visual checking. Franco and Butterworth (1996) conducted a study in which infants were presented with toys either in close proximity to the child, but out of reach, or 2.7 metres away. They found that even 10-month-olds point only to the more distant object. Visual checking with pointing increased from 50% of the time at 12 months to 65% of the time at 18 months. But what also changed was *when* the infant checked. At 12 months babies usually checked just after pointing. At 14 months, checking tended to be during the pointing, and at 16 months, checking occurred most often just before the pointing gesture – presumably to make sure the interactant was attending. This strongly suggests that infants go through different levels of understanding of pointing in the process of mastering the gesture. Similarly, Moore and D'Entremont (2001) explored differences in pointing between 1-year-olds and 2-year-olds. The children were presented with an interesting sight on the other side of the room while their parent was either looking toward that side or not. One-year-olds were more likely to point when the parent was looking at them, and their pointing did not depend on whether the parent had already seen the interesting sight. Two-year-olds, however, were more likely to point when their parent had either not seen the interesting sight or was no longer looking at the sight. Again, this supports the idea that 2-year-olds are using pointing to direct others' attention, whereas 1-year-olds seem to use pointing more to enhance interaction than to redirect others' attention.

6.3 IMITATION, CULTURE, AND POINTING

If learning to point is part of the child's everyday social experience, how exactly does it emerge? Perhaps pointing could be explained if babies watch their parents gesturing and then copy this action. It has been claimed that 'imitation would appear to be the learning process involved in the emergence of declarative pointing' (Cochet & Vauclair, 2010, p. 438). Cochet and Vauclair suggest separate origins of what appear to be similar gestures: imperative 'points' most often involve the whole hand, whereas declaratives involve the extended index finger. Although different types of pointing might have different origins, the only evidence that imitation is important is that parents start pointing before infants and the rate of pointing for both parents and infants increases in the second half of the first year. This could be explained in other ways (Lock et al., 1990). As Tomasello (2008, p. 112) suggests, pointing may not develop through imitation, but could instead emerge 'perhaps as a nonsocial orienting action that becomes socialized in interaction with others'. He considers the possibility that imitation may play a role later in mastering the skill, but here we will focus only on his view of the nature of the social and cultural processes that facilitate its development.

If pointing emerges from social interaction and interaction varies across cultures, then does this mean that pointing may not develop in all cultures? This question was explored across seven cultural groups differing from small-scale rural groups to large-scale urban populations. Pointing was elicited in a fairly natural situation of caregivers carrying their infant in a room with many interesting novel objects. The researchers found that most of the 10- to 14-month-old infants pointed with their index finger and there were no significant differences across the cultures (Liszkowski, Brown, Callaghan, Takada, & de Vos, 2012).

Liszkowski et al. (2012) also found that across cultures there was a relation between infant and caregiver pointing. When the infant or the parent pointed, about a third of the time the other responded by also pointing, and it was primarily the infant following the caregiver's pointing. This suggests the infant's actions in these episodes were not just imitative but instead part of a conversation of gestures, involving turn taking and sharing information.

The question of whether differences in social interaction influence the development of pointing was addressed by comparing infants' pointing across three cultural groups that varied widely in the amount and type of social interaction infants were exposed to (Salomo & Liszkowski, 2013). Salomo and Liszkowski compared Dutch children with Yucatec Mayan children living in small villages with large families and therefore perhaps experiencing less interaction with parents. The third group selected was Shanghai Chinese infants who had no siblings because of the one-child policy in China and were cared for by grandparents and thus experienced a great deal of interaction. In spite of the large differences in social interaction across the cultural groups, infants in all the families were observed engaging in triadic (child–adult–toy) interaction. In each setting, others gestured to the infants and the infants also used gestures such as showing, offering, and pointing. There were also differences. There was more interaction in the Dutch families than the Mayan families, and the Dutch children used more gestures than the Mayan infants. Similarly, there was more interaction in Chinese families compared to the Dutch families, and the Chinese infants used more gestures. Index finger pointing was observed in only a few of the older Mayan infants, but the majority of the Dutch infants were pointing and almost all of the Chinese infants were. It was not simply the case that the caregivers' gestures predicted the infants' gestures. Instead, the amount of time spent in joint activity with caregivers was a better predictor. Thus, pointing is influenced by the social context that infants experience, but it is unlikely to be explained by imitation because, for example, Dutch infants were exposed to more showing gestures but they used more pointing than showing. Rather, the extent of the infant's use of a gesture like pointing seems to be the product of the amount and nature of adult–child communication.

Further evidence that babies do not just copy their parents, and indeed use index finger pointing within a specific communicative context, comes from a study in which, in the context of looking at things together, the number of pointing gestures mothers used was not correlated with their infants' pointing gestures (Liszkowski & Tomasello, 2011). This fits with an account according to which pointing emerges within social practices but not just through imitation. Before infants started using index finger pointing, other forms were observed such as whole hand pointing. Those who used finger pointing did more pointing, and it was coordinated with both vocalisation and an understanding of others' pointing gestures.

To address the role of imitation experimentally, Matthews et al. (2012) conducted a study in which half the mothers were asked to spend 15 minutes per day for one month in an activity with more pointing. This involved walking around with their baby on their hip pointing to interesting things, compared to a control group doing music and nursery rhymes. They found that this training did not prompt infants to start to use the gesture. Instead the emergence of pointing was predicted by the infant's earlier ability to follow gaze. However, the training was associated with infants' gaze checking when pointing, so it might have had more general influences on the quality of joint attention. The infants' frequency of using the gesture at the end of the study was correlated with how much their mothers naturally pointed when playing with them.

If the development of pointing depends on social experience, and if forms of social interaction differ across cultures, then why do we not see large cultural variations in its use and development? We need to remember that pointing depends on a particular developmental niche. Typically developing human babies have arms and hands. They come to coordinate their reaching and learn about the action potential of objects and then reach toward them. As infants are relatively helpless, they may not be able to get what they want for themselves. At the same time caregiving arrangements for toddlers may vary across cultures and subcultural groups from parents to siblings to nursery staff. Thus, given typical human physical embodiment (including the release of the upper body and arms once walking is achieved) and the social developmental niche in which human infants develop, their forms of interaction are likely to develop to fulfil specific communicative needs (Carpendale & Wereha, 2013). These constraints are relatively consistent across all cultures. The research described in this section shows that requests and pointing of various forms emerge within family interaction and there is potential for some differences given individual infants' caregiving experiences and cultural beliefs.

SUMMARY AND CONCLUSIONS

In this chapter we have examined how the skills described in Chapter 5 develop. We started by describing two broad theoretical approaches that are popular at the moment. Explanations of the mind (and thinking) through non-social processes usually assume that infants are born with knowledge. The innate module accounts wrestle with the conundrum that it is hard to account for how knowledge emerges, and they assume that the knowledge must therefore be there from the outset. Although current versions of these approaches appear to be based in biology it seems that such claims are, in fact, not consistent with current biology (see Chapter 2). The second, weaker, form of this argument – the 'like me' perspective – does not propose an innate theory of mind but suggests the infant can relate their own movements to those of others. This approach also presupposes the mind to begin with rather than explaining it. We contrasted those approaches that rely on non-social processes with an alternative family of theories focusing on social processes in the emergence of infant social skills.

We then turned to theories of the development of gestures, specifically to the skills involved in pointing. We provided evidence in this chapter that the ability to understand and use these skills emerges within the complexity of everyday interaction. Learning how to point appropriately is a slowly acquired skill. In the next chapter we examine animal communication systems and then move on to human languages. We will consider whether early communication is a bridge to language and social understanding. The routines forming the cradle of communication lead to gestures, which then form the foundation on which words can be added, and which then gradually replace those gestures.

FURTHER READING

Bruner, J. (1975). The ontogenesis of speech acts. *Journal of Child Language, 2,* 1–19.

Carpendale, J. I. M., Atwood, S., & Kettner, V. (2013). Meaning and mind from the perspective of dualist versus relational worldviews: Implications for the development of pointing gestures. *Human Development, 56,* 381–400.

Carpendale, J. I. M., & Lewis, C. (2015). The development of social understanding. In L. Liben & U. Müller (vol. eds), *Vol. 2: Cognitive Processes,* R. Lerner (Editor-in-Chief), 7th edition of the *Handbook of Child Psychology and Developmental Science* (pp. 381–424). New York: Wiley Blackwell.

Carpendale, J. I. M., & Lewis, C. (2015). Taking natural history seriously in studying the social formation of thinking. Essay Review. *Human Development, 58,* 55–66.

7 ANIMAL COMMUNICATION AND HUMAN LANGUAGE

LEARNING OUTCOMES

By the end of this chapter you should:

- Understand how the study of animal communication informs us about the nature and sophistication of human communication.

- Be able to discuss the details of the communication patterns of vervet monkeys and honeybees.

- Know that attempts to teach apes to speak have been conducted for a hundred years and why those based on behavioural training were inconclusive.

- Be able to define what a LAD and a LASS are (and know their theoretical differences).

- Be able to discuss the differences between human and animal communication and therefore the complexity of the latter.

- Be aware of how more recent training programmes based on social interaction have changed our understanding of how apes may learn to communicate with humans as well as how they have informed our understanding of children's early language development.

Do animals use languages? Can dogs learn words? Rico, a 9-year-old border collie, was able to learn 200 words (Kaminski, Call, & Fischer, 2004). But are these really words in the same sense that humans use them? What Rico had learned was to *fetch* 200 different objects (Bloom, 2004). This is an incredibly impressive feat, but what does it tell us about human languages? When a child learns a word, more is expected than the ability to fetch the object that it identifies. Rico became an expert in the fetching game, but this is only one of the many 'games' children learn to engage in with language. Did Rico learn in the same way as children do? Is what he achieved very different from learning to obey commands such as to *sit* and *come*? These are the sorts of questions we address in attempting to learn more about human languages by studying animal communication systems. By studying one we also learn a lot about the other.

We have discussed the development of infant communication before language in the previous chapters. What do we learn by comparisons with other animals? We can ask if there is anything like human language among the complex systems of animal communication. As we suggest in Chapter 5, animals communicate at several levels. Its form, however, varies radically across species. We cited the brilliant colouring of poison dart frogs, which is highly visible. It 'communicates' or signals its deadly nature to potential predators, but this colouring has evolved; it is not intentional as in the case of an electric transformer painted yellow and black and labelled 'Danger'. Humans communicate in very different ways compared to social insects like ants and bees. However, we can also see some involuntary communication in humans such as when someone turns red with embarrassment. This communicates something to others even though it is not intentional. It is the intentional forms of communication, however, that are important in human languages.

Recent research shows that chimpanzees can look where others are looking and even follow pointing gestures, but they do not understand a human trying to show them the location of food (Call, Hare, & Tomasello, 1998; Call & Tomasello, 2008). However, 2-year-old human children have no difficulty understanding this task and, surprisingly, dogs do much better than chimps (Kaminski et al., 2004). We can learn much about the basics of human communication through these comparisons. In this chapter we describe two 'rounds' of research conducted over the past hundred years, in which researchers have attempted to teach higher-order primates to communicate. In reality there have been scores of skirmishes, as successive generations have used new strategies in trying to solve Dr Doolittle's problem of talking to the animals – and getting them to talk back. We divide these into two general rounds because recent attempts have been based on very different principles and their results have been very informative about the origins and nature of human communication – a topic we develop in the next two chapters.

7.1 THE EVOLUTION OF MEANING AND LANGUAGE

If the ability to convey meaning and learn languages is an evolved capacity we could explore its nature by considering what, if anything, humans share with closely related species.

In order to do this we first consider whether animal communications systems exist that are similar to human language. We then turn to the question of whether other species can be taught to use languages similar to human languages.

Is animal communication different from human language?

A first step in taking a comparative approach to animal communication is to see if any other species has a communication system that is similar to human language. Researching this question is not just to indulge in idle curiosity. Whether or not animals use language is related to important questions about the nature of this sophisticated human skill, and whether or not it is inborn or learned. The linguist Noam Chomsky (1965) has claimed that language is innate, that humans and only humans are able to acquire language. We will discuss further in the next two chapters Chomsky's claim that humans are born with an evolved Language Acquisition Device (LAD) that makes learning human languages possible. This is required because according to his description of language there is no way for children to be able to learn a language, given the limited input they receive. He has argued that known learning mechanisms could not account for how children learn language because he holds that children are not corrected when they make a mistake so they could not learn the rules of syntax (that is, they lack what is known as *negative evidence*, which is discussed in the next chapter). If the rules of syntax are not available to children in the language they are exposed to, but children do learn languages, then it follows that the rules must be 'pre-wired' or built into an innate language module within the child. This view has a long tradition in Western thinking dating back at least three hundred years before Plato and Aristotle, as seen, for example, in Parmenides' poem *On Nature*. That is, if children cannot learn language based on the information available, but obviously typically developing children do acquire a language, then they must already know it – in some sense. This last qualification is essential. Of course, we know that babies are not born speaking German, Mandarin, or English. A LAD is a universal grammar (UG) with parameters that can be set by exposure to a particular human language. That is, it is claimed that humans must be born with some universal ground plan, or a 'one-size-fits-all' set of rules that will form the foundation for all human languages, all five to six thousand of them – in fact, any possible human language. Therefore, acquiring a language, Chomsky assumes, is much more like maturation, more like growing an arm or a leg, than learning a skill such as arithmetic. He argues that it must be this way because he couldn't imagine how children could learn language given the input they are exposed to. This claim has been called the argument from 'lack of imagination'. Of course, this verdict is somewhat ironic, given Chomsky's brilliance. However, it does illustrate the fact that given certain starting points, particular conclusions necessarily follow.

Chomsky believes that the ability to learn and use language is unique to humans. It is an inherited, species-specific ability. The idea that some animals might be able to learn a language if they are taught to do so does not, according to Chomsky, make any biological sense. This would be like saying we might find an animal that has some very advantageous ability such as the ability to fly and has wings, but has not thought to use them for flying until researchers came along and taught it how to do so.

An important first step in determining if animals have communication systems similar to that of humans or can be taught to communicate is to *define* language. Without a clear definition of language, we have no criteria at hand to determine whether animals do have a language. And attempting to define it helps to refine our understanding of just what *human* language is. Like Rico, apes can also learn certain communication skills, but the question remains: is this what is essential about language? Other reasons for studying animal communication include the fact that it is interesting to observe how other species cooperate, coordinate efforts and convey information. This research contributes to understanding the evolution of language. One way to study the evolution of a capacity is to examine the fossil record, but language itself leaves no trace (although some physical structures, such as specialised brain structures and skeletal evidence indicating the size of the vocal chords, may leave a fossil record). Since it is not possible to study the evolution of spoken communication fully in this manner, another way is to look at the distribution of varying capacities for language in currently living species. That is, to see if closely related species communicate in a way that is similar to human language.

Before discussing the research, it is important to know something about studies of animal communication. It is a fairly unusual area of research because of the amount of controversy it has generated. It is also unusual because of the amount of public interest in this work. One of the important researchers in this area, David Premack, acknowledged that he should have anticipated the amount of interest and controversy this research would generate, but that it was hard to prepare for this because there are few areas in psychology that are similar. Most psychologists just tend to work away by themselves with little attention from the outside world, but the chimpanzee language work was different. At the time, there was a great deal of attention from major media outlets such as magazines like *Life* and *People*, and such was the publicity of this work that Premack and his wife Ann presented their most discussed analysis of chimp language in the journal *Scientific American* (Premack & Premack, 1972), which usually publishes short, popular accounts of already published work.

Research on animal communication generates a great deal of interest because the whole enterprise challenges beliefs about essential differences between other animals and humans. This research requires a large investment of time, effort and money, sometimes even personal money. Animal language research involves long-term projects that take many years, which means the pay-off in terms of data is delayed. The work is controversial because most projects just involve a few individual animals, so warm personal relationships tend to develop, which may make objectivity difficult. Furthermore, the research design tends to be different from typical studies in psychology because usually there are only one or at most a few participants in each study. This sort of research may be difficult to accept for other psychologists who are accustomed to studies with large numbers of participants and tight controls over variables. Let's examine the products of this intensive investigation.

Do animals have languages?

The first question to address is do animals talk naturally? That is, are their communication systems similar to human languages? To answer this question we need to return to the issue of defining, but this task is not as easy as might appear. One approach is to consider what is essential to human language. Hockett (1966) proposed several features to capture this. His list changed over time, and the longest one contained 16 characteristics. Here we consider three features that seem most important. The first is *semanticity or reference* (taken from the Greek word *significant* to refer to meaning). Humans use language to refer to things, but it is not clear whether other animals do this. When a hen squawks because there is a fox outside the henhouse, is the hen saying 'Watch out, danger!' or does she just automatically make this sound when she is frightened, in the way a human might involuntarily scream when he or she sees a snake? In both cases the fact that something potentially dangerous is going on would be communicated, but in these cases this communication is not intentional.

Vervet monkeys have a system of several different calls that distinguish different sorts of danger. There is one call for a snake (puff adder or cobra), another call for an eagle, a third call used for lions and leopards, and a fourth to signal the presence of a spotted hyena or Masai tribesman. Many other species of monkeys also have call systems (Fitch, 2005). Perhaps these different calls are like words as the monkeys do respond to them differently. When other monkeys hear the call warning of a snake they stand on their hind legs and look around for a snake. When they hear the call for an eagle they dive into the vegetation as if they are hiding from an airborne attack. And at the lion call they quickly climb a tree (Fitch, 2010). Many species of birds and mammals learn to eavesdrop on other species' use of alarm calls to learn about dangers (Magrath, Haff, Fallow, & Radford, 2015; Seyfarth & Cheney, 2012).

These calls may serve a *function* because they elicit particular responses from conspecifics. However, it may be that they are not intentionally used referentially – they could simply be the reaction of the utterer to a threat. For example, vervets will continue making the call even if all of their group has seen the danger and escaped. At the same time, alarm calls do not seem to be just automatic reactions because it is more likely that birds and mammals will give such calls when they are close to others of their species compared to when they are alone. Some species, such as chickens, produce alarm calls only when they are with other chickens. A question arising here is are alarm calls given depending on whether the others have not seen the predator? This has been addressed with chimpanzees who emit two kinds of calls. First, when they encounter immediate danger such as a leopard, python, or a neighbouring group of chimpanzees they give loud 'SOS' screams or barks. When the threat is less serious, however, such as poisonous vipers or evidence of leopards or other chimpanzees, they make quiet 'alert hoos'. An extensive field study was conducted by following individual chimpanzees through the forest and placing a model of a poisonous snake in its path, then waiting to see if it would give alarm calls to other approaching chimpanzees. It was found that they called more if the other chimpanzees had not seen the model snake, and alarm calls were also more likely if there was a close bond with the other chimpanzees. Also, the number of alarm calls given depended on the risk to the caller as well as to the receiver of the signals (Crockford, Wittig, Mundry, & Zuberbühler, 2012).

Humans have a sort of call system in parallel to language, such as yelps of pain, shrieks of fear, and different types of crying in babies which express different needs (that can be identified by caregivers). However, alarm calls seem to lack the productivity of human languages (i.e. the creative use of language to say new things; see below, Fitch, 2005). Thus, even though animals clearly do have communication systems that work very well for their purposes, we have to be careful before accepting the claim that animal communication is a simple form of language. We may be trying to compare systems as different as a human language like English or Japanese with a set of traffic signals, which also functions to coordinate action but in a different way.

A second important characteristic of human languages provided in Hockett's list is *displacement*. This is the ability to refer to things that are far removed in time or space. Alarm calls do not show displacement because they are only used in the presence of danger. They are not used to discuss dangers that are not present. For example, a dog may bark when a burglar is in the house, but it will not do so to tell us that there was a burglar in the house yesterday. There is, however, an example of an animal communication system that does seem to have at least a form of displacement. This is the complex communication system used by honeybees. Beekeepers had long noticed that when one worker from a hive finds a new source of nectar other bees from the same hive also start to arrive at the new source. Soon there would be a large number of bees from the same hive gathered at the new source of nectar, but bees from other hives did not tend to find the new source as quickly. And bees from hives that are quite close together often fly to different sources of nectar. So, it seems that bees are somehow communicating about the location of nectar.

Much of the important research on this issue was conducted by the ethologist Karl von Frisch (1967). He found that when a foraging bee discovers a rich source of food it is able to communicate the source of the food to the other bees in its hive. It communicates this message through a pattern of movements; that is, by doing a sort of dance on the inside walls of the hive. There are two major types of dance, depending on how far the food source is from the hive: the round dance and the tail-wagging or waggle dance. If the nectar is within 10 metres of the hive the returning bee does what is called the round dance on the wall of the hive. This involves going in a circle in one direction and then turning in

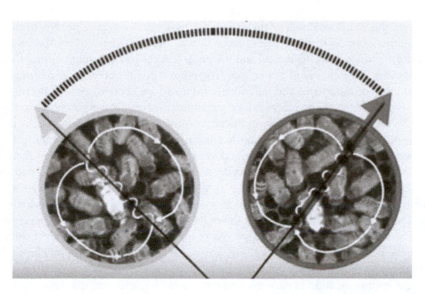

Figure 7.1 Demonstration by Georgia Tech University of Computing (www.youtube.com/watch?v=bFDGPgXtK-U)

The location of two sites is marked with a drop of green or red paint dropped onto the back of the bee who returns to dance. The two bees are dancing at different locations on the hive wall. The direction of each bee's waggle accurately identifies the location of each food source – the video is excellent and well worth a viewing.

the opposite direction. The intensity of the dance signals the richness of the food source, and the scent of the dancing bee indicates what type of food source to look for. The other bees then fly randomly around the hive until they pick up the scent they had detected on the dancing bee, and at that point they can fly directly to the rich food source.

The tail-wagging or waggle dance, however, is an even more impressive way to communicate information. Honeybees use this pattern of movements when the source of nectar is far from the hive, over 100 metres. For distances in between 10 and 100 metres bees may perform either of the two types of dance, but for the longer distances they are more likely to do the tail-wagging dance. Studies have shown that bees can accurately indicate food sources up to 11 kilometres away (almost 7 miles). With these sorts of distances it would not be efficient for bees to search randomly and try to follow scents. Thus, the tail-wagging dance contains much more information about the direction and distance the bees should fly. The structure of this dance consists of two roughly semicircular paths with a straight-line portion in between, and this is when the bee waggles. The orientation of the straight-line portion of the dance tells the other bees which direction they should fly with respect to the position of the sun. Vertical means to fly directly towards the sun, 80 degrees to the left means to fly 80 degrees to the left of the sun, and downward indicates away from the sun. The length of time spent during the tail-wagging portion of the dance tells the other bees the distance that must be flown. The bees also make a special buzzing sound during this part of the dance, and the general level of excitement during the dance communicates the richness of the source. There are some differences in dancing among different types of honeybees and individuals within a type (Frisch, 1966, 1967).

The waggle dance of honeybees is a very complex and efficient communication system, especially for an animal with a brain the size of a grass seed. And this system involves some displacement, just like a human language, because bees can communicate about food sources that are not present. But the degree of displacement is much less than that of human languages. Bees cannot communicate about the food sources they visited the day before, nor food sources that are farther away; they can't communicate about nectar in the next valley. And they also can't communicate anything about vertical distance. If the nectar source is placed at the top of a tower they can't tell the other bees because 'bees have no word for "up" in their language. There are no flowers in the clouds' (von Frisch, 1927/1966, p. 139). The other bees will just come to the base of the tower, and buzz around there before giving up and going home.

So, the communication system used by bees is fairly rigid, and this leads to the most important characteristic of human language that seems to set it apart from animal communication systems, and that is creativity which is identified by openness or productivity. This is the feature that Chomsky emphasised – it is the ability to talk about anything. Animals may be able to communicate a lot of information, but as Bertrand Russell put it no matter how eloquently a dog barks he will never be able to tell you that his parents were poor but honest. Animals have a fixed number of signals that they can employ to convey messages. Bees cannot communicate about vertical distance because they haven't needed to communicate such information: there are no food sources in the air, so there would be no selective pressure for this to evolve. In contrast, with human languages we can discuss just about anything, and if we don't have a word for something we invent one. We are constantly adding new words to our languages, and our communication is constantly changing. For example, hundreds of computer-related words have crept into everyday language over the past thirty years and dictionaries are regularly updated. Bees cannot 'dance about dancing' (i.e. use their form of communication to reflect upon the process of communicating), whereas humans can discuss communication, as we are currently doing. That is, animal communication systems, although complex and efficient, do not have the *openness or creativity* of human languages through which new messages can be created, the third of Hockett's (1966) criteria that we draw upon.

The next question, after finding that animals do not naturally use forms of communication that are comparable to human language (although this debate is not completely settled), is to ask if animals can be taught to use a human language. The most convincing evidence would be a demonstration of adult human language in animals, but this is unrealistic and instead researchers have adopted the strategy of trying to show that animals are *on the path to language*, although they may not have full human capability.

7.2 CAN ANIMALS BE TAUGHT LANGUAGES?

If animals don't naturally use communication systems similar to human languages, can they be taught a language? Much of this research has focused on Great Apes and chimpanzees in particular. There have been several waves of research addressing this question.

The first rounds in the chimp language wars

For a number of years researchers have tried to teach language to apes. One of the early studies began in 1909 when William Furness (1916) attempted to teach two young orangutans and two chimpanzees to speak. After considerable training one of the orangutans learned to produce 'papa' and 'cup'. The apes did, however, learn to understand a great deal of what was said to them. Another early attempt began in 1931 when Winthrop and Luella Kellogg (Kellogg & Kellogg, 1933) took a 7-month-old chimpanzee, Gua, into their home and brought it up alongside their own son, Donald. These researchers decided not to attempt systematically to teach words to the chimp, but rather to let Gua pick up language in the same way a child learns. The chimpanzee was well in advance of the child with things like releasing a door latch by 10 months, learning to unlock the front door by 13 months, and eating with a spoon before the child did. At around 12 to 14 months Gua and Donald were about equal in the number of different requests that they seemed to understand and respond to. These were sentences like 'supper's ready' or 'close the drawer'. Each of them understood about 20 different requests. Although the child was slower to begin with, at 19 months, when the study was ended, Donald started to learn new words quickly. Of course their son learned to speak but the chimpanzee never did, although Gua did learn to understand the meaning of over 70 single words.

A second attempt began in 1947 when Keith and Catherine Hayes (Brown, 1958; Hayes & Hayes, 1951) gave a young chimpanzee, Viki, intensive coaching in English. They made a great effort to develop vocal speech, but the chimp only learned four words – 'papa, mama, cup, and up' – and even these were not clearly articulated. Furthermore, it was not clear that she was using these words properly. This was after three years of hard training. Although it was very difficult to train her to speak, Viki did seem to grasp a large number of phrases. But the Hayes team recognised that it was very difficult to measure comprehension because failure to follow a command is not necessarily a measure of understanding since a chimp, just like a child, may not feel like obeying.

It seems, however, that chimpanzees are not able to learn to make the sounds used in human languages. This inability may be located at the neural level rather than at the level of anatomical structures. Fitch (2005, p. 200) suggests that 'the basic vocal tract anatomy of a chimp or monkey, or even a dog or goat, would clearly support many of the phonetic contrasts found in human languages, if a human brain were in control'. Thus, there was a change in research strategy in the 1960s and 1970s. Researchers shifted from teaching chimpanzees to use a vocal medium to teaching them to use a visual medium of communication.

In 1966 Allen and Beatrix Gardner acquired a female chimpanzee named Washoe. She was thought to be about one year old when they started: her age is important because it may be that language learning is easiest or only possible for young animals. The Gardners taught Washoe to use modified American Sign Language, and they tried to approach language learning in a fairly 'natural' way. That is, they kept her surrounded by humans who used signs to communicate with each other and with her. She was raised by student caretakers in a house trailer in the Gardners' backyard, and no one was allowed to use spoken language around her, only signs were allowed. There were no rigorous training schedules, and the Gardners hoped that she would pick up language in a fairly natural way. Washoe did not usually learn new signs just by observing her caretakers, as normal children would. Instead, the Gardners would teach her signs by shaping her hands in the proper way. Of course, there were some problems in trying to teach an ape a language. The following quotation gives a flavour of these problems: 'Washoe can become completely diverted from her original object, she may ask for something entirely different, run away, go into a tantrum, or even bite her tutor' (Gardner & Gardner, 1969, p. 666). But in spite of these problems she did learn a number of signs. After the first 21 months she had learned 34 signs, and a sign was only counted as learned if she used it spontaneously and appropriately on consecutive days.

Washoe sometimes combined words in new ways. For example she used 'water-bird' for swan. This seems like evidence of productivity; that is, combining words in new ways. This interpretation was controversial, however, because Washoe did see both water and a bird and might have been referring to them individually, and consecutively, so it is inconclusive whether she had devised a novel concept. She did use this combination of signs again in other contexts, but these were also inconclusive because she was heavily reinforced for the first utterance. Usually, however, when Washoe combined words she just added words like 'hurry', 'more', 'food', 'please', and 'gimme' to nouns.

A problem with assessing novel word combinations and what they mean is that the Gardners only reported a few interesting novel word combinations. They did not report how often Washoe made uninteresting combinations that were just nonsense. This is important because the apocryphal room full of monkeys typing randomly may, every so often, just by chance produce an interesting looking string of words, even if it is unlikely that they will come up with *Hamlet*.

Some of the Gardners' students employed the same approach with gorillas and orangutans. Francine Patterson (1978) worked with a gorilla named Koko. Koko was taught sign language, and she also seemed to be creative in her use of signs. She appeared to combine signs in new ways. For example, Koko used the sequence EYE HAT for 'mask', WHITE TIGER for 'zebra', and COOKIE ROCK for a sweet, stale roll. She also signed ME CRY THERE when she saw a picture of a gorilla in a bath, apparently because she didn't like having a bath (Aitchison, 1989, p. 43). These early claims were picked up by the media in programmes like *Sixty Minutes*, *20/20*, and *The Tonight Show*, and magazines like *People* and *Life*. This research in the 1960s and 1970s focused on the question of whether or not apes could learn the basic features of a grammar. This was a major interest in psycholinguistics at the time, particularly because of the claim that grammar is innate. It is why people got so excited about the possibility that these apes could produce strings of symbols. By the late 1970s many people were claiming that there was evidence that apes could create sentences. It seemed that apes were combining words to produce new meanings and it was argued that they were using simple grammatical rules. This seemed to be evidence that language was not a uniquely human capacity, and it also suggested that apes and humans shared some common ancestor with a linguistic capacity.

This claim, however, was demolished in 1979 by Herbert Terrace. In the 1970s Terrace started a research project with a chimpanzee he named Nim Chimpsky. Terrace worked with this chimpanzee for a few years and taught him to sign with American Sign Language. But it was after the project ran out of money, and the chimpanzee had to be returned to a chimpanzee colony in Oklahoma, that Terrace started carefully to analyse the videotapes he and his research team had made of Nim's signing. He analysed about 20,000 combinations of two or more signs made by Nim using this communication system. Many of these seemed to have been generated by simple grammatical rules (e.g. more + x). So this seemed to be strong support for the claim that apes can learn to use language and that they can use grammatical rules.

This, however, was not what Terrace claimed. Instead, he argued that a careful frame-by-frame analysis of the videotapes showed that Nim's signing occurred in response to his teacher who encouraged him to gesture, and thus much of Nim's repertoire was a full or partial imitation of what his teacher was signing. Nim's signing therefore seemed to be *non-spontaneous* and *imitative*. Terrace pointed out some major flaws in the research on apes' language, and he argued that even when apes had been trained to use language they did not use it spontaneously. Apes only used gestures to *get* something – to request something from their trainers, usually food. This is different from the way humans use language, because a child often just spontaneously uses words to refer to things, or to point objects out to another person with no desire to obtain them – just for the joy of sharing attention (see Chapters 5 and 6). An important function of a child's initial communication is to inform a parent that he has noticed something. Children enjoy naming things, and this is something that, at least at the time that Terrace was writing, had not been observed in apes.

Terrace (1979) also argued that Nim's signs were highly repetitive of the trainer's immediately preceding signs and also highly redundant. For example:

'Apple eat eat apple eat apple hurry apple hurry hurry.'

The Gardners never did straightforwardly deal with Terrace's critique that the combinations of signs produced by apes like Washoe were mostly imitations. This may have been because they would not have the evidence to respond to his criticism unless they had kept a record of the signs directed to Washoe, and all of her combinations of signs. So it was hard to know if Washoe was imitating the experimenter or not. And even when they replicated their work with other chimpanzees they did not address Terrace's criticism directly. Terrace's conclusion ended the first round of the chimp language wars.

The second round in the chimp language wars

After this devastating attack by Terrace, funding dried up in this area of research, and many researchers lost interest in the topic. That is how things were in the mid-1980s, but some researchers continued in this area and changed methods and objectives and used new participants. Just before these controversies emerged, Sue Savage-Rumbaugh and her colleagues had started some interesting research in which they dealt with many of the flaws that Terrace had pointed out in earlier research. They used two young male chimpanzees named Sherman and Austin, and when they weren't being trained or tested these chimps lived with other chimpanzees.

Savage-Rumbaugh's earlier work with a chimp called Lana had been criticised by Terrace who claimed that Lana's sentences were really just 'stock phrases'; that is, since she was trained to use strings of symbols she treated them as a unit and did not create them herself. Thus, in the Sherman and Austin project, the chimps were trained with single words. Second, all of the communication between the experimenters and the apes was done through lexigrams, symbols representing a word, on a keyboard which made it possible for the researchers to keep a record of all the experimenters' and chimps' utterances. This meant that they could check how many of the apes' combinations of signs were imitations. Savage-Rumbaugh and colleagues also redirected the focus of their research from analyses of syntax to questions about intentional communication, reference, and semantics. Finally, an interesting difference to previous research was that her project involved two apes communicating with each other, so the researchers investigated the apes' *comprehension* of each others' utterances. This was something that had been taken for granted, or neglected, in previous research (Savage-Rumbaugh, Rumbaugh, & Boysen, 1978). Most previous researchers had assumed that their apes like Washoe and Nim understood more than they produced but they couldn't give any empirical support for this claim (Savage-Rumbaugh, 1986).

The next major advance involved work with 'pygmy chimpanzees' (*pan paniscus*) or 'Bonobos' instead of the common chimpanzee (*pan troglodytes*). Bonobos seem to be more intelligent than common chimpanzees, and have social characteristics that appear closer to those of humans. They are smaller, less aggressive, more social, more intelligent, and more communicative than common chimpanzees. However, bonobos are also very rare. They are native to Zaire but they are not protected and are an endangered species.

The first attempt in this new line of research was made with an adult female bonobo caught in the wild. She was named Matata, and intensive efforts to teach her to use symbols were made for four years, but with no success. When she was sent to be involved in a breeding programme and her adopted son, Kanzi, was left behind, it became clear that

Figure 7.2   Kanzi, language-reared male bonobo, converses with Sue Savage-Rumbaugh in 2006 using a portable 'keyboard' of arbitrary symbols that Kanzi associates with words

he had acquired symbols just by observing the efforts to train his mother, even though he was not rewarded and no efforts were made to teach him. When he was 2 years old it also became evident that he had an understanding of spoken language. At this point the researchers decided that they would not try directly to teach Kanzi language. Instead, they would just see how much he could pick up by himself in the same natural way that children learn languages. By 5 years of age Kanzi spontaneously produced combinations of symbols that revealed a sensitivity to English word order, and he seemed to be able to invent grammatical rules.

Kanzi's training was quite different from that of other apes and it was motivated by Savage-Rumbaugh's learning approach to language. In most previous studies of ape communication animals were taught to form associations between symbols and objects. Many species can learn to do this; for example, a dolphin can be trained to retrieve a frisbee in response to symbols that the trainer uses to refer to a specific object, but does the dolphin understand such communication in the way humans do? Is reference just an association between a word and something in the world? No, words don't just refer by themselves, speakers refer with words. Rather, symbolic communication is constituted by a triadic relation among speaker, listener, and reference to the world. According to this view, reference is a social function, and words are the vehicle of the process of referring.

It is possible to train an ape to use a symbol for an apple in order to get an apple. This is done by laboriously rewarding the animal with a slice of apple if it selects the token that corresponds to it, but this simple association between a symbol and an object has very limited use. The ape may not be able to use the symbol in all the ways that humans use the word (e.g. 'You are the apple of my eye'). It is much more difficult to teach an ape to be able to use a token to describe a food that it is not allowed to eat, or a food that it sees someone else eating, or a kind of food that it does not like, and so on.

So what is it that makes an environment appropriate for learning a human language? What was it about Kanzi's experience that was different from that of other apes and animals that allowed him to learn so much more effectively? What are the critical differences between the linguistic experience of normal children and the language training given to animals? Sue Savage-Rumbaugh (1986) describes several differences that she thinks are critical. For a start, communication of new information to predict important events is crucial. This involves knowledge of what is going to happen next, which makes the world more predictable. For example, in the utterance 'Oh here comes Mummy', the information provided is important for the child, particularly in the attachment phase of development (see Chapter 5). Error correction is also important when a young child is learning language. If the child doesn't understand, her parents do not withhold rewards and keep on repeating the sentence. And adults don't throw the child a fish if she carries out a request correctly. Instead, if the child doesn't understand, the parent attempts to do something to reach a mutual understanding. For example, if a child is told to 'help carry your toys' or 'throw the ball' and she doesn't understand, then the parent would usually show how to do it. The child is involved in the flow of interaction and the linguistic cues are used to help coordinate this activity.

The child's communicative experience contrasts with the language training given to animals such as dolphins. For dolphins, linguistic experience involves associating a symbol with a behaviour in order to be rewarded with a fish. They learn that when they are given certain symbols, either visual or auditory, they should do something, like fetch a frisbee, and if they do the right thing they will get food. Under these conditions there is no need to be concerned with the intent of the speaker. What the experimenter asks is not of intrinsic interest to the dolphin; its purpose is only to help the experimenter evaluate the animal's ability to respond correctly. In contrast, the child is involved in interaction that is interesting and motivating. Her behaviour is being influenced through linguistic means and she is motivated to use language to influence her parents. For example, a toddler who hears 'Let's drink some juice' may later want to start this action herself by saying the same thing or pointing towards the jug. But the dolphin is not likely to be motivated to want to ask another dolphin to 'take the frisbee to the surfboard'.

Savage-Rumbaugh (1986) has examined the social structure that children are embedded in when they learn language and she emphasises the importance of this social support for learning. In contrast to Chomsky's LAD, this is closer to Bruner's (1985) theory of language development, which emphasises that language is learned in the context of social activity and with the support of others. To highlight the importance of the social context in his theory, Bruner came up with the acronym LASS (Language Acquisition Support System) in opposition to Chomsky's LAD. In Savage-Rumbaugh's view of language acquisition, comprehension is very important. She argues that a great deal of language learning goes on in the course of children trying to understand their parents' utterances. Most of the research on the linguistic capacity of apes, however, has focused on their ability to produce words, and there has been little concern with their comprehension, perhaps also because studying comprehension is much more difficult than studying production. It has been recognised, however, that comprehension precedes production in the language development of children (e.g. Snyder, Bates, & Bretherton, 1981). Parents know that their children understand many more words than they can produce. And when people are learning a second language they understand more than what they can produce. Typically, when children are between 1 and 2 years of age they may use about 10 words, but they can usually understand more than 50 (e.g. Snyder et al., 1981, see Chapters 8 and 9). Similarly, a 2-year-old bonobo raised in a naturalistic language environment was able to understand 70 words, but could only produce 4 words (Savage-Rumbaugh, Murphy, Brakke, Williams, & Rumbaugh, 1993).

In their research, Savage-Rumbaugh and colleagues (1993) focused on comprehension of language rather than production, and the language comprehension skills of a 2-year-old child (Ali) were compared to those of an 8-year-old bonobo (Kanzi). The bonobo was raised in a language environment that was similar to that experienced by children, but modified in ways to make it more appropriate for apes. For example, researchers went for walks in the forest with Kanzi and they found food in various places, just as they would in the wild. They also talked about anything that occurred and would be of interest to the ape. Ali's mother, Jeannine Murphy, was also a caretaker for Kanzi. Murphy worked full time as a caretaker for Kanzi, and after her daughter was born she worked half days. Thus, the research participants shared similar language environments. Although the child did not play with the apes, she did see them through a window.

The caretakers spoke to Kanzi in English, and they also used symbols on a large board, referred to as *lexigrams* (see Figure 7.2). The caretakers pointed to the symbols when they spoke. Both the child and the bonobo were tested on the same sentences and the procedure was treated like a game. Their understanding of the same 660 novel sentences was assessed. Ali and Kanzi were presented with two types of trials: non-blind and blind. The first 240 trials were non-blind – the experimenter was in the room with Ali or Kanzi. That is, Ali's mother was with Ali, and Sue Savage-Rumbaugh was with Kanzi. This was done in order to get Ali and Kanzi used to the testing procedure. Note, however, that the two experimenters were blind to the responses of the other research participant. In the blind trials, the experimenter was behind a one-way mirror and there was another person in the room with the participant, but this person had headphones on with loud music so that she could not hear the test sentence given to Ali or Kanzi. This was done so that the experimenter could not unconsciously help Ali and Kanzi.

THE CLEVER HANS EFFECT

Experimenters in this area have to be very careful because of what is called the Clever Hans phenomenon. Clever Hans was a horse a century ago who appeared to be able to count. The horse gave the answer to arithmetic problems by tapping his hoof and stopping at the correct number. The horse's performance was very convincing, and it appeared to be able to do all sorts of calculations. Clever Hans became quite an attraction and hundreds flocked to his nightly stage performance. However, it was eventually discovered that the horse was responding to unintentional cues from his owner and, indeed, some members of the public. The horse just struck the ground with his foot until the trainer, unconsciously, signalled him to stop by showing tension just before the right answer and relaxing when he reached it. All the horse had to do was to start striking the ground and stop when he sensed some cue from the trainer. Cues such as relaxing the shoulders when the correct count had been reached were enough to tell the horse it was time to stop. Thus, in research with animals it is important to include careful controls such as experimenters who are kept unaware of the animal's responses.

The following were some of the test sentences used in this study with Kanzi and Ali:

'Can you make the snake bite the doggie?'

'Take the lettuce out of the microwave.'

'Wash the hotdogs.'

'Go to the refrigerator and get a banana.'

'Take the potatoes outdoors and get the apple.'

It is important to be clear that neither Kanzi nor Ali could have heard these sorts of requests because people don't usually cook lettuce or store it in a microwave and so on. Overall, in response to these test sentences Kanzi was correct on 72% across all the trials, and Ali was correct on 66% of the trials. This rate includes counting 'partially correct' as incorrect, even though Kanzi and Ali generally responded correctly to at least a portion of the sentence. So, overall, both Ali and Kanzi showed high levels of comprehension for these types of sentences. Some of their errors, in fact, actually showed some level of understanding. For example, Kanzi was asked to 'Put some water on the carrot' on a day when it happened to be raining heavily at the time. Kanzi responded by tossing the carrot out into the rain, which worked quite well to achieve the goal, but might have been coincidental. That was the only time during the test that he threw something outside, and no one had ever shown him this way of getting carrots wet, so this could have been a novel solution. Ali also came up with interesting solutions. Even though Kanzi's and Ali's errors showed some understanding, Savage-Rumbaugh counted them as incorrect because they are ambiguous and she wanted to be very conservative.

There were also many different examples of sentences in which the word order was very important. Take, for example, the following sentences:

'Put the hat on your ball.'

'Put the ball on the hat.'

Across all the types of sentences in which key words were presented in both orders, Kanzi was correct on 88% of the sentences and Ali was correct on 66%, and their errors were not usually getting the order backwards (Kanzi made two of these errors and Ali made five in the 660 trials). Instead, when they made a mistake, it tended to be a semantic one or due to inattention. For example, when Kanzi heard 'Put the melon in the tomatoes', he put the melon in the water. Ali made similar types of mistakes: when she heard 'Pour the lemonade in the Coke' she tried to pour the lemonade (from the can) into the bowl of lemonade.

So, it seems that both Kanzi and Ali were sensitive to word order. Kanzi was slightly better than Ali at the time of the test, although neither was perfect, and of course Ali developed very rapidly after this study. Both Ali and Kanzi seemed to process the requests at the level of the sentence, because the meaning they assigned to the instruction was based on its role in the whole utterance rather than a simple dictionary definition of individual words. For example, both responded correctly to:

'Give the knife to [person]'

and to

'Can you knife the sweet potatoes' (p. 99).

Even though the word 'knife' is used in different ways in the two sentences (as an object in the first and as action in the second) both Ali and Kanzi responded correctly. These were very unusual requests and they would never have heard these sorts of sentences before. For example, Kanzi had a ball with a face on it and when he was asked to 'Feed your ball some tomato' he put the tomato to its mouth.

Kanzi's understanding of language cannot be attributed to imitation because such actions had not been demonstrated. The sentences were new and the experimenter had not responded to them, so there was nothing for Kanzi to copy. Also, in order to understand the requests, he had to be able to process the sentences at a syntactical level. He had to parse the phonemes (the components of words) and words as well as the structure of the sentence. Furthermore, his ability to understand English appeared spontaneously when he was raised in a linguistic environment that was similar to that experienced by children. Although his language skills were rudimentary, his performance is still impressive and these results present a challenge to the accepted view that language is an innate capacity of only humans.

Savage-Rumbaugh's work has also been criticised for being the product of stimulus response learning rather than the acquisition of language in all its complexity (Seidenberg & Petitto, 1987). Steven Pinker (1994, p. 341) claims that 'Kanzi's language abilities, if one is being charitable, are just above those of his common cousins by a just-noticeable difference, but not more'. Michael Tomasello (2008, pp. 252–256) points out that other non-primate species such as dolphins and parrots have shown a similar ability to understand patterns of signs. That is, they have shown comprehension but not production of communicative acts, and thus even apes like Kanzi do not appear to use syntax in their communication with humans. Tomasello suggests that the reason for this is that their communication centres around requests, which contrasts with the way human children use language for many other purposes.

These criticisms are fair but does this mean that human language is qualitatively different from that of bonobos and other higher-order species? Reviewing this divisive and passionate literature (hence the reason why we and others use the term 'chimp wars'), Caroline Rowland (2014) draws upon five of Charles Hockett's sixteen 'design features' of language to consider whether animal communication is equivalent to that of humans. She points out that even the bee dance shows '*displacement*' (the object being referred to is not physically present), that the learning of new dialects in some birds (species of finches) shows '*discreteness*' (similar sounds being linked together but are perceived as being different), and that the alarm calls of vervet monkeys illustrate '*arbitrariness*' (there is no reason for the particular sound to have this meaning, as in onomatopoeia). She continues:

> However, unlike human languages, no animal communication system demonstrates all of Hockett's design features. For example, vervet monkeys do not invent new calls for new predators or string calls together to convey different meanings (*productivity*) or use their calls to reflect on and talk about the calls themselves (*reflexiveness*). (2014, p.12)

Given that several of the examples from Savage-Rumbaugh's studies involve the use of different and novel combinations of lexigrams, the debate about whether or not great apes can learn language encourages us to think more carefully about the importance of the environment in which children develop these skills. Furthermore, research on animal communication is interesting because it encourages us to think about the very nature of language.

7.3 IMPLICATIONS OF RESEARCH ON ANIMAL COMMUNICATION: THE ROLE OF MEANING

We turn in this section to consider the implications of the chimp language wars for our understanding of the development of (human) thinking. The first attempts to train non-human primates to use something like human communication failed because the view of language that informed the research was based on the idea that words communicate by being associated with things. This is a view of meaning according to which language is conceptualised as a naming game. Therefore, the goal was just to train an animal to form associations between new signs and objects, and see if animals would combine signs and show evidence of syntax. The more successful second attempt to teach apes language, however, was based on quite a different view of language and meaning. The take-home message then is that language does not work simply through associations between words and objects or events. What is especially interesting about this second round of chimp research is the nature of the interactive and linguistic environment that made language learning possible. Words are not seen as being attached to meanings; rather that people use them to convey meaning and they are learned within shared routines or well-known patterns of activity. This approach to language learning resulted in bonobos and chimpanzees acquiring at least its rudiments.

The question of whether other species can learn human languages depends on how it is conceptualised. From the perspective of Chomsky (e.g. 2007) and Pinker (1994), language is based on knowledge of the set of rules of syntax, and since chimpanzees do not seem to be able to learn this whole system they are not considered to have a language. This approach has been referred to as Cartesian (see Chapter 1) because it is based on a search for a firm dividing line between species and contrasted with a Darwinian approach based on an expectation of continuity between species (Canfield, 1995, 2007). The Darwinian approach also fits with Wittgenstein's (1953) view of language, according to which rather than one coherent whole, language is made up of a large collection of different social activities or language games. Adults are immersed in 'playing' such games in an effortless way so it may be difficult to reflect on the nature of language. However, it can be seen developing as children learn to communicate. In the previous chapter we examined how they become engaged in everyday activities such as eating, going for a walk, playing, greeting, and so on. They gradually rely on shared knowledge of these routines to communicate. For example, a 13-month-old holding his foot over his shoe or a 16-month-old bringing her shoes to her mother is also developing the ability to request going for a walk. They do so based on shared experience with this activity. Such communication becomes even more effective when the child adds a word like 'outside'.

From this perspective, Savage Rumbaugh's research described in the previous section suggests that some other species, particularly the great apes, can learn some of the rudiments of language. However, whether they can learn the fluidity of language games is debatable. For example, the sign language-trained chimpanzee, Washoe, was alleged to have insulted her keeper. She displayed anger about being placed in a small holding cage and she made the sign for dirty as in dirty diaper and then the sign for her keeper's name. This bears the hallmarks of a human insult, but there is no record of Washoe combining signs to make similar comments. To be convincing that she had mastered the language game of insulting, we would need evidence of an expectation that her signs would hurt his feelings through belittling and humiliating him, and that she could experience being insulted herself (Canfield, 1995).

This example encourages us to think again about the differences between animal and human forms of communication. Consider the difference between a dog scratching at a door to be let in, and a person knocking at the door. What is the difference between these two examples? It appears that they have the same goal – to get in. But what differences in understanding are involved and how do these develop? We could explain the dog's behaviour as being socially shaped. Perhaps it was initially just trying to open the door with its paw with no awareness that this would result in it gaining access. The scratching has meaning for the owner but the dog was not intentionally trying to communicate (just to get in). As the scratching is responded to by the owner, gradually the dog comes to acquire expectations about what happens when he scratches at the door – that is, it often opens. But this explanation will not do for the human, at least for humans older than about 12 months. Some form of awareness or anticipation of how others typically respond must surely be involved. The dog's activity can be explained as originating in practical activity. Human communication is similarly based originally in such concrete action, but our activity does not stop there when we consider the development of conventions like door knocking (and waiting for a sufficient or 'polite' time before knocking again). At some point children develop an awareness of the effect of a signal on others. How does this happen? Our approach is that instead of simply focusing on the individual and a psychological concept like 'attention', we start from the infant's observable interaction with others. Attentiveness is an observable aspect of interpersonal engagement with others. Infants develop expectations about another person's attitudes in particular situations.

The issue of meaning has been an underlying theme in the first part of this chapter as well as the previous two chapters, on the origins of infant communication. Meaning first emerged in this book in explaining how infants develop the ability to use gestures, discussed in Chapter 5. It then cropped up later when we considered whether animal communication is similar to human language. It will be the focus of our attention in our analysis of the nature of language itself in Chapter 8 and in how children learn language in Chapter 9, where we will examine the everyday miracle of how it is that words come to have meaning.

Although the nature of meaning has been a central problem in philosophy for much of the last century, psychologists rarely concern themselves with this question. Theories in psychology, however, are built on assumptions about meaning, and it is essential to examine these because they are too often simply taken for granted. This lack of concern regarding meaning may be because it is felt that an answer is already well accepted and straightforward. However, this view of meaning on which theories in psychology and language development are based is deeply flawed, according to criticism from Ludwig Wittgenstein and others (see Chapter 9). In attempting to unpack this process the work of G. H. Mead (1934, especially pages 75–79) is helpful, although there are parts of the story that still need to be filled in because he was not interested primarily in development. Rather, he focused on how meaning exists in interactions between animals, and his approach is highly relevant to the issues that emerge from the ape studies discussed in this chapter. Mead introduced an important distinction between conversations of gestures and significant gestures. A *non-significant gesture* is an action taken by one dog that is responded to by a second animal, but there is no evidence that the first intended to evoke that response. In a dog fight, for example, one dog may take an aggressive posture and the other will assume a defensive stance or run. In contrast, *significant gestures*, which are a hallmark of higher order communication, involve the shared understanding of a gesture or utterance shown in being able to anticipate how the other will respond. That is, they demarcate the transition from a communication that is unintentional to one that is intentional:

> A … gesture … means this idea behind it and it arouses that idea in the other individual … in the present case we have a symbol which answers to a meaning in the experience of the first individual and which also calls out that meaning in the second individual. Where the gesture reaches that situation it has become what we call 'language'. It is now a significant symbol and it signifies a certain meaning. (Mead, 1934, pp. 45–46)

Savage Rumbaugh's research suggests that Kanzi's and others' use of signs contains the elements of this capability. However, there are still many questions about how non-significant gestures develop into significant gestures, how it is that humans are adapted to make this transition. Meaning is an underlying issue in dealing with the question of human thinking.

SUMMARY AND CONCLUSIONS

We have examined animal communication systems, primarily in order to learn more about human language. This topic is also relevant for reflecting on how human forms of language and cognition evolved. The first question we addressed concerned whether there are any animal communication systems that are similar to human languages. Although many species from honeybees to great apes have complex and effective systems of communication, it is less clear how aware they are of communicating, and whether there is a fixed set of events that can be communicated about, or if there is potential for generativity in the sense of communicating about new experiences. It is the generative, or productive, use of language that seems quintessentially human.

The next question was whether animals can be taught to use human languages. Based on the first round of the chimp language wars, the general evaluation of the capacity of primates to learn language is that apes imitate their caregivers, and only make requests with redundant series of signs, and hence it was widely accepted that apes cannot learn language. However, this conclusion was called into question by research conducted by Savage-Rumbaugh and her colleagues suggesting that bonobos and chimpanzees can learn to understand human languages and acquire at least rudimentary communication skills when they grow up in a linguistic environment, similar to the way in which human children learn languages. This approach to research was based on a different view of meaning. From this perspective, instead of being attached to words or sentences, meaning depends on the context within an ongoing sequence of interaction. This view of meaning is consistent with the approach introduced by G. H. Mead. From this perspective meaning is necessarily social, and therefore thinking, which is based on a system of meaning, must emerge within the child's everyday social interactions.

FURTHER READING

Savage-Rumbaugh, E. S. (1996). *Kanzi: The Ape at the Brink of the Human Mind*. New York: Wiley.

Savage-Rumbaugh, S. E., Murphy, J., Sevcik, R. A., Brakke, K. E., Williams, S. L., & Rumbaugh, D. M. (1993). Language comprehension in ape and child. *Monographs of the Society for Research in Child Development, 58* (Serial No. 233).

VIDEO LINKS

Vervet monkeys' alarm calls: www.youtube.com/watch?v=q8ZG8Dpc8mM

Honeybee dancing to communicate: www.youtube.com/watch?v=-7ijI-g4jHg

Honeybee playing soccer: www.theregister.co.uk/2017/02/27/scientists_teach_bees_to_play_football/

Kanzi the bonobo: www.youtube.com/watch?v=2Dhc2zePJFE; www.greatapetrust.org/library/video-gallery/#bonobosTab

LANGUAGE IN HUMAN COMMUNICATION AND THINKING

8

LEARNING OUTCOMES

By the end this chapter you should:

- Know the basics of Noam Chomsky's approach to language – he suggested that humans are innately endowed with a 'Universal Grammar' (UG), and that this universal grammar is applied to the particular language(s) children learn.
- Understand the main debating points over Chomsky's theory including: language and the brain, the linking problem, parental input to children, the critical period hypothesis, and why the study of pidgins and creoles such as Nicaraguan sign language has been a battleground over the validity of innate versus constructivist theories.
- Think about the development of semantic and pragmatic approaches to language development as alternatives to Chomsky, particularly the usage-based approach to language acquisition
- Consider the complexity of communication and reflect upon how it works

At this stage of the book we feel it is vital to reflect on the topic of language in order to understand how children gain the capacity for communication and how cognitive change takes place. Indeed, we feel that this chapter is central to our grasp of all the developing skills that we cover, from how infants learn about other people to the foundations of our moral reasoning. It has long been presumed that a competence in social interaction makes language possible (Bates, 1976). It is the foundation on which language is built. And so it is difficult to draw a firm line between early prelinguistic gestures and first words because they overlap in how infants use these skills to communicate. But how do words work, and how do we learn to use them? The previous chapter on chimpanzee communication showed us the importance of social interaction in the acquisition of elementary skills, but the paradox of this chapter and the next is, respectively, that 1) the fundamentals of language are complex – we argue that they fool many theoreticians of language!; yet 2) most toddlers gain access to these complexities very easily. We will focus on the relevance of language for an understanding of children's thinking, and further reading will require a specialist text. Ambridge and Lieven (2011) provide a detailed account for those wishing to study the topic in depth.

Why don't we all speak the same language? Why indeed are there so many different languages with great variations in their intonation patterns, vocabulary, and sentence structure? We are all experts in speaking and understanding at least one language, so why should it be a topic of research? Although we are embedded in communication throughout our life this does not make it any easier to understand. There are five to six thousand different human languages in use on the planet, but this number is dropping at an alarming rate as languages become extinct when the last speakers of those languages die (Davis, 2009). Papua New Guinea is one of the most linguistically diverse areas of the planet with over 850 languages. British Columbia, Canada, is also an area of great linguistic diversity, with over 60 Aboriginal languages across Canada and half of these in British Columbia coming from seven families, with two referred to as *isolates*; that is, there is no known similar language. This compares to three language families across Europe and one isolate (Basque). British Columbia has been designated a language 'hotspot' by the Living Tongues Institute, not only because there are many languages in British Columbia, but also because many of them are under severe threat of extinction because the last speakers are elderly (http://livingtongues.org/language-hotspots/; see also Thicke, 2014).

There are at least two types of reasons for studying language. First, it could be considered in its own right, because human forms of communication are interesting and they reflect the nature of different cultures, as well as being crucial for maintaining cultures. An important *practical* offshoot of this concerns being able to help people with language problems to communicate more effectively. There are many groups of children who have difficulties ranging from: those with Down syndrome, who are often delayed across the board in language skills; to those with Specific Language Impairment, where there is a problem with communication skills but not other cognitive abilities; to those with autism, which involves difficulties with the social aspects of communication; to those with rare disorders like Williams syndrome in which the basic communication skills are generally picked up but there is a specific and continuing problem with grasping the pragmatic and higher-level skills (Mervis & Velleman, 2011). Understanding the nature of language itself helps us to target specific interventions for particular groups like these. But a second reason for studying language is that it is a window into larger, fundamental questions concerning the nature of thinking and the mind. Theories about the mind can be tested against the facts of language. Philosophers from Plato and Aristotle to Wittgenstein and Quine have used language to talk about questions of meaning. More recently, cognitive scientists are using the facts of language to support and evaluate various theories about the nature of the mind.

There are different approaches to language and this chapter focuses on a basic division between two types. The first is well illustrated in the subtitle to Steven Pinker's (1994) bestselling book on language, *The Language Instinct*, namely 'how the mind creates language'. In contrast, from the perspective taken by George Herbert Mead and others the key question is just the opposite: that is, 'how language creates the mind'. This basic division illustrates how the two approaches discussed throughout this book apply to the topic of language. It might be assumed that the area of language development would be a nice quiet field in which researchers just record and describe children's language. But in fact it is a highly controversial topic. A lot depends on views of language, and the broad division we have depicted here reflects different views of the nature of mind and development.

In this chapter we start with a theory that has generated even more heated discussion than the chimp wars discussed in Chapter 7. Blood, guts, and thunder have been spilled over Noam Chomsky's claim that we are born with an innate propensity to grasp syntax. The debate between Chomsky and his critics has occupied much of the attention of developmental psychologists interested in language, and so the bulk of this chapter summarises this debate. This is followed by a brief description of an account of language that has been increasingly prominent, the idea that children initially learn elements of language in particular contexts and then generalise the 'rules' of communication as a result. This usage-based approach leads us to consider the nature of the problem that children need to understand – the nature of human communication itself.

8.1 THEORIES OF LANGUAGE

Explaining human communication is a test for any theory. In 1957 the influential behaviourist B. F. Skinner published a book in which he attempted to explain how we use language. This work, which was based on a public lecture that earned him his job at Harvard in 1947, was in part a critique of the discipline of linguistics – the study of the structure of language. Skinner's claim was that the study of 'verbal behavior' or how we come to use language would render irrelevant the linguist's focus. He drew on the principles of behaviourism and the processes of imitation, shaping, and reinforcement to account for how we come to learn language. So, for Skinner, language is a trained skill. Given that he believed that biology has only made a small contribution to language acquisition, it follows that clear and effective conditioning should lead a chimp into language. As we found in Chapter 7, attempts to train Viki in 1952 provided little support for this claim.

At that time Noam Chomsky was a young unknown linguist, but his devastating (1959) critique of Skinner's book attracted far more attention than is typical for a book review, and brought to the fore his earlier book (Chomsky, 1957). Chomsky noted that it would follow from behaviouristic principles that parents shape children's language through reinforcement. Skinner assumed that any child's utterance could be reinforced to become a distinct word. Chomsky pointed out, however, that in the US children of immigrant parents learned better English than their parents just by playing with friends on the street who were not likely to reinforce their language in the careful way that would be necessary to support a behaviourist account. Chomsky argued that there was more to sentences than associations formed between adjacent words. He illustrated this with his famous bit of nonsense:

'Colorless green ideas sleep furiously.'

The strength of association between the words in this sequence must be low or non-existent. It is not likely that children would have heard 'colorless and green' together, or 'sleep furiously' and so on. Nowadays there is talk about 'green ideas', in the sense of ideas that may help reduce greenhouse gases and so slow climate change, but this was not the case at the time when Chomsky put together this unlikely string of words. If this is recognised as a grammatical sentence, even though it is a very odd one that doesn't make any sense, then it cannot be explained through association between the words. And if we reverse the order of the words ('Furiously sleep ideas green colorless') the strength of associations should be the same, but now this does not seem to be a grammatical sentence.

In direct contrast to Skinner's analysis of learning language, Chomsky argued that it was not possible for children to learn the grammar of their native language from their experience and therefore grammar must be innate. That is, children must be born with a knowledge of language, or at least the rules of how to learn the grammar of their own tongue. This is the conclusion to Chomsky's (1980) *poverty of the stimulus argument*. It is the claim that there is just not enough information in the language children hear to account for the richness and complexity of their language. There are two aspects to this argument. The *degeneracy of the stimulus* is Chomsky's claim that the sentences children hear are often incomplete and ungrammatical. He made this assertion before there was any evidence for it and after research had been conducted it turned out that much of what children hear is grammatical (Snow, 1972; Sokolov & Snow, 1994). The second part is the *poverty of the stimulus* – that even if what children hear was completely error-free it still wouldn't provide enough evidence for them to learn the abstract principles on which the language is based. The argument is that syntactic rules are either learned or innate. They are not learned, or at least not through known learning mechanisms. Therefore, they must be innate.

Chomsky's goal was to come up with a grammar, or a set of rules, that would generate all the possible grammatical sentences in the language. He termed this the *transformational-generative grammar*. This view of language has been very influential, mainly in linguistics but also in developmental psychology. The approach is referred to as 'transformational' in that a sentence can be transformed into another sentence with the same underlying meaning, but differing in surface form. The surface form is the superficial arrangement of the words that convey this meaning. In other words, two different sentences can have the same meaning – it's obvious that there is more than one way to say something. (For example, 'The moon was jumped over by the cow' has the same meaning as the simpler, and equally improbable, although more familiar form, 'The cow jumped over the moon'.) The assumption behind this deep structure vs surface structure distinction is that the deep structure is linked to the surface structure through a sequence of transformations that change the sentence but not its meaning (Aitchison, 2008; Ambridge & Lieven, 2011). Chomsky's theory itself went through a number of transformations. These revisions were needed, in part, because it was discovered that the transformations proposed were too powerful and were actually changing the meaning of the sentences.

A student of linguistics might need to know the fine distinctions between these perspectives, but for our purposes it is sufficient to know that in each of these Chomsky was attempting to account for how the innate propensity for language may be structured and how the most simple model of this may work most efficiently. In the extended standard theory Chomsky coined the term 'Universal Grammar' to solve the poverty of the stimulus problem, and this term has been used to depict these aspects of his theory since the 1970s. Of course, children cannot be born knowing a particular language like English, French, or Hindi because there are thousands of different languages spoken in the world, all with very different grammars. Instead, what must be innate is this 'universal grammar', that is, something that is common to all human languages.

Within universal grammar there are assumed to be a number of alternative choices, or switches, that can be set one way or the other as 'either'... 'or'... . These switches are what Chomsky calls *parameters* and when children are exposed to a language these parameters become set (Aitchison, 2008; Ambridge & Lieven, 2011);

> Language learning, then, is the process of determining the values of the parameters left unspecified by Universal Grammar, of setting the switches that make the network function ... . Beyond that, the language learner must discover the lexical items of the language and their properties. To a large extent this seems to be a problem of finding what labels are used for preexisting concepts ... . (Chomsky, 1988, p. 134)

According to the idea of a Universal Grammar, 1) it is possible to apply a set of finite rules and principles which combine sets of nouns and verbs into clauses, phrases, and sentences; 2) not all grammars contain the same 'parameters' and a few are specific to one language (see Ambridge & Lieven, 20ll: Chapters 6 and 7) so there are exceptions and any structures specific to one language cannot be used to falsify the 'universality' of theory which is why it has lasted so long!; 3) there are specific principles that govern the uses of words – for example, in the binding principle the 'her' in the sentence 'Mum was feeding her' cannot refer to Mum, but to someone else (presumably mentioned earlier).

8.2 CONTINUING DEBATES BETWEEN FOLLOWERS AND CRITICS OF CHOMSKY

As well as being influential, Chomsky has also been highly controversial. According to Michael Tomasello (1996, p. 275), 'Over the last three decades the major obstacle for scientists interested in the psychological aspects of human linguistic competence has been generative grammar'. The main battle has been over the questions: 1) Is the number of different types of language so large that the exceptions 'disprove' the rule?; 2) Even if languages are similar in structure do we need a specific and self-contained (domain specific) innate propensity to construct sentences that fit both the general rules and the specifics of a particular language? In this section we outline a series of debates that have occurred, in parallel, over the past fifty years, centred on the issue of the validity of Chomsky's theory and the nature of possible alternatives.

Language and the brain

What role does biology play in language development? There is no simple answer to this question. Although everyone agrees that it plays an important function, language research-ers differ on what that role actually is. One view is from Chomsky and his colleagues who use terms like 'biolinguistic' (Chomsky, 2007), the 'language bioprogram' (Fitch, 2010), and 'the genetic endowment for the faculty of language' (Chomsky, 2007, p. 1). This sounds like it is based on biology, on hard science. But, ironically, as discussed in Chapter 2, these claims may actually be incompatible with current work in biology. Tomasello (1995, p. 131) refers to Chomsky's position as a 'curious brand of nativism' because it is not based on any empirical evidence but instead on logical arguments. Indeed, Chomsky (2011) has described the field of the evolution of language which attempts to identify the biological foundations of human language as 'total nonsense', because it is focused on a range of precursors to language including animal musicality (Fitch, 2010) and his aim is solely focused on the ability to construct syntax.

Of course, there is a biological side to the story of language development. The baby learns to talk but the family pet does not, although they are in the same environment, usually receiving the same simplified language input from adults. Humans have evolved the capacity to learn languages. But this is different from the claim that our knowledge of language is innate, i.e. Universal Grammar. As discussed in the previous chapter, other species develop forms of communication, yet fully mastering a human language seems to require a human brain as well as human ways of living together. But this does not mean, as claimed from Chomsky's perspective, that language is already present in some form in the brain. As we suggest below, researchers from other perspectives argue that human abilities enable the development of language.

This debate over the biological foundation of language raises the question of whether language is localised in particular brain areas. It has been known for some time that it tends to be localised in particular areas of the brain, usually in the left hemisphere. One important source of evidence is the loss of language after damage to the brain. Systematic evidence for the idea that problems with speech arise after injury to the left side of the brain was reported by Paul Broca in 1861 and Carl Wernicke in 1874. They studied patients with problems with language, known as aphasia. After the death of patients with language difficulties they examined their brains to locate the damaged areas responsible for the language difficulties. Areas in the brain typically related to language have been named after Broca and Wernicke.

More recently, a number of methods have been used to localise language and it has been found that although it is usually in the left hemisphere it is sometimes in the right hemisphere, especially in left-handed individuals. For example, surgeons needing to determine a patient's language dominant hemisphere do so by anaesthetising each hemisphere one at a time to see if the patient temporarily loses the ability to speak. Another method used to map regions of the brain that are involved in language processing is electrical stimulation to the exposed brain, which has no pain receptors. The stimulation is applied to the brain while the patient is conscious and it can either disrupt speech or cause the patient to utter a vowel-like cry. Neuroimaging can also be used to assess whether language is localised in the left or right hemisphere. One study used functional transcranial Doppler ultrasonography (fTCD) for measuring neural activation: fTCD is a neuroimaging tool that is comparable to functional magnetic resonance imaging (fMRI) because it also assesses changes in blood flow. Although language is located usually in the left hemisphere, in a group of 326 people it was found that in strongly right-handed individuals language was in their right hemisphere in 4% of participants, whereas the right hemisphere was dominant for language for 27% of the strongly left-handed individuals (Knecht, Dräger, Deppe, Bobe, Lohmann, Flöel, Ringelstein, & Henningsen, 2000).

When language areas of the brain are damaged in adults they have great difficulty speaking and in recovering this skill. This is referred to as *aphasia*, of which there are several different types depending on which area is damaged (e.g. Broca's area or Wernicke's area). However, when the brain areas in which language usually develops are damaged in young children they usually develop language in other areas. They reacquire language even after they have lost their entire left hemisphere! This plasticity results in other areas of the brain taking over the language function (Bates, 2005). A series of key studies have been conducted to show how this works. For example, Lucie Hertz-Pannier and her colleagues (2002) demonstrated the neural plasticity in a single child with a severe form of epilepsy. They used functional magnetic resonance imaging (fMRI) to identify typical left-hemisphere activity when the child was processing words at 6 years and 10 months old. By the age of 9 he was experiencing several seizures a day, many of which were

accompanied by falls. To relieve the seizures, he had an operation called a hemispherec-
tomy, which involves severing the hemisphere containing the language areas from the
rest of the brain. He lost his language skills but gradually regained them. At the age of 10
years and 6 months his language skills were returning and a second fMRI scan showed
that his expressive and receptive language skills prompted brain activity in the areas of the
right side of the brain that mirror normal left-brain activity. Such studies can only occur
occasionally when medical needs dictate, but this and other investigations provide clear
evidence for plasticity beyond any age when it would be expected (see the box below).

Researchers investigating the relation between language and brain functioning have
considered two possibilities. First, that language is located in particular brain regions
from birth, or that second, language can develop anywhere in the brain. Neither of
these two hypotheses seems supported by the evidence which we briefly summarise
here. The language areas of the brain are commonly, but not always, located in the left
hemisphere. And it seems that language does not develop just anywhere in the brain.
Therefore, the third option is that it seems that particular areas may be well suited for
the development of language, but if they are damaged language can develop elsewhere
in the brain. Hence language localisation appears to be the outcome of development,
in the course of which experience shapes the brain (Bates et al., 1997).

THE CRITICAL PERIOD HYPOTHESIS

At the same time as Chomsky was developing his theory, ethologists (who study the
evolutionary origins of animal behaviour) hypothesised that some innately constrained
skills develop only if they are triggered within a key period of development. William
Thorpe (1958) discovered that a chaffinch reared in isolation from an adult member of
the species, before reaching sexual maturity, failed to produce as complex and lyrical a
song as is normally displayed when attracting mates. He attributed the fact that chaf-
finches sang at all to the innate capacity for song, while he considered that exposure to
other birds' song was necessary to trigger the capacity for more complex skills. This sort
of data led to the idea that there is a critical period in development for the emergence
of a specific skill and there has since been research on these periods for skills as diverse
as visual attention and memory.

The idea of a critical period for language was first suggested by neurologists but was
taken up by the linguist Eric Lenneberg (1967), who argued that species-specific development in the preschool period was evidence for this idea. One source of evidence for a critical

(Continued)

period is from cases of children who have not been exposed to language when they were young. There have been a number of cases reported since Victor, the 'wild boy of Aveyron' in France, was found in 1800. He may have lived in the woods by himself for at least six years and he couldn't speak. Although attempts were made to teach him to talk for over six years, he only learned a few words. This has led many to speculate that he had passed the critical period when language develops. However, others have speculated that he was cast out *because* he was autistic and did not learn to speak in the way toddlers usually do.

More recently, the girl named 'Genie' was discovered in Los Angles in 1970. She had been deprived of exposure to language and had been locked in a room by herself. Over the next few years she did learn a number of words, but her grasp of syntax was very poor (Curtiss, 1977). She was studied until the early 2000s, developing a range of nonverbal communication skills, but she struggled with expressive language, particularly in forming sentences. Some have argued that Genie provides us with evidence for a critical period for language. However, these and other similar unfortunate experiences are referred to as 'forbidden experiments' – they are not real experiments because it is not known what the children were like to begin with, and Genie was severely maltreated. In contrast, 'Chelsea' grew up in a loving family, but was not exposed to language until the age of 31 when a neurologist discovered that she was deaf and provided her with hearing aids. Yet like Genie, although she learned many words, she did not develop normal syntax (Pinker, 1994).

A third source of evidence for a critical period is from research with deaf children. This line of research draws on natural experiments that arise because deaf children vary in the age at which they are exposed to American Sign Language (ASL) (Newport, 1990). About 5 to 10% of deaf children are born to deaf parents and are exposed to sign language already in infancy. But others are not taught sign language until later in their development, typically when they go to residential schools at about at four to six years of age. In the relatively recent past sign language was not formally taught at these schools even though it was the language of everyday life for the children. Some deaf children did not start residential school until age 12 or later. The three groups thus vary in age of first exposure, but at the time of testing they had all had at least thirty years of daily exposure to ASL. When the children were tested on their competence in ASL there was no difference for word order but there was a large difference for morphology (how words are formed and relate to each other in language). Native learners were highly consistent in morphology but later learners were highly variable. Thus, it seems that early exposure to language is especially important for aspects of syntax and morphology (Newport, 1990).

Criticism of Chomsky: the linking problem

Most of the debate about Chomsky's theory revolves around whether his Universal Grammar (UG) provides a viable account of how language is acquired. Let's illustrate this in terms of the concept of parameter. Michael Tomasello (2005) points out that there is no clear agreement regarding what the parameters of the proposed UG are and how many there are, but the best example may be the alleged 'head direction parameter'. For a non-linguist, the 'head' of a sentence can be understood as something roughly like the main word of the sentence. Languages vary on whether the head is first or last. Either the head is first, as in Spanish, *la casa grande* [the house big], or last, as in English, *the big house*. The idea from UG is that as the child hears her native language her 'head direction parameter' will become set through exposure to the language. In order to set the parameter the child has somehow to know (not consciously) and recognise the head in the language she is learning. How is this possible? Consider the utterance *T'eere li ráreyiht'u*. This is from Slave, an Athebaskan language from northern Canada, and it is about a 'girl', 'dog', and 'hit'. But in order to set the head direction parameter it is necessary to know which word is the main one in the sentence. How could someone who does not yet speak this language know which is the main word in the sentence? This is the linking problem. The paradox is that in order to set the head direction parameter the child must know which word in the utterance is the head, but if the child already knows this then they don't need the parameter (Tomasello, 2005; see also Ambridge & Lieven, 2011).

Evans and Levinson (2009) report the range of variations between different languages, which suggests the need for an alternative to the UG approach. Indeed their article is full of scores of examples of the variations between them. For example, some languages contain no adjectives, and many contain no morphemes for marking tense (e.g. in Chinese the same verb form for the present is used with the word *guò* or *zhe* to indicate the past), while in others, like Turkish or Korean, the origins of knowledge have to be identified using evidential markers (for a study showing the effects of language on children's understanding of others see Lucas, Lewis, Pala, Wong, & Berridge, 2013). There are now other approaches to language such as functional (how language works in everyday use: the usage hypothesis described below) and cognitive (what cognitive processes are required to generate and understand) linguistics that characterise adult linguistic competence in ways that make it possible for children to learn (Tomasello, 1995, 2003).

It has long been argued that Chomsky's goal 'is unbelievably narrow: we are not dealing here with a theory about the way language is used and understood, but rather with one which merely investigates how grammatical sentences can be differentiated from ungrammatical sentences' (Hörmann, 1986, p. 62). Development is not a question that arises for Chomsky, and that may be why in an invited address at the 1986 Boston child language conference he stated that research on children's language could be classified in three categories: wrong, trivial, or absurd (Snow, 1994).

The role of the input in language learning

According to Chomsky (1988, p. 134), 'language learning is not really something the child does; it is something that happens to the child placed in an appropriate environment, much as the child's body grows and matures in a predetermined way'. From this perspective, language is not learned; it is present innately and only 'triggered' by the language children hear. In fact, Chomsky assumes that there is not enough information available to children to enable them to learn a language. Although they have the evidence of the sentences they hear from the target language, known as *positive evidence*, Chomsky claimed that children do not receive *negative evidence* – that is, feedback on which strings of words are not grammatical sentences in the language. These could be corrections from the parents, telling the child which of her utterances are ungrammatical. This raises some key questions. Is negative evidence available to children? Are children actually corrected by their parents? And does this do any good? That is, do they pay any attention to corrections if they get them?

In an early study of the question of negative evidence Brown and Hanlon (1970) looked for explicit feedback, and they didn't find parents saying 'Well done' or 'That's right' after grammatical utterances and 'No' or 'That's wrong' after ungrammatical utterances. Instead, they found that parents' approval depended on whether the utterance was true, not on whether it was grammatical. For example, consider the following exchange from Brown and Hanlon's study (1970, p. 49):

Adam: 'Draw a boot paper.'

Mother: 'That's right. Draw a boot on paper.'

In this example, Adam's mother does not tell him that his utterance is ungrammatical, and in fact, she even says 'That's right'. So, there is no direct correction. At the time, this was the conclusion derived from the research. However Adam's mother does rephrase his utterance in a grammatically correct form, something that Brown and Hanlon had pointed out in their article, although its significance was generally overlooked. This parental feedback has become known as 'recasting'.

The view that parents do not correct their children's language has had a long shelf life, and the details of its content are still discussed in current debates on the role of negative evidence (Rowland, 2014; Schoneberger, 2010). Brown and Hanlon's (1970) research has been replicated and extended since its publication. It has been found that there are differences in the frequency with which mothers repeat, alter, question, or recast their child's well-formed versus ill-formed utterances. In two studies, Bohannon and Stanowicz (1988) found that parents and even non-parents were more likely to repeat verbatim a child's well-formed utterances compared to ill-formed utterances. They were more likely to repeat with corrections or request clarification of a sentence with mistakes. For example:

Child: 'Fix Lilly.'

Mother: 'Oh … Lilly will fix it.'

Or adults recast the utterance in a correct manner:

Child: 'That be monkey.'

Adult: 'That is a monkey.'

In other cases, adults repeated and expanded the utterance:

Child: 'Monkey climbing.'

Adult: 'The monkey is climbing to the top of the tree.'

Bohannon and Stanowicz (1988) found that about 35% of children's flawed speech received some form of differential feedback. Chouinard and Clark (2003) found that parents recast as many as two-thirds of 2- to 4-year-old children's errors, and that children were attending to this as shown by them repeating what their parent had said, or acknowledging it, or rejecting it if the parent had misunderstood.

For example, the child may repeat it:

Abe (2½):   'I want butter mine.'

Father: 'ok give it here and I'll put butter on it.'

Abe: 'I need butter on it.' (p. 656)

Of course, finding that middle-class first-born American children receive negative evidence does not provide a sufficient case. But the same finding that parents provide feedback after a child's ill-formed utterance was replicated in research with rural working-class families in the Southern US and with later-born children. In fact, the rural Southern mothers did more explicit correcting compared to middle-class mothers with first-born children (Sokolov & Snow, 1994).

So experience with exposure to language helps, but is it necessary? The definition of negative evidence has been broadened since the early idea of direct corrections. Brown and Hanlon, even in 1970, did suggest that 'repeats of ill-formed utterances usually contain corrections and so could be instructive' (p. 43). But they didn't include this in their definition of negative evidence (not until Hirsh-Pasek et al., 1984). Negative evidence is now broadened from explicit correction to include other information to correct an utterance (Sokolov & Snow, 1994).

But it is still argued that the feedback is noisy and inconsistent across mothers and age ranges, and that this feedback is really not very good negative evidence. If this were the case it would not tell the child what exactly is wrong with the utterance. That is, there could be problems in syntax, phonology, semantics, or pragmatics. So the child cannot identify which aspect she should try to fix and constantly changing the grammar of an utterance based on her parents' responses might just make things worse (Marcus, 1993; Pinker, 1994).

It is not enough to show that negative evidence is available. It is also necessary to demonstrate that it is important in getting a message across. There is some evidence for this. First, mothers who expand on their child's utterances have children who are advanced in language development (Taumoepeau, 2016). Second, it seems that children are paying attention because after parents have recast their mistakes, children tend to imitate the correct form. Third, evidence that feedback influences language development comes from various training studies in which training on specific aspects of language results in development of those aspects of language (Sokolov & Snow, 1994). Fourth, children in daycare with more one-to-one contact with caregivers learned language more rapidly than children with less contact (McCartney, 1984). Fifth, eldest children reach 50 words faster and start combining words before second- (and later-) borns, most likely because they have more exposure to language due to one-on-one time with parents (Hoff-Ginsberg, 1998). Sixth, there is also evidence of the influence of socioeconomic status (SES) on lexical development, which seems to be related to how much parents talk to their children (Fenson, Dale, Reznick, Bates, Thal, & Pethick, 1994; Hoff-Ginsberg, 1998).

Language creation: pidgins and creoles

Much of the debate between proponents of the idea of a Universal Grammar and the opposing camp of constructivists has revolved around the languages created when cultures merge or are assimilated. This research is on languages that emerge in minority cultures, often oppressed by a dominant group. A *pidgin* is a very simple language that arises when people with no common language must communicate using strings of words that are highly variable in order; that is, there is little grammar (Pinker, 1994). Some of the best-known examples are the languages in the West Indies and Hawaiian Pidgin English. These were the focus for the research of the linguist Derek Bickerton in the 1970s. Pidgin was developed on the sugar cane plantations in Hawaii during the early part of the last century (around 1900). It became profitable to ship sugar to mainland US at this time and in order to run the plantations many workers were needed. They were brought in from various countries including Japan, Korea, Philippines, Portugal, Spain, Germany, France, and Hungary. Owners of tobacco, cotton, coffee, and sugar plantations mixed labourers from different language backgrounds. These workers needed some way to communicate while working. Pidgins consist of strings of nouns and verbs like *kote, motete, awl frend, giv, no*? (Literal meaning: 'buy, take back, all friend, give, no?': Implied meaning 'They buy presents, take them back and give them to all their friends, don't they') (Bickerton, 1984, p. 174). As Bickerton suggests, pidgins do not contain the elements of grammar that convey the complexity of, for example, tense (when an event occurred), aspect (how often), modality (degree of certainty), or sub-clauses.

What is very interesting for language researchers is that from pidgins there can be a movement to *creoles*, which are more complex languages based on pidgin but containing aspects of grammar. This *creolisation* seems to be a process that creates new languages. Bickerton (1984) argued that the children of pidgin speakers transform their parents' simple language from ungrammatical pidgin to fully-fledged and grammatically complex structures. In what is termed 'the Language Bioprogram Hypothesis', he argued that this process is evidence of an innate propensity to construct a language. He suggested that evidence for this idea comes from *universality* (that the structure of different creoles seems to share clear similarities), *invention* (the language generated is not predictable from the input), and *domain specificity* (it relates to language-specific processes, not more general cognitive skills).

In response to Bickerton (1984), many commentators who did not take a nativist approach argued that 'creolisation' can take place as a result of the demands which language and communication make upon speakers. Elizabeth Bates (1984), for example, looked at how children construct linguistic rules as an example of the processes equivalent to how creolisation might take place. She noted that one Italian child explicitly stated the 'rule' that you use the word (informal second person) *tu* in the morning and *lei* (the more formal third-person mode of address) in the afternoons. The child was making an inference based on what he heard around him as he spent his mornings at home with family members but visited others with his mother in the afternoons – where more formal language was demanded. This misplaced 'rule' is one of many that children develop, not because of the formal structure of language, but because of regularities in the way in which language is used. Bates and many theoreticians since have pointed out that the way in which we use language can account for similarities between different rules – we do not have to posit an underlying genetic structure to explain the similarity between different languages. Indeed recent analyses of creoles, like the 'Jafaican' satirised by the character Ali-G in contemporary London (Sebba & Dray, 2013) illustrate the role of cultural processes in the development of new language forms. This suggests that social factors, and not a need to impose deep grammatical rules on the language that we hear in pidgins, play a crucial function in the constant changes in languages.

A more recent debate between nativism and constructivism concerns the Nicaraguan sign language. As in Western education systems in previous generations, in Nicaragua a school for the deaf grew rapidly in the late 1970s and early 1980s. It was determined that the 'best' form of learning was through the spoken language and signing was discouraged. However, the children soon developed a sign system to communicate among themselves, which started as a simple form of communication and then developed greater complexity. As Senghas (2003) noticed, every cohort of students at the school introduced features that made their communication more similar in complexity to other signing systems (e.g. British Sign Language) and, as Ambridge and Lieven (2011) suggest, spoken languages. For example, 'spatial modulation', or performing the same sign in front of the body or to the left or right, is a feature of all studied sign languages (Senghas & Coppola, 2001). Senghas and Cuppola showed how this system developed quickly over successive cohorts in the school. Shifting from the centre to one side or the other adds complexity to the communication, allowing the listener to know whether or how two signs are related in time and space, and the Nicaraguan children worked out subtle means of doing this. As you can imagine, debate has hinged upon whether the change has been so rapid that it must have been prompted by an innate propensity for grasping grammatical form (Kegl, 2002), or whether social influences are so strong that they inspire rapid change (Tomasello, 2008).

In the argument over innate propensities for language versus factors in everyday life channelling different languages to promote similar solutions to similar problems, we side with Bates (1984) who argued that we do not have to attribute the ability to learn language to innate knowledge. The signers in Nicaraguan schools and toddlers learning language show selection biases that tilt the balance in favour of a usage explanation over a genetic one. The emergence of this language shows that a single generation of children did not invent the language, and instead a gradual process over several generations and interaction between those generations were crucial (Senghas, Senghas, & Pyers, 2005).

8.3 THE CHILD'S SEARCH FOR MEANING IN LANGUAGE

The debate over the validity of Chomsky's theory continues but has been largely superseded by another over the roles of semantics (meaning) and pragmatics (the use of language in particular contexts). In this section we sketch out the main arguments before offering an account of meaning that builds on the previous chapters and fits with the rest of the chapters in this book.

Incorporating meaning into the child's grasp of language

In response to Chomsky's theory many developmental psychologists were impressed by the force of the argument that children come to learn syntax as they acquire a vocabulary, but they rejected the claims that a grasp of syntax is innate and development is unimportant. For example, Martin Braine (1963) developed an account of children's grasp and use of grammar in which he argued that they hear and gradually learn the meanings of utterances with a similar structure and as a result also learn to use syntax correctly. His ideas have gone in and out of favour. Redington, Chater, and Finch (1998) examined the 'distributional information' of words in child-directed speech. Such utterances are highly repetitive and consistent. Their study identified how a grasp of a grammatical category may be based on this repeated experience of distributional information of words in utterances. However, for this transition from the distribution of words to a grasp of grammar to work would require memory skills that are beyond the child's sophistication for co-occurrences between thousands of words – as Pinker (1979) pointed out Braine's system is unconstrained. Thus, more recent researchers, like St Clair, Monaghan, and Christiansen (2010), have developed models of early language in which only the combinations of a word with the preceding and following word are taken into account.

Others take different tacks. Steven Pinker (1984) used the term 'semantic bootstrapping' to depict an innate theory of language in which children have a predetermined grasp not only of elementary syntactic categories, like nouns and verbs, but also semantic (or thematic) roles, like 'subjects' and 'actions', and also 'innate linking rules' to map semantics onto syntax. This elaborate system was devised to overcome the poverty of the stimulus problem because the child has the ability to map semantic categories onto syntactical ones. When the child sees the family pet curl up on the carpet and hears 'The cat sat on the mat', she or he uses these innate linking rules to map the meaning of what s/he sees onto the sentence and its grammatical structure is learned by this 'bootstrapping' process. As Caroline Rowland (2014) suggests this works for English with its simple subject–verb–object structure, but in several languages in which the marking of transitive and intransitive sentences varies (particularly across tenses), the bootstrapping hypothesis suggests that young children should make errors when they do not.

Pinker's theory attempts to maintain the importance of innate factors – indeed it adds a magnitude of complexity to Chomsky by incorporating semantics and linking rules. In contrast, several accounts of language development have stressed the child's grasp of pragmatics (the use of particular utterances in particular circumstances) as an alternative route into the complexity of syntax. In the 1970s a series of hypotheses were proposed to suggest that the child's early nonverbal interactions had the same 'grammatical' structure (agent–action–object) as later verbal interactions (e.g. Bruner, 1981; Lock, 1978). An influential recent pragmatic account is Michael Tomasello's (2003, pages 3–4) 'usage-based' model. He suggests that humans have two types of skills. The first set is largely domain general (they are cognitive processes and are not restricted to language) and involve performing pattern-finding comparisons. These include the ability to group perceptual or conceptual categories, so that things that either look the same or perform the same functions fit together to make schemas of recurrent perceptions or actions. This is akin to Piaget's notion of sensory motor schemes (see Chapter 3) and the ability to reason by analogy between related domains. The second set of skills is more relevant to our discussion. This is a set of 'intention-reading' skills (or 'theory of mind, broadly conceived'; Tomasello, 2003, p. 3), which consist of the ability to share interest and attention to objects with another person, to follow another's gaze, to understand and use attentional gestures like pointing, and most importantly to 'learn the intentional actions of others' (p. 3).

Although understanding others' intentions is central in developing communicative skills, there is controversy regarding how this ability develops. In Chapter 6 we have reviewed the critical evaluation of Tomasello's account regarding how infants learn to understand others' intentions (Carpendale & Lewis, 2015b).

Pragmatics

Pragmatics concerns how language is used in social situations – that is, how sentences have meaning in particular social contexts (Levinson, 1983; Turnbull, 2003). In understanding how meaning is conveyed with language we can't overlook the social situation, because the very same word or utterance can be used to convey different meaning in different situations. For example, if we hear Romeo saying to Juliet 'I'll be there tonight', it means something quite different from a vampire saying the same thing to his next victim. Or stating 'I'd like a glass of water' to a waiter in a restaurant is quite different compared to stating it when crossing the Sahara Desert. In fact, in irony and sarcasm words can be used to convey even the opposite of their usual meaning (Levinson, 1983; Turnbull, 2003).

John Austin (1962) argued that language does not just describe the state of the world, it is used to do things. In Austin's speech act theory he argued that language is used to perform social acts such as to persuade, apologise, or make commitments. For example, the utterance 'I do' in the context of a marriage ceremony is used to make a commitment.

In addition, Paul Grice (1975) analysed how language is used to convey additional meaning beyond the level of the sentence. For example, if we ask how Harry fared in court the other day and we are told that 'he got a fine', we assume that he *only* got a fine, even though that is not what was actually said. If we find out later that in addition to the fine Harry also got a life sentence we would feel that the speaker was not cooperating with us. That is, we would assume that 1) the proper amount of information should be given; 2) in a clear manner; and that it should be 3) true; and 4) relevant. These are assumptions that we base our interpretation of sentences on, which Grice referred to as 'maxims of conversation'. Grice also recognised that these assumptions could be intentionally flouted. For example, the statement 'Queen Victoria was made of iron' is obviously false, yet the sentence is meaningful in a metaphorical way. Or when Eeyore says to Winnie the Pooh 'You're a fine friend', when it is known that this, in fact, is not the case, it can be understood as irony. Grice believed that these principles of conversation he was describing applied to cooperative interaction in general, whether it is a conversation, baking a cake together, or repairing a car.

Another dimension to conversational interaction is that in general we are concerned with the feelings of people we interact with – this is politeness (Brown & Levinson, 1987). We want to avoid embarrassment and preserve their dignity, which is referred to as *face*, and this concern about others affects how we talk. For example, it influences the way we accept or decline an invitation. If a friend asks if you would like to meet for coffee you could accept by saying 'sure', but if you want to refuse, it would be unlikely you would just say 'no', unless you intended to offend them. A refusal is more likely to be indirect and may not even include actually saying 'no' (Turnbull, 2003, p. 118). So this topic in the area of language actually is linked to social understanding. It could equally be described as competence in interaction. This provides a bridge to the topic of the two chapters on social understanding and social competence (Chapters 11 and 12). It also raises the question of how children become skilled in a system of communication. This returns us in the final section to the topic this chapter started with, the nature of language.

8.4 THE MEANING OF MEANING

What is the common view of meaning assumed in psychology? It seems to be that words are like labels for objects (Wittgenstein, 1968, §1). This view has a long history that Wittgenstein traced to *The Confessions of St Augustine* written over fifteen hundred years ago. In this book Saint Augustine describes being an infant and attempting to communicate with the people around him. This way of setting up the problem begins from the assumption that the infant is trapped in his or her own body, trying to learn how to communicate with others. Mead describes this perspective as assuming that people start off as individuals isolated in separate prison cells, attempting to find some code with which to communicate between their isolated cells.

This view of language can also be found in the writing of the seventeenth-century English philosopher John Locke (Essay, III, ix, 6). Locke seems to have assumed that the only way words can be used to communicate is if they have a fixed meaning, and thus cause the same meaning to arise in the minds of others. The computational view of the mind is based on this assumption. A similar view can be found more recently in Steven Pinker's (1994) book *The Language Instinct* (see Proudfoot, 2009). Pinker endorses the idea that meaning is transmitted from head to head through being attached to words and sentences. We encode meaning in words and transmit them to others who decode the meaning. Such a view amounts to a code model of how language works to transmit meaning (Canfield, 1995, 2007) and faces numerous problems that motivate the search for an alternative view of meaning.

What is wrong with this view of meaning?

A difficulty with the idea that meaning is attached to words is raised by the 'whatjamicallit effect' (Levinson, 1995). Even though its meaning depends on the situation it is used in, others often understand us when we say 'where is the whatjamicallit' or 'the thingima-bob'? In many situations people seem to have no difficulty at all in understanding such utterances. Many words such as 'this', 'that', 'it', 'he', and so on work this way.

Meaning depends on the social context within a sequence of interaction; that is, it is *indexical*. The same utterance can be used in different contexts to convey different meanings. It is well known that utterances can be used sarcastically, ironically, or metaphorically to mean different things. To illustrate, in Dostoyevsky's book *The Diary of a Writer*, six young drunken workmen are described holding a conversation on the walk home from the pub with only one unprintable word, yet each of them uses it to convey a different meaning (referred to by Vygotsky, 1934/1986).

There are many other ways in which different meanings can be conveyed. For example, if we say something like 'can you pass the salad' we are not usually asking if the person is physically capable of completing this task. Instead, it is used as request to do so.

Even pauses can convey meaning. For example, consider the following exchange between a husband and wife (Turnbull, 2003, p. 152):

A: 'I'm getting fat.'

B: (three-second pause)

A: 'Do you really think so?'

Don't try this at home! I (JC) had the experience of pausing after my wife asked me if I liked her new glasses, and she believed that I didn't like them. A three-second pause is a long time in a conversation. In this case, a pause means 'yes', but does it always mean this? Consider another example overheard in an art gallery as two people look at a painting. In this situation the pause means 'no' (Turnbull, 2003, p. 153).

C: 'I really like that.'

D: (three-second pause)

C: 'Well, I mean, I think it's the type of work that kinda grows on you.'

In Chapter 5 we have already described research showing that at 14- to 18-month-old infants understand that the same pointing gesture made by different people can mean different things, That is, words and gestures do not have fixed meaning. Instead, people can use words and gestures in different social situations to convey different meanings.

Think of meaning as similar to humour or friendliness or hostility. We do not think of humour as being attached to a word, phrase, or sentence. Jokes do not intrinsically have humour; whether they are funny or not depends on their use in a sequence of interaction. This is easy to discover if a joke is told in the wrong context, or if the audience already knows it.

Wittgenstein argued that meaning is not attached to representations such as words, utterances or pictures (Goldberg, 1991). For example, Wittgenstein (1968, §139) uses a picture of a man on a hill to show that it could mean that the man is climbing up the hill or sliding back down (Goldberg, 1991). As another example, Wittgenstein considers the multiple possible meanings of a picture of a boxer. It could be the way one should stand, or the way one shouldn't stand, or it might indicate a particularly famous boxer, and so on. The general point is that there are many possible meanings for any representation, image, word, utterance, or gesture.

Wittgenstein (1968) considers whether the idea of language assumed by Saint Augustine, that words are like names for things, is a primitive view of language, or whether it would be possible for a primitive language to actually work that way. Perhaps a simple language could be used by a builder and a helper in which the words are labels for the building material, such as 'slabs', 'blocks', and 'pillars'. Then they would need numbers, say up to five. An example of an utterance in the language could be 'five slabs'. Of course, such an utterance if it is going to be meaningful must convey a meaning. But what does it mean? It could be an order for five slabs, or a report about five slabs being needed or five slabs remaining, and so on. It could also be used to convey many other meanings (Canfield, 2007). Wittgenstein's point is that any utterance can have many possible meanings, and this shows that expressions and words cannot have a fixed meaning attached to them.

But language is used to convey meaning so how does it work? It works through learning social activities and what is expected to happen next. In routine situations in which the builder is constructing a section of a wall and says 'five slabs' it could be used to ask the assistant to fetch that many slabs. It would mean something different if he was taking the wall down. The meaning must be based on a shared history of interaction and recent events.

The view of meaning that Wittgenstein critiqued was also mocked by Jonathan Swift in 1726 in his book *Gulliver's Travels* (1726, Part 3, ch. 5). Gulliver travels to a town where the scholars have figured out that words are just names for things, and therefore it would be possible to save one's breath and be healthier by having conversations by showing objects instead of speaking words. Of course, a drawback of this practice is that one has to carry around a bag of objects which could get large depending on the breadth of one's planned conversation. But wealthier scholars could hire servants to carry the bags (the women in the town refused to be involved in this silliness). In Chapter 7 we stated this is the view of meaning taken for granted in the first round of the chimp language wars – that is, the chimps were trained to associate signs with objects such as food.

But how does meaning work in a view of language as activity? We tend to have a picture of meaning as located within us, perhaps in our head in some way, and we wish to transmit it to others; we try to 'get our meaning across'. And sometimes if we fail and the other person obviously misunderstands then we try again. Thus, a view of meaning as located in the individual seems to fit with our personal experience. This feeling may be the source of the code model introduced above. However, we have now encountered the problems that arise when we try to carefully think through the implications of such a view of meaning. How do we resolve this paradox? We suggest that it is helpful to think about it from a developmental perspective. Our way of thinking, our human experience, is a developmental accomplishment. That is, we need an explanation for how a skill develops, rather than assume that the skill is simply given and that it explains development. Doing so would be like setting the cart before the horse. Our adult experience of meaning and our attempts to convey meaning may be the outcome of a gradual developmental process. We don't start off that way. To understand development it is important to look at the forms of interpersonal engagement babies and children grow up embedded in, as we did in Chapters 5 and 6.

If the common fixed view of meaning has all of these problems and more, yet it is obvious that we are very good at conveying meaning, what is an alternative approach to meaning that avoids these problems? We now turn to proposing an alternative.

Shared practices

It might be thought that children first learn words like labels for objects, and then learn how to put the words together to do things like make requests. For example, they might first learn the label for juice and then learn how to ask for juice. Naming things can be one routine that some children in some families and some cultures learn to do with language. But children also want to get things done socially with language. Children may first learn routine patterns of interaction and these will then form the bedrock on which language can be built. These routines or customs are patterns of interaction such as making requests and responding, refusing, and greeting. The Nicaraguan sign language users, discussed above, created a formal communication system from their need and desire to communicate within particular contexts. Such patterns as making requests and greeting seem to be based on natural reactions that infants become familiar with and form expectations about, which may be common to all human societies (Canfield, 2007). Children then learn to graft language onto the custom. Canfield (2007) describes eight early language games or interaction patterns which form the basis for and slowly become infused with language. Refusing and making requests appear early, whereas merely naming actually appears later and may not be universal across cultures. These two natural actions become gestures as children learn the actions that follow. They represent two forms of human interaction. As discussed in Chapter 5, requests may develop from reaching, which is a natural reaction. Humans reach for objects because our hands are adapted to grasping.

To extend the idea of children learning the meaning of words through their natural reactions consider emotion words such as happy and afraid. In viewing a child's natural reactions, it is clear to adults that the child is happy when receiving a present or afraid of a large dog. Adults then talk about the child's feelings and the child can come to acquire verbal expressions for these contexts. We extend this discussion in Chapters 11 and 12 when we consider how children come to learn about the social world. Before this we consider how children grasp the meaning of words.

SUMMARY AND CONCLUSION

In introducing the topic of language we considered practical reasons for understanding its development, but there are also theoretical reasons because it raises crucial questions concerning thinking and the mind. Although this is a new topic in this book, it is linked to the other topics in multiple ways. In Chapter 3 we began a discussion of the development of children's understanding of the physical world, and then in Chapter 4 the social world, which was followed in Chapters 5 and 6 by a review of the development of communicative skills in infancy. The topic of communication was continued in Chapter 7 with a focus on animal communication systems, which we reviewed for the purpose of learning more about human communication. All of this forms the foundation for the development of language.

Language, however, has been approached from radically different theoretical perspectives, resulting in ongoing heated debates. We introduced Noam Chomsky's influential approach by contrasting it with Skinner's attempt to explain language based on behaviouristic learning principles. Chomsky argued that sentences are not just strings of words linked by associations. Instead, he described language as knowledge of a set of rules of syntax that enable individuals to produce a practically unlimited number of new grammatical sentences. The question is how do individuals learn this syntax? Chomsky argued that it is not possible to acquire this knowledge through learning because children do not receive enough corrections for mistakes, known as 'the poverty of the stimulus argument'. Therefore, for Chomsky it follows that children must already have an innate knowledge of language in the form of a Universal Grammar (UG) that works for all of the possible human languages. This UG, according to Chomsky, has a set of fixed principles and a number of variable parameters remaining to be set by the child's exposure to the local language.

Chomsky's influence has resulted in a number of theoretical debates. One important topic concerns how language is supported by the brain, and in particular whether language processing is localised in particular brain regions. It has been known for some time that language processing is usually located in the left hemisphere of the brain. More recently it is has been found that this is especially so for right-handed individuals, but sometimes it is located in the right hemisphere especially in left-handed individuals. This evidence suggests that infants are not just born with language already in their left hemisphere, but that the left hemisphere is best suited for processing language so that it typically develops there, but it can also develop in the right hemisphere, or occasionally in both (Bates, 1999, 2005).

If language processing develops in particular brain regions, is there a critical time period for such development? The critical period hypothesis is that there is an age range during which children must be exposed to everyday speech otherwise they will not develop normal language. We reviewed evidence from damage to brains, research with feral children who have not been exposed to language, and studies of deaf children who varied in age of exposure to language, all supporting the hypothesis that there is a critical period for first language development, or at least for syntax. However, this is protracted as even young adolescents with brain damage can recruit new areas of the brain to process language.

Another source of criticism of Chomsky concerns the process of getting from a UG, which it is claimed infants are born with, to the setting of the parameters for one's own language. This is known as 'the linking problem'. It has been argued that this is a paradox because setting the parameters appears to require some knowledge of the language, but the point of the UG is that it is supposed to help a child learn the language (Tomasello, 2005).

Chomsky's claim that acquiring a language is more like growing an organ than learning a skill has led to debates about the role of the language children hear in growing up.

He argued that children do not receive corrections for mistakes, known as negative evidence. It was found that parents were more concerned with truth rather than their child's correct grammar. But in follow-up research it has been found that children do experience considerable indirect feedback from parents through adults recasting what children say in a grammatical form. And it appears that children pay attention to and learn from this feedback.

Another interesting area of debate concerns pidgins and creoles. It has been argued that children exposed to pidgins (simple communication systems with little syntax) spontaneously produce more complex languages (creoles) through a process of creolisation in which this degraded input is made more complex. It has been argued that this supports the view that children are born with knowledge of language. This story is more complex, however. The more recent case of the development of Nicaraguan Sign Language suggests that the process of developing a complex language does not happen over one generation but instead is a gradual social process through which groups of children develop more complex aspects of their language. Subsequently, the next cohort of children growing up exposed to this language master it even more competently and improve it.

Chomsky has also been criticised for focusing only on the abstract knowledge of language necessary to construct new sentences, but not being concerned with how language is actually used in communicative contexts. For example, the same sentence can convey different meanings in different situations, and listeners derive additional meaning from what others say based on assumptions about communication. This is a large and interesting area of study known as pragmatics. This examination of the process through which meaning is conveyed directs attention to the more general issue of meaning.

Given these critiques of Chomsky's theory, in the final third of the chapter we presented an alternative approach to how language is constructed by the child. Martin Braine argued in the 1960s that syntax is the product of the child's communication, not the reverse. More recently Michael Tomasello has developed a theory of language based on the idea that the child needs to grasp something about the intentions of the person with whom they interact. In the final, theoretical, section we considered the assumption that communication works through meaning being attached to words that are transmitted to others who then decode the meaning. We reviewed arguments against this assumption that meaning can be attached to words or sentences or any other representation. If these arguments are accepted then an alternative view of meaning is needed, which we suggest is based on shared practices. This view is compatible with the approach to communication in Chapters 5 and 6 on infant social development and Chapter 7 on animal communication. We used this section as a build-up to the next chapter in which we examine how children come to understand the meaning of words.

FURTHER READING

Ambridge, B., & Lieven, E. V. M. (2011). *Child Language Acquisition: Contrasting Theoretical Approaches*. Cambridge: Cambridge University Press.

Rowland, C. (2014). *Understanding Child Language Acquisition*. London: Routledge.

Tomasello, M. (2003). *Constructing a Language: A Usage-based Theory of Language Acquisition*. Cambridge, MA: Harvard University Press.

9

HOW CHILDREN LEARN THE MEANING OF WORDS

LEARNING OUTCOMES

By the end this chapter you should:

- Understand how early experience tunes infants' sensitivity to particular sounds that are important in the language that they hear.

- Know what W. V. O. Quine termed the 'problem of translation' – that a word can refer to several (perhaps even infinite) aspects of the world, and that children need to home in on a speaker's intended meaning.

- Understand some of the biases in early word learning: the whole object and taxonomic assumptions, mutual exclusivity, and the shape and function biases.

- Learn the three major theoretical perspectives on how children learn words, the constraints, associative learning, and social-pragmatic approaches, and the evidence in favour and against each.

- Know that these theoretical positions have become somewhat blended in recent years and understand how the emergentist coalition model is an example of a hybrid theory.

- Consider the effect of the complexity of communication on how language is constructed.

9.1 GRASPING THE MEANING OF WORDS

We started to examine language in Chapter 8 by presenting the approach that focuses on an abstract description of language in terms of sentences. In the tradition of this approach, it is customary to study *grammar* or *syntax*, which provides a characterisation of all the rules and principles that govern language. Our conclusion was that we need to take into account other aspects of communication and three broad aspects or levels of analysis are usually recognised in linguistics. Learning a new word involves *phonology*, mapping its sounds and sound patterns onto the network of sounds involved in a language, and *semantics*, or word meaning. It is the final category of *pragmatics*, which concerns how language is used in conversational contexts, that we concluded our discussion with in Chapter 8 and which we expand on here. Any analysis of language must take into account these aspects as parts of a whole system of communication.

In order to bring together Chapters 5 and 6 on preverbal interaction and Chapter 8 on how children come to understand the flow of human speech, we move to what most texts on language development consider to be a simpler level of analysis than syntax – the individual word. This is usually dealt with as the starting point for the acquisition of speech. We first ask the question about what happens to sounds that occur in one language but not in another. We also consider the amazing feat that word learning is – infants have to unpack a stream of sounds to understand the words of their native language or languages. The second section charts the extraordinary development of children's vocabulary in order to emphasise that the crucial factor in language and its development is how we convey and grasp meaning. The expansion of an individual child's vocabulary is so rapid that researchers have long been intrigued by how human beings so effortlessly come to understand and use words. The third section of the chapter summarises the main theoretical perspectives on word learning and also the problems that children encounter in learning a language. We will explore key research supporting the three main, and competing, perspectives before returning once again to the question of meaning in communication. This, we feel, is the crux of the issue of how children learn words. We conclude the chapter by building up a picture of the nonverbal interactions and early verbal exchanges between toddlers and their caregivers to reflect on the developmental processes that facilitate language learning. Centrally, we ask how are word meanings learned?

9.2 WHAT DO BABIES NEED TO KNOW BEFORE THEY CAN LEARN WORDS?

Learning to listen: tuning into the sound system of a language

To study how children learn a language on what age group should we start to focus? That is, when do children begin to discriminate the sounds that we identify as 'words'? Well, many children start using their first words soon after their first birthday, so perhaps we should commence with 1-year-old children? The answer to this must be a resounding 'no'.

Even before they start to use words babies are already learning a great deal about language and conversation, and much of this concerns the phonology of what they hear. As we have already discussed in Chapters 5 and 6, during this time infants make significant advances in the perception and production of language, as well as in communication through gestures. So, what does a baby have to learn? There is evidence that even newborn infants prefer their mother's voice to that of another woman (DeCasper & Fifer, 1980) and they show a preference for their native language: this preference must be based on their experience with language before birth (Gervain & Mehler, 2010). They even demonstrate a preference for a story heard prenatally, suggesting that babies hear speech and learn something about language before birth (DeCasper, Lecanuet, & Busnel, 1994; MacWhinney, 2015). What can infants hear in their mother's womb? Just as they can make basic visual discriminations (Reid et al., 2017), it seems that they hear the prosodic pattern of their native language – its rhythm and intonation. We know this because babies can still tell the difference between different languages when the speech samples were filtered to leave only the prosodic pattern (Gervain & Mehler, 2010). We are not suggesting that mothers should give their unborn infants language lessons, but that infants seem to naturally pick up something about the rhythm of their native language in the uterus.

Even before encountering the problem of what words mean, babies already have to overcome a whole series of other problems. They have to learn which speech sounds are important in their native language. Out of the possible speech sounds, or *phones*, any particular human language makes use of some subset of these sounds. For example, the various versions of English use about 45 phones, while Zulu uses other types of speech sounds, several of which are different types of clicks. The speech sounds that are meaningful in a particular language are called *phonemes*. Adult speakers classify the speech they hear into the categories that are important in their native language. That is, even though sound varies on a continuous dimension, adults group speech sounds together into those categories, or phonemes, which are meaningful in their native language. This means that adults overlook distinctions between speech sounds that may be important in other languages. For example, in English the phoneme /b/ comes before the vowel /ee/ in the word 'beet', and it also comes before the vowel /oo/ in the word 'boot', but although English speakers hear these both as 'b's they are actually different sounds. So the phoneme /b/ can be different depending on the vowel that follows it. How then do English speakers deal with this variability in phonemes? Wouldn't they have trouble telling what is a /b/ and what isn't a /b/? In fact, English speakers don't notice the difference between these two types of /b/ and just group both together. That is, adults perceive speech sounds within categories and variability within a category is not even noticed, an ability that is called *categorical perception*. So, there may be different kinds of /b/ but adults perceive them all as belonging to the same category if that distinction is not important in their language (Gervain & Mehler, 2010; Werker, 1989; Werker & Tees, 1999).

The question that arises here is when can infants do this? Since they can't be asked, other methods must be used to determine if they notice the distinctions between speech sounds.

In one procedure, *high-amplitude sucking* (or 'HAS') infants have a pacifier in their mouth and when they suck on it they hear a sound. After they have heard the same sound a number of times babies get bored with it and tend to slow down with their sucking rate – in scientific terminology, they *habituate*. If infants are then presented with a different sound, and if they can tell the difference between the new sound and the old sound, they should begin sucking again (*dishabituate*). But if they cannot tell the difference they do not resume sucking. This method can be used to find out if young infants from one month to four months can tell the difference between various sounds. Research shows that their abilities are very similar to those of adults. Babies perceive speech sounds in categories: they can tell the difference between a /pa/ and a /ba/, but not between various different /pa/s. These sounds are very brief, about 25 milliseconds, and there is little to distinguish between them except that the lips are more pursed (or rigid) when the sound is made. Yet it seems that infants are able to categorise these subtle speech sounds soon after birth. In a number of studies since the first demonstration of this effect (starting with Eimas, Siqueland, Jusczyk, & Vigorito, 1971), it has been shown that infants can discriminate nearly every phonetic category on which they have been tested, but they are usually not able to discriminate the differences within a single phonemic category (Werker, 1989; Werker & Tees, 1999). This is not a uniquely human skill as categorical perception has been found in several mammals, including chinchillas (Kuhl & Miller, 1975).

What is even more interesting is that infants seem to be able to make distinctions between speech sounds that are not used in their native language. If babies can do this then it might be expected that adults can also do so. But this is something that adults usually cannot do. For example, a Japanese-speaking adult cannot tell the difference between the English /ra/ and /la/, because this is not a difference that is meaningful in Japanese (Japanese uses a single phoneme that combines the two English phonemes). English speakers have difficulty perceiving the difference between the two /p/ phones that are used as different phonemes in Thai (Werker, 1989).

Janet Werker (1989) explored how speech perception develops or becomes adult-like. In order to address this question a method was needed to work with infants between about 6 and 12 months. HAS does not work so well with older infants because they are not so interested in sucking. Furthermore, a method was needed that could be used with older children and adults as well. Her team used the *Infant Head Turn* procedure in which infants hear a series of slightly different versions of the same phoneme (e.g. /ba/) every two seconds. Then, randomly, a new phoneme is heard. For example, after repeatedly hearing 'ba', 'ba', 'ba', 'ba', 'ba', a new phoneme, 'da', 'da', is heard. Babies learn that when they hear a change from one phoneme to a new one a toy animal with sounds and lights will be turned on to the side, so they learn to turn to look in expectation of this rewarding sight. After learning this, a head turn indicates that an infant has detected a difference between the sounds. The babies are sitting on their parents' lap, but cannot be unintentionally cued because the caregiver wears sound-attenuating earphones. Older children and adults are asked simply to press a button when they hear a difference (Werker, 1989).

One of the contrasts used in this research was a difference between two types of 't' that are not distinguished in English but are in Hindi (Werker, 1989). Werker and her colleagues found that 6- to 8-month-old infants from English-speaking families, like the Hindi-speaking adults, were able to tell the difference between the two types of 't', but by about one year of age these infants no longer had this ability. Infants from Hindi-speaking families, in contrast, could still hear the difference. So the loss of ability clearly depends on the type of language that the infant hears. These results have been replicated with other languages, such as two types of 'k' from a native North American language of the Interior Salish family (called Nthlakapmx or Thompson) (Werker, 1989; Werker & Tees, 1999). Although these were cross-sectional studies the result has also been found in a longitudinal study in which six infants were tested every two months. In this study, it was found that by 12 months the babies from English-speaking families had lost the ability to tell the difference between the speech sounds that were not important in their language (Werker, 1989; Werker & Tees, 1999). Research also shows that a sensitivity to the various tones for the same vowel in Chinese Mandarin are present in 6-month-olds in English speaking cultures but this discrimination is not made in 12-month-olds (Mattock & Burnham, 2006).

This evidence suggests that young infants have the ability to tell the difference between various speech sounds, but that if this ability is not used they lose it at about one year, a process known as perceptual narrowing (Maurer, & Werker, 2014). It is possible to recover this ability but it is difficult. People who had studied Hindi for about five years or more could tell the difference between the non-English Hindi syllables, but students studying Hindi at university level for one year could not do this. Similarly, it has been found in other studies that it is only after a year of intensive English training in the United States that Japanese speakers are able to tell the difference between /ra/ and /la/ (Werker, 1989).

RELEARNING TO DISTINGUISH SPEECH SOUNDS

Interestingly, if adult English speakers are tested with shortened forms of the syllables, they are able to distinguish the different sounds (Werker, 1989). The shortened forms of the syllables do not sound like speech at all, but they do still contain the critical acoustic information regarding the difference between the phonemes. This shows that the actual physical ability to hear the difference between various sounds is not lost, but there is some difficulty when it involves speech (that is, when it sounds like speech). It is reversible with enough training. So, what seems to happen between infancy and adulthood is a sort

(Continued)

of reorganisation of the categories of speech sounds rather than the loss of the ability (Werker, 1989). Adults don't lose the ability to tell the difference between phones that are not used in their language. For example, English speakers can still tell the difference between the two types of clicks used in Zulu. These are not sounds that are used in English so reorganisation may not be necessary (Werker, 1989).

Finding words

A further source of difficulty faced by babies in learning a language is telling where one word ends and another one begins. For adults it is difficult to recognise this as a potential problem because we hear separate words and tend to assume that there must be spaces between them, just as there are on a printed page. But printing words with spaces between them is a convention in English that dates from 1400 years ago. In fact, speech is often a continuous stream of sound. If we try to find words when listening to an unfamiliar foreign language, we gain some insight into the problem faced by young children.

Generally, however, children have few problems in solving this complex task. Only occasionally do children and even adults make amusing mistakes known as 'slips of the ear', but they are surprisingly rare (Cutler, 2012). For example, one day when Hannah was listening to a song she told me (JC) that she used to think that a line in that song was 'Teenage mutant ninja turtle stew'. Later on she realised that it was actually 'Teenage mutant ninja turtles too'. In another example, Ulrich and Benjamin were looking at a picture book together and Ulrich said 'Two tulips'. Benjamin corrected him, saying 'No Daddy. One lip, two lips and three lips.'

One possibility might be that infants identify word boundaries sequentially by finding one word, and then another word should start where the first word ends and so on. This strategy requires knowing the words, and may be used when infants learn words that are presented in isolation (MacWhinney, 2015), but it wouldn't always work because words can have other words embedded in them. For example, *fundamentalism* contains fun, fund, fundament, fundamental (and men, meant, mental, and mentalism).

It appears that the strategies babies develop for breaking up speech into words depend on the rhythmic structure of the particular language they are learning. Recent analyses show they do this in part as a result of the probability of different sounds marking intonation boundaries (Saffran, Newport, & Aslin, 1996) and the distribution of sounds (Onnis, Monaghan, Richmond, & Chater, 2005) across an utterance. English and French, for example, differ in their rhythmic structure. In English this is based on a contrast between a strong and then a weak syllable, with the stress usually on the first syllable of a word (Gervain & Mehler, 2010). English speakers use this structure to find word boundaries.

But this strategy would not work in all languages because other languages may be based on different types of rhythmic structure. For example, French speakers seem to use a segmentation procedure based on the syllable (Gervain & Mehler, 2010). Japanese has a rhythmic structure based on a unit that is smaller than a syllable, a *mora*, which Japanese speakers use to segment speech (Cutler, 2012).

The wonder of words

Infants usually produce their first words after 12 months but they understand some words several months before this. That is, they will look at the correct object when an adult provides a familiar label (MacWhinney, 2015). Indeed at 6 months they will look at a picture of a named object more than a control picture, showing that understanding words occurs much earlier than word production (Bergelson & Swingley, 2012). The most common words they learn are names for specific individuals (e.g. 'Mama', 'Dadda'), objects ('car'), or substances (e.g. 'milk', 'juice'). Other common words include action verbs like 'give', adjectives like 'big', greetings like 'hi', and sanctions like 'no!' and 'hot!' (Macnamara, 1972). By 15 months infants understand about 50 words but they do not produce 50 words until 20 months. At 2 years of age children's vocabulary is about 150 words on average, but it can range from 10 up to 450 words (MacWhinney, 2015). These data tell us a lot about early word learning. First, as we note above, the child's comprehension (known as 'receptive vocabulary') is always considerably in advance of what they can say ('expressive vocabulary'). This is because it takes toddlers time to be able to articulate words and remember how to produce them. Second, children at the same age differ significantly in their language abilities. There is more variability in language development than in other areas of development, in part because language is such a multifaceted skill – involving both articulation and cognitive abilities.

At about 18 months there is what has been labelled a 'naming explosion' during which children begin rapidly learning a large number of new words. About this age their vocabularies start increasing at an amazing rate. At 30 months 569 was the median number of words children *produced* (Fenson et al., 1994). The number of words children *understand* increases from about 10,000 at age 6 to approximately 40,000 by age 10 (Anglin, 1993), so development occurs at a faster rate once children enter formal education. As a result of this, there are critics of the idea that the vocuabulary 'explosion' occurs in the second year (Bloom, 2000). Children also learn more about how to figure out the meanings of words they haven't heard before, based on their general knowledge of how words are derived from other words, and this is thought to explain the increase in the number of words learned (Anglin, 1993). It is agreed that the development of language is an extraordinary accomplishment, possibly unique to humans. So how do young children perform such an amazing feat?

Learning the names for objects might appear to be a simple case to start with, but the child has to figure out which object is being referred to. When an adult and child are attending to the same object, and the adult labels it, each needs to know that the other is attending to the same object. If the child is looking at a rabbit when an adult says 'spoon' the child might become confused, or inadvertently harm the family pet, if she heard 'put the spoon in your mouth'! But errors happen rarely and in an orderly and informative way (see below). How is it that children avoid making this sort of mistake? Achieving this 'joint attention' should be quite easy if the adult does all the work and is careful only to label objects when the child is focused on them. Research on this issue suggests that, at the beginning of the second year, parents do much of this work (making sure that they are talking about the thing their toddler is looking at). Of course, parents cannot always be consistent in doing this yet children don't seem to get confused. Toddlers soon start to play an active role in this process. By 18 months or even earlier, they are able to check what an adult is looking at when that person uses a new word (Baldwin, 1995) and by age two children can learn new words simply by overhearing someone labelling objects (Akhtar, Jipson, & Callanan, 2001).

Children certainly do learn new words quickly. To begin with parents will usually be able to keep track of which words their child knows, but around the middle of their second year children will be learning so rapidly that the parents will lose track. The complexities and difficulties of how this happens, however, tend to be masked by the apparent ease with which these young children, who cannot yet tie their own shoes or even do buttons up, add to their vocabularies. How does this happen? At first glance it all may seem straightforward. After all, what could be simpler than learning a new word? We do it all the time and it doesn't seem particularly difficult. Yet, learning words is not so straightforward. We can't give babies a definition of the new word because they wouldn't understand those words either. For example, we can't tell a 14-month-old infant that a ball is a round object that you play with, or that a rabbit is a small furry mammal that hops (not a cupped object you put in your mouth!). Even though a dictionary definition wouldn't work for a child, couldn't we just point to something like a rabbit and say 'look at the rabbit'? For a small child with a limited vocabulary this seems like the only way to teach her a word like 'rabbit', because the language needed for a verbal explanation would be useless. Yet in some cultural groups toddlers pick up terms just by watching and witnessing adults and older children in everyday conversation (Bryce Heath, 1983).

Let's reflect briefly on the commonsense explanation for how children learn language – that adults point to an object and say, for example, 'dog' or 'doggie'. Such a direct correspondence between the object and the label has been suggested by many philosophers, such as John Locke some three hundred years ago. But if a child hears 'dog' when looking at a dog, she may still not know what the word means. It could mean brown, Golden Retriever, animal, puppy, big, fast, running, nose, tail, or bad, animal, mammal, or even be the name of that particular animal. There are countless possible meanings of the word. How can a child narrow down all these possibilities (Markman, 1990)?

This question amounts to what the philosopher W. V. O. Quine (1960) calls the problem of translation (Quine is always known by his initials rather than his first name). Quine asks us to imagine that a linguist is visiting an unknown country to learn the native language and write a manual for translating it into English. Now imagine that a rabbit hops by and a native speaker says 'gavagai'. How does the linguist figure out what 'gavagai' means? At first it might appear obvious that it means 'rabbit', but if you think about this a bit more you'll see that there are actually many other things that it could mean – 'white' or 'furry' or 'ears' or 'medium-sized', or even 'fast' or 'lunch' And it is easy to make up far stranger possibilities. Some of Quine's favourite examples were 'An undetached part of a rabbit is over there', 'Rabbithood is instantiated over there', or 'A stage in the history of a rabbit is over there'.

Even for non-philosophers, the general problem here is that there appears to be an almost infinite number of possible meanings for any new word. But very young children seem to have no difficulty in unpacking intended meanings. They learn new words with ease and speed, and without seeming to consider Quine's possibilities such as 'rabbithood'. So how do they do it? Well, even though there are many possible meanings children, and adults, tend to assume that 'gavagai', used in that situation, means 'rabbit'. That is, we assume the word refers to the whole object (and is an example of a class which shares the same features).

Lexical principles

It has been proposed that children solve the problem of how to test the limitless number of hypotheses about possible meanings of new words because they possess knowledge about, or easily learn the constraints on, possible word meanings. These help to narrow down or somehow limit the possibilities. That is, children are biased language learners. There are a number of such hypothesised constraints and we summarise four of these.

One of these proposed constraints is the expectation that a new word refers to the object that is being identified and not a part or an attribute. This *whole object assumption* would cut down on the number of possible meanings, so that when an adult points to an animal and says 'look at the dog' it is clear that he is not referring to the legs or the tail or a property like muddy (Markman, 1990). A number of studies have found that children between two and five (there is even some evidence from 18-month-olds) will assume that a new word refers to a whole object, not just a part or a property, such as the material it is made out of (Bloom, 2000).

A second, related, constraint is the *taxonomic assumption*, according to which 'labels refer to objects of the same kind rather than objects that are thematically related' (Markman, 1990, p. 59). Young children's tendency to make this assumption allows them to learn labels for categories. Although young children have a tendency to sort things into groups based on thematic relations, such as putting a rabbit with a carrot and a dog with a bone, when it comes to learning new words they seem to overcome this bias and instead group together objects that are similar (Golinkoff, Mervis, & Hirsh-Pasek, 1994). This is something of a remarkable achievement given, for example, that the term 'doggie' can refer to a chihuahua and also a German shepherd.

A third type of constraint is the assumption that words will only have one meaning, which has been called 'the novel-name-nameless-category' (Mervis & Bertrand, 1994) and principle of contrast (Clark 1988), but is usually known as the *mutual exclusivity bias* (Markman & Wachtel, 1988). This, in combination with the whole object and taxonomic assumptions, can make it easier to learn new words. For example, if children are presented with a pair of objects, one familiar and one new, and then hear a new word they will tend to assume that it refers to the unfamiliar object. But they still have to learn words such as their dog's name as well as words for parts of objects such as legs, nose, tail, puppy, and brown. To do this each child must ignore or override the whole object assumption. To explain this development it has been proposed that since children assume a word can only have one meaning, once a child has learned the word 'dog' and she hears the word 'tail' she will assume it couldn't mean the same thing as 'dog' and so she must look for another meaning such as a salient part of the dog. In one study, a new word was used with 3- to 4-year-olds in the context of either an object with a known label or an object without a known label. For example, Susan Carey presented a child with two objects, one red and the other dark green, and then asked the child, 'Can you pass me the chromium one, not the red one, the chromium one?' Although technically a word which can identify colour, the word 'chromium' is not in most 3-year-olds' vocabulary (and it usually refers to a material quality). The mutual exclusivity bias helps children learn new words other than object labels, because if a child already knows the name for red and an adult points to two objects one of which is not red, the child needs to look for the object that is not red. Carey and Bartlett (1978) found that 3-year-olds could perform this task well. More recent studies show that this ability is present reliably at 24 months and develops further between that age and 30 months (Bion, Borovsky, & Fernald, 2013).

Two further constraints are the 'shape bias' and the 'function bias'. The *shape bias* refers to a tendency to give the same name to two objects that are not identical but share some qualities. For example, the label 'fork' for a preschooler's plastic dining implement can be used to identify a metal one or even a garden digging tool. This need to generalise across items with very different uses was pointed out by one of the great developmental psycholinguists of the twentieth century, Roger Brown (1957). The term 'shape bias' was used to describe this tendency by Landau, Smith, and Jones (1988). They showed children (aged 2 and 3) and adults a completely new object (made especially for the study) and then seven further novel objects. One of these was identical to the first object while the other six differed in one way, either by colour, shape, or size. They compared a 'naming' condition ('this is a dax') with a control condition where no name was mentioned. The participant was asked which of the six new objects was also a 'dax' (the 'yes or no task'), or which was like the one they had seen (the non-naming condition). The adults used shape to identify objects irrespective of whether they were named or not. The children were less accurate but selected objects that looked most like the original, but only when it was named. That 2-year-olds use shape as a guide to applying a label suggests this skill is part of the process of learning language. Shape becomes more salient over development, even into adulthood (Horst & Twomey, 2013). However, Cimpian and Markman (2005) showed the shape bias is not applied spontaneously by preschoolers when the array of objects is complex, so we must not assume shape is a dominant or exclusive influence on the connections that children make.

Similar types of experiments are conducted in which a child is shown some objects and told what they are used for. This is to test for *function bias*. Suppose that a child is presented with three objects. Two look alike while the third looks different but is described as performing the same function as one of the others. If the child chooses the pairing based on what the objects are said to do, she would display the function bias (Gentner, 1978). Again the function bias seems to emerge in the third year of life (Casler & Kelemen, 2005). An interesting question is how shape and function might compete to guide the child's attention in situations where children generalise across different objects. The evidence suggests that before the age of 5 word–object connections are made on the basis of shape, but by 6 years there is a shift in preference towards function (Merriman, Scott, & Marazita, 1993). What happens if two biases compete? The evidence suggests that demonstrating an object's function trumps the shape bias (Butler & Markman, 2014; Diesendruck, Markson, & Bloom, 2003). Having described some of the main 'constraints' on learning we need now to discuss the theoretical accounts of how these emerge in, and are used by, language learners.

9.3 THEORIES OF WORD LEARNING

In this section we compare and contrast the three prototypical accounts of word learning – the constraints, associative, and social pragmatic approaches. We explore variations within these accounts and hybrid models which attempt to combine two of the three. Much contemporary discussion of the nature of word learning, and the errors that children make, has for the past thirty years hinged on the nature of the rules that children abide by and guide development. So, descriptions of the theories usually start with the 'constraints' approach, which identifies these principles. We follow suit, but we hold back on introducing the third theoretical perspective until the end of this section.

Are constraints on word learning determined by genes?

That children seem to show similar biases to learning words according to their function, shape or membership of a taxonomic category, has led several authors to assume that we are naturally inclined to make distinctions between the identity (what the object is) and meaning (what the object does). This is called the *constraints approach*

(Markman, 1990), as each of the biases is thought to limit the possible ways in which the language learner will interpret a word. Yet, as Ambridge and Lieven (2011) point out, the term can be used in two contrasting ways. First, it can refer to the same innate principles to which we referred in Chapter 8 with reference to Chomsky's theory of grammar, just that it now refers to innate word learning principles. The second use of the term 'constraint' relies less on the idea of innate knowledge and instead reflects the belief that we are born with key attentional skills to make quick associations between aspects of the world, like associations between a sound (word) and the object to which it refers. The basic idea behind the constraints approach (particularly the first, most typical, version defined here) is that the learner tries to learn new words by creating a list of possible hypotheses about how the new word maps onto the real world, and then begins a process of eliminating incorrect hypotheses. The goal is to acquire the correct mapping between word and world. The problem that Quine pointed out is that there are just too many possible hypotheses to be tested. From this perspective, the child must somehow be given a head start in this process, and that head start is provided by children having built-in constraints that rule out some hypotheses before they are even seriously considered – that is, children must be biased learners.

It was suggested that initially language learners rely upon the ability to grasp the link between a word and an object, and then move to a stage where they make classifications of types of objects (Golinkoff et al., 1994). Over the past three decades, much of the debate concerning how children learn words has been over whether the concept of innate modules explains biases like the shape and function biases, mutual exclusivity, and the whole object assumption. Each approach has its own problems. The nativist claim rests on the principle that there is what is termed a dedicated fast-mapping system for word learning (Carey & Bartlett, 1978). Behind this idea are a number of assumptions, notably that the constraints apply only to language learning and not more general cognitive skills. To test this claim, Lori Markson and Paul Bloom (1997) looked at mutual exclusivity in preschoolers in order to examine their ability to infer a new word by reference to a known word (like the example of 'chromium' in the previous section). To test the specificity of this skill they devised a condition where the child hears information about the object but not its name. The child was told either that one object is called a 'koba' or that 'my uncle gave this to me'. They are then asked to identify the 'blicket' (another novel word) and in *both* conditions they choose the object that was not referred to. These findings suggest that the skills pinpointed by the term 'constraints' reflect more general inference skills and not dedicated modules for distinguishing between word–object associations.

Katherine Nelson (1988, 1990) has been particularly forthright in arguing against the constraints approach. One criticism has already been mentioned. This is that these assumptions are really biases, not 'constraints', because children have to overcome or abandon them sometimes to learn certain kinds of words, such as names for parts, substances, and abstract entities, or verbs, determiners ('the' or 'a'), and conjunctions ('and', 'but', 'so', etc.).

Nelson's (1988) point is that calling these 'constraints' doesn't tell us much. We can see that children's behaviour is constrained, but the question is why or how? As Ambridge and Lieven (2011) suggest, the constraints stipulated by these theorists describe only a few of the legion of problems faced in identifying the meaning of a word – for example, that a word will refer to the same object tomorrow as it does today. In addition, the constraints account cannot explain how young children come to give multiple labels to the same object – for example, that this 'cat' is also called 'Rover' and is an 'animal' (Mervis, Golinkoff, & Bertrand, 1994). Indeed, Nelson argues that these constraints are the *result* of early word learning, and therefore they cannot serve as an explanation of how children learn their first words. Some constraints theorists are open on this point. There is general agreement that these word-learning constraints by themselves could not solve the word-learning problem.

As a result, currently researchers either focus on specific 'constraints' or develop an alternative theoretical account. One popular candidate for the latter seems to be somewhat improbable, as it argues that the child learns words by association, which has been discussed and dismissed in Chapter 7 with reference to chimp communication. However, proponents of the modern associationist account argue that they are not simply repeating the mistakes and weaknesses of behaviourism (Samuelson & Smith, 1998). Samuelson and Smith's associationist approach takes into account the context in which a word is linked with an object and then remembered in this setting with particular perceptual cues. To demonstrate her case, Linda Smith conducted a preferential looking procedure in which varied groups of objects were presented to 1-year-olds over a series of trials in quick succession (Smith & Yu, 2008). In each group the infant heard over a loud speaker the novel 'word' that identified *one* of the objects. The association between word and picture was always unclear until and unless all 30 pairs of trials had been conducted. Given that infants showed a looking preference towards the labelled object, they concluded that some associational (or 'statistical') learning was taking place, and that this involved both remembering and blocking because on half the trials when it was presented the word associated with a particular picture was not uttered.

Smith's associative learning account also applies to individual constraints like the shape bias. It holds that shape provides an excellent cue for the child to link similar objects with the same identifying term (e.g. Smith, Jones, & Landau, 1996; Samuelson & Smith, 2005). An association develops following repeated co-occurrences. Therefore, she argues that the shape bias is exclusive to naming, and does not emerge until children already know a substantial number of words for objects. An early vocabulary dominated by nouns referring to solid objects in shape-based categories has been found to accentuate shape bias (Samuelson, 2002). However, other theorists take an alternative position. The shape-as-cue account of Paul Bloom (2000) blends previous theory about the role of the function of objects with the theory of mind literature (see Chapter 11). He suggests that an object's shape tells us about the referential intent of its maker. Manufactured objects (which are termed 'artifacts') look alike because we intend them to have the same purpose. A sensitivity to shape-as-cue emerges before a child develops sufficient vocabulary. Even at 15 months children will select objects on the basis of the similarity of shape to ones that are similar in terms of colour or texture (Graham & Diesendruck, 2010).

For the past twenty years there have been continuous debates between the proponents of the two perspectives we have discussed so far (constraints vs associative learning). The state of play between these has always been that some data support one theory over another, but for reasons we discuss below no evidence will completely show the superiority of one theory over the other. Two moves should be mentioned here. First, each account has acknowledged the complexity of factors that influence the child, particularly the richness of the learning environment. Proponents of the associative account also maintain that word learning takes place as a result of toddlers' attentional skills and developing memory. They refer to the cues provided by more advanced language users and suggest that the prompts they give towards labelled objects, like behavioural cues (e.g. pointing), facilitate the associations a child can make (Smith, Suanda, & Yu, 2014). They also suggest that the contrasts between stimuli enable such associations to take place (e.g. Monaghan & Mattock, 2012; Suanda, Magwanya, & Namy, 2014). Monaghan and Mattock show that learning words is even more complex than Quine suggested, as children hear many words in each utterance and only some of these serve a 'referring' function, i.e. they identify or label objects. In an analysis of a large corpus of child–adult communication Monaghan and Mattock show that children use several cues, like the grammatical structure of a sentence, to identify the referring word.

A second move to bridge the various competing hypotheses consists of the development of hybrid theories that attempt to draw upon more than one perspective and use these different approaches to explain the phenomena and changes that occur at different points in development. The most widely discussed is the *emergentist coalition model* (Golinkoff & Hirsh-Pasek, 2006; Hollich, Hirsh-Pasek, & Golinkoff, 2000). Like other models it suggests that children draw upon a mixture of social, attentional, cognitive, and linguistic skills in order to link items and actions in the world to words. The idea is that infants form correct word–object associational links, even as early as 10 months of age. As children become more competent in interactions with others, Hollich et al. (2000) argue, drawing on the research of Baldwin (1991), that social skills drive the explosion of language development from 18 months. Although the emergentist coalition model may be a valiant attempt at reconciling positions that were seen as incompatible, it might be perceived as being a fudge, in that it assumes that there is a transition from association to social cues without fully demonstrating it. We need clearer evidence to show that such a transition takes place.

In sum, neither the constraints nor associative learning positions explain the nature of early word learning. As a result, each seems to feed off each other. Ambridge and Lieven (2011, p. 63) show how even within the same theoretical account there are references to apparently contrasting positions:

Hollich, Hirsch-Pasek, Golinkoff and Bloom (2000: 10) claim that 'The solution [to Quine's problem] rests within the head of the child. The child is predisposed to make certain hypotheses over others about word-meaning.' Yet elsewhere (2000, p. 17) they claim that 'principles … are the *products* of attentional/associationistic factors in early development, which then become the *engines* of subsequent development'.

9.4 THE SOCIAL-PRAGMATIC ACCOUNT OF EARLY WORD LEARNING

We place special emphasis on a third account of word learning, which is termed the *social-pragmatic approach,* because we feel that this allows us to understand how infants unpack the flow of interaction and speech that is both directed to and spoken around them. This approach has a long history and can be traced to the work of Jerome Bruner (1983), Katherine Nelson (1985) and others in the 1970s and 1980s, and forms the basis of discussion in the more recent analyses of Paul Bloom (2000) and Michael Tomasello (2003).

The parent–child system: an ideal opportunity for word learning?

One reason why we favour the social pragmatic approach is that the infant's language-learning environment has long been identified as being structured so that a grasp of language is possible. In the first section of the chapter we summarised the research on the topic that babies have managed to break up speech into separate words, many of which have similar sounds that need to be distinguished, but their problems are still far from over. Infants still have to figure out which word, if any, in a sentence like 'look at the rabbit', actually refers to an object. They have both to coordinate attention with the adult and then grasp what is being referred to. Just as children solve so many other problems with relative ease, they also seem to encounter little difficulty here. However, the occasional mistake children make is fairly obvious. For example, when Jeremy's Hannah was about 20 months old she referred to jumping as '*much*' and stuck to this for several months. At this time Hannah had finally managed to jump and get both feet off the ground. This was a major accomplishment that she had been trying to achieve for some time, and needless to say she was very pleased about being able to do this. When she was jumping she was told encouraging things like 'You're jumping so *much*' or 'You're doing so *much* jumping'. Jeremy realised afterwards that he may have emphasised the word '*much*' and perhaps that was why she thought it was the important word in the sentence. Perhaps she relied on how her parents stressed the word or sometimes placed it at the end of a sentence? Systematic diary records have long shown that toddlers tend to use words in the same setting and context as their parents did (Harris, Barrett, Jones, & Brookes, 1988).

The example of Hannah's use of 'much' brings out an addition level of analysis – the *prosodic* level (i.e. the pattern of intonation in the sound stream). Certain words tend to be accented or stressed. In the case of learning names for objects it seems that parents sometimes say a new word by itself, or emphasise it and place it at the end of a sentence. This should usually help children, and Hannah's mistake was common among the toddlers in Margaret Harris and her colleagues' study. Adults' ways of introducing new words is one aspect of how the way adults talk to children may help with language learning. The style of speech adults use with children has been termed 'baby talk', 'motherese' ('father-ese' for dads), or 'parentese', but is now usually referred to as 'child-directed speech'. In child-directed speech, the pitch of the voice is higher and more variable and the intonation more exaggerated than in speech to adults. Given that it consists of shorter sentences with simpler words that are often repeated, adults may well do this to maximise an infant's opportunity to unpack the stream of language and learn new words, or to attract the child's attention. Even children as young as four years tend to change the way they speak when talking to a baby or younger child (Shatz & Gelman, 1973).

Just because many of us talk to children in a different way does not necessarily mean that this has an influence on language development. Longitudinal research shows that the mother's use of child-directed speech and the child's own ability to segment (i.e. separate words in) speech when the infant is 7 months predicts the extent of the child's vocabulary at 2 years (Newman, Rowe, & Ratner, 2016). The research also suggests that mothers and fathers may provide different language experiences for their children, perhaps because they interact with them in different settings (Lewis & Gregory, 1987). Fathers' child-directed speech varies across cultures. For example, in a comparison of fathers in Tanna, Vanuatu, and in North America it was found that both groups adjusted their speech and used a greater range in pitch to infants, but Vanuatu fathers use a higher pitch on aver-age, whereas North Americans slow down their speech more (Broesch & Bryant, 2017). Over forty years ago Jean Berko Gleason mused over why some studies showed that fathers use more complex language to their toddlers and why some studies seemed (and continue) to show that paternal language to infants is correlated with a child's language production. She argued that in being less sensitive fathers, paradoxically, stretched their child's skills (Gleason, 1975).

Finally, there is the issue of culture in the debate regarding the role of parental input. In the 1980s Bambi Schieffelin and Elinor Ochs (1983, 1986) reported on the language development of children in the Kaluli people of Papua New Guinea. In this culture, it was forbidden for adults to use child-directed speech, because it was felt that this would cause learning difficulties in the child. Although under this system children's language learning was slightly delayed, they did catch up with their American peers in their later preschool years. These reports were often taken to mean that child-directed speech was not common across cultures. However, more recently researchers conducting system-atic acoustic analysis found that mothers in two small-scale traditional societies in Fiji and Kenya slowed their speech and increased their pitch and variability in pitch when talking to babies compared to speaking to adults in the same way as middle-class American mothers do (Broesch & Bryant, 2015). So, the question of parental input across cultures has been reopened. Catherine Snow (1994) considered the issue of language development in cultures in which parents do not adjust their language to suit the child, or recast her statements. She suggested that language learning in a socially responsive environment is the most well-known route to acquiring language. In cultures like that of the Kaluli in Papua New Guinea, where parents believe that they should teach their children the correct adult form, there may be another pathway to language through explicit teaching of discourse structures.

Similarly, the role of the language children hear was studied cross culturally by comparing children's language environment in a Yucatec Mayan village to that of children growing up in families in the United States (Schneidman & Goldin-Meadow, 2012). Whereas on average three people were present with the US children, an average of seven people – including aunts, uncles, and other children – were present with the children in the Mayan village. For the US toddlers at 14 months, 69% of the speech they heard was directed to them. In contrast, it was found that in the Mayan village child-directed speech was 21% at 13 months, and gradually rose to 43% at 18 months and to 60% at 35 months. As reported above, it has been found that by 30 months children are proficient at learning new words from speech they overhear (Akhtar et al., 2001). The question then is do Mayan children pick up language from overheard speech? The answer appears to be no. It was still the speech from adults directed to toddlers that was correlated with the number of words the child learned. Furthermore, it was found that the type of words the children learned were those they heard from adults talking to them, and those words overheard were less often picked up (Shneidman & Goldin-Meadow, 2012). The roles of parental input and child-directed speech still need to be clarified.

The social-pragmatic account: strong and weak hypotheses

A central assumption of the social pragmatic approach is that children construct an understanding of words *within* social interactions, not simply by employing a few constraints or learning by association. Yet the social-pragmatic approach represents a variety of views and the data for each are not completely conclusive. Even the theorists who assume that the child has a natural ability to pick up the meaning of words realise that word learning cannot be solved just by constraints, because these also have to be used in conjunction with social-pragmatic cues about a person's referential intentions in specific settings. For example, even if children make (or in nativist terms 'have') a whole object assumption they still have to know which object is being referred to.

Michael Tomasello rejects the metaphor of children mapping words onto aspects of the world, which is fundamental to the approaches based on constraints or simple associations. Instead, he adopts the view that words (and other linguistic symbols) are used 'to invite others to experience situations in particular ways'. Therefore, 'attempting to map word to world will not help in situations in which the very same piece of real estate may be called: "the shore" (by a sailor), "the coast" (by a hiker), "the ground" (by a skydiver), and "the beach" (by a sunbather)' (Tomasello, 2001, p. 112). We could go on with this list – for example a biologist might talk about 'the intertidal zone'. Thus the social pragmatic approach focuses on the social nature, and use, of language: a word does not have a single abstract meaning, just as in Chapters 6 and 7 we concluded that children use nonverbal gestures and construct sentences to get a message across. From this perspective, word learning is a social communicative process, turning on what the speaker wishes the listener to attend to in a specific context. Social situations constrain the possible meanings of an utterance. For example, 'the child who knows that his mother wishes him to eat his peas (she is holding them up to his mouth and gesturing) assumes that her utterance is relevant to that intention' (Tomasello, 2001, p. 113). The problem is thus not to determine the abstract meaning of a word (to map the word onto an object), but rather to understand what the other person means to draw attention to. Children learn to attend to what is most relevant.

Not only can individual words be separated from the stream of speech by the language learner, but so too can their function be identified from the way in which they are used. Tomasello and Akhtar (1995, study 1) taught 24-month-old children a new word in two different conditions. In one condition a child watched an experimenter throw two new objects, which the child would not have words for, down a pipe. The experimenter then said 'now modi' and threw the third new object down the pipe. In this case it seems that 'modi' refers to the third object. In a second condition the experimenter did two new things with the new object, and then said 'now modi' and threw it down the pipe. Here, in contrast, it seems that the new word refers to the action not the object. The final action and object were the same in both conditions. These differed only in the preceding actions. Children were then given a comprehension test in which an experimenter said 'Show me ball'; 'Show me bounce'; 'Show me modi'. These requests could be referring to an object or an action. In the first condition described, many of the children acted as if 'modi' referred to the *object*, for example by pointing to it. In contrast, in the second condition children thought that 'modi' referred to the *action*, which they copied. The results of this research suggest that children are not learning words because of constraints, but instead are using their general social cognitive skills (i.e. reading what a particular gesture and/or utterance means in a specific setting) to figure out what the adult is referring to. The most relevant thing in that interaction depends on prior events. Thus, Tomasello (2001) suggests that lexical principles (constraints) are *products* of development. Quine's (1960) problem concerns *radical* translation where it is assumed that two people have no shared culture. But even in different cultures there still may be shared experience based on human ways of living. In the case of children learning a first language, they certainly do share a great deal of culture and understanding of everyday routines with the adults they live with, and this shared understanding can serve as the foundation on which language is based.

So for Tomasello (and we agree) there is a consistency between how children learn preverbal gestures and words. For example, Tomasello and Haberl (2003) conducted a study in which one experimenter shared a toy with a child and left. While she was out a second experimenter brought out a second toy. The first one returned and simply said 'Wow! Look at that … Give it to me please!' Eighteen-month-olds assumed that she was referring to the new toy. In these and other experiments (e.g. Moll, Koring, Carpenter, & Tomasello, 2006) the child is learning about another person's orientation to an object and not anything that is specifically related to language, but the social pragmatic account holds that these are related.

Indeed it has long been assumed that joint attention is foundational for language learning (Bates, 1979). In the second year, gaze following is used in some but not all situations in word learning. Dare Baldwin (1993) conducted a word-learning study in which in one condition, known as 'discrepant labelling', the experimenter used a new word to label a new toy she was attending to while the child was playing with another new toy. She found that 18-month-olds identified the correct object, but younger children did not learn the new word for the object at above the level of chance. They also did not systematically apply the new word to the object they were playing with. One-year-olds may learn words only when joint attention is achieved, while toddlers become proficient at realising the speaker's perspective is important and will often check where the other person is looking. In the past few years it has been possible to conduct experiments in which a small eye-tracker can identify the looking patterns of both the adult and the infant in establishing joint attention. This line of research shows that focusing on (and manipulating) a toy is even more likely to result in a shared focus than gaze in attempting to attract the attention of the other interactant (see Chapter 6) (Yu & Smith, 2013). So, there are different ways of establishing joint attention.

Why has the focus on joint attantion been taken to be important? A longitudinal study by Melinda Carpenter and her colleagues (1998) found that the amount of mother–infant joint attention in free play at 10 months correlated with the toddlers' understanding of words 12 months later. This has been replicated for mother–infant pairs in West Africa (Childers, Vaughan, & Burquest, 2007). Does this mean that mother–infant joint attention *causes* or teaches language development? While sympathetic to the idea, Ambridge and Lieven (2011) point out that a number of factors might account for the association, including general influences like social class (which, in turn, may be a proxy for a variety of more specific factors such as good nutrition), or more local influences like the mother's interest in the toddler's development (which presumably will be stable over this time period). So, we must be careful about jumping to the conclusion that mother–infant joint attention causes language development.

Does the lack of a landmark study to show the importance of the social pragmatic account over the other perspectives presented in this chapter suggest that this perspective is no better than the others? It could, for example, easily be argued that the so-called associative learning account is more parsimonious – it offers a simpler explanation and one rule in science is always to go with the simpler explanation if two are on offer. Such a simpler explanation would also be consistent with studies that show that children around their first birthdays learn the names of objects through speakers who give no pragmatic cues (Houston-Price, Plunkett, & Harris, 2005; Smith & Yu, 2008; Werker et al., 1998). However, if we consider these findings against a backdrop of research on adult–infant interaction, it may well be the case that children can learn to perform associations *because* (not despite the fact) they are developing within a highly contingent and stimulating social environment. No study could expose children just to associational cues in the manner provided by Smith and Yu (see the previous section), and we would put our money on such infants not learning any language at all.

SUMMARY AND CONCLUSION

We began this chapter by pointing out some of the difficulties infants encounter in learning a language, which tend to be overlooked by commonsense views of how children learn words. These problems begin with speech perception and learning the categories of speech sounds that are meaningful in the language that young infants experience. Even then infants must still find the boundaries between words, before encountering the problem of determining what the words refer to. Here the way parents talk to young children may play some role in helping them, but they are still faced with figuring out the meanings of new words. The problem, highlighted by Quine (1960), concerning the multiple possible meanings of any new word, has been addressed in three main ways: the constraints, associative learning, and social pragmatic approaches. These approaches are based on different underlying views of the nature of language and meaning, showing that the empirical study of language development is based on philosophical assumptions about meaning (Bruner, 1983). From the perspective of the constraints approach, the problem is viewed as how to map new words onto objects. It has been proposed that infants must have a head start in the process of learning word meaning in the form of constraints on possible word meanings. The associative perspective purports to be about more than the young child being able to make links between sounds and objects, but most of the experimental work within this newer tradition has only attempted to show such connections. In contrast, from the perspective of the social pragmatic approach, meaning depends on the context within a sequence of interaction. People can use words in different ways to convey meaning. In learning word meaning infants must draw on the social pragmatic cues in the particular social situation to figure out the adult's referential intent and thus to determine the meanings of new words. Yes, some words are learned by simple association, but the complexity of language is such that children need an equally rich communicative environment in order to learn the meaning of words. The preceding chapters form the foundation for analysing language development. Furthermore, language is linked to thinking and social understanding as well as morality, which we consider in the remaining chapters of the book.

FURTHER READING

Rowland, C. (2014). *Understanding Child Language Acquisition*. London: Routledge.

Tomasello, M. (2003). *Constructing a Language: A Usage-based Theory of Language Acquisition*. Cambridge, MA: Harvard University Press.

 HOW CHILDREN COME TO CONTROL THEIR BEHAVIOUR

LEARNING OUTCOMES

Having read this chapter you should:

- Be able to identify the components of executive function, notably working memory, set shifting and inhibitory control and how they fit together, plus an example of a test for assessing each skill.

- Be familiar with Miyake et al.'s 'unity with diversity' model of executive function and the differences between the structure of the executive system in preschoolers and elementary school-aged children.

- Be aware of measurement issues in tests of executive function, notably task impurity, test–retest reliability and ecological validity.

- Be aware of the results of twin studies in adult executive function.

- Be able to identify the evidence which shows that children's executive test performance takes place within the complexity of social interactions, thus supporting the developmental pattern proposed by Vygotsky and Luria.

Even as adults we can sometimes find ourselves in circumstances where we will fail to control the tendency toward impetuous or uncontrolled behaviour. Movie stars who pride themselves on being able to get into a role become jibbering idiots when they receive their Oscars or Emmys. In everyday life we leap to a conclusion before working out a more complex and correct means of solving a task, or blurt out a secret (and then regret it!). The historian Roger Smith (1992) pointed out that the history of psychology over the past two centuries has returned repeatedly to the study of how we control impetuous behaviour. Indeed many of the key theories focus on this very topic. Freud's (1910) psychoanalysis was concerned with how we come to control our more basic animal instincts (what he termed the 'Id'), through the process of identifying with more controlled 'love objects', our parents, and developing a 'superego' in which our parents' sanctions are internalised. Similarly the behaviourism of B. F. Skinner (1955) was centred on how societal rules are learned through the gradual shaping of operant conditioning by others around us.

For the past sixty years psychology has rejected these theories in favour of an approach based on the nature and power of thought itself. For example, in 1958 Donald Broadbent published a book entitled *Perception and Communication*. Along with others like Jerome Bruner (Bruner, Goodnow, & Austin, 1956), he identified that a cognitive 'revolution' was taking place. This depicted psychological processes in terms of the links, and flow of information, from the sense organs to an individual's response. The two aims were to describe the components of the mind–brain system and how they fit together. Self-control became an integral part of the models of these processes. This information-processing approach has witnessed constant testing and modification over the decades, with the inclusion of supervisory systems that control the flow of information and regulate behaviour. For example, in 1974 Alan Baddeley and Graham Hitch devised a model to explain the processes of very short-term memory, in the moment after we perceive a stimulus and only maintained through rehearsal (reciting the information repeatedly, as in remembering a phone number). They proposed a working memory model in which information is stored very briefly and either 'worked on' or lost. The idea is that we encounter so much information that we need a set of cognitive processes which select the important details. To do this, Baddeley and Hitch proposed that we initially process visual and auditory information through two different stores (the visuospatial scratchpad and the phonological loop) and these are operated on by a higher-order function (the central executive). The central executive is a dynamic control system that directs, divides, and modifies attention (Baddeley, 1986, 2012; Norman & Shallice, 1980). Indeed Susan Gathercole (1999) pointed out that for the working memory system to become engaged, the person must not simply recall stored information, but manipulate the information that is held in mind. Take, for example, the backward digit span task. In this task, a person is ask to repeat backwards a string of numbers. So, if I say 4 3 6 9 to you, your working memory system will need to operate on each item such that you can recall the string of numbers backwards to me (9 6 3 4) and thus there is an element of supervisory control even in the phonological loop. Such abilities, with their inherent control mechanisms, have become central to the make-up of 'executive function' and refer to a number of inter-related skills. Baddeley, Engle, and Kane (2004) suggest that the ability to control attention ('executive attention') is the central function of working memory.

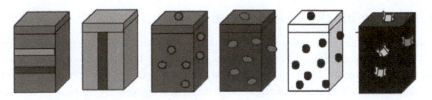

Figure 10.1   Six boxes test for working memory

The six boxes test is a measure of working memory. The memory capacity ('stationary') condition measures capacity. Here the child has to retrieve a reward (e.g. a sticker) in each of these boxes, distinguished by colour and pattern. In the working memory ('scrambled') condition the boxes are hidden and their location changed between trials, so that that child has to remember the colour and pattern of the box, not simply its location. (The figures in this chapter are courtesy of Karen Shimmon.)

In this chapter we describe the way in which the term 'executive function' has become dominant in our thinking about the development of thinking skills, not only in working memory but also in controlling our actions more generally. We start with some definitions and examples of the processes which comprise 'executive function'. These are often regarded as purely 'cognitive' in their structure and many researchers in this diverse area of research have concentrated on the processes and mechanisms of the means of thought. We will attempt to show, first, how these processes are inherently social in their origins and nature. Second, we will briefly describe how executive function skills are difficult to measure, particularly for developmental psychologists because each skill is complex and develops at a rate which may be independent of developments in the other skills. Third, we will explore executive function as a theoretical construct. There are some interesting data that show the variation in scores in a sample of children is highly influenced by genetic factors and we report the leading study that shows this. However, some researchers in developmental psychology have always defined executive functions as social-cognitive processes (not simply as brain processes) and we explore these ideas at the end the chapter.

10.1 EXECUTIVE FUNCTION: THE SKILLS AND HOW THEY FIT TOGETHER

In 2000 a key paper was published by Akira Miyake and his colleagues (Miyake, Friedman, Emerson, Witzki, Howerter, & Wager, 2000) which tested the existence of, and relationships between, a range of cognitive skills that comprise 'executive function', and these are widely discussed as being central constructs. We will describe each of these component skills before reporting on what Miyake and others found.

The building blocks of executive function

First, as we report above, *working memory* (what Miyake calls 'updating', as the memory store is continually changing) is the capacity not only to hold information in mind, but also to be able to recall it in a way that is not simply a rote repetition of what is seen or heard. The boxes task is a good example of a measure tapping the visuospatial scratchpad (see Figure 10.1). Six or eight boxes, each distinctively marked by colour and pattern, are arranged in front of the preschooler who is told that there is a sticker in each for them to win. Between each trial the boxes are hidden and moved around, so the child has to identify which she has opened from the colour/pattern to be rewarded each time.

Inhibitory control (referred to as inhibition by Miyake et al.) refers to the ability to suppress a prepotent response – like rushing to copy 'Simon' when he has not prefaced a command with 'Simon says' in the popular children's game. In one of the most widely used tasks, the Day–Night task, the child has to say 'day' when a picture of the moon and stars is turned over and 'night' when they see the picture of the sun (see Figure 10.2).

Attentional flexibility ('set shifting' in Miyake's terminology) is the ability to change from one way to solve a problem to another complementary means. There are tasks, for example, where instead of using a previously successful rule we have to use another rule. Attentional flexibility refers to the ability to switch between these. In tests for older children and adults, like the Wisconsin Card Sorting task (Berg, 1948), no warning is provided of the need to switch, and children have to pick this up from being told that they selected the wrong card. The most common task for children is the Dimension Change Cart Sort (see Figure 10.3; Frye, Zelazo, & Palfai, 1995).

Figure 10.2   Materials used for the Day–Night task (Gerstadt, Hong, & Diamond, 1994)

In the two top panels are cards representing the inhibition trials while the ones below represent the control trials (see the middle section of the chapter). The child is presented with 16 shuffled sets of cards (sun/moon or the two patterns) which she has to turn over and label.

Figure 10.3 Typical materials used for the card-sort task

The prototype cards stand in front of two boxes and the child sorts the test cards, of a different colour, into the sorting trays (represented by black rectangles here). After six trials sorting by shape (as above) the child is told 'We're not going to play the shape game now, no way, we're going to play the colour game ... you put the red ones in here and the blue ones in here'. Whether colour or shape is used first as sorting dimension is counterbalanced.

Finally, *planning* is usually regarded as the most important, or superordinate, executive skill because we need to combine memory, inhibition, and attentional flexibility in order to conduct complex operations, like writing an essay or boiling an egg. Children's planning is often tested using the Tower of London task (Shallice, 1982), in which the participant needs to move the beads on three pegs, one at a time, to copy another array and this involves moves that do not directly lead to the goal state (see Figure 10.4).

Executive function

So how do these skills fit together? Are they simply different aspects of the same ability, as is predicted by notions of intelligence, or are they discrete or separate? Miyake et al. (2000) assessed a sample of adults on tests of the various executive skills and compared a range of models, depicted in Figure 10.5, to explore how they fit together. They modelled whether there is a single underlying skill (e.g. IQ) against models depicting various combinations of the individual constructs, or no relation between them. Their final model represented in Figure 10.5 is the one that best fitted the data, using a technique known as confirmatory

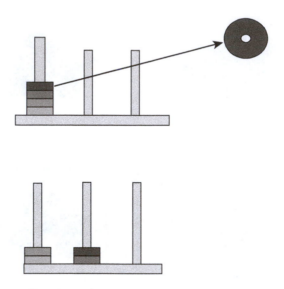

Figure 10.4   The Tower of London task

The child has to move one bead at a time from one peg to another to make her tower (above) look like the tester's (below). In this trial she has to move the blue bead onto the right-hand peg (away from the goal of end state) in order to succeed and this constitutes 'planning'. The procedure starts with two-move solutions and gets progressively more difficult until the child fails two trials with a particular number of moves. This example is a three-move solution – count how many bead moves are required.

factor analysis. This model has two (on the surface contradictory) features. It shows that each of the constituent factors was depicted as a separate component of the model.

However, the curved double arrowed lines between these three constructs were also needed to produce a 'best fit' model. This reveals that the best means of representing the data is one where individual constructs (e.g. Working Memory) each contribute unique variance to the factor 'executive function', while the relationships between each construct were also important. This is called the 'unity with diversity model' because the three skills each contribute unique variance to executive function but they overlap considerably by sharing common variance. A more recent analysis has supported the idea that once common variance between the three constructs is taken into account. Updating and shifting are separate factors, but inhibition appears not to be distinct from the other two components and does not contribute uniquely to executive function (Miyake and Friedman, 2012). The unity with diversity model still receives support, but it might initially consist of two unique contributors.

How do these factors fit together in children and how does development take place? Miyake's research methodology has been applied in several studies of children (Garon Smith, & Bryson, 2008). With preschoolers the analyses suggest that the components of

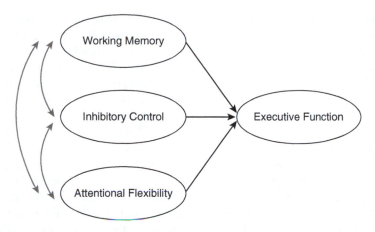

Figure 10.5 The 'unity with diversity' model of executive function (Miyake et al., 2000)

The ellipses represent 'latent variables' which are extracted from measures of the same construct. The curved double arrows depict the need to include measures of shared variance (or 'covariance') between the three predictor variables on the left.

executive function fit together into a unitary EF factor structure, but without the separated components (working memory, etc.) showing individual contributions (e.g. Hughes et al., 2010; Wiebe, Sheffield, Nelson, Clark, Chevalier, & Espy, 2011; Willoughby, Wirth, & Blair, 2012). Most of the data also fit a two-factor EF structure in which working memory and inhibitory control are separable (Miller, Giesbrecht, Müller, McInerney, & Kerns, 2012), but it is commonly agreed that these skills are more closely related in preschoolers.

School-age children show more differentiated executive function like the one in Figure 10.5, but it is not clear how this differentiation occurs and what the structure of the executive system is. Some evidence suggests the factor structure that Miyake and colleagues found for adults (Lehto, Juujarvi, Kooistra, & Pulkkinen, 2003; Rose, Feldman, & Jankowski, 2011: see Figure 9.1b). However, two studies (Huizinga et al., 2006; van der Sluis et al., 2007) distinguish a working memory and a shifting factor (but not inhibitory control which Huizinga et al. found was not related to the other skills). Two further studies found that the best fit for the data was a two-factor model with inhibition and shifting combined being separate from working memory in 6- to 8-year-olds (Van der Ven, Kroesbergen, Boom, Leseman, 2013) and 5- to 13-year-olds (Lee, Bull, & Ho, 2013). Thus, on the basis of current evidence, we may conclude that the studies suggest a gradual differentiation over development from a unitary system in the preschool years to the differentiated system ('unity with diversity') depicted in Figure 10.5 developing in the elementary school years.

However, the plot thickens when we consider that the relatively recent term 'executive function' refers to the skills depicted in Figure 10.5. As Müller and Kerns (2015) suggest, to understand how differentiation occurs we need to know which developments and experiences influence this developmental process. Future research needs to identify more clearly the emergence of a particular factor structure (e.g. why EF might be fractionated into working memory and flexibility but not, for example, into inhibitory control and planning). There is a particular problem of how we should interpret the unitary factor identified in the preschool period. This might be attributable to the abilities being driven by a common skill. Some have suggested that this might be the ability to keep a goal clearly in mind (Miyake & Friedman, 2012; Wiebe, Espy, & Charak, 2008), while others attribute the single factor to the speed at which the child processes information (an old contender for 'g' or intelligence) (Rose et al., 2011). For example, research on working memory and inhibition shows that age-linked improvements seem to be accounted for by developments in processing speed (McAuley & White, 2011). McAuley and White's research suggests that this capacity (processing speed) is subject to similar, if not the very same, developments as executive skills. However, there is other evidence to suggest that inborn individual differences may account for these links. For example, a few studies suggest that the speed in which infants (0 to 2-year-olds) habituate to novel stimuli, by turning away or not attending, predicts executive function skills in early adolescence (Rose et al., 2011).

The different component skills of executive function undergo protracted development from infancy to adolescence (Müller & Kerns, 2015). There is rapid change in children's inhibitory skills during the preschool years, followed by more gradual improvements during late childhood. With respect to working memory, the ability to hold information in mind (visuospatial short-term memory) improves significantly in the first year of life, and the central executive component of working memory emerges later during the preschool period and has a more protracted time course than the simpler abilities to hold visual and verbal information in mind. Flexibility undergoes major qualitative changes during the preschool period as children learn to switch between increasingly complex rules, but less is known about the development of flexibility during middle childhood and adolescence. Planning skills and performance on more complex measures of executive function such as the Wisconsin Card Sorting task continue to show significant age-related developments through childhood well into adolescence. Next, we consider the problems of studying executive function.

10.2 METHODOLOGICAL ISSUES IN THE ANALYSIS OF EXECUTIVE FUNCTION

Before we consider the question of how children gain control over their actions and thoughts, we need to examine the nature and validity of the tests that are commonly used to identify the components and structure of executive function. Four problems are commonly raised and we will discuss them here – task impurity, test–retest reliability, construct fractionation, and validity. In this section we describe and discuss each of these in turn. This is a sound example of the problems faced in developmental psychology – of identifying the links between theories and the methods used to test them. Simply assuming that particular tests, like those in Figures 10.1–10.4, are 'clean' measures of only one underlying skill or construct is problematic.

Researchers in the area have long been concerned about 'task impurity' (e.g. Rabbitt, 1997). This refers to the question of whether a test measures only what it sets out to assess. As Rabbitt and many others suggest, tasks designed to assess one construct, like those described in the first section, often unwittingly involve other abilities. Let's consider some examples. Tests of inhibitory control and set shifting almost necessarily involve working memory, as the child has to recall which response to make and which to inhibit. To perform the Day–Night test, illustrated in the top row of Figure 10.2, the child has to hold in mind either a simple rule, 'Say the opposite of what I see', or combine two rules, 'If I see the sun I should say "night"' and 'If I see the moon in a dark sky I should say "day"'. Whatever rule set explains how the task is solved, the child has to keep in mind the idea that there are two labels ('day' and 'night') and these have to be retained in memory and used under the appropriate circumstances. Adele Diamond and her colleagues (Gerstadt et al., 1994) were fully aware of this working memory component as well as the need to inhibit a prepotent response (seeing a sun usually implies 'day', even for the authors of this book who all live in wet northern places!). As a result they devised a control condition, depicted in the lower row of Figure 10.2. This shows two abstract patterns. The words 'day' and 'night' are arbitrarily allocated to each stimulus. In theory, this enables us to take the child's abstract pattern score away from the score from the sun vs moon pictures to distill the true effect of inhibitory control. However, most researchers do not usually apply the abstract pattern version, and 'inhibitory control' is taken to be just the score out of 16 sun vs moon pictures (i.e. inhibition plus working memory). We do not know of systematic research attempting to explore the procedure that Gerstadt et al. recommended. Our research suggests a high correlation between the two sets of pictures and the versions with two abstract patterns, thereby suggesting that there is a greater overlap in the task demands of the control and test versions than Gerstadt assumed – indeed the control version seems to contain a clear inhibitory component (Lewis, Liu, & Shimmon, in preparation). Müller and Kerns (2015) point out that factors that involve skills outside executive function, like the language used in the task, also contribute to task impurity.

Indeed, several authors have suggested that the limited language abilities of young children (Anderson & Reidy, 2012; Hughes & Graham, 2002) present us with clear problems that are specific to the assessment of their executive function. To minimise these difficulties, procedures like those in Figures 10.1 to 10.4 were designed to contain simple language and others contain even more minimal verbal demands (e.g. Garon, Smith, & Bryson, 2014; Müller et al., 2012). However, the role of language cannot be completely discarded and it is always possible that supposed developments in executive function skills may reflect improvements in language abilities (Hughes & Graham, 2002).

How can we tell whether a measure does what it sets out to assess? One way to do this is to ensure that it is reliable – that different parts of a test measure the same underlying construct, or that the same procedure produces the same results on two occasions. This latter measure, test–retest reliability, has been explored in tests like the Tower of Hanoi (similar to the Tower of London but with different-sized beads and with a rule 'a bead cannot be placed on a smaller one') and shows only moderate consistency over time (Bishop et al., 2001). In addition, the correspondence between these related tests, the Towers of Hanoi and London, has been low (Bull, Espy, & Senn, 2004). Planning is a complex skill, requiring all the other constituent skills (see Figure 10.4) so perhaps it is not surprising that reliability is low. The same applies to some assessments of these component skills. For example, retest reliabilities for measures of inhibition have been more variable, ranging from poor retest reliabilities (correlation less than .30) for some measures of inhibition (Knock Tap Game – knock with the knuckles vs tap with the palm of the hand under different instructions) to adequate retest reliability (correlation of .74) for other measures of inhibition (e.g. Luria's tapping task, where the participant has to tap once [twice] if the experimenter taps twice [once]; Nampijja et al., 2010; see also Archibald & Kerns, 1999; Kuntsi et al., 2001). By contrast, measures of working memory usually show adequate to good test–retest reliability (e.g. Alloway, Gathercole, & Pickering, 2006; Schmid et al., 2008). For example, Müller and colleagues (2012) found correlations between .70 and .84 for measures of the phonological loop and central executive that were administered to 3- to 5-year olds, with testing sessions three weeks apart.

The variations in test–retest reliability may well reflect issues to do with the complexity of the skill and the resultant task requirements in executive function. As stated above, the Tower of Hanoi is often referred to as a 'complex executive function task' because it involves numerous executive (working memory, inhibitory control and attentional flexibility) and non-executive processes, particularly language skills. As a result, the nature and development of performance on these tasks are difficult to determine (Miyake et al., 2000). Three trends have been apparent in the past two decades.

First, researchers have attempted to work with the variability of data to extract common variance between diverse measures of the same hypothesised skills. It has long been shown that several measures of the same construct can be aggregated to provide a more stable and representative overall measure than any single test (Rushton, Brainerd, & Pressley, 1983). Techniques like confirmatory factors analysis, as reported at the start of this chapter with reference to Miyake and colleagues' key study, are designed to construct latent (or hidden) variables from this variance (see Espy et al., 2016, for a recent application to preschoolers). The ellipses in Figure 10.5 represent such variables, as they are each drawn from three tests of the same construct (this is shown in Miyake et al.'s 2000 paper with the tasks displayed in rectangular boxes, in compliance with the convention of confirmatory factor analysis). However, the correlations among the executive function tasks (or variables) are typically very low, and as a result the majority of variance of each task does not contribute to the latent variable (Blair & Willoughby, 2013). Furthermore, the latent variable approach may not represent the concept of executive function accurately if it is assumed that executive function consists of a heterogeneous set of processes that are distributed over different brain networks (Willoughby, Holochwost, Blanton, & Blair, 2014). If executive function is conceptualised as a broad and heterogeneous set of processes, its measurement should include sufficient tasks that capture the multiple facets of this construct. Clearly, the measurement of executive function should be guided by the theoretical framework of the researcher.

A second approach to the problem of measuring executive function has been to construct batteries (i.e. a full set to examine a group of related abilities) of tests assessing the skills, like the National Institutes of Health (NIH) Toolbox Cognition Battery (Zelazo et al., 2013). Given the limited concentration powers of children, these batteries only test a subset of skills with a small number of measures, not all of which concern executive function. For example, the NIH Toolbox assesses only inhibition while seeking a goal and set shifting using a one card-sorting procedure. As with a similar battery for preschoolers (Willoughby & Blair, 2011) these measures show very good test–retest reliability. Indeed, Willoughby and Blair found that the test–retest reliability for latent executive function ability resulting from confirmatory factor analysis was stronger than that of individual measures of executive function. One reason for this was that these individual measures were more accurate at different ages/stages of development (Willoughby et al., 2012). So, the lesson is that to improve test–retest reliability researchers should aggregate over conceptually similar measures, but this will not explain the different developmental trajectories of each component of executive function.

NIH TOOL BOX

A video demonstration can be found on this site, so you can get an idea of how it works: www.psytoolkit.org/experiment-library/wcst.html. Be sure to perform several trials as the rule changes are not frequent.

A third recent move taken by researchers has been to attempt to construct more ecologically valid measures of executive function. 'Ecological validity' is used to refer to the link between what we study and measure and how the construct is used in everyday life. Throughout the history of studies of these higher-order skills, some researchers have suggested that the best way to get an understanding of these processes is to use the true experts on each child – her parents or teacher. As a result, they have developed parent and teacher rating scales of executive function. More recently these reflect the component skills identified in Figure 10.5. In their review of these measures, Toplak,

West, and Stanovich (2013) report that the correlation between child test scores and these parental rating measures of executive function was very low, with a median correlation of only $r = .19$. Toplak and colleagues note that the lack of correlations between test scores on executive function tasks and parental ratings could be due to a variety of reasons, including the type of behaviour elicited by each measure. Whereas the executive function tasks typically are highly structured and require relatively simple behavioural responses, the parental rating measures are less restrictive and ask parents to rate relatively broad and complex behaviours. To illustrate the relatively broad and ill-defined behaviours assessed by rating scales, take the following two items from a widely used behavioural rating scale of executive function, the BRIEF: 'acts too wild and out of control' or 'has trouble carrying out the actions needed to complete tasks'. Based on these differences, Toplak and colleagues (2013) suggest that executive function tasks and rating instruments likely tap into different aspects of functioning. So, clearly more research is required to determine the ecological validity of executive function tasks and the relation between these tasks and rating scales.

The issue of measurement will continue to occupy the attention of researchers on executive function in children. There has been a move recently to use batteries so that issues to do with task impurity can be minimised. However, it has been noted that when executive function tests are either repeatedly administered, or placed onto a computer package, the child's performance may become automatised, or may even no longer draw on executive control (Hughes & Graham, 2002). As Claire Hughes (2011) points out, the past twenty years have witnessed advances in the way in which we measure individual and combined skills, and also parallel development in attempts to integrate the cognitive and neuroscience perspectives on executive function. However, she also notes that we need more research comparing development in clinical groups, like children with autism or ADHD. Such studies will allow us to extend the measures we have developed for typically developing children and new ones for particular special groups.

10.3 THE NATURE OF EXECUTIVE FUNCTION: BIOLOGICAL AND SOCIAL EXPLANATIONS

The role of biology in executive function

We devote a chapter in this book to executive function in part because the issue of control has a long history in psychology. Some studies on this topic have become increasingly focused on the biological components of these skills, while other research suggests that the development of these skills is influenced by the child's social experience. Adult brain-scanning research, using functional magnetic resonance imaging (fMRI), has developed apace and confirms earlier suggestions that these related skills are associated with increased activity in the prefrontal cortex – those parts of the brain which are in the front of the highest of the three levels of the cortex, the most recent development of the brain in evolutionary history (the evolution of brain regions is thought to begin from the brain stem and move to the midbrain and then to the cortex).

Three areas of the cortex have been particularly associated with executive skills. First, the dorsolateral prefrontal cortex (behind the top of the forehead) is known to develop throughout childhood. It has been closely associated with the performance of tasks involving working memory, goal-directed behaviour, and the temporal sequencing of behaviour (Goldman-Rakic, 1987). It seems that this area of the cortex drives the cognitive skills which organise behaviours both in time and place. Second, the orbito-frontal cortex, just below the dorsolateral prefrontal region and behind the eyes, is responsible for monitoring activity, issues to do with rewards and social behaviours, particularly emotions (Alvarez & Emory, 2006). Third, Alvarez and Emory's meta-analysis of the studies suggests that the anterior cingulate cortex (ACC), which lies next to the dorsolateral prefrontal cortex, is also involved in the inhibition of inappropriate responses, decision making, and processing emotions. As they point out, these brain areas are often simultaneously active when a particular cognitive function (e.g. decision making) is performed, suggesting that multiple areas of the brain might be involved in any single activity or mental process. It is not simply the case that a small area of the brain is responsible for a single process.

Techniques like fMRI inform us only about increased neuronal activity in the area identified, so only tell a general story. Very few studies have used this procedure with children as it requires participants to remain very still in a confined space. So researchers use other procedures, particularly Electroencephalography (or EEG for short) or the electrical signals produced by the brain over brief periods of time, Evoked Response Potentials (ERPs). This technique is non-invasive as it requires placing a number of electrodes (8, 16, 32, 64, or 128) on the scalp and recording the electrical activity in the area below the scalp. Often children will wear a cap with the electrodes built in to keep them in place. Research is conducted on the change in electrical activity when a child performs a task. This shows a link between skills like attentional flexibility and activity in the prefrontal cortex (e.g. Espinet, Anderson, & Zelazo, 2012), but as yet the spatial resolution is not as precise as with fMRI.

A second line of primarily biologically focused research comes from studies attempting to tease apart the genetic and environmental contributions to executive function skills. Extending their methodology to a sample of twins, Miyake and his colleagues (Friedman et al., 2008) conducted a study comparing 316 monozygous (i.e. they originate from the same egg and have a perfect genetic match: 'identical twins') and 266 dizygous (i.e. 'fraternal twins', sharing 50% of their genes) pairs on the same tasks as in their earlier study (Miyake et al., 2000). The correlations between the linked measures were twice as strong for the monozygous twins than for the dizygous twins. A similar confirmatory factor analysis to that in Figure 10.5, but including the effect of heritability (the two types of twin pairs), found that, even when factors like IQ were taken into account, genetic influences predicted almost all (98%) of the model of executive function performance across pairs

Figure 10.6   An EEG net with 128 channels

Each channel records the electrical activity just below it and measures the activity in each part of the brain as the participant performs a task. (Source: Katerina Kaduk and Dave Gaskell.)

of twins, particularly the components dedicated to attentional flexibility (shifting) and working memory (updating). Thus, in keeping with the 'unity with diversity' model that we described in the first section of the chapter, their analyses suggested contribution of genes separately on the executive system as a whole and these two components. These results are impressive but the almost perfect correlation needs to be explained.

Miyake and Friedman (2012) acknowledge that the high heritability estimate does not identify the *origins* of each individual's executive function capability. Furthermore, Friedman et al.'s analyses of genetic contributions have given rise to claims that the latent variables in the studies may reflect more fundamental skills like attentional capacity or intelligence (Blair & Willoughby, 2013; Willoughby et al., 2014), and it is these fundamental skills that display high heritability, not executive function. As Müller and

Kerns (2015) suggest, heritability only tells us something about the genetic influence on the *variability* of individual performance within a population. The higher agreement of scores between monozygous twins than dizygous ones does not rule out the possibility that specific environmental influences may play their part in determining how the composite skills develop.

Indeed, Müller and Kerns identify several types of study which suggest that the social environment *is* important. For a start, many animal and human studies show that developmental differences in individuals' prefrontal cortex and executive skills are dependent on those individuals' experiences (Müller, Baker, & Yeung, 2013). Therefore, we turn now to the literature within developmental psychology to examine the nature of the social processes that give rise to executive skills.

Social processes in the production of executive function: the move to interaction

Several studies have shown broad influences of social factors upon children's executive function capabilities. At a very general level of analysis, socioeconomic status (SES, or 'social class') predicts test performance (Müller et al., 2013). For example, Sebastian Lipina and his colleagues (2013) found that 4-year-old children, in households in Argentina which were classified as barely providing for their needs, performed significantly less well on tests of inhibitory control, interference control (i.e. the ability to filter out irrelevant information; interference control is considered to be an aspect of inhibition, see Müller & Kerns, 2015), planning, and working memory, even when IQ was taken into account. Müller et al. (2013) and others (e.g. Hackman, Farah, & Meaney, 2010; Mackey, Raizada, & Bunge, 2013; Segretin et al., 2016) summarise several other studies showing the same influences. They point out that the research does not identify whether SES influences only the executive function skills or a whole range of cognitive skills.

Indeed, the research suggests that factors as broad as SES need to be considered alongside other potential influences. Clancy Blair and his colleagues (2011) examined poverty in terms of the quality of the parents' caregiving. What they termed 'positive parenting', based on the parent's view of, and sensitivity to, their 7- and 15-month-old infant, mediated between (i.e. protected against) the family's poverty and the child's executive function performance at the age of three years. Such findings raise further questions about the ways in which parents might influence these developments, and they show that something about the way in which parents and infants interact may be important.

Longitudinal research has identified a number of aspects of parenting which predict executive function skills in children. These range from the effects of poverty on family members' physiological responsivity to stress (Blair & Raver, 2012), the influence of poverty on the disorganisation of family life (Hughes & Ensor, 2009) and mother–infant attachment (see Box 6.1) (Bernier, Carlson, Deschênes, & Matte-Gagné, 2012). A lot of these and other studies have additionally considered the subtle interplay between factors as diverse as social processes, like poverty or income, and the parent's specific inter-action style. How do these factors relate to one another and are there other influences? Longitudinal studies that control for prior executive function skills need to consider the possibility that a third factor, other than parenting, may contribute to individual differ-ences in executive function. Hughes and Ensor found that prior executive function skills predicted much of the variance in later performance. Another candidate for influence may be the child's temperament, which has been shown to moderate the effects of parenting (Conway & Stifter, 2012; Kim & Kochanska, 2012).

It is also possible to identify effects of the child's daily routines on their executive skills. If we consider the Day–Night task (Figure 10.2), Gerstadt and colleagues (1994) found that social interactional factors influenced the performance of children. Preschoolers in daycare performed better than those raised only at home. This implies that peer or child–teacher interactions might facilitate the rate of acquisition of key cognitive skills, perhaps because the daycare environment is one in which children need to abide by particular rules – so they may have more experience of shifting from one rule set to another.

In examining the possible mechanisms by which social factors influence the child's developing executive function, the construct of parental scaffolding has been studied in particular. This refers to the way in which parents stage-manage a task so that it is just beyond the child's level of competence. This helps the child to achieve each goal. Sensitive parents will structure the activity so that the child performs the task but with sufficient guidance to enable her to move, step by step, towards success. In so doing the child learns the sequencing of particular cognitive skills.

Several studies show that the quality of parental scaffolding predicts better perfor-mance on executive function in preschool children (e.g. Bernier, Carlson, & Whipple, 2010; Hughes & Ensor, 2009). In one longitudinal analysis Stuart Hammond and his colleagues (2012) found that the amount of scaffolding provided by a parent in a joint problem-solving task with 2- and 3-year-olds predicted 9% of the variability in their children's performance on executive function tests once other factors, including prior executive function skills, had been taken into account. As Hammond et al. suggest, stud-ies of scaffolding could go even further by identifying which aspects of scaffolding are most effective. There are several candidates, including verbal support, verbal labelling or nonverbal guidance.

The development of executive function in (inter)action

How might scaffolding by a parent, or another person like a nursery teacher, sibling or peer, work to influence the child's control over her memory, in switching between rules and con-trolling impulsive actions? This is a very difficult question as it requires the researcher to witness development taking place and then to infer both the nature of change and its causes. In this final subsection we examine, successively, what we can learn from manipulating the way in which executive function tests are administered, training studies, and longitudinal research looking at the role of language.

The Dimension Change Card Sort (DCCS) task (Figure 10.3) provides a good example of a test which allows us to explore the dynamic of developmental change. Recall that in this task children sort cards, differentiated by shape and colour, into one of two trays. After six sorts, the sorting criteria are changed (from colour to shape or vice versa). Three-year-olds usually continue to sort cards by the first (pre-switch) rule. They do this even if only one or two pre-switch trials are completed. In contrast, 4-year-olds usually grasp the switch with ease (Frye et al., 1995). Philip Zelazo and his colleagues (e.g. Zelazo, Carter, Reznick, & Frye, 1997) understand this as a problem-solving task. They depict the procedure as setting up a series of distinct sub-functions that need to be hierarchically organised in time in order to achieve a specific goal (i.e. to follow the specific rule). This involves an articulation of the problem, planning the moves that must be made to solve the problem in sequence, execution of the plan and evaluation of when the problem has been solved. Zelazo and his colleagues argue that the ability to hold these aspects of the problem in mind and perform them requires the child to construct higher order rules that combine two lower-order rules (e.g. the shape and colour rule sets) and make them accessible to conscious control. This is known as Cognitive Complexity and Control (CCC) theory (Zelazo, Müller, Frye, & Marcovitch, 2003).

Given that the results of the DCCS show that children usually can or cannot follow the rule and that the 3- to 4-year-shift is clear, it seems likely that an account based purely upon the child's capacity to execute the problem-solving exercise should provide a sufficient explanation. However, even this simple task and its clear results are open to some change when the procedure is manipulated slightly. Yuko Munakata and her colleagues, for example, showed that a demonstration of the correct response produced more successful results in younger children than giving the standard verbal instruction ('in the shape game the cars go in there …') (Brace, Morton, & Munakata, 2006; see also Towse, Redbond, Houston-Price, & Cook, 2000). This improvement suggests that something about the experimenter–child interaction can scaffold the child's activity if it is action-based, as opposed to a simple instruction (in many versions of the test the child is reminded of the rule on each trial, e.g. 'in the shape game where does this one go', so perhaps action really does speak louder than words and we need to explain this).

Similarly, in a series of experiments Yusuke Moriguchi and his colleagues (Moriguchi, Lee, & Itakura, 2007) re-examined early research which suggested that conducting the DCCS within an interactive context, like judging the success or failure of a puppet doing the DCCS, did not produce improvements in performance at age three (Jacques et al., 1999). Moriguchi et al. asked children to watch an adult do the first part of the task. In one condition this adult model made errors on the pre-switch trials (e.g. placing the cards in the trays matched by shape when the children were asked to match by colour). The children were then asked to sort by the same rule, but they committed fewer errors in these trials. In this case the correct strategy was to use the sorting procedure that they had not seen being used and they had to instigate a change to do so. Moriguchi et al. then changed the procedure to test whether there was an effect of the actor expressing awareness of their errors or confidence in their performance. They showed that these social factors had a dramatic influence on performance. Having sorted the cards incorrectly, if the actor then said that she was right in her sorting, almost 80% of 3-year-olds failed, but when the actor says she made a mistake or 'I'm not sure', 80% of 3-year-olds' performance jumped to ceiling levels. These contrasting results suggest that the child's access to the skills required to solve set-shifting problems are facilitated by, or emerge within, social interactions with others.

If social interaction improves children's performance on tasks does this mean that executive function skills can be trained? If so what do training studies show us? There is an old adage often attributed to the social psychologist Kurt Lewin that 'If you want to truly understand something, try to change it'. This is music to the ears of the developmental psychologist as change is inherent in what we study. Training regimes usually involve repeated practice over a few sessions. If they improve a skill, then this suggests learning is about to take place and also that something about the means of training influences the mechanism of change. In addition, if training in one aspect of executive function causes improvements in another then this suggests that the two skills have some functional inter-dependence. Direct training approaches target specific components of a skill. They often involve a build-up of trials so that they become progressively harder. More indirect approaches target executive skills in more subtle ways by incorporating training into activities such as physical exercise (a healthy mind in a healthy body; Best, 2010; Lambrick, Stone, Grigg, & Faulkner, 2016), musical training (Moreno et al., 2011), and the practice of self-regulation within meditative approaches like mindfulness (Zelazo & Lyons, 2012). There is support for all these interventions but the results are patchy (see Müller & Kerns, 2015, for a review).

Direct training methods are often found to improve performance, particularly in younger children (Wass, Scerif, & Johnson, 2012) and in those who are slightly behind developmental norms (Diamond & Lee, 2011). There is very great variety in the findings from these studies and a need for meta-analyses. For example, two such meta-analyses of working memory training studies show that positive effects of interventions based on improving auditory storage (the articulatory loop) and recall led to improvements, but these were short lived and did not lead to improvements in other skills such as reading comprehension and arithmetic which arguably should involve working memory (Melby-Lervåg & Hulme, 2013). On the other hand, Melby-Lervåg, Redick, and Hulme (2016) found that training in visual short-term memory had more lasting effects (on the 'visuospatial scratchpad').

Differences like these may well help us understand the dynamics of change in the component parts of executive function, even the subcategories of working memory. In other areas there are transfer effects beyond the executive system. For example, Kloo and Perner (2003) found that training in set shifting on the Dimension Change Card Sort (Figure 10.4) led to improvements on false belief – a test of the child's grasp of mental states that we will discuss in detail in Chapter 11. It has been suggested that there are difficulties in how we interpret training studies given their varied methods to test this diverse collection of component skills, and that these have been applied to different age groups, using different types of control groups (Kray & Ferdinand, 2013). However, we feel that there is much to learn from these interventions. Training allows us to interpret possible developmental processes.

Finally, in this section, we consider one area of adult–child interaction that many consider to home in on the mechanism of change in executive function, the role of the child's developing language in the development of self-control. Longitudinal studies show that general measures of language development are predictive of later executive skills. This can be tested in a simple way, by examining the child's ability to identify named objects, in a measure of receptive vocabulary where they have to pick out one object, e.g. a 'ball', from a group of photos. The extent of a child's vocabulary predicts later executive function performance even when earlier executive test scores are taken into account. For example, Claire Hughes and Rosie Ensor (2009) found that receptive vocabulary in the preschooler at 2 and 3 years significantly predicted executive function at age 4. Indeed several studies show that the child's earlier verbal ability can protect her against known negative effects of SES on executive function (Catale et al., 2012; Noble et al., 2007).

10.4 THEORETICAL ISSUES

In this section we draw together the findings described in the previous two sections. These include the child's ability to hold information in mind and report it back in a different way (working memory), to inhibit the impetuous responses that thwart the achievement of a goal, or to learn which rule to apply in which setting. These seem to be influenced by both the nature of their interactions with others (notably adults but this represents the data collected to date) and their own previous language and executive skills which seem to predict the child's later executive functioning. So how do these skills fit together?

Before we address this question let's look at one more set of data that Stephanie Carlson and her colleagues (Carlson, Davis, & Leach, 2005) collected in an interesting study to address this cocktail of factors. They conducted a task in which preschoolers could win two or five candies and they were presented with different types of help to get the reward. In one condition the candies were on the top of a box, while in three others they were hidden inside one of two boxes. To mark where the reward of each number of candies was hidden, one of three pairs of symbolic representation was placed on the top of each to represent the contents: a few or many dots, two or five stones, or a mouse and an elephant. In each case the size of the cue provided a symbolic representation of the numbers of sweets inside. Carlson et al. showed that the mouse–elephant condition led to greatest success (even significantly more than the real treat condition). In the mouse–elephant and the dots trials children were significantly above statistical chance in identifying which box to select. These findings suggest that a symbolic cue can help preschoolers give a correct answer, but why might it be the case that the elephant–mouse comparison was so successful when it conveyed no information about the number of items in the box (there was one of each)? Carlson argued that the mouse–elephant cue gave the child a memorable symbolic link between the contents of the box and the memory of where the larger number was. These findings are in keeping with similar experiments in which the more poignant the symbolic link the more effective it is. Others like a model 'pointing hand' in a similar task have the same effect (Hala & Russell, 2001; see also Towse, Lewis, & Knowles, 2007).

Carlson et al.'s (2005) results home in on both the nature of the symbolic connection that a child uses in memory *and* the person who makes a stronger or weaker symbolic gesture. This brings us back to the issue of 'scaffolding' that we referred to above with reference to Hammond et al.'s (2012) study. Like other research (Landry, Miller-Loncar, Smith, & Swank, 2002; Matte-Gagné & Bernier, 2011), Carlson's findings fit in with the Vygotskian tradition in which it is hypothesised that the speech and symbolic gestures used by more skilled members of our culture, notably parents, structure the interaction, facilitating the child's contribution to an activity which becomes gradually internalised by the child. As we suggest in Chapter 4, Vygotsky theorised that what the child can perform in collaboration with others now, she can later perform by herself. His (1978) book *Mind in Society* is largely about how the child gains control over her actions. The notion of higher mental functions, which is central to his theory, captures all the element of executive function – particularly memory and the inhibition of prepotent responses. He describes how these are acquired through the child's learning from her interactive partners.

It is important to mention Vygotsky's collaborator Alexander Luria (1973) here, as his research on the prefrontal cortex and higher cognitive skills led to him being regarded by many as being one of the fathers of the construct executive function. Luria's (e.g. 1961, 1981) later career was devoted to the establishment of neuroscience as a subdiscipline. His approach to brain functioning was to envisage mental activity within hierarchically organised functional systems and he argued that these are rooted in social interaction. Luria agreed with Vygotsky that these higher mental functions are social in origin, and are constructed within socially mediated *sign systems*, particularly language. As Müller and Kerns (2015) point out, moves within developmental science to merge the social and cognitive processing (what is often referred to as social-affective-cognitive neuroscience) make Luria's theory highly topical.

To explore the Vygotsky/Luria argument a bit further, let's revisit the elephant–mouse condition in Carlson et al.'s study that we started this section with. From Carlson and colleagues' perspective, their findings would be seen as an example of how social conventions using the metaphors elephant = big = more and mouse = small = less drive cognitive development. This is a classic example of the ways in which we humans use symbols both to embed our interactions into historical and cultural traditions (which repeat and ritualise interactions) *and* to acquire higher order skills which are central to executive function – memory and self-control. As Vygotsky suggests, it is the grasp of symbols that 'permits humans, by the aid of extrinsic stimuli, *to control their behaviour from the outside*. The use of signs leads humans to a specific structure of behaviour that breaks away from biological development and creates new forms of a culturally-based psychological process' (Vygotsky, 1978, p. 40, original emphasis). As we have shown in this chapter, a considerable number of recent research studies provide support for this position.

SUMMARY AND CONCLUSION

We started this chapter with a description of the three cognitive skills that have been taken to be central to executive function – working memory, set shifting, and inhibitory control (see Figure 10.5). Not only do these represent areas of intense research in their own right, they also appear to fit together into an overarching construct – 'executive function'. Akira Miyake (e.g. Miyake et al., 2000) and other researchers have demonstrated that this higher-order construct is described in terms of 'unity with diversity'. By this, it is thought that the best model of the adult executive system is one where there is overlap in the ways in which participants perform the three component parts, but that they are still identifiable as making unique contributions to the overall system. The research on children shows that a system like the adult one is in place by the middle elementary school years, but this is not identifiable in the preschool period and there may be subtle differences between the system in children and adults.

Many of the cognitive psychologists who study executive function are interested in individual processes, like working memory, but do not pay too much attention to the origins of these skills or their relation to each other. Indeed, even when they do consider the group of skills together, some have been criticised for their 'inherent conflation' of the term 'executive function' with the working of the prefrontal cortex (Barkley, 2012), as if increased activity shown on an fMRI scan is sufficient for our research to understand the phenomenon. Of course, studying the neural underpinnings of each cognitive skill is important, but it does not shed much light on the *nature* of that skill. Developmental psychologists are particularly aware of the Vygotsky/Luria tradition. For example, Zelazo's Cognitive Control and Complexity Model derives its functional approach from Luria (Zelazo et al., 1997). The research that completes this chapter shows that it is the child's acquisition of skills like language which allows her to gain control over her mental functions and language itself is learned in a network of social interactions in which others (parents, teachers, siblings, etc.) facilitate self-control in stage-managed interactions.

This social interactional turn that developmental psychology has made brings us finally to wider issues to do with self-control which have been explored within psychology over the past fifty years. The term 'executive function' tends to focus on the pattern of constructs depicted in Figure 10.5, yet there are related traditions that broaden the construct to incorporate a wider focus. Two issues should be considered here. First, each construct has been considered very narrowly in this chapter (and by several studies following the Miyake model). Inhibitory control, for example, does not only include conflict inhibition as illustrated in the Day–Night test (Figure 10.2). There is an equally long tradition in another aspect of inhibition that we have not covered which is referred to as delay of gratification (e.g. Kopp, 1982). Second, each of the constructs in Figure 10.5 is focused on an abstract notion of cognition. It fails to acknowledge that emotion is involved in the development of self-control. Yet there is a parallel tradition examining developmental patterns in how children come to understand and control their displays of emotion (Saarni, 1984).

We conclude by mentioning briefly an old experiment to show how these two issues are currently being brought together in research. In the early 1970s Walter Michel carried out a series of experiments in which children were presented with a small treat (they could choose a chocolate biscuit, a pretzel, or a marshmallow). They were told that they could eat the treat now, but if they waited for 15 minutes until the experimenter returned they would receive two treats. The experimenter then left the room and the child was observed (and filmed) until she ate the treat. This has become the classic delay of gratification study. Several manipulations of the task have been performed that show that the child's interactions with the experimenter influence the amount of time that the child delayed. In Mischel's work, children waited longer when they reflected upon resisting the temptation rather than focusing on performance on the task (Patterson & Mischel, 1976) or when asked to imagine a reward as something else (e.g. Mischel & Baker, 1975). More recently Kidd, Palmeri, and Aslin (2013) showed that trust in the experimenter is important. Before the marshmallow task the experimenter said she'd go out and get some interesting art materials. In one condition the experimenter returned with these, but in the other she came back and said 'I'm sorry, but I made a mistake. We don't have any other art supplies after all', and offered the child some dull crayons that she had already played with. Kidd and colleagues found in the former condition the child waited four times longer (12 minutes) before taking the treat than in the condition when the experimenter had not produced the promised art materials (3 minutes). These results suggest that, as with the executive function measures examined in the rest of the chapter, in delay inhibition children's performance is influenced by the strategies they are helped to perform and their feelings about the trustworthiness of their interactant. So, again, social factors are important in this executive skill.

FURTHER READING

Müller, U., & Kerns, K. (2015). The development of executive function. In L. S. Liben & U. Müller (vol. eds), R. M. Lerner (series ed.), *Handbook of Child Psychology and Developmental Science, Vol. 2: Cognitive Processes* (7th edn, pp. 571–623). Hoboken, NJ: Wiley. This is a single chapter that reviews the literature in this rapidly growing area of research.

Sokol, B. F. Müller, U., Carpendale, J. I. M., Young, A. R., & Iarocci, G. (eds) (2010). *Self- and Social Regulation*. Oxford: Oxford University Press. This is a collection of essays which take a reflexive look at the area of self-regulation, of which 'executive function' forms a part.

UNDERSTANDING
THE SOCIAL WORLD

LEARNING OUTCOMES

Having read this chapter you should:

- Be aware of the history of twentieth-century approaches to social understanding, particularly the topics of perspective taking and 'theory of mind'.

- Be familiar with the false belief test and understand its importance in the development of social understanding.

- Understand the links between false belief and later transitions in children's abilities.

- Be able to distinguish the three main approaches to 'theory of mind' and the alternative social activity account of social understanding.

- Be familiar with the recent debate over the extent of infants' knowledge of the social world.

- Be able to relate work on social understanding to recent studies examining the neural circuits underpinning those skills.

- Be aware of the debates over the problems faced by children with autism spectrum disorder concerning social understanding.

- Be familiar with some of the theories on the causes of autism.

'I know you want your mummy, but your mummy's at work. She will come back.'
(Hannah at 2 years, 4 months, reassuring her doll)

This example shows a young child's use of the word 'know' and 'want', here in the context of her knowledge of other people and the causes of emotions, attributed to a doll. In this remark she appears to grasp what might upset someone as well as how to reassure that person. It could be that Hannah was simply repeating something she'd heard without a full understanding, but other examples suggest that a more complex explanation is needed. At a further level of social understanding, Max, aged 4, asked me (JC) to get out of the kitchen when I knew that he wanted a cookie. This suggests that he understood that if I didn't see him get a cookie I wouldn't know about it – brilliant! That this manoeuvre is ill-conceived seems so obvious and straightforward for adults yet it is hard to understand why this is a difficult insight that young children have to gain. Realising that young children lack this understanding helps to fathom why 3-year-olds seem to have only an incomplete grasp of how to play hide-and-seek. They may always hide in the same place, or call out 'I'm hiding in the closet. Come and find me!' They enjoy being found, but they don't seem to understand that the whole point of the game is that the seeker is not meant to know where the others are hiding.

These are some simple examples of social cognition – the thought processes required for understanding the social world. Understanding others is such an essential aspect of being human, but it involves complex skills that we take for granted in our everyday interactions. So, it is hard even to notice them. They become apparent when communication breaks down or when we encounter someone who lacks this taken-for-granted skill, such as individuals diagnosed on the autism spectrum, a disorder involving problems with language and understanding others, as well as repetitive behaviours.

Given its central importance to being human, social cognition has been a topic of great interest in developmental psychology and other disciplines for decades, from philosophy to cognitive science. It has been addressed in various literatures using labels such as *perspective taking* or *role taking*. Most recently the phrases 'theory of mind', 'mentalizing', and 'mindreading' have become popular. Since 'mindreading' actually refers to something like telepathy that psychics and magicians claim to do, and 'theory of mind' is already associated with a particular theory, we will use the more theory-neutral phrase *social understanding* (for reviews, see Carpendale & Lewis, 2006, 2010, 2015a).

In the first two sections of this chapter we present the main methods that have been used for studying social understanding, beginning with standard tasks for preschoolers and working up to less commonly studied ones which show changes throughout a child's development. In the middle two parts we introduce and analyse the three theoretical perspectives that dominated research for the two decades straddling the turn of the millennium, before focusing upon two of the more recent theoretical perspectives. Finally, we explore how the accounts of, and research into, social understanding interact with studies and theory within neuroscience, as this is a growth area. A separate box examines, in detail, the social interactional problems associated with autism spectrum disorder.

11.1 A BRIEF HISTORY: FROM PERSPECTIVE TAKING TO FALSE BELIEF UNDERSTANDING

In surveying the history of research on social understanding, an early approach was inspired by Piaget's 'three mountain task', a test of *visual-spatial* perspective taking in which children had to demonstrate an understanding that moving around an array of three mountains would result in different visual perspectives on the same tableau (Piaget & Inhelder, 1948/1967). Perspective taking was then extended to *social* perspectives, or taking others' roles in social interactions. For example, one task in this line of research involved presenting children with a story in which a young boy has just lost his coin that fell down a hole. When children were asked about how the boy would feel even 3-year-olds were able to correctly state he would feel sad. So, in this simple situation they can take another's perspective (Borke, 1971). However, then the plot thickens and the boy's friend arrives late on the scene after the coin has been lost. Young children have much more difficulty taking the perspective of this late-arriving bystander (Chandler & Greenspan, 1972). The result of years of research with many different tests of perspective taking was that many of these tests did not correlate with each other, and thus a single point at which children become able to take others' perspectives could not be easily found (Chandler, 2001). Looking back on this programme of research it can be seen that it was necessary to think about what these various tests assess. They measure different forms of social understanding in situations of increasing complexity (Carpendale & Racine, 2011). However, at the time this inconsistency across tasks led to the demise of the perspective-taking research programme.

The gap left by the perspective-taking research programme was filled by another line of research and this new line of research was considered 'a fresh start' (Harris, 2006, p. 812). The origin of this approach, labelled 'theories of mind', is usually traced to an article by Premack and Woodruff (1978) in which they addressed the question 'Does the chimpanzee have a theory of mind?' Three philosophers commenting on this target article argued that demonstrating an understanding of mind and beliefs requires understanding that beliefs can be false because this indicates an understanding of the mind. What is usually considered the first empirical work on this topic was published by Wimmer and Perner (1983, but Johnson & Maratsos, 1977, published a version of this procedure first).

In this now classic experiment, children were presented with a story in which Maxi, returning from shopping with his mother, puts his chocolate away and then goes outside to play (Wimmer & Perner, 1983). But while he is outside, unbeknownst to him, his mother moves his chocolate. When Maxi gets hungry and returns for his chocolate the test question is where will he look for it and/or where will he think it is. These types of tasks have now been used in many studies and the general finding is that children aged 5 and older understand, of course, that he will look for it where he left it, but the counterintuitive finding with 3-year-olds is that they incorrectly claim that Maxi will look in the new location where his mother has moved the chocolate. This type of false belief task is referred to as an *unexpected transfer task*. It is sometimes also called the *change of location task*.

A second type of false belief task, known as the *unexpected contents task*, involves showing a child a familiar tube containing candies known as Smarties in the UK and Canada, which are similar to M&Ms in the United States (Perner, Leekam, & Wimmer, 1987). Children are then asked what they think is in the container and, being experts on candies, they say Smarties or candies. But they are then shown that it actually contains something far less interesting, such as pencils. In the test questions, they are asked what they thought was in the tube before it was opened, and what they would think a friend who has not seen inside the tube would think it contained. Passing the task requires saying that at first they had thought the box contained Smarties, and that is also what a friend would think. But 3-year-olds tend to fail by claiming that they knew all along that the box contained pencils and that a friend would also know this. That is, they fail to realise they had a false belief and that others would also be mistaken. This finding has now been replicated in hundreds of experiments (Milligan, Astington, & Dack, 2007; Wellman, Cross, & Watson, 2001).

An additional way to assess children's understanding of false beliefs is with an appearance–reality task in which children are first presented with an object that looks like a rock and they identify it, for example, as 'a stone'. On touching it they discover that it is actually a sponge. Then, like the deceptive container task, they are asked what they first thought it was before touching it, and what another child might think about it before touching it. Again, 3-year-olds say that they thought it was a sponge all along and guess that their friend would say the same. After their fourth birthday, most children understand that an object can look like something but really be something else (Carpendale & Lewis, 2006).

One reason why researchers are interested in false belief understanding is that the whole point about beliefs is that they can be false or mistaken. Secondly, the methodological point is that asking children about true beliefs would not show if the child was answering based on her own beliefs, the story character's beliefs, or indeed the state of the world as it is currently (e.g. 'Where is the chocolate now?'). False belief understanding has been taken as a major transition point in development that indicates an understanding of the representational mind.

Three-year-olds' failure on these tasks is unexpected and seems counterintuitive. Wimmer and Perner's (1983) paper gave rise to an explosion of research in an attempt to determine what it is that is making children fail. For example, in one study the false belief story was presented to children in a storybook rather than a puppet show, and the experimenter went over the story twice before they were asked the test questions. With this additional support 3-year-olds had more success on the task (Lewis, Freeman, Hagestadt, & Douglas, 1994). Another approach was to give children an active role in planning the deception, leading to an experimenter having a false belief. When children helped to hide cookies, or played a trick on an experimenter, about 80% of 3-year-olds tended to pass the false belief question (Chandler & Hala, 1994). We return to more recent manipulations of the task below.

11.2 FURTHER DEVELOPMENT IN SOCIAL UNDERSTANDING: BEYOND (FALSE) BELIEF?

The initially narrow focus of researchers on false belief understanding has been referred to as a 'one miracle view' of development that neglects what happens before and after children develop false belief understanding (Chandler, 1988). Indeed, in the early 2000s it was common for symposia at conferences to focus on what was called the '3–5 shift', as this period witnessed a number of parallel shifts in children's grasp of the mind, language, self-control, and memory. In this section, we describe how the development of social understanding is not just about a grasp of false beliefs. We look first at emotion as a case example, then discuss social abilities in a range of domains and how each ability fits into the pattern of unfolding developments.

Although false belief understanding may be an important step in their social understanding, children still have much to learn after gaining this insight. For instance, in the example at the beginning of the chapter with Max and the cookie jar, he didn't yet realise that I might be suspicious about *why* he wanted me out of the kitchen. That is, children have to learn about the implications of false beliefs and how these may be related to emotions because fully understanding social situations would typically require a grasp of how beliefs are related to emotions and intentions (e.g. Banerjee, 2004; Dunn, 1996; de Rosnay, Pons, Harris, & Morrell, 2004; Wellman & Banerjee, 1991).

Children's grasp of emotion

As well as understanding beliefs, emotions are also a crucial aspect of human life that children need to learn about. Understanding emotions involves simple cases such as the examples used at the beginning of this chapter concerning children's understanding of when someone would feel happy, sad, or afraid. But even what might appear to be a simple emotion like happiness and sadness can be difficult to understand in more complex situations. For example, in Chandler's (Chandler & Greenspan, 1972) bystander task a girl is shown sadly waving goodbye to her father as he goes off in an airplane. Then, when the girl returns home, a mail carrier delivers a present to her. Young children can understand that she would feel happy receiving a present, but then it becomes more complex because when she opens the present it turns out to be a toy airplane: seeing this reminds the girl of her father leaving, and it makes her sad. In addition, it is difficult to understand the perspective of the mail carrier who has no knowledge of the girl's father leaving on an airplane. This task involves a range of situations of varying complexity, some of which involve the understanding that emotions can depend on beliefs (Carpendale & Lewis, 2006, 2015a).

An additional level of complexity regarding understanding emotions concerns mixed feelings when someone might feel two emotions at the same time. This is somewhat analogous to false belief understanding where the child has to contrast two views on the same event. For example, a child learning how to ride a bicycle for the first time might feel both excited and a bit scared (Dunn, 1995). Other more complex emotions seem to involve some self-consciousness, in the sense of a person being aware of how others may see her. Shame and guilt are emotions that may involve some knowledge of social norms and whether they are being conformed to (Tangney & Fischer, 1995).

A range of unfolding skills?

Other important assessments of social understanding show there are clear developments between 5 and 11 years. One concerns understanding *faux pas* situations in which some-one unintentionally insults someone else. For example, in a test of this understanding one scenario involves a child saying that he doesn't like a picture, but then realising he is standing beside the child who drew it. There were gender differences on this task, with girls showing a more advanced ability to identify why this causes embarrassment and is inappropriate than boys (Banerjee, Watling, & Caputi, 2011; Caputi, Lecce, Pagnin, & Banerjee, 2012).

A second measure of social understanding in middle childhood concerns a grasp of *strange stories* in which children have to explain why someone might act in a way that is not in keeping with their feelings. In telling a white lie, for example, the participant has to identify why a child might say that her aunt looks great in what he thinks is a really ugly hat. Originally devised by Francesca Happé (1994), a shorter version of the task is usually now administered and assesses children's grasp of deception, double bluff, white lies, and miscommunication (White, Hill, Happé, & Frith, 2009). Studies show that there are improvements in these abilities between 8 and 13 years. Some of these studies show gender differences, with girls outperforming boys (Devine & Hughes, 2013), but others show no gender differences (O'Hare, Bremner, Nash, Happe, & Pettigrew, 2009).

Gender differences in false belief understanding, with a few exceptions (Charman, Ruffman, & Clements, 2002), are rarely reported. Although minor in false belief under-standing, they are more commonly reported in research on children's understanding emotions. For example, in one longitudinal study, parents talking to daughters used more and a greater variety of emotion terms than when they were talking with their sons. Although there was no gender difference at 40 months, by 70 months girls used more and a greater variety of emotions words than boys (Kuebli, Butler, & Fivush, 1995).

In the past fifteen years researchers have taken a broader approach to evaluating social understanding, considering the transitions that might take place both before and after the development of false belief. This has been largely inspired by Henry Wellman and David Liu (2004), who combined a series of social understanding tasks to form a scale that assesses five steps of increasing complexity in social understanding: (1) grasping that different people may want different things (diverse desires); (2) understanding that different people may have and act on different beliefs about the same thing when it is not known if these beliefs are true or false (diverse beliefs); (3) appreciating that a lack of visual access results in not knowing (knowledge access); (4) false belief understanding; and (5) grasping that the emotions someone experiences may be different from what they display (hidden emotion). They have published a series of investigations, using a statistical technique known as Guttman scaling (after the statistician Louis Guttman) used to calculate the probability of the five measures unfolding in the order listed above. Their studies suggest a three-step developmental sequence: a grasp of diverse desires occurs before items 2–4 concerning beliefs and knowledge that precede a grasp of hidden emotion. This lends support to the idea that there are incremental changes in the ways proposed by Wellman and Liu.

More recently, a sixth task was added to assess understanding sarcasm, which is challenging even for 9-year-olds (Peterson, Wellman, & Slaughter, 2012). This extends the scale to age 6 when children start to show an understanding of sarcasm. However, there is still controversy about the complexity of tasks assessing sarcasm, and even 3-year-olds reveal some understanding of sarcastic comments in the context of simple and familiar social events (Rooksby & Lewis, in preparation). So, whether it is sarcasm or the complexity of the social situation being assessed remains an open question, in either case, the scale appears to indicate increasing sophistication of social understanding (Carpendale & Lewis, 2015a).

As well as having direct access to the world, children must also learn that inference can be a way of knowing what others know. For instance, in a scenario in which a child is seen leaving a candy store with a bag of something that he has purchased there, it can be inferred that the bag contains candy if that is the only thing available at the store. In one experimental procedure, either a child or the experimenter is allowed to peek into one of two boxes, one of which contains a yellow marble and the other holds a blue marble. Once someone has looked into the box containing the yellow marble he or she should be able immediately to infer that the remaining blue marble must be in the other box. If the child has seen the experimenter look into a box it is possible to infer that the experimenter knows where the two marbles are. However, even 5-year-olds have difficulty with this task and often attribute knowledge only if they have looked into the box (Varouxaki, Freeman, Peters, & Lewis, 1999). This ability is not typically mastered until the age of 9 (Pillow, 2002). So, this way of knowing about others' beliefs is a form of understanding developing after passing false belief tasks around the age of 5.

More complex beliefs

Another aspect of social understanding that is more complex than false belief understanding is thinking about others' thinking, or *recursive* thinking (Flavell, Botkin, Fry, Wright, & Jarvis, 1968; Müller & Overton, 2010). This is also called 'second order belief understanding'. It was studied by Perner and Wimmer (1985) by presenting children with a story in which John and Mary see an ice-cream van when playing at the park. While Mary goes home to get money for ice-cream, John sees the van move to the church. Mary also finds out that the van has moved, but John doesn't know this. Then Mary sets off to buy ice-cream. The question is where will John think she will go to buy ice-cream? Many 6- to 7-year-olds pass this test by realising that John would think that Mary still believes the van is at the park, but younger children do not. However, is this way in which this task is presented just too complicated? In a simplified task, a mother gets a puppy for her son Peter for his birthday, but does not tell him. However, Peter accidentally finds out about the puppy. Peter's grandmother asks Peter's mother if he knows what he is getting for his birthday. The test question here is 'What does his mother say?' Most 5½-year-olds passed the test and even 40% of 4-year-olds mastered this simplified task (Sullivan, Zaitchik, & Tager-Flusberg, 1994).

Thinking about thinking is certainly more complex than first-order false belief tasks (such as the unexpected location task), but are these types of tasks *qualitatively* different from one another? Another form of understanding beliefs does differ qualitatively because it concerns how the same information is interpreted. For example, think about watching a movie with a friend. If your friend leaves the room and misses part of the film he or she may end up with different beliefs and this would be based on different information, just like the false belief task. But even if you both watch the whole movie together you might still *interpret* it differently. Understanding this possibility involves a complex conception of how humans acquire beliefs. Specifically, it involves the understanding that different beliefs can be due to the *same* information being interpreted in different ways (Carpendale & Chandler, 1996; Chandler & Lalonde, 1996; Lalonde & Chandler, 2002). This more complex, interpretive understanding of belief may be involved in understanding irony, sarcasm, and forms of humour involving one word with different meanings.

There are two main ways in which an understanding of interpretation has been assessed. One way of assessing children's understanding that the same ambiguous stimulus can be interpreted in multiple ways is to present children with a word or a sentence that can be interpreted in two ways. Some pictures can also be interpreted in two ways such as the famous 'duck–rabbit' (see Figure 11.1) which can be seen as either a duck or a rabbit (Jastrow, 1900). Two puppets are then shown to disagree about what the picture is, one claiming that it is a duck and the other disagreeing and insisting that it is a rabbit. When children are asked about this situation 5-year-olds tend to think that one of the puppets is right, whereas 8-year-olds

Figure 11.1   Jastrow's duck–rabbit

Jastrow's duck–rabbit picture can be used to test children's ability to appreciate that the same picture can be seen as two different depictions. (Jastrow, 1900.)

easily realise that both can be right, and that it is not possible to predict how someone else would interpret this ambiguous figure. A second way to assess an early understanding of interpretation is to present children with an ambiguous stimulus that is likely to be interpreted in different ways by different people, such as a Rorschach inkblot (a 'picture' that does not obviously have a symbolic connection to an object). With this methodology it is also at about the age of 7 to 8 that children master the task, realising that given an ambiguous stimulus it is very unlikely that two people will come up with the same interpretation (Chandler & Lalonde, 1996; Lalonde & Chandler, 2002).

Another aspect of understanding interpretation is realising that there could be reasons for why individuals end up with particular perspectives, and that some people might be biased in their interpretation. This was studied with the scenario of a classroom situation in which a boy, Steve, is holding the class pet rabbit next to its cage and is seen by two other boys, Doug and Karl. The action is ambiguous because Steve could be acting help-fully by returning the rabbit or he could be naughty by taking it out of the cage. Doug and Karl have different biases because Doug likes Steve and so is likely to interpret the act positively, whereas Karl does not like him and so will probably interpret his action negatively. The understanding of *biased* interpretation develops between the ages of 5 and 8 (Pillow, 2012). Applying this insight to social situations, such as understanding the possible meanings of two children in the schoolyard looking at another child, talking among themselves and then approaching the other child, continues to develop during preadolescence from ages 9 to 11 (Bosacki & Astington, 1999).

Understanding how knowledge is acquired continues to develop through adolescence and beyond. Indeed, there is a rich history of research on college students developing their understanding of knowledge and knowing, also referred to as *epistemic development* (Perry, 1970). A number of researchers have described the development of forms of such understanding but a common pattern articulated is that younger adolescents start off thinking of knowledge as absolute, as black and white, but they then realise that, in fact, more and more of what they thought was black and white is actually open to alternative interpretations. They start to think of all knowledge as relativistic, and only gradually realise that although knowledge is not absolutely certain, decisions must still be made based on the best evidence and arguments available (e.g. Hallett, Chandler, & Krettenauer, 2002; see Carpendale & Lewis, 2006, for a further review).

11.3 THEORIES OF SOCIAL COGNITIVE DEVELOPMENT

Many theories have been proposed to explain the development of children's social understanding. During the 1980s and 1990s three theories of false belief understanding were particularly popular. Although these theories differ, they are all based on the same preconception regarding the mind (see Ratcliffe, 2007). That is, it is assumed that children experience their own private mind and are faced with the problem of trying to understand other people. In philosophy this is known as 'the problem of other minds' (see Chapter 1 and Chapter 5 for a discussion with reference to infants). In this section we will describe each of these three theories and then offer an alternative to them. On the basis of what you have read in previous chapters, you might like to guess what the theories are before we start to consider them. You will notice that these three theories have been around for some time. They have lasted a long while, in part because it is hard to test one against the others.

The first of these three solutions to the problem is known as the 'theory theory' because it is a theory that children form a theory about minds. As James Russell (1992) quipped, this theory is 'so good they named it twice'. From this perspective, mental states are conceptualised as abstract and invisible and thus they have to be inferred. In other words, we see people act but we have to infer their reasons for doing so. Children are depicted as little scientists trying to figure out other people and how their minds work (e.g. Gopnik & Wellman, 1992, 1994, 2012). To do so, children are thought to formulate a set of laws concerning belief-desire reasoning, and this provides a framework for explaining and predicting others' action. This approach is also applied in other areas such as children's understanding of physics and biology (Carey, 1985).

Another version of the theory theory focuses on children's understanding of meta-representation, thought to develop around 4 years, which allows children to compare representations (Perner, 1991). For example, in the standard false belief task the child needs to hold in mind and compare the representation of reality ('The chocolate is in the red cupboard') with the contrasting representation of Maxi's belief ('Maxi thinks the chocolate is in the blue cupboard'). According to Perner's theory what develops is the ability to compare and contrast discrepant representations like these and it is when they are about 4 that children develop a higher-order ('meta') grasp of the two representations.

A second proposed solution is that rather than each child having to formulate her own understanding, this way of thinking is claimed to have evolved in humans, and children are born with theories in the form of innate modules (or a set of modules) for 'computing' mental states, the 'Theory of Mind Mechanism' (Leslie, 1987). In addition, a series of modules or mechanisms have been proposed to explain earlier social skills: the intentionality detector, the eye direction detector, and the shared attention mechanism (Baron-Cohen, 1995). Gopnik and Wellman's (2012) most recent position seems to be a combination of theory theory and innate modules, because they claim infants are born with theories and then develop further refinements.

A third solution is that children do not need a theory to understand the mind because they have their own mind, and therefore they can imagine themselves in another's place. According to this simulation theory children get better at imagining others' perspectives when these differ from their own (e.g. Gordon, 1986; Harris, 1991, 2000; Johnson, 1988). There have also been some attempts to combine theory theory and simulation theory (Carruthers & Smith, 1996; Hurley, 2008; Perner, 1996; Stone & Davies, 1996).

We first discuss particular criticisms focusing on the three theories and then reflect on the assumptions they share. To begin with theory theory, the proposal that children are little scientists constitutes a problem for some: 'for academic investigators children are almost invariably miniature theoreticians, never miniature musicians, politicians, panel beaters, stand-up comics, or lay-abouts' (Gellatly, 1997, p. 32). But, rather than scientists, children could also be viewed as like little 'clowns, thespians and warmongers' (Russell, 1992, p. 515).

It might be thought that the theory theory is the idea that humans have general frameworks for thinking about experience, and these frameworks change with development. However, this vague idea is consistent with any approach to understanding human knowledge. The theory theory is more specific in describing knowledge in terms of laws that are formulated, tested, and applied (Campbell & Bickhard, 1993). From early on in the debate, Russell (1992, p. 515) had argued that 'theory change' merely describes 'what children say at different ages in terms of the concept of theory', but this does not provide an explanation of how children get from one theory to the next. In the philosophy of science there has also been a debate over how we can account for historical shifts in thinking. In addition, it could also be questioned whether 3-year-olds, let alone infants, can form and revise theories. Of course, the claim is not that young children go through the same reflective process that scientists do, but rather that their theorising is implicit. Accordingly, the child could act on a set of assumptions about the mind but not be able to articulate exactly (or at all) what these are. This presents us with a problem: although we know what theorising is in the sense that a scientist is required to produce a comprehensible account of what is to be explained, it is not clear what 'implicit theorising' is, so it is difficult to know what is actually being claimed by proponents of this view.

As noted above, some theory theorists assert that infants may be born with innate theories for computing mental states, and so this position converges with researchers proposing innate modules. The validity of the claim that infants are born with innate modules requires that this is biologically plausible. However, even these researchers have to acknowledge that modules must develop, so that stating that they are innate is simply deferring the developmental explanation. To date there has been no clarification regarding the biological details of how it is possible to get from the zygote, or fertilised egg, to such complex innate and modular forms of thinking. Perhaps this is too much to ask of psychologists and it should really be a task for biologists. But as Hebb, Lambert, and Tucker (1971) noted some time ago, in order to make claims of innate knowledge it is necessary that such an explanation is, in fact, possible. Furthermore, a group of researchers, taking what is referred to as a neuroconstructivist approach, argue that it is not biologically plausible to claim innate knowledge because there are not enough genes in the human genome to completely specify the incredible neural interconnectivity required for human forms of thinking, and that instead neural pathways are shaped through experience (Mareschal et al., 2007; see Chapter 5). We consider their position below.

Finally, versions of the simulation theory have been discussed for some time, and they have been criticised for decades. The view that humans understand others based on applying their own experience to those people might appear to be commonsense. As adults we can do this, although resorting to this form of understanding is likely to be fairly rare. But that adults can do this is an *outcome* of development. The problem here is to explain the development of this ability, and we cannot assume infants can already do this (Carpendale & Lewis, 2006; Scheler, 1913/1954; Zahavi, 2008).

Criticism is not limited to individual theoretical approaches, it can also apply to their shared assumptions. Even though they might appear to be quite different, in fact these apparently diverse accounts all start from the same way of thinking about the problem children are faced with in learning about other people. That they draw upon the philosophical assumption of the problem of other minds (see Chapter 2) is recognised by proponents (Meltzoff, 2011) as well as critics (Leudar & Costall, 2004). Beyond these three approaches there is another family of theories sharing the idea that the origins of human thinking emerge in social activity (e.g. Carpendale, Hammond, & Atwood, 2013; Overton, 2015) and these are the central focus of Chapter 12.

11.4 RECENT RESEARCH AND TWO CURRENT THEORETICAL DEBATES

False belief understanding in infancy?!

Until 2005 the standard view was that children learn that others, as well as themselves, can have beliefs that are false sometime between 3 to 5 years of age (Wellman et al., 2001). Evidence that even infants may already understand false beliefs has been a challenge to the field! This was first shown in an experiment that we have already described in Box 6.1 (Onishi & Baillargeon, 2005). This experiment showed that 15-month-olds look longer if an experimenter reaches where they would not expect her to reach – to a green box if they had seen her putting an object into a yellow box and the object had moved to the green one in her absence. Onishi and Baillargeon claimed that this is evidence of infants' understanding others' false beliefs. This finding has now been replicated and extended in a number of studies (Surian, Caldi, & Sperber, 2007; Surian & Geraci, 2012; for a review see Baillargeon et al., 2016). There is even evidence to suggest that at 7 months infants respond to others' beliefs (Kovács, Téglás, & Endress, 2010), but it now appears that this finding in such young infants may have been due to artifacts arising from the experimental paradigm: an 'attention check' made to ensure that the infant was paying attention (a human agent walking across the screen to attract the infant's attention). A series of later experiments showed that the timing of this check was causing this attentional bias and this was shown even when no agent was present, by using a light bulb illuminating to keep the infant's attention (Phillips, Ong, Surtees, Xin, Williams, Saxe, & Frank, 2015, Experiment 7).

Much debate has focused on how this research should be interpreted. There is a paradox here regarding why infants pass tasks that are claimed to assess false belief understanding, but 3-year-olds still fail standard verbal tests. This has been described as the 'new puzzle of theory of mind development' (Saxe, 2013), but in fact this contrast between infants' abilities and preschoolers' understanding was already present from the beginning of this research tradition. Some early researchers argued that infants already have an 'implicit' theory of mind (Bretherton, McNew, & Beeghly-Smith, 1981). Onishi and Baillargeon's (2005) interpretation of this research is that infants at this age already understand false beliefs, and the standard verbal false belief tasks underestimate children's actual knowledge. Another view is that this paradox can be explained through two systems or cognitive processes. The first system is simple, efficient, inflexible, and innate. A second, later emerging, more flexible system is needed to pass the verbal false belief tasks (Apperly & Butterfill, 2009; Leslie, 2005; Scott & Baillargeon, 2009; Sodian, 2011; Surian et al., 2007).

Another approach is to provide a different set of explanations for infants' success on these tasks. One argument is that infants form associations between an actor, object, and location, or they learn behavioural rules about what people do, such as reaching toward where they have last seen an object. Such low-level explanations do not require an understanding of the mind (Perner & Ruffman, 2005; Ruffman & Perner, 2005). A similar view is that infants learn links between behavioural patterns and goals (Ruffman, 2014; Ruffman, Taumoepeau, & Perkins, 2011). This explanation then preserves the importance of the verbal false belief task as really assessing an understanding of false beliefs, unlike the earlier implicit understanding.

At the methodological level, the research with infants is based on looking times and what is termed 'violation of expectation' – in this instance that the actor will search where she last saw the object and a reach elsewhere violates this principle. This is a method that has been critiqued because it only indicates that infants have detected a difference between the two conditions; anything beyond this is interpretation (Bremner, 1994; Haith, 1998; Sirois & Jackson, 2007). Even if the findings are accepted, claims such as Onishi and Baillargeon's (2005, p. 257) assertion that infants are born with an 'abstract computational system' for social understanding rest on several problematic assumptions. First, they assume that thinking can be understood as computation, a view that has been extensively critiqued (e.g. Heil, 1981). Second, a full biological explanation would have to show how the neural pathways presumably required for such 'computation' would operate. So presumably the claim simply assumes that infants are born with such 'computational skills'. In contrast to this requirement for fixed pathways, those who take a neuroconstructivist approach argue that neurological pathways must develop through experience (e.g. Fisher, 2006; Mareschal et al., 2007; Stiles, 2009; Stiles et al., 2015).

This debate has been characterised as the 'rich' position that infants are born with an abstract computational system versus the 'lean' perspective that they merely form associations based only on 'surface' behaviour, not 'deeper' mental states (Sodian, 2011). In fact, both these positions share the same starting assumption regarding the mind that we have discussed throughout this book – a Cartesian view that there is a separation between mental states that cause physical movements, and individuals can introspect on their own private mind that is inaccessible to others. Although this may be adults' experience (it may not!), it is an outcome of earlier development not an inborn skill.

From the perspective of an alternative relational or constructivist approach it is not surprising that there is evidence of two forms of knowledge. The constructivist view of knowledge holds that infants learn about the interactive potential of their social world just as they learn about their physical world (Allen & Bickhard, 2013; Mead, 1934; Piaget, 1936/1952; Stone et al., 2012). Infants develop a practical sensorimotor intelligence that has to do with actions and goals (e.g. Fenici, 2015; Woodward, 2005). They learn about action patterns that involve goals and intentions, and are linked to the experience of seeing or touching. The view that this is just surface behaviour that is separate from and caused by underlying mental states is a philosophical assumption that is not arrived at through empirical observation, but is instead a preconception through which empirical evidence is interpreted. Infants' experience of others is full of intentions and emotions. The practical understanding of what others do based on their previous interaction is what is assessed with infant false belief tasks. This is different from later verbal and reflective understanding (Carpendale & Lewis, 2010, 2015a, 2015b; Fenici, 2013, 2015; Stone et al., 2012).

Filling in the developmental sequence

We started with verbal false belief understanding achieved between the ages of 3 and 5 years, and then described infants' abilities to respond to others' beliefs. But we need to fill that gap. Nativist claims about infants' knowledge do not provide a developmental sequence of forms of social understanding. Here are some examples. Two-year-olds show some understanding of what others have seen because they point more for their mothers when she returns to the room having not seen a toy being moved. This suggests they have some understanding that she would not know about where the object is now located (O'Neill, 1996). In another task children watch a puppet mouse place cheese in one box and then go to bed, but while he is asleep another mouse moves the cheese to a different box. The experimenter then says 'I wonder where he will look for his cheese?' Children under 3 tend to *look* toward the correct location in this false belief situation, even though they *fail* the verbal question (Clements & Perner, 1994).

Furthermore, 18-month-olds seem to show some understanding of what others have experienced. This is suggested by a study in which 18-month-old infants play with two toys with an experimenter who then leaves the room and the infant plays with a third toy with a second experimenter. Then the first experimenter returns and says 'Wow can you give that to me?' while looking in the direction of all three toys. The infants tend to give her the toy she hadn't played with, suggesting that they know something about what she knew (Moll, Carpenter, & Tomasello, 2007). Another way to reveal 18-month-olds' knowledge of others is through how they help. Infants aged 16, 18, and 30 months were taught how to unlock two boxes. Then they watched as an experimenter placed a toy in one box and left the room. While he was out a second experimenter moved the toy to the other box and locked both boxes. Then the first experimenter returned and attempted to open the box where he had placed the toy (remember that it had been moved to the other box without his knowledge). The question is how do the children help? If they understand that he is looking for his toy, then they should help by unlocking the other box where the toy actually is. The two older age groups did just this, although the results for the 16-month-olds were not strong, suggesting that 18-month-olds show some understanding of others' false beliefs (Buttelmann, Carpenter, & Tomasello, 2009).

An alternative interpretation of this research, however, is that rather than having to reason about mental states in order to help the adult, the children might be responding based on their understanding of the social situation. This is what Allen (2015) argued and provided evidence for with an additional control condition in which one experimenter places a toy in one of two boxes. While he is out of the room another experimenter moves the toy to the other box. In the false belief condition the returning experimenter looks in the box where he left it, i.e. acting on his false belief. But in an additional condition the returning experimenter looks in the other box, where the toy it was moved to but he has no reason to know that, which is why this condition is called the 'clairvoyance condition'. If children were reasoning about his mental states they should have thought he wanted an empty box and should have helped with that goal, but instead the children tended to assume he wanted the toy and opened the box for him. Although it might be strange to want an empty box, another condition was used in which the social situation made that action understandable because the returning experimenter came back with his hands full of toys looking for a place to hide them. In this situation an empty box is a relevant goal and when he tried to open the box with the toy (which he should have thought was empty) children helped him instead with opening the empty box. These results are consistent with the possibility that rather than requiring reasoning about mental states, children's helping in these experiments could be due to their understanding of typical social situations (Allen, 2015).

Another approach to evaluating young children's grasp of beliefs is to observe their ability to be deceptive. In the context of trying to trick someone searching for a treasure, even 2½-year-olds had some success in laying false trails and erasing the footprints leading to the treasure (Chandler, Fritz, & Hala, 1989; Hala, Chandler, & Fritz, 1991). But other researchers reported mixed results (Russell, Mauthner, Sharpe, & Tidswell, 1991; Sodian, Taylor, Harris, & Perner, 1991). In naturalistic observation, young children seem to engage in deception in everyday life before they can pass a standard false belief task (Newton, Reddy, & Bull, 2000; Reddy, 2007).

In further research, Rubio-Fernández and Geurts (2013) conducted an unexpected transfer false belief task in which a banana was moved from one location to the other. They modified the standard procedure in two important ways. First (following Freeman, Lewis, & Doherty, 1991), instead of asking the usual test question they gave the doll to the child to continue acting out the story and just asked open-ended questions about what the doll might do. Second, the children did well when the doll was present but with her back turned when the banana was moved. In a different condition in which the doll was not present because it was put into a bag of toys, the 3½-year-old children tended to fail the task at a rate of 80% (Rubio-Fernández & Geurts, 2013). It is interesting that having the doll present, but with her back turned, helped children pass the test. It is possible that this is because their understanding is based on their earlier mastery of joint attention events in which they have learned that if someone is turned away from the critical events they don't respond. This research reopens a longstanding question about the criteria for competence in understanding tasks like false belief (Lewis & Mitchell, 1994).

11.5 SOCIAL COGNITIVE NEUROSCIENCE: NEURONS AND KNOWLEDGE

A complete account of social cognitive development should include the biological side to the story. All of the theories discussed have a biological dimension, yet these can differ radically. Research in neuroscience has generated a lot of excitement, both in the field and the popular press. In particular, two lines of research have been influential in social cognitive research: mirror neurons and localisation of functions in particular brain regions.

Mirror neurons

Mirror neurons are a type of neuron that have generated great excitement because it is argued by some that these neurons may explain social cognition. They were first discovered in the ventral premotor cortex (area F5) in macaque monkey brains. These neurons are activated during performance of acts such as grasping a nut, but also when the monkey observes a human experimenter performing the same act. They even fire when the action is partially hidden, or only heard (Gallese, 2007). The research with macaques was based on an invasive procedure (each nerve cell had to be tapped through surgery), but mirror neurons are now inferred in human brains through imaging research (Gallese, Gernsbacher, Heyes, Hickok, & Iacobon, 2011). Some researchers argue that this provides a neural basis for social cognition because these neurons seem to allow for understanding others' action, and that these are 'neural mechanisms (mirror mechanisms) that allow us to directly understand the meaning of the actions and emotions of others by internally replicating ("simulating") them without explicit reflective mediation' (Gallese et al., 2004, p. 396). Vittorio Gallese argues that our nervous system is equipped to make the same 'like me' comparisons which Andrew Meltzoff argued newborn humans are capable of.

Several difficulties with these claims have been pointed out, however. First, macaques don't develop false belief understanding, so simply having mirror neurons is not enough to develop a fully-fledged grasp of the mind. Second, the claim that these neurons could facilitate or underlie social understanding assumes that this system is in place very early in development, yet this assumption is problematic, and it is more likely that this system develops through experience. Third, there is a tendency to overlook the limits of what can be explained by mirror neurons. Assuming that the same neurons are activated when a child reaches or sees someone else reach (even if this results in some form of action understanding) does not help in understanding the other person, because it does not make it possible to decide among the many potential reasons why the other person reached. Furthermore, mirror neurons cannot explain children's understanding of simple communicative acts such as pointing. If the same neuron fires when a child points and when she sees someone else point, this does not aid her in understanding the multiple possible meanings. These depend on a history of shared social interaction (see Chapter 5;

Carpendale & Lewis, 2008a, 2008b, 2015a). Thus, mirror neurons may play an important role in the anticipation of action, but by themselves do not provide a complete explanation of the complex problems of conceptualising human understanding. In addition, it is necessary to be aware of the history of social experience through which neural connections are formed.

Neuroimaging and localising functions in the brain

A great deal of recent research attention has been focused on where in the brain particular functions are located. Although this is just one approach in neuroscience, it has tended to dominate the field. Neuroimaging studies use a variety of imaging technologies, but functional magnetic resonance imaging (fMRI) is perhaps the most common methodology used in research to localise neural structures active during particular forms of cognition in adults, but studies involving children are relatively rare (Byars et al., 2002). A number of different brain regions have been proposed as being important in social cognition. However, it has not been easy to reach a consensus on where thinking about other people occurs in the brain. Some of the brain regions that have been proposed as part of the system supporting social cognition include the medial prefrontal cortex, posterior cingulate/precuneus, and bilateral temporal parietal junction (Mar, 2011).

To provide a quantitative summary of previous findings, Mar conducted three meta-analyses (analyses of the data from a group of studies) of neuroimaging studies of social cognition and concluded that the brain regions involved are actually much larger than is usually assumed, and include other areas not typically mentioned (see also Gallese, 2007), notably the bilateral superior temporal sulcus, left temporal pole, left amygdala, and left superior frontal gyrus. Furthermore, the areas active in social understanding overlap with regions that are important in understanding stories. The brain regions that are shared by social cognition and narrative comprehension form a network that has been associated with various forms of thinking, such as daydreaming, autobiographical memory, and thinking about the future (Mar, 2011). As discussed in the context of language development (Chapter 8), the localisation of functions in particular parts of the brain is likely to be the outcome of development, and does not necessarily reveal much about its nature.

Neuroscience research in general, and neuroimaging in particular, have generated a great deal of excitement both in the scientific literature and the popular press. Why is it that this research is considered so exciting? Perhaps it is because neuroimaging technology gives the impression of actually being able to see into the mysterious organ that seems to hold the key to understanding who we are and how we work. Brain scans seem like hard evidence, unlike interviewing people and so on. In the popular press there is a tendency to transform neuroimaging research into somehow magically seeing thoughts. It is important to guard against such problematic thinking.

The attraction of neuroscience, and especially neuroimaging, has been examined in several studies. For example, when students were asked to rate the scientific reasoning presented in brief fictitious articles, they rated the article as making much more sense when it included a brain image compared to students who read the same article with only a bar graph or no graphic representation (McCabe & Castel, 2008). This held even for published articles, and the brain image was even given more weight by students (who are relatively less experienced) than the criticism of an expert (Crawford, 2008; McCabe & Castel, 2008; Wesiberg et al., 2008). More recently, it seems that this effect extends more broadly to the neuroscience information that is presented, even when it is irrelevant, rather than specifically to brain images (Weisberg, Taylor, & Hopkins, 2015). Fortunately, this effect was not found for experts in the field. So we must be cautious about reading too much into findings just because a study employs imaging or mentions areas of the brain.

The results from any methodology require careful and critical analysis, so it is important to be aware of discussions both inside and outside neuroscience. We need to know about what neuroimaging informs us and what it does not. If we take fMRI as an example because it is probably the most common imaging technology, then what does it indicate? The signal for fMRI indicates blood flow in parts of the brain. Based on increased blood flow it is assumed that there is increased firing of the neurons in that part of the brain. However, it is possible for areas of the brain to be active but still not transmit signals to other regions (Logothetis, 2008; Page, 2006). Furthermore, evaluating neuroimaging research requires being aware of the assumptions regarding averaging neural activity to produce the scans, and this is not as straightforward as the appealing images suggest (e.g. Tallis, 2011; see also Vul, Harris, Winkielman, & Pashler, 2009, and commentaries). Furthermore, it is not simply the case that particular regions perform only one function, because areas can be active for different functions (Kagan, 2006; Miller, 2008; Page, 2006).

Localisation and development: from information to knowledge

Researchers involved in localising functions in particular brain regions are, unfortunately, often silent regarding how the adult brain becomes specialised into areas dedicated to particular functions. Discussion of development in cognitive neuroscience is often left at the level of presenting differences in activation patterns between children and adults. What is also needed is discussion of the developmental processes involved in getting to the adult level. Using the word *maturation* is not sufficient, as this simply restates the problem. Those who take a neuroconstructivism approach argue that it is not possible simply to leap to conclusions about the origins and nature of neural interconnectivity. These authors also hold that social experience shapes neurological processes just as much as the reverse (Carpendale, Sokol, & Müller, 2010; Di Paolo & De Jaegher, 2012; Mareschal et al., 2007; Sameen, Thompson, & Carpendale, 2013).

The goal of neural imaging is to discover the neural correlates of forms of thinking; that is, finding the brain regions that are active during particular forms of thinking, in this case thinking about social matters. These neural correlates are referred to as the neural basis of the form of thinking. It sounds as if something could be learned about thinking once we find the neural processes that underlie it. But, in fact, all that is known is that those regions are more active than they normally are when they produce background activity.

Neuroscience research is interpreted from the perspectives of psychological theories and, therefore, work in neuroscience is as good as the psychological theory it is assimilated to. Neuroscience research can be interpreted from the perspectives of both of the worldviews we have discussed throughout this book. One is in terms of the information-processing approach. From this perspective, thinking is understood using the metaphor of a computer, and neural activity is depicted as its electrical processes. Thinking is assumed to occur in the brain just as processing goes on in computers. Input occurs through the senses, then the information received is processed, and the output is action. A difficulty is that the word *information* is ambiguous and can have different meanings. Light hitting the eyes is transformed and transmitted to the brain via the optic nerves. This is 'information', in one sense of the term, like a camera recording information. However, the camera doesn't know anything and it is still necessary to explain how a person knows something about what she sees (see Chapter 1). Thus, the information-processing framework appears to explain how humans acquire knowledge by slipping, unnoticed, from a definition of information as a neural activity to information as knowledge.

Another way of thinking about this issue is that our human nervous system allows us to form expectations about our interaction with the world. Neural activity enables individuals to engage in action and social interaction and gradually master this social process. According to this view, humans see the world in terms of action potential and form action plans concerning what can be done with the world (Kinsbourne & Jordan, 2009).

Clearly, neuroscience research is fascinating and it is important to learn more about the incredible complexity of synapses, and how brains enable human ways of life. However, it is also essential to be cautious about jumping to conclusions about what this research tells us. For example, it has been found that looking at a picture of a loved one who has recently died results in increased blood flow to the brain area known as the nucleus accumbens (Beck, 2010). This may be an important piece of information, but it must also be combined with a complex appreciation of the experience of extended grief. Neuroscience studies *causes*, but actions are done for *reasons*. Neurons are necessary for cognition, and enable the forms of interaction in which human thinking develops. But in order to understand human social practices such as making promises, it is necessary to understand that this emerges through social experience in human ways of life. The social and biological dimensions to the development of social understanding can also be addressed by studying cases in which development is not typical.

ATYPICAL SOCIAL DEVELOPMENT: AUTISM SPECTRUM DISORDER

Autism and Asperger Syndrome are now referred to as Autism Spectrum Disorder (ASD) (Diagnostic and Statistical Manual of the APA, 2013), in which there are continua in terms of intellectual ability, language, and communication skills. Considering these people along a spectrum of such abilities seems to be more valid than dividing them into subtypes (e.g. Mandy et al., 2014). People on the autism spectrum are of continuing interest for researchers in social cognitive development because they have difficulties with aspects of social understanding that seem to come so easily to typically developing individuals. This raises the question of what goes wrong in ASD, and whether these difficulties can inform us about typical development.

Autism was first described by Leo Kanner in 1943. His series of case studies begins with Donald, whose parents reported that he 'did not seem to notice his father's homecomings, and was indifferent to visiting relatives'. He 'even failed to pay the slightest attention to Santa Claus in full regalia' and seemed 'happiest when left alone' (p. 218). Donald was reported to pay 'no attention to persons around him. When taken into a room, he completely disregarded the people and instantly went for objects' (p. 220). Other parents described their children as 'like in a shell' and 'acting as if people weren't there' (p. 242). Donald also 'developed a mania for spinning blocks and pans and other round objects' (p. 218) and engaged in other repetitive behaviours such as shaking his head from side to side. Donald became upset and had temper tantrums when his rituals were interfered with. He also repeated words that he had heard such as 'chrysanthemum' and 'business'.

Independently, one year later, Hans Asperger also described a group of children as 'autistic', although they had high nonverbal intelligence. Autism-like difficulties in social interaction, but high intelligence and intact language skills, were until recently referred to in the DSM classification as Asperger Syndrome. The term is sometimes still used (e.g. Helles et al., 2017) but according to the 2013 version of the *Diagnostic and Statistical Manual* (APA, 2013) is now known as high-functioning ASD. The omission of the Asperger Syndrome diagnosis has not met with universal approval (Parsloe & Babrow, 2016).

ASD may co-exist with other disabilities such as intellectual disability, epilepsy, and attention deficit/hyperactive disorder (ADHD). Although some individuals on this spectrum do not use language, others do not have intellectual disabilities and can be highly intelligent. Some individuals with ASD with average or above average intelligence may develop a remarkable memory, or others may develop special skills at a level higher than their other abilities, such as in music, art, numerical calculation, reading, or doing jigsaw puzzles.

(Continued)

Some higher-functioning children on the autism spectrum may develop particular, narrow interests involving memorising facts about a specific, obscure subject such as train timetables, the names of subway stations, sport scores, or licence plate numbers (Armstrong, 2014).

Concerning the children he described, Kanner noted that 'They all come of highly intelligent families' (1943, p. 248, original emphasis), but accumulating research shows that ASD is found across diverse ethnic, cultural, and SES backgrounds. Kanner noted that before meeting Donald, the boy's father had sent a 33-page typewritten letter describing his son that was filled with 'obsessive detail'. Kanner remarked that 'for the most part, the parents, grandparents, and collaterals are persons strongly preoccupied with abstractions of a scientific, literary, or artistic nature, and limited in genuine interest in people. Even some of the happiest marriages were rather cold and formal affairs' (p. 250), and some of the marriages were 'dismal failures'. However, Kanner did not believe that the children's difficulties were due to their family life because they showed 'extreme aloneness' from early on. Interestingly, Kanner noted in this regard that it was commonly reported that these children failed to anticipate being picked up and did not adjust their body to the person holding him or her (p. 249). Therefore, Kanner suggested that 'these children have come into the world with an innate inability to form the usual, biologically provided affective contact with people' (p. 250).

It is accepted that autism is not an emotional disorder related to parenting (Rimland, 1964). Rather, it is recognised as having biological origins. It is more common in males than females; for every four boys who are affected there is one girl on the spectrum (US CDC), and this ratio can be as high as 11 to 1 for those verbally able children who used to be classed as having Asperger Syndrome (Baron-Cohen, Lombardo, Auyeung, Ashwin, Chakrabarti, & Knickmeyer, 2011).

ASD can run in families and so it seems that there is a strong link to genetics. However, it is possible that one monozygotic twin may be diagnosed with autism whereas the other may not, even though they have identical DNA. If both are diagnosed they can still differ in the level of severity of their symptoms. This indicates there is also a role for non-genetic factors in explaining ASD. Even though these twins have the same DNA their genome can be altered (e.g. methylated), resulting in the genes being expressed differently (Wong, Meaburn, Ronald, Price, Jeffries, Schalkwyk, Plomin, & Mill, 2013). Most geneticists no longer think that there is direct link to genes that can account for many cases of autism. Instead there seems to be great variability in the genes involved and combinations of genetic and environmental risks, with new mutations accounting for up to 20% of cases (Elsabbagh & Johnson, 2010).

One in 68 children is affected by ASD (US Center for Disease Control and Prevention, www.cdc.gov/ncbddd/autism/data.html), resulting in an annual societal cost of these disorders in

(Continued)

the UK alone of over 27 billion pounds (Elsabbagh & Johnson, 2010). In spite of the amount of research attention devoted to these disorders, little is still known about them. Autism was initially described as having three areas of impairment: difficulties in social understanding and interaction; problems in communication and language development; and repetitive behaviours. More recently the problems in the areas of social interaction and communication have been combined in the new *Diagnostic and Statistical Manual of Mental Disorders* (DSM-5, 2013), which followed a 14-year review of the diagnosis.

Autism spectrum disorders are so diverse in their manifestation that it is difficult or even impossible to categorise individuals with ASD simply and draw simple conclusions with respect to the causes of the disorder (Wong et al., 2013). Even in Kanner's (1943) seminal article he noted the diversity among the cases he described, each of which he believed 'merits … a detailed consideration of its fascinating peculiarities' (p. 217). In fact, some researchers have argued that autism may not be a single disorder and that the areas of difficulties in social interaction, problems in communication, and rigid and repetitive behaviours may not hang together as a single entity. Instead, some individuals may have impairment in one of these areas but not others. If it is not a single entity then there is unlikely to be a single cause (Happé, Ronald, & Plomin, 2006).

This diversity extends to the possibility of multiple pathways to the development of ASD. Two subgroups have been suggested. One pathway consists of infants who show subtle symptoms early on, around their first birthday, that become more obvious by the age of two. These infants show the following signs during their second year: deficits and delays in forms of joint attention; decreased responsiveness to their name and deficits in imitation; delays in verbal and nonverbal communication; motor delay; increased repetitive behaviours such as hand waving; extremes of temperament; and decreased flexibility in shifting their visual attention. If these children focus on a central object of interest they seem to have difficult disengaging from it to pay attention to something else. A second possible pathway is apparently typical development in early stages with surprisingly few signs of difficulties and these infants seem to interact well with their caregivers, but this is followed by what appears to be regression. This seems to be a less common pathway, and it has yet to be confirmed (Elsabbagh & Johnson, 2010). It is based mostly on parental report (Bradley, Boan, Cohen, Charles, & Carpenter, 2016).

EXPLANATIONS OF AUTISM SPECTRUM DISORDER

There are diverse approaches to explaining ASD, but they can be grouped into two families that could be characterised as 'top down' or 'bottom up'. These two approaches correspond to the two worldviews we have highlighted throughout this book. First,

(Continued)

according to the top-down approach, autism is explained through deficits in an innate module or series of modules (Baron-Cohen, 1995; Leslie, 1987). Even researchers making claims regarding innate modules must acknowledge that such modules have to develop. This theory of mind deficit hypothesis runs into problems explaining how these modules develop. Answering these questions and seeking the complex developmental stories, results in moving toward the other approach that can be characterised as 'bottom up' in the sense that small differences in biological characteristics are explored that may have large effects later in development. These small differences may appear to have nothing to do with social understanding but might still change the form of interaction that infants are drawn into, and this experience may be essential for further development (Mundy, 2016).

Simon Baron-Cohen et al.'s (2011) more recent view that ASD may be due to extreme expression of the male brain appears to fit better with a developmental account, if the idea is that autism is the extreme outcome of developmental processes that typically result in male brains. It seems that much of the current research on ASD fits best into the second approach, in the sense that these researchers are exploring factors in early development that may influence the trajectory of development. We will consider three examples of the bottom-up approach, at differing levels of analysis:

1   Peter Hobson (2002) has suggested that children who develop autism differ in *identification with others*, and this results in a different pattern of development. Stuart Shanker (2004; see also Richer, 1976) has speculated that differences in infants' emotional reactivity might result in different developmental trajectories. That is, if infants are over-reactive to the emotions aroused in face-to-face interaction they might turn away from their parents and this would deprive them of essential social experience. On the other hand, being under-reactive to emotions would also be detrimental and could result in a lack of engagement and interest in interacting with other people, a key source of social information.

Another way in which persons on the ASD spectrum appear to differ from typically developing individuals concerns *how they pay attention, particularly to social stimuli*. They appear to have a preference or bias toward focusing upon the minute detail of a stimulus rather than a whole. This may influence the way they learn about their environment (Burack et al., 2016). Ami Klin and his colleagues (2003) have used eye-tracking methods in order to explore the differential salience of types of stimuli, particularly social ones. They asked what is important for individuals with autism in terms of what they look at when presented with social stimuli. Children and adults with autism often make atypical eye contact. So how does eye contact develop in children with autism?

(Continued)

2   The sort of research needed from this perspective is to study what is happening during the first few years of life, but this is difficult in the case of autism because diagnosis is not usually made until the age of 3, making it difficult to research what leads up to it. Some attempts at early diagnosis were Baron-Cohen's Checklist for Autism in Toddlers (CHAT), which is a screening tool for use by doctors and nurses seeing toddlers. The scale has nine items such as does the child point with an index finger to indicate some-thing of interest (Baron-Cohen et al., 1992; Baron-Cohen et al., 1996)? This checklist has been revised as a parent-report screening tool (Robins, Casagrande, Barton, Chen, Thyde, & Fein, 2014). In response to the difficulties of studying development before diagnosis with ASD, research is now being conducted with the younger siblings of chil-dren with autism ('infant siblings'), who have about a 20% chance of being diagnosed with autism (Elsabbagh & Johnson, 2010).

Even two days after birth, typically developing children prefer to look at biological motion (Simion et al., 2008). This is assessed by presenting infants with a film of points of lights attached to the joints of a human actor, compared to the same film shown upside down and in reverse order. This preference is found in a wide range of other species from monkeys to birds. Two-year-olds with autism, however, do not show this preference, and instead prefer to watch non-social physical contingency such as movement followed by sound (Klin et al., 2009). This suggests these infants are already on a different developmental pathway and research suggests that children up to the age of 11 still do not attend to such arrays (Swettenham et al., 2013). From early in infancy, typically developing infants are drawn to look at human eyes and their fixations increase. However, infants who later were diagnosed with autism declined in looking at eyes from 2 to 6 months of age, suggesting that they had moved off the normal trajec-tory toward human engagement (Jones & Klin, 2013; see also Chapter 5).

Following infants at risk of autism because their older siblings were diagnosed was used in studying differential neural response to shifts in eye gaze. Elsabbagh et al. (2012) studied the response to eye gaze in infancy to see if it was related to later-emerg-ing autism. They recorded infants' event related potentials (ERPs) at 6 to 10 months to viewing faces with the eye gaze shifting either toward them or away from them. Elsabbagh et al. (2012) studied 104 infants of whom 54 were at risk for autism and 50 who had no family history of autism and followed them to age 3. The group of infants not at risk of autism showed a difference in neural activity in response to the dynamic shifts of gaze toward versus away from them, but the at-risk group did not show this response. This lack of difference was found in particular for 17 of the 54 infants in the at-risk group who were diagnosed with autism by age 3. There was some indication that some of the infants at risk for autism displayed a similar pattern, but then became

(Continued)

more like typical infants. These were all in the group who were not later diagnosed with autism (Elsabbagh et al., 2012).

We need a more complete developmental story about the characteristics of human infants' visual systems that result in this interest in eyes. The typical outcome of that experience is that babies become experts in faces and eyes, a vital source of social information (see Chapter 5 and Carpendale, Frayn, & Kurcharczyk, 2017). However, small differences in infants' biological characteristics, such as those having to do with their visual system or emotional reactivity, may set up a cascade of effects downstream, and might result in a different developmental pathway in which the infant is exposed to experience that does not facilitate typical social development.

3   Another bottom-up approach to autism focuses on *synapses and brain adaptation* (Johnson et al., 2015). Humans have an extended period of brain development, and the environment plays an important role in human brain development. In some species brain development is delayed until individuals have experienced their early environment and this can result in a great deal of flexibility. Primates, in particular, have a longer period of brain development compared to other species, and this is even more extenuated in humans in whom cortical maturation after birth takes about four times longer than in other primates. This slow rate of brain development results in a larger cortex. Furthermore, there are individual differences in the extent of this plasticity in brain development. Early experience of a predictable environment may result in the specialisation of brain structures, whereas lack of consistency in individuals' early experience of their environment may result in prolonged plasticity. This may be the case in autism because brain overgrowth has been reported (Johnson et al., 2015). The social environment may be the least predicable aspect of children's experience. Hundreds of genes have been linked to autism and many of these are involved in the function of synapses (i.e. linked to the amounts of particular receptors or transmitters). Different genes can result in inefficiencies in the function of synapses. Thus, there could be different pathways resulting in problems at the level of synapses causing inconsistency in experience and leading to autism. With a brain that is inefficient at the synaptic level, an infant may experience a less consistent environment and this may prolong plasticity. Poor processing at the level of synapses could result in less reliable experience of the environment and this could result in focusing on simple repetitive events, as seen in children diagnosed with autism. These children may withdraw from what they experience as an unpredictable social world and become overly focused on the more predictable non-social world and the precitable stimulation they produce through their repetitive action (Johnson et al., 2015).

(Continued)

CONCLUSION: A LIFE-LONG CONDITION?

It has long been known that autism is a life-long condition. After early childhood, research show that even individuals with relatively good language and social skills still fail to understand the subtleties of communication, such as following someone's gaze to see what they are attending to, or understanding that someone might speak in metaphorical terms (e.g. Brent, Rios, Happé, & Charman, 2004; Kaland et al., 2008). A meta-analysis of these abilities in adults, pooling the data from 37 studies, examined a range of tasks measuring these higher-order skills, particularly Francesca Happé's (1994) Strange Stories task (see above), which measures the ability to grasp the finer qualities of speech where meaning is communicated in a subtle way – identifying why someone might say something that is a white lie, a double bluff, coveys a subtle form of persuasion, or is caused by a misunderstanding. The analyses of this large sample showed these problems persist into adulthood (Chung, Barch, & Strube, 2014).

Do these findings suggest there is no possibility of improvement in the ability of individuals with autism to make up for their problems in social communication? This has been hotly debated since autism was first described. The hopes of individuals with the disorder and their families have repeatedly been raised and dashed, sometimes because self-professed 'experts' have irresponsibly claimed to have found a cure. However, over the past decade a number of interventions have shown that child-centred communication programmes are effective in eliciting some change in the nature of interaction and the symptoms of autism presented. This has been shown most clearly in the Preschool Autism Communication Trial (PACT) study. This is a randomised control trial of a parent-based approach involving 13 months of communication intervention. Immediately after the trial children showed fewer symptoms of autism and in interaction shared attention and engaged in more reciprocal interaction with their parent and, crucially, they initiated more social interaction (Green et al., 2010). Furthermore, this reduction in autistic symptoms was still present almost six years after the intervention had finished (Pickles et al., 2016). This study gives hope to the idea that the symptoms of autism can be reduced and has been the spur to further and more long-term relationship-based interventions.

SUMMARY AND CONCLUSION

In this chapter we have described the development of children's grasp of other people, focusing initially on the understanding that beliefs can be false. Counterintuitively, children do not master false belief understanding until sometime between the ages of 3 to 5. This finding has been explored in many studies. We discussed various theoretical explanations for this social cognitive development,

We also agreed with a longstanding view (Astington, 2001; Chandler, 1988) that there is more to social development than passing one test at around the age of 4. Beyond false belief understanding, there are additional insights regarding understanding themselves and others in psychological terms that children have still to acquire. Children also learn about emotions in a variety of situations of varying complexity. Further steps in understanding how knowledge is acquired concern beliefs about beliefs, inference, and differing interpretations of the same information.

We reviewed debate regarding the three theories of children's social understanding that have dominated discussion since the late 1970s. We have maintained that these share the same problem of depicting the child as an observer of events whose assessment of the mind is either inbuilt or learned from a detached perspective. As well as recent criticism of these theories we described an emerging perspective (or really a restatement of a long-standing view) that a grasp of the mind occurs within interactions and relationships.

We then discussed the implications of evidence that even infants may understand false beliefs. Based on studies of how infants react to someone who acts counter to their belief, some researchers have restated the claim that infants have innate knowledge of others. We have shown that this evidence could be more simply explained in terms of infants developing a practical social understanding given their anticipation of what others will do based on what they have seen. This ability is different from the later skills with verbal and reflective understanding required to pass verbal false belief tasks.

Approaches to social cognitive development in neuroscience have focused on mirror neurons and the localisation of functions in particular brain regions. We reviewed research and debate in both of these areas. Although mirror neurons may play a role in social understanding, it seems that they cannot provide a complete explanation. Considerable research has focused on localising brain regions that are active when individuals are thinking about social matters. In addition to localisation, it is essential to conceptualise the step from neural activity to an individual's understanding.

At the end of this chapter, we examined recent research on Autism Spectrum Disorder (see the box above). This is a biologically based disorder and its central diagnostic features of poor language and social skills have been linked to the areas of social understanding that we explored in this chapter. This review has led us to the conclusion that studying the development of ASD children may provide insights into the typical development of social understanding. It also provides key information to educationalists who spend a lot of their time working with these children to enhance their social skills. By breaking social skills down and working on the elementary processes, even children with severe communication difficulties can make progress in their communication (e.g. Houghton, Schuchard, Lewis, & Thompson, 2103). This reveals a clear interaction between research and practice.

FURTHER READING

Carpendale, J. I. M., & Lewis, C. (2006). *How Children Develop Social Understanding*. Oxford: Blackwell.

Carpendale, J. I. M, & Lewis, C. (2015). The development of social understanding. In L. Liben & U. Müller (vol. eds), *Vol. 2: Cognitive Processes*, R. Lerner (Editor-in-Chief), 7th edition of the *Handbook of Child Psychology and Developmental Science* (pp. 381–424). New York: Wiley Blackwell.

12 SOCIAL INTERACTION, LANGUAGE, AND SOCIAL UNDERSTANDING

LEARNING OUTCOMES

Having read this chapter you should:

- Be aware of the ways in which the development of social understanding is influenced by children's social context, including the culture they grow up in, the family context including siblings, parent–child interaction and factors within the child, including her attachment style.

- Be familiar with the role of peers in social cognitive development including play, popularity, and having a close mutual friend.

- Be aware of the effect of child characteristics such as being shy and withdrawn, as well as sensory impairments in the case of blindness and deafness.

- Be familiar with the ways in which language is linked to social understanding as a window on development as well as a context for development.

- Be able to take a position regarding the relations between language and social cognitive development.

- Be able to describe in detail the relations between social understanding and social skills and aggression.

People differ in their skill at understanding the social world. In the previous chapter we described the forms of social understanding children develop, but we presented only the average ages at which these skills are mastered because this is what researchers initially focused on. However, individual children vary widely in the rate at which they learn about others, and therefore the ages at which they reach these important milestones. Studying why some children are advanced in social understanding relative to others is one way to learn about how these skills develop. And this is a direction in which researchers have moved.

There are two groups of factors that influence the system in which children develop: the children's characteristics and their social environment. For example, parents who were advanced on a test of social understanding designed for adults in which they were asked to identify the emotions expressed in photographs of others' eyes had children who were also advanced in social understanding (Sabbagh & Seaman, 2008). This finding could be partially due to the biological characteristics that parents and their children share. However, in a large study of typically developing 60-month-old twins, most of the variability in the children's social understanding appeared to be due to environmental experience rather than genetic factors (Hughes, Jaffee, Happé, Taylor, Caspi, & Moffitt, 2005). This suggests that it is important to examine social experience and how it influences social cognitive development, and to study the way parents interact with their children.

This chapter is divided into three parts. In the first, and longest, section we map out several social processes that appear to influence the nature and rate of the development of a grasp of the social world. This has been a topic of intensive research interest over the past twenty years and the pace has been continual. These processes occur at levels as diverse as culture and social interactions. In the second section we examine theories and research concerning the role of language and communication in social understanding. The diversity of evidence on this relationship prepares us for the third section in which we consider the theoretical assumptions behind, and reflections on, how social factors channel the understanding of the mind. In the fourth and final section we examine the effect of learning about mental states. We explore a number of questions about the links with social understanding and children's behaviour, including whether having greater skills is associated with abstaining from, or committing more, acts of bullying.

12.1 THE INFLUENCE OF THE SOCIAL CONTEXT

In examining the influence of the social context on the development of social understanding some of the crucial pioneering research was a series of longitudinal studies conducted by Judy Dunn and her colleagues (e.g. Dunn, Brown, Slomkowski, Tesla, & Youngblade, 1991). For instance, they found that children who experience cooperative interaction with their siblings were more advanced in false belief understanding at 48 months. Conversely, children who lack such typical social experience because, for example, they grow up in orphanages, tend to have autism-like symptoms (Colvert et al., 2008; Rutter, Kreppner, O'Connor, & the English and Romanian Adoptees study team, 2001; Kreppner et al., 2007; Tarullo, Bruce, & Gunar, 2007; Yagmurlu, Berument, & Celimli, 2005) and these last even into adulthood (Sonuga-Barke et al., 2017). Furthermore, some studies have found that children growing up in lower socioeconomic circumstances are delayed in false belief understanding (Holmes, Black, & Miller, 1996; see also Cutting & Dunn, 1999), although this finding has not always been replicated (Hughes, Deater-Deckard, & Cutting, 1999; Ruffman, Perner, & Parkin, 1999). Such differences may be due to different amounts of parent–child talk (Cutting & Dunn, 1999). These sorts of findings led to interest in the social environments in which children learn about others (Dunn, 1996, 2004).

To investigate these general findings further what is needed are more detailed analyses of the nature of children's experience. In a series of brief subsections, we present here an analysis of nine factors that have been shown to relate to individual differences in performance on standard tests of social understanding, particularly false belief. These range from general cultural and social processes, to aspects of preschoolers' interactions, to factors within the child.

Culture and social understanding

Most broadly, children's social experience could be considered in terms of the culture in which they live. If the development of social understanding is influenced by their social experience then such development might be expected to vary across cultures that differ in the form of social experience children are exposed to. Variations in the nature of social understanding have been documented across cultures (Lillard, 1998). This question has been addressed by a number of studies, but as yet no clear answer is forthcoming (for a review see Slaughter & Perez-Zapata, 2014). A number of studies have reported a similar transition from failing false belief tasks to passing them between 3 and 5 years of age. This was found in a pioneering study with the Baka children of Cameroon, West Africa (Avis & Harris, 1991), as well as more recently across five cultures: Canada, Peru, Samoa, India, Thailand (Callaghan et al., 2005). On the other hand, other studies have reported significant delays in some cultures. The Junin Quechaun of Peru, for instance, have no words for think and refer to 'think' and 'believe' indirectly by, for example, asking 'What would he say?' Children in this culture were found to lag at least three years behind Western children (Vinden, 1996). A similar delay of three or more years in understanding false belief and belief-dependent emotions has also been reported in the Tolai and Tainae of Papua New Guinea, and the Mofu of Cameroon (Vinden, 1999). In addition, similar delays have been reported in children in Pakistan (Nawaz, Hanif & Lewis, 2015), which contrast with the data from India. Mayer and Träuble (2013) point out that in Callaghan et al.'s Samoan sample only 13 of the 18 5-year-olds passed the tasks. To investigate this finding further, they conducted a larger study of this culture with a sample of over 300 Samoan children. They reported a delay in the age at which the children passed the tests, with no significant difference between the 3- to 5-year-olds. It was not until age 8 that the majority of the children passed the tasks, with a third of the 10- to 13-year-olds still failing them (Mayer & Träuble, 2013). They pointed out that children in some cultures might be less familiar with experimental testing situations and we must keep this in mind (Mayer & Träuble, 2013).

In addition to comparing Western with non-Western children, Wellman et al. (2001) contrasted various Western cultures and found that compared to children from the US and

UK, participants from Australia and Canada did better, whereas children from Austria and Japan performed worst on false belief tasks. In a comparison of British and Italian children, the British children did better on both first- and second-order false belief tasks when controlling for age, verbal ability, maternal education, and number of siblings, but children from the two groups did not differ on tests of their understanding of mixed emotions (Lecce & Hughes, 2010).

Of course, culture must have its effect through the form of social interaction children experience, so it is essential to understand any cultural differences in terms of different family experiences such as family size and amount of talk about psychological explanations. In taking a step in this direction Vinden (2001) found that false belief understanding was negatively correlated with authoritarian parenting in European-Americans, but not in Korean-American parents. Understanding such results requires a more careful look at the form of social interaction children experience in their development.

The sibling effect

An important part of social life in many families is siblings. An intriguing finding was that having brothers and sisters is often linked to advanced understanding of false beliefs. This 'sibling effect' was first reported by researchers in the UK (Perner, Ruffman, & Leekam, 1994) who found that children with siblings were at least six months ahead of children without siblings. This finding was then extended to families in Canada, Japan, Greece, and Australia. In particular the effect was found for older siblings (Ruffman, Perner, Naito, Parkin, & Clements, 1998), but also within an age range from 12 months to 12 years (Peterson, 2000) (so younger and older than the child). Presumably this would be because it would be these children who would interact more with the child in question. In a one-year longitudinal study of children aged 3 to 5 years, those with siblings aged from 1 to 12 years were more advanced in social understanding when first assessed as well as when assessed one year later (McAlister & Peterson, 2013). This effect was also found in Greece for older kin living close by the children being studied (Lewis, Freeman, Kyriakidou, Maridaki-Kassotaki, & Berridge, 1996). The finding for older cousins was not replicated in China, however, and in fact the opposite result was found: children without older cousins did better on false belief tasks compared to those with older kin (Lewis, Huang, & Rooksby, 2007).

The sibling effect is not always replicated in all studies (Cole & Mitchell, 2000; Cutting & Dunn, 1999; Peterson & Slaughter, 2003), and no effect of having siblings has been found for twins (Cassidy, Fineberg, Brown, & Perkins, 2005). These findings suggest that it is not as simple as the number of bodies in the house, but that instead this effect is an indication of the sort of social interaction children experience, and it depends on positive quality of relationships not number of children (Hughes & Ensor, 2005). Having siblings can also change the way parents talk to their children. Four-year-olds with a brother or sister heard more discussion about what others know, think, or remember than those without siblings (Jenkins, Turrell, Kogushi, Lollis, & Ross, 2003). So, language may play a role in this effect, and this is also hinted at by the finding that the effect of having siblings is not as strong for children who are linguistically advanced (Jenkins & Astington, 1996).

There are several of possible explanations for why having siblings often leads to advanced social understanding. In families with more children there may be teasing, competing, cooperating, collaborating, playing, and so on. What is needed are more detailed explorations of the interaction children experience with siblings. Furthermore, if play is important then play with friends might also influence social development.

One suggestion is that the positive effect on social understanding is the influence of siblings on children's developing self-awareness. This possibility was evaluated in families living in New Zealand who identified as Pacific Islanders, an interdependent culture, with toddlers assessed on deception, emotion labelling, and social perspective taking at 20 and 26 months of age. A sibling effect was found, especially for children with two or more older siblings, but this effect was actually mediated by the development of the children's self-awareness. It seems that having siblings may provide more opportunities to develop a sense of self through learning how to use language such as saying 'me' or 'mine', and thus to differentiate between self and other, and that such self-awareness may facilitate the development of social understanding (Taumoepeau & Reese, 2014).

It should be noted that siblings influence one another beyond the preschool period. In one recent study Amy Paine and her colleagues examined the second order false belief skills in 229 7 year olds. They found that having a younger sibling facilitated performance on these tests, but only when the age gap was over two years. This contrasts with several studies of preschoolers who show a first order false belief advantage in children with an older sibling. The contrast at these ages reveals just how complex and changing these influences can be.

Play as a context for social development

Play may serve as an important social context for learning about others (Lillard, 1993a). Pretend play in particular may be important, especially if it involves learning about others' perspectives. Some forms of pretence have been found to be correlated with children's false belief understanding (Astington & Jenkins, 1999; Youngblade & Dunn, 1995). Those children who tended to take on roles in pretend play were advanced in false belief understanding when they were tested seven months later (Youngblade & Dunn, 1995). Making joint plans for pretend play, as well as assigning roles, were also found to be associated with false belief understanding (Astington & Jenkins, 1995). When this finding was followed up longitudinally, it was reported that the children who were advanced in false belief understanding were more involved in assigning roles and making joint plans seven months later (Jenkins & Astington, 2000). Thus, it may be that having an advanced level of social understanding might result in engaging in more pretend play, and this link between pretend play and social understanding could easily be bi-directional in nature. Play among siblings may be a factor in the sibling effect. More pretend play among sibling has been reported to be associated with increased use of psychological words (Howe et al., 2002; Youngblade & Dunn, 1995).

The role of peers

If siblings are important in development, what about peers? Children who were rated as popular by their peers were also found to be advanced in false belief understanding (Peterson & Siegal, 2002; Slaughter, Imuta, Peterson, & Henry, 2015). If interacting with other children is helpful, then it follows that the lack of such experience may be linked with slower social development. This fits with the finding that children who were rejected by their peers had lower social understanding when tested one year later with the faux pas test, which assesses children's understanding of unintended insults. This finding is consistent with the possibility that because these children were rejected they may have had less social experience and so were less advanced (Banerjee et al., 2011).

Being popular might appear to mean having friends, but this is not always the case. Some popular children lack a close mutual friend, while others who are low on popularity may have a close mutual friendship (Wellman, 2015). In one study, over half the children who were not popular had a close mutual friend, whereas almost a quarter of the popular children were friendless (Fink, Begeer, Peterson, Slaughter, & de Rosnay, 2015). Having no friends has long been associated with mental health difficulties from childhood to adulthood (Reisman, 1985), and this raises the question of what effect it might have on social cognitive development. Children who were delayed in social understanding at age 5 when they started school tended to lack friends (Fink et al., 2015). There may be a bidirectional relation between experiencing a close mutual friendship as a context for further developing social cognition, and the social skills needed to form close friendships. We return to this link between social understanding and children's social lives in a later section.

Child characteristics

If social understanding develops within interpersonal relationships then it is important to be aware of what the child brings to that relationship as well as the adult. That is, it takes two to tango. Children will influence the sort of interaction they experience – they will affect how others respond to them. There is little research, however, on the role of children's characteristics in their social cognitive development. There is some interesting work showing that infants reported to have a shy and socially fearful temperament tend to be advanced in social understanding as preschoolers (Mink, Henning, & Aschersleben, 2014). Similary Wellman, Lane, LaBounty, and Olson (2011) found that the children who were less aggressive and more shy in their interaction with others were advanced in social understanding later on in their preschool years. This might be due to such children taking a more reflective stance in thinking about others. This relation was not found, however, in a sample of younger children from 18 to 30 months (Gross, Drummond, Satlof-Bedrick, Waugh, Svetlova, & Brownell, 2015).

Infants' early social understanding seems also to be related to their later social skills. This was supported in as study by Sodian and Kristen-Antonow (2015) in which they reported correlations between declarative pointing at 12 months and later false belief understanding assessed at 50 months.

Sensory loss: blindness and deafness

Another aspect of children's characteristics that might influence their development concerns sensory loss. Some research with congenitally blind children shows a delay in false belief understanding, even until age 12 (Minter, Hobson, & Bishop, 1998; Peterson, Peterson, & Webb, 2000). This delay might be due to greater difficulty in keeping track of who has had visual access to various events, and so this may influence learning about the social and psychological consequences of such knowledge.

Delays in false belief understanding have also been reported for deaf children (Peterson & Siegal, 1995). What is especially interesting about this research is that deaf children with deaf parents are not delayed in false belief understanding. This may be because deaf parents would be fluent in sign language, and therefore their children would be exposed to a complex language from early on (de Villiers & de Villiers, 2000; Schick, de Villiers, de Villiers, & Hoffmeister, 2007; Woolfe, Want, & Siegal, 2002). This suggests that language plays an important role in false belief understanding, a topic to which we return to in a later section.

Parent–child interaction and social understanding

Reviews of several studies show that that parenting is of key importance in children's social cognitive development (see Pavarini, de Hollanda Souza, & Hawk, 2013). When parents were asked about their approach to discipline, those who reported they would talk to their offspring about others' feelings had children who were advanced in false belief understanding, suggesting that this form of talk might facilitate such development (Ruffman et al., 1999). This finding was extended beyond disciplinary situations to everyday events (Peterson & Slaughter, 2003). In contrast, when parents used assertive parenting involving yelling and spanking, this was linked to poor social understanding (Pears & Moses, 2003). Parental warmth was linked to advanced false belief understanding, but this was found only for girls (Hughes et al., 1999). What is needed are more fine-grained assessments of parenting.

Relationships: attachment style

A crucial factor in children's development is the strong emotional bond that develops between parents and their children (see Box 5.1). The form that psychological attachment

(Bowlby, 1958, 1969) takes depends on the child's experience with particular caregivers. Infants form secure attachment when they have had a history of responsive and dependable interactions. Various forms of insecure attachment can develop when parents are not responsive or are inconsistent in their responses.

One way of understanding parent–child relationship is in terms of the child's attachment style. A number of studies using different methodologies have reported that secure attachment is associated with earlier false belief understanding. Attachment style can be assessed at about one year of age with the 'Strange Situation', which is a procedure consisting of a series of situations in which infants' reactions to separations from and reunions with their caregiver are assessed. Using a longitudinal design, attachment was assessed with the Strange Situation at 11 or 13 months, and it was found that infants who were rated as securely attached were also more likely to pass false belief tasks when they were 4 years old (Meins, Fernyhough, Russell, & Clark-Carter, 1998). In another study, 3- to 6-year-olds who were found to be securely attached, as assessed with a projective measure in which children were asked to talk about pictures depicting separations between parents and children, were also advanced in their understanding of belief dependent emotions (Fonagy, Redfern, & Charman, 1997). Attachment security at age 2 has also been related to emotion understanding one year later at age 3 (Raikes & Thompson, 2006).

There are a number of possible explanations of why children who are securely attached also tend to be advanced in social understanding. It might be thought that children who are securely attached have easy temperaments and this makes it easier for parents to interact with them, which might facilitate social cognitive development. This is unlikely to be the explanation because attachment is not determined by temperament; children of various temperaments can form secure attachments. Another possibility is that security of attachment can mean that such children feel that they can go out to explore because they have a 'secure base' from which to venture forth and a 'safe haven' to return to. If this were so, such exploration might lead to further social development through facilitating social engagement in interaction compared to children who do not feel that potential to explore.

Mind mindmindedness

Elizabeth Meins (1999) has argued that the reason why securely attached children are advanced in social understanding is due to the way mothers talk to them. She suggests that mothers who think about their children as persons with minds will then interact with their children in this way rather than just caring for their physical needs. She used the term 'mindmindedness' to characterise parents' tendency to attribute mental states to their children and talk about their babies in psychological ways using terms like thinking, remembering, wanting, wondering, and so on to describe what their children are doing (Meins, 1999). Meins assesses this tendency to think about babies in this way with the simple request: 'Describe your child.' She found that some mothers described their babies in physical terms, some in terms of activity, and others in psychological terms. Meins argued that mindmindedness is a measure of parental sensitivity, which is linked to false belief understanding.

In a study of mothers and their 6-month-old infants Meins et al. (2002) found that it was the language mothers used rather than other measures of their responsiveness that was associated with their children's false belief understanding at age 4. However, this was not replicated in similar study in which Ereky-Stevens (2008) found that instead of mothers' talk it was their sensitivity to their infants at age 10 months that was correlated with their child's false belief understanding at the age of 4½ years. In a further study, mothers' comments about their 8-month-old infants in psychological terms that were judged to be accurate and appropriate were correlated with the child's social understanding assessed later at age 4, and that this way of talking to their infant was also indirectly linked to their child's later social understanding via that child's verbal ability, as assessed by his ability to correctly choose pictures matching words (Meins, Fernyhough, Arnott, Leekam, & de Rosnay, 2013). Overall, it appears to be the sensitivity or accuracy with which mothers use psychological terms to describe their infants that is directly and indirectly (via language ability) related to later false belief understanding,

12.2 LANGUAGE AND SOCIAL UNDERSTANDING

In the first section we suggested that several factors are implicated in social cognitive development and many of these hinge on the child's communicative skills. One approach is to view the language children use as a window on development. Accordingly, analysing what children say reveals their understanding of mind (Bartsch & Wellman, 1995). This can be examined by studying a collection of transcripts from young children as they learned language, available in the Child Language Data Exchange System (CHILDES) database, a publicly accessible language resource. For example, Adam (3 years, 3 months) said, 'It's a bus; I thought a taxi'. In this utterance, Adam contrasts his thought with the real world. Other children use the word 'know' in the following examples:

Ross (2;10):   'Mummy can't sing it. She doesn't know it. She doesn't understand.'

Naomi (3:5):   'I like this. Because this not your game. My game. You don't know what it is, right?'

Peter (2:5):   'I don't know where daddy is.'

But does use of such psychological words necessarily imply fully understanding them? It is important to be cautious about what children actually understand when they use particular words (Nelson, 2005; Shatz, Wellman, & Silber, 1983). At first they may only have a partial understanding of words (Nelson, 1996). In addition, mental state words have various different functions, such as the following:

Reference to mental state:	'She doesn't know this.'
Modulation of assertion:	'It's raining, I think.'
Directing interaction:	'It's a hat, you know.'
Expression of desire:	'I hope we have popcorn.'

The transcripts in the CHILDES database are provided by a relatively small sample of pre-schoolers and many are children of language researchers. The general finding is replicated with a more representative sample of children, although similar uses of these mental state words were found about a year later on average (Sabbagh & Callanan, 1998).

Words can be used in different ways and so perhaps understood differently. This can be seen with a detailed longitudinal analysis of how children and their parents use psychological words. For example, in one study children even under the age of 2 used the word *want* for making requests. Later on these same children used *want* in a more complex way to ask permission. In contrast, their mothers used the same word to clarify their child's desires (Budwig, 2002). This study is an example showing how a simple psychological term can be used in quite different ways by children and parents, and as children develop further understanding they may use the word in different ways.

MENTAL STATE TERMS: USES OF 'WANT' (BUDWIG, 2002)

Jeffrey (30 mos.) and Mum playing with blocks:

Jeffrey: 'My want something' (assertion) [refer to own desires]

Mum: 'Which – what would you like?' (inquiry)

Jeffrey (33 months) and Mum

Jeffrey: 'What's this?'

Mum: 'That's a little microphone'.

Jeffrey: 'I wanna talk in it'. (permission request) [indicates increased social competence]

Mum: 'Okay'.

Jeffrey: (talks into microphone)

Language as a context for development

Consistent correlations have been found between parents' use of mental state terms and children's social understanding, and this suggests language may form a context that facilitates social cognitive development. The research mentioned above with deaf children being delayed in false belief understanding only when their parents were not fluent in signing suggests that exposure to communication plays a role in this development (e.g. de Villiers & de Villiers, 2000; Schick et al., 2007; Woolfe et al., 2002). In addition, the helpful effect of having siblings is reduced for children who have advanced language skills (Jenkins & Astington, 1996), suggesting that communication may be more important. In the case of the links found between security of attachment and social understanding, language may mediate this relation because a meta-analysis has demonstrated that secure attachment correlates with advanced linguistic skills (Van Ijzendoorn, Dijkstra, & Bus, 1995). We should keep in mind the distinction between the influence of the language children hear from their parents and the role of children's own linguistic skills, although it could be that the language children hear facilitates their own language development.

Correlations have been reported between the psychological words children hear and their social understanding. Judy Dunn found that family talk about feelings and causes of mental states at 33 months was correlated with belief understanding at 40 months (Dunn et al., 1991). Similarly, mothers' use of belief terms correlated with their children's understanding of such terms (Moore et al., 1994; see Carpendale & Lewis, 2006, 2015a). These associations between the mental state terms that children hear and their social understanding were also found for emotion words (Garner, Jones, Gaddy, & Rennie, 1997; Kuebli, Butler, & Fivush, 1995).

Since these are correlations, the causal direction between the two factors is not clear. There are several possible causal directions. It could be that parental talk influences children's social development or, alternatively, that children's social development influences parental talk. That is, parents might be aware of their child's level of social understanding and this could elicit more of this talk from the parents. There is also the possibility of a third factor, such as the child's IQ, or how social the child is, that might elicit more mental state talk from parents. These possibilities were evaluated in a longitudinal study with three time points in which it was found that it was mothers' use of mental state talk at earlier time points that predicted children's social understanding at later time points, but not the other way around. That is, children's social understanding assessed at earlier time points did not predict their mothers' use of mental state terms (Ruffman et al., 2002). This general finding has been replicated and extended to younger children as well as older children (Adrián, Clemente, & Villanueva, 2007; Taumoepeau & Ruffman, 2006, 2008).

Other studies have found that it is not just words that children hear but also explanations and elaborations that promote false belief undersanding (Slaughter, Peterson, & Mackintosh, 2007).

As mentioned above, parents who reported talking to their children about how others might feel in disciplinary situations had children who were advanced in false belief understanding (Ruffman et al., 1999). This finding was extended beyond the social context of disciplining children to everyday interactions (Peterson & Slaughter, 2003).

Training with mental state terms

Another methodological approach to addressing the link between language and social understanding is to conduct training studies to explore whether linguistic skills facilitate social cognitive development. In one such intervention, exposure to mental state terms was explored. Children in kindergarten were read storybooks, both at school and at home, over a four-week training period (Peskin & Astington, 2004). In the experimental group children were read stories which had been 'enriched' by adding additional mental state terms, such as *know*, *think*, *guess*, *wonder*, and *figure out*. The control group were read the same storybooks but without the extra words. After the training, all the children were tested and it was found that those in the experimental group did use the mental state terms they had heard more than the other children, but they did not improve in their understanding of these words compared to the other children in the control group. In addition, and unexpectedly, it was the children in the control group who did better at explaining false beliefs rather than those in the experimental group. So it is clearly more that just being exposed to such words that is important. Both groups heard the same stories and were exposed to the same sequence of events in these stories, which involved false beliefs. Peskin and Astington (2004) suggested that the children in the control group might have improved because they had to figure out the false belief aspects of the stories, although presumably the experimental group would also have to do this since they did not have a good understanding of the mental state terms used. It should also be noted that although the control group did not hear words such as think and know, they did hear words like *look* and *hide* which are also used to talk about beliefs (see Turnbull, Carpendale, & Racine, 2009).

In another training study with a similar design, Ornaghi, Brockmeier, and Grazzani Gravazzi (2011) also read stories to children. As well as being told stories, the 70 3 to 4-year-old children were also given training twice a week for two months in using mental state words. The control group engaged in free play after hearing the stories, while the experimental group had sessions in which a teacher used a mental state term like *think* in various sentences and then asked each of the children to try making up sentences in which they also used the word. This training helped them understand the words. The 3-year-olds improved in their understanding of emotion, whereas the 4-year-olds improved in false belief understanding. A similar approach was employed with 2-year-olds who were read a series of illustrated stories. The experimental group was then engaged in conversations about the mental states of the characters in the stories, whereas the children in the control group discussed the physical characteristics of the characters and materials. After a month of such training the children in the experimental groups improved in correctly stating how someone would feel if they did or did not find what they were looking for, and in correctly predicting a character's action based on a true belief (Grazzani, Ornaghi, & Brockmeier, 2016).

This evidence is consistent with earlier training studies in which children improved in their false belief understanding after experiencing training consisting of encouragement to talk about false beliefs (Appleton & Reddy, 1996). It also fits with research suggesting that it is not simply exposure to mental state terms that is important, but also understanding the sequence of events in stories involving false beliefs (Turnbull et al., 2008). It is possible to talk about the psychological dimension of human activity without using mental state terms. For example, the events in a false belief task can be described as Maxi being outside when his mother moved his chocolate. Then he gets hungry. What will he do? It seems that it is not just mentioning psychological terms that is helpful, but rather explanatory, elaborative talk about human action that facilitates social cognitive development.

Language and relationships in social cognitive development

We have reviewed research on the role of social relationships on social cognitive development, and the associations between language and social understanding. What is the relative influence of these two factors? There have been mixed findings on this issue. Ruffman, Slade, Devitt, and Crowe (2006) studied this question by comparing mothers' use of mental state terms with their general parental style. Over a one-year longitudinal study, they reported it was mothers' use of mental state terms rather than their general parenting style that was associated with their children's social understanding, although Ruffman et al. acknowledge that the majority of the parents were toward the positive end of the parenting scale, which is not surprising given that they likely volunteered for the study because of their interest in their children. However, it seems that the parent–child relationship must be important in the child learning about the words mothers use. In another study, it was maternal engagement (i.e. interaction with the child), rather than their use of psychological terms, that was found to be associated with children's social understanding (Susswein, 2007).

Another approach to thinking about language and relationships is in terms of what Judy Dunn as referred to as the *connectedness* of conversation (Dunn & Cutting, 1999). This is the extent to which turns in a conversation are linked to the previous turn. This connectedness was evident in conversation for children who are advanced in false belief understanding (Dunn & Brophy, 2005). Such conversations were found to include more talk about thinking, desires, emotions, and intentions (Ensor & Hughes, 2008). Furthermore, this form of conversation at age 2 was found to be associated with social understanding at age 4 (Ensor & Hughes, 2008). It could be argued that this is an indication of an enriched conversation in which parent and child are each responding to each other, rather than producing a series of disconnected utterances, and so it reflects the quality of the relationship.

Children's linguistic skill

As well as the language that children hear from adults being correlated with their social understanding, children's own linguistic skill is also associated with their social understanding. That is, children who are advanced in their language skills also tend to be advanced in false belief understanding (Astington & Baird, 2005). This finding has been confirmed in a meta-analysis of 104 studies including over 9,000 participants, with linguistic skills accounting for 18% of the variance in children's performance on false belief tasks, and 10% when children's age is controlled for (Milligan et al., 2007). The child's linguistic skill may well lead to the development of false belief understanding, as this was the strongest effect in the meta-analysis (Milligan et al., 2007) and drew in part from longitudinal research in which advanced language correlated with advanced false belief understanding a year later. However, a weaker effect in the opposite direction was also found; that is, false belief understanding at an earlier age was also linked to later language development, suggesting that there may be some role that social understanding plays in learning language (Milligan et al., 2007; Slade & Ruffman, 2005).

Various theories have been proposed to explain the relations between language and social understanding. First, Harris (2005) has argued that conversation is helpful because it is a constant reminder that others have different perspectives, beliefs, desires, and intentions, and encounters with other perspectives may facilitate social cognitive development. This seems reasonable, but he does not clarify in sufficient detail how this would work. Second, Jill and Peter de Villiers (2000) propose that what is needed for children to be able to think about false beliefs is the grammar of complementation. An example of this aspect of the grammar of English is shown in the following utterance: 'Sarah thought *the world is flat*' (de Villiers & Pyers, 2002, p. 1038, original emphasis). This sentence is true even though the second clause, which is the embedded complement, is false. Complementation is the aspect of grammar that enables talk about false beliefs, thus it may follow that this ability to talk in such ways might be necessary for understanding false beliefs, or might at least facilitate such understanding. In fact, this approach is consistent with a Vygotskyian or sociogenetic approach to thinking (see Chapter 4), in which it would be suggested that the child's learning of complementation is guided within their conversations with others. There is some evidence supporting de Villiers' claims because children did improve in passing false belief tasks when they were trained with complementation (Hale & Tager-Flusberg, 2003).

An implication of de Villiers and de Villiers's (2000) position is that the reason English-speaking children understand desire before belief is that the syntax for desire is easier in English. This hypothesis can be evaluated by studying other languages with different complement structures. In Mandarin and Cantonese the same relatively simple grammatical construction is used to talk about both beliefs and desires. Therefore, de Villiers would predict that children speaking these Chinese languages would learn to talk about beliefs and desires at about the same time. However, this was not found. Instead Mandarin- and Cantonese-speaking children appeared similar to English-speaking children in that they also talked about desires earlier than beliefs (Tardiff & Wellman, 2000). German is another language that differs in complement structures because the grammatical requirements are the same for talking about wanting, saying, and thinking (Perner, Sprung, Zauner & Haider, 2003). It would seem that the de Villiers should predict that German-speaking children should be delayed in learning to talk about desire. But this was not found, and instead their ability to talk about desire was better than their ability to talk about saying and thinking (Perner et al., 2003). Again, these cross-language findings do not appear to support the de Villiers' predictions. Instead, it seems that it is general language ability that is most strongly correlated with false belief understanding. But this general ability is, of course, correlated with complementation (Cheung, Hsuan-Chih, Creed, Ng, Wang, & Mo, 2004).

One way to evaluate these various theories is with a training study. Lohmann and Tomasello (2003) conducted such an investigation. They showed 16 objects to children in a series of three training sessions. Twelve of the objects were deceptive. For example, one object looked like a flower, but it actually functioned as a pen. There were four training conditions. In a *no language* condition the experimenter used minimal language to point out the deceptive nature of the objects (i.e. 'Look!' 'But now look!'). In the *discourse only* condition the experimenter talked about the deceptive nature of the objects but without using sentences with sentential complement constructions (e.g. 'What is this?'). In the *sentential complement only* condition the experimenter told short stories about the objects with words like *think* and *know* with sentential complements, but without talking about the deceptive nature of the objects. The *full training* condition combined both discourse and training in sentential complement constructions using words like *think*, *know*, or *say* to talk about the deceptive nature of the objects (e.g. 'What do you think this is?'). After this training Lohmann and Tomasello tested the children and found significant improvement in their false belief understanding in the *discourse only* condition as well as the *sentential complement* training. But, in addition, they found that the full training condition resulted in even more improvement in the children's false belief understanding and it was better than either two separately. These results suggest that both factors are important aspects of language (Cheung et al., 2004). In fact, multiple aspects of language, including receptive vocabulary, syntax, and memory for complements, as well as general measures of language competence, were all found to facilitate the development of false belief understanding in Milligan et al.'s (2007) meta-analysis.

12.3 LANGUAGE, MINDS, AND SOCIAL UNDERSTANDING: THEORETICAL ISSUES

How we approach the relations between language and social understanding depends on our assumptions about the nature of the human mind. Ironically, in designing and interpreting empirical research, philosophical preconceptions about the mind are taken for granted and rarely examined. A common way of thinking about the mind is inherited from Descartes, or at least it is a view of the mind with a long history that was well articulated by him and hence is referred to as Cartesian (see Chapter 1). This is the view that the mind is private and accessible only to the self. Accordingly, mental states are separate from and cause behaviour. These assumptions lead to the problem of other minds, and it is assumed that children face this problem in developing social understanding. In figuring out that other people also have minds, children face the challenging problem that 'mental state terms refer to abstract, invisible referents like desires, intentions and beliefs', and that 'because of their absent and subjective reference, words for mental states and experiences are thought to be particularly difficult for young children to acquire' (Slaughter, Peterson, & Carpenter, 2009, p. 1053). That is, it is hard to learn words like think, know, remember, guess, as well as happy and sad, because what they refer to is invisible. In explaining how children do this, 'one prominent hypothesis is that mothers and other conversational partners explicitly label children's own mental states for them, and this allows them to map from the appropriate lexical items onto their internal mental experiences' (Slaughter et al., 2009, p. 1054). That is, the reason that hearing mental state terms used by parents is helpful for children is that they can map the new words they hear onto their own inner mental states that are accessible only to them through introspection on their own private mind. Another way of articulating this view is that 'mentalistic comments' facilitate children learning about the mind because such talk

> provides children with an opportunity to integrate their own behavior with an external comment that makes reference to the mental states underlying that behavior. Such comments thus offer a scaffolding context within which infants can begin to make sense of their own behavior in terms of its underlying mental states. (Meins, Fernyhough, Wainwright, Das Gupta, Fradley, & Tuckey, 2002, p. 1724)

Before discussing the problems with this view of the mind, we first mention an empirical difficulty with this claim. This approach appears to predict that hearing mental state terms will be helpful when they refer to the child's own inner states. However, this hypothesis is not supported in a training study in which children did not improve in their false belief understanding when the utterances were directed toward the child, but they did improve in their false belief understanding when they overheard others talking about someone else's mental states (Gola, 2012).

According to this view, individuals can look into their own minds which are private and inaccessible to others and so when children learn words like *think*, *remember*, *guess*, *happy*, and *sad*, these words must be labels for what is going on in their private minds. Although this might seem to make sense from an adult's perspective, this is just the view that Ludwig Wittgenstein (1968) famously disputed in his private language argument (or arguments). He argued against the possibility of a private language in the sense that words acquire their meaning through a private connection with inner mental entities. This is not a private language in the sense of the last speaker of a dying language, or a language that someone has just invented but has not yet taught to anyone else, because the phenomena mentioned in these two examples are potentially public. Instead, what Wittgenstein critiqued is the possibility that meanings are necessarily private because they are based on a connection to an inner entity that is only available to the individual.

Readers might wonder if it is really necessary to go into this difficult and controversial area. Shouldn't psychologists be out there like other scientists observing the natural world? There are two obvious responses. First, the topic of Wittgenstein's later work was exactly on learning the meaning of sensation words and psychological words, so it is highly relevant for the current area of research on the development of social understanding. Second, Wittgenstein himself advocated that we should observe what is right in front of us as our misconceptions prevent us from seeing what is actually going on in everyday contexts in which, we would add, development occurs.

WITTGENSTEIN'S PRIVATE LANGUAGE ARGUMENT AND DEVELOPMENTAL PSYCHOLOGY

In order to limber up readers before tackling the private language argument, let us sneak up on it by approaching it from the opposite direction. That is, instead of being philosophers and imposing their philosophical problems on children in the process of figuring out other minds, let us, for a moment, do what we are supposed to do as natural scientists and pay careful attention to what is right in front of us. Let us observe how infants gradually get better at communicating and coordinating their actions with the other people with whom they interact with every day.

We run into difficulty when starting from other philosophers' position on the problem of other minds. According to this, babies see other bodies moving around them and have to figure out that they also have minds. The starting point already presupposes

(Continued)

that the baby herself has a mind to begin with. This is like thinking of the baby as some-one who is already linguistically proficient and is visiting a foreign country where she cannot speak the local language. Such an infant would be faced with the problem of figuring out how to communicate with others. For many, this seems so natural that it is hard to see that it already presupposes what needs to be explained. That is why Wittgenstein thought of his work as therapeutic in the sense that he knew that our language naturally leads us toward making common mistakes about the mind, and his goal was to warn people. Think of his work as putting up signs saying 'Watch out, there is a slippery section ahead!' One such warning concerned the treatment of men-tal activity like concrete entities. When we talk about having beliefs we tend to start thinking about them as physical things, that populate our head, are potentially spatially extended, can cause other things (e.g. behaviour), and can be looked at with the mind's eye (i.e. through introspection). Thus we apply the concepts we use to describe physical objects to mental states (already this term is somewhat misleading). The problem with transferring attributes suitable for describing physical objects to mental phenomena is that it leads to confusion and nonsense. If you form a mental image of an elephant, this mental image will not be larger than the mental image of a mouse. You cannot measure the size of mental images because mental images are not the kind of things that are extended in space. It does also not make sense to expect that there would be little red puffs in your head if you formed a mental image of juicy strawberries – you can imagine something that is colourful, but the mental image itself is not an object that is coloured. Furthermore, once you start ascribing attributes of physical things to mental states, these start to take on a life on their own.

Meaning then resides inside these mental states, independent of any activity of the person. As a consequence, the person as an agent will become superfluous. Once this happens, thinking, feeling, believing, etc. become functional states within a causal machinery. But how can a scientist verify the claim that what goes on in the mind are functional states within a causal machinery? After all, the scientist herself is a cog in a wheel of causal machinery and is simply caused to make such a claim. If the scientist then provides reasons for her claim, she has left the realm of the causal machinery and can indeed lay claim to truth, at the price that her own behaviour (providing reasons) is no longer covered by her theory. In effect, the scientist's behaviour cannot be made intelligible within her own theory. To avoid such contradictions, we should avoid treat-ing mental states as some objects that exist independent of our activity. Indeed, to emphasise the active nature of mind, it might be better to replace the notion of mental states by the notion of mental acts, which are always intentional, i.e. directed toward something. And this directedness is first and foremost a directedness toward things in the context of interacting with others.

If we do away with the preconceptions about the mind described in the box and carefully observe infants in interaction (see Chapters 5 and 6), it does not seem that they are engaged in an intellectual task of attempting to figure others out. Instead they are immersed in social life, and they are learning about other people just like they learn about the physical world, but much of this activity is stage-managed by the caregivers. And for babies there is no clear separation between the physical and social worlds to begin with.

Although the point we are trying to make might seem quite difficult for readers immersed in philosophy (of certain types) or cognitive science (again, of particular types), this approach might seem completely obvious to other readers who have spent more time with babies. This is because readers of the first type already have a frame of reference, a way of conceptualising the problem, and this is the obstacle in understanding development in a different way. In fact, a solution is difficult to reach precisely because the way of conceptualising it already comes with particular solutions. It is only possible to solve the problem if that initial way of thinking about it is examined and rejected.

When babies are in pain or are experiencing discomfort, or when they are happy, what they are experiencing is quite obvious to the adults who are looking after them. Think of the glee of a 12-month-old heading as fast as he can toward the stairs when he sees that the gate has been moved. His intention and project are clearly manifest in his actions, as is his happiness. Stairs present an exciting challenge to overcome for infants. Frustration can also be obvious when an infant is attempting to reach something, or to get something that his big brother is playing with.

As described in Chapter 5, human infants encounter a problem space that naturally leads to developing various forms of requests. This is because their parents, their 'social world', respond to their attempts to get things. Once interaction patterns used to make requests are established, infants can then add words such as *want*. This word, like most others, can be used within different sorts of social situations. Its first use might be in making requests, but then, as reviewed above, it can also be used to ask permission or to talk about others' desires and so on. Words such as *think* and *know* are even more complex and can be used in many different situations; these routines are what Wittgenstein referred to as *language games*. There are routine activity patterns in which words are used.

Our goal is to understand the transition from the simple form of practical understanding of other people that infants develop first to the complex verbal world of talking about thinking, knowing, wanting, wondering, guessing, remembering, and so on. These are examples of terms that 3- to 5-year-olds gradually master. So, before tackling complex words like *know*, consider words like *look* and *see*. They have also to do with others' knowledge and it is possible to see how they are more easily built onto infants' practical social understanding. Pointing can be used to direct attention. Once these sorts of social routines are learned children can start to use words such as 'look' or 'see' as well as making and following pointing gestures and the words can later replace the gestures. These sorts of examples illustrate the bridge between the practical level of communication and the verbal level. From this perspective, psychological words refer to human activity. This activity is, of course, full of intentions, beliefs, desires, and so on. But these are not separate mental entities that cause mere surface behaviour.

Psychological words are used to talk about human activity. And they must be learned through being based on such activity (Malcolm, 1991). From this perspective, it is not a matter of learning laws about how the mind operates. Instead, social cognitive development is a gradual process involving learning partial understanding of words such as *remember*, *forget*, *look*, *see*, *happy*, *wonder*, *fear*, and *sad*. And these words are learned based on ways of acting, on natural human reactions. The meanings of psychological words like *remember* and *decide* are based on how they are used to talk about human activity. It is not that they refer to inner mental entities. For example, a 3-year-old girl watching a group of musicians discussing what song to play next turned to her father and said 'Are they deciding?' She had correctly used the mental state term based on watching their interaction.

But, people feel that they have introspective access to our own private thoughts and feelings. Introspection is possible for older children and adults; it is a developmental accomplishment. We can imagine how we might feel in various situations, but this requires the ability to talk about human activity in psychological terms. That is, this is the outcome of development, not the basis for social development. Once children can talk about the psychological world they can think about psychological matters.

Conclusions regarding language

There is clear evidence that various forms of social interaction and aspects of language are linked to social cognitive development, and likely facilitate this development. Several competing theories propose to explain these relations, and they are based on different views of mind and language.

In thinking about the relations between language and social understanding we can also broaden the definitions of these two complex phenomena beyond a focus on false belief understanding and aspects of language such a vocabulary and syntax. As discussed in Chapter 6, social understanding begins early in infancy and involves social skills such as following gaze and using gestures. These skills would be important in learning language. And language is far more than semantics and syntax. Becoming competent in communicating requires sophistication in pragmatics, the social use of language. So perhaps language and social understanding are better conceptualised as aspects of what could more broadly be considered social and communicative competence. And this is what we turn to next.

12.4 SOCIAL UNDERSTANDING AND CHILDREN'S SOCIAL LIVES

It is now time to turn to consider whether or how social understanding might influence children' social lives. That is, what is the pay-off on the playground? Does a grasp of mental states result in improvements in children's social lives? It might be expected that children who are advanced in social understanding might also be more skilled socially in other ways. There is support for this hypothesis from research on both first- and second-order false understanding. Children with greater social understanding relative to that of their classmates have been also rated by their teachers as being more socially skilled (Astington, 2003; Baird & Astington, 2004; Lalonde & Chandler, 1995). At the age of 11 to 12 years old, children who were viewed by their peers as socially skilled were also better than their age mates in social understanding, as assessed by their ability to understand that ambiguous social situations can be interpreted in multiple ways (Bosacki & Astington, 1999). In addition, children who both play cooperatively with others and have fewer conflicts with their friends were relatively advanced in understanding beliefs and emotions (Dunn & Cutting, 1999; see Dunn, 2004). Similarly, children who understand false beliefs also used more sophisticated arguments when interacting with their siblings in the sense that they included their sibling's perspective and interests in their arguments (Foote & Holmes-Lonergan, 2003). The skill in coming up with persuasive arguments, as assessed by attempts to convince a puppet to eat broccoli and brush his teeth, was correlated with children's understanding of false beliefs (Slaughter, Peterson, & Moore, 2013). Furthermore, children who were advanced in social understanding when they were assessed at the age of 5 to 6 were also more cooperative and helpful when interacting with others one year later (Caputi et al., 2012). This could be one reason that such children are accepted by their peers.

Popularity with their peers might also be associated with children's social understanding. Children who were advanced relative to their classmates in their understanding of emotions and beliefs when they were 5 were also accepted by their peers when assessed two years later (Caputi et al., 2012; see also Peterson & Siegal, 2002; Slaughter, Dennis, & Pritchard, 2002). Not only did Banerjee et al. (2011) produce similar findings, they found that children who were rejected by their peers when they were 8 to 9 years old had more difficulty on a test of their understanding of unintentional insults (the *faux pas* task). A recent meta-analysis of 20 studies including over two thousand children from 2 to 10 years old found that children who were relatively advanced in social understanding were also concurrently more popular with their peers. This effect held across this age range, but it was a small one. That is, social understanding accounted for 3.6% of variance in popularity with peers, thus many other factors must also be important in peer popularity. The effect was stronger for girls than boys (Slaughter et al., 2015).

The evidence discussed above concerns general peer popularity, but how does social understanding relate to close mutual friendships? Being delayed in false belief understanding at age 5 was correlated with lacking friends at this age and also two years later at the age of 7 (Fink et al., 2015). A possible bidirectional relation between friendship and social cognition is that some level of social skill may facilitate having a close mutual friend, and experience in this social context may promote social cognition. A grasp of mental states seems also to relate to more skilled social interactions beyond peer and close relationships. Being advanced in false belief understanding in the preschool years was found to be associated with sensitivity to teacher criticism in the first year of school. That is, children who were advanced in false belief understanding took the teacher's criticism into account when evaluating their own work (Dunn, 2004).

Children's understanding of the ambiguity of some events and that such experiences can be interpreted in multiple ways is a further level of social understanding that is also linked to children's social lives. This understanding correlated with children's understanding of siblings' conflicting interpretations (Ross, Recchia, & Carpendale, 2005), and understanding ambiguous communication – a judgment of whether an utterance conveys sufficient information to communicate what is needed (e.g. Robinson & Robinson, 1983). For example, if there are two red toys and your playmate says 'Give me the red one', this is not sufficiently precise. Advanced understanding of interpretation (that two people can have different, even contrasting, views of the same experience) in 6- to 9-year-olds correlated with their sophisticated communication regarding symbols on a map (Myers & Liben, 2012). Another dimension of children's general social competence is their understanding of humour. More complex forms of humour, in which the joke is hidden or closely relates to a literal meaning, depend on understanding that words or utterances can have multiple meanings (McGhee, 1979), and it would seem that this would require some understanding of interpretation.

If we think of morality as involving perspective taking, then it should be related to social understanding. In a longitudinal study children who were advanced in understanding emotions when they were 3½ used more reasoning about others' physical needs when responding to a prosocial moral dilemma at age 5½, and understanding beliefs was linked to reasoning about others' psychological needs. Both understanding emotions and beliefs together predicted conforming to adults' social expectations (Lane, Wellman, Olson, LaBounty, & Kerr, 2010).

If anything has been learned from Niccolò Machiavelli (1469–1527), a Florentine intellectual who famously wrote about power and politics in *The Prince* (1950), the dark side of social understanding, as potentially being used to manipulate others, should also be considered. However, when comparing children rated as skilled in social manipulation with their classmates who were less manipulative, they did not differ in false belief understanding, although they did have more negative views of others (Repacholi, Slaughter, Pritchard, & Gibbs, 2003). Are bullies skilled social manipulators or stupid oafs? Of course, both are possible. Bullies have not been found to be poorer in social understanding (Sutton, Smith, & Swettenham, 1999; see also Gini, 2006). Sutton and colleagues (1999) classified 7- to 10-year-old children into categories including ringleader bullies, followers, victims, and defenders. The bullies were not delayed in social understanding. But there were also many children in their study who were advanced in social understanding and who were not bullies.

Relations between social understanding and bullying were also evaluated in a large longitudinal study in which a sample of 2,232 twins was assessed at aged 5 with first- and second-order false belief tasks and belief-dependent emotions tasks. Those children who did poorly on these tasks were found to be at a greater risk of being involved in bullying either as a victim or as both a victim and a bully when they were followed up later at age 12 (Shakoor et al., 2012). The children who were rated as both bullies and victims and had the highest level of mental health problems were the children who had the lowest level of social understanding at age 5. However, this does not mean that being a bully or a victim is explained simply by a child's level of social understanding. This study did not distinguish bully–victims from 'ringleader bullies', which might be children who use social skills to manipulate others. There are a number of possible reasons for why poorer social understanding might increase the risk of being bullied, and then bullying others. These children might not be so skilled at picking up on social cues, they may be anxious and therefore seen as an easy target, and lower social understanding tends to be linked to other difficulties in children's family backgrounds (Shakoor et al., 2012). In this study poor social understanding was also related to family factors, such as child maltreatment and growing up in circumstances of deprivation. In a study involving almost 400 participants physical aggression at 6 years old was correlated with social understanding assessed one year earlier at 5 years old, but this relation was found only for the children who were low to average in prosocial behaviour (Renouf et al., 2010).

In considering relations between aggression and social understanding, it is important to keep in mind that types of aggression are often categorised as proactive or 'cold-blooded' unprovoked and premeditated aggression, versus reactive or 'hot-headed' provoked aggression. It was reactive aggression but not proactive aggression that was found to be correlated with poorer social understanding (Carpendale & Lewis, 2006; Jones, 2007). One possibility is that these children react impulsively when provoked, but the relationship between this form of behaviour and social understanding needs to be studied further.

Bullying is a complex social problem with far-reaching effects, and it cannot simply be explained by children's level of social understanding. Rather than simply examining relations between social understanding and bullying, it is important to take into account the children's values. There are multiple ways to attempt to reduce bullying. One approach is to change school cultures so that the practice is completely unacceptable. Programmes to help develop the social understanding of children who bully, without accompanying policies designed to discourage bullying, may be counterproductive: for a few children this might create a 'school for scoundrels' (Chandler, 1973): they might use such knowledge to bully others. Bullying can occur in many ways, including social exclusion, spreading rumours, and undermining friendships. Aggression is not always just physical. It is not restricted to children; adults continue to bully and it can be a significant problem in workplaces.

In this section, we have only scratched the surface of the vast and complex question of how children's social understanding influences their social lives. The answer is that it does so in multiple ways. Grasping how someone feels may provide the potential for compassion. We have suggested that the ability to gain such an understanding is acquired as part of the process of learning language – the pragmatics of everyday communication. As we have argued throughout this book, language is not just a matter of conveying information

(Austin, 1962). It also involves face work, showing an interest in how others feel, and treating others as persons. This links social understanding to language as well as morality. A crucial aspect of the social world involves obligations, commitment, and promises.

SUMMARY AND CONCLUSIONS

In this chapter we have looked beyond the average ages at which children develop social understanding skills, to examine individual differences in children's development. We have reviewed research on the influence of various aspects of children's social experience on their social-cognitive development. This can be studied from the perspective of culture, but mixed results have been reported concerning differences in false belief understanding between different societies, possibly because children's actual face-to-face experience will depend on their families. Such family experience will depend, at least in part, on parents' beliefs and practices. Although there are mixed findings, assertive parenting tends to be associated with poor social understanding, whereas parental warmth was associated with advanced understanding, particularly for girls.

As an aspect of family experience, the presence of siblings has been found to facilitate social cognitive development. Positive sibling relationships are themselves correlated with various factors such as the quality of parents' talk to their children. The interaction children experience with siblings may facilitate the development of their self-awareness, which in turn may result in further social cognitive development. Play may also be a factor in social cognitive development. Pretend play involving making joint plans and assigning roles has been reported to be correlated with false belief understanding. Children who have developed secure attachments with their caregivers also tend to be advanced in social understanding. Beyond the immediate family, children's experience with their peers can also play a role in development. Popular children tend to be advanced in social understanding, whereas children who were rated as rejected by their peers were relatively delayed in social understanding.

Conversely, lacking social experience tends to result in deficits in social understanding. Some children without families or adequate care grow up in institutions. Unfortunately, these children tend to be delayed in social understanding, and when they grow up in poor-quality institutions they may never catch up with typically developing children (Sonuga-Barke et al., 2017).

Within social interaction children learn about others, but the quality of the social interaction itself is influenced by their own characteristics. Although there is little work on this issue it seems that children who are sensitive and shy tend to be advanced in social understanding, perhaps because those children are keen observers of human social life. Other characteristics of children such as blindness and deafness can result in delays in social cognitive development. For deaf children this seems to be due to a lack of exposure to the nuances of communication.

Language has been shown to be linked to social understanding in various ways. It has often been claimed that what children say acts as a window on their social understanding. Yet we have argued that language also appears to act as context for development, in terms of what children hear from others. In addition, children's own linguistic skills lead to further social cognitive development. Understanding the role that language plays in the development of social understanding led us to a discussion and evaluation of the various explanations of development, as well as views of the nature of language, meaning, and mind.

As well as contexts for development, the social skills that children have acquired may enable them to engage in more complex forms of social interaction. In addition to social skills facilitating forms of social interaction, it is essential to also keep in mind the complementary influences in which social experience may result in further social cognitive development. There are bidirectional relations in which increased social understanding may make more complex forms of interaction possible within which children will learn more about their social world.

In addition, there are further topics such as trust in others' knowledge and deciding who it is best to learn from (Carpendale & Lewis, 2015a). A focus only on beliefs, desires, and intentions, however, overlooks an understanding of how human conduct is embedded in a social network of obligations, which leads to the topic of moral development, addressed the next two chapters.

FURTHER READING

Carpendale, J. I. M., & Lewis, C. (2006). *How Children Develop Social Understanding*. Oxford: Blackwell.

Carpendale, J. I. M, & Lewis, C. (2015). The development of social understanding. In L. Liben & U. Müller (vol. eds), *Vol. 2: Cognitive Processes*, R. Lerner (Editor-in-Chief), 7th edition of the *Handbook of Child Psychology and Developmental Science* (pp. 381–424). New York: Wiley Blackwell.

I3 MORAL REASONING AND ACTION

LEARNING OUTCOMES

Having read this chapter you should:

- Be aware of the ways in which a grasp of morality is fundamental to an understanding of human social conduct and the ways in which societies function.

- Be able to describe in detail the reasoning behind Piaget's theory of moral development.

- Be familiar with the main methods used by Piaget and Kohlberg (being able to describe particular studies would help).

- Be aware of the criticism of Kohlberg's theory, particularly the care–justice distinction made by Carol Gilligan.

- Be familiar with social cognitive domain theory and understand how its focus on convention relates to Piaget and Kohlberg's focus on moral principles.

- Be able to take a position on these major twentieth-century approaches to moral thinking in order to adjudicate on recent positions and evidence outlined in Chapter 14.

'People so nice you can't believe it, and people so mean you can't believe it.'

(Vonnegut, 1997, p. 12)

Morality is an essential aspect of children's understanding of their social world.[1] So what is it, and how do children come to understand it? A number of theorists have grappled with these questions. In this chapter the first two sections begin with the dilemma that Kurt Vonnegut summarises so well, in an attempt to show how hard it is to define moral action and clarify that it varies along key dimensions from selflessness to selfishness. In doing so we will show how psychologists have justified the study of the development of moral reasoning skills. The major portion of this chapter will focus on what has been referred to as a cognitive developmental approach, with special emphasis on Jean Piaget and Lawrence Kohlberg. We will look at their theories in detail as these have dominated the ways in which developmental psychology has approached the topic and examine the critiques of Kohlberg's theory. As we argue in the next chapter, Piaget's and Kohlberg's theories still have a strong influence on how we understand the child's developing grasp of the moral world. It is for this reason that this chapter dwells on arguments and evidence that are of more than historical interest. We argue that the work of Piaget, in particular, is still of major importance, and in the last few years researchers have been returning to his insights, as we will show at the end of the following chapter.

13.1 WHAT IS MORALITY?

The answer to this question may seem quite obvious. Surely everyone knows?! Even though we tend to feel that we know what morality is, it turns out to be difficult to define. It could be said, for example, that morality has to do with concern for others. Some would argue that it extends beyond that, but that concern for others at least is a place to start. Readers might object, however, that there is not much evidence of concern for others when we look at events in the news and witness the oppression and injustice in the world. As Kurt Vonnegut pointed out, there are plenty of people who are nastier than you can believe. The events of the twentieth century provide many unfortunate examples. Take, for instance, Adolf Eichmann who played a role in the Holocaust during which six million people were killed. He claimed that he loved children, yet as a leading figure in the Third Reich he ordered half a million of them killed. He thought that these children were different because they were Jewish. His later defence was that he was just following orders.

Unfortunately, this is just one example of genocide. Digging deep enough into the history of just about any country is likely to reveal evidence of other genocides. Mentioning the names of Rwanda and Yugoslavia brings to mind some of the other horrendous events of the twentieth century and indeed horrible events are occurring in Syria as we write. In Cambodia the genocide known as the 'Killing Fields' from 1976 to 1978 is another

---

[1] Although ethics is sometimes used narrowly to refer to codes of behaviour, the words 'morality' and 'ethics' are often used interchangeably, which is what we will do.

horrendous example, prompting Vonnegut's comment on 'people so mean you can't believe it'. The Khmer Rouge led by Pol Pot killed at least 1.5 million people from a population of 7 million. Those responsible for these atrocities were eventually charged with genocide and crimes against humanity, including some of the high-ranking leaders of the Khmer Rouge who were finally brought to trial in 2012. But this process had taken so long that at 87 years of age one of these leaders, Mr Ieng Sary, fell asleep while listening to Pech Srey Phal explaining to the court how she had to watch her child starve to death because the Khmer Rouge deprived them of food and shelter (*The Globe and Mail*, 7 December 2012). Another recent example of the 'failure of humanity' is the genocide in Rwanda during which 800,000 people were murdered and millions more were injured or displaced. A further dimension of this tragedy was the failure of the international community to intervene (Dellaire, 2003).

We could go on listing crimes against humanity, so it might seem there is little morality in our world. Indeed you might think there is nothing left to explain in this chapter and that we should stop right here. But how is it that we can realise these events are wrong? How can we recognise injustice? This requires an explanation. The questions we must grapple with concerning morality involve how children come to think about rights and obligations involving themselves and other people. How do individuals make decisions about conflicting rights? What should, or shouldn't, they do? Why are some people like Gandhi and Martin Luther King Jr., but others are not?

In the discussion so far our focus on morality seems restricted to crucial life and death issues. But how about a simple act like buying a cup of coffee or tea? How could that be moral?! Well, consider the consequences of that action for other people involved. Is the act supporting oppression of the farmers through unfair payment and environmental degradation? Is the coffee organic and shade-grown in order to make the agriculture sustainable? Is it fairly traded so that the farmers were adequately compensated for their work? Is it in your own cup or a paper cup drawn from trees in an old growth forest or with a non-biodegradable plastic coating?

In addition to the far-reaching social consequences of such simple acts, what about the everyday level of interpersonal interaction and the manner in which we treat others? It could be argued that even our everyday conversation is built on moral principles. For example, many consider lying to be wrong in general, although not always. But it is only possible to lie because people usually tell the truth. Truth telling is a norm that is necessary for conversation to get off the ground. In fact, if everyone randomly lied or told the truth normal conversation would not be possible. Thus conversation is based on the moral principle of telling the truth. It is built into the foundations of typical social interaction (Holiday, 1988). The morality of lying is further complicated by the potential for white lies to protect others' feelings.

Morality is also evident in the area of human rights. For example, Liu Xiaobo won the 2010 Nobel Peace Prize, but in China he was given an 11-year jail sentence for 'inciting subversion' because he helped to write a document promoting democracy. Although his wife, Liu Xia, had not been charged with anything, in 2012 she had not been allowed to leave her home for two years. Morality extends into politics, and the number of examples could easily be expanded by considering more countries.

At the same time that Vonnegut commented on the extent of human nastiness, he also pointed out that there are also lots of people who are *nicer* than you can believe. How can we explain the extent of human kindness and compassion? This is just as large a problem, and it might be even more difficult to explain. One way to address questions like these regarding morality is through the study of moral development. There are various aspects of the topic that can be studied which we have noted here, such as moral feelings, moral action, and moral reasoning. We will start with moral reasoning, although of course it is moral action that is ultimately important.

13.2 THE DIMENSIONS OF MORALITY

One common definition of morality is that it is simply the way of doing things in a particular culture, a set of social norms. Clearly cultures do differ in beliefs about ways to behave such as the colour to wear at funerals – black or white. Before we address issues in developmental psychology, it is important to set out some of the wider dimensions of the topic of morality. The key issues concern whether moral judgments are relative to a specific time and culture, or whether there are universal pan-cultural moral principles. This section outlines some of the complexities of the argument pertinent to these two positions, and the next chapter continues to explore a third option – the idea of a general process for resolving moral conflicts.

According to the socialisation perspective, morality consists of conforming to the local social rules that are imposed by the previous generation. Following this view, children learn about morality from their parents who teach them what is right and wrong. Children become moral because their parents teach them the correct ways to behave. This way of defining morality would explain differences between cultures and is consistent with the key idea of social learning theory that learning occurs through imitation and reinforcement.

Children certainly are influenced by their parents. This will be part of the story of moral development, but in itself it is an incomplete story because, as readers likely know, either from having parents or being a parent, kids and adults don't always obey their parents. And this is not necessarily a bad thing. In fact, it can lead to important social changes. Also, this explanation does not tell us where moral norms came from originally, or how they change. Some might claim that moral norms come from religious texts and divine instruction. But many people are less convinced by this now, and religious texts, such as the Bible and the Koran, still have to be interpreted.

From this socialisation perspective, morality seems to imply conformity to cultural rules, so that according to this view morality equals conformity. But is this really what we mean by morality? Many of the people often considered most moral have defied authority and even broken laws because they believed that those laws were not moral and needed to be changed. Leaders such as Martin Luther King and Nelson Mandela defied the moral and legal standards of their countries. But according to a socialisation account we would expect people to obey authority, to *conform* to the norms of their society. The majority, however, are not always right. For example, a brother and sister, Hans and Sophie Scholl, living in Munich during the Second World War, joined the Hitler Youth but then started questioning what they were being told. They left the Hitler Youth and started their own group called the White Rose. They printed pamphlets critical of the Nazi regime but they were caught, quickly tried, and beheaded along with four other students. More generally, many adolescents start questioning the moral standards of their parents, as it happened, for example, during the movement against apartheid in South Africa. The calling into question of societal norms and practices, which requires autonomous thinkers and not clones, is an important dimension of morality that is in need of an explanation.

Another implication of the idea that morality is just the way of doing things in a particular culture is that it does not seem possible to say that one moral norm is better than another. All that is left to say is that moral norms are just all different. Therefore, one culture should not impose views on another group. Throughout history there have been many tragic cases of this occurring. For example, there is the shameful example of residential schools in Canada. This government-funded, church-run programme was an explicit attempt to 'kill the Indian in the child'. These residential schools started in the 1870s with the last one closing as recently as 1996. During those 130 years more than 150,000 First Nations, Inuit, and Metis children, some as young as 5, were sent to over 130 schools scattered across Canada. Some of these children were physically and sexually abused by the Christian clergy who ran the schools, and some died at the schools. The United Church acknowledged that Aboriginal children were 'victims of evil acts that cannot under any circumstances be justified or excused'. This experience continues to influence future generations because while attending these schools they were deprived of learning how to be a parent from their own parents (see the Truth and Reconciliation Commission of Canada, www.trc.ca/websites/trcinstitution/index.php?p=39; Sunday edition, May 4, August 10, 2014, Michael Enright, interview with Judge Murray Sinclair, Chair of the Truth and Reconciliation Commission, Manitoba's first aboriginal judge; CBC *The Sunday Edition*, 2014). From this and many other terrible examples around the world we are gun-shy, as we should be, of any hint at imposing values on other cultures.

But can we do without judging some moral norms and practice as better and others as worse? Notice that already our discussion of residential schools relied on such an evaluation. There is now a general consensus that what happened to children in residential schools was terribly wrong. So how is that we can evaluate this practice as unethical? The notion of moral relativism – the view that it is not possible to judge one moral position as any better than another – makes such evaluation impossible. According to this position, it would be possible to say that what the Canadian government did was *different*, but not *right* or *wrong*. However, there is now agreement that this was, in fact, clearly wrong, and the Canadian government finally did apologise in 2008. This conclusion does not fit with moral relativism.

Another case pertinent to the issue of moral relativism is that against Warren Jeffs, the leader of a polygamist religious group. In 2006 he was charged in Utah for forcing a 14-year-old girl to marry her 19-year-old cousin and have sex with him. Arizona was waiting to charge him with other cases of forcing under-age girls to marry, and the government of British Columbia was also considering charges. Jeffs' defence was that charging him would be religious persecution because he claimed to be part of a different culture, and that what he had done was acceptable in that culture. According to moral relativism, his reasons should be legitimate.

Is this a legitimate defence? Jeffs' claim can be examined by considering the issue of the *size* of cultures. If a family is a mini-culture, then what could be said if a wife beats her husband and her defence is that this is what they do in their culture? Is there any response to this? What could be said if in that culture (i.e. family) the children are told that it is good to beat up other kids and steal their lunches at school? This would just be the way things are done in that culture (i.e. that family). There is something wrong about this.

These examples show that moral relativism is problematic because it does not explain why we judge certain moral norms and practices as better than others. But what is the basis for these judgments? For example, giving more citizens the right to vote might be considered to be better than having fewer citizens voting. Women were given the right to vote in New Zealand in 1893. In Australia it was 1902, but aboriginal men and women could not vote until 1962. Similarly in Canada, although most women could vote in 1920, First Nations men and women could not vote until 1960. In Saudi Arabia women were able to vote in 2015, but only in local government elections. This seems like an improvement. But we are not suggesting that progress is natural and inevitable. Rather, we suggest that this is the struggle toward improvement because unfairness is recognised. However, democracy is a complex issue and depends on individuals actually using their right to vote, and the assumption that these votes actually result in representation in a government. Unfortunately, archaic voting systems like the UK's and Canada's do not result in proportional representation, unlike voting systems in many other countries such as Germany.

These are some of the issues addressed in the approaches to moral development. We begin with Piaget's (1932/1965) theory, partly for historical reasons to set the context for the research, but also because he introduced insights that are just recently being recognised as crucial for a comprehensive account of morality, and current research is returning to his insights (Carpendale et al., 2013; Göckeritz, Schmidt, & Tomasello, 2014; Schmidt, Rakoczy, Meitzsch, & Tomasello, 2016).

13.3 JEAN PIAGET'S THEORY OF MORAL DEVELOPMENT

Although he is best known for his work on cognitive development, in one of his early books, *The Moral Judgement of the Child* (1932/1965), Jean Piaget presented an influential approach to moral development. He studied moral development in two main ways: first by researching children's understanding of the rules of games, and second by evaluating their judgments about bad behaviours. His first chapter opens with an unusual approach to studying moral development. Piaget observed boys playing the game of marbles and talked to them about the rules of the game. He argued that this was an appropriate way to study moral development because the rules of the game were handed down from older children to younger children, similar to adult morality (Piaget, 1932/1965).

Piaget's (1932/1965) book on moral development, like many of his other books, is filled with detailed accounts of particular children taken from the transcripts of his conversations with them, used to illustrate different types of reasoning. Piaget played marbles with boys from 3 to 13 and asked them questions about the game such as 'Can the rules be changed?', 'Can you make up a new rule?', 'Would it be real?', 'Where do rules come from?' Based on the children's answers, he described stages in the *practice* of rules, i.e. how children of different ages actually apply them. The youngest children, aged 3, were unaware of the rules and played with the marbles without conforming to any rules. Between the ages of 3 and 6 children did apply the rules of the game but they were inconsistent in how they did so. In this stage of idiosyncratic application (a form of egocentrism according to Piaget – see below) the child attempts to imitate older children. At this second stage two children might play together but when asked 'Who won?' they might say that they both won. They are each playing on their own even if they are side by side. That is, they may both shoot at the same time and it doesn't matter if one of them makes up different rules. Finally, in the third stage, beginning at about age 7, their play begins to be coordinated by rules, but these rules are not codified. Now winning has a social definition; that is, winning is doing better than others while observing common rules. According to Piaget, at this point the game becomes social in the sense that the participants are conforming to the same principles, objectives, and criteria for success. The difference between stages 3 and 4 is just one of degree – that is, how well the children know the rules. They play a simplified game at stage 3, whereas 11- to 13-year-old children at stage 4 have thoroughly mastered the rules, and they are like lawyers in their understanding of their details.

Piaget also described stages in *understanding* rules and this is where moral reasoning comes in. At stage 1 (premoral), approximately 3 to 6 years, children did not treat the rules as obligatory and felt no obligation to follow them. At stage 2, beginning at about 6 to 9 years, Piaget described a *morality of constraint* during which children treated the rules as sacred and untouchable. They stated the rules were passed on from their fathers, or the elders of the community, and ultimately from God. That is, rules are imposed from the outside and cannot be changed. Of course Piaget realised it is unlikely that these children had actually pondered the origin of rules before he asked them, but he argued that their answers reveal their feeling that these rules come from others and are not open to negotiation. Then, beginning at about age 9, the children Piaget interviewed radically changed their conception of rules and they now stated that the rules originate in mutual consent. In this stage of *cooperation* they treated the rules as the outcome of a free decision, and the rules should be respected if they are based on mutual consent, but not otherwise. Children agree to a change in the rules if everyone agrees. As one child put it, 'So as not to be always quarrelling you must have rules, and then play properly' (Piaget, 1932/1965, p. 71). Piaget noted that the stages he described in the development of moral practice and understanding were for the sake of convenience, and that moral development is actually continuous. Furthermore, the ages that he reported for the different stages were not meant to indicate general age norms but were meant to describe just his particular sample of children (Carpendale, 2009; Piaget, 1932/1965).

For Piaget, the advances in children's moral understanding raised the question of, in his words, 'How is it that democratic practice is so developed in the games of marbles played by boys of 11 to 13, whereas it is still so unfamiliar to the adult in many spheres of life?' (Piaget, 1932/1965, p. 76).[2] Piaget's answer was that these boys experienced relationships of cooperation among equals because their slightly older peers (14- to 15-year-olds) no longer played the game so there was no one with greater authority imposing rules them. Thus what is of importance here is not age, but instead the structure of the relationship the children experienced.

Piaget acknowledged that one aspect of morality is that rules are imposed on children from parents and culture. He referred to this as *heteronomous* morality – the imposition of rules is associated with relationships of constraint and unequal power. Many approaches to morality are concerned only with this dimension of conforming to moral rules handed down from one generation to the next. However, Piaget did not agree that all moral knowledge is acquired from parents. Some moral knowledge is constructed and he was interested in the question of how *new* moral knowledge develops. He argued that the morality of constraint based on unilateral respect between one generation and the next is only one kind of moral code. He made the case that morality is not just imposed by the group on the individual, nor imposed by parents on children, and argued that adult authority can reinforce constraint because children cannot take the perspective of adults due to the inequality in such relationships. Constructing morality requires relationships of equality, and this is usually among peers because they can take each other's perspective.

---

[2] Piaget has been criticised for just studying boys in this context (Gilligan, 1982), but here we wish to draw out his broad insights that are useful in studying moral development in general. It is true that he studied boys in the context of playing marbles in one chapter in his book, but in the rest of the chapters he studied both boys and girls.

When individuals are among equals they are obliged to listen to each other and present their own position in a way that is understandable. Thus, relationships of cooperation are best suited to reaching mutual understanding. Such relationships are the breeding ground for the emergence of autonomous morality in which rules come from mutual discussion rather than from the outside. This point applies beyond moral understanding to knowledge in general, and therefore has implications for education.

A second method that Piaget employed in studying moral development was to present children with pairs of stories and ask for their judgments about the story characters. His best-known example contrasts actors' differing intentions with contrasting material outcomes. For example, John accidentally breaks 15 cups while trying to help his parents, whereas Henry breaks one cup while disobeying his parents as he tries to reach the jam when his mother is out. In another pair of stories, Piaget contrasts Marie, who wants to give her mother a nice surprise but accidently cuts a big hole in her dress, with Margret, who plays with scissors one day when her mother is out and intentionally cuts a small hole in her dress. Children were then asked if the story characters were equally guilty and which of the two was the naughtiest. Based on their responses, Piaget described a gradual shift from *moral realism*, that is judging action based on the material consequences (breaking 15 cups verus one) and not the child's intentions, to *subjective responsibility*, that is considering the intentions involved (trying to help).

A common criticism of this research regarding intentions and moral judgments is that Piaget 'underestimated' children's abilities because at this age they would understand intentions. In fact he was clear that these children did talk about intentions, but they did not apply this understanding in these situations because in their experience adults failed to consider intentions and only reacted to consequences.

Piaget introduced the idea of relationships of constraint in the context of parent–child relationships and the idea of relationships of cooperation in the context of peer relationships. But he stated that any relationship is, in fact, some mixture of the two, and it is clear that peer relationships can involve constraint in the context of bullying, and parent–child relationships can vary in how cooperative they are.

Understanding lying

Piaget also explored the development of children's understanding of lying. He told children stories about various lies and asked which of the lies were worse. Using this method he found that young children thought it was worse to tell a lie that a child had seen a dog as big as a cow compared to lying about getting a good mark at school. Their reason for this judgment was that their mother might believe that they got a good mark in school and so they would not get punished, but their mother would never believe that they had seen a dog as big as a cow and so they would be reprimanded. This showed that their understanding of how bad a lie was depended on whether they would be punished.

They did not understand why lying is bad; they experienced being punished for saying certain things but they didn't understand why. They even thought that making a mistake was the same as a lie. Thus, the young children thought that lying to an adult was worse than lying to a child because they would be punished when lying to an adult but not when lying to a child.

For the older children, however, it was exactly the opposite. They thought that telling a lie that one's mother would believe was far worse that telling one she would not believe. This was because she would be taken in and deceived. They also thought that sometimes you just couldn't avoid lying to an adult because of their rules, but to lie to a friend was really bad! In order to learn this about lying, Piaget argued that it was not enough just to be told by adults that lying was wrong because children did not understand why. Instead, they had to experience relationships among equals in order to learn about the interpersonal consequences of lying (Piaget, 1932, p. 164).

The origin of a sense of justice

According to Piaget, the notion of justice is not imposed on children by adults, nor does it pre-exist in the child. Rather, children develop this understanding in particular forms of interaction involving cooperation among equals – its emergence depends on experiencing a particular form of social life. What is needed for its development, according to Piaget, are relationships of mutual affection (1932/1965). Within relationships among equals children develop a practical way of interacting to get along with each other. The principles that structure cooperative relationships are *constitutive* rules. These principles are the 'logic of action' (Piaget, 1932/1965, p. 398), and children work this out at a practical level before gradually becoming aware of these principles that structure their interaction. Piaget described this as a process of *conscious realisation* through which children become aware of and can then talk about what was previously implicit in their interaction with others. Conscious realisation transfers to the level of thought what was already worked out at the level of interaction with others. Piaget described a lag of a couple of years between the practical level and the verbal level (Piaget, 1932/1965). *Constituted* rules, on the other hand, are those rules that are formulated within cooperative relationships (Carpendale, 2009; Piaget, 1932/1965).

Research assessing Piaget's view of moral development was conducted in the 1960s and 1970s, and this generally supported his view of the development of moral judgment (Lickona, 1976). The belief at that time was that Piaget's approach should be extended in the direction taken by Lawrence Kohlberg (Lickona, 1976). Although it should be recognised that Piaget's work on morality is incomplete (Wright, 1982), it is not simply the case that it leads seamlessly into more recent work (Carpendale, 2000, 2009; Wright, 1982). Rather, central points of Piaget's work have been ignored or misconstrued, a point we return to in the next chapter.

13.4 LAWRENCE KOHLBERG'S THEORY OF MORAL DEVELOPMENT

Lawrence Kohlberg (1969, 1981, 1984) is one of the most well-known theorists working on the topic of moral development. Although it is usually assumed that he built on and extended Piaget's work, it is more correct to say that Kohlberg was inspired by his Swiss predecessor, as there are also important differences in their approaches. Piaget was concerned with the emergence of a practical level of moral understanding in children's interaction, and the process through which children come to a conscious realisation of these principles. Instead, Kohlberg focused on the forms of moral reasoning that individuals use to resolve more complex moral dilemmas and developmental changes in these forms of moral reasoning. Thus, although they both studied moral development, Piaget and Kohlberg approached it from different directions (Wright, 1982).

Kohlberg's theory dominated the study of morality in psychology for many years, and many approaches have been proposed in reaction to it. Introducing his theory is facilitated by contrasting it with an early approach to the study of morality. Hartshorne and May (1928–1930) conducted a large study on cheating in an attempt to determine whether there were certain types of children who cheated. Children between the ages of 9 and 14 were given opportunities to cheat on a classroom achievement test (e.g. they had an opportunity to look at the answers to the test or to keep working) or cheat on a test of athletic ability and strength. Hartshorne and May did not find that only certain children cheat, rather that many cheated depending on the situation. The study was criticised, however, because the physical skill was so difficult that it almost required cheating, and there were no apparent consequences for others if a child cheated on the test. The experimenter seemed uninterested. This is not like everyday events in which if one person cheats there are consequences for others – like looking at another's hand in a card game. In fact, it could be argued that the study was not really about morality at all. The experimental procedure involved the experimenter deceiving the children because it was set up to elicit cheating (Kohlberg, 1966).

From Kohlberg's perspective, it is not just the behaviour but also the reasons for it that are important. Reasons are important because action itself cannot be moral (i.e. the same action could be either moral or immoral depending on the reasons). Consider the example of not paying one's income tax. This could be done for the *selfish* reason of wanting to keep the money for oneself, or for a *moral* reason if one is opposed to a war one's government is waging.

Kohlberg claimed that, whether it is acknowledged or not, schooling is a moral enterprise, and thus it is not value-neutral. Instead, implicit values are embedded in school life, with its rules and norms about conduct such as obedience (Kohlberg & Hersh, 1977). He contrasted his definition of morality with two approaches to moral education: *values clarification* and *character education*.

The *values clarification* approach is based on the idea that people have different values concerning, for example, whether to give one's seat on a bus to an elderly person or follow the rule 'first come first served'. The goal, from this perspective, is to help the child explore and clarify her own values. It is based on the idea that there is no single correct answer, instead values are just different (Higgins, 1995). It follows then that a teacher has no moral basis for imposing any particular set of values. However, the view that values should not be imposed is a value itself. A bully may be clear about his values but this does not make them right.

Kohlberg referred to *character education* as the *bag of virtues* approach. These are values held by teachers and the culture that are imposed on the child. Consider the Scout/Guide principles of being honest, loyal, reverent, clean, brave, and so on. The Hartshorne and May goal of assessing children's tendency to cheat is based on this 'bag of virtues' approach. Although in general it is usually right to be honest and not to lie or steal, this is not always the case. There could be situations in which lying would be necessary to save someone, or stealing might be necessary to feed someone, so this might be the right thing to do. Kohlberg's dilemmas are based on conflicts between two moral rules, and so the dilemma cannot just be solved by appealing to the solution in a rule-book – you have to weigh up the relative merits and demerits of, for example, feeding the starving person versus stealing. Thus, Kohlberg was concerned with how people make decisions when two moral rules are in conflict.

Kohlberg used Piaget's interview method but he presented his research participants with a series of moral dilemmas in which he set two moral principles in conflict, so that there was no easy answer that could be arrived at by following a rule. He also asked participants a number of questions to clarify the reasons for their decisions. Kohlberg's most well-known moral dilemma involves a character named Heinz attempting to save his dying wife who desperately needs a drug made by a 'druggist' (pharmacist) who is selling it for $4,000, although his production cost is only $400. Heinz can only raise $2,000 but the druggist refuses to budge on his price. In his desperation Heinz considers stealing the drug.

Research participants are first asked if Heinz should or should not steal the drug, and then, more importantly, they are asked for their reasons. This is followed by a series of probing questions such as 'should he steal the drug if he doesn't love his wife?', or should he steal the drug for a stranger, or a pet, as well as questions about whether the law should be obeyed in general, and why or why not. The story then continues with further dilemmas involving a policeman who suspects Heinz of stealing the drug and must decide whether or not to arrest him, and a judge who faces the decision of whether or not Heinz should be sentenced or given a suspended sentence (Colby & Kohlberg, 1987). Kohlberg used these and other hypothetical dilemmas in order to assess the highest stage of moral reasoning presented by each participant. It is unlikely that people would have encountered these dilemmas so they could not rely on previous experience or a rule but had to work out a decision.

This dilemma might seem like an abstract hypothetical story completely unrelated to anything likely to be encountered in daily lives, but think of the AIDS/HIV epidemic in Africa and the prices charged by pharmaceutical companies for medication. In 2012 Stephen Lewis, Canada's former ambassador to the UN on AIDS, pointed out that the epidemic was 'like all the wars of the twentieth century wrapped into one. Thirty million people have died; 34 million live with the virus. There were two and half million new infections last year, of which 330,000 are children. More then 50% of those infected in Africa are women' (Postcard, Stephen Lewis Foundation). In a related case, the patent for a 62-year-old drug, Daraprim, was purchased by Martin Shkreli and he immediately raised the price from $13.50 to $750 per pill! Even the price of $13.50 was a recent increase from $1.00 per pill. This 5000% increase in price is, unfortunately, not an uncommon business strategy (*New York Times*, 20 September 2015).

Kohlberg also used a dilemma involving euthanasia in which a doctor is asked by a patient dying in pain to help her to die. This dilemma pits caring for others against following the law. This issue is now being debated by courts and governments, and assisted dying is available in some countries. Kohlberg was interested not just in what people thought was right or wrong in particular situations, but even more in the reasons behind their decisions, because he thought that it is the reasons, not the behaviour, that make it right or wrong. Kohlberg distinguished the specific moral belief or opinion (i.e. whether or not to steal the drug) from the general organising principles or patterns of thought. He believed that the form of thinking exhibits *developmental regularity* and *generalisability*. That is, although individuals might make different decisions on different dilemmas, Kohlberg expected that their reasoning should be of the same form.

> Think-point or class exercise: Before reading on, discuss with your classmates (or yourself!) whether and in what circumstances it would be acceptable to help a patient end his or her life. Write down your reasons for your decision.

In one of the studies for his PhD dissertation, Kohlberg (1958) interviewed 72 males between the ages of 10 and 16 and recorded their responses to a series of moral dilemmas. He then followed these participants longitudinally. From these interviews he concluded that there were six qualitatively different ways of viewing moral issues. Each stage of reasoning depends on the form of reasoning an individual uses, not the decision made. That is, the decision, for example, of whether Heinz should or should not steal the drug for his wife, can be justified with reasons that fall into different stages of moral reasoning. For some of the dilemmas, however, there tends to be convergence at Stage 5 on particular decisions such as the view that the law in the Heinz dilemma is wrong.

Kohlberg initially described six stages of moral reasoning. There are now five stages of moral reasoning in Kohlberg's extensive 1,200-page scoring manual (Colby & Kohlberg, 1987), subdivided into three levels. These stages differ in how perspectives are coordinated.

KOHLBERG'S STAGES OF MORAL DEVELOPMENT

Reasoning at Stage 1, the preconventional level, focuses on punishment and obedience. The social order is understood in terms of power and status differences, and weaker individuals are expected to obey stronger ones. Punishment is expected for those who deviate from this. Participants at this stage state that Heinz should (or should not) steal the drug, and use relatively simple justifications like 'Because it's against the law'. At Stage 2 the perspective is concrete and individualistic. The concern is to act to serve one's own needs or interests in a world where others are expected to do the same. So stealing a drug to save a friend's life might be chosen as the course of action 'because you may need him to do the same for you someday'. This mindset is captured by the Stage 2 understanding of the Golden Rule: 'Do unto others so that they will do unto you; or Do unto others what they have done unto you.' At Stage 3 the understanding of this rule is transformed to 'Do unto others as if the others were the self' (Lapsley, 1996, p. 73).

Stage 3 marks the onset of what is termed the 'conventional level', and individuals' moral judgments focus on conformity to social norms. Individuals are concerned about approval from friends, family, and community. They think about feelings, interpersonal relationships, and others' expectations. There is a need to be a good person in one's own eyes and those of others. The perspective is of the individual in relationships with other individuals, aware of shared feelings, agreements, and expectations, which are more important than individual interests. At Stage 3 society is viewed as a collection of close relationships such as family and friends, and moral reasoning does not go beyond these smaller groups to consider a more general system (e.g. all citizens of a country).

At Stage 4 this is generalised, and conduct is not just regulated by shared relational expectations but rather by legal codes that apply impartially. Rules at Stage 4 are shared and accepted by the community in order to avoid a breakdown of the system. The point of view taken at this stage is that of the system as a whole. From this perspective, laws should be upheld in order to maintain the system. They should only be broken in extreme circumstances. The right thing to do is to fulfil the duties one has accepted such as being a physician or judge, or wife or husband.

Stage 5 reasoning, at the postconventional level, is based on a 'prior-to-society' perspective. It is concerned with values such as liberty and human dignity which anyone would

(Continued)

want in order to build an ideally just society (Colby & Kohlberg, 1987, p. 73). But societies are not ideal so it is possible to criticise and improve existing societies if they fail to protect citizens. The thinking is based on the assumption that there are fundamental human rights that laws cannot remove, and that laws are only valid if they serve to protect such rights when circumstances change – like the pandemic of HIV/AIDS. Thus at Stage 4 the emphasis is on maintaining society and laws, whereas at Stage 5 the focus is on creating a society based on social cooperation (Lapsley, 1996, p. 74). So at Stage 4 the question might be whether an act is legal, and but at Stage 5 the question is whether the current law is moral, and if it isn't then that law needs to be changed, such as introducing a new law that grants individuals the right to end one's own life in certain situations.

Although Stage 6 is no longer in the scoring manual, because it is very rare and not clearly distinguishable from Stage 5, it is still important in Kohlberg's theory. The difference between Stage 5 and Stage 6 is not so much in perspective and consists more in the use of procedures to ensure a moral process by considering all perspectives involved. This is 'the moral point of view' according to which everyone affected by a decision should contribute to the decision-making process, and thus the outcome is based on respect for persons. Kohlberg's 'moral musical chairs' in which all positions are considered is one procedure used to check if a decision is fair from all the perspectives involved. Kohlberg's moral point of view is similar to John Rawls's (1971) idea of a 'veil of ignorance' when designing a society that blinds individuals to self-interest because they do not know what position they might take in the society. That is, they wouldn't know whether they would be rich or poor, or male or female, and so on. Therefore, it would not make sense to construct a society with slavery or oppression of any kind (Colby & Kohlberg, 1987). These procedures are also similar to Habermas's (1983/1990) ideal communication situation in which there is no coercion and everyone has the potential to present their view, and Piaget's (1932/1965) cooperative relationships among equals in which everyone explains their position and listens to those of others.

Kohlberg's assumptions about stages

Kohlberg claimed that these types of moral reasoning form stages similar to Piaget's stages of cognitive development. Each stage is a qualitatively different form of thinking about moral conflicts, and these stages form an invariant sequence. Although social and cultural factors may speed up or slow down an individual's development, according to Kohlberg there can be no regression, skipping, or reverting to a prior stage. He assumed that everyone goes through the same sequence, but not everyone reaches Stage 5 and there may be different rates of development. The most common stages in adults are 3 or 4 and few reach Stage 5.

Each stage or way of thinking forms a 'structured whole' – a coherent and organised perspective or 'worldview' that is used to resolve various kinds of moral dilemmas. This assumption implies consistency in the form of moral reasoning that individuals use. That is, individuals are expected to use a similar style of reasoning, and therefore be at the same stage, on different moral dilemmas. Kohlberg based his theory on the 'received view' of Piaget's stages (see Chapter 3 and Chapman, 1988, for a critique of this view; also Carpendale, 2000). In fact, Piaget (1932/1965) did not think that children's moral reasoning could be described in terms of stages.

Stages fit together in a hierarchy of increasing complexity; each is more advanced than the previous one. A more advanced stage should be able to resolve conflicts more adequately and fairly. To test this idea Kohlberg and his colleagues conducted a longitudinal study, and then re-tested participants every few years to see if they had advanced through the hierarchy of stages in an orderly fashion and their expectation was confirmed (Colby, Kohlberg, Gibbs, & Leiberman, 1983).

What causes moral development?

Kohlberg believed that what stimulates moral development are events that evoke moral reasoning and encourage people to take the role of others. This follows from the Piagetian idea of disequilibrium. That is, complex social situations may raise moral issues that are not easily resolved, and individuals may realise that their current way of thinking is inadequate. According to Kohlberg, the 'scientific theory as to why people factually *do* move upward from stage to stage, and why they factually *do* prefer a higher stage to a lower, is broadly the same as a moral theory as to why people *should* prefer a higher stage to a lower' (Kohlberg, 1981, p. 179, original emphasis). In other words, the idea is that individuals develop through stages because higher ones are more adequate for solving moral dilemmas, and if they realise their current way of thinking is incomplete this will motivate further development.

In addition, Kohlberg thought that stages of cognitive development are required but are not enough by themselves for stages of social perspective taking, and these are in turn necessary but not sufficient for stages of moral development. There is some empirical support for this claim from studies by Lawrence Walker (1983). He presented participants with reasoning that was either one or two stages higher than their own stage of reasoning. He found what when they were re-tested later there was some developmental advance, but if they changed it was only by one stage. That is, the participants who were presented with reasoning that was two stages above their own did not just copy or model that type of reasoning. This suggests an inability simply to internalise higher-stage reasoning in a rote way. He found that what stimulated the most moral growth was exposure to moral reasoning that was one stage higher and advanced a conflicting point of view. But even higher-stage reasoning that was in agreement with the child's view, or same stage reasoning between adults who disagreed with each other, stimulated moderate development. This shows the important role cognitive conflict (what followers of this tradition term 'disequilibrium') plays in the development of moral reasoning.

Just community schools

A less well-known aspect of Kohlberg's research programme is his work in schools and his idea of a *just community*. Kohlberg initially thought that the development of moral reasoning was a gradual process. But one of his graduate students wanted to try to increase children's moral reasoning through discussion of moral dilemmas. Kohlberg was initially sceptical about whether this would work. In a 12-week study based on discussing moral dilemmas, a third of the 12- to 14-year-old children had moved up one stage on his test. After replicating this research to confirm the finding, Kohlberg and his colleagues tried this approach in other settings. They conducted a study in a prison and found that talking about moral dilemmas did improve prisoners' trust for each other, but it did not have much effect on moral reasoning. They concluded that this was because the institutional structure of prisons was at Stage 2, which constrained individuals' thinking (Higgins, 1995).

Following the prison study, Kohlberg was asked to be involved in a school in a very low-income area. He developed a 'just community' school and then later two more. Kohlberg wanted the structure of the school to be based on equality – a just community. This meant that the students had to have a significant role in school decisions, resulting in an institutional structure that could facilitate higher-stage reasoning. They naturally moved from discussion of hypothetical moral dilemmas to actual dilemmas that had occurred, such as dealing with a situation in which someone's money had been stolen. As well as community meetings with all students and teachers, a committee of 10 to 12 students and one teacher was formed to deal with moral issues that arose in the school, and decide on what should be done. The just community approach deserves further development; it has practical as well as moral implications for schools and society more broadly.

13.5 CRITICISMS OF KOHLBERG'S THEORY

As well as being influential by stimulating the study of moral development through the teenage years and into adulthood and for its focus on principles of justice, Kohlberg's theory has also been extensively criticised. We review this criticism in order to elaborate further on our presentation of his theory, and because he and his colleagues developed the theory progressively, partly in response to criticism. It is important to be aware of Kohlberg's work and the reactions to it in order to understand current research on morality that we present in the next chapter. We will see that some of the issues raised by Piaget and Kohlberg are overlooked in some current approaches, resulting in incomplete accounts.

Consistency in moral reasoning

One prediction that follows from Kohlberg's view of stages is that once someone has developed a way of thinking about a particular moral issue – that is, is at a stage of moral reasoning – they should apply that way of thinking to all the moral conflicts they encounter. There should be no regression (i.e. slippage down to a lower level of reasoning) in the stage of moral reasoning and people should consistently apply the same form of reasoning. A number of studies have evaluated this claim and it has not been supported. For example, in one study participants were presented either with Kohlberg's standard moral dilemmas, or modifications set in the context of business decisions (Carpendale & Krebs, 1992). The participants justified their decisions with reasons that could be scored with Colby and Kohlberg's (1987) scoring manual, and some participants provided Stage 4 judgments on the business dilemmas. But the modal stage of reasoning in the context of business decisions was Stage 2, even though these participants used Stages 3 to 4 on Kohlberg's moral dilemmas. This finding of inconsistency in the stage of moral reasoning used across different moral dilemmas has been replicated in many studies (Carpendale & Krebs, 1995; Krebs, Denton, Vermeulen, Carpendale, & Bush, 1991), and it challenges Kohlberg's conception of stages.

Are Kohlberg's stages found in all cultures?

Kohlberg (1981, 1984) argued that his dilemmas deal with issues that would be encountered in all societies of sufficient complexity because they concern problems that arise in human ways of living together. There is some support for this claim from cross-cultural studies. Longitudinal studies in the USA, Turkey, and Israel provide support for the sequence of stages and show no evidence of regression. Other cross-sectional studies have been conducted in India, Indonesia, Guatemala, Iran, Nigeria, Pakistan, Yucatan, Thailand, and Zambia. Stage 5 reasoning is rare in all populations but it has been found in research with participants from non-Western societies, but not in traditional tribal or village folk societies (Snarey, 1985). Kohlberg (1981) argued that this is because a particular level of societal complexity is needed for the development to higher stages of moral reasoning.

Kohlberg identified a set of moral concepts and values that are included in his scoring manual, but acknowledged that they might not be exhaustive (Kohlberg, Levine, & Hewer, 1983). A concept that came up in a number of cross-cultural studies in research with the Kipsigis people of Kenya, and the Maisin people of Papua New Guinea, involves social equilibrium, harmony, or peace in the community. A similar idea was found among young people in an Israeli kibbutz, who were concerned with social solidarity, cooperation and equality, and happiness. Harmony in relationships, empathy, concern for others' welfare, and a deep affection that extended to all people are also found in Chinese Confucian morality. This suggests that Kohlberg's theory may be incomplete and could potentially be expanded (Boyes & Walker, 1988).

Moral reasoning and moral action: from thinking to acting

The reason for studying moral development is, of course, to understand moral action. Therefore, the question is whether the hypothetical moral reasoning Kohlberg and his colleagues studied is related to moral action. A number of studies have found correlations between individuals' stage of moral reasoning and their moral behaviour – the higher the stage of moral reasoning the more likely individuals are to behave morally (Blasi, 1980). But Kohlberg's theory had little to say about this relationship to moral action, except that if someone *knows* what is right they should *do* what is right (Kohlberg, 1981).

Kohlberg acknowledged that the relationship between moral reasoning and moral action is complex, but he believed that the former causes the latter because reasoning leads to the choice of action. According to his model, the first step from moral reasoning to moral action is what he referred to as a *deontic choice*; that is, reaching a conclusion about what is right in a situation. After people decide what is right they make a judgment of responsibility concerning whether they have a personal moral obligation to carry out their decision. But even if they do feel a sense of responsibility to carry out what they think is right, they still may lack what Kohlberg and Candee (1984) call 'nonmoral skills' such as intelligence, attention, and delay of gratification that may be required to carry out the moral decision.

Another approach to linking moral reasoning and action is to study people who are generally considered to be highly moral. This approach conceptualises moral understanding as being integrated with personal identity and emotions (Blasi, 1983; Krettenauer & Hertz, 2015). It has been found that these highly principled individuals, known as 'moral exemplars', do not all reason at Stage 5. Those involved in helping others and showing devotion to the poor tended to use Stage 3 or 4 reasoning. But individuals involved in social justice and legal issues generally did use Stage 5, because this involves fundamental human rights that are prior to current laws (Colby & Damon, 1993). For some issues, such as helping others, figuring out the right thing to do is not a big problem and so does not require sophisticated moral reasoning. However, for other issues such as human rights, more complex moral reasoning may be required to work out what is right.

Piaget and Kohlberg approached the issue of the relations between thought and action from opposite directions. Piaget was concerned with how moral understanding arises first in children's practical interaction with others, and then progresses to a verbal and conscious level in the process of the child's conscious realisation of her own moral activity.

Theoretical moral reflection is 'a progressive conscious realization of moral activity' (Piaget, 1932/1965, p. 176). In contrast, Kohlberg was concerned with the development of reasoning about morality, then how reasoning becomes more complex, and how such reasoning influences individuals' actions.

Justice and care: are there gender differences in moral reasoning?

Whether men and women differ in their orientation to morality has been a longstanding issue that was resurrected in the debate between Lawrence Kohlberg and Carol Gilligan. Gilligan (1982) described two 'voices' or orientations to morality: one focused on care and the other on justice. She suggested that a focus on care is more common in girls and women and that because women were more likely to use care reasoning, which may be based on interpersonal reasons, their moral reasoning is more likely to be scored at Stage 3 in Kohlberg's stages. Because interpersonal moral reasoning is claimed to be more characteristic of women than men, Kohlberg's theory would be biased against women because they would be scored at Stage 3 on his test.

According to Gilligan, variation in moral orientation is not due to a biological sex difference; it is based on early socialisation depending on differences between boys and girls in their experience of attachment and equality (Gilligan & Wiggins, 1987). Gilligan argued that these different moral orientations arise due to boys and girls having differing experiences of inequality and attachment. They both experience these two dimensions of relationships, but to different degrees. Girls identify with their mothers and therefore are less aware of inequality. Instead, their experience of attachment and connecting with others is more central to their self-definition. On the other hand, it is argued that boys are attached to their mothers but identify with their fathers, so the experience inequality and a feeling powerless would be more salient for them and thus the need for norms of fairness and justice to try to overcome this (Brown, Tappan, & Gilligan, 1995). Gilligan's developmental explanation, however, appears to presuppose inequality between parents.

A first question concerns whether there are differences in moral orientation (i.e. care vs justice) between men and women. Gilligan and Attanucci (1988) asked participants to discuss a moral dilemma they had experienced in their own life because they argued that moral orientation is best revealed in reasoning about real-life dilemmas. Out of the 80 participants, 55 (or 69%) used both care and justice in discussing the dilemma, and only 31% used only care or justice. Men and women used both care and justice in their reasoning but Gilligan found differences in focus. Using one 'voice' was defined as 75% or more of the considerations individuals raised being representative of the care or justice perspectives, suggesting that they preferred one perspective. Out of the 22 women with a dominant focus, 12 focused on care. In contrast, out of the 31 men with a dominant focus, 30 used justice.

However, in a meta-analysis of studies assessing care and justice reasoning, 73% of studies assessing care orientation and 72% of studies assessing justice orientation found no significant differences between men and women, and the effect size found in the other studies was very small, accounting for only a very small percentage of the variance. Thus, care and justice orientations do not seem to be strongly associated with gender. It seems that most people are likely to use both orientations (Walker, 2006). Walker tested the claim that the care orientation would be associated with lower-stage reasoning than the justice orientation, but in contrast he found that in real-life dilemmas it was actually associated with *higher*-stage reasoning.

A second question concerning Gilligan's claims is whether there are gender differences in the stage of moral reasoning achieved. In his meta-analysis Walker examined 80 studies with 152 samples including a total of 10,637 participants. He found that in most cases (85%) there were no differences between men and women. In the remaining studies, females scored higher than males in 6%, and males scored higher than females in 9%. This is a very small and insignificant effect, accounting for less than a twentieth of 1% of the variance. In those studies in which men scored higher than women there were differences in education and occupation. In studies without such variations in background no gender differences were found, suggesting that any gender differences occasionally found in studies may be due to level of education (Walker, 2006). Based on this meta-analysis there is no empirical evidence that women score lower than men on Kohlberg's test (Walker, 2006). In fact, when women used care reasoning their stage on Kohlberg's test was higher, not lower (Walker, 2006).

Although it is important to consider real-life dilemmas, there is a key methodological problem. If participants are asked to reason about a dilemma they have experienced personally, then, necessarily, they all discuss different dilemmas (e.g. Gilligan & Attanucci, 1988), so perhaps differences in the forms of reasoning they use are due to the fact they are responding to different dilemmas. In fact, there is evidence that reasoning depends on the type of dilemma. Care reasoning is more common regarding dilemmas categorised as personal or relational involving conflicts with people in close ongoing relationships, whereas justice reasoning is more common in response to impersonal or non-relational dilemmas with strangers or institutions. Men and women may encounter or choose to relate different types of dilemma, and this, rather than their moral orientation, may account for gender difference in moral reasoning. There are few or no sex differences in moral orientation on a standard stimulus (i.e. when everyone discusses the same dilemma, like the Heinz problem described above) (Walker, 1995, 2006).

Many have assumed that Gilligan is proposing a feminist perspective. However, some feminists suggest that she is supporting traditional stereotypes of males as being rational and females as being emotive (e.g. Moller Okin, 1996).

Can justice and care stand alone as separate approaches? Consider, for example, moral dilemmas that teachers may encounter when dealing with students. Teachers could take two approaches. One is to make decisions based on caring about particular students.

Another is to impose fixed rules that are applied equally to all the students. Both of these approaches might result in problems. If a teacher has favourite pupils she cares about those favourites, but that is not fair to the rest of the class because the pupils were not all being treated in the same way. On the other hand, simply imposing fixed rules may not actually be fair because this might not take into account the circumstances particular students might face.

Care and justice may be compatible and interdependent, and it may not be necessary to choose between caring and being fair. Piaget wrote about this issue of love and justice long before the debate between Kohlberg and Gilligan. He acknowledged a difference between focusing on either of these dimensions, but argued that 'between the more refined forms of justice, such as equity and love properly so called, there is no longer any real conflict' (Piaget, 1932/1965, p. 324).

A crucially important point to be drawn from this debate is that care is essential in understanding morality and it is central to many of the theories discussed in the next chapter. Caring about others cannot simply be added later in development. The idea that we should care about others cannot be reached through reasoning (Wright, 1982). Instead, caring about others is needed as part of the foundation that structures the relationships in which children develop – a point that was central to Piaget (1932/1965). The ethic of care approach continues to be applied in various areas such as social work and social policy (Hankivsky, 2004).

13.6 SOCIAL-COGNITIVE DOMAIN THEORY

Moral rules are just one of the types of social rules that children encounter in their every-day lives. There are also social conventional rules, such as whether children must formally address their teacher as 'Mrs Smith' or are allowed to use their teacher's first name. Social convention concerns expectations involving modes of dress, forms of address, and eating habits. In contrast to social convention, moral issues involve concepts of welfare, justice, and rights; it concerns inflicting harm, theft, and unequal treatment. Many studies have now shown that young children, sometimes even as young as three, can distinguish between these social domains (Smetana, 2006; Turiel, 1983, 2002, 2015). When children are asked whether a rule can be changed by an authority, they agree that teachers can allow children to call them by their first name, or that a certain day will be designated pyjama day at school, when children can wear pyjamas, altering the usual social convention. Children's answers reflect their judgment that social conventions are arbitrary and can be changed. In contrast, they understand that moral norms are not changeable by authority figures and apply across situations. For example, children believe that teachers cannot announce that on some days children are allowed to hit others; one is obliged to not hit others, regardless of whether the teacher is present or not.

Domain theorists argue that children learn about these two dimensions of social rules separately within different types of social interaction. These domains of social interaction result in distinct developmental pathways (Nucci, 2004; Turiel, 1983). Hitting someone has consequences – the person being hit gets hurt. But there are no obvious consequences that result from addressing one's teacher as Lisa instead of Mrs Smith. This approach has stimulated a great deal of research. Much of this has focused on the distinctions between the domains. In addition to these two social domains, Nucci (e.g. 2004) added the personal domain as a further area of social knowledge. The personal domain subsumes issues that are considered to be a matter of personal choice that do not affect the welfare or rights of others, such as the particular clothes one wears (Nucci, 2004; Turiel, 2015). Turiel (1983) presented domain theory as a challenge to Kohlberg and Piaget. He rejects their claim that development starts from a fusion of social concepts such that moral issues and social concerns are initially entangled, and that moral development consists of the gradual differentiation between these concepts.

Not all social events can be neatly classified into either the moral domain or the social-conventional domain. Many situations may involve aspects of convention and morality, as well as prudence and personal issues. Prudential issues concern harm to one's self, but the line between personal choice and safety may not be clear. Children try to assert their personal choice, actively resisting parental power on issues they feel they should have choice over and should not be subject to parents' control. For example, if a child wants to wear a T-shirt in the winter, or no raincoat in the rain because he wants to look 'cool' he may consider this just a personal decision but his parents may be concerned about safety.

We started this chapter with the example of dress code, such as wearing white or black to a funeral. This is a convention that depends on one's culture. But if someone is offended by how another person dresses then this could be a moral issue related to respect. What about waiting in a line (queue)? Is this a moral issue or a social convention? It seems to be largely a social convention and it varies across cultures, but it is also related to fairness, because it concerns people having their turn and being treated as persons. So any social event may not fit neatly into a single domain, and require coordination between domains. Making decisions in such situations means considering and coordinating the various moral and non-moral aspects. Research on such complex situations suggests that although young children may distinguish morality and social conventions in simple situations, when situations get more complex they may give greater weight to the law and social convention than morality. For example, they apply moral criteria more consistently to hitting and hurting others than to fairness, such as sharing a toy, and psychological harm (Smetana, 2006; Turiel, 2015).

Older children are more consistent in understanding the distinction between morality and conventions. Children's ability to understand the distinction between morality and convention was not found in a study in which the transgressions of moral and social-conventional norms were more complex. The moral transgression consisted of breaking a promise, which is more difficult for children to understand because it does not have an obvious consequence of hurting someone. The social conventional transgression involved going into the opposite gender's bathroom. In these situations, children aged 8 to 11 years old did not think that the moral transgression was less changeable than the social convention (Lourenço, 2014).

Turiel (1983) outlined development within domains, but the domain approach has been criticised as being non-developmental because there has not been much research on development within the domains (Lourenço, 2014). On the question of how children's knowledge develops, Turiel endorses a constructivist view of knowledge, as do Piaget and Kohlberg. That is, children construct knowledge of social domains through their interaction with their social environment. Social Domain Theory still has much in common with Kohlberg. Turiel still assumes that reason plays a central role in moral judgment. The role of reason, however, has been challenged by researchers who argue that emotions play a more important role in morality than reasons (e.g. Haidt, 2001). We turn to this issue in the next chapter.

SUMMARY AND CONCLUSIONS

In studying the development of morality, a first step is to describe what is being investigated. This is no easy task because morality is central to being human and permeates many aspects of human interaction, from life and death issues such as genocide to everyday social interactions concerning how we treat others. Understanding the breadth of morality leads to the question of how children learn about it. One common answer is that parents teach their children what is right and wrong. Although there is something to this socialisation view, the idea that morality is imposed on children by previous generations does not explain where it originates, nor how it changes. This approach is also linked to the idea that morality is different across cultures and there is no way to evaluate different moral norms, resulting in the view that morality is relative to particular cultures (moral relativism). But the idea that morality is imposed by others implies that morality consists of conforming to the local norms. Both Piaget and Kohlberg argued there is more to morality than conformity. A more complete theory needs to account for individuals thinking for themselves about moral issues and making autonomous decisions.

Piaget described two forms of morality developing within two types of relationships children experience. He noted that a *heteronomous* morality consisted of rules from the outside imposed on the child, which originated in relationships of constraint exemplified by parent–child relationships of inequality and one-sided respect. In contrast, children also experience peer relationships of cooperation based on mutual respect among equals. These cooperative relationships are best suited to reaching a mutual understanding, and therefore for moral development through understanding others' perspectives. In this context, *autonomous* morality can develop. Piaget was clear that although he introduced the two types of relationships in the context of parents and peers, any actual relationship was some mixture of the two.

For Piaget, children are not born with moral knowledge, nor is it imposed by others, but rather, morality emerges as ways of acting within cooperative relationships. Children first develop a practical morality that is implicit within their interactions with others, and they then gradually become aware of this through a process of *conscious realisation* and can talk about and reflect on what was previously evident at the level of activity.

Kohlberg is generally viewed as building on Piaget, but his theory differs from Piaget's in important ways. Piaget was interested in children's practical moral activity which they later become aware of, whereas Kohlberg was concerned with the development of verbal reasoning about moral issues that then might be translated into action. For Kohlberg, morality cannot consist merely of conforming to rules because sometimes these rules are in conflict. Making a moral choice might sometimes actually mean lying or stealing. Kohlberg was interested in how people figure out what to do when facing dilemmas in which moral rules are pitted against each other. In these situations such moral rules cannot just be followed because they are in conflict – you have to decide whether to obey the law and not steal a drug or to save a life by stealing, and Kohlberg was interested in how individuals justify their decision. Through many studies he and his colleagues found that the forms of reasoning people use in justifying their decisions develop, and they documented a sequence of five stages of moral reasoning, with a possible sixth stage. Kohlberg viewed these stages as different ways of thinking about moral dilemmas that he claimed form an invariant sequence with no regression or skipping of stages. Development through these stages depends on social experience and realising the inadequacy of the current stage, which motivates movement toward a more adequate form of thinking. Kohlberg applied his way of thinking about moral development to research in prisons and schools, forming what he called 'just' community schools.

Kohlberg was very influential but he was also extensively criticised. His model of stages results in the prediction that individuals should be consistent in their stage of reasoning when they resolve different moral dilemmas, but this prediction has not been supported. In cross-cultural research, Kohlberg's stages and sequence of development have been replicated, but it may be that additional moral concepts found in other cultures, such as social harmony, need to be added to his conception of morality. Although Kohlberg focused on the development of moral reasoning, he was, of course, concerned with moral action. He outlined a model of how moral reasoning led to moral action by beginning with reasoning about the right choice of action, followed by judging whether one is personally obliged to carry it out. The final step involves the non-moral factors needed to actually carry out the decision (Kohlberg & Candee, 1984).

Kohlberg has also been criticised by Gilligan (1982) for focusing on justice and neglecting care in the way he conceptualised morality. She argued that women usually focus on care and men on justice. Walker (1995) found little empirical support for

Gilligan's claims. Furthermore, although care and justice can be separated, at higher levels it seems that they are intertwined.

According to social-cognitive domain theory, from early in development children understand the distinctions between moral, social conventional, and personal domain. Morality concerns the welfare of others and fairness. Moral rules cannot be changed. On the other hand, social conventions are arbitrary rules that can be changed. Finally, the personal domain concerns individual choices that do not affect others. In the next chapter we go on to discuss theories of morality highlighting the importance of emotions and biology; these theories have been formulated partly in reaction to the theories introduced in this chapter. We also return to some overlooked insights from Piaget that are relevant for the contemporary debate.

FURTHER READING

Piaget, J. (1965). *The Moral Judgment of the Child*. New York: The Free Press. (Original work published 1932.)

14 RECENT ISSUES IN MORAL DEVELOPMENT

LEARNING OUTCOMES

Having read this chapter you should:

- Be aware of the various views regarding the role of emotions in morality.

- Be able to describe in detail Jonathan Haidt's social intuitionist model.

- Be familiar with claims regarding infants' understanding of morality, as well as criticism of such claims.

- Be aware of research on children's early prosocial development, and helping in particular.

- Understand the different perspectives on the origin of moral norms.

'Morality, like art, means drawing a line somewhere'.

A statement often attributed to Oscar Wilde or G. K. Chesterton

At midnight on 1 August, 2008, Chhiring Dorje, a Sherpa climber, was descending K2 in Nepal, the second highest mountain in the world. He was climbing down during the night because the climbers he was accompanying had reached the summit at 6.00 p.m. that day. He was on 'the deadliest stretch of the most dangerous mountain' (Zuckerman & Padoan, 2012, p. 1) when he met another Sherpa, Pasang Lama, who had left his ice axe further up in order to help other climbers descend the mountain. Pasang Lama thought that he wouldn't need his ice axe going down the mountain because he would use the fixed ropes left by the climbers on the way up that morning. Tragically, however, the ropes had been swept away by an avalanche, so that he couldn't descend without an ice axe. He was convinced he would die on the mountain because it was too risky for others to help him. Another Sherpa had already gone by and left him behind. But Chhiring risked his own life to help Pasang Lama down the mountain, even though it was quite likely that they might both die in the attempt. Miraculously, they both survived the descent that night.

What is the balance between reasons and emotions in such heroic situations? Concern for another person might make it seem that the right thing to do would be to help, but there is also the possibility of losing one's own life in a rescue attempt. In addition, Chhiring Dorje had an obligation to protect his own life in order to return to help care for his family. Psychologists disagree regarding the role of emotions in morality and moral development (e.g. Maibom, 2010, 2014). This controversy, as with many other current controversies in psychology, can be traced back hundreds of years to the debates between Jean-Jacques Rousseau's emphasis on reason and education and David Hume's emphasis on the role of emotion in moral conduct. In this chapter we describe various views of the contributions of emotions and biology to morality. We discuss approaches that suggest emotions affect moral development through the empathic sharing of emotions with others (Paulus, 2014). We review Haidt's (2001) social intuitionist model, according to which moral judgments are rooted in evolved intuitive emotional reactions. Furthermore, with the surge of interest in neuroscience over the last two decades, the view that morality is rooted in particular regions of the brain has become increasingly popular. We consider this new research.

We also examine the development of a variety of prosocial behaviours and discuss what they tell us about the emergence of morality. An alternative view of the role of emotions from a developmental perspective is that they form the interpersonal relationships of mutual affection in which morality develops as a way of treating each other as persons in actual practice. That is, emotions play a key role in structuring the human relations in which morality develops (Piaget, 1932/1965). Finally, we present a relational developmental systems, or constructivist, account that firmly grounds moral development in social relationships. From this perspective, morality emerges first as practical ways of interacting with each other within relationships of mutual affection and respect. The principles that underlie this lived way of treating each other as persons gradually become conscious and verbal processes. These develop into a method of resolving moral conflicts through considering the viewpoints involved.

14.1 EMOTIONS AND MORALITY

How selfish soever man may be supposed, there are evidently some principles in his nature, which interest him in the fortune of others, and render their happiness necessary to him, though he derives nothing from it except the pleasure of seeing it. ... That we often derive sorrow from the sorrow of others, is a matter of fact too obvious to require any instances to prove it; for this sentiment, like all the other original passions of human nature, is by no means confined to the virtuous and humane. ... The greatest ruffian, the most hardened violator of the laws of society, is not altogether without it. (Smith, 1759/1982, p. 9)

In this quotation from more than two hundred and fifty years ago Adam Smith provides a powerful characterisation of the essential role that feelings about others play in human life. These feelings are an important dimension of what it means to be human. To agree on the importance of emotions in human life does not, however, settle the question of exactly *how* emotions influence moral development, decision making, and conduct. Smith is describing empathy, which seems like an essential aspect of human experience that is especially important for understanding morality. After all, most people are concerned about others and so act to help them. Ironically, defining empathy is hotly debated (e.g. Cuff et al., 2016; Maibom, 2014) and the issue is how best to conceptualise it. A distinction is often made between empathy, viewed as feeling similar to another, and sympathy, which is thought of as being concerned about the other but not necessarily sharing the other's feelings (Hobson & Hobson, 2014; Maibom, 2014; Spinrad & Eisenberg, 2014). Another recurring theme concerns whether empathy involves understanding others at an emotional level or a conceptual level. It seems that there are both affective and cognitive aspects to empathy, but if it is restricted to the cognitive dimension to understanding others then the ideal torturer would understand how his victim feels but wouldn't care. Yet caring about others is an essential part of empathy, so it generally refers to a basic human capacity to understand and care about others (Maibom, 2014; Zahavi & Rochat, 2015).

One view of how empathy is involved in moral action is that we feel what others are feeling, and because we share emotions like pain or sadness we must act in order to relieve this discomfort. Although this may appear to make sense, there are problems with this view. It emphasises painful experience, and does not explain why individuals don't just move away for the person feeling pain, or ignore her in some way in order to decrease the discomfort felt. Also, an emotion such as discomfort may interfere with helping others (Zahavi & Rochat, 2015).

A question in understanding empathy is whether a conceptual understanding of others is required in order to grasp their feelings. This is an example of the approach discussed throughout this book, which starts out from the assumption of individual minds. Empathy then becomes a problem because it concerns how to connect individuals, and how the child must figure out others' feelings from their facial and bodily expressions. This is a 'joining together' approach (Hobson, 2002). It is neither helpful for explaining how the individual develops, nor is it a theory that can account for origins. In contrast, from a relational-process approach, interaction with others is the starting point. That is, early emotional connection or responsiveness to others is part of the process through which infants develop a more conceptual understanding of others' feelings. Children do not have to infer emotions; they see others as experiencing emotions (Hobson &

Hobson, 2014; see Chapters 11 and 12). So, empathy is not a simple solution to the problem of explaining morality, but instead requires an explanation. Empathy is a part of the typical human developmental system, and the task is to explain how increasingly complex forms of empathy develop.

In an early observation, Darwin (1877) had noted that his son at 6 months and 11 days responded with a melancholic face when his nurse pretended to cry. This reaction to others' distress becomes more complex as children come to understand others as separate from them and can understand others' feelings when they are different from their own. Based on his theory, Hoffman (2000, 2008) described a series of stages in the development of empathy, beginning with newborn infants' reactive crying in response to a peer's crying (Stage 1: 'Global empathic distress'). By the age of 11 to 12 months infants still cry in response to a peer's crying but also show a different behaviour in which they do things that would soothe themselves such as going to their mother (Stage 2: 'Egocentric empathic distress'). A month or two after this infants begin attempting to soothe the distressed child, starting with patting and touching and progressing to hugging, reassuring, and getting help from someone else (Stage 3: 'Quasi-egocentric empathic distress'). Beginning at the end of the second year when children are developing a more complete conception of themselves as an independent self and an understanding of others, they now start to do things such as bring the distressed child's teddy bear instead of their own (Stage 4: 'Veridical empathy for another's distress'). In more complex forms of empathy, children at 6 to 9 years old can show empathic distress beyond the current situation, and in middle childhood can express emotion for distressed groups (Hoffman, 2000, 2008; Spinrad & Eisenberg, 2014).

In the first study of concern for others before the infant's first birthday, Roth-Hanania, Davidov, and Zahn-Waxler (2011) explored empathy longitudinally from 8 to 16 months by examining infants' responses to their mothers' expression of distress after they pretended to hurt themselves by hitting their finger and bumping their knee. Contrary to Hoffman's theory, these researchers found some evidence of facial and vocal expression of concern for others even at 8 to 10 months which increased into the second year. They also reported that self-distress in response to the distress of their mothers was rare even at 8 months.

It is also important to study how empathy develops. It has been found that parents who encourage taking the perspective of other people have children who are advanced in empathy skills (Farrant, Devine, Mayberry, & Fletcher, 2012; see also Ruffman et al., 1999). Ross Thompson (2010) further clarified that what is important about parent–child conversations in the development of morality and conscience is not just telling children about rules and what happens if they are not obeyed, but instead to help young children become aware of how their actions affect others' feelings. This raises the question of children's feelings of responsibility regarding others' distress. It was this feeling of responsibility, not just children's experience of emotional arousal, that was found to give rise to helping (Chapman, Zahn-Waxler, Cooperman, & Iannotti, 1987).

From this debate on empathy, we can infer that emotions do play a crucial role in morality, but exactly what that role is and which emotions are focused on is controversial. If we take a developmental systems approach, there must be an emotional connection influencing the changes that occur. According to Piaget, emotions are essential because mutual affection is the foundation for relationships in which morality develops. For Piaget (1932/1965) emotions play an essential role in structuring the relationships based on mutual respect and affection in which children learn about morality through having to coordinate their desires with others (e.g. Carpendale, 2009; Turiel, 2006). Equality can be rooted in ways of living together that are saturated with emotions; it is not a value that is figured out rationally or imposed by others. We return to this point below, but first consider other theorists who focus on the roles of different emotions in morality.

The Social Intuitionist Model

In contrast to Kohlberg's focus on reasoning in making moral decisions, Jonathan Haidt cites David Hume's view that reason is the slave of the passions. Here we focus on Haidt's interpretation of Hume (1751), whose views are complex and nuanced. Key to Haidt's (2001, 2013) Social Intuitionist Model is the claim that moral decisions are typically the result of intuitions based on evolved emotional reactions that are justified after the fact. Rather than being like judges using moral reasoning to make decisions about what to do, as assumed by Kohlberg, Haidt claims that people are really more like lawyers using moral reasoning to justify decisions already made based on evolved intuitive reactions. Moral intuitions are claimed to be rapid, effortless, and automatic. For example, one of his topics of research concerns reactions to incest, which he suggests have evolved because inbreeding may result in biological risks. In his research, he uses scenarios of consensual incest between a brother and a sister and asks participants to evaluate incest. Research participants typically disapprove of this, although they have difficulty justifying why. Moral reasoning, according to Haidt, is rarely the cause of moral judgments. Instead the decision is based on a gut response and the reasoning is used to justify the decision to the self and others. Reasoning is also used to influence others, to persuade and rationalise. So reasoning is secondary; it is a justification for an intuitive judgment (Haidt & Bjorklund, 2008). Haidt (2007) recognises that intuitions can also be shaped by culture, and he acknowledges that moral reasoning can in some cases correct affect-laden intuitions, but he claims that it is typically used by individuals to get what they want rather than figure out the moral thing to do.

Haidt draws support for his theory from research in social psychology. This sort of research shows that a number of contextual factors may influence prosocial behaviour. For example, experimental manipulations ranging from giving participants cookies to eat or coffee to smell tend to increase the chance that they will help others (Haidt & Kesebir, 2010). Furthermore, some contextual factors can also influence moral reasoning. For example, individuals at a particular Kohlbergian stage of moral reasoning can be influenced by whether the same moral dilemmas are set in a business or a philosophical social setting (Carpendale & Krebs, 1992), or whether people had already made a selfish choice (Carpendale & Krebs, 1995). Research participants tend to use lower stages of moral reasoning in business contexts and to justify a previously made selfish choice (Krebs, 2011).

Criticism of the Social Intuitionist Model

Haidt's model has not gone unchallenged. His focus on evolved intuitions rather than active thinking means that his is a deterministic theory: we are driven by our impetuous responses. His approach is framed as a response to Kohlberg's emphasis on reasoning, but ironically Kohlberg and Piaget were both reacting to the earlier deterministic theories of Freud, Durkheim, and Skinner (Turiel, 2015). Current deterministic perspectives on morality have been referred to as the 'people-are-stupid' school of psychology because the focus is on non-conscious, automatic, and non-rational processes rather than persons conceptualised as actively considering choices (Turiel, 2015).

Turiel (2006) has argued that Haidt uses selective examples such as incest in claiming that such intuitive responses might have evolved and could now be innate. However, although taboos against incest are common, they are not universal across cultures; some societies allow certain forms of incest in particular circumstances (Prinz, 2009). Furthermore, Turiel asks us to imagine the following situations in the southern US during the 1920s to 1950s: 'a Black man and a White woman decide to get married; a Black person wants to eat in a restaurant reserved for Whites: a Black boy who is 15 years old drinks from a water fountain designated "for Whites only"' (Turiel, 2006, p. 19). At that time, many White people might have had gut reactions of disapproval, but it cannot be argued that these are evolved responses. Furthermore, Black people and many White people would not have had these responses. In fact, they would have an immediate reaction that it is wrong to consider these acts wrong, and that reaction is not based on gut feelings, rather on reasoning about rights and fairness (Turiel, 2006).

Haidt's distinction between effortful reasoning and automatic, effortless gut reactions may also be simplistic, largely due to the fact that he does not take a developmental view. In fact from a developmental perspective children often slowly and consciously acquire an understanding in a variety of social and cognitive domains, but once such understanding has been acquired it becomes automatic (Karmiloff-Smith, 2009, 2015; Turiel, 2006, 2010, 2015). Watching a preschooler trying to count or understand family relations shows how effortful this is to begin with. Thus, reasoning can have a role in shaping intuitions. In fact, the philosopher David Hume (1751) thought that reasoning educates our intuitions and he argued that intitutions are not innate. Furthermore, in considering moral reasoning to be more like a lawyer's justification than a judge's deliberations, Haidt downplays the role that lawyers can play in supporting a fair process of decision making (Turiel, 2010).

Turiel (2006) has argued that Haidt's theory is paradoxical because it does not account for his own behaviour. This is because Haidt describes people as merely justifying their self-interested actions with whatever justification appears convincing. Yet, at the same time in making scientific inferences he is making statements he claims to be true, because he is concerned with presenting good reasons for his position. Therefore, in the process of engaging in science, he considers himself exempt from his description of other people (Carpendale et al., 2010; Turiel, 2006). According to the Social Intuitionist Model, arguments tend to be used to justify self-interests, not to convince readers of a position. Haidt's own writings thus put him in the predicament that he cannot explain his own behaviour without contradiction (Turiel, 2006).

A final question that can be raised with respect to Haidt's theory is how much of human social life does it explain? Even if he can describe some aspects of human social activity, other moral decisions have no quick intuitive answer, such as the moral dilemmas involving conflicts between the values that Kohlberg used in research. Haidt argues that reasoning is involved in only a tiny fraction of all moral decisions, but those few deliberate reflections may be crucial in structuring our lives and identities. Here it is useful to take into consideration that Haidt is a social psychologist, trying to explain everyday interaction and how people justify their actions. For this goal, his theory may be useful. However, this does not mean that he accounts for everything we think of as morality. Nor is he addressing the problem of the construction of moral norms addressed by Kohlberg and Piaget. This is simply assumed or overlooked by Haidt. Even if he is correct that people sometimes justify their actions without using reasoning about morality, it is still possible to evaluate such actions and recognise whether or not they are just. So recognising injustice seems to be presupposed by Haidt, but it is smuggled in without an explanation.

Perhaps part of the problem here is that emotions, morality, and rationality are vast and diverse domains with a great deal of overlap. Particular theorists may focus on some aspects of each of these domains, and particular emotions. For Haidt the focus is on disgust or disapproval, and these sorts of emotions result in an evaluation, which is then justified after the judgment has been made. But Haidt's intuitionist theory does not give a satisfactory account of other ways that emotions may play crucial roles in moral judgment. We now turn to explore morality at the level of neuroscience.

14.2 MORALITY AND NEUROSCIENCE

Can morality be studied within neuroscience? On one hand, it is clear that human brains and the whole nervous system are obviously required for morality so neuroscience is required for a full explanation of morality. But, on the other hand, the fact that neurons are needed for moral norms does not mean that it is possible to study a sense of moral obligation, such as to keep a promise, purely at the level of neural activity without also keeping in mind the human relations in which interaction is based (Carpendale et al., 2010).

Where is morality? Localising thinking about morality

Are there particular areas of the brain devoted to thinking about morality? One approach to this question is to study individuals who have experienced damage to particular brain regions. The example used in many textbooks is the unfortunate case of Phineas Gage who at the age of 25 was reportedly a model citizen before he had an accident in 1848 while working as a foreman on a railway track. A tamping iron was fired through his brain, apparently through the medial frontal cortex. Although he miraculously survived and was even conscious when a doctor arrived, it was reported that his personality changed radically after this damage and that he engaged in anti-social behaviour. Although the case of Phineas Gage has become somewhat of a myth, there are few facts available. Either the change in his personality was not as extreme as claimed or he may have recovered somewhat because he spent some years employed in the demanding occupation of driving a stagecoach in Chile, before experiencing epileptic seizures beginning in the last few months of his life in 1860 (Macmillan, 2008). Since that time, case studies of brain lesions have been reported suggesting that damage to the prefrontal cortex in early childhood is linked to severe problems in moral judgment and behaviour (Anderson, Bechara, Damasio, Tranel, & Damasio, 1999; Eslinger, Flaherty-Craig, & Benton, 2004; Price, Daffner, Stone, & Mesulam, 1990). This line of research suggests that an intact prefrontal cortex is necessary for moral development, but it does not show exactly what kind of role the prefrontal cortex plays in moral development, nor does it imply that the prefrontal cortex determines moral development – after all, the development of the prefrontal cortex is experience-dependent (Müller et al., 2013).

Another way to localise brain regions that are active when people think about morality is to use neuroimaging techniques such as fMRI. Various studies have attempted to find brain regions that are active when individuals are given tasks designed to elicit such thinking. However, it has been argued that these brain regions are also involved in non-moral processes, and the general conclusion seems to be that many brain regions are involved, and that 'Moral cognition is distributed. … it involves more-or-less the entire brain' (Casebeer, 2003, p. 846). In other words, 'Many brain areas make important contributions to moral judgment' (Greene & Haidt, 2002, p. 517). The conclusion of this line of research is that morality is located almost everywhere in the brain (Young & Dungan, 2012), and this should not be surprising because of the way morality is linked to much of human social life.

As with any methodology it is important to be aware of the advantages and disadvantages of neuroimaging (e.g. Slaby, 2010; and Chapter 2). The methodology is necessarily linked to how morality is defined. One definition of morality used in neuroimaging studies is that 'Morality is considered as the set of customs and values that are embraced by a cultural group to guide social conduct' (Moll et al., 2005). But, as discussed in the previous chapter, this definition reduces morality to conformity, which is different from the normative dimension of morality studied by other researchers, so it is always essential to be aware of what is being studied under the label of morality.

One line of neuroscience research uses philosophical dilemmas involving train accidents. In the *trolley car* dilemma an observer watches a runaway trolley car approach five people working on the tracks. They will all be killed unless the observer moves a switch directing the trolley car to a sidetrack, where there is just one person working. The dilemma is whether to save five people by sacrificing one person. Is the observer morally obliged to move the switch? Many people have the intuition that this is the right thing to do.

A related dilemma is known as the *footbridge* dilemma. In this case the observer is standing on a footbridge watching a runaway trolley car approach five people on the track. The observer realises that the only way to stop the trolley is to push a large person who is also standing on the footbridge onto the tracks below in order to stop the trolley car. The observer is not large enough to serve this function so self-sacrifice will not work. In this case, is the observer morally obliged to push the large person? The arithmetic is the same – five to one –but in this case many people have the intuition that the observer is not morally obliged to push the other person onto the tracks. (Given the interest in these trolley car incidents some philosophy students now wear t-shirts emblazoned with 'The Metaphysical Transit Authority', depicting an onrushing trolley car approaching a fork in the tracks leading to either five people or one person).

Joshua Greene and colleagues (2001) characterise these types of dilemmas as impersonal in the case of the trolley car and personal in the case of the footbridge (Greene, Sommerville, Nystrom, Darley, & Cohen, 2001). Another personal dilemma used in the research involves helping an injured hiker on the roadside, which would result in blood ruining one's car seats at the cost of $200 to fix them, versus an impersonal dilemma consisting of receiving a request for a donation to help a family in a far-off country, also at the cost of $200. Participants are asked to indicate whether they felt the actions were appropriate or inappropriate. For the trolley car dilemma, it was found that most participants approve of moving the switch and disapprove of pushing the person. When the brain scans of these participants were examined, Greene and colleagues (2001) found that responding to personal moral dilemmas (as compared with impersonal dilemmas) produced increased brain activity in areas that are typically associated with social-emotional processing (e.g. the medial frontal gyrus, posterior cingulate gyrus, and bilateral superior temporal sulcus). By contrast, impersonal dilemmas (as compared with personal dilemmas) were associated with increased activity in areas typically linked to cognitive (working memory) processes (e.g. the dorsolateral prefrontal cortex). Furthermore, Greene and colleagues found that reactions to personal dilemmas were slow when participants approved of the action, but very fast when they disapproved of the action. Reaction times to impersonal dilemmas did not differ depending on whether participants approved or disapproved of the action. The reaction time data suggest that for a personal dilemma participants had to overcome some sort of internal conflict (Greene & Haidt, 2002; see also Greene, Morelli, Lowenburg, Nystrom, & Cohen, 2008; Greene, Nystrom, Engell, Darley, & Cohen, 2004).

Greene has argued that the impersonal dilemma requires utilitarian judgment because participants need to reason carefully about how to maximise 'utility' (i.e. select the scenario with the lowest death toll). By contrast, the personal dilemma invokes deontological judgment because participants here evaluate the actions according to their intrinsic moral value (i.e. another person can never be a means to an end). According to Greene, the brain imaging findings and reaction time data suggest that utilitarian and deontological judgments are based on different systems: whereas the deontological judgments are based on affectively charged ('hot'), fast, automatic processes, the utilitarian judgments are based on cognitive ('cool'), slow, and consciously controlled processes.

Greene (2003) argues that his empirical findings have ethical implications. The strong emotional response to personal dilemmas evolved in the context of face-to-face interactions that our ancestors encountered in small-scale societies. By contrast, they had little opportunity to encounter the situation of providing famine relief in distant countries:

> What does this mean for ethics? Again, we are tempted to assume that there must be 'some good reason' why it is monstrous to ignore the needs of someone like the bleeding hiker, but perfectly acceptable to spend our money on unnecessary luxuries while millions starve and die of preventable diseases. Maybe there is 'some good reason' for this pair of attitudes, but the evolutionary account given above suggests otherwise: we ignore the plight of the world's poorest people not because we implicitly appreciate the nuanced structure of moral obligation, but because, the way our brains are wired up, needy people who are 'up close and personal' push our emotional buttons, whereas those who are out of sight languish out of mind. (Greene, 2003, p. 849)

Greene's research and his claims have been criticised for both empirical and conceptual reasons (Miller, 2008; for further analysis and criticism see, e.g., Berker, 2009; Birnbacher, 2016; Kahane & Shackel, 2010; Sauer, 2012; Schleim & Schirmann, 2011). For example, the function of the brain regions that Greene identifies as being specialised for emotional processing seems to be rather unspecific, barring the inference that the activation of these brain regions in personal dilemmas is evidence for the involvement of emotional processes. The dilemmas Greene uses in his research have also been criticised (Kahane & Shackel, 2010; Sauer, 2012). Many of these do not present a genuine conflict between utilitarian and deontological considerations, and some dilemmas are not moral at all. A further methodological critique is that the question participants were asked with respect to the action ('Is the action appropriate?') is at best ambiguous, and might not even be understood to refer to a moral property. It could instead be interpreted to refer to compliance with a conventional rule (Kahane & Shackel, 2010). The brief discussion of the problems of neuroscientific studies on morality should have illustrated that this research depends on sound psychological methods, and presupposes (rather than provides) an answer to the question of what morality is and how it develops. For such an answer we thus need to look elsewhere, and we suggest that the study of the development of morality within social and emotional relationships is a good direction to take to find these answers.

14.3 EVOLUTION AND MORALITY

Although there must be an evolutionary side to accounting for the origins of morality, it is sometimes assumed that morality and cooperation are difficult to explain from a Darwinian perspective because individuals should act in their self-interest in trying to pass on their genes, and therefore they should not help others unless it is to their advantage (e.g. Tomasello, 2016; Tomasello & Vaish, 2013). This long-held view is attributed to Thomas Hobbes (*The Leviathan*, 1651) who believed that humans are not naturally social. It was later assumed by Thomas Henry Huxley, known for his role as 'Darwin's bulldog' in defending the theory of evolution. Huxley focused on the struggle for survival and the view of nature as 'red in tooth and claw', a line from Tennyson's poem *In Memoriam* (Gould, 1992). There seemed to be no room in this view of nature for being nice and helpful – for altruism and morality. Like Hobbes, Huxley viewed human ethics as imposed to control a naturally selfish human nature. This idea of a thin layer of culture imposed over a selfish animal nature is what Frans de Waal (2006) labelled a 'veneer theory'. Huxley did not elaborate on where such human ethics might come from. There is a sleight of hand here in removing ethics from nature, yet somehow smuggling it back in, even though it has no place in evolutionary theory.

A different view of evolution was proposed by Kropotkin (1902/1989), according to which cooperation or 'mutual aid' is viewed as widespread in the animal kingdom. This was similar to the approach taken by Darwin in *The Descent of Man* (1871) based on observations of cooperation in many species. Instead of presupposing that human nature is selfish, Darwin – in some of his work – and Kropotkin documented detailed observations of the extensive cooperation in many species. In contrast to Huxley's interpretation of Darwin which was developed in an overcrowded, industrialised England, Kropotkin formed his ideas as a young naturalist on long trips in the vast wilderness of northern Russia, where the struggle for survival in a harsh environment seemed to require cooperation among species (Glassman, 2000). The dog-eat-dog view of human nature was popular in the 1970s with books such as Richard Dawkins' (1976) *The Selfish Gene*. But, more recently, an alternative view of human nature as cooperative and helpful is on the rise due to researchers such as Frans de Waal (2006; see also Meloni, 2013).

How can altruism have evolved given its cost to the self? One possible solution is kin selection. It would make sense to help others who share one's genes, so a tendency to altruism could be selected for, particularly given the tendency for humans to live with or near to their kin. But how do individuals know who they share genes with? Loving thy neighbour could result in making mistakes by helping someone who is familiar but unrelated (Tomasello et al., 2012). Another suggestion is that individuals may have selected mates (sexual selection) based partly on their altruistic tendencies and this could result in more offspring for individuals with such traits, leading to the evolution of altruistic tendencies (Krebs, 2011). A third possibility is group selection, according to which those groups with more altruistic individuals would likely be more successful than others resulting in more offspring and the evolution of such traits (Krebs, 2011).

In 1975 E. O. Wilson predicted a 'new synthesis' for a full understanding of human morality involving the integration of an understanding of evolution and neural processes, as well as social meanings and institutions. Haidt and Kesebir (2010) revived this perspective. Although this makes sense, there is plenty of debate concerning exactly *how* to integrate these levels. It is not clear that Wilson and Haidt have a new way of integrating these dimensions. Instead, a relational developmental systems perspective puts back together levels of understanding that should not be separated because they do not exist independently.

Various claims have been made about the biological basis and the evolution of human morality. A number of approaches propose innate moral knowledge. Since morality is often thought of as a set of rules, some philosophers and psychologists have linked grammatical rules to moral rules that work like Chomsky's notion of Universal Grammar. The claim is that morality is based on a Universal Moral Grammar (UMG), an innate structure that underlies the various human moral systems (Dwyer, 2006; Hauser, 2006; Mikhail, 2007). As evidence for UMG, Mikhail (2007) lists the fact that 3- to 4-year-olds can distinguish moral rules from social conventions, and that every language has words for moral obligations and duties. However, by 3 years of age children have learned about many aspects of their culture that are not innate. Furthermore, it is likely that all languages have words for social acts such as greetings, but this does not mean that humans have an innate grammar for greeting just that this is a typical aspect of human life. In addition, this account faces the problem of how theoretical analysis can be translated from a genetic level to explaining human morality (see Chapter 2).

DeScioli and Kurzban (2012) proposed an alternative solution to what they describe as the 'mysteries of morality'. They claim that moral cognition is a computational system that evolved to help individuals choose which side it would be best to be on in a moral conflict. This is not which side is *right* or *just* in a moral sense, but simply which is more *advantageous* for the individual. Although this may be an aspect of social life for some people, it is precisely what morality is *not*.

In proposing an explanation for prosociality, Chudek and Henrich (2011, p. 218) argue that what has evolved is a 'norm-psychology', which is 'a suite of psychological adaptations' for learning, remembering, following, and enforcing 'the shared behavioral standards of one's community'. These skills for conformity form an important aspect of human social life, but like the computational perspective just described, the account overlooks previous discussions about what morality is (reviewed in Chapter 13). An aspect of morality concerns questioning whether current standards are right or wrong, why they emerged, and how those standards change or develop. Morality may sometimes lead to *disobedience* rather than obedience and conformity. Similarly, Kohlberg was inspired to study morality at least partially because of the events surrounding the Holocaust in which conformity resulted from a *lack* of morality. That is, in addition to obedience, it is crucially important to study *disobedience* because there may be times when the moral choice is to act against current practices when those practices need to be changed. So 'norm-psychology' is a description of an aspect of human life, but not an explanation for it. Human life is structured around the norms that children have to learn. As humans have evolved, it could be said that in a sense this human way of life is part of that process. However, this claim requires an explanation regarding how it develops.

To present the perspective of Evolutionary Psychology (see Chapter 2), let us return to Pinker's (1997) and Tooby and Cosmides' (2013) claims that human minds are made up of many modules that have evolved to solve particular problems and that forms of thinking are due to genetically specified computational systems. Does this theory account for morality? Steven Pinker (2008) suggests that 'we are born with a universal moral grammar that forces us to analyze human action in terms of its moral structure' in the same way that we have a universal grammar for language (see Chapters 7, 8, and 9). Yet, elsewhere Pinker (1997) is not so sure. He endorses a strong biological position when it comes to language and the mind, but when it comes to human qualities like altruism his position is different. Richard Hamilton (2008) points out that elsewhere Pinker states that 'happiness and virtue have nothing to do with what natural selection designed us to do in the ancestral environment. They are for us to determine' (Pinker, 1997, p. 52). Hamilton is opposed to the idea of there being a modular explanation for moral reasoning as proposed by Evolutionary Psychology. Other people take a mixed approach. From an evolutionary perspective it has been argued that mental mechanisms for dealing with morality have evolved (Krebs, 2011). But it is still necessary to explain how children develop ways of interacting and thinking that enable living together smoothly – that is, morality. For this task a developmental approach is needed. Modularity theorists acknowledge that these modules must develop, but they do not discuss how. Researchers have emphasised that it is an exceedingly complex route to get from genes to modules to thinking (Karmiloff-Smith, 2009).

14.4 THE DEVELOPMENT OF PROSOCIAL BEHAVIOUR: HELPING AND COOPERATING

One approach to moral development is to study the development of children's prosocial behaviour. This generally refers to actions one person engages in for the benefit of another, often in response to a need that is perceived in that person. Different types of prosocial behaviour can be distinguished depending on the specific need to which that behaviour is a response. It has been found that various prosocial behaviours in toddlers such as comforting, sharing, and helping are not correlated, suggesting different patterns in development (Paulus, 2014). In this section we focus on helping – both infants' reactions to others' helping and their own engagement in helping – before examining cooperation.

Are babies born moral?

There have been recent claims that babies are born already knowing something about morality (Bloom, 2014; Hamlin, 2013). Paul Bloom (2010, p. 46), writing in the *New York Times*, asserted that 'some sense of good and evil seems to be bred in the bone'. This claim is based on research in which infants watched characters helping or hindering others. For example, in one of these simple morality plays, 6- and 10-month-old infants watch a red ball apparently attempting to go up a hill. Then a yellow square, the 'good guy', helps the hapless ball up the hill. In another scenario a green triangle, the 'bad guy', instead pushes the red ball down the hill, hindering its progress toward its goal. After watching these hill-climbing situations, 6- to 10-month-olds were presented with both the helper and the hinderer and they tended to reach toward the helper character rather than the hinderer. Infants also looked longer when the protagonist approached the hinderer compared to the helper, and this longer looking time was interpreted as indicating surprise (Hamlin, Wynn, & Bloom, 2007). Similar results were found when infants watched characters helping or hindering another character attempting to open a box (for a review see Hamlin, 2013).

Hamlin et al. (2007, p. 559) interpreted these results as follows: 'the capacity to evaluate individuals on the basis of their social interactions is universal and unlearned', and 'at least some aspects of human morality are innate' (Hamlin, 2013, p. 191). These claims have attracted a great deal of attention in the popular press, but the process of science should be based on careful evaluation, in both methodological and conceptual terms. At the methodological level, Scarf, Imuta, Colombo, and Hayne (2012a) argued that the effects might be an artifact (i.e. caused by a factor not considered by the researchers). They claimed that infants might make simple perceptual associations between the protagonist's happy bouncing at the top of the hill in the helping condition compared to an aversive collision in the hindering condition. When controlling for these perceptual level factors they did not replicate Hamlin's effect. In response Hamlin (2015) reproduced the original effect without the bouncing, and also reported that what is important in finding the effect is that the eyes on the 'protagonist object' should be pointed toward the top of the hill, presumably indicating their goal. Two other studies have also failed to replicate infants' preference for helping over hindering (Cowell & Decety, 2015; Salvadori, Biazsekova, Volein, Karap, Tatone, Mascaro, & Csibra, 2015). It has also been suggested that Hamlin's results could be explained by infants' tendency to associate good outcomes with characters, rather than showing innate knowledge and the ability to determine preference for characters based on moral grounds (Scarf, Imuta, Colombo, & Hayne, 2012b). The effect was replicated in a study with 12-, 24-, and 36-month-old infants (Scola et al., 2016), but at this age it does not support claims that infants are born knowing about helping and hindering.

Even when research is conducted with 6- to 10-month-old infants, this does not necessarily test a nativist claim. Hamlin, Wynn, and Bloom (2010) extended their procedure to 3-month-old infants. Infants do not reliably reach at this age so the researchers used looking time methodology instead. At 3 months the infants looked longer at a neutral character compared to a hinderer, but they did not differ in looking time between a neutral character versus the helper. The longer looking time toward the neutral character was interpreted as showing aversion to the hinderer, so in this study looking time was viewed as indicating preference. However, as mentioned above, in other studies longer looking time is often assumed to indicate surprise (e.g. Hamlin et al., 2007). This research with 3-month-old infants has yet to receive critical examination at the methodological level. The looking time methodology is controversial because although it indicates that infants have detected a difference between conditions how they understand that difference is based on interpretation (see e.g. Aslin, 2007; Haith, 1998).

In arguing for innate moral knowledge, Bloom (2010, p. 63) noted that infants 'smile and clap during good events and frown, shake their heads and look sad during the naughty events'. Clapping, however, is not innate; it is not 'built-in', babies are not born knowing how to clap. This is a cultural convention that is gradually learned. Also, shaking one's head to indicate *no* is actually a relatively late-developing gesture (Kettner & Carpendale, 2013; see Chapter 5). In this case the head shaking seems to indicate disapproval, a somewhat different use of the gesture than indicating *no*.

Claims of innate knowledge can also be evaluated in terms of the biological implications presupposed. As we have discussed throughout this book (see Chapter 2), innateness accounts do not encourage research and are really just an IOU ('I owe you') for a more complete account of how skills develop. From a developmental systems perspective there are many levels of interacting factors. Consider the metaphor of ecological transitions. Biological adaptations set up the infant for the kinds of social interaction in which human development occurs, and neurological structures are shaped by social interaction. Newborn infants have capacities such as a sensitivity to eyes, and a tendency to look at eyes and faces, as well as an interest in looking at biological motion. These biological characteristics do not comprise innate knowledge, and especially not moral knowledge, but they may set infants up for engagement in interaction in which they learn about others and eventually develop moral principles.

Claims of innate moral knowledge should also be examined at the conceptual level concerning the implications drawn from the research results (Tafreshi, Thompson, & Racine, 2014). The nativist claim is that infants are born with the understanding of the actions of helping and hindering and that they prefer helping. This requires understanding goals. Hamlin (2015) now suggests that the effect is driven by the protagonist's gaze toward the goal, and therefore seems to depend on some understanding not only of gaze, but also the goals directing this looking. But in Chapter 5 we discussed evidence that suggested infants' understanding of gaze does not seem to be innate. Research also shows that some understanding of goal-directed reaching develops by about 6 months (Woodward, 2013), especially if the action is in an infant's own motor repertoire (Ambrosini, Reddy, de Looper, Costantini, Lopez, & Sinigaglia, 2013). Furthermore, the development of this skill is advanced if the infant's mother is emotionally available (Licata et al., 2014). Even at 2 months infants are already learning about others' actions and how to coordinate with them. For example, when parents are about to pick up their infant, typically developing infants will stiffen their body in anticipation (Reddy et al., 2013). These researchers do not claim that infants are born with these skills. Instead they document their gradual development.

The questions should be how does this ability develop and what does it lead to? In one of the failed attempts to replicate infants' preference for helping over hindering no effect was found at the behavioural level, but neurophysiological differences were found between the helping versus hindering conditions. The researchers interpreted this as indicating neural activity linked to withdrawal and avoidance when watching hinderers, whereas there appeared to be a reduction in this withdrawal when observing helping (Cowell & Decety, 2015). Further careful analysis of this line of research is needed at both the methodological and conceptual levels in order fully to evaluate its implications. We have contrasted the different ways to interpret this evidence – we can either interpret it as innate knowledge or as learning about patterns of interaction. We now turn from infants' reactions to others' helping to their own helping behaviour.

Toddlers' helping

The research discussed above concerns infants watching episodes involving helping and hindering, but there is also accumulating evidence that young children at the age of 14 to 18 months old already like to participate in helping their parents with everyday activities (Warneken, 2015, 2016). They like to help with folding laundry, sweeping, unloading dishwashers, and so on (Hammond, 2014). This characteristic of young children has been noted for some time in baby diaries (see Hay, 2009), but with the exception of one seminal study (Rheingold, 1982), it has not been the topic of systematic research. This situation has recently changed with a flurry of studies on prosocial behaviour in general and helping in particular.

The early research on helping by Rheingold (1982) has been extended by Warneken and Tomasello and others in a number of recent studies. The experimental tasks used are based on everyday situations such as an experimenter dropping objects like clothes pegs. Toddlers will often help by picking up the object and giving it back to the experimenter. They will open a cupboard door when the experimenter cannot do it because he has his arms full with a stack of books. At the age of 2 children will help in situations where the adult is not even aware that she has dropped something (Warneken, 2013). Toddlers will actually stop their own playing or climb over obstacles in order to help. This is considered 'costly' helping, and therefore toddlers' helping has been described as 'some of the earliest manifestations of altruism in human ontogeny: children acting on behalf of others without a benefit for themselves' (Warneken & Tomasello, 2009, p. 459).

Warneken and Tomasello (2014) found that giving 20-month-old toddlers a reward undermines their helping but praise or no reward did not. Thus, Warneken and Tomasello (2013, p. 366) claim that helping is not influenced by parental encouragement, and that this suggests helping is a natural 'biological predisposition' and children are 'equipped with prosocial tendencies with deep evolutionary roots'. Warneken and Tomasello seem to have a particular conception of 'socialisation' in terms of parents rewarding toddlers' helpful behaviour.

In contrast, there is evidence that toddlers ranging in age from 11 to 25 months old are encouraged in their helping and supported in the home (Brownell, 2016; Dahl, 2015). Furthermore, parents' encouragement of helping at home is positively linked to advanced social understanding, and helping at home is associated with instrumental helping in the lab (Gross et al., 2015). Gross and colleagues found that toddlers from 18 to 30 months old who were more advanced in social understanding also tended to help at home and in lab tasks where they needed to help an experimenter who was cold or upset, but not on instrumental tasks such as picking up dropped objects. They reported that children's temperament was not related to helping.

Intentionally helping someone requires understanding the person's goal and the situation. But goals can vary greatly in complexity. For example, a 12-month-old infant watching his mother rub his father's back could easily participate in this simple activity (Carpendale, Kettner, & Audet, 2015). On the other hand, toddlers may understand the goal of picking up objects and putting them in a box, but not the larger goal of tidying the house. This is evident in that they might enjoy the activity of putting toys in a box, but then happily dump them out so that they can do it again (Carpendale et al., 2015). Parents report that their children are so 'helpful' that they often try to distract them with other tasks or resort to doing the chores while their children are asleep because it is easier (Hammond & Carpendale, 2015). Children's enjoyment of helping is rarely mentioned in this research literature. It could be that rather than altruism it may well be that toddlers' helping is due to their interest in participating in the activity of others (Carpendale et al., 2015; Hammond, 2014; Rheingold, 1982). If helping is due to toddlers' interest in participating in the activity of adults and this tends to emerge within human ways of living together, then giving children opportunities to participate and encouraging and supporting them may facilitate their helping (Carpendale et al., 2015).

The research on helping documents the early steps in a complex developmental sequence. For many people helping others continues to be an important activity which provides a purpose to their lives. There are diverse ways to help others and contribute to moving the world in a better direction. How to best help an individual, however, is not always straightforward, because doing something for someone may not always be the best way to help in the longer term. Helping is one form of cooperative behaviour, which we turn to next.

Cooperation

One approach to explaining cooperation has been to argue that particular cognitive abilities are required in order for children to engage in this activity, especially the ability to understand and coordinate with others' intentions. But this may imply that infants and other species lacking such cognitive abilities could not cooperate. We return to this issue below. In this section we outline the development of cooperation in the first few years of life, as well as link cooperation to cognitive skills that predict and influence its presentation. The infant's ability to evaluate his or her social environment will be discussed, as well as the environmental influences that result in increased cooperation.

The development of cooperation has been found to be linked to cognitive factors, such as self–other differentiation (Brownell & Carriger, 1990) and joint attention (Brownell, Ramani, & Zerwas, 2006; Kärtner, Schuhmacher, & Collard, 2014; Wu, Pan, Su, & Gros-Louis, 2013). It has been hypothesised that the ability to differentiate self and other is necessary for an infant to cooperate successfully and this ability increases with age (Brownell & Carriger, 1990). Brownell and Carriger (1990) examined the infant's level of self-other differentiation as it related to cooperation in a study with play-scenarios. Self-other differentiation systematically increased between 12 and 30 months old, and those infants who displayed high levels of self–other differentiation were more successful in a follow-up task requiring cooperation with a peer. The infants who understood the self as separate from others could successfully coordinate their behaviour in order to achieve a shared goal. This study highlights that self–other differentiation is related to cooperation; however, it does not demonstrate whether self–other differentiation is a prerequisite for cooperative behaviours.

Although self–other differentiation relates to cooperation, social understanding and joint attention are also predictive of cooperative abilities in infants (e.g. Kärtner et al., 2014; Wu et al., 2013). To understand the development of social understanding as it relates to cooperation, Brownell and colleagues (2006) investigated the differences in cooperative ability in peer-to-peer tasks. They hypothesised that advanced social understanding and joint attention skills would be positively correlated with cooperative abilities. Toddlers were assessed on their ability to cooperate with a peer. To assess social understanding, the researchers first hypothesised that toddlers who used pronouns to describe themselves and others would have higher levels of social understanding. Second, in consequence, they predicted that these toddlers would be better able to cooperate with a peer. The results showed that 19-month-olds attempted to cooperate on the task irregularly and mostly by chance. In contrast, 23- and 27-month-old children could cooperate with a peer, and this ability was correlated with their joint attention skills and pronoun use. This study suggests that in order to become a competent social partner it may be important to be able to understand another's goals and intentions and successfully share attention with that person (Tomasello et al., 2005).

Although children get better with age at coordinating their actions in cooperative tasks (Brownell & Carriger, 1990), early forms of interaction could be described as forms of cooperation. Even the simple act of pointing to inform others at 12 months seems to constitute communicative behaviour used to cooperate with others (Liszkowski, 2005). Given that sharing attention with someone requires the infant to share information, joint attention skills can be hypothesised to be a precursor of cooperative behaviour in infants. To investigate the role of joint attention in infant cooperation further, Wu et al. (2013) examined infants' ability to respond to, and initiate, joint attention bids. Children who were better at responding in this context (i.e. to find a visual object in response to pointing) were more cooperative in tasks that required similar roles at the same time – each pressing a button at a different end of a long box to turn on a music and light display. In contrast, children who were better at initiating joint attention (i.e. pointing to an object) were more cooperative in tasks that required different and independent roles enacted one after the other. This evidence provides support for the hypothesis that different aspects of joint attention are differentially related to cooperation.

Although self–other differentiation and joint-attention skills seem to be related to infant cooperation, the coordination of activity is also indicative of cooperative skills (Warneken & Tomasello, 2007). Warneken and Tomasello (2007) observed that as infants get older, they were more likely to coordinate their positions to cooperate successfully in a shared task. Fourteen-month-old infants displayed low levels of coordination, but there was increased coordination in 18-month-olds. In this study, the researchers also examined the communicative acts infants used during cooperative tasks. Fourteen-month-old infants tended to communicate their desire to continue the cooperative task through eye contact, 18-month-olds commonly used pointing gestures, and 24-month-olds verbalised their intent. This observation highlights how communicative skills and coordinated actions increase with age.

A problem with the view that cooperation requires understanding others' mental states is that some elementary forms can be observed in early infancy and are common among many other species such as social insects like ants and bees, and even between species. For example, coral trout – a species of grouper – learn how to collaborate with moray eels to hunt. By shaking its head a trout recruits a moray eel for hunting, and then it shakes its head again over narrow chambers in the coral in which small prey may be hiding. They also learn which eels are good collaborators, and they do so at a rate very similar to that of chimpanzees (Vail Manica, & Bshary, 2014). Such forms of coordination of activity are ubiquitous in nature. In their first year, human infants are already showing some ability to coordinate their actions with their parents' action. During infancy these forms of cooperation become increasingly complex (Carpendale & Lewis, 2015a; Fantasia, De Jaegher, & Fasulo, 2014).

SUMMARY AND OVERALL CONCLUSIONS

In the two parts of this section we draw the discussion of moral development, and indeed the whole book, to a close. The first part summarises the main points and themes of the chapter. The second draws the main points from Chapters 13 and 14 together on the basis of recent research, longstanding theoretical debates, and the resonance between the issues discussed in these chapters and those raised in the rest of the book. In order to attempt to show these connections, we finish with a list of learning achievements that we hope we have made clear along the way.

Summary of the chapter

This chapter has reviewed many current approaches to morality, starting with accounts based on emotions and biology. In evaluating these different views it is important to keep in mind the aspect of morality being studied. Topics like conformity to rules or justifying self-interested action are aspects of human social interaction related to morality, but other dimensions such as obligation and commitment are equally as relevant, and may be overlooked by approaches focusing on self-interested action. Perhaps no one has defined morality in a way that is completely satisfactory, but this may be because it is such an integral part of human life, and it is difficult to separate it from other aspects of our life, or to capture all of its facets.

We started this discussion with major dilemmas involving life and death, but morality also permeates our lives at much more mundane levels including the way we treat each other in everyday encounters. For example, if a friend or acquaintance greets us and we fail to respond, they may interpret this as a snub, unless it is obvious that we didn't hear them. Morality is rooted in communicative practices. The way we live also has broader implications for many others, and so morality is also present in our daily decisions, as well as at the larger scale of politics.

Although many theories assume the importance of emotions and biology in understanding morality, these approaches can still differ radically. The view that an emotional connection to others is important in morality has a long history, although there is disagreement regarding exactly how to conceptualise this connection. There is controversy regarding whether empathy (sharing another's emotion) explains morality as the reason we are concerned about others, or if this emotional connection is a problem that requires a developmental explanation. In understanding empathy, various forms of increasingly complex emotional connection to others have been described. It has been found that parents have a role in helping their children become more aware of others' feelings. A general lesson to be learned is that caring about others cannot be added later to human interaction through rationally figuring this out. Instead, mutual affection structuring human relationships is likely to be the foundation on which morality develops.

An approach that focuses on the role of emotions is Jonathon Haidt's influential Social Intuitionist Model. In contrast to Kohlberg's view that moral reasoning is a process through which moral decisions are reached (see Chapter 13), he claims that the primary process begins with an evolved intuitive response of approval or disapproval that is then justified with moral reasoning. Haidt's model has been extensively criticised for restricting the focus of his research to examples that fit with his theory, and neglecting the issue of whether intuitions have evolved or developed (Turiel, 2015). Although Haidt may describe aspects of human social life, the question remains of whether he has provided a complete account of morality.

The neuroscience approach has attempted to identify brain regions that might be specialised for processing moral issues. Researchers have used neuroimaging to locate areas that are active when an individual is solving a particular task. The general conclusion from this area of research, however, is that many brain regions are involved in moral thinking. This should not be too surprising given its complexity and links to many aspects of social life. Neuroimaging methods have also been used to support the view that, compared to impersonal moral situations, conflicts that are more personal in nature activate brain regions devoted to emotions (Greene et al., 2001). This position, however, has been criticised because the brain is not so neatly divided into regions dealing with particular functions such as emotions; rather each region serves multiple purposes (Miller, 2008).

Any account of human morality must be grounded in evolution, but evolutionary perspectives differ greatly. One view is that only selfishness could evolve (e.g. Dawkins, 1976), but a contrasting position is that a species can evolve to be naturally good (de Waal, 2006). Claims about a human nature, however, whether good or bad, should be based on knowledge of modern developmental biology. As reviewed in Chapter 2 there has been a shift in thinking in the last forty years, from the view that the development of brains is specified by genes to the understanding that genes have a less deterministic influence on development. This new view holds that neurological development is the outcome of a system of interacting factors through which experience shapes neurological development (Stiles, 2009; Stiles et al., 2015).

We have reviewed a number of claims about which skills humans have evolved that might explain our capacity for morality. We discussed particular difficulties with each theory as well as the general problem of explaining the biological processes in connecting genes to thinking. Claims of innate moral knowledge represent one view of the role of biology in moral development. Some researchers presuppose human infants are born with innate moral knowledge about, for example, the evaluation of the actions of helping versus hindering (e.g. Bloom, 2010; Hamlin, 2013). The empirical findings regarding this claim are still mixed, so the conceptual issues are still under debate.

In the longest section of the chapter we reviewed the recent and exciting literature on the development of toddlers' helping. Research has revealed prosocial behaviour very early in development underlining the importance of cooperation with others. The early onset of prosocial behaviour can be accounted for in two ways. One claim is that such behaviour is a biological predisposition (e.g. Warneken, 2016). But every aspect of being human has biological foundations, so this is not a complete explanation. We still need a developmental account. Infants' understanding of helping and hindering, as well as their own helping and cooperation in general, are important aspects of human moral development that require a developmental explanation. A second view is that the infant's biological characteristics set up the process of interaction in which moral development occurs. It is this latter view that we develop in the next section.

Moral development: a relational developmental systems account

Humans live in systems of cooperation and webs of obligations. We help each other when we can, such as assisting with a friend's house move, or spending time with a friend who is unhappy. Although this can sometimes feel like a burden, it is more commonly part of the joy of a mutual friendship. Infants grow up in this social world full of expectations and obligations. Yet, the complexity of thinking required to solve moral dilemmas has to be achieved gradually. A key feature of morality that is generally agreed on is some sense of obligation or sense of *ought*. In Darwin's words (1871, p. 70, original emphasis), this is 'summed up in that short but imperious word *ought*, so full of high significance'.

We have suggested that although cultural views and biology will play some role in explaining morality, by themselves they are incomplete. We have argued throughout this book that it is important to spell out the role of biology in human functioning. In all areas it is also necessary to be aware of the various parts of the developmental system in which children grow up. Social relations are a stable and expectable part of children's developmental niche, the crucible of learning. Jean Piaget (1932/1965) focused on early cooperative relationships with peers or parents. He did so because these presuppose mutual affection, which structures relationships among those who treat each other as equals. Within such relationships individuals must find a way of coordinating their actions. Children gradually become aware of the rules that constitute such cooperative interaction and then can verbalise and reflect on them.

From this perspective, what has to be explained is how the process of social interaction begins and becomes more complex. To understand this we need to examine how forms of cooperative relationships emerge. We feel that the recent research on helping behaviour shows the start of a process by which toddlers construct an understanding of norms and cooperation within interaction. This process occurs earlier than Piaget intimated and within a wider network of interactions. In Warneken's (2006) studies the person helped is often a stranger adult. Across the second year of life children have had plenty of experience of cooperative activity just as they have also experienced teasing others within cooperative interaction (Reddy & Mireault, 2015), which leads to the establishment of norms and affects the infant's thinking about relationships.

It might be asked that if morality develops from social activity, and such social interaction and resulting norms differ across cultures, then is morality also different in different societies? Conventions do differ across cultures, but these are followed in order to show our caring and respect for others. We have argued that similar values can emerge, even though there are differences among cultures, because relationships of mutual caring are based on natural human forms of interaction that arise due to our biological characteristics. This is not a claim that knowledge of morality is innate. We have reviewed arguments against that position. Instead, examples of biological characteristics have been used throughout the book to demonstrate this. For example, infants' visual capabilities draw them into an interest in others' eyes and faces, and they develop enjoyment in interacting with others and sharing attention. Emotional exchange plays a key role in drawing the infant into this interaction. Neural pathways develop within such social interaction, and as infants develop the ability to anticipate others' actions, these social skills can enable them to elicit more complex social activity from the other interactant, and as a consequence, social exchange will occur in an increasingly bidirectional manner. Of course, these are just a few simple examples of factors in a complex developmental system, and there are alternative ways to the same developmental endpoints as we see in the development of blind or deaf infants. What may be universal across human ways of life is not a set of rules, but instead a set of social processes which make interaction possible and provide us with a medium for reaching moral decisions.

As Piaget (1932/1965) suggested, peer interactions play a part in this process, particularly when the child enters preschool. Consider the following quotation from a 3½-year-old girl: 'It's not so much fun playing by your own.' This comment expresses the common experience that it is more fun to play with other kids. If a child wants to play with other children then she has to learn to treat them properly, with respect as persons. Children discover that if they take all the toys and always want to have it their own way, they will find out they do not have friends to play with. That is, they learn the social consequences of their actions, and they may do so by making mistakes and learning from negative outcomes (Dahl, Campos, & Witherington, 2011). Thus, there is a practical, lived morality that structures their interaction. Of course, this won't always be the case, and adults often need to play some role in facilitating this through helping children learn, but it still has to arise in the context of children's lives.

We have discussed this early development in terms of communication and social understanding but there is also a moral dimension to treating others as persons – as someone not something (Spaemann, 1996/2006). This is the development of enjoying interacting with and caring about others. This can be seen in turn taking in conversation; that is, responding to others and giving them an opportunity to respond. Thus human ways of being, intelligence, and morality have their roots in emotional interpersonal engagement. Given all of this, we can return to the insights discussed in the previous chapter regarding morality emerging with interpersonal agreement, and the role of reasoning in more complex forms built onto prior, lived morality (Carpendale, 2017). This Piagetian idea – that interpersonal agreement may be a source of moral norms – has recently become a topic of research (Göckeritz et al., 2014; Schmidt et al., 2016; see Carpendale et al., 2013). This latter form of thinking must be explained from a developmental perspective because it cannot be reduced to separate biological or social influences. Instead, we have argued that it emerges within certain forms of cooperative human interaction that enable reaching an interpersonal understanding and consensus. We then had to explain how those forms of interaction develop. All of the topics covered in this book come together to understand the nature and development of morality. And these human developments make culture, history, and politics possible, and culture, in turn, influences child development.

Piaget (1932/1965) began with a practical, lived morality that children later become aware of and can reflect on. He concentrated on negotiations between peers and the problem of how children change rules. Although Piaget started his exploration of moral development in his description of heteronomous morality (rules coming from the outside), what is more important from his perspective is the idea that norms may emerge through interpersonal agreement. This resonates with George Herbert Mead's (1934, p. 379) argument that there is a universality of the process of making moral judgments through considering all perspectives in a conflict, 'from the fact that we take the attitude of the entire community, of all rational beings … that is, everyone who can rationally appreciate the situation agrees'. This is what Mead labelled 'the method of morality' – a process through which moral decisions can be reached. According to Mead, norms do not pre-exist in the individual or the culture but emerge in relations.

Kohlberg approached the problem from another direction in terms of verbal reasoning (Wright, 1982) and levels of complexity that are not negotiated in everyday interactions. In Chapter 13 we discussed his theory and its focus on stages defined by principles for resolving moral dilemmas. At its highest level, Kohlberg's Stage 6 consists of a procedure for making moral decisions, based on understanding and coordinating all of the perspectives involved in a moral conflict, a process he called 'moral musical chairs'. This level of abstraction is so complex that few of us ever achieve it. However, the principle shares common ground with Mead's moral method and the thinking of the philosopher Jürgen Habermas (1983/1990). Habermas located the foundation of ethics in discourse, and he developed the notion of an ideal form of discourse in which there is no coercion, so that everyone can state their position without fear of oppression and will listen to others. For Habermas morality is already presupposed in the principles that guide everyday communication in conversation, in listening to and responding to others. The goal is to reach an understanding based on equality and respect. In keeping with Mead and Piaget this method requires equality.

Beyond Piaget's practical level of lived morality, the processes discussed by Mead, Kohlberg, and Habermas involve giving reasons. So, it is also necessary to explain the emergence of reasons in the causal world of natural science. Humans live in a world in which explanations and reasons are expected (Forst, 2005). Reasons emerge socially because we give reasons to others and expect reasons; that is, reasons are initially for others. Giving and expecting reasons for unexpected actions is an aspect of human ways of life. It is social in its origin before becoming an individual skill (Piaget, 1928). In Mead's words, 'Man is a rational being because he is a social being' (Mead, 1934, p. 379).

This brief sketch is further filled in throughout the chapters in this book. But even so we have barely scratched the surface of the incredibly complex human developmental system within which persons develop. Still, the examples we have given illustrate the relational developmental system approach. The point we have repeatedly made is that instead of thinking of biology and socialisation as separable factors, the more we learn the more we see that multiple biological levels mutually create and are created by social activity in a bidirectional manner throughout development. Social activity, in turn, takes place within a larger sociocultural context, and even though this larger social-cultural context was not the focus of our discussion, our approach could easily be extended in that direction.

We close this chapter and the book by again emphasising the centrality of morality in human life. This extends from the interpersonal level of conversation and how we treat others to politics and decisions about how we live our lives, because the way we live affects others in our immediate circle as well as those who are more distant in time and place.

HAVE YOU ACHIEVED THE LEARNING OBJECTIVES OF THE BOOK?

Having read this book you should now be aware of:

- How we understand the development of children's thinking is greatly influenced by the worldviews (introduced in Chapter 1), ranging from genetic to environmental determinism to relational approaches.

- The developmental systems view of biology (reviewed in Chapter 2), which suggests that genetic influences are more complex and malleable than is suggested by contemporary 'modular' accounts of development.

- The constructivist view of knowledge outlined (in Chapter 3) which takes a child-centred view of development.

- The sociocultural idea that people develop within relationships of cooperation (in Chapter 4) and that the child's social relationships form the basis of thinking.

- The emergence of communication in the increasing inter-coordination of adults and infants, and how these form the foundation for language (Chapters 5 and 6).

(Continued)

- Research on animal communication systems as a way to understand the nature and development of human language (Chapter 7).

- How children's grasp of the structure of language and individual words is a consequence of the processes by which they construct meaning in everyday interactions (Chapters 8 and 9).

- The nature of social understanding and children's understanding of thinking as well as the social process involved in how this knowledge develops (Chapters 11 and 12).

- How moral reasoning is embedded in the child's coordinated social interactions (Chapters 13 and 14): these interactions, thinking, and moral reasoning are intricately related.

FURTHER READING

Carpendale, J. I. M., Hammond, S. I., & Atwood, S. (2013). A relational developmental systems approach to moral development. In R. M. Lerner & J. B. Benson (eds), *Embodiment and Epigenesis: Theoretical and Methodological Issues in Understanding the Role of Biology within the Relational Developmental System* (pp. 105–133). Advances in Child Development and Behavior, vol. 45.

REFERENCES

Adrián, J. E., Clemente, R. A., & Villanueva, L. (2007). Mothers' use of cognitive state verbs in picture-book reading and the development of children's understanding of mind: A longitudinal study. *Child Development*, *78*, 1052–1067.

Aitchison, J. (1989). *The Articulate Mammal: An Introduction to Psycholinguistics* (3rd edn). London: Routledge. (2008 is the 5th edition)

Akhtar, N., & Gernsbacher, M. A. (2008). On privileging the role of gaze in infant social cognition. *Child Development Perspectives*, *2*, 59–65.

Akhtar, N., Jipson, J., & Callanan, M. A. (2001). Learning words through overhearing. *Child Development*, *72*, 416–430.

Allen, J. W. P. (2015). How to help: Can more active behavioural measures help transcend the infant false-belief debate? *New Ideas in Psychology*, *39*, 63–72.

Allen, J., & Bickhard, M. (2013). Transcending the nativist-empiricist debate: Methodological and conceptual issues regarding infant development. *Cognitive Development*, *28*, 96–133.

Alloway, T. P., Gathercole, S. E., & Pickering, S. J. (2006). Verbal and visuospatial short-term and working memory in children: Are they separable? *Child Development*, *77*, 1698–1716.

Alvarez, J. A., & Emory, E. (2006). Executive function and the frontal lobes: A meta-analytic review. *Neuropsychology Review*, *16*, 17–42.

Ambridge, B., & Lieven, E. V. M. (2011). *Child Language Acquisition: Contrasting Theoretical Approaches*. Cambridge: Cambridge University Press.

Ambrosini, E., Reddy, V., de Looper, A., Costantini, M., Lopez, B., & Sinigaglia, C. (2013). Looking ahead: Anticipatory gaze and motor ability in infancy. *PLOS One*, *8*(7), e67916.

Anderson, M. L. (2003). Embodied cognition: A field guide. *Artificial Intelligence*, *149*, 91–130.

Anderson, P. J., & Reidy, N. (2012). Assessing executive function in preschoolers. *Neuropsychological Review*, *22*, 345–360.

Anderson, S. W., Bechara, A., Damasio, H., Tranel, D., & Damasio, A. R. (1999). Impairment of social and moral behavior related to early damage in human prefrontal cortex. *Nature Neuroscience*, *2*, 1032–1037.

Anglin, J. M. (1993). Vocabulary development: A morphological analysis. *Monographs of the Society for Research in Child Development*, *58*, No.10 (Serial No. 238).

Anisfeld, M. (1991). Neonatal imitation. *Developmental Review*, *11*, 60–97.

Anisfeld, M. (1996). Only tongue protrusion modeling is matched by neonates. *Developmental Review*, *16*, 149–161.

Anisfeld, M., Turkewitz, G., & Rose, S. (2001). No compelling evidence that newborns imitate oral gestures. *Infancy*, *2*, 111–122.

APA (2013). *Diagnostic and Statistical Manual of Mental Disorders: DSM-5*. Washington, DC: American Psychiatric Association.

Appel, H. M., Fescemyer, H., Ehlting, J., Weston, D., Rehrig, E., Joshi, T., Xu, D., Bohlmann, J., & Schultz, J. (2014). Transcriptional responses of *Arabidopsis thaliana* to chewing and sucking insect herbivores. *Frontiers of Plant Science, 5*.

Apperly, I. A., & Butterfill, S. A. (2009). Do humans have two systems to track beliefs and belief-like states? *Psychological Review, 116*, 953–970.

Appleton, M., & Reddy, V. (1996). Teaching three year-olds to pass false belief tests: A conversational approach. *Social Development, 5*, 275–291.

Archibald, S. J., & Kerns, K. A. (1999). Identification and description of new tests of executive functioning in children. *Child Neuropsychology, 5*, 115–129.

Archives Piaget. (1989). *Bibliographie Jean Piaget*. Geneva: Foundation Archives Jean Piaget.

Armstrong, K. A. (2014). *Interests in Adults with Autism Spectrum Disorder*. Unpublished Doctoral Dissertation, Simon Fraser University.

Aslin, R. N. (2007). What's in a look? *Developmental Science, 10*, 48–53.

Astington, J. W. (2001). The future of theory-of-mind research: Understanding motivational states, the role of language, and real-world consequences. *Child Development, 72*, 685–687.

Astington, J. W., & Baird, J. A. (eds) (2005). *Why Language Matters for Theory of Mind*. New York: Oxford University Press.

Astington, J. W., & Jenkins, J. M. (1995). Theory of mind development and social understanding. *Cognition and Emotion, 9*, 151–165.

Astington, J. W., & Jenkins, J. M. (1999). A longitudinal study of the relations between language and theory-of-mind development. *Developmental Psychology, 35*, 1311–1320.

Austin, J. L. (1962). *How to Do Things with Words*. Oxford: Clarendon Press.

Avis, J., & Harris, P. L. (1991). Belief-desire reasoning among Baka children: Evidence for a universal conception of mind. *Child Development, 62*, 460–467.

Aziz, S. A., Fletcher, J., & Bayliss, D. M. (2016). The effectiveness of self-regulatory speech training for planning and problem solving in children with specific language impairment. *Journal of Abnormal Child Psychology, 44*, 1045–1059.

Azmitia, M. (1992). Expertise, private speech, and the development of self-regulation. In R. M. Diaz & L. E. Berk (eds), *Private Speech: From Social Interaction to Self-regulation* (pp. 101–122). Hove: Lawrence Erlbaum Associates.

Baddeley, A. (1986). Oxford psychology series, No. 11. Working Memory.

Baddeley, A. (2012). Working memory: Theories, models, and controversies. *Annual Review of Psychology, 63*, 1–29.

Baddeley, A. D., & Hitch, G. (1974). Working memory. *Psychology of Learning and Motivation, 8*, 47–89.

Baddeley, Engle Kane 2014

Baillargeon, R. (1987). Object permanence in 3½- and 4½-month old infants. *Developmental Psychology, 23*, 655–664.

Baillargeon, R. (2000). Reply to Bogartz, Shinskey, and Schilling; Schilling; and Cashon and Cohen. *Infancy, 1*, 447–462.

Baillargeon, R. (2004). Infants' reasoning about hidden objects: Evidence for event-general and event-specific expectation. *Developmental Science, 7*, 391–414.

Baillargeon, R. (2008). Innate ideas revisited: For a principle of persistence in infants' physical reasoning. *Perspectives on Psychological Science, 3*, 2–12.

Baillargeon, R., Scott, R. M., & Bain, L. (2016). Psychological reasoning in infancy. *Annual Reviews in Psychology, 67*, 159–186.

Baillargeon, R., Scott, R. M., & Bian, L. (2016). Psychological reasoning in infancy. *Annual Review of Psychology*, *67*, 159–186.

Baillargeon, R., Scott, R. M., & He, Z. (2010). False-belief understanding in infants. *Trends in Cognitive Sciences*, *14*, 110–118.

Baird, J. A., & Astington, J. W. (2004). The role of mental state understanding in the development of moral cognition and moral action. In J. A. Baird & B. W. Sokol (eds), *Connections between Theory of Mind and Sociomoral Development*. New Directions for Child and Adolescent Development, 103, 37–49.

Baldwin, D. A. (1991). Infants' contributions to the achievement of joint reference. *Child Development*, *62*, 875–890.

Baldwin, D. A. (1991). Infants' contributions to the achievement of joint reference. *Child Development*, *62*, 875–890.

Baldwin, D. A. (1993). Early referential understanding – infants' ability to recognize referential acts for what they are. *Developmental Psychology*, *29*, 832–843.

Baldwin, D. A. (1995). Understanding the link between joint attention and language. In C. Moore & P. J. Dunham (eds), *Joint Attention: Its Origins and Role in Development* (pp. 131–158). Hillsdale, NJ: Erlbaum.

Baldwin, D. A., & Moses, L. J. (1996). The ontogeny of social information gathering. *Child Development*, *67*, 1915–1933.

Baldwin, J. M. (1897). *Social and Ethical Interpretations in Mental Development: A Study in Social Psychology*. London: Macmillan.

Baldwin, J. M. (1906). *Thoughts and Things, Vol. 1: Functional Logic*. New York: The Macmillan Company.

Baldwin, J. M. (1911). *The Individual and Society*. Boston: The Durham Press.

Bandura, A. (1977). Self-efficacy: Toward a unifying theory of behavioral change. *Psychological Bulletin*, *84*, 191–215.

Banerjee, R. (2004) The role of social experience in advanced social understanding. *Behavioral and Brain Sciences*, *27*, 97–98.

Banerjee, R., Watling, D., & Caputi, M. (2011). Peer relations and the understanding of faux pas: Longitudinal evidence for bidirectional associations. *Child Development*, *82*, 1887–1905.

Barkley, R. A. (2012). *Executive functions: What They Are, How They Work, and Why They Evolved*. New York: Guilford Press.

Baron-Cohen, S. (1995). *Mindblindness: An Essay on Autism and Theory of Mind*. Cambridge, MA: MIT Press.

Baron-Cohen, S. (2008). Theories of the autistic mind. *The Psychologist*, *21*(2), 112–116.

Baron-Cohen, S., Allen, J., & Gillberg, C. (1992). Can autism be detected at 18 months? The needle, the haystack, and the CHAT. *British Journal of Psychiatry*, *161*, 839–843.

Baron-Cohen, S., Cox, A., Baird, G., Swettenham, J., Nightingale, N., Morgan, K., Drew, A., & Charman, T. (1996). Psychological markers in the detection of autism in infancy in a large population. *British Journal of Psychiatry*, *168*, 158–163.

Baron-Cohen, S., Lombardo, M. V., Auyeung, B., Ashwin, E., Chakrabarti, B., & Knickmeyer, R. (2011). Why are autism spectrum conditions more prevalent in males? *PLOS Biology*, *9*, 1–10.

Barresi, J., & Moore, C. (1996). Intentional relations and social understanding. *Behavioral and Brain Sciences*, *19*, 107–154.

Barrett, L. (2011). *Beyond the Brain: How Body and Environment Shape Animal and Human Minds*. Princeton, NJ: Princeton University Press.

Barsalou, L. W. (2008). Grounded cognition. *Annual Review of Psychology*, *59*, 617–645.

Bartsch, K., & Wellman, H. M. (1995). *Children Talk about the Mind*. Oxford: Oxford University Press.

Bates, E. (1976). *Language and Context*. New York: Academic Press.

Bates, E. (1979). *The Emergence of Symbols: Cognition and Communication in Infancy*. New York: Academic Press.

Bates, E. (1984). Bioprograms and the innateness hypothesis: Response to D. Bickerton. *Behavioral and Brain Sciences*, *7*(2), 188–190.

Bates, E. (1999). Plasticity, localization and language development. In S. H. Broman & J. M. Fletcher (eds), *The Changing Nervous System: Neurobehavioral Consequences of Early Brain Disorders* (pp. 214–253). New York: Oxford University Press.

Bates, E. (2005). Plasticity, localization, and language development. In S. T. Taylor, J. Langer, & C. Milbrath (eds), *Biology and Knowledge Revisited: From Neurogenesis to Psychogenesis* (pp. 205–253). Mahwah, NJ: Erlbaum.

Bates, E., Camaioni, L., & Volterra, V. (1975). The acquisition of performatives prior to speech. *Merrill-Palmer Quarterly*, *21*, 205–226.

Bates, E., Thal, D., Trauner, D., Fenson, J., Aram, D., Eisele, J., & Nass, R. (1997). From first words to grammar in children with focal brain injury. *Developmental Neuropsychology*, *13*(3), 275–343.

Baum, S., & Titone, D. (2014). Moving toward a neuroplasticity view of bilingualism, executive control, and aging. *Applied Psycholinguistics*, *35*, 875–894.

Beach, F. A. (1955). The descent of instinct. *Psychology Review*, *62*, 401–410.

Beck, D. M. (2010). The appeal of the brain in the popular press. *Perspectives on Psychological Science*, *5*, 762–766.

Begus, K., & Southgate, V. (2012). Infant pointing serves an interrogative function. *Developmental Science*, *15*, 611–617.

Behne, T., Liszkowski, U., Carpenter, M., & Tomasello, M. (2012). Twelve-month-olds' comprehension and production of pointing. *British Journal of Developmental Psychology*, *30*, 359–375.

Behrend, D.A., Rosengren, K.S., & Perlmutter, M. (1989). A new look at children's private speech: The effects of age, task difficulty, and parent presence. *International Journal of Behavioral Development*, *12*, 305–320.

Beilin, H. (1992). Piaget's enduring contribution to developmental psychology. *Developmental Psychology*, *28*, 191–204.

Bell, S. M., & Ainsworth, M. D. S. (1972). Infant crying and maternal responsiveness. *Child Development*, *43*, 1171–1190.

Berg, E.A. (1948). A simple objective technique for measuring flexibility in thinking. *Journal of Experimental Psychology*, *38*, 404–411.

Bergelson, E., & Swingley, D. (2012). At 6–9 months, human infants know the meanings of many common nouns. *Proceedings of the National Academy of Sciences*, *109*, 3253–3258.

Berger, P. L., & Luckman, T. (1966). *The Social Construction of Reality: A Treatise in the Sociology of Knowledge*. Garden City, NY: Anchor Books.

Berk, L. E. (1992). Children's private speech: An overview of theory and the status of research. In R. M. Diaz & L. E. Berk (eds), *Private Speech: From Social Interaction to Self-regulation* (pp. 17–54). Hillsdale, NJ: Lawrence Erlbaum.

Berker, S. (2009). The normative insignificance of neuroscience. *Philosophy and Public Affairs*, *37*, 293–329.

Bernier, A., Carlson, S. M., & Whipple, N. (2010). From external regulation to self-regulation: Early parenting precursors of young children's executive functioning. *Child Development*, *81*, 326–339.

Bernier, A., Carlson, S. M., Deschênes, M., & Matte-Gagné, C. (2012). Social factors in the development of early executive functioning: A closer look at the caregiving environment. *Developmental Science*, *15*, 12–24.

Bernstein, R. J. (2010). *The Pragmatic Turn*. Malden, MA: Polity.

Best, J. R. (2012). Exergaming immediately enhances children's executive function. *Developmental Psychology, 48*, 1501–1510.

Best, J. R., & Miller, P. H. (2010). A developmental perspective on executive function. *Child Development, 81*, 1641–1660.

Bialystok, E. (2009). Bilingualism: The good, the bad, and the indifferent. *Bilingualism: Language and Cognition, 12*, 3–11.

Bialystok, E. (2015). Bilingualism and the development of executive function: The role of attention. *Child Development Perspectives, 9*, 117–121.

Bibok, M. B., Carpendale, J. I. M., & Lewis, C. (2008). Social knowledge as social skill: An action based view of social understanding. In U. Müller, J. I. M. Carpendale, N. Budwig, & B. Sokol (eds), *Social Life and Social Knowledge: Toward a Process Account of Development* (pp. 145–169). New York: Taylor & Francis.

Bibok, M. B., Carpendale, J. I. M., & Müller, U. (2009). Social interactive quality of parent–child scaffolding as a predictor of children's executive function. In C. Lewis, & J. I. M. Carpendale (eds), *Social Interaction and the Development of Executive Function*. New Directions in Child and Adolescent Development, *123*, 17–34. (Series editors R. Larson & L. Jensen). New York: Jossey Bass.

Bibok, M. B., Müller, U., & Carpendale, J. I. M. (2009). Childhood. In U. Müller, J. I. M. Carpendale, & L. Smith (eds), *The Cambridge Companion to Piaget* (pp. 229–254). Cambridge: Cambridge University Press.

Bickerton, D. (1984). The language bioprogram hypothesis. *Behavioral and Brain Sciences, 7*, 173–188.

Bickhard, M. H. (1999). Interaction and representation. *Theory & Psychology, 9*, 435–458.

Bigelow, A. E. (2003). The development of joint attention in blind infants. *Development and Psychopathology, 15*, 259–275.

Bion, R. A., Borovsky, A., & Fernald, A. (2013). Fast mapping, slow learning: Disambiguation of novel word–object mappings in relation to vocabulary learning at 18, 24, and 30 months. *Cognition, 126*, 39–53.

Birnbacher, D. (2016). Where and when ethics needs empirical facts. In C. Brand (ed.), *Dual-Process Theories in Moral Psychology: Interdisciplinary Approaches to Theoretical, Empirical and Practical Considerations* (pp. 41–55). Wiesbaden: Springer Verlag.

Bishop, D. V. M., Aadmodt-Leeper, G., Cresswell, C., McGurk, R., & Skuse, D. (2001). Individual differences in cognitive planning on the Tower of Hanoi task: Neuropsychological maturity or measurement error? *Journal of Child Psychology and Psychiatry, 42*, 551–556.

Bivens, J. A., & Berk, L. E. (1990). A longitudinal study of the development of elementary school children's private speech. *Merrill-Palmer Quarterly, 36*, 443–463.

Blair, C., & Raver, C. C. (2012). Individual development and evolution: Experiential canalization of self-regulation. *Developmental Psychology, 48*, 647–657.

Blair, C., & Willoughby, M. (2013). Rethinking executive functions: Commentary on 'The contribution of executive function and social understanding to preschoolers' letter and math skills' by M. R. Miller, U. Müller, G. F. Giesbrecht, J. I. M. Carpendale, and K. A. Kerns. *Cognitive Development, 28*, 350–353.

Blair, C., Granger, D., Willoughby, M., Mills-Koonce, R., Cox, M., Greenberg, M. T., & the FLP Investigators (2011). Salivary cortisol mediates effects of poverty and parenting on executive functions in early childhood. *Child Development, 82*, 1970–1984.

Blake, J., O'Rourke, P., & Borzellino, G. (1994). Form and function in the development of pointing and reaching gestures. *Infant Behavior and Development, 17*, 195–203.

Blasi, A. (1980). Bridging moral cognition and moral action: A critical review of the literature. *Psychological Bulletin, 88*, 1–45.

Bloom, P. (2000). *How Children Learn the Meaning of Words*. Cambridge, MA: MIT Press.

Bloom, P. (2004). Can a dog learn a word? *Science, 304*, 1605–1606.

Bloom, P. (2010). The moral life of babies. *New York Times*, 5 May.

Bloom, P. (2014). Horrible children: The limits of natural morality. In M. R. Banaji & S. A. Gelman (eds), *Navigating the Social World: What Infants, Children and Other Species Can Teach Us* (pp. 348–351). New York: Oxford University Press.

Bogartz, R. S., Shinskey, J. L., & Schilling, T. H. (2000). Object permanence in five-and-a-half-month-old infants? *Infancy, 1*, 403–428.

Bogartz, R. S., Shinskey, J. L., & Speaker, C. J. (1997). Interpreting infant looking: The event set x event set design. *Developmental Psychology, 33*, 408–422.

Bohannon, M., & Stanowicz, L. (1988). The issue of negative evidence: Adult responses to children's language errors. *Developmental Psychology, 24*, 684–689.

Borke, H. (1971). Interpersonal perception of young children. *Developmental Psychology, 5*, 263–269.

Bosaki, S., & Astington, J. W. (1999). Theory of mind in preadolescence: Relations between social understanding and social competence. *Social Development, 8*, 237–255.

Bowers, J. S., & Davis, C. J. (2012). Bayesian just-so stories in psychology and neuroscience. *Psychological Bulletin, 138*, 389–414.

Bowlby, J. (1958). The nature of the child's tie to his mother. *International Journal of Psychoanalysis, 39*, 350–373.

Bowlby, J. (1969). *Attachment and Loss: Volume 1, Attachment*. London: Penguin Books.

Boyes, M. C., & Walker, L. J. (1988). Implications of cultural diversity for the universality claims of Kohlberg's theory of moral reasoning. *Human Development, 31*, 44–59.

Brace, J. J., Morton, B. J., & Munakata, Y. (2006). When actions speak louder than words: Improving children's performance on a card-sorting task. *Psychological Science, 17*, 665–669.

Bradley, C. C., Boan, A. D., Cohen, A. P., Charles, J. M., & Carpenter, L. A. (2016). Reported history of developmental regression and restricted, repetitive behaviors in children with autism spectrum disorders. *Journal of Developmental and Behavioral Pediatrics, 37*, 451–456.

Braine, M. D. S. (1963). On learning the grammatical order of words. *Psychological Review, 70*(4), 323.

Brainerd, C. (1978). *Piaget's Theory of Intelligence*. Englewood Cliffs, NJ: Prentice-Hall.

Bremner, J. G. (1994). *Infancy*. Oxford: Blackwell.

Brent, E., Rios, P., Happé, F., & Charman, T. (2004). Performance of children with autism spectrum disorder on advanced theory of mind tasks. *Autism, 8*, 283–299.

Bretherton, I., McNew, S., & Beeghly-Smith, M. (1981). Early person knowledge as expressed in gestural and verbal communication: When do infants acquire a 'theory of mind'? In M. E. Lamb & L. R. Sherrod (eds), *Infant Social Cognition: Empirical and Theoretical Considerations* (pp. 333–373). Hillsdale, NJ: Lawrence Erlbaum.

Bringuier, J.-C. (1980). *Conversations with Jean Piaget*. Chicago: University of Chicago Press.

Broadbent, D. E. (1958). *Perception and Communication*. London: Pergamon.

Broca, P. (1861). Sur le principe des localisations cérébrales. *Bulletin de la Société d'Anthropologie, 2*, 190–204.

Broesch, T. L., & Bryant, G. A. (2015). Prosody in infant-directed speech is similar across western and traditional cultures. *Journal of Cognition and Development, 16*, 31–43.

Broesch, T. L., & Bryant, G. A. (2017). Fathers' infant-directed speech in a small-scale society. *Child Development*, Wiley Online Library, doi: 10.1111/cdev.12768

Brooks, R., & Meltzoff, A. N. (2008). Infant gaze following and pointing predict accelerated vocabulary growth through two years of age: A longitudinal, growth curve modeling study. *Journal of Child Language, 35,* 207–220.

Brown, L. M., Tappan, M., & Gilligan, C. (1995). Listening to different voices. In W. M. Kurtines & J. L. Gewirtz (eds), *Moral Development: An Introduction* (pp. 311–335). Boston, MA: Allyn & Bacon.

Brown, P., & Levinson, S. C. (1987). *Politeness: Some Universals in Language Use.* Cambridge: Cambridge University Press.

Brown, R. (1957). Linguistic determination and the part of speech. *Journal of Abnormal and Social Psychology, 55,* 1–5.

Brown, R. (1958). How shall a thing be called? *Psychological Review, 65,* 14–21.

Brown, R., & Hanlon, C. (1970). Derivational complexity and order of acquisition in child speech. In J. R. Hayes (ed.), *Cognition and the Development of Language* (pp. 11–53). New York: Wiley.

Brownell, C. A. (2016). Prosocial behavior in infancy: The role of socialization. *Child Development Perspectives, 10,* 222–227.

Brownell, C. A., Ramini, G. B., & Zerwas, S. (2006). Becoming a social partner with peers: Cooperation and social understanding in one- and two-year-olds. *Child Development, 77,* 803–821.

Brownell, C., & Carriger, M. (1990). Changes in cooperation and self-other differentiation during the second year. *Child Development, 61,* 1164–1174.

Bruner, J. (1975). The ontogenesis of speech acts. *Journal of Child Language, 2,* 1–19.

Bruner, J. S. (1981). The social context of language acquisition. *Language & Communication, 1*(2–3), 155–178.

Bruner, J. S. (1983). *Child's Talk: Learning to Use Language.* New York: Norton.

Bruner, J. S. (1985). The role of interaction formats in language acquisition. In J. P. Forgas (ed.), *Language and Social Situations* (pp. 31–46).

Heidelberg: Springer. Springer Series in Social Psychology.

Bruner, J. S., Goodnow, J. J., & Austin, G. A. (1956) *A Study of Thinking.* London: Chapman & Hall.

Bruner, J., & Sherwood, V. (1976). Peek-a-boo and the learning of rule structures. In J. S. Bruner, A. Jolly, & K. Sylva (eds), *Play: Its Role in Evolution and Development.* Harmondsworth: Penguin.

Bryce Heath, S. (1983). *Ways with Words: Language, Life, and Work in Communities and Classrooms.* Cambridge: Cambridge University Press.

Budwig, N. (2002). A developmental-functionalist approach to mental state talk. In E. Amsel & J. P. Byrnes (eds), *Language, Literacy, and Cognitive Development: The Development and Consequences of Symbolic Communication* (pp. 59–86). Mahwah, NJ: Lawrence Erlbaum Associates.

Bull, R., Espy, K. A., & Senn, T. E. (2004) A comparison of performance on the Towers of London and Hanoi in young children. *Journal of Child Psychology & Psychiatry, 45,* 743–754.

Buller, D. J. (2005a). Evolutionary psychology: The emperor's new paradigm. *Trends in Cognitive Sciences, 9,* 277–283.

Buller, D. J. (2005b). *Adapting Minds: Evolutionary Psychology and the Persistent Quest for Human Nature.* Cambridge, MA: MIT Press.

Burack, J. A., Russo, N., Kovshoff, H., Frenandes, T. P., Ringo, J., Landry, O., & Iarocci, G. (2016). How I attend – not how well do I attend: Rethinking developmental frameworks of attention and cognition in autism spectrum disorder and typical development. *Journal of Cognition and Development, 17,* 553–567.

Butler, L. P., & Markman, E. M. (2014). Preschoolers use pedagogical cues to guide radical reorganization of category knowledge. *Cognition, 130,* 116–127.

Buttelmann, D., Carpenter, M., & Tomasello, M. (2009). Eighteen-month-old infants show false belief understanding in an active helping paradigm. *Cognition*, *112*, 337–342.

Butterworth, G. (2001). Joint visual attention in infancy. In G. Bremner & A. Fogel (eds), *Blackwell Handbook of Infant Development* (pp. 213–240). Oxford: Blackwell.

Butterworth, G. (2003). Pointing is the royal road to language for babies. In S. Kita (ed.), *Pointing: Where Language, Culture, and Cognition Meet* (pp. 9–33). Mahwah, NJ: Lawrence Erlbaum.

Byars, A. W., Holland, S. K., Strawsburg, R. H., Schmithorst, V. J., Dunn, R. S., & Ball, W. S. (2002). Practical aspects of conducting large scale fMRI studies in children. *Journal of Child Neurology*, *17*(12), 885–890.

Byers-Heinlein, K., Burns, T. C., & Werker, J. F. (2010). The roots of bilingualism in newborns. *Psychological Science*, *21*, 343–348.

Call, J., & Tomasello, M. (2008). Does the chimpanzee have a theory of mind? 30 years later. *Trends in Cognitive Sciences*, *12*(5), 187–192.

Call, J., & Tomasello, M. (2008). Does the chimpanzee have a theory of mind? 30 years later. *Trends in Cognitive Sciences*, *12*(5), 187–192.

Call, J., & Tomasello, M. (2008). Does the chimpanzee have a theory of mind? 30 years later. *Trends in Cognitive Sciences*, *12*(5), 187–192.

Call, J., Hare, B. A., & Tomasello, M. (1998). Chimpanzee gaze following in an object-choice task. *Animal Cognition*, *1*, 89–99.

Call, J., Hare, B. A., & Tomasello, M. (2008). Does the chimpanzee have a theory of mind? 30 years later. *Trends in Cognitive Sciences*, *12*, 187–192.

Callaghan, T., Rochat, P., Lillard, A., Claux, M. L., Odden, H., Itakura, S. T., & Singh, S. (2005). Synchrony in the onset of mental-state reasoning. *Psychological Science*, *16*, 378–384.

Cameron-Faulkner, T., Theakston, A., Lieven, E., & Tomasello, M. (2015). The relationship between infant holdout and gives, and pointing. *Infancy*, *20*, 576–586.

Campbell, R. L. (2009). Constructive process: Abstraction, generalization, and dialectics. In U. Müller, J. I. M. Carpendale, & L. Smith (eds), *The Cambridge Companion to Piaget* (pp. 150–170). Cambridge: Cambridge University Press.

Campbell, R. L., & Bickhard, M. H. (1993). Knowing levels and the child's understanding of mind. *Behavioral and Brain Sciences*, *16*, 33–34.

Campbell, R. L., Christopher, J. C., & Bickhard, M. H. (2002). Self and values: An interactivist foundation for moral development. *Theory & Psychology*, *12*, 795–823.

Canfield, J. V. (1995). The rudiments of language. *Language and Communication*, *15*, 195–211.

Canfield, J. V. (2007). *Becoming Human: The Development of Language, Self, and Self-consciousness*. New York: Palgrave Macmillan.

Caputi, M., Lecce, S., Pagnin, A., & Banerjee, R. (2012). Longitudinal effects of theory of mind on later peer relations: The role of prosocial behavior. *Developmental Psychology*, *48*, 257–270.

Carey, S. (1985). *Conceptual Change in Childhood*. Cambridge, MA: MIT Press.

Carey, S., & Bartlett, E. (1978). Acquiring a single new word. *Stanford University Papers and Reports on Child Language Development*, 15, 17–29.

Carlson, S. M., Davis, A. C., & Leach, J. G. (2005). Less is more: Executive function and symbolic representation in preschool children. *Psychological Science*, *16*, 609–616.

Carpendale, J. I. M, & Lewis, C. (2015a). The development of social understanding. In L. Liben & U. Müller (vol. eds; Editor-in-Chief, R. M. Lerner)), *Vol. 2: Cognitive Processes*, 7th edition of the *Handbook of Child Psychology and Developmental Science* (pp. 381–424). New York: Wiley Blackwell.

Carpendale, J. I. M. & Carpendale, A. B. (2010). The development of pointing: From personal directedness to interpersonal direction. *Human Development*, *53*, 110–126.

Carpendale, J. I. M. & Chandler, M. J. (1996). On the distinction between false belief understanding and subscribing to an interpretive theory of mind. *Child Development*, *67*, 1686–1706.

Carpendale, J. I. M. (2000). Kohlberg and Piaget on stages and moral reasoning. *Developmental Review*, *20*, 181–205.

Carpendale, J. I. M. (2009). Piaget's theory of moral development. In U. Müller, J. I. M Carpendale, & L. Smith (eds), *The Cambridge Companion to Piaget* (pp. 270–286). Cambridge: Cambridge University Press.

Carpendale, J. I. M. (2017). Communication as the coordination of activity: The implications of philosophical preconceptions for theories of the development of communication In A. Dick & U. Müller (eds), *Advancing Developmental Science: Philosophy, Theory, and Method*. New York: Taylor & Francis.

Carpendale, J. I. M., & Lewis, C. (2004). Constructing an understanding of mind: The development of children's social understanding within social interaction. *Behavioral and Brain Sciences*, *27*, 79–151.

Carpendale, J. I. M., & Lewis, C. (2006). *How Children Develop Social Understanding*. Oxford: Blackwell.

Carpendale, J. I. M., & Lewis, C. (2008a). Imitation cannot explain understanding. *Behavioral and Brain Sciences*, *31*, 23–24.

Carpendale, J. I. M., & Lewis, C. (2008b). More smoke than mirror neurons. *Human Development: Letters to the Editor* (invited letter).

Carpendale, J. I. M., & Lewis, C. (2010). The development of social understanding: A relational perspective. In W. F. Overton (ed.; Editor-in-Chief, R. M. Lerner), *Handbook of Lifespan Development*. Chichester: Wiley.

Carpendale, J. I. M., & Lewis, C. (2015). Taking natural history seriously in studying the social formation of thinking: Critical analysis of a natural history of human thinking by Michael Tomasello. *Human Development*, *58*(1).

Carpendale, J. I. M., & Lewis, C. (in preparation). *What Makes Us Human?*

Carpendale, J. I. M., & Müller, U. (2004). Social interaction and the development of rationality and morality: An introduction. In J. I. M. Carpendale & U. Müller (eds), *Social Interaction and the Development of Knowledge* (pp. 1–18). Mahwah, NJ: Lawrence Erlbaum Associates.

Carpendale, J. I. M., & Racine, T. P. (2011). Intersubjectivity and egocentrism: Insights from the relational perspectives of Piaget, Mead, and Wittgenstein. *New Ideas in Psychology*, *29*, 346–354.

Carpendale, J. I. M., & Wereha, T. J. (2013). Understanding common developmental timetables across cultures from a developmental systems perspective. *Human Development*, *56*, 207–212.

Carpendale, J. I. M., Atwood, S., & Kettner, V. (2013). Meaning and mind from the perspective of dualist versus relational worldviews: Implications for the development of pointing gestures. *Human Development*, *56*, 381–400.

Carpendale, J. I. M., Frayn, M., & Kucharczyk, P. (2017). The social formation of human minds. In J. Kiverstein (ed.), *Routledge Handbook of the Philosophy of the Social Mind* (pp. 189–207). New York: Routledge.

Carpendale, J. I. M., Hammond, S. I., & Atwood, S. (2013). A relational developmental systems approach to moral development. In R. M. Lerner & J. B. Benson (eds), *Embodiment and Epigenesis: Theoretical and Methodological Issues in understanding the Role of Biology within the Relational Developmental System* (pp. 105–133). Advances in Child Development and Behavior, vol. 45.

Carpendale, J. I. M., Kettner, V. A., & Audet, K. N. (2014). On the nature of toddlers' helping: Helping or interest in others' activity? *Social Development*, *24*, 357–366. doi:10.1111/sode. 12094

Carpendale, J. I. M., Müller, U., & Bibok, M. (2008). Piaget's theory of cognitive development. In N. J. Salkind (ed.), *Encyclopedia of Educational Psychology*, Vol. 2 (pp. 798–804). Thousand Oaks, CA: Sage.

Carpendale, J. I. M., Sokol, B., & Müller, U. (2010). Is a neuroscience of morality possible? In P. Zelazo, M. Chandler, & E. Crone (eds), *Developmental Social Cognitive Neuroscience* (pp. 289–311). New York: Psychology Press.

Carpendale, J. I., & Krebs, D. L. (1995). Variations in level of moral judgment as a function of type of dilemma and moral choice. *Journal of Personality*, *63*, 289–313.

Carpendale, J., & Krebs, D. L. (1992). Situational variation in moral judgment: In a stage or on a stage? *Journal of Youth and Adolescence*, *21*, 203–224.

Carpenter, M., Nagell, K., & Tomasello, M. (1998). Social cognition, joint attention, and communicative competence from 9 to 15 months of age. *Monographs of the Society for Research in Child Development*, *63* (Serial No. 255).

Carruthers, P. (2009). How we know our own minds: The relationship between mindreading and metacognition. *Behavioral & Brain Sciences*, *32*, 121–182.

Carruthers, P., & Smith, P. K. (eds) (1996). *Theories of Theories of Mind*. Cambridge: Cambridge University Press.

Casebeer, W. D. (2003). Moral cognition and its neural constituents. *Nature Reviews Neuroscience*, 4 (10), 840–846.

Casler, K., & Kelemen, D. (2005). Young children's rapid learning about artifacts. *Developmental Science*, *8*, 472–480.

Cassidy, K. W., Fineberg, D. S., Brown, K., & Perkins, A. (2005). Theory of mind may be contagious, but you don't catch it from your twin. *Child Development*, *76*, 97–106.

Catale, C., Willems, S., Lejeune, C., & Meulemans, T. (2012). Parental educational level: Influence on memory and executive performance in children. *Revue Européenne de Psychologie Appliquée*, *62*, 161–171.

Chandler, M. J. (1973). Egocentrism and antisocial behavior: The assessment and training of social perspective-taking skills. *Developmental Psychology*, *9*, 326–332.

Chandler, M. J. (1988). Doubt and developing theories of mind. In J. W. Astington, P. L. Harris, & D. R. Olson (eds), *Developing Theories of Mind* (pp. 387–413). New York: Cambridge University Press.

Chandler, M. J. (1997). Stumping for progress in a post-modern world. In E. Amsel & K. A. Renninger (eds), *Change and Development: Issues of Theory, Method, and Application* (pp. 1–26). Mahwah, NJ: Erlbaum.

Chandler, M. J. (2001). Perspective taking in the aftermath of theory-theory and the collapse of the social role-taking literature. In A. Tryphon & J. Voneche (eds), *Working with Piaget: In Memoriam – Barbel Inhelder* (pp. 39–63). Hove: Psychology Press.

Chandler, M. J., & Greenspan, S. (1972). Ersatz egocentrism: A reply to Borke. *Developmental Psychology*, *7*, 104–106.

Chandler, M. J., & Hala, S. (1994). The role of personal involvement in the assessment of early false belief skills. In C. Lewis & P. Mitchell (eds), *Children's Early Understanding of Mind: Origins and Development* (pp. 403–425). Hove: Erlbaum.

Chandler, M. J., & Lalonde, C. (1996). Shifting to an interpretive theory of mind: 5- to 7-year-olds' changing conceptions of mental life. In A. Sameroff & M. Haith (eds), *Reason and Responsibility: The Passage Through Childhood* (pp. 111–139). Chicago: University of Chicago Press.

Chandler, M. J., Fritz, A. S., & Hala, S. (1989). Small scale deceit: Deception as a marker of 2-, 3- and 4-year-olds' theories of mind. *Child Development*, *60*, 1263–1277.

Chapman, M. (1988). *Constructive Evolution: Origins and Development of Piaget's Thought*. New York: Cambridge University Press.

Chapman, M. (1991). The epistemic triangle: Operative and communicative components of cognitive development. In M. Chandler & M. Chapman (eds), *Criteria for Competence: Controversies in the Conceptualization and Assessment of Children's Abilities* (pp. 209–228). Hillsdale, NJ: Erlbaum.

Chapman, M. (1992). Equilibration and the dialectics of organization. In H. Beilin & P. Pufall (eds), *Piaget's Theory: Prospects and Possibilities* (pp. 39–59). Hillsdale, NJ: Erlbaum.

Chapman, M. (1999). Constructivism and the problem of reality. *Journal of Applied Development Psychology*, 20, 31–43.

Chapman, M., Zahn-Waxler, C., Cooperman, G., & Iannotti, R. (1987). Empathy and responsibility in the motivation of children's helping. *Developmental Psychology*, *23*, 140–145.

Charman, T., Ruffman, T., & Clements, W. (2002). Is there a gender difference in false belief development? *Social Development*, *11*, 1–10.

Charney, E. (2013). Cytoplasmic inheritance redux. In R. M. Lerner & J. B. Benson (eds), *Embodiment and Epigenesis: Theoretical and Methodological Issues in Understanding the Role of Biology within the Relational Developmental System* (pp. 225–256). Advances in Child Development and Behavior, vol. 44.

Cheung, H., Hsuan-Chih, C., Creed, N., Ng, L., Wang, S. P., & Mo, L. (2004). Relative roles of general and complementation language in theory-of-mind development: Evidence from Cantonese and English. *Child Development*, 75, 1155–1170.

Childers, J. B., Vaughan, J., & Burquest, D. A. (2007). Joint attention and word learning in Ngas-speaking toddlers in Nigeria. *Journal of Child Language*, *34*(2), 199–225.

Chomsky, N. (1957). *Syntactic Structures*. The Hague: Mouton.

Chomsky, N. (1959). A review of B. F. Skinner's 'Verbal Behavior'. *Language*, *35*, 26–58.

Chomsky, N. (1965). *Aspects of the Theory of Syntax*. Cambridge, MA: MIT Press.

Chomsky, N. (1968). *Language and Mind*. New York: Harcourt, Brace & World, Inc.

Chomsky, N. (1980). *Rules and Representations*. New York: Columbia University Press.

Chomsky, N. (1988). *Language and Problems of Knowledge*. Cambridge, MA: MIT Press.

Chomsky, N. (2007). Biolinguistic explorations: Design, development, evolution. *International Journal of Philosophical Studies*, *15*, 1–21.

Chomsky, N. (2011). On the poverty of the stimulus. Lecture presented at University College London, 10 October. Available at www.ucl.ac.uk/psychlangsci/research/linguistics/news-events/latest-news/n_chomsky (accessed 15 June 2017).

Chouinard, M. M., & Clark, E. V. (2003). Adult reformulations of child errors as negative evidence. *Journal of Child Language*, *30*, 637–669.

Christen, M., & Müller, S. (2014). Effects of brain lesions on moral agency: Ethical dilemmas in investigating moral behavior. *Current Topics in Behavioral Neuroscience*, *19*, 159–188.

Chudek, M., & Henrich, J. (2011) Culture-gene coevolution, norm-psychology and the emergence of human prosociality. *Trends in Cognitive Sciences*, *15*(5), 218–226.

Chung, Y. S., Barch, D., & Strube, M. (2014). A meta-analysis of mentalizing impairments in adults with schizophrenia and autism spectrum disorder. *Schizophrenia Bulletin*, *40*(3), 602–616.

Cimpian, A., & Markman, E. M. (2005). The absence of a shape bias in children's word learning. *Developmental Psychology*, *41*, 1003–1019.

Clark, E. V. (1988). On the logic of contrast. *Journal of Child Language, 15*, 317–335.

Clark, R. A. (1978). The transition from action to gesture. In A. Lock (ed.), *Action, Gesture and Symbol* (pp. 231–257). New York: Academic Press.

Clements, W. A., & Perner, J. (1994). Implicit understanding of belief. *Cognitive Development*, 9, 377–395.

Cochet, H., & Vauclair, J. (2010). Pointing gestures produced by toddlers from 15 to 30 months: Different functions, hand shapes and laterality patterns. *Infant Behavior and Development, 33*, 431–441.

Colby, A., & Damon, W. (1993). The uniting of self and morality in the development of extraordinary moral commitment. In G. G. Noam & T. E. Wren (eds), *The Moral Self* (pp. 149–174). Cambridge, MA: MIT Press.

Colby, A., & Kohlberg, L. (1987). *The Measurement of Moral Judgment: Volume 1, Theoretical Foundations and Research Validation.* New York: Cambridge University Press. (pp. 1–40).

Colby, A., Kohlberg, L., Gibbs, J. C., & Lieberman, M. (1983). A longitudinal study of moral judgment. *Monographs of the Society for Research in Child Development, 48*(1–2, Serial No. 200).

Cole, K., & Mitchell, P. (2000). Siblings in the development of executive control and a theory of mind. *British Journal of Developmental Psychology*, 18, 279–295.

Cole, M. (2010). Vygotsky and context: Toward a resolution of theoretical disputes. In S. Kirschner & J. Martin (eds) *The Sociocultural Turn in Psychology: The Contextual Emergence of Mind and Self* (pp. 253–280). New York: Columbia University Press.

Colonnesi, C., Stam, G. J. J. M., Koster, I., & Noom, M. J. (2010). The relation between pointing and language development: A meta-analysis. *Developmental Review, 30*, 352–366.

Colvert, E., Rutter, M., Kreppner, J., Beckett, C., Castle, J., Groothues, C., Hawkins, A., Stevens, S., Sonuga-Barke, E. J. S. (2008). Do theory of mind and executive function deficits underlie the adverse outcomes associated with profound early deprivation? Findings from the English and Romanian adoptees study. *Journal of Abnormal Child Psychology, 36*, 1057–1068.

Comparini, L., Douglas, E. M., & Perez, S. N. (2014). The development of social cognition: Preschoolers' use of mental state talk in peer conflicts. *Early Education and Development*, 25, 1083–1101.

Conway, A., & Stifter, C. A. (2012). Longitudinal antecedents of executive function in preschoolers. *Child Development, 83*, 1022–1036.

Corkum, V., & Moore, V. (1995). Development of joint visual attention in infants. In C. Moore & P. Dunham (eds), *Joint Attention: Its Origins and Role in Development* (pp. 61–83). Hillsdale, NJ: Erlbaum.

Corkum, V., & Moore, V. (1998). The origins of joint visual attention in infants. *Developmental Psychology*, 34, 28–38.

Corkum, V., & Moore, V. (1998). The origins of joint visual attention in infants. *Developmental Psychology*, 34, 28–38.

Cosmides, L. & Tooby, J. (2003). Evolutionary psychology: Theoretical foundations. In L. Nadel (ed.), *Encyclopedia of Cognitive Science* (pp. 54–64). London: Macmillan.

Cosmides, L., & Tooby, J. (2013). Evolutionary psychology: New perspectives on cognition and motivation. *Annual Review of Psychology, 64*, 201–229.

Cowell, J. M., & Decety, J. (2015). Precursors to morality in development as a complex interplay between neural, socioenvironmental, and behavioral facets. *PNAS, 112*, 12657–12662.

Crawford, M. B. (2008). The limits of neuro-talk. *The New Atlantis*, Winter, 65–78.

Crockford, C., Wittig, R. M., Mundry, R., & Zuberbühler, K. (2012). Wild chimpanzees inform ignorant group members of danger. *Current Biology*, *22* (2), 142–146. doi: 10.10 16/j.cub.2011.11.053

Cuff, B., Brown, S. J., Taylor, L., & Howat, D. J. (2016). Empathy: A review of the concept. *Emotion Review*, *8*(2), 144–153.

Curtiss, S. (1977). *Genie: A Psycholinguistic Study of a Modern-Day "Wild Child"*, Perspectives in Neurolinguistics and Psycholinguistics (pp. 319–328). Boston, MA: Academic.

Cutler, A. (2012). *Native Listening: Language Experience and the Recognition of Spoken Words*. Cambridge, MA: The MIT Press.

Cutting, A. L., & Dunn, J. (1999). Theory of mind, emotion understanding, language, and family background: Individual differences and interrelations. *Child Development*, *70*, 853–865.

D'Entremont, B. (2000). A perceptual-attentional explanation of gaze-following in 3- and 6-month-olds. *Developmental Science*, *3*, 302–311.

Dahl, A. (2015). The developing social context of infant helping in two U.S. samples. *Child Development*, *83*, 1080–1093.

Dahl, A., Campos, J. J., & Witherington, D. C. (2011). Emotional action and communication in early moral development. *Emotion Review*, *3*(2), 147–157.

Danziger, K. (1985). The problem of imitation and early explanatory models in developmental psychology. In G. Eckardt, W. G. Bringmann and L. Sprung (eds), *Contributions to a History of Developmental Psychology*. The Hague and New York: Mouton.

Darwin, C. (1877). A biographical sketch of an infant. *Mind*, *2*, 285–294.

Darwin, C. (1981). *The Descent of Man, and Selection in Relation to Sex*. Princeton, NJ: Princeton University Press. (Original work published 1871.)

Darwin, C. (1998). *The Expression of the Emotions in Man and Animals,* 3rd edn. London: HarperCollins Publishers. (Original work published 1872.)

Davis, W. (2009). *The Wayfinders: Why Ancient Wisdom Matters in the Modern World*. Toronto: House of Anansi Press.

Dawkins, R. (1989). *The Selfish Gene*. New York: Oxford University Press.

Day, J. M., & Tappan, M. B. (1996). The narrative approach to moral development: From the epistemic subject to dialogical selves. *Human Development*, *39*, 67–82.

de Barbaro, K., Johnson, C. M., & Deák G. O. (2013). Twelve-month 'social revolution' emerges from mother–infant sensorimotor coordination: A longitudinal investigation. *Human Development*, *56*, 223–248.

de Barbaro, K., Johnson, C. M., Forster, D., & Deák, G. O. (2015). Sensorimotor decoupling contributes to triadic attention: A longitudinal investigation of mother–infant–object interactions. *Child Development*, *87*(2).

De Rosnay, M., Pons, F., Harris, P. L., & Morrell, J. M. B. (2004). A lag between understanding false belief and emotion attribution in young children: Relationships with linguistic ability and mothers' mental-state language. *British Journal of Developmental Psychology*, *22*, 197–218.

de Villiers J. G., & de Villiers, P. A. (2000). Linguistic determinism and the understanding of false beliefs. In P. Mitchell & K. J. Riggs (eds), *Children's Reasoning and the Mind* (pp. 191–228). Hove: Psychology Press.

de Villiers, J. G., & Pyers, J. E. (2002). Complements to cognition: A longitudinal study of the relationship between complex syntax and false-belief-understanding. *Cognitive Development*, *17*, 1037–1060.

de Waal, F. (2006). *Primates and Philosophers: How Morality Evolved*. Princeton, NJ: Princeton University Press.

DeCasper, A. J., & Fifer, W. P. (1980). Of human bonding: Newborns prefer their mothers' voices. *Science*, *208*, 1174–1176.

DeCasper, A. J., Lecanuet, J., & Busnel, M. (1994). Fetal reactions to recurrent mother speech. *Infant Behavior and Development*, *17*, 159–164.

Dellaire, R. (2003). *Shake Hands with the Devil: The Failure of Humanity in Rwanda*. Toronto: Random House.

Descartes, R. (1960). *Discourse on Method and Meditations*. Trans. Laurence Lafleur. Upper Saddle River, NJ: Prentice-Hall. (Original work published in 1641.)

Descartes, R. (1960). The meditations concerning first philosophy. In R. Descartes (ed.), *Discourse on Method and Meditations* (pp. 67–141). Indianapolis, IN: Bobbs-Merrill Educational Publishing. (Original work published in 1641.)

DeScioli, P., & Kurzban, R. (2012). A solution to the mysteries of morality. *Psychological Bulletin, 139*, 477–496.

Desrochers, S., Morissette, P., & Ricard, M. (1995). Two perspectives on pointing in infancy. In C. Moore & P. J. Dunham (eds), *Joint Attention: Its Origins and Role in Development* (pp. 85–101). Hillsdale, NJ: Erlbaum.

Devine, R. T., & Hughes, C. (2013). Silent films and strange stories: Theory of mind, gender, and social experiences in middle childhood. *Child Development, 84*, 989–1003.

Di Paolo, E., & De Jaegher, H. (2012). The interactive brain hypothesis. *Frontiers in Human Neuroscience, 6*, article 163.

Diamond, A., & Lee, K. (2011). Interventions shown to aid executive function development in children 4 to 12 years old. *Science, 333*, 959–964.

Diaz, R. M., & Berk, L. E. (eds) (1992). *Private Speech: From Social Interaction to Self-regulation*. Hillsdale, NJ: Lawrence Erlbaum.

Diesendruck, G., Markson, L., & Bloom, P. (2003). Children's reliance on creator's intent in extending names for artifacts. *Psychological Science, 14*(2), 164–168.

Donaldson, M. (1978). *Children's Minds*. London: Fontana.

Duncan, R.M., & Cheyne, J.A. (2002). Private speech in young adults: Task difficulty, self-regulation, and psychological predication. *Cognitive Development, 16*, 889–906.

Dunn, J. (1995). Children as psychologists: The later correlates of individual differences in understanding of emotions and other minds. *Cognition and Emotion, 9*, 187–201.

Dunn, J. (1996). Children's relationships: Bridging the divide between cognitive and social development. *Child Psychology and Psychiatry, 37*, 507–518.

Dunn, J. (2004). *Children's Friendships: The Beginnings of Intimacy*. Oxford: Blackwell.

Dunn, J., & Brophy, M. (2005). Communication, relationships, and individual differences in children's understanding of mind. In J. W. Astington & J. A. Baird (eds), *Why Language Matters for Theory of Mind* (pp. 50–69). New York: Oxford University Press.

Dunn, J., & Cutting, A. L. (1999). Understanding others, and individual differences in friendship interactions in young children. *Social Development, 8*, 201–219.

Dunn, J., & Kendrick, C. (1982). *Siblings: Love, Envy and Understanding*. Oxford: Blackwell.

Dunn, J., Brown, J., Slomkowski, C., Tesla, C., & Youngblade, L. (1991). Young children's understanding of other people's feelings and beliefs: Individual differences and their antecedents. *Child Development, 62*, 1352–1366.

Dupré, J. (2012). *Processes of Life*. New York: Oxford University Press.

Dwyer, S. (2006). How good is the linguistic analogy? In P. Caruthers, S. Laurence, & S. Stich (eds), *The Innate Mind* (pp. 237–256). Vol. 2. New York: Oxford University Press.

Eimas, P. D., Siqueland, E. R., Jusczyk, P. W., & Vigorito, J. (1971). Speech perception in infants. *Science, 171*, 303–306.

Eklund, A., Nichols, T. E., & Knutsson, H. (2016). Cluster failure: Why fMRI inferences for spatial extent have inflated false-positive rates. *PNAS, 113*, 7900–7905.

Elsabbagh, M., & Johnson, M. H. (2010). Getting answers from babies about autism. *Trends in Cognitive Sciences, 14*, 8187.

Elsabbagh, M., Mercure, E., Hudry, K., Chandler, S., Pasco, G., Charman, T., Pickles, A., Baron-Cohen, S., Bolton, P., Johnson, M. H., & the

BASIS Team (2012). Infant neural sensitivity to dynamic eye gaze is associated with later emerging autism. *Current Biology*, *22*, 338–342.

Emery, N. J., & Clayton, N. S. (2009). Comparative social cognition. *Annual Review of Psychology*, *60*, 87–113.

Ensor, R. & Hughes, C. (2008). Content or connectedness? Mother–child talk and early social understanding. *Child Development*, *79*, 201–216.

Ereky-Stevens, K. (2008). Associations between mothers' sensitivity to their infants' internal states and children's later understanding of mind and emotion. *Infant and Child Development*, *17*, 527–543.

Eslinger, P. J., Flaherty-Craig, C. V., & Benton, A. L. (2004). Developmental outcomes after early prefrontal cortex damage. *Brain and Cognition*, *55*, 84–103.

Espinet, S. D., Anderson, J. E., and Zelazo, P. D. (2012). N2 amplitude as a neural marker of executive function in young children: An ERP study of children who switch versus perseverate on the dimensional change card sort. *Developmental Cognitive Neuroscience*, *2*, 49–58.

Espy, K. A. (ed) (2016). The changing nature of executive control in preschool. *Monographs of the Society for Research in Child Development*, serial no. 323.

Evans, N., & Levinson, S. C. (2009). The myth of linguistic universals: Linguistic diversity and its importance for cognitive science. *Behavioral and Brain Sciences*, *35*, 429–492.

Fantasia, V., De Jaegher, H., & Fasulo, A. (2014). We can work it out: An enactive look at cooperation. *Frontiers in Psychology*, *5*, 1–11.

Fantz, R. (1961). The origin of form perception. *Scientific American*, 204, 66–72.

Farrant, B. M., Devine, T. A., Maybery, M. T., & Fletcher, J. (2012). Empathy, perspective taking and prosocial behaviour: The importance of parenting practices. *Infant and Child Development*, *21*, 175–188.

Farroni, T., Massaccesi, S., Pividori, D., & Johnson, M. H. (2004). Gaze following in newborns. *Infancy*, *5*, 39–60.

Fenici, M. (2013). Social cognitive abilities in infancy: Is mindreading the best explanation?, *Philosophical Psychology*, *28*(3).

Fenici, M. (2015). A simple explanation of apparent early mindreading: Infants' sensitivity to goals and gaze direction. *Phenomenology and the Cognitive Sciences*, *14*(3), 497–515.

Fenson, L., Dale, P. S., Reznick, J. S., Bates, E., Thal, D. J., & Pethick, S. J. (1994). Variability in early communication. *Monographs of the Society for Research in Child Development*, *59* (Serial No. 242).

Fernyhough, C. (2008). Getting Vygotskian about theory of mind: Mediation, dialogue, and the development of social understanding. *Developmental Review*, *28*, 225–262.

Fernyhough, C., & Fradley, E. (2005). Private speech on an executive task: Relations with task difficulty and task performance. *Cognitive Development*, *20*, 103–120.

Filippova, E. and Astington, J. W. (2008). Further development in social reasoning revealed in discourse irony understanding, *Child Development*, *79*, 126–138.

Fink, E., Begeer, S., Peterson, C. C., Slaughter, V., & de Rosnay, M. (2015). Friendlessness and theory of mind: A prospective longitudinal study. *British Journal of Developmental Psychology*, *33*, 1–17.

Fisher, S. E. (2006). Tangled webs: Tracing the connections between genes and cognition. *Cognition*, *101*, 270–297.

Fitch, W. T. (2005). The evolution of language: A comparative review. *Biology and Philosophy*, *20*, 193–230.

Fitch, W. T. (2005). The evolution of language: A comparative review. *Biology and Philosophy*, *20*, 193–230.

Fitch, W. T. (2010). *The Evolution of Language*. Cambridge: Cambridge University Press.

Flavell, J. H., Botkin, P. T., Fry, C., Wright, J., & Jarvis, P. (1968). *The Development of Role-taking and Communication Skills in Children*. New York: Wiley.

Flom, R., Lee, K., & Muir, D. (eds) (2007). *Gaze-following: Its Development and Significance*. Mahwah, NJ: Lawrence Erlbaum.

Flynn, E., Pine, K., & Lewis, C. (2007). Using the microgenetic method to investigate cognitive development: An introduction. *Infant and Child Development*, *16*, 1–6.

Fodor, J. A. (1983). *The Modularity of Mind*. Cambridge, MA: The MIT Press.

Fodor, J. A. (2000). *The Mind Doesn't Work That Way*. Cambridge, MA: MIT Press.

Fogel, A., & Hannan, T. E. (1985). Manual actions of nine- to fifteen-week-old human infants during face-to-face interaction with their mothers. *Child Development*, *56*, 1271–1279.

Fonagy, P., Redfern, S., & Charman, T. (1997). The relationship between belief-desire reasoning and a projective measure of attachment security (SAT). *British Journal of Developmental Psychology*, 15, 51–61.

Foote, R. C., & Holmes-Lonergan, H. A. (2003). Sibling conflict and theory of mind. *British Journal of Developmental Psychology*, *21*, 45–58.

Forst, R. (2005). Moral autonomy and the autonomy of morality: Toward a theory of normativity after Kant. *Graduate Faculty Philosophy Journal*, *26*, 65–88.

Franco, F., & Butterworth, G. E. (1996). Pointing and social awareness: Declaring and requesting in the second year. *Journal of Child Language*, *23*, 307–336.

Frauenglass, M.H., & Diaz, R.M. (1985). Self-regulatory functions of children's private speech: A critical analysis of recent challenges to Vygotsky's theory. *Developmental Psychology*, *21*, 357–364.

Freeman, N. H., Lewis, C., & Doherty, M. (1991). Preschoolers' grasp of a desire for knowledge in false-belief reasoning: Practical intelligence and verbal report. *British Journal of Developmental Psychology*, 9, 139–157.

Freud, S. (1910). The origin and development of psychoanalysis. *American Journal of Psychology*, *21*, 181–218.

Friedman, N. P., Miyake, A., Young, S. E., DeFries, J. C., Corley, R. P., & Hewitt, J. K. (2008). Individual differences in executive functions are almost entirely genetic in origin. *Journal of Experimental Psychology General*, *137*, 201–225.

Frisch, K., von. (1966). *The Dancing Bees: An Account of the Life and Senses of the Honey Bee*. London: Methuen & Co. Ltd. (Original work published 1927.)

Frisch, K., von. (1967). *The Dance Language and Orientation of Bees*. Cambridge, MA: Belknap.

Frodi, A. M., Lamb, M. E., Leavitt, L. A., & Donovan, W. L. (1978). Fathers' and mothers' responses to infant smiles and cries. *Infant Behavior and Development*, *1*, 187–198.

Frodi, A. M., Lamb, M. E., Leavitt, L. A., Donovan, W. L., Neff, C., & Sherry, D. (1978). Fathers' and mothers' responses to the faces and cries of normal and premature infants. *Developmental Psychology*, *14*, 490–498.

Frydman, O., and Bryant, P. (1988). Sharing and understanding of number equivalence by young children. *Cognitive Development*, *3*, 323–339.

Frye, D., Zelazo, P. D., & Palfai, T. (1995). Inference and action in early causal reasoning. *Cognitive Development*, *10*, 120–131.

Furness, W. H. (1916). Observations on the mentality of chimpanzees and orang-utans. *Proceedings of the American Philosophical Society*, *55*, 281–290.

Gallese, V. (2007). Before and below 'theory of mind': Embodied simulation and the neural correlates of social cognition. *Philosophical Transactions of the Royal Society B: Biological Sciences*, *362*(1480), 659–669.

Gallese, V., Gernsbacher, M. A., Heyes, C., Hickok, G., & Iacoboni, M. (2011). Mirror neuron forum. *Perspectives on Psychological Science*, *6*(4), 369–407.

Gallese, V., Keysers, C., & Rizzolatti, G. (2004). A unifying view of the basis of social cognition. *Trends in Cognitive Sciences*, *8*(9), 396–403.

Galton, F. (1869). *Hereditary Genius*. London: Macmillan.

Gardner, R. A., & Gardner, B. T. (1969). Teaching sign language to chimpanzees. *Science, 165*, 664–672.

Gardner, R. A., & Gardner, B. T. (1969). Teaching sign language to chimpanzees. *Science, 165*, 664–672.

Garner, P., Jones, D., Gaddy, D., & Rennie, K. (1997). Low income mothers' conversations about emotion and their children's emotional competence. *Social Development, 6*, 125–142.

Garon, N., Smith, I. M., & Bryson, S. E. (2008). Executive function in preschoolers: A review using an integrative framework. *Psychological Bulletin, 134*, 31–60.

Garon, N., Smith, I. M., & Bryson, S. E. (2014). A novel executive function battery for pre-schoolers: Sensitivity to age differences. *Child Neuropsychology, 20*, 713–736.

Gauvain, M., & Perez, S. (2015). Cognitive development and culture. In L. Liben & U. Müller (vol. eds), *Vol. 2: Cognitive processes*, R. Lerner (editor-in-chief), 7th edition of the *Handbook of Child Psychology and Developmental Science* (pp. 854–896). New York: Wiley Blackwell.

Gehlen, A. (1940/1988). *Man, his Nature and Place in the World*. New York: Columbia University Press. (Original work published in 1940.)

Gellatly, A. (1997). Why the young child has neither a theory of mind nor a theory of anything else. *Human Development, 40*, 32–50.

Gelman, R., & Baillargeon, R. (1983). A review of some Piagetian concepts. In E. Mussen (ed.), *Handbook of Child Psychology* (Vol. 4, pp. 167–230). New York: Wiley.

Gentner, D. (1978). A study of early word meaning using artificial objects: What looks like a jiggy but acts like a zimbo? *Papers and Reports on Child Language Development, 15*, 1–6.

Gerstadt, C.L., Hong, Y.J., & Diamond, A. (1994). The relationship between cognition and action—performance of children 3 ½–7 years old on a stroop-like day–night test. *Cognition, 53*, 129–153.

Gervain, J., & Mehler, J. (2010). Speech perception and language acquisition in the first year of life. *Annual Review of Psychology, 61*, 191–218.

Gesell, A. (1945). *The Embryology of Behaviour: The Beginnings of the Human Mind*. Westport, CT: Greenwood Press.

Gibbs, J. C. Basinger, K. S., Grime, R. L., & Snarey, J. R. (2007). Moral judgment development across cultures: Revisiting Kohlberg's universality claims. *Developmental Review, 27*, 443–500.

Gilligan, C. (1982). *In a Different Voice: Psychological Theory and Women's Development*. Cambridge, MA: Harvard University Press.

Gilligan, C., & Attanucci, J. (1988). Two moral orientations: Gender differences and similarities. *Merrill-Palmer Quarterly, 34*, 223–237.

Gilligan, C., & Wiggins, G. (1987). The origins of morality in early childhood relationships. In J. Kagan & S. Lamb (eds), *The Emergence of Morality in Young Children* (pp. 277–305). Chicago: The University of Chicago Press.

Gini, G., (2006). Social cognition and moral cognition in bullying: What's wrong? *Aggressive Behavior, 32*, 528–539.

Glasersfeld, E., von (1995). *Radical Constructivism: A Way of Knowing and Learning*. London: Falmer Press.

Glassman, M. (2000). Mutual aid theory and human development: Sociability as primary. *Journal for the Theory of Social Behaviour, 30*, 391–412.

Gleason, J. B. (1975). Fathers and other strangers: Men's speech to young children. In D. P. Dato (ed.), *Developmental Psycholinguistics: Theory and Applications* (pp. 289–297). Washington, DC: Georgetown University Press.

Glenberg, A. M., & Gallese, V. (2012). Action-based language: A theory of language acquisition, comprehension, and production. *Cortex, 48*, 905–922.

Glenberg, A. M., & Kaschak, M. P. (2002). Grounding language in action. *Psychonomic Bulletin & Review*, *9*, 558–565.

Göckeritz, S., Schmidt, M. F. H., & Tomasello, M. (2014). Young children's creation and transmission of social norms. *Cognitive Development*, *30*, 81–95.

Goffman, E. (1969). *The Presentation of Self in Everyday Life*. Harmondsworth: Penguin. (Original work published 1959.)

Gola, A. A. H. (2012). Mental verb input for promoting children's theory of mind: A training study. *Cognitive Development*, *27*, 64–76.

Goldberg, B. (1991). Mechanism and meaning. In J. Hyman (ed.), *Investigating Psychology: Sciences of the Mind after Wittgenstein* (pp. 48–66). New York: Routledge.

Goldin-Meadow, S. (2007). Pointing sets the stage for learning language – and creating language. *Child Development*, *78*(3), 741–745.

Goldman-Rakic, P. S. (1987). Development of cortical circuitry and cognitive function. *Child Development*, *58*, 601–622.

Golinkoff, R. M., & Hirsh-Pasek, K. (2006). Baby wordsmith: From associationist to social sophisticate. *Current Directions in Psychological Science*, *15*(1), 30–33.

Golinkoff, R. M., Mervis, C., & Hirsh-Pasek, K. (1994). Early object labels: The case for a developmental lexical principles framework. *Journal of Child Language*, *21*, 125–155.

Goodwyn, S. W., Acredolo, L. P., & Brown, C. A. (2000). Impact of symbolic gesturing on early language development. *Journal of Nonverbal Behavior*, *24*, 81–103.

Gopnik M (1990). Feature blind grammar and dysphasia. *Nature*, *344* (6268), 715.

Gopnik, A. (1996). The child as scientist. *Philosophy of Science*, *63*, 485–514.

Gopnik, A., & Wellman, H. M. (1992). Why the child's theory of mind really is a theory. *Mind and Language*, *7*, 145–171.

Gopnik, A., & Wellman, H. M. (1994). The theory theory. In L. A. Hirschfeld & S. A. Gelman (eds), *Mapping the Mind: Domain Specificity in Cognition and Culture* (pp. 257–293). New York: Cambridge University Press.

Gopnik, A., & Wellman, H. M. (2012). Reconstructing constructivism: Causal models, Bayesian learning mechanisms, and the theory theory. *Psychological Bulletin*, *136*.

Gordon, R. M. (1986). Folk psychology as simulation. *Mind and Language*, *1*, 156–171.

Gottlieb, G. (1991). Experiential canalization of behavioral development: Theory. *Developmental Psychology*, *27*, 4–13.

Gottlieb, G. (1997). *Synthesizing Nature–Nurture: Prenatal Roots of Instinctive Behaviour*. Mahwah, NJ: Erlbaum.

Gottlieb, G. (2007). Probablistic epigenesis. *Developmental Science*, *10*, 1–11.

Gould, S. J. (1992). Red in tooth and claw. *Natural History*, *101* (11), 14.

Graham, S., & Diesendruck, G. (2010). Fifteen-month-old infants attend to shape over other perceptual properties in an induction task. *Cognitive Development*, *25*, 111–123.

Grandin, T. (1986). *Emergence: Labeled Autistic*. Novato, CA: Academic Therapy Publications.

Grazzani, I., Ornaghi, V., & Brockmeier, J. (2016). Conversations on mental states in nursery: Promoting social cognition in early childhood. *European Journal of Developmental Psychology*, *13*(5).

Grazzani, I., Ornaghi, V., & Brockmeier, J. (2016). Conversations on mental states at nursery: Promoting social cognition in early childhood. *European Journal of Developmental Psychology*, *13*, 563–581.

Green, J., Charman, T., McConachie, H., Aldred, C., Slonims, V., Howlin, P., Le Couteur, A., Leadbitter, K., Hudry, K., Byford, S., & Barrett, B. (2010). Parent-mediated communication-focused treatment in children with autism (PACT): A randomised controlled trial. *The Lancet*, *375*, 2152–2160.

Greenberg, A., Bellana, B., & Bialystok, E. (2013). Perspective-taking ability in bilingual children: Extending advantages in executive control to spatial reasoning. *Cognitive Development, 28,* 41–50.

Greenberg, G. (2014a). Emergence, self-organization, and developmental science. *Research in Human Development, 11,* 1–4.

Greenberg, G. (2014b). How new ideas in physics and biology influence developmental science. *Research in Human Development, 11,* 5–21.

Greene, J. (2003). From then neural 'is' to moral 'ought': What are the moral implications of neuroscientific moral psychology? *Nature Reviews: Neuroscience, 4,* 847–850.

Greene, J. D., Morelli, S. A., Lowenburg, K., Nystrom, L. E., & Cohen, J. D. (2008). Cognitive load selectively interferes with utilitarian moral judgment. *Cognition, 107,* 1144–1154.

Greene, J. D., Nystrom, L. E., Engell, A. D., Darley, J. M., & Cohen, J. D. (2004). The neural bases of cognitive conflict and control in moral judgment. *Neuron, 44,* 389–400.

Greene, J. D., Sommerville, R. B., Nystrom, L. E., Darley, J. M., & Cohen, J. D. (2001). An fMRI investigation of emotional engagement in moral judgment. *Science, 293,* 2105–2107.

Greene, J., & Haidt, J. (2002). How (and where) does moral judgment work? *Trends in Cognitive Sciences, 6*(12), 517–523.

Grice, H. P. (1975). Logic and conversation. In P. Cole & J. L. Morgan (eds), *Syntax and Semantics. Vol 3: Speech Acts.* London: Academic Press.

Griffiths, P. E., & Tabery, J. (2013). Developmental systems theory: What does it explain, and how does it explain it? In R. M. Lerner & J. B. Benson (eds), *Embodiment and Epigenesis: Theoretical and Methodological Issues in Understanding the Role of Biology within the Relational Developmental System.* Volume 44 of Advances in Child Development and Behavior, pp. 65–94.

Gross, L. (2009). Broken trust: Lessons from the vaccine-autism wars. *PLOS Biology, 7,* 1–7.

Gross, R. L., Drummond, J., Satlof-Bedrick, E., Waugh, W. E., Svetlova, M., & Brownell, C. A. (2015). Individual differences in toddlers' social understanding and prosocial behavior: Disposition or socialization? *Frontiers in Psychology, 6,* 1–11.

Guillaume, P. (1971). *Imitation in Children.* Chicago: The University of Chicago Press. (Original work published 1926; translated by Elaine P. Halperin.)

Habermas, J. (1990). *Moral Consciousness and Communicative Action.* Cambridge, MA: The MIT Press. (Original work published 1983.)

Hackman, D. A., Farah, M. J., & Meaney, M. J. (2010). Socioeconomic status and the brain: Mechanistic insights from human and animal research. *Nature Reviews Neuroscience, 11,* 651–659.

Haidt, J. (2001). The emotional dog and its rational tail: A social intuitionist approach to moral judgment. *Psychological Review, 108,* 814–834.

Haidt, J. (2007). The new synthesis in moral psychology. *Science, 316,* 998–1002.

Haidt, J. (2008a). The emotional dog and its rational tail: A social intuitionist approach to moral judgment. *Psychological Review, 108,* 814–834.

Haidt, J. (2008b). The new synthesis in moral psychology. *Science, 316,* 998–1002.

Haidt, J. (2008c). Morality. *Perspectives on Psychological Science, 3,* 65–72.

Haidt, J. (2013). Moral psychology for the twenty-first century. *Journal of Moral Education, 42,* 281–297.

Haidt, J., & Bjorklund, F. (2008). Social intuitionists answer six questions about moral psychology. In W. Sinnott-Armstrong (ed.), *Moral Psychology, Volume 2: The Cognitive Science of Morality: Intuition and Diversity.* Cambridge, MA: MIT Press.

Haidt, J., & Kesebir, S. (2010). Morality. In S. Fiske, D. Gilbert, & G. Lindzey (eds),

Handbook of Social Psychology, 5th edn (pp. 797–832). Hoboken, NJ: Wiley.

Haith, M. M. (1998). Who put the cog in infant cognition? Is rich interpretation too costly? *Infant Behavior and Development, 21*, 167–179.

Haith, M. M., & Benson, J. B. (1998). Infant cognition. In W. Damon (series ed.), D. Kuhn & R. Siegler (vol. eds), *Handbook of Child Psychology, Vol. 2: Cognition, Perception, and Language* (5th edn., pp. 199–254). New York: Wiley.

Hakuta, K., Bialystok, E., & Wiley, E. (2003). Critical evidence: A test of the critical-period hypothesis for second-language acquisition. *Psychological Science, 14*, 31–38.

Hala, S., & Russell, J. (2001). Executive control within strategic deception: A window on early cognitive development? *Journal of Experimental Child Psychology, 80*, 112–141.

Hala, S., Chandler, M. J., & Fritz, A. (1991). Fledgling theories of mind: Deception as a marker of 3-year-olds' understanding of false belief. *Child Development, 62*, 83–97.

Hale, C. M., & Tager-Flusberg, H. (2003). The influence of language on theory of mind: A training study. *Developmental Science, 6*, 346–359.

Halina, M., Rossano, F., & Tomasello, M. (2013). The ontogenetic ritualization of bonobo gestures. *Animal Cognition, 16*, 653–666.

Hallett, D., Chandler, M. J., & Krettenauer, T. (2002). Disentangling the course of epistemic development: Parsing knowledge by epistemic content. *New Ideas in Psychology, 20*, 285–307.

Hamilton, R. (2008). The Darwinian cage: Evolutionary Psychology as moral science. *Theory, Culture & Society, 25*, 105–125. doi: 10.1177/0263276407086793

Hamlin, J. K. (2013). Moral judgment and action in preverbal infants and toddlers: Evidence for an innate moral core. *Current Directions in Psychological Science, 22*, 186–193.

Hamlin, J. K. (2015). The case for social evaluation in preverbal infants: Gazing toward one's goal drives infants' preferences for helpers over hinders in the hill paradigm. *Frontiers in Psychology, 5*, article 1563, 1–9. doi: 10.3389/fpsyg.2014.01563.

Hamlin, J. K., Wynn, K., & Bloom, P. (2007). Social evaluation by preverbal infants. *Nature, 450*, 557–559.

Hamlin, J. K., Wynn, K., & Bloom, P. (2010). Three-month-olds show a negativity bias in their social evaluations. *Developmental Science, 13*, 923–929.

Hammond, S. I. (2014). Children's early helping in action: Piagetian developmental theory and early prosocial behavior. *Frontiers in Psychology, 5*, article 759.

Hammond, S. I., & Carpendale, J. I. M. (2015). Helping children help: The relation between maternal scaffolding and children's early help. *Social Development, 24*, 367–383.

Hammond, S. I., & Carpendale, J. I. M. (2015). Helping children help: The relation between maternal scaffolding and children's early help. *Social Development, 24*, 367–383.

Hammond, S. I., Müller, U., Carpendale, J. I. M., Bibok, M. B., & Liebermann-Finestone, D. P. (2012). The effects of parental scaffolding on preschoolers' executive function. *Developmental Psychology, 48*, 271–281.

Hankivsky, O. (2004). *Social Policy and the Ethic of Care*. Vancouver: UBC Press.

Happé, F. (1994). An advanced test of theory of mind: Understanding of story characters' thoughts and feelings by able autistic, mentally handicapped, and normal children and adults. *Journal of Autism and Developmental Disorders, 24*, 129–154.

Happé, F., Ronald, A., & Plomin, R. (2006). Time to give up on a single explanation for autism. *Nature Neuroscience, 9*, 1218–1220.

Harris, M., Barrett, M., Jones, D., & Brookes, S. (1988). Linguistic input and early word meaning. *Journal of Child Language, 15*, 77–94.

Harris, P. L. (1991). The work of the imagination. In A. Whiten (ed.), *Natural Theories of Mind* (pp. 283–304). Oxford: Blackwell.

Harris, P. L. (2000). *The Work of the Imagination.* Oxford: Blackwell.

Harris, P. L. (2005). Conversation, pretense, and theory of mind. In J. W. Astington & J. A. Baird (eds), *Why Language Matters for Theory of Mind* (pp. 70–83). New York: Oxford University Press.

Harris, P. L. (2006). Social cognition. In D. Kuhn & R. Sielgler (vol. eds), (W. Damon & R. M. Lerner, Editors-in-Chief), *Handbook of Child Psychology*, 6th edn, *Vol. Two: Cognition, Perception, and Language* (pp. 811–858). Hoboken, NJ: Wiley.

Harris, P. L. (1974). Perseverative search at a visibly empty place by young infants. *Journal of Experimental Child Psychology*, *18*, 535–542.

Hartshorne, H., & May, M. A. (1928–1930). *Studies in the Nature of Moral Character* (3 vols.). New York: Macmillan & Co.

Hauser, M. D. (2006). *Moral Minds: How Nature Designed our Universal Sense of Right and Wrong.* New York: HarperCollins.

Hay, D. (2009). The roots and branches of human altruism. *British Journal of Psychology*, *100*, 473–479.

Hayes, K. J., & Hayes, C. (1951). The intellectual development of a home-raised chimpanzee. *Proceedings of the American Philosophical Society*, *95*, 105.

Hayes, K. J., & Hayes, C. (1951). The intellectual development of a home-raised chimpanzee. *Proceedings of the American Philosophical Society*, *95*,105.

Hebb, D. O., Lambert, W. E., & Tucker, G. R. (1971). Language, thought and experience. *Modern Language Journal*, *55*, 212–222.

Heil, J. (1981). Does cognitive psychology rest on a mistake? *Mind*, *90*, 321–342.

Held, R., & Hein, A. (1963). Movement-produced stimulation in the development of visually guided behavior. *Journal of Comparative and Physiological Psychology*, *56*, 872–876.

Helles, A., Gillberg, I. C., Gillberg, C., & Billstedt, E. (2017). Asperger syndrome in males over two decades: Quality of life in relation to diagnostic stability and psychiatric comorbidity. *Autism*, *21*(4), 458–469.

Henrich, J., & Boyd, R. (2002). Culture and cognition: Why cultural evolution does not require replication of representations. *Culture and Cognition*, *2*, 87–112.

Herder, J. G. (1966). Essay on the origin of language. In J. H. Moran, & A. Gode (eds), *On the Origin of Language* (pp. 87–166). New York: Frederick Ungar Publishing, Co. (Original work published 1772.)

Hertz-Pannier, L., Chiron, C., Jambaqué, I., Renaux-Kieffer, V., Van de Moortele, P.-F., Delalande, O., Fohlen, M., Brunelle, F., & Le Bihan, D. (2002). Late plasticity for language in a child's non-dominant hemisphere: a pre- and post-surgery fMRI study. *Brain*, *125*, 361–372.

Higgins, A. (1995). Just community. In W. M. Kurtines & J. L. Gewirtz (eds), *Moral Development: An Introduction.* Boston, MA: Allyn & Bacon.

Hirsh-Pasek, K., Treiman, R., & Schneiderman, M. (1984) Brown & Hanlon revisited: Mothers' sensitivity to ungrammatical forms. *Journal of Child Language*, *11*, 81–89.

Ho, M. W. (2010). Development and evolution revisited. In K. E. Hood, C. T. Halpern, G. Greenberg, & R. M. Lerner (eds), *Handbook of Developmental Systems, Behavior and Genetics* (pp. 61–109). Malden, MA: Wiley Blackwell.

Hobson, P. (2002). *The Cradle of Thought: Explorations of the Origins of Thinking.* Macmillan: London. (ch. 3, pp. 61–94; ch. 9, pp. 239–274.)

Hobson, R. P. (1993). *Autism and the Development of Mind.* Hove: Erlbaum.

Hobson, R. P. (2007). Communicative depth: Soundings from developmental psychopathology. *Infant Behavior & Development*, *30*, 267–277.

Hobson, R. P., & Hobson, J. (2011). Joint attention or joint engagement? Insights from autism. In A. Seemann (ed.), *Joint Attention* (pp. 115–135). Cambridge, MA: The MIT Press.

Hobson, R. P., & Hobson, J. A. (2014). On empathy: A perspective from developmental psychopathology. In H. L. Maibom (ed.), *Empathy and Morality* (pp. 172–192). New York: Oxford University Press.

Hockett, C. F. (1966). The problem of universals in language. In J. H. Greenberg (ed.), *Universals of Language*, 2nd edn (pp. 1–29). Cambridge, MA: MIT Press.

Hoff-Ginsberg, E. (1998). The relation of birth order and socioeconomic status to children's language experience and language development. *Applied Psycholinguistics*, *19*(4), 603–629.

Hoffman, M. (2000). *Empathy and Moral Development: Implications for Caring and Justice*. Cambridge: Cambridge University Press.

Hoffman, M. L. (2008). Empathy and prosocial behavior. In M. Lewis, J. M. Haviland-Jones, & L. Feldman-Barrett (eds), *Handbook of emotions*, (3rd ed., pp. 440–455). New York: Guilford Press.

Hoffman, M.L. (2000). *Empathy and Moral Development: Implications for Caring and Justice*. New York: Cambridge University Press.

Holiday, A. (1988) *Moral Powers: Normative Necessity in Language and History*. New York: Routledge.

Hollich, G. J., Hirsh-Pasek, K., Golinkoff, R. M., Brand, R. J., Brown, E., Chung, H. L., ... & Bloom, L. (2000). Breaking the language barrier: An emergentist coalition model for the origins of word learning. *Monographs of the Society for Research in Child Development*, i–135.

Holmes, H. A., Black, C., & Miller, S. A. (1996). A cross-task comparison of false-belief understanding in a Head Start population. *Journal of Experimental Child Psychology*, *63*, 263–285.

Hörmann, H. (1986). *Meaning and Context*. New York: Plenum. (Original work published 1981.)

Horst, J. S., & Twomey, K. E. (2013). It's taking shape: Shared object features influence novel noun generalizations. *Infant and Child Development*, *22*, 24–43.

Houghton, K., Schuchard, J., Lewis, C., & Thompson, C. K. (2013). Promoting child-initiated social-communication in children with autism: Son-Rise program intervention effects. *Journal of Communication Disorders*, *48*(5–6), 495–506.

Houston-Price, C., Plunkett, K., and Harris, P. (2005). 'Word-learning wizardry' at 1;6. *Journal of Child Language*, 32(1): 175–189.

Howe, N., Rinaldi, C., Jennings, M., & Petrakos, H. (2002). 'No! The lambs can stay out because they got cosies': Constructive and destructive sibling conflict, pretend play, and social understanding. *Child Development*, *73*, 1460–1473.

Hughes, C. (2011). Changes and challenges in 20 years of research into the development of executive functions. *Infant and Child Development*, *20*, 251–271.

Hughes, C., & Ensor, R. (2005). Executive function and theory of mind in 2 year olds: A family affair? *Developmental Neuropsychology*, *28*, 645–668.

Hughes, C., & Ensor, R. (2009). How do families help or hinder the emergence of early executive function? *New Directions in Child and Adolescent Development*, *123*, 35–60. doi:10.1002/cd.234

Hughes, C., & Graham, A. (2002). Measuring executive functions in childhood: Problems and solutions? *Child and Adolescent Mental Health*, *7*, 131–142.

Hughes, C., Deater-Deckard, K., & Cutting, A. L. (1999). 'Speak roughly to your little boy'? Sex differences in the relations between parenting and preschoolers' understanding of mind. *Social Development*, *8*, 143–160.

Hughes, C., Ensor, R., Wilson, A., & Graham, A. (2010). Tracking executive function across the transition to school: A latent variable approach. *Developmental Neuropsychology*, *35*, 20–36.

Hughes, C., Jaffee, S. R., Happé, F., Taylor, A., Caspi, A., & Moffitt, T. E. (2005). Origins of individual differences in theory of mind: From nature to nurture? *Child Development*, *76*, 356–370.

Huizinga, M., Dolan, C. V., & van der Molen, M. W. (2006). Age-related change in executive function: Developmental trends and a latent variable analysis, *Neuropsychologia*, *44*, 2017–2036.

Hume, D. (1751). *An Enquiry Concerning the Principles of Morals*. London: A. Millar.

Hurley, S. (2008). The shared circuits model (SCM): How control, mirroring, and simulation can enable imitation, deliberation, and mindreading. *Behavioral and Brain Sciences*, *31*, 1–58.

Hutto, D. D., & Myin, E. (2013). *Radicalizing Enactivism: Basic Minds Without Content*. Cambridge, MA: The MIT Press.

Inhelder, B., & Piaget, J. (1969). The early growth of logic in the child. New York: W. W. Norton & Company. (Original work published in 1959.)

Jablonka, E., & Lamb, M. J. (2005). *Evolution in Four Dimensions: Genetic, Epigenetics, Behavioral, and Symbolic Variation in the History of Life*. Cambridge, MA: MIT Press.

Jablonka, E., & Lamb, M. J. (2007). Précis of *evolution in four dimensions. Behavioral and Brain Sciences*, *30*, 353–392.

Jacques, S., Zelazo, P. D., Kirkham, N. Z., & Semcesen, T. K. (1999). Rule selection versus rule execution in preschoolers: An error-detection approach. *Developmental Psychology*, *35*, 770–780.

James, W. (1950). *The Principles of Psychology*, Vol. 1. New York: Dover Publications, Inc. (Original work published 1890.)

Janet, P. (1928). *L'évolution de la mémoire et de la notion du temps*. Paris: Chachine.

Jastrow, J. (1900). *Fact and Fable in Psychology*. Boston, MA: Houghton-Mifflin.

Jenkins, J. M., & Astington, J. W. (1996). Cognitive factors and family structure associated with theory of mind development in young children. *Developmental Psychology*, *32*, 70–78.

Jenkins, J. M., Turrell, S. L., Kogushi, Y., Lollis, S., & Ross, H. S. (2003). A longitudinal investigation of the dynamics of mental state talk in families. *Child Development*, *74*, 905–920.

Johansson, E. (2008). Empathy or intersubjectivity? Understanding the origins of morality in young children. *Studies in the Philosophy of Education*, *27*, 33–47.

Johnson, C. N. (1988). Theory of mind and the structure of conscious experience. In J. W. Astington, P. L. Harris & D. R. Olson (eds), *Developing Theories of Mind* (pp. 47–63). New York: Cambridge University Press.

Johnson, C. N., & Maratsos, M. P. (1977). Early comprehension of mental verbs: Think and know. *Child Development*, *48*, 1743–1747.

Johnson, J. S., & Newport, E. L. (1989). Critical period effects in second language learning: The influence of maturational state on the acquisition of English as a second language. *Cognitive Psychology*, *21*, 60–99.

Johnson, M. H., Jones, E. J. H., & Gliga, T. (2015). Brain adaptation and alternative developmental trajectories. *Development and Psychopathology*, *27*, 425–442.

Jones, C. P. (2007). *Executive and social-cognitive functioning in reactive- and proactive-aggressive young boys*. Unpublished Doctoral Dissertation, Simon Fraser University.

Jones, S. (2008). Nature and nurture in the development of social smiling. *Philosophical Psychology*, *21*, 349–357.

Jones, S. S. (1996). Imitation or exploration? Young infants' matching of adults' oral gestures. *Child Development*, *67*, 1952–1969.

Jones, S. S. (2006). Exploration or imitation? The effect of music on 4-week-old infants' tongue protrusions. *Infant Behavior & Development*, *29*, 126–130.

Jones, S. S. (2007). Imitation in infancy: The development of mimicry. *Psychological Science*, *18*, 593–599.

Jones, S. S. (2009). The development of imitation in infancy. *Philosophical Transactions of the Royal Society, B, 364*, 2325–2335.

Jones, W., & Klin, A. (2013). Attention to eyes is present but in decline in 2–6-month-old infants later diagnosed with autism. *Nature*, *504*, 427–431.

Jopling, D. (1993). Cognitive science, other minds, and the philosophy of dialogue. In U. Neisser (ed.), *The Perceived Self* (pp. 290–309). Cambridge, MA: MIT Press.

Judge, B. (1985). *Thinking About Things: A Philosophical Study of Representation*. Edinburgh: Scottish Academic Press.

Kagan, J. (2006). Biology's useful contribution: A comment. *Human Development*, *49*, 310–314.

Kahane, G., & Shackel, N. (2010). Methodological issues in the neuroscience of moral judgement. *Mind & Language*, *25*, 561–582.

Kahn, P. H. (2006). Nature and moral development. In M. Killen & J. Smetana (eds), *Handbook of Moral Development* (pp. 461–480). Mahwah, NJ: Erlbaum.

Kail, R., & Bisanz, J. (1992). The information-processing perspective on cognitive development in childhood and adolescence. In R. J. Sternberg & C. A. Berg (eds), *Intellectual Development* (pp. 229–260). New York: Cambridge University Press.

Kaland, N., Callesen, K., Møller-Nielsen, A., Mortensen, E. L., & Smith, L. (2008). Performance of children and adolescents with Asperger syndrome or high-functioning autism on advanced theory of mind tasks. *Journal of Autism and Developmental Disorders*, *38*, 1112–1123.

Kaminski, J., Call, J., & Fischer, J. (2004). Word learning in a domestic dog: Evidence for 'fast mapping'. *Science*, *304*, 1682–1683.

Kaminski, J., Call, J., & Fischer, J. (2004). Word learning in a domestic dog: Evidence for 'fast mapping'. *Science*, *304*, 1682–1683.

Kaminski, J., Riedel, J., Call, J., & Tomasello, M. (2005). Domestic goats, *Capra hircus*, follow gaze direction and use social cues in an object choice task. *Animal Behaviour*, *69*, 11–18.

Kanner, L. (1943). Autistic disturbances of affective contact. *Nervous Child*, *2*, 217–250.

Kapa, L. L., & Colombo, J. (2013). Attentional control in early and later bilingual children. *Cognitive Development*, *28*, 233–246.

Karmiloff-Smith, A. (2009). Nativism versus neuroconstructivism: Rethinking the study of developmental disorders. *Developmental Psychology*, *45*, 56–63.

Karmiloff-Smith, A. (2015). An alternative to domain-general or domain-specific frameworks for theorizing about human evolution and ontogenesis. *AIMS Neuroscience*, *2*, 91–104.

Kartner, J., Schuhmacher, N., & Collard, J. (2014). Socio-cognitive influences on the domain-specificity of prosocial behaviour in the second year. *Infant Behavior and Development*, *37*, 665–675.

Kaye, K. (1982). *The Mental and Social Life of Babies*. Hemel Hempstead: Harvester Wheatsheaf.

Kegl, J. (2002). Language emergence in a language-ready brain. In G. Morgan and B. Woll (eds), *Directions in Sign Language Acquisition* (pp. 207–254). Amsterdam: John Benjamins.

Kellogg, W. N., & Kellogg, L. A. (1933). *The Ape and the Child: A Comparative Study of Environmental Influence Upon Early Behavior*. New York: Hafner.

Kettner, V., & Carpendale, J. I. M. (2013). Developing gestures for no and yes: Head shaking and nodding in infancy. *Gesture*, *13*, 193–209.

Kidd, C., Palmeri, H., & Aslin, R. N. (2013). Rational snacking: Young children's decision-making on the marshmallow task is moderated by beliefs about environmental reliability. *Cognition*, *126*, 109–114.

Killen, M., & Smetana, J. G. (eds) (2014). *Handbook of Moral Development*, 2nd edn. New York: Psychology Press.

Kim, S., & Kochanska, G. (2012). Child temperament moderates effects of parent–child mutuality on self-regulation: A relationship-based path for emotionally negative infants. *Child Development, 83,* 1275–1289.

Kinsbourne, M., & Jordan, J. S. (2009). Embodied anticipation: A neurodevelopmental interpretation. *Discourse Processes, 46,* 103–126.

Kipling, R. (1962). *Just So Stories.* London: Macmillan. (Original work published 1902.)

Kirk, E., Howlett, N., Pine, K. J., & Fletcher, B. (2013). To sign or not to sign? The impact of encouraging infants to gesture on infant language and maternal mind-mindedness. *Child Development, 84,* 574–590.

Klahr, D. (1982). Non-monotone assessment of monotone development: An information processing analysis. In S. Strauss & R. Stavy (eds), *U-shaped Behavioral Growth* (pp. 63–86). New York: Academic.

Klahr, D. (1995) Computational models of cognitive change: The state of the art. In T. Simon & G. Halford (eds), *Developing Cognitive Competence: New Approaches to Process Modeling* (pp. 355–375). Hillsdale, NJ: Erlbaum.

Klin, A., Jones, W., Schultz, R., & Volkmar, F. (2003). The enactive mind, or from actions to cognition: Lessons from autism. *Philosophical Transactions of the Royal Society, London B, 358,* 345–360.

Klin, A., Lin, D. J., Gorrindo, P., Ramsay, G., & Jones, W. (2009). Two-year-olds with autism orient to non-social contingencies rather than biological motion. *Nature, 459,* 257–261.

Kloo, D., & Perner, J. (2003). Training transfer between card sorting and false belief understanding: Helping children apply conflicting descriptions. *Child Development, 74,* 1823–1839.

Kluckhohn, C. (1949). *Mirror For Man: The Relation of Anthropology to Modern Life.* New York: McGraw-Hill.

Knecht, S., Dräger, B., Deppe, M., Bobe, L., Lohmann, H., Flöel, A., Ringelstein, E.-B., & Henningsen, H. (2000). Handedness and hemispheric language dominance in healthy humans. *Brain, 123,* 2512–2518.

Kobayashi, H., & Kohshima, S. (1997). Unique morphology of the human eye. *Nature, 387,* 767–768.

Kobayashi, H., & Kohshima, S. (2001). Unique morphology of the human eye and its adaptive meaning: Comparative studies of external morphology of the primate eye. *Journal of Human Evolution, 40,* 419–435.

Kohlberg, L. (1958). *The Development of Modes of Moral Thinking and Choice in the years 10 to 16.* Unpublished Doctoral Dissertation, University of Chicago.

Kohlberg, L. (1966). Moral education in the schools: A developmental view. *The School Review, 74*(1), 1–30.

Kohlberg, L. (1969). Stage and sequence: The cognitive-developmental approach to socialization. In D. A. Goslin (ed.), *Handbook of Socialization Theory and Research* (pp. 347–480). Chicago: Rand McNally & Company.

Kohlberg, L. (1981). *Essays in Moral Development: The Philosophy of Moral Development,* vol. 1. San Francisco, CA: Harper & Row.

Kohlberg, L. (1984). *Essays on Moral Development, Vol. 2: The Psychology of Moral Development.* San Francisco, CA: Harper & Row.

Kohlberg, L., & Candee, D. (1984). On the relationship of moral judgment to moral action. In W. M. Kurtines & J. L. Gewirtz (eds), *Morality, Moral Behavior, and Moral Development* (pp. 52–73). New York: Wiley.

Kohlberg, L., & Candee, D. (1984). On the relationship of moral judgment to moral action. In W. M. Kurtines & J. L. Gewirtz (eds), *Morality, Moral Behavior, and Moral Development* (pp. 52–73). New York: John Wiley & Sons.

Kohlberg, L., & Hersh, R. H. (1977). Moral development: A review of the theory. *Theory into Practice, 16,* 53–59.

Kohlberg, L., Levine, C., & Hewer, A. (1983). *Moral Stages: A Current Formulation and a Response to Critics.* Basel: Krager.

Kopp, C. (1982). Antecedents of self-regulation: A developmental perspective. *Developmental Psychology, 18*, 199–214.

Korner, A. F., & Thoman, E. B. (1970). Visual alertness in neonates as evoked by maternal care. *Journal of Experimental Child Psychology, 10*(1), 67–78.

Korner, A. F., & Thoman, E. B. (1970). Visual alertness in neonates as evoked by maternal care. *Journal of Experimental Child Psychology, 10*, 67–78.

Kovács, Á. M., Téglás, E, & Endress, A. D. (2010). The social sense: Susceptibility to others' beliefs in human infants and adults. *Science, 330*, 1830–1834.

Kray, J., & Ferdinand, N. K. (2013). How to improve cognitive control in development during childhood: Potentials and limits of cognitive interventions. *Child Development Perspectives, 7*, 121–125.

Krebs, D. L. (2011). *The Origins of Morality: An Evolutionary Account.* New York: Oxford University Press.

Krebs, D., & Van Hesteren, F. (1994). The development of altruism: Toward an integrated model. *Developmental Review, 14*, 103–158.

Krebs, D., Denton, K., Vermeulen, S., Carpendale, J., & Bush, J. (1991). The structural flexibility of moral judgment. *Journal of Personality and Social Psychology, 61*, 1012–1023.

Kreppner, J. M., Rutter, M., Beckett, C., Castle, J., Colvert, E., Grothues, C., Hawkins, A., O'Connor, T. G., Stevens, S. and Sonuga-Barke, E. J. S. (2007). Normality and impairment following profound early institutional deprivation: a longitudinal examination through childhood. *Developmental Psychology, 43*(4), 931–946.

Krettenauer, T., & Hertz, S. (2015). What develops in moral identities? A critical review. *Human Development, 58*, 137–153.

Kropotkin, P. (1989). *Mutual Aid: A Factor in Evolution.* Montreal: Black Rose Books. (Original work published 1902.)

Kuebli, J., Butler, S., & Fivush, R. (1995). Mother–child talk about past emotions: Relations of maternal language and child gender over time. *Cognition and Emotion, 9*, 265–283.

Kuhl, P. K., & Miller, J. D. (1975). Speech perception by the Chinchilla: Voiced-voiceless distinction in alveolar plosive consonants, *Science, 190*(4209), 69–72.

Kuhn, T. (1962). *The Structure of Scientific Revolutions.* Chicago: University of Chicago Press.

Kuntsi, J., Stevenson, J., Osterlaan, J., & Sonuga-Barke, E. J. S. (2001). Test–retest reliability of a new delay aversion task and executive function measures. *British Journal of Developmental Psychology, 19*, 339–348.

Kuo, Z. Y. (1930). The genesis of the cat's response to the rat. *Journal of Comparative Psychology, 11*, 30–35.

Kuo, Z. Y. (1938). Further study of the behavior of the cat towards the rat. *Journal of Comparative Psychology, 25*, 1–8.

Kuo, Z.-Y. (1967). Emergence, self-organization, and developmental science. *The Dynamics of behavior development.* New York: Random House.

Laland, K. N., & Brown, G. R. (2011). *Sense and Nonsense: Evolutionary Perspectives on Human Development* (2nd edn). New York: Oxford University Press.

Laland, K. N., Odling-Smee, F. J., & Feldman, M. W. (1999). Evolutionary consequences of niche construction and their implications for ecology. *Proceedings of the National Academy of Sciences, 96*, 10242–10247.

Lalonde, C. E. & Chandler, M. J. (1995). False belief understanding goes to school: On the social-emotional consequences of coming early or late to a first theory of mind. *Cognition and Emotion, 9*, 167–185.

Lalonde, C. E., & Chandler, M. J. (2002). Children's understanding of interpretation. *New Ideas in Psychology, 20*, 163–198.

Lambrick, D., Stoner, L., Grigg, R., & Faulkner, J. (2016). Effects of continuous and intermittent exercise on executive function in children aged 8–10 years. *Psychophysiology*, *53*(9), 1335–1342.

Landau, B., Smith, L. B., & Jones, S. S. (1988). The importance of shape in early lexical learning. *Cognitive Development*, *3*, 299–321.

Landry, S. H., Miller-Loncar, C. L., Smith, K. E., & Swank, P. R. (2002). The early parenting in children's development of executive processes. *Developmental Neuropsychology*, *21*, 15–41.

Lane, J. D., Wellman, H. M., Olson, S. L., LaBounty, J., & Kerr, D. C. R. (2010). Theory of mind and emotion understanding predict moral development in early childhood. *British Journal of Developmental Psychology*, *28*, 871–889.

Lapsley, D. K. (1996). *Moral Psychology*. Boulder, CO: Westview Press.

Lawrence, J. A. (2017). Developing persons, clashing cultures. To appear in A. S. Dick & U. Müller (eds), *Advancing Developmental Science: Philosophy, Theory, and Method*. New York: Psychology Press.

Leavens, D. A. (2011). Joint attention: Twelve myths. In A. Seemann (ed.), *Joint Attention: New Developments in Psychology, Philosophy of Mind, and Social Neuroscience* (pp. 43–72). Cambridge, MA: MIT Press.

Leavens, D. A., Sansone, J., Burfield, A., Lightfoot, S., O'Hara, S., & Todd, B. K. (2014). Putting the "joy" in joint attention: Affective-gestural synchrony by parents who point for their babies. *Frontiers in Psychology*, *5*, 1–7.

Lecce, S., & Hughes, C. (2010). 'The Italian job?': Comparing theory of mind performance in British and Italian children. *British Journal of Developmental Psychology*, *28*, 747–766.

Lee, K., Bull, R., & Ho, R. M. H. (2013). Developmental changes in executive functioning. *Child Development*, *84*, 1933–1953.

Lehrman, D. S. (2001). A critique of Konrad Lorenz's theory of instinctive behavior. In S. Oyama, P. E. Griffiths, & R. D. Gray (eds), *Cycles of Contingency: Developmental Systems and Evolution* (pp. 25–39). Cambridge, MA: The MIT Press. (Original work published 1953.)

Lehto, J. E., Juujarvi, P., Kooistra, L., & Pulkkinen, L. (2003). Dimensions of executive functioning: Evidence from children. *British Journal of Developmental Psychology*, *21*, 59–80.

Lenneberg, E. H. (1967). *Biological Foundations of Language*. New York: Wiley.

Leontiev, A. N. (1981). The problem of activity in psychology. In J. V. Wertsch (ed.), *The Concept of Activity in Soviet Psychology* (pp. 37–71). Armonk, NY: Sharpe.

Lerner, R. M., Agans, J. P., DeSouza, L. M., & Hershberg, R. M. (2014). Developmental science in 2025: A predictive review. *Research in Human Development*, *11*, 255–272.

Leslie, A. M. (1987). Pretense and representation: The origins of 'theory of mind'. *Psychological Review*, *94*, 412–426.

Leslie, A. M. (2005). Developmental parallels in understanding minds and bodies. *Trends in Cognitive Sciences*, *9*, 459–462.

Leslie, A. M., Friedman, O., & German, T. P. (2004). Core mechanisms in 'theory of mind'. *Trends in Cognitive Sciences*, *8*, 528–533.

Leudar, I., & Costall, A. (2004). On the persistence of the 'problem of other minds' in psychology: Chomsky, Grice and theory of mind. *Theory & Psychology*, *14*, 601–621.

Levinson, S. C. (1983). *Pragmatics*. Cambridge: Cambridge University Press.

Levinson, S. C. (1995). Interactional biases in human thinking. In E. N. Goody (ed.), *Social Intelligence and Interaction* (pp. 221–260). Cambridge: Cambridge University Press.

Lewis, C. (1979). *Infancy in north-west Ecuador*. M. A. thesis, University of Nottingham.

Lewis, C., & Gregory, S. (1987). Parents' talk to their infants: The importance of context. *First Language, 7*(21), 201–216.

Lewis, C., & Mitchell, P. (eds) (1994). *Children's Early Understanding of Mind: Origins and Development*. Hove: Erlbaum.

Lewis, C., Freeman, N. H., Kyriakidou, C., Maridaki-Kassotaki, K., & Berridge, D. M. (1996). Social influences on false belief access: Specific sibling influences or general apprenticeship? *Child Development, 67,* 2930–2947.

Lewis, C., Freeman, N., Hagestadt, C., & Douglas, H. (1994). Narrative access and production in preschoolers' false belief reasoning. *Cognitive Development, 9*(4), 397–424.

Lewis, C., Huang, Z. & Rooksby, M. (2007). Chinese preschoolers' false belief understanding: Is social knowledge underpinned by parental styles, social interactions or executive functions? *Psychologia, 49,* 252–266.

Lewis, C., Huang, Z. & Rooksby, M. (2007). Chinese preschoolers' false belief understanding: Is social knowledge underpinned by parental styles, social interactions or executive functions? *Psychologia, 49,* 252–266.

Lewis, C., Liu J., & Shimmon, K. (in preparation). Using random-effects item response theory models to grasp executive function skills in pre-schoolers. Manuscript in preparation.

Lewkowicz, D. J. (2011). The biological implausibility of the nature–nurture dichotomy and what it means for the study of infancy. *Infancy, 16,* 331–367.

Lewontin, R. C. (2001). Gene, organism and environment. In S. Oyama, P. E. Griffiths, & R. D. Gray (eds), *Cycles of Contingency: Developmental Systems and Evolution* (pp. 55–66). Cambridge, MA: The MIT Press. (Original work published 1983.)

Licata, M., Paulus, M., Thoermer, C., Kirsten, S., Woodward, A. L., & Sodian, B. (2014). Mother–infant interaction quality and infants' ability to encode action as goal-directed. *Social Development, 23,* 340–356.

Lickliter, R. (2008). Representing development: Models, meaning, and the challenge of complexity. *Behavioral and Brain Sciences, 31,* 342–343.

Lickliter, R., & Honeycutt, H. (2009). Rethinking epigenesis and evolution in light of developmental science. In M. Blumberg, J. Freeman & S. Robinson (eds), *Oxford Handbook of Developmental Behavioral Neuroscience* (pp. 30–50). New York: Oxford University Press.

Lickliter, R., & Honeycutt, H. (2015). Biology, development, and human systems. In W. F. Overton & P. C. M. Molenaar (vol. eds), *Vol. 1: Theory and Method*, R. Lerner (editor-in-chief), 7th edition of the *Handbook of Child Psychology and Developmental Science*. Oxford: Wiley Blackwell.

Lickona, T. (1976). Research on Piaget's theory of moral development. In T. Lickona (ed.), *Moral Development and Behavior: Theory, Research, and Social Issues* (pp. 219–240). New York: Holt, Rinehart & Winston.

Liebal, K., Behne, T., Carpenter, M., & Tomasello, M. (2009). Infants use shared experience to interpret pointing gestures. *Developmental Science, 12*(2): 264–271.

Lieven, E., & Stoll, S. (2013). Early communicative development in two cultures: A comparison of the communicative environments of children from two cultures. *Human Development, 56,* 178–206.

Lillard, A. (1998). Ethnopsychologies: Cultural variations in theories of mind. *Psychological Bulletin, 123,* 3–32.

Lillard, A. S. (1993a). Pretend play skills and the child's theory of mind. *Child Development, 64,* 348–371.

Lipina, S. J., Segretin, S., Hermida, J., Prats, L., Fracchia, C., Camelo, J. L., & Colombo, J. (2013). Linking childhood poverty and cognition: Environmental mediators of non-verbal executive control in an Argentine sample. *Developmental Science, 16,* 697–707.

Liszkowski, U. (2005). Human twelve-month-olds point cooperatively to share interest and helpfully provide information for a communicative partner. *Gesture, 5*, 135–154.

Liszkowski, U., & Tomasello, M. (2011). Individual differences in social, cognitive, and morphological aspects of infant pointing. *Cognitive Development, 26*, 16–29.

Liszkowski, U., Brown, P., Callaghan, T., Kakada, A., & de Vos, C. (2012). A prelinguistic gestural universal of human communication. *Cognitive Science*, 1–16.

Liszkowski, U., Carpenter, M., Striano, T., & Tomasello, M. (2006). Twelve- and 18-month-olds point to provide information for others. *Journal of Cognition and Development, 7*, 173–187.

Llewellyn, J. (2016). A relational approach to justice: Implications for the law. Invited talk, President's Dream Colloquium, Simon Fraser University, Burnaby, BC Canada, 10 November.

Lock, A. (1978). The emergence of language. In A. Lock (ed.), *Action, Gesture and Symbol* (pp. 3–18). New York: Academic.

Lock, A., Young, A., Service, V., & Chandler, P. (1990). Some observations on the origins of the pointing gesture. In V. Volterra & C. J. Erting (eds), *From Gesture to Language in Hearing and Deaf Children* (pp. 42–55). New York: Springer Verlag.

Logothetis, N. (2008). What we can and what we cannot do with fMRI. *Nature, 453*, 869–878.

Lourenço, O. (2014). Domain theory: A critical review. *New Ideas in Psychology, 32*, 1–17.

Lourenço, O., & Machado, A. (1996). In defense of Piaget's theory: A reply to 10 common criticisms. *Psychological Review, 103*, 143–164.

Lucas, A. J., Lewis, C., Pala, F. C., Wong, K., & Berridge, D. (2013). Social-cognitive processes in preschoolers' selective trust: Three cultures compared. *Developmental Psychology, 49*(3), 579–590. 10.1037/a0029864

Luria, A. R. (1961). *The Role of Speech in the Regulation of Normal and Abnormal Behavior*. Oxford: Pergamon.

Luria, A. R. (1981). *Language and Cognition*. Chichester: Wiley.

Machiavelli, N. (1950). *The Prince*. New York: Random House.

Mackey, A. P., Raizada, R. D. S., & Bunge, S. A. (2013). Environmental influences on prefrontal development. In D. T. Stuss & R. T. Knight (eds), *Principles of Frontal Lobe Function*, 2nd edn (pp. 145–163). New York: Oxford University Press.

Macmillan, M. (2008). Phineas Gage: Unravelling the myth. *The Psychologist, 21*: 828–839.

Macnamara, J. (1972). Cognitive basis of language learning in infants. *Psychological Review, 79*, 1–13.

MacWhinney, B. (2015). Language development. In L. Liben & U. Müller (vol. eds), *Vol. 2: Cognitive Processes*, R. Lerner (Editor-in-Chief), 7th edition of the *Handbook of Child Psychology and Developmental Science* (pp. 296–338). New York: Wiley Blackwell.

Magrath, R. D., Haff, T. M., Fallow, P. M., & Radford, A. N. (2015). Eavesdropping on heterospecific alarm calls: From mechanisms to consequences. *Biological Reviews, 90*(2), 560–586.

Maher B. (2008). Personal genomes: the case of the missing heritability. *Nature, 456*(7218), 18–21.

Maibom, H. L. (2010). What experimental evidence shows us about the role of emotions in moral judgement. *Philosophy Compass, 5*(11), 999–1012.

Maibom, H. L. (2014). Introduction: (Almost) everything you ever wanted to know about empathy. In H. L. Maibom (ed.) *Empathy and Morality* (pp. 1–40). New York: Oxford University Press.

Malcolm, N. (1991). The relation of language to instinctive behaviour. In J. Hyman (ed.), *Investigating Psychology: Sciences of the Mind after Wittgenstein* (pp. 27–47). New York: Routledge.

Mameli, M., & Bateson, P. (2006). Innateness and the sciences. *Biology and Philosophy, 21*(2), 155–188.

Mameli, M., & Bateson, P. (2011). An evaluation of the concept of innateness. *Philosophical Transactions of the Royal Society B*, *366*, 436–443.

Mandy, W., Charman, T., Puura, K., & Skuse, D. (2014). Investigating the cross-cultural validity of DSM-5 autism spectrum disorder: Evidence from Finnish and UK samples. *Autism*, *18*, 45–54.

Manfra, L., Tyler, S. L., & Winsler, A. (2016). Speech monitoring and repairs in preschool children's social and private speech. *Early Childhood Research Quarterly*, *37*, 94–105.

Manuck, S. B., & McCaffery, J. M. (2014). Gene–environment interaction. *Annual Review of Psychology*, *65*, 41–70.

Mar, R. A. (2011). The neural bases of social cognition and story comprehension. *Annual Review Psychology*, *62*, 103–134.

Marcus, G. (1993). Negative evidence in language acquisition. *Cognition*, *46*, 53–85.

Mareschal, D., Johnson, M. H., Sirois, S., Spratling, M. W., Thomas, M. S. C., & Westermann, G. (2007). *Neuroconstructivism: How the Brain Constructs Cognition* (vol. 1). New York: Oxford University Press.

Margolis, E., & Laurence, S. (2013). In defense of nativism. *Philosophical Studies*, *165*, 693–718.

Marian, V., Spivey, M., & Hirsch, J. (2003). Shared and separate systems in bilingual language processing: Converging evidence from eyetracking and brain imaging. *Brain and Language*, *86*, 70–82.

Markman, E. M. (1990). Constraints children place on word meanings. *Cognitive Science*, *14*, 57–77.

Markman, E. M., & Wachtel, G. F. (1988). Children's use of mutual exclusivity to constrain the meanings of words. *Cognitive Psychology*, *20*, 121–157.

Markson, L., & Bloom, P. (1997). Evidence against a dedicated system for word learning in children. *Nature*, *385*, 813–15.

Marshall, P. J. (2009). Relating psychology and neuroscience: Taking up the challenges. *Perspectives on Psychological Science*, *4*, 113–125.

Marshall, P. J. (2009). Relating psychology and neuroscience: Taking up the challenges. *Perspectives on Psychological Science*, *4*, 113–125.

Marshall, P. J. (2014). Beyond different levels: Embodiment and the developmental system. *Frontiers in Psychology*, *5*, 929.

Marshall, P. J. (2015). Neuroscience, embodiment, and development. In W. F. Overton & P. C. M. Molenaar (vol. eds), *Vol. 1: Theory and Method*, R. Lerner (editor-in-chief), 7th edition of the *Handbook of Child Psychology and Developmental Science* (pp. 244–283). Wiley Blackwell.

Marshall, P. J. (2016). Embodiment and human development. *Child Development Perspectives*, *10*, 245–250.

Masataka, N. (2003). From index-finger extension to index-finger pointing: Ontogenesis of pointing in preverbal infants. In S. Kita (ed.), *Pointing: Where Language, Culture, and Cognition Meet* (pp. 69–84). Mahwah, NJ: Erlbaum.

Mascolo, M. F., & Fischer, K. W. (2015). Dynamic development of thinking, feeling, and acting. In W. F. Overton & P. C. M. Molenaar (vol. eds), *Vol. 1: Theory and Method*, R. Lerner (editor-in-chief), 7th edition of the *Handbook of Child Psychology and Developmental Science*, (pp. 113–161). Wiley Blackwell.

Matte-Gagné, C., & Bernier, A. (2011). Prospective relations between maternal autonomy support and child executive functioning: Investigating the mediating role of child language ability. *Journal of Experimental Child Psychology*, *110*, 611–625.

Matthews, D., Behen, T., Lieven, E., & Tomasello, M. (2012). Origins of the human pointing gesture: A training study. *Developmental Science*, *15*, 817–829.

Mattock, K., & Burnham, D. (2006). Chinese and English infants' tone perception: Evidence for perceptual reorganization. *Infancy*, *10*, 241–265.

Maturana, H., & Varela, F. (1992). *The Tree of Knowledge: The Biological Roots of Human Understanding*. Boston, MA: Shambhala.

Maurer, D., & Werker, J. F. (2014). Perceptual narrowing during infancy: A comparison of language and faces. *Developmental Psychobiology*, *56*, 154–178.

Mayer, A., & Träuble, B. E. (2013). Synchrony in the onset of mental state understanding across cultures? A study among children in Samoa. *International Journal of Behavioral Development*, *37*, 21–28.

McAlister, A. R., & Peterson, C. C. (2013). Siblings, theory of mind, and executive functioning in children aged 3–6 years: New longitudinal evidence. *Child Development*, *84*, 1442–1458.

McAuley, T., & White, D. A. (2011). A latent variables examination of processing speed, response inhibition, and working memory during typical development. *Journal of Experimental Child Psychology*, *108*, 453–468.

McCabe, D. P., & Castel, A. D. (2008). Seeing is believing: The effect of brain images on judgments of scientific reasoning. *Cognition*, *107*, 343–352.

McCartney, K. (1984). Effect of quality of day care environment on children's language development. *Developmental Psychology*, *20*(2), 244.

McDonough, R. (1989). Towards a non-mechanistic theory of meaning. *Mind*, *98*, 1–21.

McGhee, P. E. (1979). *Humor: Its Origin and Development*. San Francisco, CA: W. H. Freeman and Company.

Mcquaid, N., Bibok, M., & Carpendale, J. I. M. (2009). Relationship between maternal contingent responsiveness and infant social expectation. *Infancy*, *14*, 390–401.

Mead, G. H. (1922). A behavioristic account of the significant symbol. *Journal of Philosophy*, *19*, 157–163.

Mead, G. H. (1934). *Mind, Self and Society: From the Standpoint of a Social Behaviorist*. Chicago: University of Chicago Press. http://www.brocku.ca/MeadProject/Mead/pubs2/mindself/Mead_1934_46.html

Meaney, M. J. (2010). Epigenetics and the biological definition of gene x environment interactions. *Child Development*, *81*, 41–79.

Meins, E. (1999). Sensitivity, security and internal working models: Bridging the transmission gap. *Attachment & Human Development*, *1*, 325–342.

Meins, E., Fernyhough, C., Arnott, B., Leekam, S. R., & de Rosnay, M. (2013). Mind-mindedness and theory of mind: Mediating roles of language and perspectival play. *Child Development*, *84*, 1777–1790.

Meins, E., Fernyhough, C., Russell, J., & Clark-Carter, D. (1998). Security of attachment as a predictor of symbolic and mentalising abilities: A longitudinal study. *Social Development*, *7*, 1–24.

Meins, E., Fernyhough, C., Wainwright, R., Das Gupta, M., Fradley, E., & Tuckey, M. (2002). Maternal mind-mindedness and attachment security as predictors of theory of mind understanding. *Child Development*, *73*, 1715–1726.

Melby-Lervåg, M., & Hulme, C. (2013). Is working memory training effective? A meta-analytic review. *Developmental Psychology*, *49*, 270–291.

Melby-Lervåg, M., Redick, T. S., & Hulme, C. (2016). Working memory training does not improve performance on measures of intelligence or other measures of 'far transfer' evidence from a meta-analytic review. *Perspectives on Psychological Science*, *11*(4), 512–534.

Meloni, M. (2013). Moralizing biology: The appeal and limits of the new compassionate view of nature. *History of the Human Sciences*, *26*(3), 82–106.

Meltzoff, A. N. (2011). Social cognition and the origin of imitation, empathy, and theory of mind. In U. Goswami (ed.), *Wiley-Blackwell Handbook of Childhood Cognitive Development*, 2nd edn (pp. 49–75). Malden, MA: Wiley-Blackwell.

Meltzoff, A. N., & Brooks R. (2007). Eyes wide shut: The importance of eyes in infant gaze-following and understanding other minds. In R. Flom, K. Lee, & D. Muir (eds), *Gaze-following: Its Development and Significance* (pp. 217–241). Mahwah, NJ: Erlbaum.

Meltzoff, A. N., & Moore, M. K. (1977). Imitation of facial and manual gestures by human neonates. *Science*, *198*(4312), 75–78.

Merriman, W. E., Scott, P. D., & Marazita, J. (1993). An appearance-function shift in children's object naming. *Journal of Child Language*, *20*, 101–118.

Mervis, C. B., & Bertrand, J. (1994). Acquisition of the novel name-nameless category (N3C) principle. *Child Development*, *65*, 1646–1662.

Mervis, C. B., & Velleman, S. L. (2011). Children with Williams Syndrome: Language, cognitive, and behavioral characteristics and their implications for intervention. *Perspectives on Language Learning and Education*, *18*(3), 98–107. doi.org/10.1044/lle18.3.98.

Mervis, C. B., Golinkoff, R. M., & Bertrand, J. (1994). Two-year-olds readily learn multiple labels for the same basic-level category. *Child Development*, *65*, 1163–1177.

Mikhail, J. (2007). Universal moral grammar: Theory, evidence and the future. *Trends in Cognitive Science*, *11*(4), 143–152.

Miller, G. (2008). Growing pains for fMRI. *Science*, *320*, 1412–1414.

Miller, M. R., Giesbrecht, G., Müller, U., McInerney, R., & Kerns, K. A. (2012). A latent variable approach to determining the structure of executive function in preschool children. *Journal of Cognition and Development*, *13*, 395–423.

Miller, S. A., Shelton, J. & Flavell, J. H. (1970). A test of Luria's hypotheses concerning the development of self-regulation. *Child Development*, *41*, 651– 665.

Miller, S.A. (2009). Children's understanding of second-order mental states. *Psychological Bulletin*, *135*, 749–773.

Milligan, K., Astington, J. W., & Dack, L. A. (2007). Language and theory of mind: Meta-analysis of the relations between language ability and false-belief understanding. *Child Development*, *78*, 622–646.

Mink, D., Henning, A., & Aschersleben, G. (2014). Infant shy temperament predicts preschoolers theory of mind. *Infant Behavior & Development*, *37*(1), 66–75.

Minter, M., Hobson, R. P., & Bishop, M. (1998). Congenital visual impairment and 'theory of mind'. *British Journal of Developmental Psychology*, *16*, 183–196.

Mischel, W., & Baker, N. (1975) Cognitive transformations of reward objects through instructions. *Journal of Personality and Social Psychology*, *31*, 254–261.

Mischel, W., & Ebbesen, E. B. (1970). Attention in delay of gratification. *Journal of Personality and Social Psychology*, *16*, 329–337.

Mistry, J. & Dutta, R. (2015). Human development and culture. In W. F. Overton & P. C. M. Molenaar (vol. eds), R. M. Lerner (series ed.), *Handbook of Child Development and Developmental Science, Vol. 1: Theory and Method* (pp. 369–406). Hoboken, NJ: Wiley.

Miyake, A., & Friedman, N. P. (2012). The nature and organization of individual differences in executive functions: Four general conclusions. *Current Directions in Psychological Science*, *8*, 8–14.

Miyake, A., Friedman, N. P., Emerson, M. J., Witzki, A. H., Howerter, A., & Wager, T. D. (2000). The unity and diversity of executive functions and their contributions to complex 'frontal lobe' tasks: A latent variable analysis. *Cognitive Psychology*, *41*, 49–100.

Moll, H., & Tomasello, M. (2004). 12- and 18-month-old infants follow gaze to spaces behind barriers. *Developmental Science, 7,* F1–F9.

Moll, H., Carpenter, M., & Tomasello, M. (2007). Fourteen-month-olds know what others have experienced only in joint engagement with them. *Developmental Science, 10,* 826–835.

Moll, J., Zahn, R., de Oliveira-Souza, R., Krueger, F., & Grafman, J. (2005). The neural basis of human moral cognition. *Neuroscience, 6,* 799–809.

Moller Okin, S. (1996). The gendered family and the development of a sense of justice. In E. S. Reed, E. Turiel, & T. Brown (eds), *Values and Knowledge* (pp. 61–74). Mahwah, NJ: Erlbaum.

Monaghan, P., & Mattock, K. (2012). Integrating constraints for learning word–referent mappings. *Cognition, 123,* 133–143.

Moore, C. (1996). Evolution and the modularity of mindreading. *Cognitive Development, 11,* 605–621.

Moore, C. (1998). Social cognition in infancy. In M. Carpenter, K. Nagell, & M. Tomasello (eds), *Social Cognition, Joint Attention and Communicative competence from 9 to 15 Months of Age*. Monographs of the Society for Research in Child Development, *63,* 167–174.

Moore, C. (1999). Intentional relations and triadic interaction. In P. D. Zelazo, J. W. Astington, & D. R. Olson (eds), *Developing Theories of Intention* (pp. 43–61). Mahwah, NJ: Erlbaum.

Moore, C. (2006). *The Development of Commonsense Psychology*. Mahwah, NJ: Erlbaum.

Moore, C. (2008). The development of gaze following. *Child Development Perspectives, 2,* 66–70.

Moore, C., & Corkum, V. (1994). Social understanding at the end of the first year of life. *Developmental Review, 14,* 349–372.

Moore, C., & D'Entremont, B. (2001). Developmental changes in pointing as a function of parent's attentional focus. *Journal of Cognition and Development, 2,* 109–129.

Moore, C., Furrow, D., Chiasson, L., & Patriquin, M. (1994). Developmental relationships between production and comprehension of mental terms. *First Language, 14,* 1–17.

Moore, L. K., Persaud, T. V. N., & Torchia, M. G. (2008). *Before We Are Born: Essentials of Embryology and Birth Defects*. Philadelphia, PA: Saunders/Elsevier.

Moreno, S., Bialystok, E., Barac, R., Schellenberg, E. G., Cepeda, N. J., & Chau, T. (2011). Short-term music training enhances verbal intelligence and executive function. *Psychological Science, 22,* 425–433.

Moriguchi, Y., Lee, K., & Itakura, S. (2007) Social transmission of disinhibition in young children. *Developmental Science, 10,* 481–491.

Morton, B. J. (2014). Sunny review casts a foreboding shadow over status quo bilingual advantage research. *Applied Psycholinguistics, 35,* 929–931.

Morton, J., & Johnson, M. H. (1991). CONSPEC and CONLERN: A two-process theory of infant face recognition. *Psychological Review, 98,* 164–181.

Muldoon, K., Lewis, C., & Berridge, D. (2007). Predictors of early numeracy: Is there a place for mistakes when learning about number? *British Journal of Developmental Psychology, 25,* 543–558.

Muldoon, K., Lewis, C., & Francis, B. (2007). Using cardinality to compare quantities: The role of social-cognitive conflict in early numeracy. *Developmental Science, 10,* 691–711.

Muldoon, K., Lewis, C., & Freeman, N. H. (2009). Why set-comparison is vital in early number learning. *Trends in Cognitive Science, 13,* 203–208.

Muldoon, K., Lewis, C., & Towse, J. (2005). Because it's there! Why some children count, rather than infer numerical relationships. *Cognitive Development, 20,* 472–491.

Müller, U. (2009). Infancy. In U. Müller, J. I. M. Carpendale, & L. Smith (eds), *The Cambridge*

Companion to Piaget (pp. 200–228). Cambridge: Cambridge University Press.

Müller, U., & Carpendale, J. I. M. (2004). From joint activity to joint attention: A relational approach to social development in infancy. In J. I. M. Carpendale & U. Müller (eds), *Social Interaction and the Development of Knowledge* (pp. 215–238). Mahwah, NJ: Erlbaum.

Müller, U., & Giesbrecht, G. (2008). Methodological and epistemological issues in the interpretation of infant cognitive development. *Child Development, 79*, 1654–1658.

Müller, U., & Kerns, K. (2015). The development of executive function. In L. S. Liben & U. Müller (vol. eds), R. M. Lerner (series ed.), *Handbook of Child Psychology and Developmental Science, Vol. 2: Cognitive Processes*, 7th edn (pp. 571–623). Hoboken, NJ: Wiley.

Müller, U., & Overton, W. F. (1998). How to grow a baby: A reevaluation of image-schema and Piagetian action approaches to representation. *Human Development, 41*, 71–111.

Müller, U., & Overton, W. F. (1999)

Müller, U., & Overton, W. F. (2010). Thinking about thinking—thinking about measurement: A Rasch analysis of recursive thinking. *Journal of Applied Measurement, 11*, 78–90.

Müller, U., & Runions. K. (2003). The origins of understanding of self and other: James Mark Baldwin's theory. *Developmental Review, 23*, 29–54.

Müller, U., Baker, L., & Yeung, E. (2013). A developmental systems approach to executive function. In R. M. Lerner & J. B. Benson (eds), *Embodiment and Epigenesis: Theoretical and Methodological Issues in Understanding the Role of Biology within the Relational Develop- mental System. Part B — Ontogenetic dimensions. Advances in child development and behavior* (Vol. 45, pp. 39–66). London: Elsevier.

Müller, U., Carpendale, J. I. M., & Smith, L. (eds) (2009). *The Cambridge Companion to Piaget*. Cambridge: Cambridge University Press.

Müller, U., Carpendale, J. I. M., Budwig, N., & Sokol B. (2008). Developmental relations between forms of social interaction and forms of thought: An introduction. In U. Müller, J. I. M. Carpendale, N. Budwig, & B. Sokol, (eds), *Social Life and Social Knowledge: Toward a Process Account of Development* (pp. 1–16). New York: Taylor & Francis.

Müller, U., Kerns, K. A., & Konkin, K. (2012). Test–retest reliability and practice effects of executive function tasks in preschool children. *Clinical Neuropsychologist, 26*, 271–287.

Müller, U., Sokol, B., & Overton, W. F. (1998). Reframing a constructivist model of the development of mental representations: The role of higher-order operations. *Developmental Review, 18*, 155–201.

Müller, U., Yeung, E., & Baker, L. (2013). A dynamic systems approach to executive function. *Advances in Child Development and Behavior, 45*, 39–66.

Munakata, Y. (2006). Information processing approaches to development. In D. Kuhn & R. Siegler (vol. eds), W. Damon & R. Lerner (series eds), *Handbook of Child Psychology, Vol 2: Cognition, Perception and Language* (6th ed., pp. 426–463). Hoboken, NJ: Wiley.

Mundy, P., Block, J., Vaughan Van Hecke, A., Delgado, C., Parlade, M., & Pomeras, Y. (2007). Individual differences in the development of joint attention in infancy. *Child Development, 78*, 938–954.

Mundy, P. C. (2016). *Autism and Joint Attention: Development Neuroscience, and Clinical Fundamentals*. New York: The Guilford Press.

Mundy, P., Block, J., Delgado, C., Pomares, Y., Van Hecke, A. V., & Parlade, M. V. (2007). Individual differences and the development of joint attention in infancy. *Child Development, 78*(3), 938–954.

Muñetón, M. A., & Rodrigo, M. J. (2011). Functions of the pointing gesture in mothers and their 12 to 36-month-old children during everyday activities. *The Spanish Journal of Psychology*, *14*(2), 619–629.

Murphy, C. M., & Messer, D. J. (1977). Mothers, infants and pointing: A study of gesture. In H. R. Schaffer (ed.), *Studies in Mother–Infant Interaction* (pp. 325–354). London: Academic Press.

Myers, L. J., & Liben, L. S. (2012). Graphic symbols as 'the mind on the paper': Links between children's interpretive theory of mind and symbol understanding. *Child Development*, *83*, 186–202.

Nadel, J., Carchon, I., Kervella, C., Marcelli, D., & Réserbat-Plantey, D. (1999). Expectancies for social contingency in 2-month-olds. *Developmental Science*, *2*, 164–173. DOI: 10.1111/1467-7687.00065

Nagy, E., Pilling, K., Orvos, H., & Molnar, P. (2013). Imitation of tongue protrusion in human neonates: Specificity of the response in a large sample. *Developmental Psychology*, *49*(9), 1628.

Nagy, E., Pilling, K., Orvos, H., & Molnar, P. (2013). Imitation of tongue protrusion in human neonates: Specificity of the response in a large sample. *Developmental Psychology*, *49*, 1628–1638.

Nampijja, M., Apule, B., Lule, S., Akurut, H., Muhangi, L., Elliott, A. M., & Alcock, K. J. (2010). Adaptation of Western measures of cognition for assessing 5-year-old semi-urban Ugandan children. *British Journal of Educational Psychology*, *80*(1), 15–30.

Nawaz, S., Hanif, R., & Lewis, C. (2015). 'Theory of mind' development of Pakistani children: Do preschoolers acquire an understanding of desire, pretence and belief in a universal sequence? *European Journal of Developmental Psychology*, *12*, 177–188.

Nee, P. (2005). The great chain of being. *Nature*, *435*, 429.

Nelson, K. (1974). Variations in children's concepts by age and category. *Child Development*, *45*, 577–84.

Nelson, K. (1985). *Making Sense: The Acquisition of Shared Meaning*. New York: Academic.

Nelson, K. (1988). Constraints on word learning? *Cognitive Development*, *3*(3), 221–246.

Nelson, K. (1990). Remembering, forgetting, and childhood amnesia. In R. Fivush & J. A. Hudson (eds.), *Emory Symposia in Cognition, Vol. 3. Knowing and Remembering in Young Children* (pp. 301–316). New York: Cambridge University Press.

Nelson, K. (1996). *Language in Cognitive Development: The Emergence of the Mediated Mind*. New York: Cambridge University Press.

Nelson, K. (2005). Language pathways into the community of minds. In J. W. Astington & J. Baird (eds), *Why Language Matters for Theory of Mind* (pp. 26–49). Oxford: Oxford University Press.

Nelson, L. H., White, K. R., & Grewe, J. (2012). Evidence for website claims about the benefits of teaching sign language to infants and toddlers with normal hearing. *Infant and Child Development*, *21*, 474–502.

Newman, R. S., Rowe, M. L., & Ratner, N. B. (2016). Input and uptake at 7 months predicts toddler vocabulary: The role of child-directed speech and infant processing skills in language development. *Journal of Child Language*, *43*, 1158–1173.

Newport, E. L. (1990). Maturational constraints on language learning. *Cognitive Science*, *14*, 11–28.

Newson, J. (1974). Towards a theory of infant understanding. *Bulletin of the British Psychological Society*, *27*, 251–257.

Newton, P., Reddy, V., & Bull, R. (2000). Children's everyday deception and performance on false-belief tasks. *British Journal of Developmental Psychology*, *18*, 297–317.

Nguyen, T.-K., & Astington, J. W. (2013). Reassessing the bilingual advantage in theory of mind and its cognitive underpinnings. *Bilingualism: Language and Cognition, 17*, 396–409.

Ninio, A. and Bruner, J. (1978). The achievement and antecedents of labelling. *Journal of Child Language, 5*, 1–15.

Noble, K. G., McCandliss, B. D., & Farah, M. J. (2007). Socioeconomic gradients predict individual differences in neurocognitive abilities. *Developmental Science, 10*, 464–480.

Norman, D.A., & Shallice, T. (1980). *Attention to Action: Willed and Automatic Control of Behavior*. University of California at San Diego, CHIP Report 99.

Nucci, L. (2004). Social interaction and the construction of moral and social knowledge. In J. I. M. Carpendale & U. Muller (eds), *Social Interaction and the Development of Knowledge* (pp. 195–213). Mahwah, NJ: Erlbaum.

Nunes, T., & Bryant, P. (2015). The development of mathematical reasoning. In L. Liben & U. Müller (vol. eds.), *Vol. 2: Cognitive Processes*, R. Lerner (editor-in-chief), 7th edition of the *Handbook of Child Psychology and Developmental Science* (pp. 715–762). New York: Wiley Blackwell.

O'Hare, A. E, Bremner, L., Nash, M., Happé, F., Pettigrew, L. M. (2009). A clinical assessment tool for advanced theory of mind performance in 5 to 12 year olds. *Journal of Autism and Developmental Disorders, 39*, 916–928.

O'Neill, D. K. (1996). Two-year-old children's sensitivity to a parent's knowledge state when making requests. *Child Development, 67*, 659–677.

Odling Smee, F. J., Laland, K. N. & Feldman, M. W. (2003) *Niche Construction: The Neglected Process in Evolution*. Princeton, NJ: Princeton University Press.

Oller, D. K., Pearson, B. Z., & Cobo-Lewis, A. B. (2007). Profile effects in early bilingual language and literacy. *Applied Psycholinguistics, 28*, 191–230.

Onishi, K., & Baillargeon, R. (2005). Do 15-month-old infants understand false beliefs? *Science, 308*, 255–258.

Onnis, L., Monaghan, P., Richmond, K., & Chater, N. (2005). Phonology impacts segmentation in online speech processing. *Journal of Memory and Language, 53*, 225–237.

Ornaghi, V., Brockmeier, J., & Grazzani Gavazzi, I. (2011). The role of language games in children's understanding of mental states: A training study. *Journal of Cognition and Development, 12*, 239–259.

Overton, W. F. (1991). Historical and contemporary perspectives on developmental theory and research strategies. In R. Downs, L. Liben and D. Palermo (eds), *Visions of Aesthetics, the Environment, and Development: The Legacy of Joachim Wohlwill* (pp. 263–311). Hillsdale, NJ: Erlbaum.

Overton, W. F. (2015). Processes, relations, and relational-developmental-systems. In W. F. Overton & P. C. M. Molenaar (vol. eds), *Vol. 1: Theory and Method*, R. Lerner (Editor-in-Chief), 7th edition of the *Handbook of Child Psychology and Developmental Science* (pp. 9–62). New York: Wiley Blackwell.

Overton, W. F., & Reese, H. W. (1973). Models of development: Methodological implications. In J. R. Nesselroade and H. W. Reese (eds), *Life-span Developmental Psychology; Methodological Issues* (pp. 65–86). New York: Academic Press.

Oyama, S. (2000). *The Ontogeny of Information: Developmental Systems and Evolution*. Durham, NC: Duke University Press.

Page, M. P. A. (2006). What can't functional neuroimaging tell the cognitive psychologist? *Cortex, 42*, 428–443.

Paine A. L., Pearce, H., van Goozen S. H. M., de Sonneville L. M. J., & Hay, D. F. (2018). Late, but not early, arriving younger siblings foster firstborns' understanding of second-order false belief. *Journal of Experimental Child Psychology, 66*, 251–265.

Parsloe, S. M., & Babrow, A. S. (2016). Paine et al here Removal of Asperger's syndrome from the DSM V: Community response to uncertainty. *Health Communication*, *31*(4), 485–494.

Patterson, C. J., & Mischel, W. (1976). Effects of temptation-inhibiting and task-facilitating plans on self-control. *Journal of Personality and Social Psychology*, *33*, 209–217.

Patterson, F. G. (1978). The gestures of a gorilla: Language acquisition in another pongid. *Brain and Language*, *5*(1), 72–97.

Paul, R. (2009). Parents ask: Am I risking autism if I vaccinate my children? *Journal of Autism and Developmental Disorders*, *39*, 962–963.

Paulus, M. (2014). The emergence of prosocial behavior: Why do infants and toddlers help, comfort, and share? *Child Development Perspectives*, *8*, 77–81.

Paulus, M., Becker, E., Scheub, A., & König, L. (2015). Preschool children's attachment security is associated with their sharing with others. *Attachment and Human Development*, *18*(1).

Pavarini, G., de Hollanda Souza, D., & Hawk, C. K. (2013). Parental practices and theory of mind development. *Journal of Child and Family Studies*, *22*, 844–853.

Peal, E., & Lambert, W. (1962). The relation of bilingualism to intelligence. *Psychological Monographs*, *76*, 1–23.

Pears, K. C., & Moses, L. J. (2003). Demographics, parenting, and theory of mind in preschool children. *Social Development*, *12*, 1–20.

Pentland, L., Todd, J. A., & Anderson, V. (1998). The impact of head injury severity on Planning ability in adolescence: A functional analysis. *Neuropsychological Rehabilitation: An International Journal*, *8*, 301–317.

Perner, J. (1991). *Understanding the Representational Mind*. Cambridge, MA: The MIT Press.

Perner, J. (1996). Simulation as explication of predication – implicit knowledge of the mind. In P. Carruthers & P. K. Smith (eds), *Theories of Theories of Mind* (pp. 90–104). Cambridge: Cambridge University Press.

Perner, J., & Ruffman, T. (2005). Infants' insight in the mind: How deep? *Science*, *308*, 214–216.

Perner, J., & Wimmer, H. (1985). 'John thinks that Mary thinks that …': Attribution of second-order beliefs by 5- to 10-year-old children. *Journal of Experimental Child Psychology*, *39*, 437–471.

Perner, J., Leekam, S. R., & Wimmer, H. (1987). 3-year-olds difficulty with false belief – the case for a conceptual deficit. *British Journal of Developmental Psychology*, *5*, 125–137.

Perner, J., Ruffman, T., & Leekam, S. R. (1994). Theory of mind is contagious: You catch it from your sibs. *Child Development*, *65*, 1228–1238.

Perner, J., Sprung, M., Zauner, P., & Haider, H. (2003). Want that is understood well before say that, think that, and false belief: A test of de Villiers's linguistic determinism on German-speaking children. *Child Development*, *74*, 179–188.

Perry, W.G., Jr. (1970). *Forms of Intellectual and Ethical Development in the College Years: A Scheme*. New York: Holt, Rinehart, & Winston.

Peskin, J., & Astington, J. W. (2004). The effects of adding metacognitive language to story texts. *Cognitive Development*, *19*, 253–273.

Peterson, C. C. (2000). Kindred spirits: Influences of siblings' perspectives on theory of mind. *Cognitive Development*, *15*, 435–455.

Peterson, C. C., & Siegal, M. (2002). Mindreading and moral awareness in popular and rejected preschoolers. *British Journal of Developmental Psychology*, *20*, 205–224.

Peterson, C. C., Peterson, J. L., & Webb, J. (2000). Factors influencing the development of a theory of mind in blind children. *British Journal of Developmental Psychology*, *18*, 431–447.

Peterson, C. C., Wellman, H. M., & Slaughter, V. (2012). The mind behind the message: Advancing theory-of-mind scales for typically developing children, and those with deafness, autism, or Asperger syndrome. *Child Development*, *83*, 469–485.

Peterson, C., & Slaughter, V. (2003). Opening windows into the mind: Mothers' preferences for mental state explanations and children's theory of mind. *Cognitive Development, 18,* 399–429.

Phillips, J., Ong, D. C., Surtees, A. D. R., Xin, Y., Williams, S., Saxe, R., & Frank, M. C. (2015). A second look at automatic theory of mind: Reconsidering Kovács, Téglás, and Endress (2010). *Psychological Science, 26,* 1353–1367.

Piaget, J. (1928). *Judgment and Reasoning in the Child.* London: Routledge & Kegan Paul. (Original work published 1924).

Piaget, J. (1952). *The Origins of Intelligence in the Child.* London: Routledge & Kegan Paul. (Original work published in 1936).

Piaget, J. (1954). *The Construction of Reality in the Child.* New York: Basic Books. (Original work published in 1937.)

Piaget, J. (1955). *The Language and Thought of the Child.* Cleveland, OH: Meridian. (Original work published 1923.)

Piaget, J. (1962). *Play, Dreams and Imitation in Childhood.* New York: W. W. Norton & Co. (Original work published in 1945.)

Piaget, J. (1965). *The Moral Judgment of the Child.* New York: The Free Press. (Original work published 1932.). Chapter 2: Adult constraint and moral realism (pp. 109–196).

Piaget, J. (1970). Piaget's theory. In P. H. Mussen (ed.), *Carmichael's Manual of Child Psychology,* 3rd edn, vol. 1 (pp. 703–732). New York: Wiley.

Piaget, J. (1971). *Biology and Knowledge.* Edinburgh: Edinburgh University Press. (Original work published in 1967.)

Piaget, J. (1977). Problems of equilibration. In M. H. Appel & L. S. Goldberg (eds), *Topics in Cognitive Development. Vol. 1 Equilibration: Theory, Research and Application* (pp. 3–13). New York: Plenum.

Piaget, J. (1985). *Equilibration of Cognitive Structures.* Chicago: University of Chicago Press. (Original work published in 1975.)

Piaget, J. (1995). *Sociological Studies.* London: Routledge. (Original work published 1977.)

Piaget, J. (2000). Commentary on Vygotsky's criticisms of *Language and Thought of the Child* and *Judgement and Reasoning in the Child. New Ideas in Psychology, 18,* 241–259. (Original work published 1962).

Piaget, J. (2008). Intellectual evolution from adolescence to adulthood. *Human Development, 51,* 40–47. (Original work published 1972.)

Piaget, J., & Inhelder, B. (1967). *The Child's Conception of Space.* New York: Norton. (Original work published 1948.)

Pickles, A., Le Couteur, A., Leadbitter, K., Salomone, E., Cole-Fletcher, R., Tobin, H., ... & Aldred, C. (2016). Parent-mediated social communication therapy for young children with autism (PACT): Long-term follow-up of a randomised controlled trial. *The Lancet, 388,* 2501–2509.

Pika, S., & Bugnyar, T. (2011). The use of referential gestures in ravens (*Corvus corax*) in the wild. *Nature Communications, 2,* 560.

Pillow, B. H. (2002). Children and adults' evaluation of the certainty of deductive inferences, inductive inferences, and guesses. *Child Development, 73,* 779–792.

Pillow, B. H. (2012). *Children's Discovery of the Active Mind: Phenomenological Awareness, Social Experience, and Knowledge about Cognition.* New York: Springer.

Pinker, S. (1979). Formal models of language learning. *Cognition, 7*(3), 217–283.

Pinker, S. (1984) *Language Learnability and Language Development.* Cambridge, MA: Harvard University Press.

Pinker, S. (1994). *The Language Instinct.* New York: HarperPerennial.

Pinker, S. (1997). *How the Mind Works.* New York: W. W. Norton & Company.

Pinker, S. (2002). T*he Blank Slate: The Modern Denial of Human Nature.* New York: Viking.

Pinker, S. (2008). The moral instinct. *New York Times Magazine,* 8 September. Available at www.nytimes.com/2008/01/13/magazine/ 13Psychology-t.html (accessed 18 June 2017).

Plomin, R. S., & Simpson, M. A. (2013). The future of genomics for developmentalists. *Development and Psychopathology*, *25*, 1263–1278.

Plooij, F. X. (1978). Some basic traits of language in wild chimpanzees? In A. Lock (ed.), *Action, Gesture and Symbol* (pp. 111–131). New York: Academic Press.

Popper, K. (1959). *The Logic of Scientific Discovery*. London: Routledge & Kegan Paul. (Published first in German in 1934.)

Portmann, A. (1990). *A Zoologist Looks at Humankind*. New York: Columbia University Press. (Original work published 1944.)

Poulin-Dubois, D., Blaye, A., Coutya, J., & Bialystok, E. (2011). The effects of bilingualism on toddlers' executive functioning. *Journal of Experimental Child Psychology*, *108*(3), 567–579.

Premack, A. J., & Premack, D. (1972). Teaching language to an Ape. *Scientific American*, *227*(4), 92–99.

Premack, D., & Woodruff, G. (1978). Does the chimpanzee have a theory of mind? *Behavioral and Brain Sciences*, *4*, 515–526.

Pribram, K. H. (1973). The primate frontal cortex: Executive of the brain. In K. H. Pribram & A. R. Luria (eds), *Psychophysiology of the Frontal Lobes* (pp. 293–314). New York: Academic Press.

Price, B. H., Daffner, K. R., Stowe, R. M., & Mesulam, M. M. (1990). The comportmental learning disabilities of early frontal lobe damage. *Brain*, *113*, 1383–1393.

Prinz, J. J. (2006). Is the mind really modular? In R. Stainton (ed.), *Contemporary Debates in Cognitive Science* (pp. 22–36). Oxford: Blackwell.

Prinz, J. J. (2009). Against moral nativism. In D. Murphy & M. Bishop (eds). *Stich and His Critics* (pp. 167–189). Oxford: Wiley-Blackwell.

Proudfoot, D. (2009). Meaning and mind: Wittgenstein's relevance for the 'does language shape thought?' debate. *New Ideas in Psychology*, *27*, 163–183.

Quine, W. V. O. (1960). *Word and Object*. Cambridge, MA: MIT Press.

Rabbitt, P. (1997). Introduction: Methodologies and models in the study of executive function. In P. Rabbitt (ed.), *Methodology of Frontal and Executive Function*. Hove: Psychology Press.

Racine, T. P., & Carpendale, J. I. M. (2007a). The role of shared practice in joint attention. *British Journal of Developmental Psychology*, *25*, 3–25.

Racine, T. P., & Carpendale, J. I. M. (2007b). Shared practices, understanding, language and joint attention. *British Journal of Developmental Psychology*, *25*, 45–54.

Raikes, H. A., & Thompson, R. A. (2006). Family emotional climate, attachment security, and young children's emotion understanding in a high-risk sample. *British Journal of Developmental Psychology*, *24*(1), 89–104.

Ramscar, M., Dye, M., & Mccauley, S. M. (2013). Error and expectation in language learning: The curious absence of mouses in adult speech. *Language*, *89*(4), 760–793.

Ratcliffe, M. (2007). From folk psychology to commonsense. In D. D. Hutto & M. Ratcliffe (eds), *Folk Psychology Re-assessed* (pp. 223–243). Heidelberg: Springer.

Rawls, J. (1971). *A Theory of Justice*. Cambridge, MA: Harvard University Press.

Ray, E., & Heyes, C. (2011). Imitation in infancy: The wealth of the stimulus. *Developmental Science*, *14*, 92–105.

Reddy, V. (2007). Getting back to rough ground: Deception and 'social living'. *Philosophical Transactions of the Royal Society*, *B*, *362*, 621–637.

Reddy, V., & Mireault, G. (2015). Teasing and clowning in infancy. *Current Biology*, *25*, R20–R23.

Reddy, V., Markova, G., & Wallot, S. (2013). Anticipatory adjustments to being picked up in infancy. *PLOS One*, *8*, 1–9.

Redington, M., Chater, N., & Finch, S. (1998). Distributional information: A powerful cue for acquiring syntactic categories. *Cognitive Science*, *22*, 425–469.

Reid, V., & Striano, T. (2005). Adult gaze influences infant attention and object processing: Implications for cognitive neuroscience. *European Journal of Neuroscience*, *21*(6), 1763–1766.

Reid, V.M., Dunn, K.J., Young, R.J., Amu, J., Donovan, T., & Reissland, N. (2017). The human fetus preferentially engages with face-like visual stimuli. *Current Biology*, *27*, 1825–1828.

Reisman, J. M. (1985). Friendship and its implications for mental health or social competence. *Journal of Early Adolescence*, *5*, 383–391.

Renouf, A., Brendgen, M., Parent, S., Vitaro, F., Zelazo, P., Boivin, M., & Séguin, J. R. (2010). Relations between theory of mind and indirect and physical aggression in kindergarten: Evidence of the moderating role of prosocial behaviors. *Social Development*, *19*, 535–555.

Repacholi, B. M., Slaughter, V., Pritchard, M., & Gibbs, V. (2003). Theory of mind, Machiavellianism, and social functioning in childhood. In B. Repocholi & V. Slaughter (eds), *Individual Differences in Theory of Mind: Implications for Typical and Atypical Development* (pp. 67–97). New York: Psychology Press.

Rheingold, H. L. (1982). Little children's participation in the work of adults, a nascent prosocial behavior. *Child Development*, *53*, 114–125.

Richardson, R. (2007). *Evolutionary Psychology as Maladapted Psychology*. Cambridge, MA: MIT Press.

Richer, J. (1976). The social-avoidance behaviour of autistic children. *Animal Behaviour*, *24*, 898–906.

Richerson, P. J., & Boyd, R. (2001). Built for speed, not for comfort: Darwinian theory and human culture. *History and Philosophy of the Life Sciences*, *23*, 425–465.

Ricketts J., Nation K., & Bishop D. V. M. (2007). Vocabulary is important for some, but not all reading skills. *Scientific Studies of Reading*, *11*, 235–257.

Rimland, B. (1964). *Infantile Autism: The Syndrome and its Implications for a Neural Theory of Behaviour*. New York: Appleton-Century-Crofts.

Rivera, S. M., Wakeley, A., & Langer, J. (1999). The drawbridge phenomenon: Representational reasoning or perceptual preference? *Developmental Psychology*, *35*, 427–435.

Rizzolatti, G., & Kalaska, J. F. (2012). Voluntary movement: The parietal and premotor cortex. In E. R. Kandel, J. H. Schwarts, T. M. Jessel, S. A. Siegelbaum, & A. J. Hudspeth (eds), *Principles of Neural Science*, 5th edn (pp. 865–893). New York: McGraw-Hill.

Robins, D. L., Casagrande, K., Barton, M., Chen, C.-M., Thyde, D.-M., & Fein, D. (2014). Validation of the modified checklist for autism in toddlers, revised with follow-up (M-CHAT-R/F). *Pediatrics*, *133*, 37–45.

Robinson, E. J., & Robinson, W. P. (1983). Children's uncertainty about the interpretation of ambiguous messages. *Journal of Experimental Child Psychology*, 36, 81–96.

Rodríguez, C. (2009). The 'circumstances' of gestures: proto-interrogatives and private gestures. *New Ideas in Psychology*, *27*, 288–303.

Rogoff, B. (1990). *Apprenticeship in Thinking: Cognitive Development in Social Context*. New York: Oxford University Press.

Rogoff, B. (2003). *The Cultural Nature of Human Development*. New York: Oxford University Press.

Rooksby, M., & Lewis, C. (in preparation). The origins of a grasp of ironic criticism: Do preschoolers understand the intent of sarcasm?

Rose, S. A., Feldman, J. F., & Jankowski, J. J. (2011). Modeling a cascade of effects: The role of speed and executive functioning in preterm/full-term differences in academic achievement. *Developmental Science*, *14*, 1161–1175.

Ross, H. S., Recchia, H. E., & Carpendale, J. I. M. (2005). Making sense of divergent interpretations of conflict and developing an interpretive understanding of mind. *Journal of Cognition and Development, 6*, 571–592.

Ross, R. (2006). *Returning to the Teachings: Exploring Aboriginal Justice*. Penguin Canada.

Rosslenbroich, B. (2006). The notion of progress in evolutionary biology – the unresolved problem and an empirical suggestion. *Biology and Philosophy, 21*, 41–70.

Rossmanith, N., Costall, A., Reichelt, A. F., López, B., & Reddy, V. (2014). Jointly structuring triadic spaces of meaning and action: Book sharing from 3 months on. *Frontiers in Psychology, 5*, December.

Roth-Hanania, R., Davidov, M., & Zahn-Waxler, C. (2011). Empathy development from 8 to 16 months: Early signs of concern for others. *Infant Behavior and Development, 34*, 447–458.

Rottman, J., Kellemen, D., & Young, L. (2015). Hindering harm and preserving purity: How can moral psychology save the planet? *Philosophy Compass, 10*, 134–144.

Rowland, C. (2014). *Understanding Child Language Acquisition*. London: Routledge.

Rubio-Fernández, P., & Geurts, B. (2013). How to pass the false-belief task before your fourth birthday. *Psychological Science, 24*(1), 27–33. doi:10.1177/0956797612447819

Ruffman, T. (2014). To belief or not belief: Children's theory of mind. *Developmental Review, 34*(3), 265–293.

Ruffman, T., & Perner, R. (2005). Do infants really understand false belief? *Trends in Cognitive Sciences, 9*, 462–463.

Ruffman, T., Perner, J., & Parkin, L., (1999). How parenting style affects false belief understanding. *Social Development, 8*, 395–411.

Ruffman, T., Perner, J., Naito, M., Parkin, L., & Clements, W. A. (1998). Older (but not younger) siblings facilitate false belief understanding. *Developmental Psychology, 34*, 161–174.

Ruffman, T., Slade, L., & Crowe, E. (2002). The relation between children's and mothers' mental state language and theory-of-mind understanding. *Child Development, 73*, 734–751.

Ruffman, T., Slade, L., Devitt, K., & Crowe, E. (2006). What mothers say and what they do: The relation between parenting, theory of mind, language and conflict/cooperation. *British Journal of Developmental Psychology, 24*, 105–124.

Ruffman, T., Taumoepeau, M., & Perkins, E. (2011). Statistical learning as a basis for social understanding in children. *British Journal of Developmental Psychology, 30*, 87–104.

Rushton, J. P., Brainerd, C. J., & Pressley, M. (1983). Behavioral development and construct validity: The principle of aggregation. *Psychological Bulletin, 94*, 18–38.

Russell, J. (1978). *The Acquisition of Knowledge*. London: Macmillan.

Russell, J. (1992). The theory theory: So good they named it twice? *Cognitive Development, 7*, 485–519.

Russell, J., Mauthner, N., Sharpe, S., & Tidswell, T. (1991). The windows task as a measure of strategic deception in preschoolers and autistic subjects. *British Journal of Developmental Psychology, 9*, 331–349.

Rutter, M. L., Kreppner, J. M., O'Connor, T. B., & the English and Romanian Adoptees study team. (2001). Specificity and heterogeneity in children's responses to profound institutional privation. *British Journal of Psychiatry, 179*, 97–103.

Saarni, C. (1984). An observational study of children's attempts to monitor their expressive behavior. *Child Development, 55*, 1504–1513.

Sabbagh, M. A., & Callanan, M. A. (1998). Metarepresentation in action: 3-, 4-, and 5-year-olds' developing theories of mind in parent-child conversations. *Developmental Psychology, 34*, 491–502.

Sabbagh, M. A., & Seamans, E. L. (2008). Intergenerational transmission of theory-of-mind. *Developmental Science*, *11*, 354–360.

Sachdeva, J., & Mazar, N. (2015). Green consumerism: Moral motivations to a sustainable future. *Current Opinion in Psychology*, *6*, 60–65.

Saffran, J. R., Newport, E. L., & Aslin, R. N. (1996). Word segmentation: The role of distributional cues. *Journal of Memory and Language*, *35*, 606–621.

Salomo, D., & Liszkowski, U. (2013). Sociocultural settings influence the emergence of prelinguistic deictic gestures. *Child Development*, *84*, 1296–1307.

Salvadori, E., Biazsekova, T., Volein, A., Karap, Z. Tatone, D., Mascaro, O., & Csibra, G. (2015). Probing the strength of infants' preference for helpers over hinders: Two replication attempts of Hamlin and Wynn (2011). *PLOS One*, *10*(11).

Sameen, N., Thompson, J., & Carpendale, J. I. M. (2013). Further steps toward a second-person neuroscience. *Behavioral and Brain Sciences*, *36*, 437.

Samuelson, L. K. (2002). Statistical regularities in vocabulary guide language acquisition in connectionist models and 15–20-month-olds. *Developmental Psychology*, *38*(6), 1016.

Samuelson, L. K. and Smith, L. B. (1998). Memory and attention make smart word learning: An alternative account of Akhtar, Carpenter and Tomasello. *Child Development*, *1*, 94–104.

Samuelson, L. K., & Smith, L. B. (2005). They call it like they see it: spontaneous naming and attention to shape. *Developmental Science*, *8*, 182–198.

Sanders, P. T. (2013). Evolutionary psychology: A house built on sand. In R. M. Lerner & J. B. Benson (eds), *Embodiment and Epigenesis: Theoretical and methodological issues in understanding the role of biology within the relational developmental system* (pp. 257–284). Advances in Child Development and Behavior, vol. 44.

Sauer, H. (2012). Morally irrelevant factors: What's left of the dual process-model of moral cognition. *Philosophical Psychology*, *25*, 783–811.

Savage-Rumbaugh, E. S. (1986). *Ape Language: From Conditioned Response to Symbol*. New York: Columbia University Press.

Savage-Rumbaugh, E. S., Rumbaugh, D. M., & Boysen, S. (1978). Symbolic communication between two chimpanzees (Pan troglodytes). *Science*, *201*(4356), 641–644.

Savage-Rumbaugh, E. S., Murphy, J., Sevcik, R. A., Brakke, K. E., Williams, S. L., & Rumbaugh, D. M. (1993). Language comprehension in ape and child. *Monographs of the Society for Research in Child Development*, *58* (Serial No. 233).

Saxe, G. B. (2012). *Cultural Development of Mathematical Ideas: Papua New Guinea Studies*. Cambridge: Cambridge University Press.

Saxe, G. B., Guberman, S. R., & Gearhart, M. (1987). Social processes in early number development. *Monographs of the Society for Research in Child Development*, *52*(2).

Saxe, R. (2013). The new puzzle of theory of mind development. In M. R. Banaji & S. A. Gelman (eds), *Navigating the Social World: What Infants, Children, and Other Species Can Teach Us* (pp. 107–112). Oxford: Oxford University Press.

Scaife, M. & Bruner, J. (1975). Capacity for joint visual attention in infant. *Nature*, *253*, 256–266.

Scarf, D., Imuta, K., Colombo, M., & Hayne, H. (2012a). Social evaluation or simple association? Simple associations may explain moral reasoning in infants. *PLoS ONE*, *7*(8): e42698. doi:10.1371/journal.pone.0042698

Scarf, D., Imuta, K., Colombo, M., & Hayne, H. (2012b). Golden rule or valence matching? Methodological problems in Hamlin et al. *Proc. Natl. Acad. Sci. U.S.A.*, 109: E1426; author reply E1427. doi: 10.1073/pnas.1204123109

Scheler, M. (1954). *The Nature of Sympathy* (translated by P. Heath). Hamden, CT: Archon Books. (Original work published 1913.)

Schick, B., De Villiers, P., De Villiers, J., & Hoffmeister, R. (2007). Language and theory of mind: A study of deaf children. *Child Development*, *78*(2), 376–396.

Schieffelin, B., & Ochs, E. (1983). Cultural perspectives on the transition from pre-linguistic to linguistic communication. In R. Golinkoff (ed.), *The Transition from Pre-linguistic to Linguistic Communication*. Hillsdale, NJ: Lawrence Erlbaum.

Schieffelin, B., & Ochs, E. (1986). *Language Socialization Across Cultures*. Cambridge: Cambridge University Press.

Schleim, S., & Schirmann, F. (2011). Philosophical implications and multidisciplinary challenges of moral physiology. *Trames: A Journal of the Humanities & Social Sciences*, *15*(2), 127–146.

Schmid, C., Zoelch, C., & Roebers, C. M. (2008). Das Arbeitsgedächtnis von 4- bis 5-jährigen Kindern: Theoretische und empirische Analyse seiner Funktionen. *Zeitschrift für Entwicklungspsychologie und Pädagogische Psychologie*, *40*, 2–12.

Schmidt, M. F. H., & Sommerville, J. A. (2011). Fairness expectations and altruistic sharing in 15-month-old human infants. *PLoS ONE*, *6*, 1–7.

Schmidt, M. F., Rakoczy, H., Meitzsch, T., & Tomasello, M. (2016). Young children understand the role of agreement in establishing arbitrary norms – but unanimity is key. *Child Development*, PMID 26990417. doi: 10.1111/cdev.12510

Scholl, B. J., & Leslie, A. M. (2001). Minds, modules, and meta-analysis. *Child Development*, *72*, 696–701.

Schoneberger, T. (2010). Three myths from the language acquisition literature. *The Analysis of Verbal Behavior*, *26*(1), 107–131.

Scola, C., Holvoet, C., Arciszewski, T., & Picard, D. (2016). Further evidence for infants' preference for prosocial over antisocial behaviors. *Infancy*, *20*, 684–692.

Scott, R. M., & Baillargeon, R. (2009). Which penguin is this? Attributing false beliefs about identity at 18 months. *Child Development*, *80*, 1172–1196.

Sebba, M., & Dray, S. (2013). Making it real: 'Jamaican', 'Jafaican' and authenticity in the language of British youth. *Zeitschrift für Anglistik und Amerikanistik*, *60*(3), 255–273.

Segretin, M. S., Hermida, M. J., Prats, L. M., Fracchia, C. S., Ruetti, E., & Lipina, S. J. (2016). Childhood poverty and cognitive development in Latin America in the 21st century. *New Directions for Child and Adolescent Development*, *152*, 9–29.

Seidenberg, M. S., & Petitto, L. A. (1987). Communication, symbolic communication, and language: Comment on Savage-Rumbaugh, McDonald, Sevcik, Hopkins, and Rupert (1986). *Journal of Experimental Psychology: General*, *116*(3), 279–287. doi.org/10.1037/0096-3445.116.3.279

Senghas, A. (2003) Intergenerational influence and ontogenetic development in the emergence of spatial grammar in Nicaraguan Sign Language. *Cognitive Development*, *18*(4), 511–531.

Senghas, A., & Coppola, M. (2001). Children creating language: How Nicaraguan sign language acquired a spatial grammar. *Psychological Science*, *12*(4), 323–328.

Senghas, R. J., Senghas, A., & Pyers, J. E. (2005). The emergence of Nicaraguan Sign Language: Questions of development, acquisition, and evolution. In S. T. Taylor, J. Langer, & C. Milbrath (eds), *Biology and Knowledge Revisited: From Neurogenesis to Psychogenesis* (pp. 287–306). Mahwah, NJ: Erlbaum.

Seo, H. S., Hirano, M., Shibato, J., Rakwal, R., Hwang, I. K., & Masuo, Y. (2008). Effects of coffee bean aroma on the rat brain stressed by sleep deprivation: A selected transcript- and

2D gel-based proteome analysis. *Journal of Agricultural and Food Chemistry*, *56*, 4665–4673.

Service, V., Lock, A., & Chandler, P. (1989). Individual differences in early communicative development: A social constructivist perspective. In S. von Tetzchner, L. S. Siegal, & L. Smith (eds), *The Social and Cognitive Aspects of Normal and Atypical Language Development* (pp. 21–49). New York: Springer-Verlag.

Seyfarth, R. M., & Cheney, D. L. (2012). Animal cognition: Chimpanzees alarm calls depend on what others know. *Current Biology*, *22*(2), R51–R52.

Shakoor, S., Jaffee, S. R., Bowes, L., Ouellet-Morin, I., Andreou, P., Happé, F., Moffitt, T. E., & Arseneault, L. (2012). A prospective longitudinal study of children's theory of mind and adolescent involvement in bullying. *Journal of Child Psychology and Psychiatry*, *53*(3), 254–261.

Shallice, T. (1982). Specific impairments of planning. Philosophical Transactions of the Royal Society of London. *Series B, Biological Sciences*, *298*(1089), 199–209.

Shanker, S. G. (2004). Autism and the dynamic developmental model of emotions. *Philosophy, Psychiatry & Psychology*, *11*, 219–233.

Shatz, M., & Gelman, R. (1973). The development of communication skills: Modifications in the speech of young children as a function of listener. *Monographs of the Society for Research in Child Development*, 1–38.

Shatz, M., Wellman, H. M., & Silber, S. (1983). The acquisition of mental verbs: A systematic investigation of the first reference to mental state. *Cognition*, *14*, 301–321.

Shing, Y. L., Lindenberger, U., Diamond, A., Li, S.-C., & Davidson, M. C. (2010). Memory maintenance and inhibitory control differentiate from early childhood to adolescence. *Developmental Neuropsychology*, *35*, 679–687.

Shinn, M. W. (1900). *The Biography of a Baby*. Boston and New York: Mifflin Company. (Re-published 1975.)

Shneidman, L. A., & Goldin-Meadow, S. (2012). Language input and acquisition in Mayan village: How important is directed speech? *Developmental Science*, *15*, 659–673.

Siegler, R. S., & Shrager, J. (1984). Strategy choices in addition and subtraction: How do children know what to do? In C. Sophian (ed.), *Origins of Cognitive Skills* (pp. 229–293). Hillsdale, NJ: Erlbaum.

Simion, F., Regolin, L. & Bulf, H. A. (2008). Predisposition for biological motion in the newborn baby. *Proc. Natl Acad. Sci. USA*, *105*, 809–813.

Sirois, S., & Jackson, I. (2007). Social cognition in infancy: A critical review of research on higher order abilities. *European Journal of Developmental Psychology*, *4*, 46–64.

Sirois, S., Spratling, M., Thomas, M.S.C., Westermann, G., Mareschal, D., & Johnson, M. H. (2008). Précis of Neuroconstructivism. *Behavioral and Brain Sciences*, *31*(3), 321–331.

Skinner, B. F. (1955). The control of human behavior. *Transactions of the New York Academy of Sciences*, *17*, 547–551.

Skinner, B. F. (1957). *Verbal Behavior*. New York: Appleton-Century-Crofts.

Skinner, B. F. (1957). *Verbal Behavior*. New York: Appleton-Century-Crofts.

Slaby, J. (2010). Steps toward a critical neuroscience. *Phenomenology and the Cognitive Sciences*, *9*, 397–416.

Slade, L., & Ruffman, T. (2005). How language does (and does not) relate to theory-of-mind: A longitudinal study of syntax, semantics, working memory and false belief. *British Journal of Developmental Psychology*, *23*, 117–141.

Slaughter, V., & McConnell, D. (2003). Emergence of joint attention: Relationships between gaze following, social referencing, imitation, and naming in infancy. *Journal of Genetic Psychology*, *164*, 54–71.

Slaughter, V., & Perez-Zapata, D. (2014). Culture variations in the development of mind reading. *Child Development Perspectives*, *8*(4), 237–241. doi:10.1111/cdep.12091–1241

Slaughter, V., Dennis, M. J., & Pritchard, M. (2002). Theory of mind and peer acceptance in preschool children. *British Journal of Developmental Psychology*, *20*, 545–564.

Slaughter, V., Imuta, K., Peterson, C. C., & Henry, J. D. (2015). Meta-analysis of theory of mind and peer popularity in preschool and early school years. *Child Development*, *86*, 1159–1174.

Slaughter, V., Peterson, C. C., & Carpenter, M. (2009). Maternal mental state talk and infants' early gestural communication. *Journal of Child Language*, *36*, 1053–1074.

Slaughter, V., Peterson, C. C., & Mackintosh, E. (2007). Mind what mother says: Narrative input and theory of mind in typical children and those on the autism spectrum. *Child Development*, *78*, 839–858.

Slaughter, V., Peterson, C. C., & Moore, C. (2013). I can talk you into it: Theory of mind and persuasion behavior in young children. *Developmental Psychology*, *49*, 227–231.

Slavich, G. M., & Cole, S. W. (2013). The emerging field of human social genomics. *Clinical Psychological Science*, *1*, 331–348.

Slotnick, S. D. (2013). *Controversies in Cognitive Neuroscience*. Basingstoke: Palgrave Macmillan.

Smetana, J. G. (2006). Social-cognitive domain theory: Consistencies and variations in children's moral and social judgments. In M. Killen & J. Smetana (eds), *Handbook of Moral Development* (pp. 119–153). Mahwah, NJ: Erlbaum.

Smetana, J. G., Jambon, M., & Ball, C. (2014). The social domain approach to children's moral and social judgments. In M. Killen & J. G. Smetana (eds), *Handbook of Moral Developmen*, 2nd edn (pp. 3–22). New York: Psychology Press.

Smith, A. (1982). *The Theory of Moral Sentiments*. Indianapolis: Liberty Fund. (Original work published 1759.)

Smith, L. (1993). Necessary knowledge: Piagetian perspectives on constructivism. Hove: Erlbaum.

Smith, L. (1996a). The social construction of rational understanding. In A. Tryphon & J. Vonèche (eds), *Piaget–Vygotsky: The Social Genesis of Thought* (pp. 107–123). Hove: Psychology Press.

Smith, L. (1996b). With knowledge in mind: Novel transformations of the learner or transformation of novel knowledge. *Human Development*, *39*, 257–263.

Smith, L. (2009). Introduction II: Jean Piaget: From boy to man. In U. Müller, J. I. M. Carpendale, & L. Smith (eds), *The Cambridge Companion to Piaget* (pp. 18–27). Cambridge: Cambridge University Press.

Smith, L. B., & Yu, C. (2008). Infants rapidly learn word-referent mappings via cross-situational statistics. *Cognition*, *106*, 1558–1568.

Smith, L. B., Jones, S. S., & Landau, B. (1996). Naming in young children: A dumb attentional mechanism? *Cognition*, *60*, 143–171.

Smith, L. B., Suanda, S. H., & Yu, C. (2014). The unrealized promise of infant statistical word–referent learning. *Trends in Cognitive Sciences*, *18*, 251–258.

Smith, R. (1992). *Inhibition: History and Meaning in the Sciences of Mind and Brain*. Berkeley and Los Angeles: University of California Press.

Snarey, J. R. (1985). Cross-cultural universality of social-moral development: A critical review of Kohlbergian research. *Psychological Bulletin*, *97*, 202–232.

Snow, C. E. (1972). Mothers' speech to children learning language. *Child Development*, *43*, 549–565.

Snow, C. E. (1994). Beginning from baby talk: Twenty years of research on input and interaction. In C. Gallaway & B. J. Richards (eds), *Input and Interaction in Language Acquisition* (pp. 3–12). Cambridge: Cambridge University Press.

Snyder, L., Bates, E., & Bretherton, I. (1981). Content and context in early lexical development. *Journal of Child Language, 8,* 565–582.

Sodian, B. (2011). Theory of mind in infancy. *Child Development Perspectives, 5,* 39–43.

Sodian, B., & Kristen-Antonow, S. (2015). Declarative joint attention as a foundation of theory of mind. *Developmental Psychology, 51,* 1190–1200.

Sodian, B., Taylor, M., Harris, P. L., & Perner, J. (1991). Early deception and the child's theory of mind – false trails and genuine markers. *Child Development, 62,* 468–483.

Sokolov, J. L., & Snow, C. E. (1994). The changing role of negative evidence in theories of language development. In C. Gallaway & B. J. Richards (eds), *Input and Interaction in Language Acquisition* (pp. 38–55). Cambridge: Cambridge University Press.

Sonuga-Barke, E. J., Kennedy, M., Kumsta, R., Knights, N., Golm, D., Rutter, M., Maughan, B., Schlotz, W., and Kreppner, J. (2017). Child-to-adult neurodevelopmental and mental health trajectories after early life deprivation: The young adult follow-up of the longitudinal English and Romanian adoptees study. *The Lancet,* 23 May, 1–10.

Spaemann, R. (2006). *Persons: The Difference between 'Someone' and 'Something'.* New York: Oxford University Press. (Original work published 1996.)

Spelke, E. S., & Kinzler, K. D (2007). Core knowledge. *Developmental Science, 10,* 89–96.

Spelke, E. S., Bernier, E. P., & Skerry, A. E. (2014). Core social cognition. In M. R. Banaji & S. A. Gelman (eds), *Navigating the Social World: What Infants, Children and Other Species Can Teach Us* (pp. 11–16). New York: Oxford University Press.

Spencer, J. P., Blumberg, M. S., McMurray, B., Robinson, S. R., Samuelson, L. K., & Tomblin, J. B. (2009). Short arms and talking eggs: Why we should no longer abide the nativist–empiricist debate. *Child Development Perspectives, 3,* 79–87.

Sperber, D. (1994). The modularity of thought and the epidemiology of representations. In L. A. Hirschfeld & S. A. Gelman (eds), *Mapping the Mind: Domain Specificity in Cognition and Culture* (pp. 39–67). New York: Cambridge University Press.

Spinrad, T. L., & Eisenberg, N. (2014). Empathy and morality: A developmental perspective. In H. L. Maibom (ed.), *Empathy and Morality* (pp. 58–70). New York: Oxford University Press.

Spitz, R. A. (1957). *No and Yes: On the Genesis of Human Communication.* New York: International Universities Press, Inc.

Sprintzen, D. (2009). *Critique of Western Philosophy and Social Theory.* New York: Palgrave Macmillan.

St Clair, M. C., Monaghan, P., & Christiansen, M. H. (2010). Learning grammatical categories from distributional cues: Flexible frames for language acquisition. *Cognition, 116,* 341–360.

Stack, J., & Lewis, C. (2008). Steering towards a developmental account of infant social understanding. *Human Development, 51,* 229–234.

Stiles, J. (2009). On genes, brains, and behavior: Why should developmental psychologists care about brain development? *Child Development Perspectives, 3,* 196–202.

Stiles, J., Brown, T. T., Haist, F., & Jernigan, T. L. (2015). Brain and cognitive development. In L. Liben & U. Müller (vol. eds), *Vol. 2: Cognitive Processes,* R. Lerner (Editor-in-Chief), 7th edition of the *Handbook of Child Psychology and Developmental Science* (pp. 9–62). New York: Wiley Blackwell.

Stone, J. E., Carpendale, J. I. M., Sugarman, J., & Martin, J. (2012). A Meadian account of false belief understanding: Taking a non-mentalistic approach to social understanding. *New Ideas in Psychology*, *30*, 166–178.

Stone, T., & Davies, M. (1996). *Theories of Theories of Mind: The Mental Simulation Debate*. Cambridge: Cambridge University Press.

Striano, T., Stahl, D., & Cleveland, A. (2009). Taking a closer look at social and cognitive skills: A weekly longitudinal assessment between 7 and 10 months of age. *European Journal of Developmental Psychology*, *6*, 567–591.

Striano, T., Vaish, A., & Benigno, J. P. (2006). The meaning of infants' looks: Information seeking and comfort seeking? *British Journal of Developmental Psychology*, *24*, 615–630.

Suanda, S. H., Mugwanya, N., & Namy, L. L. (2014). Cross-situational statistical word learning in young children. *Journal of Experimental Child Psychology*, *126*, 395–411.

Sullivan, K., Zaitchik, D., & Tager-Flusberg, H. (1994). Preschoolers can attribute second-order beliefs. *Developmental Psychology*, *30*, 395–402.

Surian, L., & Geraci, A. (2012). Where will the triangle look for it? Attributing false beliefs to a geometric shape at 17 months. *British Journal of Developmental Psychology*, *30*, 30–44.

Surian, L., Caldi, S., & Sperber, D. (2007). Attribution of beliefs by 13-month-old infants. *Psychological Science*, *18*, 580–586.

Susswein, N. (2007). *Maternal Engagement, Mental State Terms, and Children's Understanding of the Mind*. Masters Thesis, Simon Fraser University.

Sutton, J., Smith, P. K., & Swettenham, J. (1999). Bullying and 'theory of mind': A critique of the 'social skills deficit' view of anti-social behaviour. *Social Development*, *8*, 117–127.

Swettenham, J., Remington, A., Laing, K., Fletcher, R., Coleman M., & Gomez, J.-C. (2013). Perception of pointing from biological motion point-light displays in typically developing children and children with autism spectrum disorder. *Journal of Autism and Developmental Disorders*, *43*, 1437–1446.

Swift, J. (1968). *Gulliver's Travels*. Toronto: Macmillan of Canada. (Original work published 1726.)

Tafreshi, D., Thompson, J., & Racine, T. (2014). An analysis of the conceptual foundations of the infant preferential looking paradigm. *Human Development*, *57*, 222–240.

Tallerman, M. (2013). Join the dots: A musical interlude in the evolution of language? *Journal of Linguistics*, *49*, 455–487. doi:10.1017/S0022226713000017

Tallis, R. (2011). *Aping Mankind: Neuromania, Darwinitis and the Misrepresentation of Humanity*. London: Routledge.

Tangney, J. P., & Fischer, K. W. (eds) (1995). *Self-conscious Emotions*. New York: Guilford.

Tappan, M. (2006a). Mediated moralities: Sociocultural approaches to moral development. In M. Killen & J. Smetana (eds), *Handbook of Moral Development*. Hillsdale, NJ: Lawrence Erlbaum.

Tappan, M. (2006b). Moral functioning as mediated action. *Journal of Moral Education*, *35*, 1–118.

Tardiff T., & Wellman, H. M. (2000). Acquisition of mental state language in Mandarin- and Cantonese-speaking children. *Developmental Psychology*, *36*, 25–43.

Tarullo, A. R., Bruce, J., & Gunnar, M. R. (2007). False belief and emotion understanding in post-institutionalized children. *Social Development*, *16*, 57–78.

Taumoepeau, M. (2016). Maternal expansions of child language relate to growth in children's vocabulary. *Language Learning and Development*, *12*(4), 429–446.

Taumoepeau, M., & Reese, E. (2014). Understanding the self through siblings: Self-awareness mediates the sibling effect on social understanding. *Social Development*, *23*, 1–18.

Taumoepeau, M., & Ruffman, T. (2006). Mother and infant talk about mental states relates to desire language and emotion understanding. *Child Development*, *77*, 465–481.

Taumoepeau, M., & Ruffman, T. (2008). Stepping stones to others' minds: Maternal talk relates to child mental state language and emotion understanding at 15, 24, and 33 months. *Child Development*, *79*, 284–302.

Terrace, H. S. (1979). *Nim*. New York: Knopf.

Thicke, L. (2014). Vanishing voices. *Trek Magazine*, *36*.

Thompson, R. A. (2010). Feeling and understanding through the prism of relationships. In S. D. Calkins & M. A. Bell (eds), *Child Development at the Intersection of Emotion and Cognition* (pp. 79–95). Washington, DC: American Psychological Association.

Thorpe, W. (1958). The learning of song patterns by birds, with special reference to the song of the chaffinch, 'Fringilla coelebs'. *Ibis*, *100*, 535–570.

Tomasello, M. (1995a). Joint attention as social cognition. In C. Moore & P. J. Dunham (eds), *Joint Attention: Its Origins and Role in Development* (pp. 103–130). Hillsdale, NJ: Lawrence Erlbaum.

Tomasello, M. (1995b). Language is not an instinct. *Cognitive Development*, *10*, 131–156.

Tomasello, M. (1996). The cultural roots of language. In B. M. Velichkovsky & D. M. Rumbaugh (eds), *Communicating Meaning: The Evolution and Development of Language* (pp. 275–307). Mahwah, NJ: Lawrence Erlbaum.

Tomasello, M. (1999). *The Cultural Origins of Human Cognition*. Cambridge, MA: Harvard University Press.

Tomasello, M. (2001). Perceiving intentions and learning words in the second year of life. In M. Tomasello & E. Bates (eds), *Language Development: The Essential Readings* (pp. 111–128). Oxford: Blackwell.

Tomasello, M. (2003). *Constructing a Language: A Usage-based Theory of Language Acquisition*. Cambridge, MA: Harvard University Press.

Tomasello, M. (2005). Beyond formalities: The case of language acquisition. *The Linguistic Review*, *22*, 183–197.

Tomasello, M. (2008). *Origins of Human Communication*. Cambridge, MA: The MIT Press.

Tomasello, M. (2009). *Why We Cooperate*. Cambridge, MA: The MIT Press.

Tomasello, M. (2014a) *A Natural History of Human Thinking*. Cambridge, MA: Harvard University Press.

Tomasello, M. (2014b). The ultra-social animal. *European Journal of Social Psychology*, *44*, 187–194. doi: 10.1002/ejsp.2015

Tomasello, M. (2016). *A Natural History of Human Morality*. Cambridge, MA: Harvard University Press.

Tomasello, M. and Akhtar, N. (1995). Two-year-olds use pragmatic cues to differentiate reference to objects and actions. *Cognitive Development*, *10*, 201–24.

Tomasello, M. and Haberl, K. (2003). Understanding attention: 12 and 18 month olds know what is new for other persons. *Developmental Psychology*, *39*, 906–12.

Tomasello, M., & Carpenter, M. (2007). Shared intentionality. *Developmental Science*, *10*, 121–125.

Tomasello, M., & Carpenter, M. (2013). Dueling dualists: Commentary on Carpendale, Atwood, and Kettner. *Human Development*, *56*, 401–405.

Tomasello, M., & Vaish, A. (2013). Origins of human cooperation and morality. *Annual Review of Psychology*, *64*, 231–255.

Tomasello, M., Call, J., & Hare, B. (2003). Chimpanzees understand psychological states: The question is which ones and to what extent. *Trends in Cognitive Science*, *7*, 153–156.

Tomasello, M., Carpenter, M., & Liszkowski, U. (2007). A new look at infant pointing. *Child Development*, *78*, 705–722.

Tomasello, M., Carpenter, M., Call, J., Behne, T., & Moll, H. (2005). Understanding and sharing intentions: The origins of cultural cognition. *Behavioral and Brain Sciences*, *28*, 675–735.

Tomasello, M., Hare, B., Lehmann, H., & Call, J. (2007). Reliance on head versus eyes in the gaze following of great apes and human infants: The cooperative eye hypothesis. *Journal of Human Evolution*, *52*, 314–320.

Tomasello, M., Melis, A. P., Tennie, C., Wyman, E., & Herrmann, E. (2012). Two key steps in the evolution of human cooperation: The interdependence hypothesis. *Current Anthropology*, *53*, 673–692.

Toplak, M. E., West, R. F., & Stanovich, K. E. (2013). Practitioner review: Do performance-based measures and ratings of executive function assess the same construct? *The Journal of Child Psychology and Psychiatry*, *54*(2), 131–143.

Towse, J. N., Redbond, J., Houston-Price, C. M. T., & Cook, S. (2000). Understanding the dimensional change card sort: Perspectives from task success and failure. *Cognitive Development*, *15*, 347–365.

Towse, J., Lewis, C., & Knowles, M. (2007). When knowledge is not enough: The phenomenon of goal neglect in preschool children. *Journal of Experimental Child Psychology*, *96*, 320–332.

Trevarthen, C. (1977). Descriptive analyses of infant communicative behaviour. In H. R. Schaffer (ed.), *Studies in Mother–Infant Interaction* (pp. 227–270). London: Academic.

Trevarthen, C. (1979). Communication and cooperation in early infancy: A description of primary intersubjectivity. In M. M. Bullowa (ed.), *Before Speech: The Beginning of Interpersonal Communication*. New York: Cambridge University Press.

Turiel, E. (1983). *The Development of Social Knowledge: Morality and Convention*. Cambridge: Cambridge University Press.

Turiel, E. (2002). *The Culture of Morality: Social Development, Context, and Conflict*. Cambridge: Cambridge University Press.

Turiel, E. (2006). Thought, emotions, and social interactional processes in moral development. In M. Killen & J. Smetana (eds), *Handbook of Moral Development* (pp. 7–35). Mahwah, NJ: Erlbaum.

Turiel, E. (2008). The development of children's orientations toward moral, social, and personal orders: More than a sequence in development. *Human Development*, *51*, 21–39.

Turiel, E. (2015). Moral development. In W. F. Overton & P. C. M. Molenaar (vol. eds), *Vol. 1: Theory and Method*, R. Lerner (Editor-in-Chief), 7th edition of the *Handbook of Child Psychology and Developmental Science* (pp. 484– 522). New York: Wiley Blackwell.

Turnbull, W. (2003). *Language in Action: Psychological Models of Conversation*. Hove: Psychology Press.

Turnbull, W., Carpendale, J. I. M., & Racine, T. P. (2008). Relations between mother–child talk and 3- to 5-year-old children's understanding of belief: Beyond mental state terms to talk about the mind. *Merrill-Palmer Quarterly*, *54*, 367–385.

Turnbull, W., Carpendale, J. I. M., & Racine, T. (2009). Talk and children's understanding of the mind. *Journal of Consciousness Studies*, *16*, 140–166.

Usai, M. C., Viterbori, P., Traverso, L., & De Franchis, V. (2014). Latent structure of executive function in five- and six-year-old children: A longitudinal study. *European Journal of Developmental Psychology*, *11*, 447–462.

Vail, A. L., Manica, A., & Bshary, R. (2014). Fish choose appropriately when and with whom to collaborate. *Current Biology*, *24*(17), R791–R793.

Vainio, L., Symes, E., Ellis, R., Tucker, M., & Ottoboni, G. (2008). On the relations between action planning, object identification, and motor representations of observed actions and objects. *Cognition*, *108*, 444–465.

Vallotton, C. D. (2012). Infant signs as intervention? Promoting symbolic gestures for preverbal children in low-income families to support responsive parent–child relationships. *Early Childhood Research Quarterly*, *27*, 401–415.

Valsiner, J. (2000). *Culture and Human Development*. London: Sage.

Valsiner, J. (2014). *An Invitation to Cultural Psychology*. Los Angeles: Sage.

Valsiner, J., & Lawrence, J. A. (1997). Human development in culture across the life span. In J. W. Berry, P. R. Dasen, & T. S. Saraswathi (eds), *Handbook of Cross-Cultural Psychology: Vol. 2, Basic Processes and Developmental Psychology* (2nd ed., pp. 69–106). Boston, MA: Allyn & Bacon.

Valsiner, J., & van de Veer, R. (2000). *The Social Mind: Construction of the Idea*. New York: Cambridge University Press.

Van de Vondervoort, J. W., & Hamlin, J. K. (2016). Evidence for intuitive morality: Preverbal infants make sociomoral evaluations. *Child Development Perspectives*, *10*(3), 143–148.

van der Sluis, S., de Jong, P. F., & van der Leij, A. (2007). Executive functioning in children, and its relations with reasoning, reading, and arithmetic. *Intelligence*, *35*, 427–449.

Van der Veer, R., & Valsiner, J. (1988). Lev Vygotsky and Pierre Janet: On the origin of the concept of sociogenesis. *Developmental Review*, *8*, 52–65.

Van der Ven, S. H. G., Kroesbergen, E. H., Boom, J., & Leseman, P. P. M. (2012). The development of executive functions and early mathematics: A dynamic relationship. *British Journal of Educational Psychology*, *82*, 100–119.

Van der Ven, S. H. G., Kroesbergen, E. H., Boom, J., & Leseman, P. P. M. (2013). The structure of executive functions in children: A closer examination of inhibition, shifting, and updating. *British Journal of Developmental Psychology*, *31*, 70–87.

van IJzendoorn, M. H., Bakermans-Kranenburg, M. J., & Ebstein, R. P. (2011). Methylation matters in child development: Toward developmental behavioral epigenetics. *Child Development Perspectives*, *5*, 305–310.

van IJzendoorn, M. H., Dijkstra, J., & Bus, A. G. (1995). Attachment, intelligence, and language: A meta-analysis. *Social Development*, *4*(2), 115–128.

Varouxaki, A., Freeman, N. H., Peters, D., & Lewis, C. (1999). Inference neglect and inference denial. *British Journal of Developmental Psychology*, *17*, 483–499.

Vidal, F. (1994). *Piaget Before Piaget*. Cambridge, MA: Harvard University Press.

Vinden, P. G. (1996). Junin Quechua children's understanding of mind. *Child Development*, *67*, 1701–1716.

Vinden, P. G. (1999). Children's understanding of mind and emotion: A multi-cultural study. *Cognition and Emotion*, *13*, 19–48.

Vinden, P. G. (2001). Parenting attitudes and children's understanding of mind: A comparison of Korean American and Anglo-American families. *Cognitive Development*, *16*, 793–809.

Vocate, D. R. (1987). *The Theory of A. R. Luria*. Hillsdale, NJ: Lawrence Erlbaum.

Von Foerster, H. (2003). *Understanding Understanding: Essays on Cybernetics and Cognition*. New York: Springer Verlag.

Vonnegut, K. (1991). *Fates Worse than Death*. New York: G. P. Putnam's Sons.

Vonnegut, K. (1997). *Timequake*. New York: G. P. Putnam's Sons.

Vul, E., Harris, C., Winkielman, P., & Pashler, H. (2009). Puzzlingly high correlations in fMRI studies of emotion, personality, and social cognition. *Perspectives on Psychological Science*, *4*(3), 274–290.

Vygotsky, L. S. (1978). *Mind in Society: The Development of Higher Psychological Processes*. Cambridge, MA: Harvard University Press.

Vygotsky, L. S. (1981). The instrumental method in psychology. In J. V. Wertsch (ed.), *The Concept of Activity in Soviet Psychology* (pp. 134–143). Armonk, NY: Sharpe.

Vygotsky, L. S. (1986). *Thought and Language*. Cambridge: MIT Press. (Original work published 1934.)

Vygotsky, L. S. (1997). Genesis of higher mental functions. In R. Rieber and A. Carton (eds),

The Collected Works of L. S. Vygotsky, Vol. 4. New York: Plenum Press.

Walden, T., & Ogan, T. (1988). The development of social referencing. *Child Development*, 59, 1230–1240.

Walker, L. J. (1983). Sources of cognitive conflict for stage transition in moral development. *Developmental Psychology*, *19*, 103–110.

Walker, L. J. (1995). Sexism in Kohlberg's moral psychology? In W. M. Kurtines & J. L. Gewirtz (eds), *Moral Development: An Introduction* (pp. 83–107). Boston, MA: Allyn & Bacon.

Walker, L. J. (2006). Gender and morality. In M. Killen & J. G. Smetana (eds), *Handbook of Moral Development* (pp. 93–115). Mahwah, NJ: Erlbaum.

Walker, L. J. (2014). Moral personality, motivation, and identity. In M. Killen & J. G. Smetana (eds), *Handbook of Moral Development*, 2nd edn (pp. 497–519). New York: Psychology Press.

Wallace, G. L., Silvers, J. A., Martin, A., & Kenworthy, L. E. (2009). Further evidence for inner speech deficits in autism spectrum disorders. *Journal of Autism and Developmental Disorders*, *39*(12), 1735–1739.

Warneken, F. (2006). Altruistic helping in human infants and young chimpanzees. *Science, 311*(5765), 1301–1303.

Warneken, F. (2013). Young children proactively remedy unnoticed accidents. *Cognition*, *126*, 101–108.

Warneken, F. (2015). Precocious prosociality: Why do young children help? *Child Development Perspectives*, *9*, 1–6.

Warneken, F. (2016). Insights into the biological foundation of human altruistic sentiments. *Current Opinion in Psychology*, *7*, 51–56.

Warneken, F., & Tomasello, M. (2007). Helping and cooperation at 14 months of age. *Infancy*, *11*, 271–294.

Warneken, F., & Tomasello, M. (2009). The roots of human altruism. *British Journal of Psychology*, *100*, 455–471.

Warneken, F., & Tomasello, M. (2013). Parental presence and encouragement do not influence helping in young children. *Infancy*, *18*(3), 345–368.

Warneken, F., & Tomasello, M. (2014). Extrinsic rewards undermine altruistic tendencies in 20-month-olds. *Motivational Science*, *1*, 43–48.

Wass, S. V., Scerif, G., & Johnson, M. H. (2012). Training attentional control and working memory in memory – Is younger, better? *Developmental Review*, *32*, 360–387.

Watson, J. B. (1970). *Behaviorism*. New York: W. W. Norton & Company Inc. (Original work published in 1924.)

Weisberg, D. S., Keil, F. C., Goodstein, J., Rawson, E., & Gray, J. R. (2008). The seductive allure of neuroscience explanations. *Journal of Cognitive Neuroscience*, *20*(3), 470–477.

Weisberg, D. S., Taylor, J. C. V., & Hopkins, E. J. (2015). Deconstructing the seductive allure of neuroscience explanations. *Judgment and Decision Making*, *10*, 429–441.

Wellman, H. M. & Liu, D. (2004). Scaling of theory of mind tasks. *Child Development*, *75*, 523–541.

Wellman, H. M. (1990). *The Child's Theory of Mind*. Cambridge, MA: MIT Press.

Wellman, H. M. (2015). Friends, friendlessness, and social cognition. *British Journal of Developmental Psychology*, *33*, 24–26.

Wellman, H. M., & Banerjee, M. (1991). Mind and emotions: Children's understanding of the emotional consequences of beliefs and desires. *British Journal of Developmental Psychology*, *9*, 191–214.

Wellman, H. M., Cross, D., & Watson, J. (2001). Meta-analysis of theory of mind development: The truth about false belief. *Child Development*, *72*, 655–684.

Wellman, H. M., Lane, J. D., LaBounty, J., & Olson, S. L. (2011). Observant, nonaggressive temperament predicts theory-of-mind development. *Developmental Science*, *14*, 319–326.

Werker, J. F. & Tees, R. C. (1999). Influences on infant speech processing: Toward a new synthesis. *Annual Review of Psychology*, *50*, 509–535.

Werker, J. F. (1989). Becoming a native listener. *American Scientist*, *77*, 54–59.

Werker, J. F., Cohen, L. B., Lloyd, V. L., Casasola, M. and Stager, C. L. (1998). Acquisition of word-object associations by 14-month-old infants. *Developmental Psychology*, *34*, 1289–1309.

Werner, H., & Kaplan, B. (1963). *Symbol Formation*. New York: Wiley.

Wernicke, C. (1874). *Der Aphasische Symptomen complex. Eine Psychologische Studie auf Anatomischer*. Breslau: Crohn und Weigert.

Wertsch, J. V. (1985). *Vygotsky and the Social Formation of Mind*. Cambridge, MA: Harvard University Press.

Wertsch, J. V. (1991). *Voices in the Mind*. Cambridge, MA: Harvard University Press.

Wertsch, J. V., & Tulviste, P. (1992). L. S. Vygotsky and contemporary developmental psychology. *Developmental Psychology*, *28*, 548–557.

West, M. J., & King, A. P. (1987). Settling nature and nurture into an ontogenetic niche. *Developmental Psychobiology*, *20*, 549–562.

Westermann, G., Mareschal, D., Johnson, M. H., Sirois, S., Spratling, M. W., & Thomas, M. S. C. (2007). Neuroconstructivism. *Developmental Science*, *10*, 75–83.

White, S., Hill, E., Happé, F., & Frith, U. (2009). Revisiting the strange stories: revealing mentalizing impairments in autism. *Child Development*, *80*, 1097–1117.

Wiebe, S. A., Espy, K. A., & Charak, D. (2008). Using confirmatory factor analysis to understand executive control in preschool children: I. Latent structure. *Developmental Psychology*, *44*, 575–587.

Wiebe, S. A., Sheffield, T., Nelson, J. M., Clark, C. A. C., Chevalier, N., & Espy, K. A. (2011). The structure of executive function in 3-year-olds. *Journal of Experimental Child Psychology*, *108*, 436–452.

Wiley, E. W., Bialystok, E., & Hakuta, K. (2005). New approaches to using census data to test of the critical-period hypothesis for second-language acquisition. *Psychological Science*, *16*, 341–343.

Wilkins, D. (2003). Why pointing with the index finger is not a universal (in sociocultural and semiotic terms). In S. Kita (ed.), *Pointing: Where Language, Culture, and Cognition Meet* (pp. 171–215). Mahwah, NJ: Erlbaum.

Willoughby, M. T., & Blair, C. B. (2011). Test–retest reliability of a new executive function battery for use in early childhood. *Child Neuropsychology*, *17*, 564–579.

Willoughby, M. T., Wirth, R. J., & Blair, C. B. (2012). Executive function in early childhood: Longitudinal measurement invariance and developmental change. *Psychological Assessment*, *24*, 418–431.

Willoughby, M., Holochwost, S. J., Blanton, Z. E., & Blair, C. B. (2014). Executive functions: Formative versus reflective measurement. *Measurement: Interdisciplinary Research and Perspectives*, *12*, 69–95.

Wills, G. (2001). *Saint Augustine's Childhood: Confessions Book One*. New York: Viking.

Wilson, E. O. (1975). *Sociobiology*. Cambridge, MA : Harvard University Press.

Wilson, M. (2002). Six views of embodied cognition. *Psychonomic Bulletin & Review*, *9*(4), 625–636.

Wilson, R. A., & Foglia, L. (2015). Embodied cognition. *Stanford Encyclopedia of Philosophy*. https://plato.stanford.edu/entries/embodied-cognition/

Wimmer, H., & Perner, J. (1983). Beliefs about beliefs: Representation and constraining function of wrong beliefs in young children's understanding of deception. *Cognition*, *13*, 103–128.

Winnicott, D. W. (1964). *The Child, the Family, and the Outside World*. Harmondsworth: Penguin.

Winsler, A. (2009). Still talking to ourselves after all of these years: A review of current research on private speech. In A. Winsler, C. Fernyhough, & I. Montero (eds), *Private Speech, Executive Function, and the Development of Self-regulation* (pp. 3–41). New York: Cambridge University Press.

Winsler, A., Abar, B., Feder, M. A., Schunn, C. D., & Rubio, D. A. (2007). Private speech and executive functioning among high-functioning children with autistic spectrum disorders. *Journal of Autism and Developmental Disorders*, *37*, 1617–1635.

Wittgenstein, L. (1968). *Philosophical Investigations*. Oxford: Blackwell.

Wong, C. C. Y., Meaburn, E. L., Ronald, A., Price, T. S., Jeffries, A. R., Schalkwyk, L. C., Plomin, R., & Mill, J. (2013). Methylomic analysis of monozygotic twins discordant for autism spectrum disorder and related behavioural traits. *Molecular Psychiatry*, *19*(4), 495–503..

Wood, D., Bruner, J. S., & Ross, G. (1976). The role of tutoring in problem solving. *Journal of Child Psychology and Psychiatry*, *17*, 89–100.

Woodward, A. L. (1998). Infants selectively encode the goal object of an actor's reach. *Cognition*, *69*(1), 1–34. http://doi.org/10.1016/S0010-0277(98)00058-4

Woodward, A. L. (2003). Infants' developing understanding of the link between looker and object. *Developmental Science*, *6*(3), 297–311. http://doi.org/10.1111/1467-7687.00286

Woodward, A. L. (2005). The infant origins of intentional understanding. *Advances in Child Development and Behavior*, *33*, 229–262.

Woodward, A. L. (2013). Infant foundations of intentional understanding. In M. R. Banaji & S. A. Gelman (eds), *Navigating the Social World: A Developmental Perspective* (pp. 75–80). Oxford: Oxford University Press.

Woolfe, T., Want, S. C., & Siegal, M. (2002). Signposts to development: Theory of mind in deaf children. *Child Development*, *73*, 768–778.

Wörmann, V., Holodynski, M., Kärtner, J., & Keller, H. (2014). The emergence of social smiling: The interplay of maternal and infant imitation during the first three months in cross-cultural comparison. *Journal of Cross-Cultural Psychology*, *45*(3), 339–361.

Wright, D. (1982). Piaget's theory of moral development. In S. Modgil & C. Modgil (eds), *Jean Piaget: Consensus and Controversy* (pp. 207–217). London: Holt, Rinehart & Winston.

Wu, Z., Pan, J., Su, Y., & Gros-Louis, J. (2013). How joint attention relates to cooperation in 1-and 2-year-olds. *International Journal of Behavioral Development*, *37*, 542–548.

Wundt, W. (1973). *The Language of Gestures*. The Hague: Mouton.

Wynn, K. (1992). Addition and subtraction by human infants. *Nature*, *358*, 749–750.

Yagmurlu, B., Berument, S. K., & Celimli, S. (2005). The role of institution and home contexts in theory of mind development. *Applied Developmental Psychology*, *26*, 521–537.

Yasui, M., & Lewis, C. (2005) 'Oh great!' can mean nasty: a message from three-year-olds' understanding of sarcasm. Paper presented at the biennial meeting of the Society for Research in Child Development, Atlanta, GA, 7 April.

Yoshioka, J. G. (1929). A study of bilingualism. *Journal of Genetic Psychology*, *36*, 473–479.

Young, L., & Dungan, J. (2012). Where in the brain is morality? Everywhere and maybe nowhere. *Social Neuroscience*, *7*, 1–10.

Youngblade, L. M., & Dunn, J. (1995). Individual differences in young children's pretend play with mothers and siblings: Links to relationships and understanding other people's feelings and beliefs. *Child Development*, *66*, 1472–1492.

Yu, C., & Smith, L. B. (2013). Joint attention without gaze following: Human infants and their parents coordinate visual attention to objects through eye–hand coordination. *PLoS ONE*, *8*(11), e79659. https://doi.org/10.1371/journal.pone.0079659

Zahavi, D. (2008). Simulation, projection and empathy. *Consciousness and Cognition*, *17*, 514–522.

Zahavi, D., & Rochat, P. (2015). Empathy ≠ sharing: Perspectives from phenomenology and developmental psychology. *Consciousness and Cognition*, *36*, 543–553.

Zelazo, P. D., & Lyons, K. E. (2012). The potential benefits of mindfulness training in early childhood: A developmental social cognitive neuroscience perspective. *Child Development Perspectives*, *6*, 154–160.

Zelazo, P. D., Anderson, J. A., Richler, J., Wallner-Allen, K., Beaumont, J. L., & Weintraub, S. (2013). NIH Toolbox Cognition Battery (CB): Measuring executive function and attention. *Monographs of the Society for Research in Child Development*, *78*, 16–33.

Zelazo, P. D., Carter, A., Reznick, J. S., & Frye, D. (1997). Early development of executive function: A problem solving framework. *Review of General Psychology*, *1*, 198–226.

Zelazo, P. D., Müller, U., Frye, D., & Marcovitch, S. (2003). The development of executive function in early childhood. *Monographs of the Society for Research in Child Development*, *68* (Serial No. 274).

Zuckerman, P., & Padona, A. (2012). *Buried in the Sky: The Extraordinary Story of the Sherpa Climbers on K2's Deadliest Day*. New York: Norton.

SUBJECT INDEX

Note: Page numbers in *italics* indicate figures.

abbreviated speech 68
accommodation 39–41
action-based approach *see* constructivism
aggression 27, 265
analogical argument 106
animals
    communication 122, 123–128, 139–141
    language learning 121–122, 129–138
aphasia 149
appearance-reality task 216
arms up gesture 92, 107
Asperger Syndrome *see* autism spectrum disorder
    (ASD)
assimilation 39–41, 47, 59
    generalised assimilation 115
associative approach to word learning 179–180
attachment styles 249–250, 253
attachment theory 84–85
attention task (Woodward) 90, *91*
attentional flexibility 192, 196
autism spectrum disorder (ASD) 71–72, 84, 93, 214,
    233–239

baby signing 96
bees 126–128, *127*
behaviour, innate 20–21
behaviour control *see* executive function
behaviour genetics 16, 22
biological motion 84
biology 8–9
    role in executive function 200–203
    genetics, epigenetics and developmental
        psychobiological systems 26–29
    role in language learning 148–151

and the social environment 15–26
    role in social understanding 229–232
    see also brain; neuroscience
blindness 30, 249
bonobos, language learning in 132–134, 135–138
    role of meaning 139–141
bottle study 42
brain
    role in executive function 200–203
    role in language learning 148–151
    localising functions in 230–232, 301–305
    neuroconstructivism 29–31
    thinking 14–15
    see also neuroscience
bullying 264–265

canonical pointing gesture 93
card-sort task *see* Dimension Change Card Sort task
    (DCCS)
care-justice distinction 288–290
Cartesian perspective 5–6
change of location task 216
character education 280
cheating 279
child characteristics 248–249
Child Language Data Exchange System (CHILDES)
    251–252
child-as-scientist 6
child-directed speech 182–183
chimpanzees,
    language learning in 129–138
    role of meaning 139–141
Clever Hans Effect 136
cognition, embodied 32–33

Cognitive Complexity and Control (CCC)
    theory 205
cognitivism 6, 14, 15, 31–32, 55
communication
    infant-caregiver interaction 83–87
    preverbal 81–97
        development of 99–120
        gaze following 82, 89–92, *91*
        gestures 92–96, 102, 107. *see also* pointing
        joint (visual) attention 82–83, 87–89, *88*,
            106–107, 185
    see also animals: communication; language
computational theory of mind 17
conceptual knowledge 32
concrete operational thinking 49–50
conservation 50, 56-57, 78
constraints approach to word learning 177–179
construct fractionation 198–199
constructivism 10, 38–42, 110, 226
    see also Piaget, Jean
conversation 67–69, 159-162, 168-169, 174,
    254–258, 271, 317-319
connectedness of 255–256
cooperation 276, 277, 278, 305, 312–313
copy theory of knowledge 10
creative thinking 69
creoles 155–156
critical period hypothesis 150–151
culture
    and biology 25–26
    and individuals 73
    and language learning 182–183, 184–185
    and moral development 286–287
    and morality 272–274
    and pointing 117–119
    and social understanding 245–246

Day-Night task 192, *192*, 197, 204
deafness 72, 151, 156–157, 249, 253
delay of gratification study 210
desire 256–257
developmental perspective *see* "relational develop-
    mental systems perspective"
Developmental Systems Theory 8–9, 22–23
dilemmas 303–304
Dimension Change Card Sort task (DCCS) 192, *193*,
    205–206, 207
domain theory 290–292
duck-rabbit 220–221, *221*

ecological validity 199–200
ecosystems, regular development in 24

education 279–280
egocentric speech 67–68, 69
elementary mental functions 66
embodied cognition 32–33
emotions 114–115, 217–218, 250, 296–301
empathy 297–298
empiricism 5–6, 38
enculturation 73
environmental factors 26–28
epigenetics 28, 29
epilepsy 149–150
epistemic development 222
epistemic triangle 78–79
epistemology 37
equilibration theory 43–44
ethics *see* morality
Evolutionary Psychology 17–19
evolution 25–26, 41, 122–128, 305–307
executive function 190–196
    problems of studying 196–200
    role of biology 200–203
    role of social processes 203–207
    theoretical issues 207–209
    "unity with diversity model" *195*
experience, role in brain development 29–31

false belief tasks 215–217
false belief theories 222–224
false belief understanding 225–227
    and bullying 264–265
    connectedness of conversation 255
    and culture 245–246
    effect of language on 245, 253–257
    effect of parent-child interaction on 249–251
    and friendship 263
    and play 247
    role of peers 248
    and sensory impairment 249
    sibling effect 246–247, 263
    and teacher criticism 263–264
fathers 182
faux pas situations 218
footbridge dilemma 303
formal operational thinking 51–52
friendship 248, 263
function bias 177

gaze following 82, 89–92, *91*
gender 218, 234, 288–290
gene-centred approach to biology 17
general genetic law of cultural
    development 63–65

genetic epistemology 37–42
genetics 16, 22, 26–28
genome-wide association (GWA) study 16
gestures 92–96, 102, 107
    see also pointing
grammar 146–148, 157

habituation-dishabituation technique 53, 87–88
head movements for communication 94–95, 309
helping 310–312
heredity 25
heritability 201–203
heteronomous morality 276
high-amplitude sucking (HAS) 170
higher mental functions 66
honeybees 126–128, *127*
horizontal décalage 56–57
human rights 271–272
humour 264

imagery 69
imitation 104–105, *104*, 117–119
impairment *see* blindness; deafness
impersonal dilemmas 303–304
in jokes 68
incest 299, 300
individualist perspective *see* cognitivism
Infant Head Turn procedure 170
infant-caregiver interaction 83–87
 see also parental input
inference 219
information processing 74–76
information visualization 66, 69
inheritance systems 25
inhibitory control 192, 197, 198
innateness 15
innate behaviour 20–21
innate knowledge 14, 18–21, 76, 224
innate module account of social understanding
        100–103
innate morality 308–310
instincts 19–20
intelligence 65–66
intentionality, shared 108–109
interaction *see* social interaction
"internalisation" 64
interpretation 220–221, 264

joint attention 82–83, 87–89, *88*, 106–107, 185
joint action 110–111
just community schools 285
justice 278, 288–290

kittens' experience study 38
knowledge
    conceptual 32
    innate 14, 18–21, 76, 224
    logical-mathematical 43
    physical 42–43
    theories of 10

language 143–145
    characteristics 125, 126, 128
    effect on social understanding 251–257
        assumptions about the mind 258–262
    evolution of 122–128
    and executive function 197
    and false belief understanding 245, 253–257
    innate knowledge 18–19
    private 259–260
    see also communication; language learning
Language Acquisition Device (LAD) 123, 134, 135
Language Acquisition Support System (LASS) 135
language comprehension 32
language creation 155–157
language families 144
language learning 123–124
    animals 121–122, 129–138
    and attachment 253
    and meaning 157–163
    parental input 152–155, 181–183
    role of biology in 149–151
    sibling effect 247, 253
    speech sounds 168–171
    word boundaries 172–173
    word learning 64, 173–177
        associative approach 179–180
        constraints approach 177–179
        emergentist coalition model 180
        social-pragmatic account 181–186
lexical principles 175–177
"like me" account of social understanding
        103–108, *104*
linkage analysis 16
linking problem 151–152
logical-mathematical knowledge 43
lying 271, 277–278

manipulation 264
mathematics 73–77, 136
meaning 5, 122–128, 139–141, 157–163
memory 66
mental functions 66
mental logic 56–57
mental state talk 253

mental state terms 251–252, 254–255, 258
metarepresentation 223
mind 258–262
mindmindedness 250–251
mirror neurons 229–230
modularity 18–19
molecular genetics 16
monkeys, alarm calls 125, 138
moral action 287–288
moral development 316–319
   pro-social behaviour 307–313
moral education 279–280
moral realism 277
moral reasoning 286, 287–290
moral relativism 274
morality 264, 270–272
   and culture 272–274
   and emotions 296–301
   and evolution 305–307
   innate 308–310
   and neuroscience 301–305
   versus social convention 290–292
mutual exclusivity bias 176

National Institute of Health (NIH) Toolbox
      Cognition Battery 199
nativism 5–6, 38
nature versus nurture 15–26
negative evidence 153–155
neonatal imitation 104–105, 104
neonativism 52–55, 76
neuroconstructivism 29–31
neuroimaging 230–232, 302–303
neurons 229–230
neuroscience 31–33, 229–232, 301–305
nodding 94–95
norm-psychology 306–307
numbers, understanding of 73–77
nurture see nature versus nurture

object concept 47–48, 52–55
operational thinking 49–52
orangutans, language learning in 129

parental input 152–155, 181–183, 249–251,
      255–257, 298
   see also infant-caregiver interaction
peers 248, 263, 276–277, 312–313, 317
pendulum task 51
personal dilemmas 303–304
personal domains 291
perspective taking 215

phonology 168–171
physical knowledge 42–43
pidgins 155–156
planning 193, 196
play 247, 275–276
pointing 92–95, 102, 107, 111–119, 313
positive evidence 153
pragmatics 158–159
preoperational thinking 49
pretend play 247
preverbal communication 81–97
   development of 83–87, 99–120
      innate module account 100–103
      "like me" account 103–108, 104
      relational framework 109–118
      shared intentionality 108–109
   gaze following 82, 89–92, 91
   gestures 92–96, 102, 107. see also pointing
   joint attention 82–83, 87–89, 88, 106–107, 185
private language argument 259–260
private speech 70–72, 80
   see also egocentric speech
probabilistic epigenesis 28
problem of other minds 6, 8
procedural décalage 56
process-relational worldview 7, 14, 15
pro-declarative pointing 94
pro-imperative pointing 93–94
pro-social behaviour 307–313
prosodic level of analysis 182

quantitative genetics see behaviour genetics

recursive thinking 220
relational developmental systems perspective 7, 9,
      14, 15, 226
relational framework of social understanding
      109–118
relationships 249–250, 255–257
   see also peers; sibling effect
representation 55
role play see pretend play
rule-based play 275–276

sarcasm 219
scaffolding 72–73, 204, 205
schemes 39–40
   secondary 47
schooling 279–280
self-awareness 247
self-organising systems 39
self-other differentiation 312

semantics 157–158
sensorimotor actions 38
sensorimotor development 45–47
sensorimotor experience 32
sensorimotor intelligence 45, 115
sensory impairment *see* blindness; deafness
serotonin 26–27
set shifting *see* attentional flexibility
sex 27
shape bias 176–177, 179–180
shared intentionality 108–109
sibling effect 246–247, 253
sign language 72, 96, 151, 156–157, 249, 253
simulation theory *see* "like me" account of social
   understanding
six boxes test for working memory *191*, 192
smiling 24–25, 85
social class 203
social cognition *see* social understanding
social context 244–251
social conventions 290–292
social experience 28
social factors 58
social genomics 28
Social Institutionist Model 299–301
social interaction 9, 43, 83–87, 203–207
social learning theory 64
social perspectives 215
social referencing 88, 91–92
social understanding 82, 213–214
   and cooperation 312–313
   development
      innate module account 100–103
      "like me" account 103–108, *104*
      relational framework 109–118
      shared intentionality 108–109
   developmental sequence 219, 227–228
   effect of child characteristics on 248–249
   effect of language on 251–257
      assumptions about the mind 258–262
   effect of social context on 244–251
      culture 245–246
      parent-child relationship 249–251, 255–257
      peers 248, 263
      play 247
      sibling effect 246–247
   emotions 217–218
   epistemic development 222
   false belief understanding 225–227
   faux pas situations 218
   and helping 311
   history of approaches 215–217

   impact on children's social lives 262–266
   inference 219
   interpretation 220–221
   problem of other minds 8
   recursive thinking 220
   role of biology 229–232
   sarcasm 219
   strange stories 218
   theories of 222–224
social-cognitive domain theory 290–292
social-pragmatic account of word learning
   181–186
sociocultural approach to cognitive
   development 73
socioeconomic status 203
sociogenesis 61–62
spectator theory of knowledge 10
speech
   abbreviated 68
   "child-directed speech" 182–183
   "egocentric" 67–68, 69
   see also language; language learning
speech sounds 168–172
split position 6
Strange Situation 250
strange stories 218
structures 42
subjective responsibility 277
symbols 208, 209
sympathy 297
syntax 157
   see also grammar

task impurity 197
taxonomic assumption 175–176
test-retest reliability 198–199
theory of mind 17–18, 215
   see also false belief tasks; social
      understanding
Theory of Mind Mechanism 223
theory theory 222–224
three mountain task (Piaget) 215
Tower of Hanoi task 198
Tower of London task 193, *194*
transformational-generative grammar 146–147
triadic interaction 87–88
trolley car dilemma 303
trust 210
twins 29, 201–203, 234

unexpected contents task 216
unexpected transfer task 216

"unity with diversity model" of executive function
194–196, *195*
Universal Grammar 147–148, 152
Universal Moral Grammar (UMG) 305

validity 199–200
values clarification 280
violation of expectation 226
visual checking 116

waving 92
"we" intentionality *see* shared intentionality

whole object assumption 175
word boundaries 172–173
word learning 64, 173–186
associative approach 179–180
constraints approach 177–179
emergentist coalition model 180
social-pragmatic account 181–186
working memory 192, 191, 196, 198, 206
worldviews 5–10

zone of proximal development (ZPD)
65–66

AUTHOR INDEX

Aadmodt-Leeper, G. 198
Abar, B. 72
Acredolo, L. P. 96
Adrián, J. E. 253
Agans, J. P. 7, 9
Ainsworth, M. D. S. 86
Aitchison, J. 130
Akhtar, N. 89, 174, 183, 184
Akurut, H. 198
Alcock, K. J. 198
Aldred, C. 239
Allen, J. 93
Allen, J. W. P. 22, 54, 226, 228, 237
Alloway, T. P. 198
Alvarez, J. A. 201
Ambridge, B. 144, 147, 152, 156, 178–180, 185
Ambrosini, E. 310
Amu, J. 84, 169
Anderson, J. A. 199
Anderson, J. E. 201
Anderson, M. L. 32
Anderson, P. J. 197
Anderson, S. W. 302
Anderson, V. 36
Andreou, P. 265
Anglin, J. M. 173
Anisfeld, M. 105
APA 233
Appel, H. M. 28
Apperly, I. A. 225
Appleton, M. 255
Apule, B. 198
Aram, D. 150
Archibald, S. J. 198
Archives Piaget 36

Arciszewski, T. 309
Armstrong, K. A. 234
Arnott, B. 251
Arseneault, L. 265
Aschersleben, G. 248
Ashwin, E. 234, 236
Aslin, R. N. 172, 210, 309
Astington, J. W. 216, 222, 240, 247, 253, 254, 256, 257, 263
Attanucci, J. 288, 289
Atwood, S. 94, 102, 111, 224, 274, 318
Audet, K. N. 311
Austin, G. A. 190
Austin, J. L. 159, 266
Auyeung, B. 234, 236
Avis, J. 245
Aziz, S. A. 72
Azmitia, M. 71

Babrow, A. S. 233
Baddeley, A. D. 190
Baillargeon, R. 19, 36, 53, 54, 55, 101–102, 225, 226
Bain, L. 101, 225
Baird, G. 93, 237
Baird, J. A. 256, 263
Baker, L. 203, 302
Baker, N. 210
Bakermans-Kranenburg, M. J. 23, 29
Baldwin, D. A. 88, 174, 180, 185
Baldwin, J. M. 36, 62, 85, 106, 109
Ball, W. S. 230
Bandura, A. 64
Banerjee, M. 217
Banerjee, R. 217, 218, 248, 263

Barac, R. 206
Barch, D. 239
Barkley, R. A. 209
Baron-Cohen, S. 93, 223, 234, 236, 237, 238
Barresi, J. 110
Barrett, B. 239
Barrett, L. 20
Barrett, M. 181
Barsalou, L. W. 32
Bartlett, E. 176, 178
Barton, M. 237
Bartsch, K. 251
BASIS Team 237, 238
Bates, E. 82, 93, 112–116, 135, 144, 149, 150, 155, 156, 157, 164, 173, 185
Bateson, P. 15
Bayliss, D. M. 72
Beach, F. A. 19
Beaumont, J. L. 199
Bechara, A. 302
Beck, D. M. 232
Beckett, C. 244
Beeghly-Smith, M. 225
Begeer, S. 248, 263
Begus, K. 94
Behen, T. 116, 118
Behne, T. 94, 106, 107, 108, 313
Behrend, D. A. 71
Beilin, H. 36
Bell, S. M. 86
Benigno, J. P. 88
Benson, J. B. 54
Benton, A. L. 302
Berg, E. A. 192
Bergelson, E. 173
Berger, P. L. 41
Berk, L. E. 70, 71
Berker, S. 304
Bernier, A. 203, 204, 208
Bernier, E. P. 17
Bernstein, R. J. 9, 10
Berridge, D. 77, 152, 246
Bertrand, J. 176, 179
Berument, S. K. 244
Best, J. R. 206
Bialystok, E. 206
Biazsekova, T. 308
Bibok, M. 25, 49, 85
Bibok, M. B. 49, 73, 76, 110, 204, 208
Bickerton, D. 155, 156
Bickhard, M. 22, 54, 55, 223, 226
Bigelow, A. E. 89

Billstedt, E. 233
Bion, R. A. 176
Birnbacher, D. 304
Bisanz, J. 75
Bishop, D. V. M. 198
Bishop, M. 249
Bivens, J. A. 71
Bjorklund, F. 299
Black, C. 245
Blair, C. 198, 202, 203
Blair, C. B. 195, 199, 202
Blake, J. 93
Blanton, Z. E. 199, 202
Blasi, A. 287
Block, J. 107
Bloom, L. 180
Bloom, P. 19, 122, 173, 175, 177, 178, 179, 181, 308, 309, 315
Blumberg, M. S. 15
Boan, A. D. 235
Bobe, L. 149
Bogartz, R. S. 54
Bohannon, M. 153, 154
Bohlmann, J. 28
Boivin, M. 265
Bolton, P. 237, 238
Boom, J. 195
Borke, H. 215
Borovsky, A. 176
Borzellino, G. 93
Bosacki, S. 222, 263
Botkin, P. T. 220
Bowes, L. 265
Bowlby, J. 84, 250
Boyd, R. 26
Boyes, M. C. 287
Boysen, S. 132
Brace, J. J. 205
Bradley, C. C. 235
Braine, M. D. S. 157
Brainerd, C. 36, 198
Brakke, K. E. 135
Brand, R. J. 180
Bremner, J. G. 226
Bremner, L. 218
Brendgen, M. 265
Brent, E. 239
Bretherton, I. 135, 225
Bringuier, J.-C. 50, 52
Broadbent, D. E. 190
Broca, P. 149
Brockmeier, J. 254, 255

Broesch, T. L. 182, 183
Brookes, S. 181
Brooks, R. 89, 107
Brophy, M. 255
Brown, C. A. 96
Brown, E. 180
Brown, G. R. 20
Brown, J. 244, 253
Brown, K. 246
Brown, L. M. 288
Brown, P. 93, 117, 159
Brown, R. 129, 153, 154, 176
Brown, S. J. 297
Brown, T. T. 20, 29, 30, 226, 315
Brownell, C. 312, 313
Brownell, C. A. 248, 311, 312
Bruce, J. 244
Brunelle, F. 149
Bruner, J. 72, 86, 90, 107, 114, 134, 158, 181, 186, 190
Bryant, G. A. 182, 183
Bryant, P. 76
Bryce Heath, S. 174
Bryson, S. E. 194, 197
Bshary, R. 313
Budwig, N. 62, 252
Bugnyar, T. 114
Bulf, H. A. 83–84, 237
Bull, R. 195, 198, 228
Buller, D. J. 18
Bunge, S. A. 203
Burack, J. A. 236
Burfield, A. 114
Burnham, D. 171
Burquest, D. A. 185
Bus, A. G. 253
Bush, J. 286
Busnel, M. 169
Butler, L. P. 177
Butler, S. 218, 253
Buttelmann, D. 227
Butterfill, S. A. 225
Butterworth, G. 90, 93, 116
Byars, A. W. 230
Byford, S. 239

Caldi, S. 225
Call, J. 89, 106, 108, 121, 122, 313
Callaghan, T. 93, 117, 245
Callanan, M. A. 174, 183, 252
Callesen, K. 239
Camaioni, L. 93, 112–116

Camelo, J. L. 203
Cameron-Faulkner, T. 114
Campbell, R. L. 44, 223
Campos, J. J. 317
Candee, D. 287, 293
Canfield, J. V. 102, 111, 115, 139, 140, 160, 162, 163
Caputi, M. 218, 248, 263
Carchon, I. 85
Carey, S. 58, 176, 178, 222
Carlson, S. M. 203, 204, 207, 208
Carpendale, A. B. 94, 96, 112, 113, 115, 116
Carpendale, J. I. M. 25, 44, 49, 62, 73, 76, 85, 89, 90, 93–96, 100, 102, 106, 109–113, 115, 116, 119, 204, 208, 214, 215, 216, 218, 219, 220, 222, 224, 226, 227, 229–230, 232, 253, 254, 255, 264, 265, 267, 274, 276, 278, 284, 286, 299, 300, 301, 309, 311, 313, 317, 318
Carpenter, L. A. 235
Carpenter, M. 93, 94, 106, 107, 108, 111, 115, 185, 227, 258, 313
Carriger, M. 312, 313
Carruthers, P. 67, 223
Carter, A. 205, 209
Casagrande, K. 237
Casasola, M. 186
Casebeer, W. D. 302
Casler, K. 177
Caspi, A. 244
Cassidy, K. W. 246
Castel, A. D. 231
Castle, J. 244
Catale, C. 207
Celimli, S. 244
Cepeda, N. J. 206
Chakrabarti, B. 234, 236
Chandler, M. J. 215, 217, 220, 221, 222, 228, 240, 263, 265
Chandler, P. 93, 107, 117
Chandler, S. 237, 238
Chapman, M. 37, 38, 44, 47, 48, 50, 52, 56, 57, 59, 74, 78, 87, 284, 298
Charak, D. 196
Charles, J. M. 235
Charman, T. 93, 218, 233, 237, 238, 239, 250
Charney, E. 29
Chater, N. 157, 172
Chau, T. 206
Chen, C.- M. 237
Cheney, D. L. 125
Cheung, H. 257
Chevalier, N. 195

Cheyne, J. A. 71
Chiasson, L. 253
Childers, J. B. 185
Chiron, C. 149
Chomsky, N. 20, 123–124, 139, 146–148, 151–152
Chouinard, M. M. 154
Christiansen, M. H. 157
Chudek, M. 306
Chung, H. L. 180
Chung, Y. S. 239
Cimpian, A. 177
Clark, C. A. C. 195
Clark-Carter, D. 250
Clark, E. V. 154, 176
Clark, R. A. 113
Claux, M. L. 245
Clayton, N. S. 89
Clemente, R. A. 253
Clements, W. 218
Clements, W. A. 227, 246
Cleveland, A. 107
Cochet, H. 117
Cohen, A. P. 235
Cohen, J. D. 303, 304, 315
Cohen, L. B. 186
Colby, A. 280, 282, 283, 284, 286, 287
Cole-Fletcher, R. 239
Cole, K. 246
Cole, S. W. 28
Coleman, M. 237
Collard, J. 312
Colombo, J. 203
Colombo, M. 308, 309
Colonnesi, C. 93
Colvert, E. 244
Conway, A. 204
Cook, S. 205
Cooperman, G. 298
Coppola, M. 156
Corkum, V. 90, 109, 110
Corley, R. P. 16, 201
Cosmides, L. 17, 22, 101, 307
Costall, A. 83, 86, 224
Costantini, M. 310
Cowell, J. M. 308, 310
Cox, A. 93, 237
Cox, M. 203
Crawford, M. B. 231
Creed, N. 257
Cresswell, C. 198
Crockford, C. 126
Cross, D. 216, 225, 245

Crowe, E. 253, 255
Csibra, G. 308
Cuff, B. 297
Curtiss, S. 151
Cutler, A. 172, 173
Cutting, A. L. 245, 246, 249, 255, 263

Dack, L. A. 216, 256, 257
Daffner, K. R. 302
Dahl, A. 311, 317
Dale, P. S. 155, 173
Damasio, A. R. 302
Damasio, H. 302
Damon, W. 287
Danziger, K. 64
Darley, J. M. 303, 304, 315
Darwin, C. 95, 298, 305, 316
Das Gupta, M. 251, 258
Davidov, M. 298
Davies, M. 223
Davis, A. C. 207, 208
Davis, W. 144
Dawkins, R. 305, 315
de Barbaro, K. 83, 86, 110, 333
de Hollanda Souza, D. 249
De Jaegher, H. 232, 313
de Jong, P. F. 195
de Looper, A. 310
de Oliveira-Souza, R. 302
De Rosnay, M. 217, 248, 251, 263
de Sonneville, L. M. J. 247
de Villiers, J. G. 249, 253, 256
de Villiers, P. A. 249, 253, 256
de Vos, C. 93, 117
de Waal, F. 305, 315
Deák, G. O. 83, 86, 110, 333
Deater-Deckard, K. 245, 249
DeCasper, A. J. 169
Decety, J. 308, 310
DeFries, J. C. 16, 201
Delalande, O. 149
Delgado, C. 107
Dellaire, R. 271
Dennis, M. J. 263
Denton, K. 286
D'Entremont, B. 90, 116
Deppe, M. 149
Descartes, R. 5, 6
Deschênes, M. 203
DeScioli, P. 306
DeSouza, L. M. 7, 9
Desrochers, S. 107

Devine, R. T. 218
Devine, T. A. 298
Devitt, K. 255
Di Paolo, E. 232
Diamond, A. 192, 197, 204, 206
Diaz, R. M. 70, 71
Diesendruck, G. 177, 180
Dijkstra, J. 253
Doherty, M. 228
Dolan, C. V. 195
Donaldson, M. 56
Donovan, T. 84, 169
Donovan, W. L. 86
Douglas, H. 216
Dräger, B. 149
Dray, S. 156
Drew, A. 93, 237
Drummond, J. 248, 311
Duncan, R. M. 71
Dungan, J. 302
Dunn, J. 217, 218, 244, 245, 246, 247, 253, 255, 263, 264
Dunn, K. J. 84, 169
Dunn, R. S. 230
Dupré, J. 18
Dutta, R. 73
Dwyer, S. 306

Ebstein, R. P. 23, 29
Ehlting, J. 28
Eimas, P. D. 170
Eisele, J. 150
Eisenberg, N. 297, 298
Elliott, A. M. 198
Ellis, R. 32
Elsabbagh, M. 234, 235, 237, 238
Emerson, M. J. 191, 193, 195, 198, 201, 209
Emery, N. J. 89
Emory, E. 201
Endress, A. D. 225
Engell, A. D. 304
English and Romanian Adoptees study team 244
Ensor, R. 195, 203, 204, 207, 246, 255
Ereky-Stevens, K. 251
Eslinger, P. J. 302
Espinet, S. D. 201
Espy, K. A. 195, 196, 198
Evans, N. 152

Fallow, P. M. 125
Fantasia, V. 313
Fantz, R. 84

Farah, M. J. 203, 207
Farrant, B. M. 298
Farroni, T. 84, 89
Fasulo, A. 313
Faulkner, J. 206
Feder, M. A. 72
Fein, D. 237
Feldman, J. F. 195, 196
Feldman, M. W. 25, 26
Fenici, M. 226, 227
Fenson, J. 150
Fenson, L. 155, 173
Ferdinand, N. K. 207
Fernald, A. 176
Fernyhough, C. 69, 71, 250, 251, 258
Fescemyer, H. 28
Fifer, W. P. 169
Finch, S. 157
Fineberg, D. S. 246
Fink, E. 248, 263
Fischer, J. 121, 122
Fischer, K. W. 110, 218
Fisher, S. E. 14, 102, 226
Fitch, W. T. 125, 126, 129, 148
Fivush, R. 218, 253
Flaherty-Craig, C. V. 302
Flavell, J. H. 220
Fletcher, B. 96
Fletcher, J. 72, 298
Fletcher, R. 237
Flöcl, A. 149
Flom, R. 100
FLP Investigators 203
Flynn, E. 71
Fodor, J. A. 18
Fogel, A. 93
Foglia, L. 32
Fohlen, M. 149
Fonagy, P. 250
Foote, R. C. 263
Forst, R. 318
Forster, D. 333
Fracchia, C. S. 203
Fradley, E. 69, 71, 251, 258
Francis, B. 77
Franco, F. 116
Frank, M. C. 225
Frauenglass, M. H. 71
Frayn, M. 89
Freeman, N. 216
Freeman, N. H. 77, 79, 219, 228, 246
Frenandes, T. P. 236

Freud, S. 190
Friedman, N. P. 16, 191, 193, 194, 195, 196, 198, 201, 202, 209
Friedman, O. 19, 101, 103
Frisch, K. von 126, 128
Frith, U. 218
Fritz, A. 228
Frodi, A. M. 86
Fry, C. 220
Frydman, O. 76
Frye, D. 192, 205, 209
Furness, W. H. 129
Furrow, D. 253

Gaddy, D. 253
Gallese, V. 32, 229, 230
Galton, F. 65
Gardner, B. T. 130
Gardner, R. A. 130
Garner, P. 253
Garon, N. 194, 197
Gathercole, S. E. 198
Gauvain, M. 73
Gearhart, M. 72
Gehlen, A. 41
Gellatly, A. 223
Gelman, R. 36, 182
Gentner, D. 177
Geraci, A. 102, 225
German, T. P. 19, 101, 103
Gernsbacher, M. A. 89, 229
Gerstadt, C. L. 192, 197, 204
Gervain, J. 169, 172, 173
Gesell, A. 19
Geurts, B. 228
Gibbs, J. C. 284
Gibbs, V. 264
Giesbrecht, G. 54, 55, 56, 195
Gillberg, C. 93, 233, 237
Gillberg, I. C. 233
Gilligan, C. 276, 288, 289, 293
Gini, G. 264
Glasersfeld, E. von 36
Glassman, M. 305
Gleason, J. B. 182
Glenberg, A. M. 32
Gliga, T. 30, 238
Göckeritz, S. 274, 318
Gola, A. A. H. 258
Goldberg, B. 102, 161
Goldin-Meadow, S. 93, 183
Goldman-Rakic, P. S. 201

Golinkoff, R. M. 176, 178, 179, 180
Golm, D. 244, 266
Gomez, J-C. 237
Goodnow, J. J. 190
Goodstein, J. 231
Goodwyn, S. W. 96
Gopnik, A. 6, 19, 222, 223
Gopnik, M. 16
Gordon, R. M. 223
Gorrindo, P. 84, 237
Gottlieb, G. 15, 26–29
Gould, S. J. 305
Grafman, J. 302
Graham, A. 195, 197, 200
Graham, S. 180
Grandin, T. 8
Granger, D. 203
Gray, J. R. 231
Grazzani Gavazzi, I. 254
Grazzani, I. 255
Green, J. 239
Greenberg, G. 14, 21
Greenberg, M. T. 203
Greene, J. D. 303, 304, 315
Greenspan, S. 215, 217
Gregory, S. 182
Grewe, J. 96
Grice, H. P. 69, 159
Griffiths, P. E. 28
Grigg, R. 206
Groothues, C. 244
Gros-Louis, J. 312, 313
Gross, R. L. 248, 311
Grothues, C. 244
Guberman, S. R. 72
Guillaume, P. 112
Gunnar, M. R. 244

Haberl, K. 185
Habermas, J. 318
Hackman, D. A. 203
Haff, T. M. 125
Hagestadt, C. 216
Haider, H. 257
Haidt, J. 292, 299–302, 304, 306
Haist, F. 20, 29, 30, 226, 315
Haith, M. M. 54, 55, 226, 309
Hala, S. 208, 217, 228
Hale, C. M. 256
Halina, M. 113
Hallett, D. 222
Hamilton, R. 307

Hamlin, J. K. 19, 308, 309, 315
Hammond, S. I. 73, 204, 208, 224, 310, 311
Hanif, R. 245
Hankivsky, O. 9, 290
Hanlon, C. 153, 154
Hannan, T. E. 93
Happé, F. 218, 235, 239, 244, 265
Hare, B. 89
Hare, B. A. 122
Harris, C. 231
Harris, M. 181
Harris, P. 186
Harris, P. L. 48, 215, 217, 223, 228, 245, 256
Hartshorne, H. 279
Hauser, M. D. 306
Hawk, C. K. 249
Hawkins, A. 244
Hay, D. 310
Hay, D. F. 247
Hayes, C. 129
Hayes, K. J. 129
Hayne, H. 308, 309
Hebb, D. O. 20, 224
Heil, J. 18, 55, 226
Hein, A. 38
Held, R. 38
Helles, A. 233
Henning, A. 248
Henningsen, H. 149
Henrich, J. 26, 306
Henry, J. D. 248, 263
Herder, J. G. 41
Hermida, J. 203
Hermida, M. J. 203
Herrmann, E. 306
Hersh, R. H. 279
Hershberg, R. M. 7, 9
Hertz-Pannier, L. 149
Hertz, S. 287
Hewer, A. 286
Hewitt, J. K. 16, 201
Heyes, C. 105, 229
Hickok, G. 229
Higgins, A. 280
Hill, E. 218
Hirano, M. 28
Hirsh-Pasek, K. 154, 176, 178, 180
Hitch, G. 190
Ho, M. W. 28
Ho, R. M. H. 195
Hobson, J. A. 106, 297–298
Hobson, R. P. 82, 106, 109, 236, 249, 297–298

Hockett, C. F. 125
Hoff-Ginsberg, E. 155
Hoffman, M. 298
Hoffman, M. L. 298
Hoffmeister, R. 249, 253
Holiday, A. 271
Holland, S. K. 230
Hollich, G. J. 180
Holmes, H. A. 245
Holmes-Lonergan, H. A. 263
Holochwost, S. J. 199, 202
Holodynski, M. 25
Holvoet, C. 309
Honeycutt, H. 14, 19, 21, 27, 28
Hong, Y. J. 192, 197, 204
Hopkins, E. J. 231
Hörmann, H. 152
Horst, J. S. 177
Houghton, K. 240
Houston-Price, C. 186
Houston-Price, C. M. T. 205
Howat, D. J. 297
Howe, N. 247
Howerter, A. 191, 193, 195, 198, 201, 209
Howlett, N. 96
Howlin, P. 239
Hsuan-Chih, C. 257
Huang, Z. 246
Hudry, K. 237, 238, 239
Hughes, C. 195, 197, 200, 203, 204, 207, 218, 244, 245, 246, 249, 255
Huizinga, M. 195
Hulme, C. 206
Hume, D. 299, 300
Hurley, S. 223
Hutto, D. D. 36
Hwang, I. K. 28

Iacoboni, M. 229
Iannotti, R. 298
Iarocci, G. 236
Imuta, K. 248, 263, 308, 309
Inhelder, B. 38, 215
Itakura, S. 205–206
Itakura, S. T. 245

Jablonka, E. 25, 26, 28
Jackson, I. 226
Jacques, S. 205
Jaffee, S. R. 244, 265
Jambaqué, I. 149
James, W. 19

Janet, P. 62
Jankowski, J. J. 195, 196
Jarvis, P. 220
Jastrow, J. 220
Jeffries, A. R. 234–235
Jenkins, J. M. 246, 247, 253
Jennings, M. 247
Jernigan, T. L. 20, 29, 30, 226, 315
Jipson, J. 174, 183
Johnson, C. M. 83, 86, 110, 333
Johnson, C. N. 215, 223
Johnson, M. H. 29–30, 84, 89, 102, 206, 224, 226,
    232, 234, 235, 237, 238
Jones, C. P. 265
Jones, D. 181, 253
Jones, E. J. H. 30, 238
Jones, S. 24, 25, 105, 176, 179
Jones, W. 84, 89, 236, 237
Jopling, D. 102
Jordan, J. S. 32, 232
Joshi, T. 28
Judge, B. 5
Jusczyk, P. W. 170
Juujarvi, P. 195

Kagan, J. 231
Kahane, G. 304
Kail, R. 75
Kakada, A. 93, 117
Kaland, N. 239
Kaminski, J. 89, 121, 122
Kanner, L. 233, 234
Kaplan, B. 93, 109, 112
Karap, Z. Tatone, D. 308
Karmiloff-Smith, A. 15, 30, 300, 307
Kartner, J. 25, 312
Kaschak, M. P. 32
Kegl, J. 157
Keil, F. C. 231
Kelemen, D. 177
Keller, H. 25
Kellogg, L. A. 129
Kellogg, W. N. 129
Kennedy, M. 244, 266
Kenworthy, L. E. 71
Kerns, K. 195, 196, 197, 198, 202–203,
    206, 208
Kerr, D. C. R. 264
Kervella, C. 85
Kesebir, S. 299, 306
Kettner, V. 94, 95, 96, 102, 111, 274, 309,
    311, 318

Keysers, C. 229
Kidd, C. 210
Kim, S. 204
King, A. P. 15
Kinsbourne, M. 32, 232
Kinzler, K. D. 17, 52, 53
Kipling, R. 18
Kirk, E. 96
Kirkham, N. Z. 205
Kirsten, S. 87, 310
Klahr, D. 40
Klin, A. 84, 89, 236, 237
Kloo, D. 207
Kluckhohn, C. 2
Knecht, S. 149
Knickmeyer, R. 234, 236
Knights, N. 244, 266
Knowles, M. 208
Kobayashi, H. 89
Kochanska, G. 204
Kogushi, Y. 246
Kohlberg, L. 279–290, 293
Kohshima, S. 89
Konkin, K. 197, 198
Kooistra, L. 195
Kopp, C. 210
Korner, A. F. 86
Koster, I. 93
Kovács, Á. M. 225
Kovshoff, H. 236
Kray, J. 207
Krebs, D. L. 286, 300, 306, 307
Kreppner, J. 244, 266
Kreppner, J. M. 244
Krettenauer, T. 222, 287
Kristen-Antonow, S. 249
Kroesbergen, E. H. 195
Kropotkin, P. 305
Krueger, F. 302
Kucharczyk, P. 89
Kuebli, J. 218, 253
Kuhl, P. K. 170
Kuhn, T. 5
Kumsta, R. 244, 266
Kuntsi, J. 198
Kuo, Z. Y. 21
Kurzban, R. 306
Kyriakidou, C. 246

LaBounty, J. 248, 264
Laing, K. 237
Laland, K. N. 20, 25, 26

Lalonde, C. E. 220, 221, 263
Lamb, M. E. 86
Lamb, M. J. 25, 26, 28
Lambert, W. E. 20, 224
Lambrick, D. 206
Landau, B. 176, 179
Landry, O. 236
Landry, S. H. 208
Lane, J. D. 248, 264
Langer, J. 54
Lapsley, D. K. 282, 283
Laurence, S. 16
Lawrence, J. A. 64, 73
Le Bihan, D. 149
Le Couteur, A. 239
Leach, J. G. 207, 208
Leadbitter, K. 239
Leavens, D. A. 86, 114
Leavitt, L. A. 86
Lecanuet, J. 169
Lecce, S. 218, 246, 263
Lee, K. 100, 195, 205–206
Leekam, S. R. 216, 246, 251
Lehmann, H. 89
Lehrman, D. S. 19
Lehto, J. E. 195
Lejeune, C. 207
Lenneberg, E. H. 150
Leontiev, A. N. 64
Lerner, R. M. 7, 9
Leseman, P. P. M. 195
Leslie, A. M. 19, 101, 103, 223, 225, 236
Leudar, I. 224
Levine, C. 286
Levinson, S. C. 152, 158, 159, 160
Lewis, C. 71, 77, 79, 86, 90, 100, 102, 106, 109,
       110, 152, 182, 197, 208, 214, 216, 218, 219,
       222, 224, 227–230, 240, 245, 246, 253, 265,
       267, 313
Lewkowicz, D. J. 28
Lewontin, R. C. 18
Liben, L. S. 264
Licata, M. 87, 310
Lickliter, R. 14, 19, 21, 27, 28, 31
Lickona, T. 278
Liebal, K. 94
Lieberman, M. 284
Liebermann-Finestone, D. P. 73, 204, 208
Lieven, E. 93, 114, 116, 118, 144, 147, 152, 156,
       178, 179, 180, 185
Lightfoot, S. 114
Lillard, A. 245

Lillard, A. S. 247
Lin, D. J. 84, 237
Lipina, S. J. 203
Liszkowski, U. 93, 94, 107, 111, 117, 118, 313
Liu, D. 219
Liu, J. 197
Llewellyn, J. 9
Lloyd, V. L. 186
Lock, A. 92, 93, 107, 117, 158
Logothetis, N. 231
Lohmann, H. 149
Lollis, S. 246
Lombardo, M. V. 234, 236
Lopez, B. 83, 86, 310
Lourenço, O. 36, 57, 292
Lowenburg, K. 304
Lucas, A. J. 152
Luckman, T. 41
Lule, S. 198
Luria, A. R. 208
Lyons, K. E. 206

Machado, A. 36, 57
Machiavelli, N. 264
Mackey, A. P. 203
Mackintosh, E. 253
Macmillan, M. 302
Macnamara, J. 173
MacWhinney, B. 169, 172, 173
Magrath, R. D. 125
Maher, B. 16
Maibom, H. L. 296, 297
Malcolm, N. 262
Mameli, M. 15
Mandy, W. 233
Manfra, L. 70
Manica, A. 313
Manuck, S. B. 16
Mar, R. A. 230
Maratsos, M. P. 215
Marazita, J. 177
Marcelli, D. 85
Marcovitch, S. 205
Marcus, G. 155
Mareschal, D. 29–30, 102, 224, 226, 232
Margolis, E. 16
Maridaki-Kassotaki, K. 246
Markman, E. M. 174–178
Markova, G. 86, 310
Markson, L. 177, 178
Marshall, P. J. 2, 29, 32, 33, 36
Martin, A. 71

Martin, J. 226, 227
Masataka, N. 93
Mascaro, O. 308
Mascolo, M. F. 110
Massaccesi, S. 84, 89
Masuo, Y. 28
Matte-Gagné, C. 203, 208
Matthews, D. 116, 118
Mattock, K. 171, 180
Maturana, H. 36
Maughan, B. 244, 266
Maurer, D. 171
Mauthner, N. 228
May, M. A. 279
Maybery, M. T. 298
Mayer, A. 245
McAlister, A. R. 246
McAuley, T. 196
McCabe, D. P. 231
McCaffery, J. M. 16
McCandliss, B. D. 207
McCartney, K. 155
McConachie, H. 239
McConnell, D. 107
McDonough, R. 111
McGhee, P. E. 264
McGurk, R. 198
McInerney, R. 195
McMurray, B. 15
McNew, S. 225
Mcquaid, N. 25, 85
Meaburn, E. L. 234–235
Mead, G. H. 109, 111, 141, 226, 319
Meaney, M. J. 14, 16, 23, 26, 102, 203
Mehler, J. 169, 172, 173
Meins, E. 250, 251, 258
Meitzsch, T. 274, 318
Melby-Lervåg, M. 206
Melis, A. P. 306
Meloni, M. 305
Meltzoff, A. N. 89, 101–105, 107, 224
Mercure, E. 237, 238
Merriman, W. E. 177
Mervis, C. 176, 178
Mervis, C. B. 144, 176, 179
Messer, D. J. 107
Mesulam, M. M. 302
Meulemans, T. 207
Mikhail, J. 306
Mill, J. 234–235
Miller, G. 231, 304, 315
Miller, J. D. 170

Miller-Loncar, C. L. 208
Miller, M. R. 195
Miller, P. H. 206
Miller, S. A. 245
Milligan, K. 216, 256, 257
Mills-Koonce, R. 203
Mink, D. 248
Minter, M. 249
Mireault, G. 316
Mischel, W. 210
Mistry, J. 73
Mitchell, P. 228, 246
Miyake, A. 16, 191, 193, 194, 195, 196, 198, 201, 202, 209
Mo, L. 257
Moffitt, T. E. 244, 265
Moll, H. 90, 106, 108, 227, 313
Moll, J. 302
Møller-Nielsen, A. 239
Moller Okin, S. 289
Molnar, P. 105
Monaghan, P. 157, 172, 180
Moore, C. 19, 90, 107, 109, 110, 116, 253, 263
Moore, L. K. 23
Moore, M. K. 104, 105
Moore, V. 90, 110
Morelli, S. A. 304
Moreno, S. 206
Morgan, K. 93, 237
Moriguchi, Y. 205–206
Morissette, P. 107
Morrell, J. M. B. 217
Mortensen, E. L. 239
Morton, B. J. 205
Morton, J. 84, 89
Moses, L. J. 88, 249
Mugwanya, N. 180
Muhangi, L. 198
Muir, D. 100
Muldoon, K. 77, 79
Müller, U. 36, 38, 44, 47, 49, 54, 55, 56, 59, 62, 73, 76, 106, 195–198, 202–206, 208, 220, 232, 301, 302
Munakata, Y. 75, 205
Mundry, R. 126
Mundy, P. 107, 236
Muñetón, M. A. 94
Murphy, C. M. 107
Murphy, J. 135
Myers, L. J. 264
Myin, E. 36

Nadel, J. 85
Nagell, K. 93, 106, 107, 185
Nagy, E. 105
Naito, M. 246
Nampijja, M. 198
Namy, L. L. 180
Nash, M. 218
Nass, R. 150
Nawaz, S. 245
Nee, P. 2
Neff, C. 86
Nelson, J. M. 195
Nelson, K. 178, 181, 251
Nelson, L. H. 96
Newman, R. S. 182
Newport, E. L. 151, 172
Newton, P. 228
Ng, L. 257
Nightingale, N. 93, 237
Ninio, A. 72
Noble, K. G. 207
Noom, M. J. 93
Norman, D. A. 190
Nucci, L. 291
Nunes, T. 76
Nystrom, L. E. 303, 304, 315

Ochs, E. 182
O'Connor, T. B. 244
O'Connor, T. G. 244
Odden, H. 245
Odling Smee, F. J. 25, 26
Ogan, T. 88
O'Hara, S. 114
O'Hare, A. E. 218
Olson, S. L. 248, 264
O'Neill, D. K. 227
Ong, D. C. 225
Onishi, K. 19, 101–102, 225, 226
Onnis, L. 172
Ornaghi, V. 254, 255
O'Rourke, P. 93
Orvos, H. 105
Osterlaan, J. 198
Ottoboni, G. 32
Ouellet-Morin, I. 265
Overton, W. F. 3, 6, 7, 9, 36, 38, 54, 56,
    220, 224
Oyama, S. 22, 30

Padona, A. 295
Page, M. P. A. 231

Pagnin, A. 218, 263
Paine, A. L. 247
Pala, F. C. 152
Palfai, T. 192, 205
Palmeri, H. 210
Pan, J. 312, 313
Parent, S. 265
Parkin, L. 245, 246, 249, 254, 298
Parlade, M. 107
Parlade, M. V. 107
Parsloe, S. M. 233
Pasco, G. 237, 238
Pashler, H. 231
Patriquin, M. 253
Patterson, C. J. 210
Patterson, F. G. 130
Paulus, M. 87, 296, 308, 310
Pavarini, G. 249
Pearce, H. 247
Pears, K. C. 249
Pentland, L. 36
Perez, S. 73
Perez-Zapata, D. 245
Perkins, A. 246
Perkins, E. 226
Perlmutter, M. 71
Perner, J. 207, 215, 216, 220, 223, 226, 227, 228,
    245, 246, 249, 254, 257, 298
Perner, R. 226
Perry, W. G., Jr. 222
Persaud, T. V. N. 23
Peskin, J. 254
Peters, D. 219
Peterson, C. 219, 246, 248, 249, 253, 254,
    258, 263
Peterson, J. L. 249
Pethick, S. J. 155, 173
Petitto, L. A. 138
Petrakos, H. 247
Pettigrew, L. M. 218
Phillips, J. 225
Piaget, J. 10, 17, 36–58, 67, 69, 74, 77–79, 109, 145,
    146, 215, 226, 275–278, 284, 288, 290, 296,
    298, 299, 316–319
Picard, D. 309
Pickering, S. J. 198
Pickles, A. 237, 238, 239
Pika, S. 114
Pilling, K. 105
Pillow, B. H. 219, 221
Pine, K. 71
Pine, K. J. 96

Pinker, S. 17, 22, 138, 139, 151, 155, 157, 158, 307
Pividori, D. 84, 89
Plomin, R. 16, 234–235
Plooij, F. X. 113
Plunkett, K. 186
Pomares, Y. 107
Pons, F. 217
Popper, K. 5
Portmann, A. 85
Prats, L. 203
Prats, L. M. 203
Premack, A. J. 124
Premack, D. 124, 215
Pressley, M. 198
Price, B. H. 302
Price, T. S. 234–235
Prinz, J. J. 18, 300
Pritchard, M. 263, 264
Proudfoot, D. 160
Pulkkinen, L. 195
Puura, K. 233
Pyers, J. E. 157, 256

Quine, W. V. O. 175, 186

Rabbitt, P. 197
Racine, T. 100, 215, 254, 255, 309
Radford, A. N. 125
Raikes, H. A. 250
Raizada, R. D. S. 203
Rakoczy, H. 274, 318
Rakwal, R. 28
Ramini, G. B. 312
Ramsay, G. 84, 237
Ratcliffe, M. 222
Ratner, N. B. 182
Raver, C. C. 203
Rawls, J., 283
Rawson, E. 231
Ray, E. 105
Recchia, H. E. 264
Redbond, J. 205
Reddy, V. 83, 86, 228, 255, 310, 316
Redfern, S. 250
Redick, T. S. 206
Redington, M. 157
Reese, E. 247
Reese, H. W. 3
Regolin, L. 83–84, 237
Rehrig, E. 28
Reichelt, A. F. 83, 86

Reid, V. 84, 88, 90, 169
Reidy, N. 197
Reisman, J. M. 248
Reissland, N. 84, 169
Remington, A. 237
Renaux-Kieffer, V. 149
Rennie, K. 253
Renouf, A. 265
Repacholi, B. M. 264
Réserbat-Plantey, D. 85
Reznick, J. S. 155, 173, 205, 209
Rheingold, H. L. 310, 311
Ricard, M. 107
Richardson, R. 18
Richer, J. 236
Richerson, P. J. 26
Richler, J. 199
Richmond, K. 172
Riedel, J. 89
Rimland, B. 234
Rinaldi, C. 247
Ringelstein, E.-B. 149
Ringo, J. 236
Rios, P. 239
Rivera, S. M. 54
Rizzolatti, G. 229
Robins, D. L. 237
Robinson, E. J. 264
Robinson, S. R. 15
Robinson, W. P. 264
Rochat, P. 245, 297
Rodrigo, M. J. 94
Rodríguez, C. 94
Roebers, C. M. 198
Rogoff, B. 73
Ronald, A. 234–235
Rooksby, M. 219, 246
Rose, S. 105
Rose, S. A. 195, 196
Rosengren, K. S. 71
Ross, G. 72
Ross, H. S. 246, 264
Ross, R. 9
Rossano, F. 113
Rosslenbroich, B. 2
Rossmanith, N. 83, 86
Roth-Hanania, R. 298
Rowe, M. L. 182
Rowland, C. 138, 153, 158
Rubio, D. A. 72
Rubio-Fernández, P. 228
Ruetti, E. 203

Ruffman, T. 102, 218, 226, 245, 246, 249, 253, 254, 255, 256, 298
Rumbaugh, D. M. 132, 135
Runions. K. 62, 106
Rushton, J. P. 198
Russell, J. 45, 55, 208, 222, 223, 228, 250
Russo, N. 236
Rutter, M. 244, 266

Saarni, C. 210
Sabbagh, M. A. 244, 252
Saffran, J. R. 172
Salomo, D. 117
Salomone, E. 239
Salvadori, E. 308
Sameen, N. 232
Samuelson, L. K. 15, 179
Sanders, P. T. 18
Sansone, J. 114
Satlof-Bedrick, E. 248, 311
Sauer, H. 304
Savage-Rumbaugh, E. S. 132, 134, 135
Saxe, G. B. 72, 74
Saxe, R. 225
Scaife, M. 90
Scarf, D. 308, 309
Scerif, G. 206
Schalkwyk, L. C. 234–235
Scheler, M. 106, 224
Schellenberg, E. G. 206
Schick, B. 249, 253
Schieffelin, B. 182
Schilling, T. H. 54
Schirmann, F. 304
Schleim, S. 304
Schlotz, W. 244, 266
Schmid, C. 198
Schmidt, M. F. 274, 318
Schmithorst, V. J. 230
Schneiderman, M. 154
Scholl, B. J. 101
Schoneberger, T. 153
Schuchard, J. 240
Schuhmacher, N. 312
Schultz, J. 28
Schultz, R. 236
Schunn, C. D. 72
Scola, C. 309
Scott, P. D. 177
Scott, R. M. 101, 225
Seamans, E. L. 244
Sebba, M. 156

Segretin, M. S. 203
Segretin, S. 203
Séguin, J. R. 265
Seidenberg, M. S. 138
Semcesen, T. K. 205
Senghas, A. 156, 157
Senghas, R. J. 157
Senn, T. E. 198
Seo, H. S. 28
Service, V. 93, 107, 117
Sevcik, R. A. 135
Seyfarth, R. M. 125
Shackel, N. 304
Shakoor, S. 265
Shallice, T. 190, 193
Shanker, S. G. 85, 236
Sharpe, S. 228
Shatz, M. 182, 251
Sheffield, T. 195
Sherry, D. 86
Sherwood, V. 86
Shibato, J. 28
Shimmon, K. 197
Shinn, M. W. 112, 115
Shinskey, J. L. 54
Shneidman, L. A. 183
Shrager, J. 75
Siegal, M. 248, 249, 253, 263
Siegler, R. S. 75
Silber, S. 251
Silvers, J. A. 71
Simion, F. 83–84, 237
Simpson, M. A. 16
Singh, S. 245
Sinigaglia, C. 310
Siqueland, E. R. 170
Sirois, S. 29–30, 102, 224, 226, 232
Skerry, A. E. 17
Skinner, B. F. 145, 190
Skuse, D. 198, 233
Slaby, J. 302
Slade, L. 253, 255, 256
Slaughter, V. 107, 219, 245, 246, 248, 249, 253, 254, 258, 263, 264
Slavich, G. M. 28
Slomkowki, C. 244, 253
Slonims, V. 239
Slotnick, S. D. 31
Smetana, J. G. 290, 291
Smith, A. 297
Smith, I. M. 194, 197
Smith, K. E. 208

Smith, L. 37, 44, 57, 77, 78, 239
Smith, L. B. 176, 179, 180, 185, 186
Smith, P. K. 223, 264
Smith, R. 190
Snarey, J. R. 286
Snow, C. E. 146, 152, 154, 155, 183
Snyder, L. 135
Sodian, B. 87, 225, 226, 228, 249, 310
Sokol, B. 38, 56, 62, 232, 301
Sokolov, J. L. 146, 154, 155
Sommerville, R. B. 303, 315
Sonuga-Barke, E. J. 198, 244, 266
Southgate, V. 94
Spaemann, R. 317
Speaker, C. J. 54
Spelke, E. S. 17, 52, 53
Spencer, J. P. 15
Sperber, D. 18, 225
Spinrad, T. L. 297, 298
Spitz, R. A. 95
Spratling, M. W. 29–30, 102, 224, 226, 232
Sprintzen, D. 9
Sprung, M. 257
St Clair, M. C. 157
Stack, J. 102
Stager, C. L. 186
Stahl, D. 107
Stam, G. J. J. M. 93
Stanovich, K. E. 199–200
Stanowicz, L. 153, 154
Stevens, S. 244
Stevenson, J. 198
Stifter, C. A. 204
Stiles, J. 20, 28, 29, 30, 226, 315
Stoll, S. 93
Stone, J. E. 226, 227
Stone, T. 223
Stoner, L. 206
Stowe, R. M. 302
Strawsburg, R. H. 230
Striano, T. 88, 90, 94, 107
Strube, M. 239
Su, Y. 312, 313
Suanda, S. H. 180
Sugarman, J. 226, 227
Sullivan, K. 220
Surian, L. 102, 225
Surtees, A. D. R. 225
Susswein, N. 255
Sutton, J. 264
Svetlova, M. 248, 311
Swank, P. R. 208
Swettenham, J. 93, 237, 264

Swift, J. 162
Swingley, D. 173
Symes, E. 32

Tabery, J. 28
Tafreshi, D. 309
Tager-Flusberg, H. 220, 256
Tallis, R. 231
Tangney, J. P. 218
Tappan, M. 288
Tardiff, T. 257
Tarullo, A. R. 244
Taumoepeau, M. 155, 226, 247, 253
Taylor, A. 244
Taylor, J. C. V. 231
Taylor, L. 297
Taylor, M. 228
Tees, R. C. 169, 170, 171
Téglás, E. 225
Tennie, C. 306
Terrace, H. S. 131
Tesla, C. 244, 253
Thal, D. J. 150, 155, 173
Theakston, A. 114
Thicke, L. 144
Thoermer, C. 87, 310
Thoman, E. B. 86
Thomas, M. S. C. 29–30, 102, 224, 226, 232
Thompson, C. K. 240
Thompson, J. 232, 309
Thompson, R. A. 250, 298
Thorpe, W. 150
Thyde, D-M. 237
Tidswell, T. 228
Tobin, H. 239
Todd, B. K. 114
Todd, J. A. 36
Tomasello, M. 25, 82, 89, 90, 93, 94, 106, 107, 108,
    111, 113–118, 122, 138, 148, 152, 157, 158, 164,
    181, 184, 185, 227, 274, 305, 306, 311, 313, 318
Tomblin, J. B. 15
Tooby, J. 17, 22, 101, 307
Toplak, M. E. 199–200
Torchia, M. G. 23
Towse, J. 77, 208
Towse, J. N. 205
Tranel, D. 302
Träuble, B. E. 245
Trauner, D. 150
Treiman, R. 154
Trevarthen, C. 82
Tucker, G. R. 20, 224
Tucker, M. 32

Tuckey, M. 251, 258
Turiel, E. 290, 291, 292, 299, 300, 301, 315
Turkewitz, G. 105
Turnbull, W. 158, 159, 161, 254, 255
Turrell, S. L. 246
Twomey, K. E. 177
Tyler, S. L. 70

Vail, A. L. 313
Vainio, L. 32
Vaish, A. 88, 305
Vallotton, C. D. 96
Valsiner, J. 62, 63, 64, 73
Van de Moortele, P-. F. 149
van de Veer, R. 62, 63
van der Leij, A. 195
van der Molen, M. W. 195
van der Sluis, S. 195
van der Veer, R. 62
Van der Ven, S. H. G. 195
van Goozen, S. H. M. 247
Van Hecke, A. V. 107
van IJzendoorn, M. H. 23, 29, 253
Varela, F. 36
Varouxaki, A. 219
Vauclair, J. 117
Vaughan, J. 185
Vaughan Van Hecke, A. 107
Velleman, S. L. 144
Vermeulen, S. 286
Vidal, F. 37
Vigorito, J. 170
Villanueva, L. 253
Vinden, P. G. 245, 246
Vitaro, F. 265
Vocate, D. R. 65
Volein, A. 308
Volkmar, F. 236
Volterra, V. 93, 112–116
Von Foerster, H. 32
Vonnegut, K. 2, 269
Vul, E. 231
Vygotsky, L. S. 62–79, 109, 112, 160, 208, 209

Wachtel, G. F. 176
Wager, T. D. 191, 193, 195, 198, 201, 209
Wainwright, R. 251, 258
Wakeley, A. 54
Walden, T. 88
Walker, L. J. 284, 287, 289, 293
Wallace, G. L. 71
Wallner-Allen, K. 199
Wallot, S. 86, 310

Wang, S. P. 257
Want, S. C. 249, 253
Warneken, F. 310, 311, 313, 316
Wass, S. V. 206
Watling, D. 218, 248, 263
Watson, J. 216, 225, 245
Watson, J. B. 19
Waugh, W. E. 248, 311
Webb, J. 249
Weintraub, S. 199
Weisberg, D. S. 231
Wellman, H. M. 19, 216, 217, 219, 222, 223, 225,
    245, 248, 251, 257, 264
Wereha, T. J. 93, 111, 119
Werker, J. F. 169, 170, 171, 172, 186
Werner, H. 93, 109, 112
Wernicke, C. 149
Wertsch, J. V. 65
West, M. J. 15
West, R. F. 199–200
Westermann, G. 29–30, 102, 224, 226, 232
Weston, D. 28
Whipple, N. 204
White, D. A. 196
White, K. R. 96
White, S. 218
Wiebe, S. A. 195, 196
Wiggins, G. 288
Wilkins, D. 93
Willems, S. 207
Williams, S. 225
Williams, S. L. 135
Willoughby, M. 195, 198, 199, 202, 203
Wills, G. 6
Wilson, A. 195
Wilson, E. O. 306
Wilson, M. 32
Wilson, R. A. 32
Wimmer, H. 215, 216, 220
Winkielman, P. 231
Winnicott, D. W. 7
Winsler, A. 70, 71, 72
Wirth, R. J. 195, 199
Witherington, D. C. 317
Wittgenstein, L. 38, 102, 111, 160, 161, 259
Wittig, R. M. 126
Witzki, A. H. 191, 193, 195, 198, 201, 209
Wong, C. C. Y. 234–235
Wong, K. 152
Wood, D. 72
Woodruff, G. 215
Woodward, A. L. 86, 87, 90, 91, 226, 310
Woolfe, T. 249, 253

Wörmann, V. 25
Wright, D. 278, 279, 290, 318
Wright, J. 220
Wu, Z. 312, 313
Wundt, W. 112
Wyman, E. 306
Wynn, K. 76, 308, 309

Xin, Y. 225
Xu, D. 28

Yagmurlu, B. 244
Yeung, E. 203, 302
Young, A. 93, 117
Young, L. 302

Young, R. J. 84, 169
Young, S. E. 16, 201
Youngblade, L. 244, 247, 253
Yu, C. 179, 180, 185, 186

Zahavi, D. 106, 224, 297
Zahn, R. 302
Zahn-Waxler, C. 298
Zaitchik, D. 220
Zauner, P. 257
Zelazo, P. D. 192, 199, 201, 205, 206, 209, 265
Zerwas, S. 312
Zoelch, C. 198
Zuberbühler, K. 126
Zuckerman, P. 295